Essentials of Strategic Management

Second Edition

Charles W. L. Hill
University of Washington

Gareth R. Jones
Texas A&M University

SOUTH-WESTERN
CENGAGE Learning

Australia • Brazil • Japan • Korea • Mexico • Singapore • Spain • United Kingdom • United States

![South-Western Cengage Learning logo] SOUTH-WESTERN
CENGAGE Learning™

Essentials of Strategic Management,
Second Edition
Charles W. L. Hill, Gareth R. Jones

For my children: Elizabeth,
Charlotte, and Michelle
Charles W. L. Hill

For Nicholas and Julia
and Morgan and Nia
Gareth R. Jones

President: Jonathan Hulbert

Vice President/Editorial Director:
Jack Calhoun

Editor-in-Chief: Melissa Acuña

Vice President/Director of Marketing:
Bill Hendee

Senior Acquisitions Editor:
Michele Rhoades

Developmental Editor: Suzanna Bainbridge

Editorial Assistant: Ruth Belanger

Media Editor: Rob Ellington

Executive Marketing Manager:
Brian Joyner

Marketing Manager: Nathan Anderson

Marketing Coordinator: Suellen Ruttkay

Senior Marketing Communications
Manager: Jim Overly

Senior Content Project Manager:
Margaret Park Bridges

Art and Design Manager: Jill Haber

Senior First Print Buyer: Diane Gibbons

Senior Rights Acquisition Account
Manager: Katie Huha

Text Researcher: Michael Farmer

Production Service: Lifland et al.,
Bookmakers

Senior Photo Editor: Jennifer Meyer Dare

Cover Design Manager: Anne Katzeff

Cover Image: Image Copyright
Jonny McCullagh, 2008, used under
license from Shutterstock.com

Compositor: Progressive Information
Technologies

For product information and technology assistance, contact us at
Cengage Learning Customer & Sales Support, 1-800-354-9706.
For permission to use material from this text or product,
submit all requests online at **www.cengage.com/permissions.**
Further permissions questions can be e-mailed to
permissionrequest@cengage.com.

Library of Congress Control Number: 2008929479

ISBN-13: 978-0-547-19432-5
ISBN-10: 0-547-19432-3

South-Western
5191 Natorp Blvd.
Mason, OH 45040
USA

Cengage Learning is a leading provider of customized learning solutions with office locations around the globe, including Singapore, the United Kingdom, Australia, Mexico, Brazil, and Japan. Locate your local office at **international.cengage.com/region.**

Cengage Learning products are represented in Canada by Nelson Education, Ltd.

For your course and learning solutions, visit **academic.cengage.com.**

Purchase any of our products at your local college store or at our preferred online store **www.ichapters.com.**

Printed in Canada
1 2 3 4 5 6 7 12 11 10 09 08

Brief Contents

PART 1   INTRODUCTION TO STRATEGIC MANAGEMENT

Chapter 1   The Strategy-Making Process   1
Chapter 2   Stakeholders, the Mission, Governance, and
            Business Ethics   26

PART 2   THE NATURE OF COMPETITIVE ADVANTAGE

Chapter 3   External Analysis: The Identification of Opportunities
            and Threats   52
Chapter 4   Building Competitive Advantage   77

**PART 3   BUILDING AND SUSTAINING LONG-RUN
            COMPETITIVE ADVANTAGE**

Chapter 5   Business-Level Strategy and Competitive Positioning   109
Chapter 6   Strategy in the Global Environment   137
Chapter 7   Corporate-Level Strategy and Long-Run Profitability   162

PART 4   STRATEGY IMPLEMENTATION

Chapter 8   Strategic Change: Implementing Strategies to Build and
            Develop a Company   188
Chapter 9   Implementing Strategy Through Organizational Design   214

PART 5   CASES IN STRATEGIC MANAGEMENT

Case 1   Boeing Commercial Aircraft: Comeback?   C1
Case 2   Apple Computer   C17
Case 3   Amazon.com   C33
Case 4   Blockbuster's Challenges in the Video Rental Industry   C44
Case 5   Whole Foods Market: Will There Be Enough Organic Food to
            Satisfy the Growing Demand?   C60
Case 6   3M in 2006   C69
Case 7   Philips versus Matsushita: A New Century, a New Round   C85
Case 8   Mired in Corruption—Kellogg Brown & Root in Nigeria   C100

Contents

Preface   xiii

PART 1   INTRODUCTION TO STRATEGIC MANAGEMENT

Chapter 1   The Strategy-Making Process   1

Competitive Advantage and Superior Performance   2
Strategic Managers   3
● **Running Case:** *Wal-Mart's Competitive Advantage*   4
   Corporate-Level Managers   4
   Business-Level Managers   6
   Functional-Level Managers   6
The Strategy-Making Process   7
   A Model of the Strategic Planning Process   7
   The Feedback Loop   10
Strategy as an Emergent Process   10
   Strategy Making in an Unpredictable World   11
   Autonomous Action: Strategy Making by Lower-Level Managers   11
● **Strategy in Action:** *A Strategic Shift at Microsoft*   12
   Serendipity and Strategy   12
   Intended and Emergent Strategies   13
Strategic Planning in Practice   14
   Scenario Planning   14
   Decentralized Planning   15
   Strategic Intent   16
Strategic Decision Making   17
   Cognitive Biases   17
   Improving Decision Making   18
Strategic Leadership   19
   Vision, Eloquence, and Consistency   19
   Commitment   19
   Being Well Informed   20
   Willingness to Delegate and Empower   20
   The Astute Use of Power   20
   Emotional Intelligence   20
Summary of Chapter ● Discussion Questions
● **Practicing Strategic Management**   22
   Small-Group Exercise: Designing a Planning System ●
   Exploring the Web: Visiting 3M
● **Closing Case:** *The Best-Laid Plans—Chrysler Hits the Wall*   23
Test Prepper   25

Chapter 2   **Stakeholders, the Mission, Governance, and Business Ethics   26**

Stakeholders   27
The Mission Statement   28
　　The Mission   28
　　Vision   30
　　Values   30
　　Major Goals   30
Corporate Governance and Strategy   31
　　The Agency Problem   32
● **Strategy in Action:** *The Agency Problem at Tyco*   35
　　Governance Mechanisms   36
Ethics and Strategy   40
　　Ethical Issues in Strategy   40
● **Running Case:** *Working Conditions at Wal-Mart*   42
　　The Roots of Unethical Behavior   44
　　Behaving Ethically   45
　　Final Words   47
Summary of Chapter   ● Discussion Questions
● **Practicing Strategic Management**   49
　　Small-Group Exercise: Evaluating Stakeholder Claims ●
　　Exploring the Web: Visiting Merck
● **Closing Case:** *Google's Mission, Ethical Principles, and Involvement in China*   49
Test Prepper   51

PART 2　　**THE NATURE OF COMPETITIVE ADVANTAGE**

Chapter 3   **External Analysis: The Identification of Opportunities and Threats   52**

Analyzing Industry Structure   53
　　Risk of Entry by Potential Competitors   54
● **Strategy in Action:** *Circumventing Entry Barriers into the Soft Drink Industry*   56
　　Rivalry Among Established Companies   57
　　The Bargaining Power of Buyers   60
　　The Bargaining Power of Suppliers   61
● **Running Case:** *Wal-Mart's Bargaining Power over Suppliers*   62
　　Threat of Substitute Products   63
　　Summary   63
Strategic Groups Within Industries   63
　　Implications of Strategic Groups   64
　　The Role of Mobility Barriers   65
Industry Life Cycle Analysis   65
　　Embryonic Industries   66
　　Growth Industries   66
　　Industry Shakeout   67
　　Mature Industries   68
　　Declining Industries   68
　　Summary   68

The Macroenvironment   69
   Macroeconomic Forces   69
   Global Forces   70
   Technological Forces   70
   Demographic Forces   71
   Social Forces   71
   Political and Legal Forces   71
Summary of Chapter   ● Discussion Questions
● **Practicing Strategic Management**   73
   Small-Group Exercise: Competing with Microsoft   ●
   Exploring the Web: Visiting Boeing and Airbus
● **Closing Case:** *The Pharmaceutical Industry*   74
Test Prepper   75

Chapter 4   Building Competitive Advantage   77

Competitive Advantage: Value Creation, Low Cost, and Differentiation   78
The Generic Building Blocks of Competitive Advantage   80
   Efficiency   80
   Quality as Excellence and Reliability   81
   Innovation   83
   Customer Responsiveness   83
The Value Chain   84
   Primary Activities   84
   Support Activities   86
Functional Strategies and the Generic Building Blocks of
Competitive Advantage   86
   Increasing Efficiency   87
● **Strategy in Action:** *Learning Effects in Cardiac Surgery*   89
● **Running Case:** *Human Resource Strategy and Productivity at Wal-Mart*   91
   Increasing Quality   94
   Increasing Innovation   96
   Achieving Superior Customer Responsiveness   99
Distinctive Competences and Competitive Advantage   100
   Resources and Capabilities   101
   The Durability of Competitive Advantage   102
Summary of Chapter   ● Discussion Questions
● **Practicing Strategic Management**   105
   Small-Group Exercise: Analyzing Competitive Advantage   ●
   Exploring the Web: Visiting Johnson & Johnson
● **Closing Case:** *Starbucks*   105
Test Prepper   107

**PART 3   BUILDING AND SUSTAINING LONG-RUN
COMPETITIVE ADVANTAGE**

Chapter 5   Business-Level Strategy and Competitive Positioning   109

The Nature of Competitive Positioning   110
   Customer Needs and Product Differentiation   110

    Customer Groups and Market Segmentation 110
    Distinctive Competences 111
Choosing a Business-Level Strategy 111
    Cost-Leadership Strategy 111
● **Running Case:** *How Wal-Mart Became a Cost Leader* 113
    Differentiation Strategy 114
    Cost Leadership and Differentiation 116
    Focus Strategy 117
    Stuck in the Middle 119
Competitive Positioning in Different Industry Environments 120
    Strategies in Fragmented and Growing Industries 121
    Strategies in Mature Industries 123
    Strategies in Declining Industries 128
● **Strategy in Action:** *How to Make Money in the Vacuum Tube Business* 130
Summary of Chapter ● Discussion Questions
● **Practicing Strategic Management** 133
    Small-Group Exercise: How to Keep the Salsa Hot ●
    Exploring the Web: Visiting the Luxury-Car Market
● **Closing Case:** *Nike's Business-Level Strategies* 134
Test Prepper 135

Chapter 6 **Strategy in the Global Environment** 137

The Global Environment 138
Increasing Profitability Through Global Expansion 139
● **Running Case:** *Wal-Mart's Global Expansion* 140
    Expanding the Market: Leveraging Products and Competences 140
    Realizing Economies of Scale 142
    Realizing Location Economies 142
    Leveraging the Skills of Global Subsidiaries 143
Cost Pressures and Pressures for Local Responsiveness 144
    Pressures for Cost Reductions 145
    Pressures for Local Responsiveness 145
Choosing a Global Strategy 147
    Global Standardization Strategy 148
● **Strategy in Action:** *The Evolution of Strategy at Procter & Gamble* 149
    Localization Strategy 149
    Transnational Strategy 150
    International Strategy 151
    Changes in Strategy over Time 151
Choices of Entry Mode 152
    Exporting 152
    Licensing 153
    Franchising 154
    Joint Ventures 155
    Wholly Owned Subsidiaries 155
    Choosing an Entry Strategy 156
Summary of Chapter ● Discussion Questions

● **Practicing Strategic Management**   159
  Small-Group Exercise: Developing a Global Strategy ●
  Exploring the Web: Visiting IBM
● **Closing Case:** *IKEA—The Global Retailer*   160
Test Prepper   161

Chapter 7   Corporate-Level Strategy and Long-Run Profitability   162

Concentration on a Single Industry   163
  Horizontal Integration   164
  Benefits and Costs of Horizontal Integration   164
  Outsourcing Functional Activities   167
Vertical Integration   168
  Arguments for Vertical Integration   170
  Arguments Against Vertical Integration   173
  Vertical Integration and Outsourcing   174
Entering New Industries Through Diversification   175
  Creating Value Through Diversification   175
● **Strategy in Action:** *Diversification at 3M: Leveraging Technology*   178
  Related versus Unrelated Diversification   180
Restructuring and Downsizing   181
  Why Restructure?   181
  Exit Strategies   182
Summary of Chapter ● Discussion Questions
● **Practicing Strategic Management**   184
  Small-Group Exercise: Comparing Vertical Integration Strategies ●
  Exploring the Web: Visiting Motorola
● **Closing Case:** *United Technologies Has an ACE in Its Pocket*   185
Test Prepper   186

PART 4   STRATEGY IMPLEMENTATION

Chapter 8   Strategic Change: Implementing Strategies to Build and Develop a Company   188

Strategic Change   189
  Types of Strategic Change   189
  A Model of the Change Process   190
Analyzing a Company as a Portfolio of Core Competences   193
  Fill in the Blanks   194
  Premier Plus 10   194
  White Spaces   194
  Mega-Opportunities   195
Implementing Strategy Through Internal New Ventures   195
  Pitfalls with Internal New Ventures   196
  Guidelines for Successful Internal New Venturing   198
● **Running Case:** *Wal-Mart Internally Ventures a New Kind of Retail Store*   199

Implementing Strategy Through Acquisitions   200
    Pitfalls with Acquisitions   200
    Guidelines for Successful Acquisition   202
● **Strategy in Action:** *News Corp's Successful Acquisition Strategy*   203
Implementing Strategy Through Strategic Alliances   204
    Advantages of Strategic Alliances   204
    Disadvantages of Strategic Alliances   205
    Making Strategic Alliances Work   206
Summary of Chapter ● Discussion Questions
● **Practicing Strategic Management**   210
    Small-Group Exercise: Identifying News Corp's Strategies ●
    Exploring the Web: Visiting UTC
    General Task   210
● **Closing Case:** *Oracle's Growing Portfolio of Businesses*   210
Test Prepper   212

Chapter 9   **Implementing Strategy Through Organizational Design**   214

The Role of Organization Structure   215
    Building Blocks of Organization Structure   216
Vertical Differentiation   216
    Problems with Tall Structures   217
    Centralization or Decentralization?   219
● **Strategy in Action:** *How to Flatten and Decentralize Structure*   220
Horizontal Differentiation   221
    Functional Structure   221
    Product Structure   223
    Product-Team Structure   224
    Geographic Structure   225
    Multidivisional Structure   226
Integration and Organizational Control   230
    Forms of Integrating Mechanisms   231
    Differentiation and Integration   233
The Nature of Organizational Control   234
    Strategic Controls   234
    Financial Controls   236
    Output Controls   238
    Behavior Controls   238
● **Running Case:** *Sam Walton's Approach to Implementing Wal-Mart's Strategy*   242
Summary of Chapter ● Discussion Questions
● **Practicing Strategic Management**   244
    Small-Group Exercise: Speeding Up Product Development ●
    Exploring the Web: Visiting Google's Control System
● **Closing Case:** *Ford Has a New CEO and a New Global Structure*   244
Test Prepper   246

PART 5   **CASES IN STRATEGIC MANAGEMENT**

Case 1   **Boeing Commercial Aircraft: Comeback?**   C1
    Charles W. L. Hill, *University of Washington*
    Has Boeing's turnaround in 2005–2006 been merely cosmetic, or has it
    fundamentally improved its strategic position?

Case 2	**Apple Computer C17**

Charles W. L. Hill, *University of Washington*

The rise, fall, and resurrection of Apple Computer, focusing on its core competences and resources.

Case 3   **Amazon.com   C33**

Gareth R. Jones, *Texas A&M University*

The business model and strategy of one of the most profitable Internet-based businesses and its emerging competitive challenges.

Case 4   **Blockbuster's Challenges in the Video Rental Industry   C44**

Gareth R. Jones, *Texas A&M University*

Blockbuster faces disruptive technologies and serious questions about the continued viability of its business model.

Case 5   **Whole Foods Market: Will There Be Enough Organic Food to Satisfy the Growing Demand?   C60**

Patricia Harasta and Alan N. Hoffman, *Bentley College*

How an entrepreneurial idea takes on a life of its own, grows rapidly into a multi-country phenomenon, and faces issues of stability and consolidation of growth, without destroying its roots and culture.

Case 6   **3M in 2006   C69**

Charles W. L. Hill, *University of Washington*

A company known for innovation uses new products as the basis of its corporate strategy, providing insight into its culture and evolving global strategy.

Case 7   **Philips versus Matsushita: A New Century, a New Round   C85**

Christopher A. Bartlett, *Harvard Business School*

A contrast of the strategy development and operations of a European and a Japanese electronic conglomerate.

Case 8   **Mired in Corruption—Kellogg Brown & Root in Nigeria   C100**

Charles W. L. Hill, *University of Washington*

A profile of the difference between legal and ethical acts and an evaluation of KBR's actions and systems with regard to ethical and legal conduct.

Notes   N1

Test Prepper Answers   A1

Index   I1

Preface

The first edition of *Essentials of Strategic Management* was well received by instructors and students alike. Based on the feedback of users and reviewers, we revised our book in ways that help students understand the importance of strategic management in today's global world. It is clear that strategic management instructors share with us a concern for currency in text and examples to ensure that cutting-edge issues and new developments in strategic management are addressed. And, in the revision, we have updated all the text material and the cases at the end of the book to present a clear and current account of strategic management.

Our goal in this revision is to explain in a clear, comprehensive, but concise way why strategic management is important to people, the companies they work for, and the societies in which they live. Often people are unaware of how the strategy-making process affects them. We are all used to going to work and visiting companies such as restaurants, stores, and banks to buy the goods and services we need to satisfy our many needs. However, the actual strategic management activities and processes that are required to make these goods and services available to us commonly go unappreciated. Similarly, we know that companies exist to make a "profit," but what is profit, how is it created, and what is it used for? Moreover, what are the actual strategic management activities involved in the creation of goods and services, and why is it that some companies seem to be more effective and more "profitable" than others? Our goal is to provide the "big picture" of what strategic management is, what strategic managers do, and how the strategy-making process affects company performance. The book provides a focused, integrated approach that gives students a solid understanding of the nature, functions, and main building blocks of strategic management.

Organization of the Book

The book presents a broad overview of the nature and functions of strategic management in nine chapters. Part 1, *Introduction to Strategic Management,* explains what strategic management is and provides a framework for understanding what strategic managers do. Chapter 1 discusses the relationship between strategic management and strategic leadership and shows how competitive advantage results in superior performance. It also describes the plan of this book and discusses the principal functions of strategic managers. Chapter 2 discusses the ways in which companies affect their stakeholders and why it is necessary to create corporate governance mechanisms that ensure that strategic managers work to further the interests of stakeholders and behave ethically.

In Part 2, *The Nature of Competitive Advantage,* we discuss the factors and forces both external and internal to an organization that determine its choice of strategies for creating a competitive advantage and achieving above-average profitability.

Chapter 3 looks at opportunities, threats, and competition in the external environment. Chapter 4 examines how a company can build competitive advantage by achieving superior efficiency, quality, innovation, and responsiveness to customers. It also discusses how managers can craft functional-level strategies that will allow an organization to achieve these goals.

In Part 3, *Building and Sustaining Long-Run Competitive Advantage,* we provide a streamlined discussion of the different levels of strategy that must be developed to build and sustain a long-term competitive advantage. Chapter 5 considers how to use business-level strategies to optimize competitive positioning and outperform industry rivals. Chapter 6 discusses how to strengthen competitive advantage by expanding globally into new national markets. Chapter 7 then examines the various corporate-level strategies, such as vertical integration, diversification, and outsourcing, that are used to protect and strengthen competitive advantage and sustain long-run profitability.

Finally, in Part 4, *Strategy Implementation,* we examine the many operational issues involved in putting all these strategies into action simultaneously. Chapter 8 first discusses the importance of strategic change in today's fast-moving global environment and the issues and problems involved in managing the change process effectively. Then it outlines how to build and develop a company's business through the use of internal new venturing, acquisitions, and strategic alliances and considers the pros and cons of these different methods. Chapter 9 discusses how to implement strategy through the design of organization structure and the operational issues involved in selecting structures to match the needs of particular strategies. It also looks at the organizational control systems necessary to fit strategy to structure and the role of organizational culture in developing competitive advantage.

As you can see by perusing the table of contents, the approach we take in *Essentials of Strategic Management* parallels that of our other book, *Strategic Management: An Integrated Approach.* Our goal is to offer a contemporary, integrated account of strategic management, but one that is streamlined and focused only on the essentials of this complex and fascinating subject.

Learning Features

Nothing makes the practice of strategic management come alive more than vivid stories and examples about people and companies that demonstrate clearly the meaning of the chapter material. Hands-on exercises offer students the opportunity to actively think about and engage in strategic-management issues and decision making. We paid considerable attention to creating and developing both in-chapter and end-of-chapter features and exercises that would offer the most learning value to students while economizing on their valuable learning time.

Each of the chapters has been revised. Several new *Strategy in Action* boxes have been carefully selected and written to raise students' interest; these have been integrated seamlessly into the text so as not to disrupt its flow. Many books have examples that disrupt students' thought processes or distract them with enormous amounts of unnecessary detail; *Essentials of Strategic Management* avoids these pitfalls.

Similarly, in the revised edition, the end-of-chapter learning features include four types of exercises, each of which offers additional insight into the chapter material to build students' learning experience. Exercises are designed to create lively discussion at the level of either the whole class, small groups, or the individual. In practice, instructors will have to decide which of these exercises to use in any particular class period and which to use as homework assignments. Frequently, instructors find that varying the exercises they use over the semester is the best way to engage students.

- *Discussion Questions.* Among these chapter-related questions and points for reflection are some that ask students to research actual management issues and learn firsthand from practicing managers.

- *Small-Group Exercise.* Each interactive experiential exercise is designed to be utilized in groups of three to four students. The instructor calls on students to break up into small groups simply by turning to people around them, and all students participate in the exercise in class. In each chapter, the exercise deals with a chapter-related issue guaranteed to lead to debate among students. A mechanism is provided for the different groups to share what they have learned with one another.

- *Exploring the Web.* This exercise asks the student to visit the website of a company and use the information contained on that website to answer a series of chapter-related questions.

Each chapter also ends with a short case, which can be used for further analysis of chapter issues. These cases have been carefully chosen to reflect contemporary issues and problems in strategic management and to offer further information on chapter issues. The accompanying discussion questions encourage students to read about and analyze how managers approach real problems in the strategic management world.

Finally, in the revised edition, a new set of eight longer cases is included at the end of the book to allow students to perform an in-depth analysis of the way a company has formulated and implemented its strategy. These cases are often focused on a specific strategic management topic—for example, analyzing the competitive environment (Blockbuster's Challenges in the Video Rental Industry; Whole Foods Market: Will There Be Enough Organic Food to Satisfy the Growing Demand?); building competitive advantage (3M in 2006); developing business-level strategy (Apple Computer; Amazon.com); changing corporate and global strategy over time (Boeing Commercial Aircraft: Comeback?; Philips versus Matsushita: A New Century, a New Round); and evaluating ethical and legal conduct (Mired in Corruption—Kellogg Brown & Root in Nigeria). Students can be asked to collect additional information on the companies in these cases, both to bring the analysis up to date and to see how managers have worked to increase competitive advantage and performance over time.

Acknowledgments

Finding a way to integrate and present an overview of the rapidly changing world of strategic management and strategic management activities and make it interesting and meaningful for students is not an easy task. In writing *Essentials of Strategic Management,* we have been fortunate to have had the assistance of several people who contributed greatly to the book's final form. First, we are grateful to Michele Rhoads, our acquisitions editor, for her support and commitment to the project, which led to its realization, and for finding ways to provide the resources that are needed to continually improve and refine a new product. Then we are grateful to Suzanna Bainbridge for taking on the task of ensuring that the book would meet the needs of its users and satisfy students and for providing us with useful feedback and information from professors and reviewers that have allowed us to shape the book to meet the needs of its intended market. Third, we are grateful to Margaret Bridges for so ably coordinating the book's progress. All these people have been instrumental in creating a product we hope will meet its goal of helping students better understand strategic management and the many ways in which it affects companies and the people who work in them.

Finally, we are indebted to the many colleagues and reviewers who provided us with useful and detailed feedback, perceptive comments, and valuable suggestions for improving the manuscript.

Kevin Banning, *Auburn University*
Robert D'Intino, *Rowan University*
Scott Droege, *Western Kentucky University*
Deborah Francis, *Brevard College*
Sanjay Goel, *University of Minnesota*
Leslie Haugen, *University of St. Thomas*
Todd Hostager, *University of Wisconsin—Eau Claire*
John Humphreys, *Eastern New Mexico University*
Deborah Johnson, *Franklin University*
Kevin L. Johnson, *Baylor University*
Elene Kent, *Capital University*
Subodh Kulkarni, *Howard University*
Kamalesh Kumar, *University of Michigan—Dearborn*
Paul Mallette, *Colorado State University*
Josetta McLaughlin, *Roosevelt University*
Tom Morris, *Radford University*
David Olson, *California State—Bakersfield*
William Ritchie, *Florida Gulf Coast University*
Tim Rogers, *Ozarks Technical College*
Stuart Rosenberg, *Dowling College*
Manjula Salimath, *University of North Texas*
Thomas Sgritta, *University of North Carolina—Charlotte*
Chanchai Tangpong, *North Dakota State University*
Michael Wakefield, *Colorado State University—Pueblo*
Edward Ward, *St. Cloud State University*
Kenneth Wendeln, *University of San Diego*
Garland Wiggs, *Hamline University*
Jun Zhao, *Governors State University*

Charles W. L. Hill, *Seattle, Washington*
Gareth R. Jones, *College Station, Texas*

Chapter 1

The Strategy-Making Process

Learning Objectives

After reading this chapter, you should be able to

1. Explain what is meant by "competitive advantage"

2. Discuss the strategic role of managers at different levels in an organization

3. Identify the main steps in a strategic planning process

4. Discuss the main pitfalls of planning, and how those pitfalls can be avoided

5. Outline the cognitive biases that might lead to poor strategic decisions, and explain how these biases can be overcome

6. Discuss the role played by strategic leaders in the strategy-making process

Chapter Outline

I. Competitive Advantage and Superior Performance
II. Strategic Managers
  a. Corporate-Level Managers
  b. Business-Level Managers
  c. Functional-Level Managers
III. The Strategy-Making Process
  a. A Model of the Strategic Planning Process
  b. The Feedback Loop
IV. Strategy as an Emergent Process
  a. Strategy Making in an Unpredictable World
  b. Autonomous Action: Strategy Making by Lower-Level Managers
  c. Serendipity and Strategy
  d. Intended and Emergent Strategies
V. Strategic Planning in Practice
  a. Scenario Planning
  b. Decentralized Planning
  c. Strategic Intent
VI. Strategic Decision Making
  a. Cognitive Biases
  b. Improving Decision Making
VII. Strategic Leadership
  a. Vision, Eloquence, and Consistency
  b. Commitment
  c. Being Well Informed
  d. Willingness to Delegate and Empower
  e. The Astute Use of Power
  f. Emotional Intelligence

Overview

Why do some companies succeed while others fail? In the fast-evolving world of the Internet, for example, how is it that companies like Yahoo!, Amazon.com, eBay, and Google have managed to attract millions of customers, while others like online grocer Webvan, software retailer Egghead.com, and the online pet supplies retailer Pets.com all went bankrupt? Why has Wal-Mart been able to do so well in the fiercely competitive retail industry, while others like Kmart have struggled? In the personal computer industry, what distinguishes Dell from less successful companies such as Gateway? In the airline industry, how has Southwest Airlines managed to keep increasing its revenues and profits through both good times and bad, while rivals such as US Airways and United Airlines have had to seek bankruptcy protection? What explains the persistent growth and profitability of Nucor Steel, now the largest steel maker in America, during a period when many of its once larger rivals have disappeared into bankruptcy?

strategy

A set of actions that managers take to increase their company's performance relative to rivals.

In this book, we argue that the strategies a company's managers pursue have a major impact on its performance relative to rivals. A **strategy** is a set of actions that managers take to increase their company's performance relative to rivals. If a company's strategy does result in superior performance, it is said to have a *competitive advantage.*

Much of this book is about identifying and describing the strategies that managers can pursue to achieve superior performance. A central aim of this book is to give you a thorough understanding of the analytical techniques and skills necessary to identify and implement strategies successfully. The first step toward achieving this objective is to describe in more detail what *superior performance* and *competitive advantage* mean.

Competitive Advantage and Superior Performance

profitability

The return that a company makes on the capital invested in the enterprise.

Superior performance is typically thought of in terms of one company's profitability relative to that of other companies in the same or a similar kind of business or industry. The **profitability** of a company can be measured by the return that it makes on the capital invested in the enterprise.[1] The return on invested capital that a company earns is defined as its profit over the capital invested in the firm (profit/capital invested). By *profit,* we mean after-tax earnings. By *capital,* we mean the sum of money invested in the company—that is, stockholders' equity plus debt owed to creditors. This capital is used to buy the resources a company needs to produce and sell goods and services. A company that uses its resources efficiently makes a positive return on invested capital. The more efficient a company is, the higher are its profitability and return on invested capital.

A company's profitability—its return on invested capital—is determined by the strategies its managers adopt. For example, Wal-Mart's strategy of focusing on the realization of cost savings from efficient logistics and information systems, and then passing on the bulk of these cost savings to customers in the form of lower prices, has enabled the company to gain ever more market share, reap significant economies of scale, and further lower its cost structure, thereby boosting profitability (for details, see the Running Case on Wal-Mart).

competitive advantage

The advantage over rivals achieved when a company's profitability is greater than the average profitability of all firms in its industry.

sustained competitive advantage

The competitive advantage achieved when a company is able to maintain above-average profitability for a number of years.

A company is said to have a **competitive advantage** over its rivals when its profitability is greater than the average profitability for all firms in its industry. The greater the extent to which a company's profitability exceeds the average profitability for its industry, the greater is its competitive advantage. A company is said to have a **sustained competitive advantage** when it is able to maintain above-average profitability for a number of years. Companies like Wal-Mart, Southwest, and Dell have had a significant and sustained competitive advantage because they have pursued firm-specific strategies that result in superior performance.

It is important to note that, in addition to its strategies, a company's performance is also determined by the characteristics of the industry the company competes in. Different industries are characterized by different competitive conditions. In some, demand is growing rapidly, while in others it is contracting. Some might be beset by excess capacity and persistent price wars, others by excess demand and rising prices. In some, technological change might be revolutionizing competition. Others might be characterized by a lack of technological change. In some industries, high profitability among incumbent companies might induce new companies to enter the industry, and these new entrants might depress prices and profits. In other industries, new entry might be difficult, and periods of high profitability might persist for a considerable time. Thus, average profitability is higher in some industries and lower in other industries because competitive conditions vary from industry to industry.[2]

Strategic Managers

general managers

Managers who bear responsibility for the overall performance of the company or for that of one of its major self-contained subunits or divisions.

functional managers

Managers responsible for supervising a particular function—that is, a task, activity, or operation like accounting, marketing, R&D, information technology, or logistics.

multidivisional company

A company that competes in several different businesses and has created a separate self-contained division to manage each of them.

Managers are the linchpin in the strategy-making process. It is individual managers who must take responsibility for formulating strategies to attain a competitive advantage and putting those strategies into effect. They must lead the strategy-making process. Here we look at the strategic roles of different types of managers. Later in the chapter, we discuss strategic leadership, which is how managers can effectively lead the strategy-making process.

In most companies, there are two main types of managers: **general managers,** who bear responsibility for the overall performance of the company or for one of its major self-contained subunits or divisions, and **functional managers,** who are responsible for supervising a particular function—that is, a task, activity, or operation like accounting, marketing, R&D, information technology, or logistics.

A company is a collection of functions or departments that work together to bring a particular product or service to the market. If a company provides several different kinds of products or services, it often duplicates these functions and creates a series of self-contained divisions (each of which contains its own set of functions) to manage each different product or service. The general managers of these divisions then become responsible for their particular product line. The overriding concern of general managers is the health of the whole company or division under their direction; they are responsible for deciding how to create a competitive advantage and achieve high profitability with the resources and capital they have at their disposal. Figure 1.1 shows the organization of a **multidivisional company**—that is, a company that competes in several different businesses and has created a separate self-contained division to manage each of these. As you can see, there are three main

Figure 1.1

Levels of Strategic Management

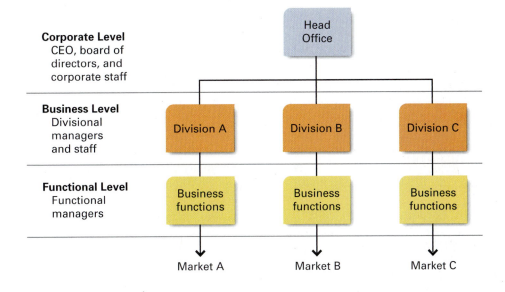

RUNNING CASE

Wal-Mart's Competitive Advantage

Wal-Mart is one of the most extraordinary success stories in business history. Started in 1962 by Sam Walton, Wal-Mart has grown to become the world's largest corporation. In the financial year ending January 31, 2007, the discount retailer, whose mantra is "everyday low prices," had sales of nearly $345 billion, 7,600 stores in fifteen countries (some 4,600 are in the United States), and 1.9 million employees. Some 8% of all retail sales in the United States are made at a Wal-Mart store. Wal-Mart is not only large; it is also very profitable. In 2006, the company earned a return on invested capital of 14.1%, doing better than its well-managed rivals Costco and Target,

which earned 11.9% and 12.6%, respectively (another major rival, Kmart, emerged from bankruptcy protection in 2004). As shown in the accompanying figure, Wal-Mart has been consistently more profitable than its rivals for years, although of late its rivals have been closing the gap.

Wal-Mart's persistently superior profitability reflects a competitive advantage that is based upon a number of strategies. Back in 1962, Wal-Mart was one of the first companies to apply the self-service supermarket business model developed by grocery chains to general merchandise (two of its rivals, Kmart and Target, were established in the same year). Unlike its rivals,

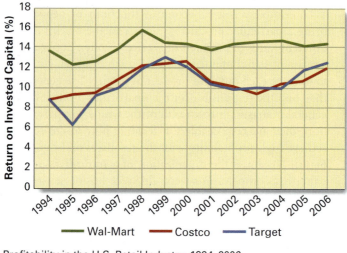

Profitability in the U.S. Retail Industry, 1994–2006

Source: Data from Value Line Investment Survey.

levels of management: corporate, business, and functional. General managers are found at the first two of these levels, but their strategic roles differ depending on their sphere of responsibility.

● **Corporate-Level Managers**   The corporate level of management consists of the chief executive officer (CEO), other senior executives, the board of directors, and corporate staff. These individuals occupy the apex of decision making within the organization. The CEO is the principal general manager. In consultation with other senior executives, the role which focused on urban and suburban locations, Sam Walton's Wal-Mart concentrated on small southern towns. Wal-Mart grew quickly by pricing lower than local mom-and-pop retailers, often putting them out of business. By the time Kmart and Target realized that small towns could support a large discount general merchandise store, Wal-Mart had already pre-empted them. These towns, which were large enough to support one discount retailer, but not two, provided a secure profit base for Wal-Mart.

The company was also an innovator in information systems, logistics, and human resource practices. Taken together, these strategies resulted in higher productivity and lower costs, which enabled the company to earn a high profit while charging low prices. Wal-Mart led the way among American retailers in developing and implementing sophisticated product tracking systems using bar-code technology and checkout scanners. This information technology enabled Wal-Mart to track what was selling and adjust its inventory accordingly, so that the products found in a store matched local demand. By avoiding overstocking, Wal-Mart did not have to hold periodic sales to shift unsold inventory. Over time, Wal-Mart linked this information system to a nationwide network of distribution centers, where inventory was stored and then shipped to stores within a 400-mile radius on a daily basis. The combination of distribution centers and information centers enabled Wal-Mart to reduce the amount of inventory it held in stores, thereby devoting more of that valuable space to selling and reducing the amount of capital it had tied up in inventory.

With regard to human resources, the tone was set by Sam Walton, who held a strong belief that employees should be respected and rewarded for helping to improve the profitability of the company. Underpinning this belief, Walton referred to employees as "associates." He established a profit-sharing scheme for all employees and, after the company went public in 1970, a program that allowed employees to purchase Wal-Mart stock at a discount to its market value. Wal-Mart was rewarded for this approach by high employee productivity, which translated into lower operating costs and higher profitability.

As Wal-Mart grew larger, the sheer size and purchasing power of the company enabled it to drive down the prices that it paid suppliers. Passing on those savings to customers in the form of lower prices enabled Wal-Mart to gain more market share and hence demand even lower prices. To take the sting out of the persistent demands for lower prices, Wal-Mart shared its sales information with suppliers on a daily basis, enabling them to gain efficiencies by configuring their own production schedules to sales at Wal-Mart.

By the time the 1990s came along, Wal-Mart was already the largest general seller of general merchandise in America. To keep its growth going, Wal-Mart started to diversify into the grocery business, opening 200,000-square-foot supercenter stores that sold groceries and general merchandise under the same roof. Wal-Mart also diversified into the warehouse club business with the establishment of Sam's Club. The company began expanding internationally in 1991 with its entry into Mexico.

For all its success, however, Wal-Mart is now encountering very real limits to profitable growth. The U.S. market is approaching saturation, and growth overseas has proved more difficult than the company had hoped. The company was forced to exit Germany and South Korea after losing money there, and it has found it tough going in several other developed nations such as Britain. Moreover, rivals Target and Costco have continued to improve their performance and are now snapping at Wal-Mart's heels.[a]

of *corporate-level managers* is to oversee the development of strategies for the whole organization. This role includes defining the goals of the organization, determining what businesses it should be in, allocating resources among the different businesses, formulating and implementing strategies that span individual businesses, and providing leadership for the entire organization.

Consider General Electric (GE) as an example. GE is active in a wide range of businesses, including lighting equipment, major appliances, motor and transportation equipment, turbine generators, construction and engineering services, industrial electronics, medical systems, aerospace, aircraft engines, and financial services.

The main strategic responsibilities of its CEO, Jeffrey Immelt, are setting overall strategic goals, allocating resources among the different business areas, deciding whether the firm should divest itself of any of its businesses, and determining whether it should acquire any new ones. In other words, it is up to Immelt to develop strategies that span individual businesses; his concern is with building and managing the corporate portfolio of businesses to maximize corporate profitability.

It is *not* Immelt's specific responsibility to develop strategies for competing in the individual business areas, such as financial services. The development of such strategies is the responsibility of the general managers of these different businesses, or *business-level managers.* However, it *is* Immelt's responsibility to probe the strategic thinking of business-level managers to make sure that they are pursuing strategies that will contribute toward the maximization of GE's long-run profitability, to coach and motivate those managers, to reward them for attaining or exceeding goals, and to hold them to account for poor performance.

Corporate-level managers also provide a link between the people who oversee the strategic development of a firm and those who own it (the shareholders). Corporate-level managers, and particularly the CEO, can be viewed as the agents of shareholders.[3] It is their responsibility to ensure that the corporate and business strategies that the company pursues are consistent with maximizing profitability and profit growth. If they are not, then ultimately the CEO is likely to be called to account by the shareholders.

● Business-Level Managers

business unit

A self-contained division (with its own functions— for example, finance, purchasing, production, and marketing departments) that provides a product or service for a particular market.

A **business unit** is a self-contained division (with its own functions—for example, finance, purchasing, production, and marketing departments) that provides a product or service for a particular market. The principal general manager at the business level, or the business-level manager, is the head of the division. The strategic role of these managers is to translate the general statements of direction and intent that come from the corporate level into concrete strategies for individual businesses. Thus, whereas corporate-level general managers are concerned with strategies that span individual businesses, business-level general managers are concerned with strategies that are specific to a particular business. At GE, a major corporate goal is to be first or second in every business in which the corporation competes. Then the general managers of each division work out for their business the details of a business model that is consistent with this objective.

● Functional-Level Managers

Functional-level managers are responsible for the specific business functions or operations (human resources, purchasing, product development, customer service, and so on) that constitute a company or one of its divisions. Thus, a functional manager's sphere of responsibility is generally confined to *one* organizational activity, whereas general managers oversee the operation of a *whole* company or division. Although they are not responsible for the overall performance of the organization, functional managers nevertheless have a major strategic role: to develop functional strategies in their area that help fulfill the strategic objectives set by business- and corporate-level general managers.

In GE's aerospace business, for instance, manufacturing managers are responsible for developing manufacturing strategies consistent with the corporate objective of being first or second in that industry. Moreover, functional managers provide most of the information that makes it possible for business- and corporate-level general managers to formulate realistic and attainable strategies. Indeed, because they are closer to the customer than the typical general manager is, functional managers themselves may generate important ideas that subsequently become major strategies for the company. Thus, it is important for general managers to listen closely to the ideas of their functional managers. An equally great responsibility for managers at the operational level is strategy implementation: the execution of corporate- and business-level plans.

The Strategy-Making Process

Now that we know something about the strategic roles of managers, we can turn our attention to the process by which managers formulate and implement strategies. Many writers have emphasized that strategy is the outcome of a formal planning process and that top management plays the most important role in this process.[4] Although this view has some basis in reality, it is not the whole story. As we shall see later in the chapter, valuable strategies often emerge from deep within the organization without prior planning. Nevertheless, a consideration of formal, rational planning is a useful starting point for our journey into the world of strategy. Here we consider what might be described as a typical formal strategic planning model for making strategy.

● **A Model of the Strategic Planning Process**

The formal strategic planning process has five main steps:

1. Select the corporate mission and major corporate goals.

2. Analyze the organization's external competitive environment to identify *opportunities* and *threats.*

3. Analyze the organization's internal operating environment to identify the organization's *strengths* and *weaknesses.*

4. Select strategies that build on the organization's strengths and correct its weaknesses in order to take advantage of external opportunities and counter external threats. These strategies should be consistent with the mission and major goals of the organization. They should be congruent and constitute a viable business model.

5. Implement the strategies.

strategy formulation

Analyzing the organization's external and internal environments and then selecting appropriate strategies.

strategy implementation

Putting strategies into action.

The task of analyzing the organization's external and internal environments and then selecting appropriate strategies is known as **strategy formulation.** In contrast, **strategy implementation** involves putting the strategies (or plan) into action. This includes taking actions consistent with the selected strategies of the company at the corporate, business, and functional levels, allocating roles and responsibilities among managers (typically through the design of organization structure), allocating resources (including capital and people), setting short-term objectives, and designing the organization's control and reward systems. These steps are illustrated in Figure 1.2 (which can also be viewed as a plan for the rest of this book).

Each step in Figure 1.2 constitutes a *sequential* step in the strategic planning process. In step 1, each round or cycle of the planning process begins with a statement of the corporate mission and major corporate goals. As shown in Figure 1.2, this statement is shaped by the existing business model of the company. The mission statement is followed by the foundation of strategic thinking: external analysis, internal analysis, and strategic choice. The strategy-making process ends with the design of the organization structure, culture, and control systems necessary to implement the organization's chosen strategy.

Figure 1.2

A Model of the Strategic
Management Process

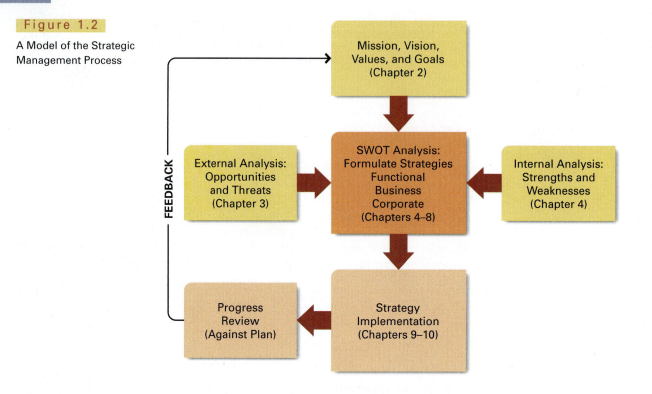

Some organizations go through a new cycle of the strategic planning process every year. This does not necessarily mean that managers choose a new strategy each year. In many instances, the result is simply to modify and reaffirm a strategy and structure already in place. The strategic plans generated by the planning process generally look out over a period of one to five years, with the plan being updated, or *rolled forward,* every year. In most organizations, the results of the annual strategic planning process are used as input into the budgetary process for the coming year so that strategic planning is used to shape resource allocation within the organization.

Mission Statement The first component of the strategic management process is crafting the organization's mission statement, which provides the framework or context within which strategies are formulated. A mission statement has four main components: a statement of the *raison d'être* of a company or organization—its reason for existence—which is normally referred to as the *mission*; a statement of some desired future state, usually referred to as the *vision*; a statement of the *key values* that the organization is committed to; and a statement of *major goals.*

For example, the current mission of Microsoft is "to enable people and businesses throughout the world to realize their full potential." The vision of the company—the overarching goal—is to be the major player in the software industry. The key values that the company is committed to include "integrity and honesty," "passion for our customers, our partners, and our technology," "openness and respectfulness," and "taking on big challenges and seeing them through." Microsoft's mission statement has absolutely set the context for strategy formulation within the company. Thus, the company's perseverance—first with Windows and now with Xbox, both of which took a long time to bear fruit—exemplifies the idea of "taking on big challenges and seeing them through."[5]

We shall return to this topic and discuss it in depth in the next chapter.

EXTERNAL ANALYSIS   The second component of the strategic management process is an analysis of the organization's external operating environment. The essential purpose of the external analysis is to identify strategic *opportunities* and *threats* in the organization's operating environment that will affect how it pursues its mission. Three interrelated environments should be examined at this stage: the *industry environment* in which the company operates, the country or *national environment,* and the wider socioeconomic environment or *macroenvironment.*

Analyzing the industry environment requires an assessment of the competitive structure of the company's industry, including the competitive position of the company and its major rivals. It also requires analysis of the nature, stage, dynamics, and history of the industry. Because many markets are now global markets, analyzing the industry environment also means assessing the impact of globalization on competition within an industry. Such an analysis may reveal that a company should move some production facilities to another nation, that it should aggressively expand in emerging markets such as China, or that it should beware of new competition from emerging nations. Analyzing the macroenvironment consists of examining macroeconomic, social, governmental, legal, international, and technological factors that may affect the company and its industry. We consider these issues in Chapter 3 and Chapter 6 (where we discuss global issues).

INTERNAL ANALYSIS   Internal analysis, the third component of the strategic planning process, serves to pinpoint the *strengths* and *weaknesses* of the organization. Such issues as identifying the quantity and quality of a company's resources and capabilities and ways of building unique skills and company-specific or distinctive competencies are considered here when we probe the sources of competitive advantage. Building and sustaining a competitive advantage requires a company to achieve superior efficiency, quality, innovation, and responsiveness to its customers. Company strengths lead to superior performance in these areas, whereas company weaknesses translate into inferior performance. We discuss these issues in Chapter 4.

SWOT ANALYSIS   The next component of strategic thinking requires the generation of a series of strategic alternatives, or choices of future strategies to pursue, given the company's internal strengths and weaknesses and its external opportunities and threats. The comparison of strengths, weaknesses, opportunities, and threats is normally referred to as a **SWOT analysis.**[6] Its central purpose is to identify the strategies that will create a company-specific business model that will best *align, fit,* or *match* a company's resources and capabilities to the demands of the environment in which it operates. Managers compare and contrast the various alternative possible strategies against each other with respect to their ability to achieve a competitive advantage. Thinking strategically requires managers to identify the set of strategies that will create and sustain a competitive advantage:

SWOT analysis

The comparison of strengths, weaknesses, opportunities, and threats.

- *Functional-level strategy,* directed at improving the effectiveness of operations, such as manufacturing, marketing, materials management, product development, and customer service, within a company. We consider functional-level strategies in Chapter 4.

- *Business-level strategy,* which encompasses the business's overall competitive theme, the way it positions itself in the marketplace to gain a competitive advantage, and the different positioning strategies that can be used in different industry settings—for example, *cost leadership, differentiation, focusing on a particular niche or segment of the industry,* or some combination of these. We consider business-level strategies in Chapter 5.

- *Global strategy,* which addresses how to expand operations outside the home country to grow and prosper in a world where competitive advantage is determined at a global level. We consider global strategies in Chapter 6.

- *Corporate-level strategy,* which answers these primary questions: What business or businesses should we be in to maximize the long-run profitability and profit growth of the organization? How should we enter and increase our presence in these businesses to gain a competitive advantage? We consider corporate-level strategies in Chapters 7 and 8.

The strategies identified through a SWOT analysis should be congruent with each other. Thus, functional-level strategies should be consistent with, or support, the business-level strategy and global strategy of the company. Moreover, as we explain later in this book, corporate-level strategies should support business-level strategies.

STRATEGY IMPLEMENTATION   Having chosen a set of congruent strategies to achieve a competitive advantage and increase performance, managers must put those strategies into action: strategy has to be implemented. Strategy implementation involves taking actions at the functional, business, and corporate levels to execute a strategic plan. Thus, implementation can include, for example, putting quality improvement programs into place, changing the way a product is designed, positioning the product differently in the marketplace, segmenting the marketing and offering different versions of the product to different consumer groups, implementing price increases or decreases, expanding through mergers and acquisitions, or downsizing by closing down or selling off parts of the company. All of this and much more is discussed in detail in Chapters 4 through 8.

Strategy implementation also entails designing the best organization structure, culture, and control systems to put a chosen strategy into action. We discuss the organization structure, culture, and controls required to implement strategy in Chapters 9 and 10.

- **The Feedback Loop**   The feedback loop in Figure 1.2 indicates that strategic planning is ongoing; it *never* ends. Once a strategy has been implemented, its execution must be monitored to determine the extent to which strategic goals and objectives are actually being achieved and to what degree competitive advantage is being created and sustained. This knowledge is passed back up to the corporate level through feedback loops and becomes the input for the next round of strategy formulation and implementation. Top managers can then decide whether to reaffirm existing strategies and goals or suggest changes for the future. For example, a strategic goal may prove to be too optimistic, and so the next time a more conservative goal is set. Or feedback may reveal that the strategy is not working, so managers may seek ways to change it.

Strategy as an Emergent Process

The basic planning model suggests that a company's strategies are the result of a plan, that the strategic planning process itself is rational and highly structured, and that the process is orchestrated by top management. Several scholars have criticized the formal planning model for three main reasons: the unpredictability of the real world, the role that lower-level managers can play in the strategic management process, and the fact that many successful strategies are often the result of serendipity, not rational strategizing. They have advocated an alternative view of strategy making.[7]

Strategy Making in an Unpredictable World

Critics of formal planning systems argue that we live in a world in which uncertainty, complexity, and ambiguity dominate and in which small chance events can have a large and unpredictable impact on outcomes.[8] In such circumstances, they claim, even the most carefully thought-out strategic plans are prone to being rendered useless by rapid and unforeseen change. In an unpredictable world, there is a premium on being able to respond quickly to changing circumstances, altering the strategies of the organization accordingly.

A dramatic example of this occurred in 1994 and 1995 when Microsoft CEO Bill Gates shifted the company strategy after the unanticipated emergence of the World Wide Web (see the Strategy in Action feature). According to critics of formal systems, such a flexible approach to strategy making is not possible within the framework of a traditional strategic planning process, with its implicit assumption that an organization's strategies need to be reviewed only during the annual strategic planning exercise.

Autonomous Action: Strategy Making by Lower-Level Managers

autonomous action

Action taken by lower-level managers who, on their own initiative, formulate new strategies and work to persuade top-level managers to alter the strategic priorities of a company.

Another criticism leveled at the rational planning model of strategy is that too much importance is attached to the role of top management, and particularly the CEO.[9] An alternative view now widely accepted is that individual employees deep within an organization can and often do exert a profound influence over the strategic direction of the firm.[10] Writing with Robert Burgelman of Stanford University, Andy Grove, the former CEO of Intel, noted that many important strategic decisions at Intel were initiated not by top managers but by the **autonomous action** of lower-level managers deep within Intel—that is, by lower-level managers who, on their own initiative, formulated new strategies and worked to persuade top-level managers to alter the strategic priorities of the firm.[11] At Intel, strategic decisions that were initiated by the autonomous action of lower-level managers included the decision to exit an important market (the DRAM memory chip market) and develop a certain class of microprocessors (RISC-based microprocessors) in direct contrast to the stated strategy of Intel's top managers. The Strategy in Action feature tells how autonomous action by two young employees drove the evolution of Microsoft's strategy toward the Internet. In addition, the prototype for another Microsoft product, the Xbox video game system, was developed by four lower-level engineering employees on their own initiative. They subsequently successfully lobbied top managers to dedicate resources to commercialize their prototype.

Autonomous action may be particularly important in helping established companies to deal with the uncertainty created by the arrival of a radical new technology that changes the dominant paradigm in an industry.[12] Top managers usually rise to preeminence by successfully executing the established strategy of the firm. Thus, they may have an emotional commitment to the status quo and are often unable to see things from a different perspective. In this sense, they are a conservative force that promotes inertia. Lower-level managers, however, are less likely to have the same commitment to the status quo and have more to gain from promoting new technologies and strategies within the firm. Thus, they may be first to recognize new strategic opportunities (as was the case at Microsoft) and lobby for strategic change.

Strategy in Action

A Strategic Shift at Microsoft

The Internet has been around since the 1970s, but prior to the early 1990s it was a drab place, lacking the color, content, and richness of today's environment. What changed the Internet from a scientific tool to a consumer-driven media environment was the invention of hypertext markup language (HTML) and the related invention of a browser for displaying graphics-rich webpages based on HTML. The combination of HTML and browsers effectively created the World Wide Web (WWW). This was a development that was unforeseen.

A young programmer at the University of Illinois in 1993, Mark Andreesen, had developed the first browser, known as Mosaic. In 1994, he left Illinois and joined a start-up company, Netscape, which produced an improved browser, the Netscape Navigator, along with software that enabled organizations to create webpages and host them on computer servers. These developments led to a dramatic and unexpected growth in the number of people connecting to the Internet. In 1990, the Internet had 1 million users. By early 1995, the number had exceeded 80 million and was growing exponentially.

Prior to the emergence of the Web, Microsoft did have a strategy for exploiting the Internet, but it was one that emphasized set-top boxes, video on demand, interactive TV, and an online service, MSN, modeled after AOL and based on proprietary standards. In early 1994, Gates received emails from two young employees, Jay Allard and Steve Sinofsky, who argued that Microsoft's current strategy was misguided and ignored the rapidly emerging Web. In companies with a more hierarchical culture, such action might have been ignored, but at Microsoft, which operates as a meritocracy in which good ideas trump hierarchical position, it produced a very different response. Gates convened a meeting of senior executives in April 1994, then wrote a memo to senior executives arguing that the Internet represented a sea change in computing and that Microsoft had to respond.

What ultimately emerged was a 180-degree shift in Microsoft's strategy. Interactive TV was placed on the back burner, and MSN was relaunched as a Web service based on HTML. Microsoft committed to developing its own browser technology and within a few months had issued Internet Explorer to compete with Netscape's Navigator (the underlying technology was gained by an acquisition). Microsoft licensed Java, a computer language designed to run programs on the Web, from a major competitor, Sun Microsystems. Internet protocols were built into Windows 95 and Windows NT, and Gates insisted that henceforth Microsoft's applications, such as the ubiquitous Office, embrace the WWW and have the ability to convert documents into an HTML format. The new strategy was given its final stamp of approval on December 7, 1995, Pearl Harbor Day, when Gates gave a speech arguing that the Internet was now pervasive in everything Microsoft was doing. By then, Microsoft had been pursuing the new strategy for a year. In short, Microsoft quickly went from a proprietary standards approach to one that embraced the public standards on the WWW.[b]

● **Serendipity and Strategy** Business history is replete with examples of accidental events that helped to push companies in new and profitable directions. What these examples suggest is that many successful strategies are not the result of well-thought-out plans but of serendipity—that is, stumbling across good things unexpectedly. One such example occurred at 3M during the 1960s. At that time, 3M was producing fluorocarbons for sale as coolant liquid in air-conditioning equipment. One day, a researcher working with fluorocarbons in a 3M lab spilled some of the liquid on her shoes. Later that day, when she spilled coffee over her shoes, she watched with interest as the coffee formed into little beads of liquid and then ran off her shoes without leaving a stain. Reflecting on this phenomenon, she realized that a fluorocarbon-based liquid might turn out to be useful for protecting fabrics from liquid stains, and so the idea for Scotchgard was born. Subsequently, Scotchgard became one of 3M's most profitable products and took the company into the fabric protection business, an area it had never planned to participate in.[13]

Serendipitous discoveries and events can open up all sorts of profitable avenues for a company. But some companies have missed out on profitable opportunities because serendipitous discoveries or events were inconsistent with their prior (planned) conception of what their strategy should be. In one of the classic examples of such myopia, a century ago the telegraph company Western Union turned down an opportunity to purchase the rights to an invention made by Alexander Graham Bell. The invention was the telephone, a technology that subsequently made the telegraph obsolete.

● Intended and Emergent Strategies

Henry Mintzberg has proposed a model of strategy development that provides a more encompassing view of what strategy actually is. According to this model, illustrated in Figure 1.3, a company's *realized strategy* is the product of whatever planned strategies are actually put into action (the company's deliberate strategies) *and* of any unplanned, or emergent, strategies.[14] In Mintzberg's view, many planned strategies are not implemented owing to unpredicted changes in the environment (they are unrealized). **Emergent strategies** are the unplanned responses to unforeseen circumstances. They arise from autonomous action by individual managers deep within the organization, from serendipitous discoveries or events, or from an unplanned strategic shift by top-level managers in response to changed circumstances. They are *not* the product of formal top-down planning mechanisms. Mintzberg maintains that emergent strategies are often successful and may be more appropriate than intended strategies. Moreover, as Mintzberg has noted, strategies can take root virtually wherever people have the capacity to learn and the resources to support that capacity.

emergent strategies

Strategies that "emerge" in the absence of planning.

In practice, the strategies of most organizations are probably a combination of the intended (planned) and the emergent. The message for management is that it needs to recognize the process of emergence and to intervene when appropriate, killing off bad emergent strategies but nurturing potentially good ones.[15] To make such decisions, managers must be able to judge the worth of emergent strategies. *They must be able to think strategically.* Although emergent strategies arise from within the organization without prior planning—that is, without going through the steps illustrated in Figure 1.3 in a *sequential* fashion—top management still has to evaluate emergent strategies. Such evaluation involves comparing each emergent

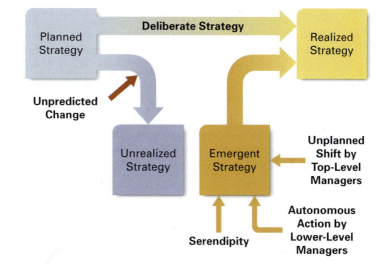

Figure 1.3

Emergent and Deliberate Strategies

Source: Adapted from H. Mintzberg and A. McGugh, "Strategy Formulation in an Adhocracy," *Administrative Science Quarterly* 30:2 (June 1985).

strategy with the organization's goals, external environmental opportunities and threats, and internal strengths and weaknesses. The objective is to assess whether the emergent strategy fits the company's needs and capabilities. In addition, Mintzberg stresses that an organization's capability to produce emergent strategies is a function of the kind of corporate culture that the organization's structure and control systems foster. In other words, the different components of the strategic management process are just as important from the perspective of emergent strategies as they are from the perspective of intended strategies.

Strategic Planning in Practice

Despite criticisms, research suggests that formal planning systems do help managers make better strategic decisions.[16] For strategic planning to work, however, it is important that top-level managers not just plan in the context of the *current* competitive environment but also try to find the strategy that will best allow them to achieve a competitive advantage in the *future* competitive environment. To try to forecast what that future will look like, managers can use scenario-planning techniques to plan for different possible futures. They can also involve operating managers in the planning process and seek to shape the future competitive environment by emphasizing strategic intent.

● **Scenario Planning**

scenario planning

Formulating plans that are based on "what if" scenarios about the future.

One reason that strategic planning may fail over the long run is that managers, in their initial enthusiasm for planning techniques, may forget that the future is inherently unpredictable. Even the best-laid plans can fall apart if unforeseen contingencies occur, and that happens all the time in the real world. Scenario planning is based upon the realization that the future is inherently unpredictable, and that an organization should plan for not just one future, but a range of possible futures. **Scenario planning** involves formulating plans that are based upon "what if" scenarios about the future. In the typical scenario-planning exercise, some scenarios are optimistic and some pessimistic. Teams of managers are asked to develop specific strategies to cope with each scenario. A set of indicators is chosen, and the indicators are used as "signposts" to track trends and identify the probability that any particular scenario will come to pass. The idea is to get managers to understand the dynamic and complex nature of their environment, to think through problems in a strategic fashion, and to generate a range of strategic options that might be pursued under different circumstances.[17] Use of the scenario approach to planning has spread rapidly among large companies. One survey found that over 50% of the *Fortune* 500 companies use some form of scenario-planning methods.[18]

The oil company Royal Dutch Shell has perhaps done more than most to pioneer the concept of scenario planning and its experience demonstrates the power of the approach.[19] Shell has been using scenario planning since the 1980s. Today, it uses two main scenarios to refine its strategic planning. The scenarios relate to future demand for oil. One, called "Dynamics as Usual," sees a gradual shift from carbon fuels, such as oil and natural gas, to renewable energy. The second scenario, "The Spirit of the Coming Age," looks at the possibility that a technological revolution will lead to a rapid shift to new energy sources.[20] Shell is making investments that will ensure the profitability of the company whichever scenario comes to pass, and it is carefully tracking technological and market trends for signs of which scenario is becoming more likely over time.

The great virtue of the scenario approach to planning is that it can push managers to think outside of the box, to anticipate what they might have to do in differ-

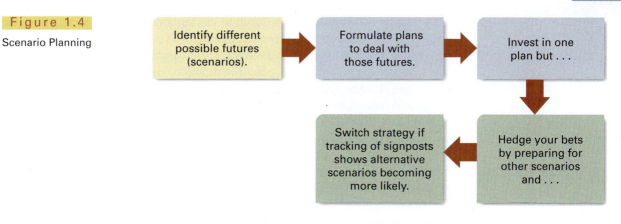

Figure 1.4

Scenario Planning

ent situations, and to learn that the world is a complex and unpredictable place that places a premium on flexibility, rather than inflexible plans based on assumptions about the future that may turn out to be incorrect. In many cases, as a result of scenario planning organizations might pursue one dominant strategy, related to the scenario that is judged to be most likely, but make some investments that will pay off if other scenarios come to the fore (see Figure 1.4). Thus the current strategy of Shell is based on the assumption that the world will only gradually shift away from carbon-based fuels (its "Dynamics as Usual" scenario), but the company is also hedging its bets by investing in new energy technologies and mapping out a strategy to pursue should its second scenario come to pass.

● **Decentralized Planning**

A mistake that some companies have made in constructing their strategic planning process has been to treat planning exclusively as a top management responsibility. This *ivory tower* approach can result in strategic plans formulated in a vacuum by top managers who have little understanding or appreciation of current operating realities. Consequently, top managers may formulate strategies that do more harm than good. For example, when demographic data indicated that houses and families were shrinking, planners at GE's appliance group concluded that smaller appliances were the wave of the future. Because they had little contact with homebuilders and retailers, they did not realize that kitchens and bathrooms were the two rooms that were *not* shrinking. Nor did they appreciate that working women wanted big refrigerators to cut down on trips to the supermarket. GE ended up wasting a lot of time designing small appliances with limited demand.

The ivory tower concept of planning can also lead to tensions between corporate-, business-, and functional-level managers. The experience of GE's appliance group is again illuminating. Many of the corporate managers in the planning group were recruited from consulting firms or top-flight business schools. Many of the functional managers took this pattern of recruitment to mean that corporate managers did not think they were smart enough to think through strategic problems for themselves. They felt shut out of the decision-making process, which they believed to be unfairly constituted. Out of this perceived lack of procedural justice grew an us-versus-them mindset that quickly escalated into hostility. As a result, even when the planners were right, operating managers would not listen to them. For example, the planners correctly recognized the importance of the globalization of the appliance market and the emerging Japanese threat. However, operating managers, who then saw Sears Roebuck as the competition, paid them little heed.

Finally, ivory tower planning ignores the important strategic role of autonomous action by lower-level managers and serendipity.

Correcting the ivory tower approach to planning requires recognizing that successful strategic planning encompasses managers at *all* levels of the corporation. Much of the best planning can and should be done by business and functional managers who are closest to the facts; planning should be decentralized. The role of corporate-level planners should be that of *facilitators* who help business and functional managers do the planning by setting the broad strategic goals of the organization and providing the resources required to identify the strategies that might be necessary to attain those goals.

● **Strategic Intent**   The formal strategic planning model has been characterized as the *fit model* of strategy making. This is because it attempts to achieve a fit between the internal resources and capabilities of an organization and external opportunities and threats in the industry environment. Gary Hamel and C. K. Prahalad have criticized the fit model because it can lead to a mindset in which management focuses too much on the degree of fit between the *existing* resources of a company and *current* environmental opportunities, and not enough on building *new* resources and capabilities to create and exploit *future* opportunities.[21] Strategies formulated with only the present in mind, argue Prahalad and Hamel, tend to be more concerned with today's problems than with tomorrow's opportunities. As a result, companies that rely exclusively on the fit approach to strategy formulation are unlikely to be able to build and maintain a competitive advantage. This is particularly true in a dynamic competitive environment, where new competitors are continually arising and new ways of doing business are constantly being invented.

As Prahalad and Hamel note, again and again, companies using the fit approach have been surprised by the ascent of competitors that initially seemed to lack the resources and capabilities needed to make them a real threat. This happened to Xerox, which ignored the rise of Canon and Ricoh in the photocopier market until they had become serious global competitors; to General Motors, which initially overlooked the threat posed by Toyota and Honda in the 1970s; and to Caterpillar, which ignored the danger Komatsu posed to its heavy earth-moving business until it was almost too late to respond.

The secret of the success of companies like Toyota, Canon, and Komatsu, according to Prahalad and Hamel, is that they all had bold ambitions that outstripped their existing resources and capabilities. All wanted to achieve global leadership, and they set out to build the resources and capabilities that would enable them to attain this goal. Consequently, top management created an obsession with winning at all levels of the organization that was sustained over a ten- to twenty-year quest for global leadership. It is this obsession that Prahalad and Hamel refer to as strategic intent. They stress that strategic intent is more than simply unfettered ambition. It encompasses an active management process, which includes "focusing the organization's attention on the essence of winning; motivating people by communicating the value of the target; leaving room for individual and team contributions; sustaining enthusiasm by providing new operational definitions as circumstances change; and using intent consistently to guide resource allocations."[22]

Thus, underlying the concept of strategic intent is the notion that strategic planning should be based on setting an ambitious vision and goals that stretch a company and then finding ways to build the resources and capabilities necessary to attain the vision and goals. As Prahalad and Hamel note, in practice the two approaches to strategy formulation are not mutually exclusive. All the components of the strategic management process that we discussed earlier (see Figure 1.2) are important.

In addition, say Prahalad and Hamel, the strategic management process should begin with a challenging vision, such as attaining global leadership, which stretches the organization. Throughout the subsequent process, the emphasis should be on finding ways (strategies) to develop the resources and capabilities necessary to achieve these goals rather than on exploiting *existing* strengths to take advantage of *existing* opportunities. The difference between strategic fit and strategic intent, therefore, may just be one of emphasis. Strategic intent is more internally focused and is concerned with building new resources and capabilities. Strategic fit focuses more on matching existing resources and capabilities to the external environment.

Strategic Decision Making

Even the best-designed strategic planning systems will fail to produce the desired results if managers do not use the information at their disposal effectively. Consequently, it is important that strategic managers learn to make better use of the information they have and understand the reasons they sometimes make poor decisions. One important way in which managers can make better use of their knowledge and information is to understand and manage their emotions during the course of decision making.[23]

● **Cognitive Biases**

cognitive biases

Systematic errors in human decision making that arise from the way people process information.

The rationality of human decision makers is bounded by our own cognitive capabilities.[24] It is difficult for us absorb and process large amounts of information effectively. As a result, when making decisions we tend to fall back on certain rules of thumb, or *heuristics,* that help us to make sense out of a complex and uncertain world. These heuristics can be quite useful, but sometimes their application can result in severe and systematic errors in the decision-making process.[25] Systematic errors are those that appear time and time again. They seem to arise from a series of **cognitive biases** in the way that human decision makers process information and reach decisions. Because of cognitive biases, many managers end up making poor decisions, even when they have good information at their disposal and use a good decision-making process that is consistent with the rational decision-making model.

prior hypothesis bias

A cognitive bias that occurs when decision makers who have strong prior beliefs tend to make decisions on the basis of these beliefs, even when presented with evidence that their beliefs are wrong.

Several biases have been verified repeatedly in laboratory settings, so we can be reasonably sure that they exist and that we are all prone to them.[26] The **prior hypothesis bias** refers to the fact that decision makers who have strong prior beliefs about the relationship between two variables tend to make decisions on the basis of these beliefs, even when presented with evidence that their beliefs are wrong. Moreover, they tend to seek and use information that is consistent with their prior beliefs, while ignoring information that contradicts these beliefs. To put this bias in a strategic context, it suggests that a CEO who has a strong prior belief that a certain strategy makes sense might continue to pursue that strategy, despite evidence that it is inappropriate or failing.

escalating commitment

A cognitive bias that occurs when decision makers, having already committed significant resources to a project, commit even more resources if they receive feedback that the project is failing.

Another well-known cognitive bias, **escalating commitment,** occurs when decision makers, having already committed significant resources to a project, commit even more resources if they receive feedback that the project is failing.[27] This may be an irrational response; a more logical response would be to abandon the project and move on (that is, to cut your losses and run), rather than escalate commitment. Feelings of personal responsibility for a project apparently induce decision makers to stick with a project despite evidence that it is failing.

reasoning by analogy

A cognitive bias that
involves the use of simple
analogies to make sense
out of complex problems.

A third bias, **reasoning by analogy,** involves the use of simple analogies to make sense out of complex problems. The problem with this heuristic is that the analogy may not be valid. A fourth bias, **representativeness,** is rooted in the tendency to generalize from a small sample or even a single vivid anecdote. This bias violates the statistical law of large numbers, which says that it is inappropriate to generalize from a small sample, let alone from a single case. In many respects, the dot-com boom of the late 1990s was based on reasoning by analogy and representativeness. Prospective entrepreneurs saw some of the early dot-com companies such as Amazon and Yahoo! achieve rapid success, at least as judged by some metrics. Reasoning by analogy from a very small sample, they assumed that any dot-com could achieve similar success. Many investors reached similar conclusions. The result was a massive wave of start-ups that jumped into the Internet space in an attempt to capitalize on the perceived opportunities. That the vast majority of these companies subsequently went bankrupt is testament to the fact that the analogy was wrong and the success of the small sample of early entrants was no guarantee that other dot-coms would succeed.

representativeness

A cognitive bias rooted in
the tendency to generalize
from a small sample or
even a single vivid
anecdote.

illusion of control

A cognitive bias rooted
in the tendency to
overestimate one's ability
to control events.

Another cognitive bias is known as the **illusion of control,** which is the tendency to overestimate one's ability to control events. People seem to have a tendency to attribute their success in life to their own good decision making and their failures to bad luck.[28] General or top managers seem to be particularly prone to this bias: having risen to the top of an organization, they tend to be overconfident about their ability to succeed.[29] According to Richard Roll, such overconfidence leads to what he has termed the *hubris hypothesis* of takeovers.[30] Roll argues that top managers are typically overconfident about their abilities to create value by acquiring another company. Hence, they end up making poor acquisition decisions, often paying far too much for the companies they acquire. Subsequently, servicing the debt taken on to finance such an acquisition makes it all but impossible to make money from the acquisition.

● Improving Decision Making

The existence of cognitive biases raises the issue of how to bring critical information to bear on the decision mechanism so that a company's strategic decisions are realistic and based on thorough evaluation. Two techniques known to enhance strategic thinking and counteract groupthink and cognitive biases are devil's advocacy and dialectic inquiry.[31] **Devil's advocacy** requires the generation of both a plan and a critical analysis of the plan. One member of the decision-making group acts as the devil's advocate, bringing out all the reasons that might make the proposal unacceptable. In this way, decision makers can become aware of the possible perils of recommended courses of action.

devil's advocacy

A technique in which one
member of a decision-
making group acts as a
devil's advocate, bringing
out all the considerations
that might make the
proposal unacceptable.

Dialectic inquiry is more complex, for it requires the generation of a plan (a thesis) and a counterplan (an antithesis) that reflect *plausible but conflicting* courses of action.[32] Strategic managers listen to a debate between advocates of the plan and counterplan and then make a judgment about which plan will lead to higher performance. The purpose of the debate is to reveal problems with definitions, recommended courses of action, and assumptions of both plans. As a result of this exercise, strategic managers are able to form a new and more encompassing conceptualization of the problem, which becomes the final plan (a synthesis). Dialectic inquiry can promote thinking strategically.

dialectic inquiry

The generation of a plan
(a thesis) and a counterplan
(an antithesis) that reflect
plausible but conflicting
courses of action.

Another technique for countering cognitive biases, championed by Nobel Prize winner Daniel Kahneman and his associates, is known as the outside view.[33] The outside view requires planners to identify a reference class of analogous past strategic initiatives, determine whether those initiatives succeeded or failed, and evaluate the project at hand against those prior initiatives. According to Kahneman, this technique is particularly useful for countering biases such as the illusion of control (hubris), reasoning by analogy, and representativeness. Thus, for example, when considering a potential acquisition, planners should look at the track record of acquisitions made by other enterprises (the reference class), determine if they succeeded or failed, and objectively evaluate the potential acquisition against that reference class. Kahneman argues that such a "reality check" against a large sample of prior events tends to constrain the inherent optimism of planners and produce more realistic assessments and plans.

Strategic Leadership

One of the key strategic roles of both general and functional managers is to use all their knowledge, energy, and enthusiasm to provide strategic leadership for their subordinates and develop a high-performing organization. Several authors have identified a few key characteristics of good strategic leaders that do lead to high performance: (1) vision, eloquence, and consistency, (2) commitment, (3) being well informed, (4) willingness to delegate and empower, (5) astute use of power, and (6) emotional intelligence.[34]

● **Vision, Eloquence, and Consistency**
One of the key tasks of leadership is to give an organization a sense of direction. Strong leaders seem to have a clear and compelling vision of where the organization should go, are eloquent enough to communicate this vision to others within the organization in terms that energize people, and consistently articulate their vision until it becomes part of the culture of the organization.[35]

Examples of strong business leaders include Microsoft's Bill Gates; Jack Welch, the former CEO of General Electric; and Sam Walton, Wal-Mart's founder. For years, Bill Gates's vision of a world in which there would be a Windows-based personal computer on every desk was a driving force at Microsoft. More recently, the vision has evolved into one of a world in which Windows-based software can be found on any computing device—from PCs and servers to video game consoles (Xbox), cell phones, and hand-held computers. At GE, Jack Welch was responsible for articulating the simple but powerful vision that GE should be first or second in every business in which it competed or exit from that business. Similarly, it was Sam Walton who established and articulated the vision that has been central to Wal-Mart's success—passing on cost savings from suppliers and operating efficiencies to customers in the form of everyday low prices.

● **Commitment**
Strong leaders demonstrate their commitment to their vision and business model by actions and words, and they often lead by example. Consider Nucor's former CEO, Ken Iverson. Nucor is a very efficient steel maker with perhaps the lowest cost structure in the steel industry. Because of a relentless focus on cost minimization, it has turned in thirty years of profitable performance in an industry where most other companies have lost money. In his tenure as CEO, Iverson set the example: He answered his own phone, employed only one secretary, drove an old car, flew coach class, and was proud of the fact that his base salary was the lowest in the *Fortune 500* (Iverson made most of his money from performance-based pay bonuses). This commitment was a powerful signal to employees that Iverson was serious about doing everything possible to minimize costs. It earned him the respect of Nucor employees, which made them more willing to work hard. Although Iverson has retired, his legacy lives on in the cost-conscious organizational culture that has been built at Nucor, and like that of all other great leaders, his impact will extend beyond his tenure as a leader.

Being Well Informed

Effective strategic leaders develop a network of formal and informal sources who keep them well informed about what is going on within their company. Herb Kelleher at Southwest Airlines, for example, was able to find out a lot about the health of his company by dropping in unannounced on aircraft maintenance facilities and helping workers there to perform their tasks; McDonald's Ray Kroc and Wal-Mart's Sam Walton routinely dropped in unannounced to visit their restaurants and stores. Using informal and unconventional ways to gather information is wise because formal channels can be captured by special interests within the organization or by gatekeepers—managers who may misrepresent the true state of affairs within the company to the leader, as may have happened at Enron. People like Kelleher, who regularly interact with employees at all levels, are better able to build informal information networks than leaders who closet themselves and never interact with lower-level employees.

Willingness to Delegate and Empower

High-performance leaders are skilled at delegation. They recognize that unless they learn how to delegate effectively, they can quickly become overloaded with responsibilities. They also recognize that empowering subordinates to make decisions is a good motivation tool. Delegating also makes sense when it results in decisions being made by those who must implement them. At the same time, astute leaders recognize that they need to maintain control over certain key decisions. Thus, although they will delegate many *important* decisions to lower-level employees, they will not delegate those that they judge to be of *critical importance* to the future success of the organization under their leadership—such as articulating the vision and business model.

The Astute Use of Power

In a now classic article on leadership, Edward Wrapp noted that effective leaders tend to be very astute in their use of power.[36] He argued that strategic leaders must often play the power game with skill and attempt to build consensus for their ideas rather than use their authority to force ideas through; they act as members or democratic leaders of a coalition rather than as dictators. Jeffery Pfeffer has articulated a similar vision of the politically astute manager who gets things done in organizations by the intelligent use of power.[37] In Pfeffer's view, power comes from control over resources: budgets, capital, positions, information, and knowledge that is important to the organization. Politically astute managers use these resources to acquire another critical resource: critically placed allies who can help a manager attain preferred strategic objectives. Pfeffer stresses that one does not need to be a CEO to assemble power in an organization. Sometimes quite junior functional managers can build a surprisingly effective power base and use it to influence organizational outcomes.

Emotional Intelligence

Emotional intelligence is a term that Daniel Goldman coined to describe a bundle of psychological attributes that many strong and effective leaders exhibit:[38]

- Self-awareness—the ability to understand one's own moods, emotions, and drives, as well as their effect on others

- Self-regulation—the ability to control or redirect disruptive impulses or moods (i.e., to think before acting)

- Motivation—a passion for work that goes beyond money or status and a propensity to pursue goals with energy and persistence

- Empathy—understanding the feelings and viewpoints of subordinates and taking those into account when making decisions

- Social skills—friendliness with a purpose

According to Goldman, leaders who possess these attributes—who exhibit a high degree of emotional intelligence—tend to be more effective than those who lack these attributes. Their self-awareness and self-regulation help to elicit the trust and confidence of subordinates. In Goldman's view, people respect leaders who, because they are self-aware, recognize their own limitations and, because they are self-regulating, consider decisions carefully. Goldman also argues that self-aware and self-regulating individuals tend to be more self-confident and therefore better able to cope with ambiguity and more open to change. A strong motivation exhibited in a passion for work can also be infectious, helping to persuade others to join together in pursuit of a common goal or organizational mission. Finally, strong empathy and social skills can help leaders earn the loyalty of subordinates. Empathetic and socially adept individuals tend to be skilled at managing disputes between managers, better able to find common ground and purpose among diverse constituencies, and better able to move people in a desired direction than leaders who lack these skills. In short, Goldman's arguments are that the psychological makeup of a leader matters.

Summary of Chapter

1. A strategy is an action that a company takes to attain one or more of its goals.

2. A company has a competitive advantage over its rivals when it is more profitable than the average for all firms in its industry. It has a sustained competitive advantage when it is able to maintain above-average profitability over a number of years. In general, a company with a competitive advantage will grow its profits more rapidly than rivals.

3. General managers are responsible for the overall performance of the organization or for one of its major self-contained divisions. Their overriding strategic concern is for the health of the total organization under their direction.

4. Functional managers are responsible for a particular business function or operation. Although they lack general management responsibilities, they play a very important strategic role.

5. Formal strategic planning models stress that an organization's strategy is the outcome of a rational planning process. The major components of the strategic management process are defining the mission, vision, and major goals of the organization; analyzing the external and internal environments of the organization; choosing strategies that align or fit an organization's strengths and weaknesses with external environmental opportunities and threats; and adopting organization structures and control systems to implement the organization's chosen strategy.

6. Strategy can emerge from deep within an organization in the absence of formal plans, as lower-level managers respond to unpredicted situations.

7. Strategic planning often fails because executives do not plan for uncertainty and because ivory tower planners lose touch with operating realities.

8. The fit approach to strategic planning has been criticized for focusing too much on the degree of fit between existing resources and current opportunities and not enough on building new resources and capabilities to create and exploit future opportunities.

9. Strategic intent refers to an obsession with achieving an objective that stretches the company and requires it to build new resources and capabilities.

10. In spite of systematic planning, companies may adopt poor strategies if their decision-making processes are vulnerable to the intrusion of individual cognitive biases.

11. Devil's advocacy, dialectic inquiry, and the outside view are techniques for enhancing the effectiveness of strategic decision making.

12. Good leaders of the strategy-making process have a number of key attributes: vision, eloquence, and consistency; commitment; being well informed; a willingness to delegate and empower; political astuteness; and emotional intelligence.

Discussion Questions

1. What do we mean by *strategy*? How is a business model different from a strategy?

2. What do you think are the sources of sustained superior profitability?

3. What are the strengths of formal strategic planning? What are its weaknesses?

4. Discuss the accuracy of this statement: Formal strategic planning systems are irrelevant for firms competing in high-technology industries where the pace of change is so rapid that plans are routinely made obsolete by unforeseen events.

5. Pick the current or a past president of the United States and evaluate his performance against the leadership characteristics discussed in the text. On the basis of this comparison, do you think that the president was/is a good strategic leader? Why?

Practicing Strategic Management

SMALL-GROUP EXERCISE

Designing a Planning System

Break up into groups of three to five people and discuss the following scenario. Appoint one group member as a spokesperson who will communicate your findings to the class when called upon to do so by the instructor.

You are a group of senior managers working for a fast-growing computer software company. Your product allows users to play interactive role-playing games over the Internet. In the past three years, your company has gone from being a start-up enterprise with 10 employees and no revenues to a company with 250 employees and revenues of $60 million. It has been growing so rapidly that you have not had time to create a strategic plan, but now your board of directors is telling you that they want to see a plan, and they want it to drive decision making and resource allocation at the company. They want you to design a planning process that will have the following attributes:

1. It will be democratic, involving as many key employees as possible in the process.

2. It will help to build a sense of shared vision within the company about how to continue to grow rapidly.

3. It will lead to the generation of three to five key strategies for the company.

4. It will drive the formulation of detailed action plans, and these plans will be subsequently linked to the company's annual operating budget.

Design a planning process to present to your board of directors. Think carefully about who should be included in this process. Be sure to outline the strengths and weaknesses of the approach you choose, and be prepared to justify why your approach might be superior to alternative approaches.

EXPLORING THE WEB

Visiting 3M

Go to the website of 3M (**www.3m.com**) and visit the section that describes its history (**www.3m.com/profile/looking/index .jhtml**). Using the information contained there, map out the evolution of strategy at 3M from its establishment to the present day. To what degree do you think that this evolution was the result of detailed long-term strategic planning, and to what degree was it the result of unplanned actions taken in response to unpredictable circumstances?

General Task   Search the Web for a company site with sufficient information to map out the evolution of that company's strategy over a significant period of time. What drove this evolution? To what degree was it the result of detailed long-term strategic planning, and to what degree was it the result of unplanned actions taken in response to unpredictable circumstances?

CLOSING CASE

The Best-Laid Plans—Chrysler Hits the Wall

In 1998, after Germany's Daimler-Benz acquired Chrysler, the third-largest U.S. automobile manufacturer, to form Daimler-Chrysler, many observers thought that Chrysler would break away from its troubled U.S. brethren, Ford and General Motors, and join ranks with the Japanese automobile makers. The strategic plan was to emphasize bold design, better product quality, and higher productivity by sharing designs and parts between the two companies. Jurgen Schrempp, the CEO of the combined companies, told shareholders to "expect the extraordinary" and went on to say that DaimlerChrysler "has the size, profitability and reach to take on everyone."

The grand scheme proved extraordinary, but for all of the wrong reasons. In 2006, Chrysler saw its market share fall to 10.6%, and the company announced that it would lose $1.26 billion. This shocked shareholders, who had been told a few months earlier that the Chrysler unit would break even in 2006.

What went wrong? First, Schrempp and his planners may have overestimated Chrysler's competitiveness prior to the merger. Chrysler was the most profitable of the three U.S. auto companies in the late 1990s, but the U.S. economy was very strong and the company's core offering of pickup trucks, SUVs, and minivans provided the right products for a time of low gas prices. After the merger, the Germans discovered that Chrysler's factories were in worse shape than they had thought and product quality was poor. Second, sharing design and engineering resources and parts between Daimler's Mercedes-Benz models and Chrysler proved to be very difficult. Mercedes was a luxury car maker, Chrysler a mass market manufacturer, and it would take years to redesign Chrysler cars so that they could use Daimler parts and benefit from Daimler engineering. In addition, Daimler's engineers and managers were not enthusiastic about helping Chrysler, which many saw as a black hole into which the profitable Mercedes-Benz line would pour billions of euros.

To be fair, the new cars that Chrysler did produce, including the 300C sedan and the PT Cruiser, garnered good reviews. Sales of the 300C were strong, but not strong enough to shift the balance of Chrysler's business away from the small truck segment.

Despite several years of financial struggle, by 2004 it looked as if things might finally be turning around at Chrysler. In 2004, and then again in 2005, the company made good money. The company actually gained market share in 2005.

Dieter Zetsche, then Chrysler's German CEO, hoped to capitalize on this with the introduction of a new SUV, the seven-seat Jeep Commander. The timing of the Commander, launched in mid-2005, could not have been worse. In 2005, the price of oil surged dramatically, as strong demand from developed nations and China combined with tight supplies (which were made worse by supply disruptions caused by Hurricane Katrina). By mid-2006, oil had reached $70 a barrel, up from half that just 18 months earlier, and gas prices hit $3 a gallon.

To make matters worse, Ford and General Motors, which themselves were hemorrhaging red ink, were engaged in an aggressive price war, offering deep incentives to move their own excess inventory, and Chrysler was forced to match prices or lose market share. Meanwhile, Japanese manufacturers, and particularly Toyota and Honda, which had been expanding their U.S. production facilities for fifteen years, were gaining share with their smaller fuel-efficient offerings and popular hybrids.

In September 2006, Chrysler announced that due to a build-up of inventory on dealers' lots, it would cut production by 16%, double the planned figure announced in June 2006. In addition to slumping sales, the new CEO, Thomas LaSorda, revealed that the company was facing sharply higher costs for its raw materials and parts, some of which were up as much as 60%. Chrysler was also suffering from high health care costs and pension liabilities for its unionized workforce. Scrambling to fill the gap in its product line, Chrysler announced that it might enter into a partnership with China's Chery Motors, to produce small fuel-efficient cars in China, which would then be imported into the United States.

Chrysler's woes, however, continued, and in February 2007 Chrysler announced a dramatic restructuring plan, including the closing down of a factory and laying off of 13,000 employees. Executives at Daimler concluded that its plans for Chrysler had failed and announced that the company might be sold. This transpired in May 2007, when Chrysler was purchased by Cerberus, a private equity group, for $4.7 billion. Cerberus brought in a new CEO for Chrysler, Bob Nardelli, formally CEO at Home Depot and before that a senior executive at General Electric. Under Nardelli, Chrysler is exploring potential alliances with foreign car makers to design cars that Chrysler will build, the company is taking steps to merge its Chrysler and

Dodge brands, poorly performing dealers have been culled from the company's network, the powerful Jeep brand is being refocused on its rugged outdoor image, and Chrysler struck a deal with the United Auto Workers union under which retiree health care liabilities, a major source of costs, have been transferred to an independent trust.[c]

Case Discussion Questions

1. What was the planned strategy at Daimler-Benz for Chrysler in 1998?

2. In retrospect, Daimler-Benz's plans for Chrysler seem overly optimistic. What decision-making errors might Daimler-Benz have made in its evaluation of Chrysler? How might those errors have been avoided?

3. What opportunities and threats was Chrysler facing in 2005 and 2006? What were Chrysler's strengths and weaknesses? Did its product strategy make sense, given these?

4. Why did Chrysler get its forecasts for product sales and earnings so badly wrong in 2006? What does this teach you about the nature of planning?

5. What must Chrysler do now if it is to regain its footing in this industry?

TEST PREPPER

True/False Questions

_____ 1. A strategy is a set of actions that managers take to increase their company's performance relative to rivals.

_____ 2. The profitability of a company can be measured by the return that it makes on the capital invested in the enterprise.

_____ 3. General managers are responsible for supervising a particular function—that is, a task, activity, or operation like accounting, marketing, R&D, information technology, or logistics.

_____ 4. The chief executive officer (CEO) is the principal general manager of the organization.

_____ 5. A business unit is a self-contained division (with its own functions—for example, finance) that provides a product or service for a particular market.

_____ 6. Emergent strategies are planned responses to unforeseen circumstances.

_____ 7. Scenario planning involves formulating plans that are based upon "what if" scenarios about the future.

Multiple-Choice Questions

8. _____ refers to the fact that decision makers who have strong prior beliefs about the relationship between two variables tend to make decisions on the basis of these beliefs, even when presented with evidence that their beliefs are wrong.
   a. Reasoning by analogy
   b. Representativeness
   c. Prior hypothesis bias
   d. Escalating commitment
   e. Cognitive biases

9. The first step of the strategic planning process is _____.
   a. to select the corporate mission and major corporate goals
   b. to analyze the organization's internal operating environment
   c. to analyze the organization's external competitive environment to identify opportunities and threats
   d. to select strategies that build on the organization's strengths and correct its weaknesses
   e. to implement the strategies

10. According to Henry Mintzberg, emergent strategies _____.
   a. are less likely to be successful than the intended strategies
   b. arise from autonomous action by individual managers deep within the organization
   c. are exactly the same as the intended strategies
   d. are usually developed by the top management team
   e. are less useful when the future is uncertain

11. _____ involves formulating plans that are based upon asking "what if . . . ?" about the future.
   a. Scenario planning
   b. Cognitive bias
   c. Ivory tower planning
   d. Planning under uncertainty
   e. Strategic fit

12. A well-known cognitive bias, _____, occurs when decision makers, having already committed significant resources to a project, commit even more resources if they receive feedback that the project is failing.
   a. reasoning by analogy
   b. representativeness
   c. escalating commitment
   d. prior hypothesis bias
   e. illusion of control

13. _____ is one of the techniques for enhancing the effectiveness of strategic decision making.
   a. Dialectic inquiry
   b. Sustained superior performance
   c. Formal strategic planning
   d. Commitment
   e. A willingness to delegate

14. _____ bear responsibility for the overall performance of the company or for that of one of its major self-contained subunits or divisions.
   a. Functional managers
   b. Business managers
   c. General managers
   d. Supervisors
   e. none of the above

15. The task of analyzing the organization's external and internal environment and then selecting appropriate strategies is known as _____.
   a. strategy implementation
   b. strategy formulation
   c. SWOT
   d. emergent strategies
   e. scenario planning

Chapter 2

Stakeholders, the Mission, Governance, and Business Ethics

Learning Objectives

After reading this chapter, you should be able to

1. Explain why managers need to take stakeholder claims into account

2. Discuss the components of a corporate mission statement

3. Explain the role played by corporate governance mechanisms in the management of a company

4. Review the causes of poor business ethics

5. Discuss how managers can ensure that the strategic decisions they make are consistent with good ethical principles

Chapter Outline

I. Stakeholders
II. The Mission Statement
   a. The Mission
   b. Vision
   c. Values
   d. Major Goals
III. Corporate Governance and Strategy
   a. The Agency Problem
   b. Governance Mechanisms
IV. Ethics and Strategy
   a. Ethical Issues in Strategy
   b. The Roots of Unethical Behavior
   c. Behaving Ethically
   d. Final Words

Overview

stakeholders

Individuals or groups with an interest, claim, or stake in the company, in what it does, and in how well it performs.

corporate governance

The mechanisms that exist to ensure that managers pursue strategies in the interests of an important stakeholder group, the shareholders.

An important part of the strategy-making process is ensuring that the company maintains the support of the key constituencies—or stakeholders—upon which it depends for its functioning and ultimate survival. A company's **stakeholders** are individuals or groups with an interest, claim, or stake in the company, in what it does, and in how well it performs.[1] We begin by looking at the relationship between stakeholders and a company. Then we move on to consider the corporate mission statement, which is the first key indicator of how an organization views the claims of its stakeholders. The purpose of the mission statement is to establish the guiding principles for strategic decision making. As we shall see, these guiding principles should recognize the claims of important stakeholder groups. Next we explore the issue of corporate governance.

By **corporate governance,** we mean the mechanisms that exist to ensure that managers pursue strategies that are in the interests of an important stakeholder group—shareholders. The chapter closes with a discussion of the ethical implications of strategic decisions. We consider how managers can make sure that their strategic decisions are founded on strong principles that treat all stakeholders in an ethical manner.

Stakeholders

internal stakeholders

Stockholders and employees, including executive officers, other managers, and board members.

external stakeholders

Individuals and groups outside the company that have some claim on the company.

A company's stakeholders can be divided into internal stakeholders and external stakeholders (see Figure 2.1). **Internal stakeholders** are stockholders and employees, including executive officers, other managers, and board members. **External stakeholders** are all other individuals and groups that have some claim on the company. Typically, this group comprises customers, suppliers, creditors (including banks and bondholders), governments, unions, local communities, and the general public.

All stakeholders are in an exchange relationship with the company. Each stakeholder group supplies the organization with important resources (or contributions), and in exchange each expects its interests to be satisfied (by inducements).[2] Stockholders provide the enterprise with risk capital and in exchange expect management to try to maximize the return on their investment. Creditors such as bondholders provide the company with capital in the form of debt, and they expect to be repaid on time with interest. Employees provide labor and skills and in exchange expect commensurate income, job satisfaction, job security, and good working conditions. Customers provide a company with its revenues and in exchange want high-quality reliable products that represent value for money. Suppliers provide a company with inputs and in exchange seek revenues and dependable buyers. Governments provide a company with rules and regulations that govern business practices and maintain fair competition. In exchange they want companies that adhere to these rules and pay their taxes. Unions help to provide a company with productive employees, and in exchange they want benefits for their members in proportion to their contributions to the company. Local communities provide companies with local infrastructure and in exchange want companies that are responsible citizens. The general public provides companies with national infrastructure and in exchange seeks some assurance that the quality of life will be improved as a result of the company's existence.

A company should take these claims into account when formulating its strategies. If it does not, stakeholders may withdraw their support. Stockholders may sell their shares, bondholders demand higher interest payments on new bonds, employees leave their jobs, and customers buy elsewhere. Suppliers may seek more dependable buyers. Unions may engage in disruptive labor disputes. Government may take civil or criminal action against the company and its top officers, imposing fines and in some cases jail terms. Communities may oppose the company's attempts to locate

Figure 2.1

Stakeholders and the Enterprise

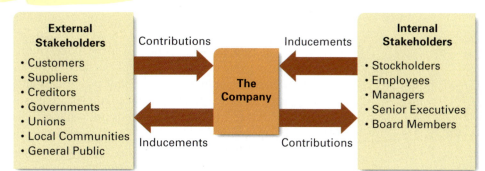

its facilities in their area, and the general public may form pressure groups, demanding action against companies that impair the quality of life. Any of these reactions can have a damaging impact on an enterprise.

Managers cannot always satisfy the claims of all stakeholders. The goals of different groups may conflict, and in practice few organizations have the resources to satisfy all stakeholder claims.[3] For example, union claims for higher wages can conflict with consumer demands for reasonable prices and stockholder demands for acceptable returns. Often the company must make choices. To do so, it must identify the most important stakeholders and give highest priority to pursuing strategies that satisfy their needs. Stakeholder impact analysis can provide such identification. Typically, stakeholder impact analysis follows these steps:

1. Identify stakeholders.

2. Identify stakeholders' interests and concerns.

3. As a result, identify what claims stakeholders are likely to make on the organization.

4. Identify the stakeholders who are most important from the organization's perspective.

5. Identify the resulting strategic challenges.[4]

Such an analysis enables a company to identify the stakeholders most critical to its survival and to make sure that the satisfaction of their needs is paramount. Most companies that have gone through this process have quickly come to the conclusion that three stakeholder groups must be satisfied above all others if a company is to survive and prosper: customers, employees, and stockholders.[5]

The Mission Statement

As noted above, a company's mission statement is a key indicator of how an organization views the claims of its stakeholders. You will also recall that in Chapter 1 we stated that the mission statement represents the starting point of the strategic planning process. Although corporate mission statements vary, the most comprehensive include four main elements; the mission, vision, values, and major goals of a corporation.

● The Mission

mission

What it is that a company exists to do.

The **mission** describes what it is that the company does. For example, the mission of Kodak is to provide "customers with the solutions they need to capture, store, process, output and communicate images—anywhere, anytime."[6] Kodak is a company that exists to provide imaging solutions to consumers. This mission focuses on the customer need that the company is trying to satisfy (the need for imaging), as opposed to the products that the company produces (film and cameras). This is a customer-oriented rather than product-oriented mission.

An important first step in the process of formulating a mission is to come up with a definition of the organization's business. Essentially, the definition should answer these questions: "What is our business? What will it be? What should it be?"[7] The responses guide the formulation of the mission. To answer the question, "What is our business?" a company should define its business in terms of three dimensions: who is being satisfied (what customer groups), what is being satisfied (what customer needs), and how customer needs are being satisfied (by what skills, knowledge, or competences).[8] Figure 2.2 illustrates these dimensions.

This approach stresses the need for a *customer-oriented* rather than a *product-oriented* business definition. A product-oriented business definition focuses on the

Figure 2.2

Defining the Business

Source: D. F. Abell, *Defining the Business: The Starting Point of Strategic Planning* (Englewood Cliffs, NJ: Prentice-Hall, 1980), p. 7.

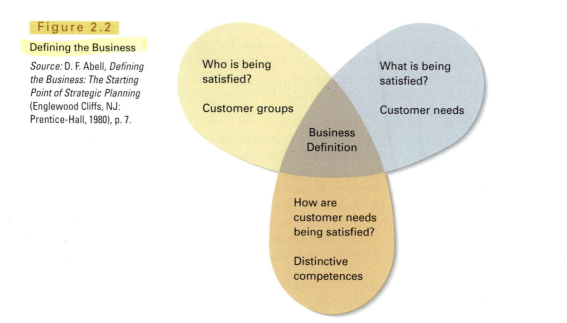

characteristics of the products sold and markets served, not on which kinds of customer needs the products are satisfying. Such an approach obscures the company's true mission because a product is only the physical manifestation of applying a particular skill to satisfy a particular need for a particular customer group. In practice, that need may be served in many different ways, and a broad customer-oriented business definition that identifies these ways can safeguard companies from being caught unaware by major shifts in demand.

By helping anticipate demand shifts, a customer-oriented mission statement can also assist companies in capitalizing on changes in their environment. It can help answer the question "What will our business be?" Recall that Kodak's mission emphasizes the company's desire to provide *customers* with the *solutions* they need to capture, store, process, output, and communicate images. This is a customer-oriented mission statement that focuses on customer needs, as opposed to a particular product (or solution) for satisfying those needs—such as chemical film processing. This customer-oriented business definition is helping to drive Kodak's current investment in digital-imaging technologies, which are starting to replace its traditional business based on chemical film processing.

The need to take a customer-oriented view of a company's business has often been ignored. History is littered with the wreckage of once-great corporations that did not define their business or defined it incorrectly so ultimately they declined. In the 1950s and 1960s, there were many office equipment companies, such as Smith Corona and Underwood, that defined their businesses as being the production of typewriters. This product-oriented definition ignored the fact that they were really in the business of satisfying customers' information-processing needs. Unfortunately for those companies, when a new technology came along that better served customer needs for information processing (computers), demand for typewriters plummeted. The last great typewriter company, Smith Corona, went bankrupt in 1996, a victim of the success of computer-based word-processing technology.

In contrast, IBM correctly foresaw what its business would be. In the 1950s, IBM was a leader in the manufacture of typewriters and mechanical tabulating equipment using punch-card technology. However, unlike many of its competitors, IBM defined its business as *providing a means for information processing and storage,* rather than just supplying mechanical tabulating equipment and typewriters.[9] Given this definition, the company's subsequent moves into computers, software systems, office systems, and printers seem logical.

● Vision

vision

The desired future state of a company.

The **vision** of a company lays out some desired future state; it articulates, often in bold terms, what the company would like to achieve. For example, the vision of RS Information Systems, a company specializing in information systems integration for federal and state government agencies, is to "become the leading African-American owned information technology (IT), scientific support, engineering services, and management consulting provider in the United States."[10] This vision represents a stretch, but it is an attainable goal for a company that already has revenues in excess of $330 million. Good vision statements are meant to stretch a company by articulating some ambitious but attainable future state that will help to motivate employees at all levels and drive strategies.[11]

● Values

values

Beliefs about how managers and employees of a company should conduct themselves, how they should do business, and what kind of organization they should build to help the company achieve its mission.

organizational culture

The set of values, norms, and standards that control how employees work to achieve an organization's mission and goals.

The **values** of a company state how managers and employees should conduct themselves, how they should do business, and what kind of organization they should build to help the company achieve its mission. Insofar as they help drive and shape behavior within a company, values are commonly seen as the bedrock of a company's **organizational culture:** the set of values, norms, and standards that control how employees work to achieve an organization's mission and goals. An organization's culture is often seen as an important source of its competitive advantage.[12] (We discuss the issue of organizational culture in depth in Chapter 9.) For example, Nucor Steel is one of the most productive and profitable steel firms in the world. Its competitive advantage is based in part on the extremely high productivity of its work force, something, the company maintains, that is a direct result of its cultural values, which shape how it treats its employees. These values are as follows:

- "Management is obligated to manage Nucor in such a way that employees will have the opportunity to earn according to their productivity."
- "Employees should be able to feel confident that if they do their jobs properly, they will have a job tomorrow."
- "Employees have the right to be treated fairly and must believe that they will be."
- "Employees must have an avenue of appeal when they believe they are being treated unfairly."[13]

At Nucor, values emphasizing pay for performance, job security, and fair treatment for employees help to create an atmosphere within the company that leads to high employee productivity. In turn, this productivity has helped to give Nucor one of the lowest cost structures in its industry, which helps to explain the company's profitability in a very price-competitive business.

● Major Goals

goal

A precise and measurable desired future state that a company attempts to realize.

Having stated the mission, vision, and key values, strategic managers can take the next step in the formulation of a mission statement: establishing major goals. A **goal** is a *precise* and *measurable* desired future state that a company attempts to realize. In this context, the purpose of goals is to specify with precision what must be done if the company is to attain its mission or vision.

Well-constructed goals have four main characteristics:[14]

1. They are *precise and measurable.* Measurable goals give managers a yardstick or standard against which they can judge their performance.

2. They *address crucial issues.* To maintain focus, managers should select a limited number of goals on which to assess the performance of the company. The goals that are selected should be crucial or important ones.

3. They *are challenging but realistic.* Goals give all employees an incentive to look for ways of improving the operations of an organization. If a goal is unrealistic in the challenges it poses, employees may give up; a goal that is too easy may fail to motivate managers and other employees.[15]

4. They *specify a time period* in which they should be achieved, when that is appropriate. Time constraints tell employees that success requires a goal to be attained by a given date, not after that date. Deadlines can inject a sense of urgency into goal attainment and act as a motivator. However, not all goals require time constraints.

Well-constructed goals also provide a means by which the performance of managers can be evaluated.

Although most companies operate with a variety of goals, the central goal of most corporations is to maximize shareholder returns, and maximizing shareholder returns requires high profitability and profit growth.[16] Thus, most companies operate with goals for profitability and profit growth. However, it is important that top managers not make the mistake of overemphasizing current profitability to the detriment of long-term profitability and profit growth.[17] The overzealous pursuit of current profitability to maximize short-term performance can encourage such misguided managerial actions as cutting expenditures judged to be nonessential in the short run—for instance, expenditures for research and development, marketing, and new capital investments. Although cutting current expenditures increases current profitability, the resulting underinvestment, lack of innovation, and diminished marketing can jeopardize long-run profitability and profit growth. These expenditures are vital if a company is to pursue its long-term mission and sustain its competitive advantage and profitability over time. Despite these negative consequences, managers may make such decisions because the adverse effects of a short-run orientation may not materialize and become apparent to shareholders for several years or because they are under extreme pressure to hit short-term profitability goals.[18]

It is also worth noting that pressures to maximize short-term profitability may result in managers' acting in an unethical manner. This apparently occurred during the late 1990s at a number of companies including Enron Corporation, Tyco, WorldCom, and Computer Associates. In these companies profits were systematically inflated by managers who manipulated financial accounts in a manner that misrepresented the true performance of the firm to shareholders.

To guard against short-run behavior, managers need to ensure that they adopt goals whose attainment will increase the *long-run* performance and competitiveness of their enterprise. Long-term goals are related to such issues as product development, customer satisfaction, and efficiency, and they emphasize specific objectives or targets concerning such things as employee and capital productivity, product quality, and innovation.

Corporate Governance and Strategy

We noted that a central goal of most companies is to provide their stockholders with a good rate of return on their investment. There are good reasons for this. Stockholders are the legal owners of a company and the providers of risk capital. The

risk capital

Equity capital for which there is no guarantee that stockholders will ever recoup their investment or earn a decent return.

agency problem

A problem that arises when managers pursue strategies that are not in the interests of stockholders.

● **The Agency Problem**

agency theory

A theory dealing with the problems that can arise in a business relationship when one person delegates decision-making authority to another.

agency relationship

A relationship that arises whenever one party delegates decision-making authority or control over resources to another.

principal

A person delegating authority to an agent, who acts on the principal's behalf.

agent

A person to whom authority is delegated by a principal.

information asymmetry

A situation in which one party to an exchange has more information about the exchange than the other party.

capital that stockholders provide to a company is seen as **risk capital** because there is no guarantee that stockholders will ever recoup their investment or earn a decent return (publicly held corporations can and do go bankrupt, in which case stockholders will lose their capital investment).

In publicly held corporations, stockholders delegate the job of controlling the company and selecting its strategies to professional managers, who become the *agents* of the stockholders.[19] As the agents of stockholders, managers should pursue strategies that maximize *long-run* returns to stockholders (subject to the constraint that they do so in a manner that is both legal and ethical). Although most managers are diligent about doing so, not all act in this fashion. This failure gives rise to what is known as the **agency problem,** where managers pursue strategies that are not in the interests of stockholders.

A branch of economics known as **agency theory** looks at the agency problems that can arise in a business relationship when one person delegates decision-making authority to another. Agency theory offers a way of understanding why managers do not always act in the best interests of stakeholders and also why they might sometimes engage in actions that are unethical and perhaps also illegal.[20] Although agency theory was originally formulated to capture the relationship between management and stockholders, the basic principles have also been extended to cover the relationship with other key stakeholders, such as employees, as well as between different layers of management within a corporation.[21] While the focus of attention in this section is on the relationship between senior management and stockholders, it should not be forgotten that some of the same language can be applied to the relationship between other stakeholders and top managers and between top management and lower levels of management.

The basic propositions of agency theory are relatively straightforward. First, an **agency relationship** is held to arise whenever one party delegates decision-making authority or control over resources to another. The **principal** is the person delegating authority, and the **agent** is the person to whom authority is delegated. The relationship between stockholders and senior managers is the classic example of an agency relationship. Stockholders, who are the *principals,* provide the company with risk capital, but they delegate control over that capital to senior managers, and particularly the CEO, who as their *agent* is expected to use that capital in a manner that is consistent with the best interests of stockholders. This means using that capital to maximize the company's long-run profitability and profit growth rate.

While agency relationships often work well, problems arise if agents and principals have different goals and if agents take actions that are not in the best interests of their principals. Agents may be able to do this because there is **information asymmetry** between the principal and the agent; agents almost always have more information about the resources they are managing than the principal does. Unscrupulous agents can take advantage of any information asymmetry to mislead principals and maximize their own interests at the expense of principals.

In the case of stockholders, information asymmetry arises because they delegate decision-making authority to the CEO, their agent, who by virtue of his or her position inside the company is likely to know far more than stockholders do about the company's operations. The information asymmetry between principals and agents is not necessarily a bad thing, but it can make it difficult for principals to measure how well an agent is performing and thus hold the agent accountable for how well he or she is using the entrusted resources. There is a certain amount of performance ambiguity inherent in the relationship between a principal and an agent. Principals cannot know for sure if the agent is acting in their best interests. They cannot know for sure if the agent is using the resources with which he or she has been entrusted as effectively and efficiently as possible. To an extent, principals have to *trust* the agent to do the right thing.

This trust is not blind: principals do put *governance mechanisms* in place whose purpose is to monitor agents, evaluate their performance, and if necessary, take corrective action. As we shall see shortly, the board of directors is one such governance mechanism, for in part the board exists to monitor and evaluate senior managers on behalf of stockholders. Other mechanisms serve a similar purpose. In the United States, the requirement that publicly owned companies regularly file with the Securities and Exchange Commission (SEC) detailed financial statements that are in accordance with generally agreed-on accounting principles (GAAP) exists to give stockholders consistent and detailed information about how well management is using the capital with which they have been entrusted.

Despite the existence of governance mechanisms and comprehensive measurement and control systems, a degree of information asymmetry will always remain between principals and agents, and there is always an element of trust involved in the relationship. Unfortunately, not all agents are worthy of this trust. A minority will deliberately mislead principals for personal gain, sometimes behaving unethically or breaking laws in the process. The interests of principals and agents are not always the same; they diverge, and some agents may take advantage of information asymmetries to maximize their own interests at the expense of principals and to engage in behaviors that the principals would never condone.

For example, some authors have argued that, like many other people, senior managers are motivated by desires for status, power, job security, and income.[22] By virtue of their position within the company, certain managers, such as the CEO, can use their authority and control over corporate funds to satisfy these desires at the cost of returns to stockholders. CEOs might use their position to invest corporate funds in various perks that enhance their status—executive jets, lavish offices, and expense-paid trips to exotic locations—rather than investing those funds in ways that increase stockholder returns. Economists have termed such behavior *on-the-job consumption*.[23] For an example, see the Strategy in Action, which describes the on-the-job consumption that occurred at Tyco under the leadership of Dennis Kozlowski.

Besides engaging in on-the-job consumption, CEOs, along with other senior managers, might satisfy their desires for greater income by using their influence or control over the board of directors to get the compensation committee of the board to grant them substantial pay increases. Critics of U.S. industry claim that extraordinary pay has now become an endemic problem and that senior managers are enriching themselves at the expense of stockholders and other employees. They point out that CEO pay has been increasing far more rapidly than the pay of average workers, primarily because of very liberal stock option grants that enable a CEO to earn huge pay bonuses in a rising stock market, even if the company underperforms the market and competitors.[24] In 1950, when *Business Week* started its annual survey of CEO pay, the highest-paid executive was General Motors CEO Charles Wilson, whose $652,156 pay packet translated into $4.7 million in inflation-adjusted dollars in 2005. In contrast, the highest-paid executive in 2005, Lee Raymond of Exxon, earned $405 million![25] In 1980, the average CEO in *Business Week*'s survey of CEOs of the largest 500 American companies earned 42 times what the average blue-collar worker earned. By 1990, this figure had increased to 85 times. Today, the average CEO in the survey earns more than 350 times the pay of the average blue-collar worker.[26]

What rankles critics is the size of some CEO pay packages and their apparent lack of relationship to company performance.[27] For example, in May 2006 shareholders of Home Depot complained bitterly about the compensation package for CEO Bob Nardelli at the company's annual meeting. Nardelli, who was appointed in 2000, had received $124 million in compensation, despite mediocre financial performance at Home Depot and a 12 percent decline in the company's stock price since he joined. When unexercised stock options were included, his compensation exceeded $250 million.[28] Another target of complaints was Pfizer CEO Hank McKinnell, who garnered an $83 million lump sum pension and $16 million in compensation in 2005, despite a 40+% decline in Pfizer's stock price since he took over as CEO.[29] Critics feel that the size of pay awards such as these is out of all proportion to the achievement of the CEOs. If so, this represents a clear example of the agency problem.

A further concern is that in trying to satisfy a desire for status, security, power, and income, a CEO might engage in *empire building,* buying many new businesses in an attempt to increase the size of the company through diversification.[30] Although such growth may depress the company's long-run profitability, and thus stockholder returns, it increases the size of the empire under the CEO's control and, by extension, the CEO's status, power, security, and income (there is a strong relationship between company size and CEO pay).

Instead of trying to maximize stockholder returns by seeking to maximize profitability, some senior managers may trade long-run profitability for greater company growth by buying new businesses. Figure 2.3 graphs long-run profitability against the rate of growth in company revenues. A company that does not grow is probably missing out on some profitable opportunities.[31] A moderate revenue growth rate of G^* allows a company to maximize long-run profitability, generating a return of Π^*. Thus, a growth rate of G_1 in Figure 2.3 (zero growth) is not consistent with maximizing profitability ($\Pi_1 < \Pi^*$). By the same token however, attaining growth *greater than* G^* requires diversification into areas that the company knows little about. Consequently, it can be achieved only by sacrificing profitability (i.e.,

Figure 2.3

The Tradeoff Between Profitability and Revenue Growth Rates

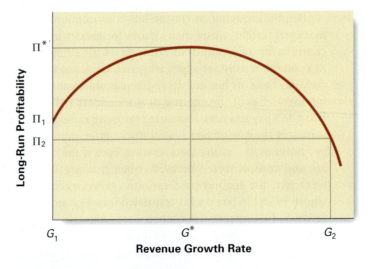

Strategy in Action

The Agency Problem at Tyco

Under the leadership of Dennis Kozlowski, who became CEO of Tyco in 1990, the company's revenues expanded from $3.1 billion in 1992 to $38 billion in 2001. Most of this growth was due to a series of acquisitions that took Tyco into a diverse range of unrelated businesses. Tyco financed the acquisitions by taking on significant debt commitments, which by 2002 exceeded $23 billion. As Tyco expanded, some questioned Tyco's ability to service its debt commitments and claimed that the company was engaging in "accounting tricks" to pad its books and make the company appear more profitable than it actually was. These criticisms, which were ignored for several years, were finally shown to have some validity in 2002, when Kozlowski was forced out by the board and subsequently charged with tax evasion by federal authorities.

Among other charges, federal authorities claimed that Kozlowski treated Tyco as his personal treasury, drawing on company funds to purchase an expensive Manhattan apartment and a world-class art collection that he obviously thought befitted the CEO of a major corporation. Kozlowski even used company funds to help pay for an expensive birthday party for his wife—which included toga-clad ladies, gladiators, a naked-woman-with-exploding-breasts birthday cake, and a version of Michelangelo's David that peed vodka! Kozlowski was replaced by a company outsider, Edward Breen. In 2003, Tyco took a $1.5 billion charge against earnings for accounting errors made during the Kozlowski era (i.e., Tyco's profits had been overstated by $1.5 billion during Kozlowski's tenure). Breen also set about dismantling parts of the empire that Kozlowski had built, divesting several businesses.

After a lengthy criminal trial, in June 2005 Dennis Kozlowski and Mark Swartz, the former chief financial officer of Tyco, were convicted of twenty-three counts of grand larceny, conspiracy, securities fraud, and falsifying business records in connection with what prosecutors described as the systematic looting of millions of dollars from the conglomerate (Kozlowski was found guilty of looting $90 million from Tyco). Both were set to serve significant jail time. As for Tyco, in 2006 CEO Ed Breen announced that the company would be broken up into three parts, a testament to the strategic incoherence of the conglomerate that Kozlowski had built.[a]

past G^*, the investment required to finance further growth does not produce an adequate return and the company's profitability declines). Yet G_2 may be the growth rate favored by an empire-building CEO, for it will increase his or her power, status, and income. At this growth rate, profitability is equal only to Π_2. Because $\Pi^* > \Pi_2$, a company growing at this rate is clearly not maximizing its long-run profitability or the wealth of its stockholders. However, a growth rate of G_2 may be consistent with attaining managerial goals of power, status, and income. Tyco International, which is profiled in the Strategy in Action feature, provides us with an example of this kind of growth.

Just how serious agency problems can be was emphasized in the early 2000s when a series of scandals swept through the corporate world, many of which could be attributed to self-interest seeking by senior executives and a failure of corporate governance mechanisms to hold the excesses of those executives in check. Between 2001 and 2004, accounting scandals unfolded at a number of major corporations, including Enron, WorldCom, Tyco, Computer Associates, Health South, Adelphia Communications, Dynergy, Royal Dutch Shell, and the major Italian food company Parmalat. At Enron, for example, some $27 billion in debt was hidden from shareholders, employees, and regulators in special partnerships that were kept off the balance sheet. In all of these cases, the prime motivation seems to have been an effort to present a more favorable view of corporate affairs to shareholders than was actually the case, thereby securing senior executives significantly higher pay packets.[32]

Confronted with agency problems, the challenge for principals is to (1) shape the behavior of agents so that they act in accordance with the goals set by principals, (2) reduce the information asymmetry between agents and principals, and (3) develop mechanisms for removing agents who do not act in accordance with the goals of principals, and mislead principals. Principals try to deal with these challenges through a series of governance mechanisms.

● **Governance Mechanisms**

governance mechanisms

Mechanisms that principals put in place to align incentives between principals and agents and to monitor and control agents.

Governance mechanisms are mechanisms that principals put in place to align incentives between principals and agents and to monitor and control agents. The purpose of governance mechanisms is to reduce the scope and frequency of the agency problem: to help ensure that agents act in a manner that is consistent with the best interests of their principals.

There are four main types of governance mechanisms for aligning stockholder and management interests: the board of directors, stock-based compensation, financial statements and auditors, and the takeover constraint.

THE BOARD OF DIRECTORS   The board of directors is the centerpiece of the corporate governance system in the United States and the United Kingdom. Board members are directly elected by stockholders, and under corporate law they represent the stockholders' interests in the company. Hence, the board can be held legally accountable for the company's actions. Its position at the apex of decision making within the company allows it to monitor corporate strategy decisions and ensure that they are consistent with stockholder interests. If the board's sense is that a company's strategies are not in the best interests of stockholders, it can apply sanctions, such as voting against management nominations to the board of directors or submitting its own nominees. In addition, the board has the legal authority to hire, fire, and compensate corporate employees, including, most importantly, the CEO.[33] The board is also responsible for making sure that audited financial statements of the company present a true picture of its financial situation. Thus, the board exists to reduce the information asymmetry between stockholders and managers and to monitor and control management actions on behalf of stockholders, ensuring that managers pursue strategies that are in the best interests of stockholders.

The typical board of directors is composed of a mix of inside and outside directors. *Inside directors* are senior employees of the company, such as the CEO. They are required on the board because they have valuable information about the company's activities. Without such information, the board cannot adequately perform its monitoring function. But because insiders are full-time employees of the company, their interests tend to be aligned with those of management. Hence, outside directors are needed to bring objectivity to the monitoring and evaluation processes. *Outside directors* are not full-time employees of the company. Many of them are full-time professional directors who hold positions on the boards of several companies. The need to maintain a reputation as competent outside directors gives them an incentive to perform their tasks as objectively and effectively as possible.[34]

There is little doubt that many boards perform their assigned functions admirably, but not all perform as well as they should. The board of now-bankrupt energy company Enron signed off on that company's audited financial statements, which were later shown to be grossly misleading.

Critics of the existing governance system charge that inside directors often dominate the outsiders on the board. Insiders can use their position within the management hierarchy to exercise control over what kind of company-specific information the board receives. Consequently, they can present information in a way that puts them in a favorable light. In addition, insiders have the advantage of intimate knowledge of the company's operations. Because their superior knowledge and control over information are sources of power, they may be better positioned than outsiders to influence boardroom decision making. The board may become the captive of insiders and merely rubber-stamp management decisions instead of guarding stockholder interests.

Some observers contend that many boards are dominated by the company CEO, particularly when the CEO is also the chairman of the board.[35] To support this view, they point out that both inside and outside directors are often the personal nominees of the CEO. The typical inside director is subordinate to the CEO in the company's hierarchy and therefore unlikely to criticize the boss. Because outside directors are frequently the CEO's nominees as well, they can hardly be expected to evaluate the CEO objectively. Thus, the loyalty of the board may be biased toward the CEO, not the stockholders. Moreover, a CEO who is also chairman of the board may be able to control the agenda of board discussions in such a manner as to deflect any criticisms of his or her leadership.

In the aftermath of a wave of corporate scandals that hit the corporate world in the early 2000s, there are clear signs that many corporate boards are moving away from merely rubber-stamping top management decisions and are beginning to play a much more active role in corporate governance. In part they have been prompted by new legislation, such as the 2002 Sarbanes-Oxley Act in the United States which tightened rules governing corporate reporting and corporate governance. Also important has been a growing trend on the part of the courts to hold directors liable for corporate misstatements. Powerful institutional investors such as pension funds have also been more aggressive in exerting their power, often pushing for more outside representation on the board of directors and for a separation between the roles of chairman and CEO, with the chairman role going to an outsider. As a result, over 50% of big companies had outside directors in the chairman's role by the mid-2000s, up from less than half of that number in 1990.

STOCK-BASED COMPENSATION   According to agency theory, one of the best ways to reduce the scope of the agency problem is for principals to establish incentives for agents to behave in their best interests through pay-for-performance systems. In the case of stockholders and top managers, stockholders can encourage top managers to pursue strategies that maximize a company's long-run profitability and profit growth, and thus the gains from holding its stock, by linking the pay of those managers to the performance of the stock price.

The most common pay-for-performance system has been to give managers stock options: the right to buy the company's shares at a predetermined (strike) price at some point in the future, usually within ten years of the grant date. Typically, the strike price is the price that the stock was trading at when the option was originally granted. The idea behind stock options is to motivate managers to adopt strategies that increase the share price of the company, for in doing so they will also increase the value of their own stock options.

Some research studies suggest that stock-based compensation schemes for executives, such as stock options, can align management and stockholder interests. For instance, one study found that managers were more likely to consider the effects of their acquisition decisions on stockholder returns if they themselves were significant shareholders.[36] According to another study, managers who were significant stockholders were less likely to pursue strategies that would maximize the size of the company rather than its profitability.[37] More generally, it is difficult to argue with the proposition that the chance to get rich from exercising stock options is the primary reason for the fourteen-hour days and six-day workweeks that many employees of fast-growing companies put in.

However, the practice of granting stock options in particular has become increasingly controversial. Many top managers often earn huge bonuses from exercising stock options that were granted several years previously. While not denying that these options do motivate managers to improve company performance, critics claim that they are often too generous. A particular cause for concern is that stock options are often granted at such low strike prices that senior managers can hardly fail to make a significant amount of money by exercising them, even if the company underperforms the stock market by a significant margin. Indeed, serious examples of the agency problem emerged in 2005 and 2006, when the Securities and Exchange Commission started to investigate a number of companies where stock options granted to senior executives had apparently been "back-dated" to a time when the stock price was lower, enabling the executive to earn more money than if those options had simply been dated on the day they were granted.[38] By 2007, the SEC was investigating some 130 companies for possible fraud relating to stock option dating. Included in the list were some major corporations including Apple Computer, Jabil Circuit, United Health, and Home Depot.[39]

Other critics of stock options, including the famous investor Warren Buffett, complain that huge stock option grants increase the outstanding number of shares in a company and therefore dilute the equity of stockholders; accordingly, they should be shown in company accounts as an expense against profits (a practice that was not required until mid-2005).

To summarize, in theory, stock options and other stock-based compensation methods are a good idea; in practice, they have been abused. To limit the abuse, accounting rules now require that stock options be treated as an expense that must be charged against profits. Some companies took matters into their own hands even before the change in accounting rules. Microsoft, for example, stopped issuing options to employees in 2003, replacing them with smaller stock grants. Since 2002, Boeing has expensed options in its accounts. The aerospace company has also gone an important step further in an effort to align management and stockholder interests, issuing what it calls "performance share" units that are convertible into common stock only if its stock appreciates at least 10% annually for five years. What these companies are trying to do in their own way is to limit the free ride that many holders of stock options enjoyed during the boom of the 1990s, while continuing to maintain a focus on aligning management and stockholder interests through stock-based compensation schemes.[40]

FINANCIAL STATEMENTS AND AUDITORS Publicly traded companies in the United States are required to file quarterly and annual reports with the SEC that are prepared according to GAAP. The purpose of this requirement is to give consistent, detailed, and accurate information about how efficiently and effectively the agents of stockholders—the managers—are running the company. To make sure that managers do not misrepresent this financial information, the SEC also requires that the accounts be audited by an independent and accredited accounting firm. Similar regulations exist in most other developed nations. If the system works as intended, stockholders can have a lot of faith that the information contained in financial statements accurately reflects the state of affairs at a company. Among other things, such information can enable a stockholder to calculate the profitability of a company in which she or he invests and to compare its profitability against that of competitors.

Unfortunately, in the United States at least, this system has not been working as intended. Although the vast majority of companies do file accurate information in their financial statements and although most auditors do a good job of reviewing that information, there is evidence that a minority of companies have abused the system, aided in part by the compliance of auditors. This was clearly an issue at bankrupt energy trader Enron, where the CFO and others misrepresented the true financial state of the company to investors by creating off-balance-sheet partnerships that hid the true state of Enron's indebtedness from public view. Enron's auditor, Arthur Andersen, also apparently went along with this deception, in direct violation of its fiduciary duty. The complacency of Arthur Andersen with financial fraud at Enron appears to have been due to the fact that Arthur Anderson also had lucrative consulting contracts with Enron that it did not want to jeopardize by questioning the accuracy of the company's financial statements. The losers in this mutual deception were shareholders who had to rely upon inaccurate information to make their investment decisions.

There have been numerous examples in recent years of managers' gaming financial statements to present a distorted picture of their company's finances to investors. The typical motive has been to inflate the earnings or revenues of a company, thereby generating investor enthusiasm and propelling the stock price higher, which gives managers an opportunity to cash in stock option grants for huge personal gain, at the expense of stockholders who have been misled by the reports.

The gaming of financial statements by companies raises serious questions about the accuracy of the information contained in audited financial statements. In response, in 2002 the United States Congress passed into law the Sarbanes-Oxley bill, which represents the biggest overhaul of accounting rules and corporate governance procedures since the 1930s. Among other things, Sarbanes-Oxley set up a new oversight board for accounting firms, required CEOs and CFOs to endorse their company's financial statements, and barred companies from hiring the same accounting firm for auditing and consulting services.

THE TAKEOVER CONSTRAINT   Given the imperfections in corporate governance mechanisms, it is clear that the agency problem may still exist at some companies. However, stockholders still have some residual power, for they can always sell their shares. If they start doing so in large numbers, the price of the company's shares will decline. If the share price falls far enough, the company might be worth less on the stock market than the book value of its assets. At this point, it may become an attractive acquisition target and runs the risk of being purchased by another enterprise, against the wishes of the target company's management.

The threat arising from the risk of being acquired by another company is known as the **takeover constraint.** The takeover constraint limits the extent to which managers can pursue strategies and take actions that put their own interests above those of stockholders. If they ignore stockholder interests and the company is acquired, senior managers typically lose their independence and probably their jobs as well. So the threat of takeover can constrain management action and limit the worst excesses of the agency problem.

takeover constraint

The threat arising from the risk of being acquired by another company.

Ethics and Strategy

The term **ethics** refers to accepted principles of right or wrong that govern the conduct of a person, the behavior of members of a profession, or the actions of an organization. **Business ethics** are the accepted principles of right or wrong governing the conduct of businesspeople. Ethical decisions are those that are in accordance with accepted principles of right and wrong, whereas an unethical decision is one that violates accepted principles. This is not as straightforward as it sounds. Managers may be confronted with **ethical dilemmas,** which are situations where there is no agreement about exactly what the accepted principles of right and wrong are or where none of the available alternatives seems ethically acceptable.

In our society, many accepted principles of right and wrong are not only universally recognized but are also codified into law. In the business arena, there are laws governing product liability *(tort laws)*, contracts and breaches of contract *(contract law)*, the protection of intellectual property *(intellectual property law)*, competitive behavior *(antitrust law)*, and the selling of securities *(securities law)*. Not only is it unethical to break these laws; it is illegal.

It is important to realize, however, that behaving ethically goes beyond staying within the bounds of the law. There are many cases of strategies and actions that, while legal, do not seem to be ethical. For example, in their quest to boost profitability, during the 1990s managers at Nike contracted out the production of sports shoes to producers in the developing world. Unfortunately for Nike, the working conditions at several of these producers were very poor and the company was subsequently attacked for using "sweatshop labor." Typical of the allegations were those detailed in the CBS news program *48 Hours.* The report told of young women at a Vietnamese subcontractor who worked six days a week, in poor working conditions with toxic materials, for only 20 cents an hour. The report also stated that a living wage in Vietnam was at least $3 a day, an income that could not be achieved without working substantial overtime. Nike was not breaking any laws, nor were its subcontractors, but this report, and others like it, raised questions about the ethics of using sweatshop labor. It may have been legal. It may have helped the company to increase its profitability. But was it ethical to use subcontractors who, by Western standards, exploited their work force? Nike's critics thought not, and the company found itself the focus of a wave of demonstrations and consumer boycotts.[41]

In this section, we take a closer look at the ethical issues that managers may confront when developing strategy and at the steps managers can take to ensure that strategic decisions are not only legal but also ethical.

● **Ethical Issues in Strategy**

The ethical issues that managers confront cover a wide range of topics, but most arise because of a potential conflict between the goals of the enterprise or the goals of individual managers and the fundamental rights of important stakeholders, including stockholders, customers, employees, suppliers, competitors, communities, and the general public. Stakeholders have basic rights that should be respected, and it is unethical to violate those rights.

Stockholders have the right to timely and accurate information about their investment (in accounting statements), and it is unethical to violate that right. Customers have the right to be fully informed about the products and services they purchase, including the right to information about how those products might cause harm to them or others, and it is unethical to restrict their access to such informa-

How many different governance mechanism do we have for!
There are for.

CHAPTER 2 Stakeholders, the Mission, Governance, and Business Ethics **41**

tion. Employees have the right to safe working conditions, fair compensation for the work they perform, and to be treated in a just manner by managers. Suppliers have the right to expect contracts to be respected, and the firm should not take advantage of a power disparity between itself and a supplier to opportunistically rewrite a contract. Competitors have the right to expect that the firm will abide by the rules of competition and not violate the basic principles of antitrust laws. Communities and the general public, including their political representatives in government, have the right to expect that a firm will not violate the basic expectations that society places on enterprises—for example, by dumping toxic pollutants into the environment or overcharging for work performed on government contracts.

Those who take the stakeholder view of business ethics often argue that it is in the enlightened self-interest of managers to behave in an ethical manner that recognizes and respects the fundamental rights of stakeholders, because doing so will ensure the support of stakeholders, which ultimately benefits the firm and its managers. Others go beyond this instrumental approach to ethics to argue that in many cases, acting ethically is simply the right thing to do. They argue that businesses need to recognize the principle of *noblesse oblige* and give something back to the society that made their success possible. *Noblesse oblige* is a French term that refers to honorable and benevolent behavior considered the responsibility of people of high (noble) birth. In a business setting, it is taken to mean benevolent behavior that is the moral responsibility of successful enterprises.

Oftentimes, unethical behavior arises in a corporate setting when managers decide to put the attainment of their own personal goals or the goals of the enterprise above the fundamental rights of one or more stakeholder groups (in other words, unethical behavior may arise from agency problems). The most common examples of such behavior involve self-dealing, information manipulation, anticompetitive behavior, opportunistic exploitation of other players in the value chain in which the firm is embedded (including suppliers, complement providers, and distributors), the maintenance of substandard working conditions, environmental degradation, and corruption.

Self-dealing occurs when managers find a way to feather their own nests with corporate monies; we have already discussed several examples in this chapter (e.g., at Tyco). **Information manipulation** occurs when managers use their control over corporate data to distort or hide information in order to enhance their own financial situation or the competitive position of the firm. As we have seen, many of the recent accounting scandals involved the deliberate manipulation of financial information. Information manipulation can also occur with regard to nonfinancial data. This occurred when managers at the tobacco companies suppressed internal research that linked smoking to health problems, violating the rights of consumers to accurate information about the dangers of smoking. When evidence of this came to light, lawyers bought class action suits against the tobacco companies, claiming that they had intentionally caused harm to smokers—they had broken tort law by promoting a product that they knew did serious harm to consumers. In 1999, the tobacco companies settled a lawsuit, brought by the states, that sought to recover health care costs associated with tobacco-related illnesses; the total payout to the states—$260 billion!

Anticompetitive behavior covers a range of actions aimed at harming actual or potential competitors, most often by using monopoly power, thereby enhancing the long-run prospects of the firm. For example, in the 1990s the Justice Department claimed that Microsoft used its monopoly in operating systems to force PC makers

self-dealing

In a business context, managers' efforts to find a way to feather their own nests with corporate monies.

information manipulation

In a business context, managers' efforts to use their control over corporate data to distort or hide information in order to enhance their own financial situation or the competitive position of the firm.

anticompetitive behavior

Actions aimed at harming actual or potential competitors, most often by using monopoly power, thereby enhancing the long-run prospects of the firm.

RUNNING CASE

Working Conditions at Wal-Mart

When Sam Walton founded Wal-Mart, now the world's largest retailer, one of his core values was that if you treated employees with respect, tied compensation to the performance of the enterprise, trusted them with important information and decisions, and provided ample opportunities for advancement, they would repay the company with dedication and hard work. For years the formula seemed to work. Employees were called "associates" to reflect their status within the company, even the lowest-paid hourly employee was eligible to participate in profit-sharing schemes and could use profit-sharing bonuses to purchase company stock at a discount from its market value, and the company made a virtue of promoting from within (two-thirds of managers at Wal-Mart started as hourly employees). At the same time, Walton and his successors always demanded loyalty and hard work from employees—managers, for example, were expected to move to a new store on very short notice—and base pay for hourly workers was very low. Still, as long as the upside was there, little grumbling was heard from employees.

In the last ten years, however, relationships between the company and its employees have been strained by a succession of lawsuits claiming that Wal-Mart pressures hourly employees to work overtime without compensating them, systematically discriminates against women, and knowingly uses contractors who hire undocumented immigrant workers to clean its stores, paying them below minimum wage.

For example, a class action lawsuit in Washington State claims that Wal-Mart routinely (1) pressured hourly employees not to report all their time worked, (2) failed to keep true time records, sometimes shaving hours from employee logs, (3) failed to give employees full rest or meal breaks, (4) threatened to fire or demote employees who would not work off the clock, and (5) required workers to attend unpaid meetings and computer training. Moreover, the suit claims that Wal-Mart has a strict "no overtime" policy, punishing employees who work more than forty hours a week, but that the company also gives employees more work than can be completed in a forty-hour week. The Washington suit is one of more than thirty suits that have been filed around the nation in recent years.

With regard to discrimination against women, complaints date back to 1996, when an assistant manager in a California store, Stephanie Odle, came across the W2 of a male assistant manager who worked in the same store. The W2 showed that he was paid $10,000 more than Odle. When she asked her boss

---

to bundle Microsoft's web browser, Internet Explorer, with Windows and to display Internet Explorer prominently on the computer desktop (the screen you see when you start a personal computer). Microsoft reportedly told PC makers that it would not supply them with Windows unless they did this. Since the PC makers had to have Windows to sell their machines, this was a powerful threat. The alleged aim of the action, which is an example of "tie-in sales," illegal under antitrust laws, was to drive a competing browser maker, Netscape, out of business. The courts ruled that Microsoft was indeed abusing its monopoly power in this case, and under a 2001 consent decree the company agreed to stop the practice.

Putting the legal issues aside, action such as that allegedly undertaken by managers at Microsoft is unethical on at least three counts. First, it violates the rights of end consumers by unfairly limiting their choices. Second, it violates the rights of downstream participants in the industry value chain, in this case PC makers, by forcing them to incorporate a particular product in their design. Third, it violates the rights of competitors to free and fair competition.

Opportunistic exploitation of other players in the value chain in which the firm is embedded is another example of unethical behavior. **Opportunistic exploitation** of this kind typically occurs when the managers of a firm seek to unilaterally rewrite the

opportunistic exploitation

In a business context, managers' efforts to unilaterally rewrite the terms of a contract with suppliers, buyers, or complement providers in a way that is more favorable to the firm, often using their power to force the revision through.

to explain the disparity, she was told that her coworker had "a wife and kids to support." When Odle, who is a single mother, protested, she was asked to submit a personal household budget. She was then granted a $2,080 raise. Subsequently Odle was fired, she claims, for speaking up. In 1998, she filed a discrimination suit against the company. Others began to file suits around the same time, and by 2004 the legal action had evolved into a class action suit that covered 1.6 million current and former female employees at Wal-Mart. The suit claims that Wal-Mart did not pay female employees the same as their male counterparts and did not provide them with equal opportunities for promotion.

In the case of both undocumented overtime and discrimination, Wal-Mart admits to no wrongdoing. The company does recognize that with some 1.6 million employees, some problems are bound to arise, but it claims that there is no systematic companywide effort to get hourly employees to work without pay or to discriminate against women. Indeed, the company claims that this could not be the case, since hiring and promotion decisions are made at the store level.

For their part, critics charge that while the company may have no policies that promote undocumented overtime or discrimination, the hard-driving cost containment culture of the company had created an environment where abuses can thrive.

Store managers, for example, are expected to meet challenging performance goals, and in an effort to do so they may be tempted to pressure subordinates to work additional hours without pay. Similarly, company policy requiring managers to change stores on short notice unfairly discriminates against women, who lack the flexibility to quickly uproot their families and move them to another state.

To compound matters, in the early 2000s Wal-Mart was hit by charges from the U.S. Immigration and Customs Enforcement Agency, which claimed that the company hired hundreds of illegal immigrants at low pay to clean floors at sixty stores around the country. Wal-Mart paid an $11 million fine and promised that the practice would stop, but the successful suit was yet another embarrassment for the company.

While the pay and discrimination lawsuits are still ongoing and may take years to resolve (there are some forty lawsuits in progress at the time of writing), Wal-Mart has taken steps to change its employment practices. For example, the company has created the position of director of diversity and a diversity compliance team, and it has restructured its pay scales to promote equal pay regardless of gender. In 2006, the company also created a panel, which has independent outside experts in addition to company insiders, charged with developing policies for extending work force diversity at Wal-Mart.[b]

---

terms of a contract with suppliers, buyers, or complement providers in a way that is more favorable to the firm, often using their power to force the revision through. For example, in the late 1990s Boeing entered into a $2 billion contract with Titanium Metals Corporation to buy certain amounts of titanium annually for ten years. In 2000, after Titanium Metals had already spent $100 million to expand its production capacity to fulfill the contract, Boeing demanded that the contract be renegotiated, asking for lower prices and an end to minimum purchase agreements. As a major purchaser of titanium, managers at Boeing probably thought they had the power to push this contract revision through, and the investment by Titanium Metals meant that they would be unlikely to walk away from the deal. Titanium Metals promptly sued Boeing for breach of contract. The dispute was settled out of court, and under a revised agreement Boeing agreed to pay monetary damages to Titanium Metals (reported to be in the $60 million range) and entered into an amended contract to purchase titanium. Irrespective of the legality of this action, it is arguably unethical since it violates the rights of suppliers to buyers who deal with them in a fair and open way.

substandard working conditions

Conditions created when managers underinvest in working conditions or pay employees below market rates, in order to reduce their costs of production.

Substandard working conditions arise when managers underinvest in working conditions or pay employees below market rates, in order to reduce their costs of production. The most extreme examples of such behavior occur when a firm

environmental degradation

In a business context, pollution or other forms of environmental harm that result directly from a firm's actions.

corruption

In a business context, payment of bribes or other unethical acts by managers in an effort to gain access to lucrative business contracts.

establishes operations in countries that lack the workplace regulations found in developed nations such as the United States. The example of Nike falls into this category. However, examples of substandard working conditions also occur within developed nations. As documented in the Running Case, for example, Wal-Mart has been accused of promoting substandard working conditions in its U.S. operations.

Environmental degradation occurs when a firm takes actions that directly or indirectly result in pollution or other forms of environmental harm. Environmental degradation can violate the rights of local communities and the general public to clean air and water and land that is free from pollution by toxic chemicals. Excessive deforestation, which results in land erosion and floods (forests absorb rainfall and limit flooding), is considered environmental degradation.

Finally, **corruption** can arise in a business context when managers pay bribes or otherwise act unethically to gain access to lucrative business contracts. Corruption is clearly unethical, since it violates a bundle of rights, including the right of competitors to a level playing field when bidding for contracts and, when government officials are involved, the right of citizens to expect that government officials will act in the best interest of the local community or nation and not in response to corrupt payments that feather their own nests.

● The Roots of Unethical Behavior

Why do some managers behave unethically? While there is no simple answer to this question, a few generalizations can be made. First, it is important to recognize that business ethics are not divorced from *personal ethics,* which are the generally accepted principles of right and wrong governing the conduct of individuals. As individuals, we are taught that it is wrong to lie and cheat—it is unethical—and that it is right to behave with integrity and honor and to stand up for what we believe to be right and true. The personal ethical code that guides our behavior comes from a number of sources, including our parents, our schools, our religion, and the media. Our personal ethical code will exert a profound influence on the way we behave as businesspeople. An individual with a strong sense of personal ethics is less likely to behave in an unethical manner in a business setting; in particular, he or she is less likely to engage in self-dealing and more likely to behave with integrity.

Second, many studies of unethical behavior in a business setting have come to the conclusion that businesspeople sometimes do not realize that they are behaving unethically, primarily because they simply fail to ask the relevant question: Is this decision or action ethical? Instead, they apply a straightforward business calculus to what they perceive to be a business decision, forgetting that the decision may also have an important ethical dimension. The fault here lies in processes that do not incorporate ethical considerations into business decision making. This may have been the case at Nike when managers originally made decisions about subcontracting. Those decisions were probably made on the basis of good economic logic. Subcontractors were probably chosen on the basis of business variables such as cost, delivery, and product quality, and the key managers simply failed to ask, "How does this subcontractor treat its work force?" If they thought about the question at all, they probably reasoned that it was the subcontractor's concern, not theirs.

Unfortunately, the climate in some businesses does not encourage people to think through the ethical consequences of business decisions. This brings us to the third cause of unethical behavior in businesses—an organizational culture that deemphasizes business ethics, reducing all decisions to the purely economic. A fourth cause of unethical behavior that is related to this may be pressure from top management to meet performance goals that are unrealistic and can be attained only by cutting corners or acting in an unethical manner. An organizational culture can "legitimize" behavior that society would judge as unethical, particularly when it is mixed with a focus on unrealistic performance goals, such as maximizing short-term economic performance, no matter what the costs. In such circumstances, there is a greater than average probability that managers will violate their own personal ethics and engage in behavior that is unethical. By the same token, an organizational culture can do just the opposite and reinforce the need for ethical behavior. At Hewlett-Packard, for example, Bill Hewlett and David Packard, the company's founders, propagated a set of values known as The HP Way. These values, which shape the way business is conducted both within and by the corporation, have an important ethical component. Among other things, they stress the need for confidence in and respect for people, open communication, and concern for the individual employee.

This brings us to a fifth root cause of unethical behavior—*leadership.* Leaders help to establish the culture of an organization, and they set the example that others follow. Other employees in a business often take their cue from business leaders, and if those leaders do not behave in an ethical manner, neither might they. It is not what leaders say that matters, but what they do.

Behaving Ethically

What is the best way for managers to make sure that ethical considerations are taken into account when making business decisions? There are no easy answers to this question, for many of the most vexing ethical problems arise because there are very real dilemmas inherent in them and no obvious right course of action. However, as discussed below, managers can do a number of things to make sure that ethical issues are considered in business decisions.

HIRING AND PROMOTION It seems obvious that businesses should strive to hire people who have a strong sense of personal ethics and would not engage in unethical or illegal behavior. Similarly, you would rightly expect a business to not promote people, and perhaps fire people, whose behavior does not match generally accepted ethical standards. But when you think about it, doing so is actually very difficult. After all, how do you know that someone has a poor sense of personal ethics? In our society, immoral individuals have an incentive to hide a lack of personal ethics from public view. Once people realize that someone is unethical, they no longer trust that person.

Is there anything that businesses can do to make sure that they do not hire people who subsequently turn out to have poor personal ethics, particularly given that people have an incentive to hide this from public view (indeed, unethical people may well lie about their nature)? Businesses can give potential employees psychological tests to try to discern their ethical predisposition, and they can check with prior employers regarding an applicant's reputation (e.g., by asking for letters of reference and talking to people who have worked with the prospective employee). The latter is certainly not uncommon and does indeed influence the hiring process. As for promoting people who have displayed poor ethics, that should not occur in a company where the organizational culture places a high value on the need for ethical behavior and where leaders act accordingly.

ORGANIZATIONAL CULTURE AND LEADERSHIP To foster ethical behavior, businesses need to build an organizational culture that places a high value on ethical behavior. Three things are particularly important in building such a culture. First, the business must explicitly articulate values that place a strong emphasis on ethical behavior. Many companies now do this by drafting a **code of ethics,** which is a formal statement of the ethical priorities a business adheres to. Others have incorporated ethical statements into documents that articulate the values or mission of the business. The food and consumer products giant Unilever has a code of ethics that includes the following points: "We will not use any form of forced, compulsory or child labor" and "No employee may offer, give or receive any gift or payment which is, or may be construed as being, a bribe. Any demand for, or offer of, a bribe must be rejected immediately and reported to management." Unilever's principles send a very clear message about the appropriate ethics to managers and employees within the organization.

Having articulated values in a code of ethics or some other document, leaders in the business must give life and meaning to those words by repeatedly emphasizing their importance *and then acting on them.* This means using every relevant opportunity to stress the importance of business ethics and making sure that key business decisions not only make good economic sense but also are ethical. Many companies have gone a step further, hiring independent firms to audit the company and make sure that they are behaving in a manner consistent with their ethical code. Nike, for example, has in recent years hired independent auditors to make sure that subcontractors used by the company are living up to Nike's code of conduct.

Finally, building an organizational culture that places a high value on ethical behavior requires incentive and promotional systems that reward people who engage in ethical behavior and sanction those who do not.

DECISION-MAKING PROCESSES   In addition to establishing the right kind of ethical culture in an organization, businesspeople must be able to think through the ethical implications of decisions in a systematic way. To do this, they need a moral compass. Some experts on ethics have proposed a straightforward practical guide—or ethical algorithm—to determine whether a decision is ethical. A decision is acceptable on ethical grounds if a businessperson can answer "yes" to each of these questions:

1. Does my decision fall within the accepted values or standards that typically apply in the organizational environment (as articulated in a code of ethics or some other corporate statement)?

2. Am I willing to see the decision communicated to all stakeholders affected by it—for example, by having it reported in newspapers or on television?

3. Would the people with whom I have a significant personal relationship, such as family members, friends, or even managers in other businesses, approve of the decision?

ETHICS OFFICERS   To make sure that a business behaves in an ethical manner, a number of firms now have ethics officers. These are individuals who are responsible for making sure that all employees are trained to be ethically aware, that ethical considerations enter the business decision-making process, and that the company's code of ethics is adhered to. Ethics officers may also be responsible for auditing decisions to make sure that they are consistent with this code. In many businesses, an ethics officer acts as an internal ombudsperson with responsibility for handling confidential inquiries from employees, investigating complaints from employees or others, reporting findings, and making recommendations for change.

United Technologies, a large aerospace company with worldwide revenues of over $28 billion, has had a formal code of ethics since 1990. There are now some 160 business practice officers within United Technologies (this is the company's name for ethics officers) who are responsible for making sure that the code is adhered to. United Technologies also established an ombudsperson program in 1986 that lets employees inquire anonymously to business practice officers about ethics issues. The program has received some 56,000 inquiries since 1986, and 8,000 cases have been handled by an ombudsperson.

STRONG CORPORATE GOVERNANCE Strong corporate governance procedures are needed to make sure that managers adhere to ethical norms, and in particular to make sure that senior managers do not engage in self-dealing or information manipulation. The key to strong corporate governance procedures is an independent board of directors that is willing to hold top managers to account for self-dealing and is able to question the information provided to them by managers. If companies like Tyco, WorldCom, and Enron had had a strong board of directors, it is unlikely that they would have been subsequently wracked by accounting scandals, and top managers would not have been able to view the funds of these corporations as their own personal treasuries.

MORAL COURAGE It is important to recognize that, on occasion, managers may need significant *moral courage*. It is moral courage that enables managers to walk away from a decision that is profitable but unethical. It is moral courage that gives an employee the strength to say no to a superior who instructs her or him to pursue actions that are unethical. And it is moral courage that gives employees the integrity to go public to the media and blow the whistle on persistent unethical behavior in a company. Moral courage does not come easily—there are well-known cases where individuals have lost their jobs because they blew the whistle on corporate behaviors that they thought were unethical by telling the media about what was occurring.

Companies can strengthen the moral courage of employees by committing themselves to not take retribution on employees who exercise moral courage, say no to superiors or otherwise complain about unethical actions. For example, consider the following extract from Unilever's code of ethics:

> Any breaches of the Code must be reported in accordance with the procedures specified by the Joint Secretaries. The Board of Unilever will not criticize management for any loss of business resulting from adherence to these principles and other mandatory policies and instructions. The Board of Unilever expects employees to bring to their attention, or to that of senior management, any breach or suspected breach of these principles. Provision has been made for employees to be able to report in confidence and no employee will suffer as a consequence of doing so.

This statement gives "permission" to employees to exercise moral courage. Companies can also set up ethics hotlines, allowing employees to anonymously register a complaint with a corporate ethics officer.

● **Final Words** All of the steps discussed here can help to make sure that when managers make business decisions, they are fully cognizant of the ethical implications and do not violate basic ethical prescripts. At the same time, it must be recognized that not all ethical dilemmas have an obvious solution—indeed, that is why they are dilemmas. At the end of the day, there are things that a business clearly should not do, and things that it should do, but there are also actions that present managers with true dilemmas. In these cases, a premium is placed on the ability of managers to make sense out of complex messy situations and make balanced decisions that are as just as possible.

Summary of Chapter

1. Stakeholders are individuals or groups that have an interest, claim, or stake in a company, in what it does, and in how well it performs.

2. A company cannot always satisfy the claims of all stakeholders. The goals of different groups may conflict. The company must identify the most important stakeholders and give highest priority to pursuing strategies that satisfy their needs.

3. The mission statement can be used to incorporate stakeholder demands into the strategy-making process of a company. The mission statement includes the mission itself and statements of corporate vision, values, and goals.

4. A company's stockholders are its legal owners and the providers of risk capital, a major source of the capital resources that allow a company to operate its business. Maximizing long-run profitability is the route to maximizing returns to stockholders.

5. An agency relationship is held to arise whenever one party delegates decision-making authority or control over resources to another.

6. The essence of the agency problem is that the interests of principals and agents are not always the same, and some agents may take advantage of information asymmetries to maximize their own interests at the expense of principals.

7. A number of governance mechanisms serve to limit the agency problem. These include the board of directors, stock-based compensation schemes, financial statements and auditors, and the threat of a takeover.

8. The term *ethics* refers to accepted principles of right or wrong that govern the conduct of a person, the behavior of members of a profession, or the actions of an organization. Business ethics are the accepted principles of right or wrong governing the conduct of businesspeople, and an ethical strategy is one that does not violate these accepted principles.

9. Unethical behavior is rooted in poor personal ethics, a failure to incorporate ethical issues into strategic and operational decision making, a dysfunctional organizational culture, and the failure of business leaders to act in an ethical manner.

10. To make sure that ethical issues are considered in business decisions, managers should (1) favor hiring and promoting people with a well-developed sense of personal ethics, (2) build an organizational culture that places a high value on ethical behavior, (3) make sure that leaders within the business not only articulate the principles of ethical behavior but also act in a manner that is consistent with those principles, (4) put decision-making processes in place that require people to consider the ethical dimension of business decisions, and (5) be morally courageous and encourage others to do the same.

Discussion Questions

1. How prevalent was the agency problem in corporate America during the late 1990s?

2. Who benefited the most from the late-1990s boom in initial public offerings of Internet companies: investors (stockholders) in those companies, managers, or investment bankers?

3. How might a company configure its strategy-making processes to reduce the probability that managers will pursue their own self-interest, at the expense of stockholders?

4. Under what conditions is it ethically defensible to outsource production to producers in the developing world who have much lower labor costs when such actions also involve laying off long-term employees in the firm's home country?

Practicing Strategic Management

SMALL-GROUP EXERCISE
Evaluating Stakeholder Claims

Break up into groups of three to five people, and discuss the following questions. Appoint one group member as a spokesperson who will communicate your findings to the class when called upon to do so by the instructor.

1. Identify the key stakeholders of your educational institution. What claims do they place on the institution?

2. Strategically, how is the institution responding to those claims? Do you think the institution is pursuing the correct strategies, in view of these claims? What might it do differently, if anything?

3. Prioritize the stakeholders in order of their importance for the survival and health of the institution. Do the claims of different stakeholder groups conflict with each other? If claims conflict, whose claims should be tackled first?

EXPLORING THE WEB
Visiting Merck

Visit the website of Merck, the world's largest pharmaceutical company, and read the Mission and Values statements posted there (**www.merck.com/about/mission.html**). Then answer the following questions:

1. Evaluate this mission statement in light of the material contained in this chapter. Does it clearly state what Merck's basic strategic goal is? Do the values listed provide a good guideline for managerial action at Merck? Do those values recognize stakeholder claims?

2. Read the section on Merck's corporate responsibility and code of conduct (**www.merck.com/cr**). How does Merck attempt to balance the goals of providing stockholders with an adequate rate of return on their investment, while at the same time developing medicines that benefit humanity and that can be acquired by people in need at an affordable price? Do you think that Merck does a good job of balancing these goals?

3. In late September 2004, Merck recalled one of its best-selling drugs, Celebrex, after research showed that people who used Celebrex had an elevated risk of suffering a heart attack. To what extent do you think that Merck's values and code of conduct played a part in this decision? Do you think the company pulled the drug from the market quickly enough? (You may want to take a look at press reports on this issue.)

General Task   Using the Web, find an example of a company where there was overt conflict between principals and agents over the future strategic direction of the organization.

CLOSING CASE

Google's Mission, Ethical Principles, and Involvement in China

Google, the fast-growing Internet search engine company, was established with a clear mission in mind: *to organize the world's information and make it universally acceptable and useful.* This mission has driven Google to create a search engine that, on the basis of key words entered by the user, will scan the Web for text, images, videos, news articles, books, and academic journals, among other things. Google has built a highly profitable advertising business on the back of its search engine, which is by far the most widely used in the world. Under the pay-per-click business model, advertisers pay Google every time a user of its search engine clicks on one of the paid links typically listed on the right-hand side of Google's results page.

Google has long operated with the mantra "Don't be evil." When this phrase was originally formulated, the central message was that Google should never compromise the integrity of its search results. For example, Google decided not to let commercial considerations bias its rankings. This is why paid links are not included in its main search results, but listed on the right-hand side of the results page. The mantra "Don't be evil," however, has become more than that at Google; it has become a central organizing principle of the company and an ethical touchstone by which managers judge all of its strategic decisions.

Google's mission and mantra raised hopes among human rights activists that the search engine would be an unstoppable tool for circumventing government censorship, democratizing information, and allowing people in heavily censored societies to gain access to information that their governments were trying to suppress, including the largest country on earth, China.

Google began a Chinese language service in 2000, although the service was operated from the United States. In 2002, the site was blocked by the Chinese authorities. Would-be users of Google's search engine were directed to a Chinese rival. The blocking took Google's managers totally by surprise. Reportedly, cofounder Sergey Brin immediately ordered half a dozen books on China and quickly read them in an effort to understand this vast country. Two weeks later, for reasons that have never been made clear, Google's service was restored. Google said that it did not change anything about its service, but Chinese users soon found that they could not access politically sensitive sites that appeared in Google's search results, suggesting that the government was censoring more aggressively. (The Chinese government has essentially erected a giant firewall between the Internet in China and the rest of the world, allowing its censors to block sites outside of China that are deemed subversive.)

By late 2004, it was clear to Google that China was a strategically important market. To exploit the opportunities that China offered, however, the company realized that it would have to establish operations in China, including its own computer servers and a Chinese homepage. Serving Chinese users from the United States was too slow, and the service was badly degraded by the censorship imposed. This created a dilemma for the company given the "Don't be evil" mantra. Once it established Chinese operations, it would be subject to Chinese regulations, including those censoring information. For perhaps eighteen months, senior managers inside the company debated the pros and cons of entering China directly, as opposed to serving the market from its U.S. site. Ultimately, they decided that the opportunity was too large to ignore. With over 100 million users, and that number growing fast, China promised to become the largest Internet market in the world and a major source of advertising revenue for Google. Moreover, Google was at a competitive disadvantage relative to its U.S. rivals, Yahoo! and Microsoft's MSN, which had already established operations in China, and relative to China's homegrown company, Baidu, which leads the market for Internet search in China (in 2006, Baidu had around 40% of the market for search in China, compared to Google's 30% share).

In mid-2005, Google established a direct sales presence in China. In January 2006, Google rolled out its Chinese homepage, which is hosted on servers based in China and maintained by Chinese employees in Beijing and Shanghai. Upon launch, Google stated that its objective was to give Chinese users "the greatest amount of information possible." It was immediately apparent that this was not the same as "access to all information." In accordance with Chinese regulations, Google had decided to engage in self-censorship, excluding results on such politically sensitive topics as democratic reform, Taiwanese independence, the banned Falun Gong movement, and references to the notorious Tiananmen Square massacre of democratic protestors that occurred in 1989. Human rights activists quickly protested, arguing that Google had abandoned its principles in order to make greater profits. For its part, Google's managers claimed that it was better to give Chinese users access to a limited amount of information than to none at all or to serve the market from the United States and allow the government to continue proactively censoring its search results, which would result in a badly degraded service. Brin justified the Chinese decision by saying that "it will be better for Chinese Web users, because ultimately they will get more information, though not quite all of it." Moreover, Google argued that it was the only search engine in China that let users know if search results had been censored (which is done by the inclusion of a bullet at the bottom of the page indicating censorship).[c]

Case Discussion Questions

1. How does Google's mission drive strategy at the company?

2. Is Google's stance toward Internet search in China consistent with its mission?

3. Do you think that Google should have entered China and engaged in self-censorship, given the company's long-standing mantra "Don't be evil"? Is it better to engage in self-censorship than to have the government censor for you?

4. If all foreign search engine companies declined to invest directly in China owing to concerns over censorship, what do you think the results would be? Who would benefit most from this action? Who would lose the most?

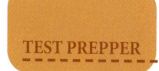

TEST PREPPER

True/False Questions

_____ **1.** A company's stakeholders are individuals or groups with an interest, claim, or stake in the company, in what it does, and in how well it performs.

_____ **2.** Internal stakeholders are customers, suppliers, creditors, governments, unions, local communities, and the general public.

_____ **3.** The mission of a company lays out some desired future state—it articulates, often in bold terms, what the company would like to achieve.

_____ **4.** Insofar as they help drive and shape behavior within a company, values are commonly seen as the bedrock of a company's organizational culture.

_____ **5.** A goal is a precise and measurable desired future state that a company attempts to realize.

_____ **6.** Inside directors are senior employees of the company, such as the chief executive officer (CEO).

_____ **7.** Business ethics are the accepted principles of right or wrong governing the conduct of businesspeople.

Multiple-Choice Questions

8. A _____ business definition focuses on the characteristics of the products sold and markets served.
   a. product-oriented
   b. customer-oriented
   c. strategic-oriented
   d. management-oriented
   e. profit-oriented

9. _____ occurs when managers use their control over corporate data to distort or hide information in order to enhance their own financial situation or the competitive position of the firm.
   a. Self-dealing
   b. Anticompetitive behavior
   c. Information manipulation
   d. Opportunistic exploitation
   e. Corruption

10. It is _____ that enables managers to walk away from a decision that is profitable but unethical.
   a. corporate governance
   b. a code of ethics
   c. moral courage
   d. a vision statement
   e. a mission statement

11. The capital that stockholders provide to a company is seen as _____ because there is no guarantee that stockholders will ever recoup their investment or earn a decent return.
   a. long-run returns
   b. risk capital
   c. short-run returns
   d. all of the above
   e. none of the above

12. _____ offers a way of understanding why managers do not always act in the best interests of stakeholders, and also why they might sometimes engage in actions that are unethical and perhaps also illegal.
   a. Agency theory
   b. Information asymmetry
   c. The agency problem
   d. The governance mechanism
   e. Stock-based compensation

13. _____ in the United States are required to file quarterly and annual reports with the SEC that are prepared according to GAAP.
   a. Publicly traded companies
   b. Private companies
   c. Mom-and-pop companies
   d. Sole-owner companies
   e. none of the above

14. _____ covers a range of actions aimed at harming actual or potential competitors, most often by using monopoly power, thereby enhancing the long-run prospects of the firm.
   a. Anticompetitive behavior
   b. Self-dealing behavior
   c. Information manipulation behavior
   d. Opportunistic exploitation
   e. Corruption

15. _____ can arise in a business context when managers pay bribes to gain access to lucrative business contracts.
   a. Corruption
   b. Environmental degradation
   c. Unethical behavior
   d. Inducements
   e. Self-dealing

Chapter 3

External Analysis: The Identification of Opportunities and Threats

Learning Objectives

After reading this chapter, you should be able to

1. Review the main technique used to analyze competition in an industry environment, the five forces model

2. Explore the concept of strategic groups and illustrate its implications for industry analysis

3. Discuss how industries evolve over time, with reference to the industry life cycle model

4. Show how trends in the macroenvironment can shape the nature of competition in an industry

Chapter Outline

I. Analyzing Industry Structure
  a. Risk of Entry by Potential Competitors
  b. Rivalry Among Established Companies
  c. The Bargaining Power of Buyers
  d. The Bargaining Power of Suppliers
  e. Threat of Substitute Products
  f. Summary

II. Strategic Groups Within Industries
  a. Implications of Strategic Groups
  b. The Role of Mobility Barriers

III. Industry Life Cycle Analysis
  a. Embryonic Industries
  b. Growth Industries
  c. Industry Shakeout
  d. Mature Industries
  e. Declining Industries
  f. Summary

IV. The Macroenvironment
  a. Macroeconomic Forces
  b. Global Forces
  c. Technological Forces
  d. Demographic Forces
  e. Social Forces
  f. Political and Legal Forces

Overview

opportunities

Conditions in a company's environment that it can take advantage of to formulate and implement strategies that will enable it to become more profitable.

The starting point of strategy formulation is an analysis of the forces that shape competition in the industry in which a company is based. The goal of such an analysis is to gain an understanding of the opportunities and threats confronting the firm and to use this understanding to identify strategies that will enable the company to outperform its rivals. **Opportunities** arise when a company can take advantage of conditions in its environment to formulate and implement strategies that enable it to become more profitable. **Threats** arise when conditions in the external environment endanger the integrity and profitability of the company's business.

This chapter begins with an analysis of the industry environment. First, it examines concepts and tools for analyzing the competitive structure of an industry and identifying industry opportunities and threats. Second, it analyzes the competitive implications that arise when groups of companies *within* an industry pursue similar and different kinds of competitive strategies. Third, it explores the way an industry

threats

Conditions in the external environment that endanger the integrity and profitability of a company's business.

evolves over time and the accompanying changes in competitive conditions. Fourth, it looks at the way in which forces in the macroenvironment affect industry structure and influence opportunities and threats. By the end of the chapter, you will understand that, to succeed, a company must either fit its strategy to the external environment in which it operates or be able to reshape the environment to its advantage through its chosen strategy.

Analyzing Industry Structure

industry

A group of companies offering products or services that are close substitutes for each other—that is, products or services that satisfy the same basic customer needs.

competitors

Enterprises that serve the same basic customer needs.

An **industry** can be defined as a group of companies offering products or services that are close substitutes for each other—that is, products or services that satisfy the same basic customer needs. A company's closest **competitors,** its rivals, are those that serve the same basic customer needs. For example, carbonated drinks, fruit punches, and bottled water can be viewed as close substitutes for each other because they serve the same basic customer needs for refreshing and cold nonalcoholic beverages. Thus, we can talk about the soft drink industry, whose major players are Coca-Cola, PepsiCo, and Cadbury Schweppes. Similarly, desktop computers and notebook computers satisfy the same basic need that customers have for computer hardware on which to run personal productivity software, browse the Internet, send email, play games, and store, display, and manipulate digital images. Thus, we can talk about the personal computer industry, whose major players are Dell, Hewlett-Packard, IBM, Gateway, and Apple Computer.

The starting point of external analysis is to identify the industry that a company competes in. To do this, managers must begin by looking at the basic customer needs their company is serving—that is, they must take a customer-oriented view of their business, as opposed to a product-oriented view (see Chapter 2). *The basic customer needs that are served by a market define an industry's boundary.* It is important for managers to realize this, for if they define industry boundaries incorrectly, they may be caught flat-footed by the rise of competitors that serve the same basic customer needs with different product offerings. For example, Coca-Cola long saw itself as being in the *carbonated* soft drink industry, whereas in fact it was in the soft drink industry, which includes noncarbonated soft drinks. In the mid-1990s, Coca-Cola was caught by surprise by the rise of customer demand for bottled water and fruit drinks, which began to cut into the demand for sodas. Coca-Cola moved quickly to respond to these threats, introducing its own brand of water, Dasani, and acquiring orange juice maker Minute Maid. By defining its industry boundaries too narrowly, Coca-Cola almost missed the rapid rise of the noncarbonated soft drinks segment of the soft drinks market.

Once the boundaries of an industry have been identified, the task facing managers is to analyze competitive forces in the industry environment to identify opportunities and threats. Michael E. Porter's well-known framework, known as the five forces model, helps managers with this analysis.[1] His model, shown in Figure 3.1, focuses on five forces that shape competition within an industry: (1) the risk of entry by potential competitors, (2) the intensity of rivalry among established companies within an industry, (3) the bargaining power of buyers, (4) the bargaining power of suppliers, and (5) the threat of substitutes to an industry's products.

Figure 3.1

Porter's Five Forces Model

Porter argues that the stronger each of these forces, the more limited the ability of established companies to raise prices and earn greater profits. Within Porter's framework, a *strong* competitive force can be regarded as a threat because it depresses profits. A *weak* competitive force can be viewed as an *opportunity* because it allows a company to earn greater profits. The strength of the five forces may change through time as industry conditions change. The task facing managers is to recognize how changes in the five forces give rise to new opportunities and threats and to formulate appropriate strategic responses. In addition, it is possible for a company, *through its choice of strategy,* to alter the strength of one or more of the five forces to its advantage.

• Risk of Entry by Potential Competitors

Potential competitors are companies that are not currently competing in an industry but have the capability to do so if they choose. For example, cable TV companies have recently emerged as potential competitors to traditional phone companies. This is because new digital technologies have allowed cable companies to offer consumers telephone service over the same cables that are used to transmit TV shows.

Established companies already operating in an industry often attempt to discourage potential competitors from entering the industry because the more companies that enter, the more difficult it becomes for established companies to protect their share of the market and generate profits. A high risk of entry by potential competitors represents a threat to the profitability of established companies. If the risk of new entry is low, established companies can take advantage of this opportunity to raise prices and earn greater returns.

The risk of entry by potential competitors is a function of the height of **barriers to entry**—that is, factors that make it costly for companies to enter an industry. The greater the costs that potential competitors must bear to enter an industry, the greater are the barriers to entry and the *weaker* this competitive force. High entry barriers may keep potential competitors out of an industry even when industry profits are high. Important barriers to entry include economies of scale, brand loyalty, absolute cost advantages, strategic preemption, customer switching costs, and government regulation.[2] It should be noted that a significant aspect of strategy is about building barriers to entry (in the case of incumbent firms) or finding ways to

potential competitors

Companies that are not currently competing in an industry but have the capability to do so if they choose.

barriers to entry

Factors that make it costly for companies to enter an industry.

[handwritten: re would be competitors]

[handwritten: Barrier to entry inhwele]

circumvent those barriers (in the case of new entrants). We shall discuss this in more detail in subsequent chapters.

economies of scale

Reductions in unit costs attributed to a larger output.

ECONOMIES OF SCALE **Economies of scale** arise when unit costs fall as a firm expands its output. Sources of scale economies include (1) cost reductions gained through mass-producing a standardized output, (2) discounts on bulk purchases of raw material inputs and component parts, (3) the advantages gained by spreading fixed production costs over a large production volume, and (4) the cost savings associated with spreading marketing and advertising costs over a large volume of output. If these cost advantages are significant, a new company that enters the industry and produces on a small scale suffers a significant cost disadvantage relative to established companies. If the new company decides to enter on a large scale in an attempt to obtain these economies of scale, it has to raise the capital required to build large-scale production facilities and bear the high risks associated with such an investment (which will drive up its cost of capital). A further risk of large-scale entry is that the increased supply of products will depress prices and result in vigorous retaliation by established companies. For these reasons, the threat of entry is reduced when established companies have economies of scale.

brand loyalty

Preference of consumers for the products of established companies.

BRAND LOYALTY **Brand loyalty** exists when consumers have a preference for the products of established companies. A company can create brand loyalty through continuous advertising of its brand-name products and company name, patent protection of products, product innovation achieved through company research and development programs, an emphasis on high product quality, and good after-sales service. Significant brand loyalty makes it difficult for new entrants to take market share away from established companies. Thus, it reduces the threat of entry by potential competitors, since they may see the task of breaking down well-established customer preferences as too costly. In the market for colas, for example, consumers have a strong preference for the products of Coca-Cola and PepsiCo, which makes it difficult for other enterprises to enter this market. (Despite this, the Cott Corporation has succeeded in entering the soft drink market—see the next Strategy in Action.)

absolute cost advantage

A cost advantage that is enjoyed by incumbents in an industry and that new entrants cannot expect to match.

ABSOLUTE COST ADVANTAGES Sometimes established companies have an **absolute cost advantage** relative to potential entrants, meaning that entrants cannot expect to match the established companies' lower cost structure. Absolute cost advantages arise from three main sources: (1) superior production operations and processes due to accumulated experience in an industry, patents, or secret processes; (2) control of particular inputs required for production, such as labor, materials, equipment, or management skills, that are limited in their supply; and (3) access to cheaper funds because existing companies represent lower risks than new entrants, and therefore face a lower cost of capital.[3] If established companies have an absolute cost advantage, the threat of entry as a competitive force is weaker.

switching costs

Costs that consumers must bear to switch from the products offered by one established company to the products offered by a new entrant

CUSTOMER SWITCHING COSTS **Switching costs** arise when it costs a customer time, energy, and money to switch from the products offered by one established company to the products offered by a new entrant. When switching costs are high, customers can be *locked into* the product offerings of established companies, even if new entrants offer better products.[4] A familiar example of switching costs concerns the costs associated with switching from one computer operating system to another. If a person currently uses Microsoft's Windows operating system and has a library of related

Strategy in Action

Circumventing Entry Barriers into the Soft Drink Industry

The soft drink industry has long been dominated by two companies, Coca-Cola and PepsiCo. Both companies have historically spent large sums of money on advertising and promotion, which has created significant brand loyalty and made it very difficult for prospective new competitors to enter the industry and take market share away from these two giants. When new competitors do try to enter, both companies have shown themselves capable of responding by cutting prices, forcing the new entrant to curtail expansion plans.

However, in the early 1990s the Cott Corporation, then a small Canadian bottling company, worked out a strategy for entering the soft drink market. Cott's strategy was deceptively simple. The company initially focused on the cola segment of the soft drink market. Cott signed a deal with Royal Crown Cola for exclusive global rights to its cola concentrate. RC Cola was a small player in the U.S. cola market. Its products were recognized as having a high quality, but RC Cola had never been able to effectively challenge Coke or Pepsi. Next, Cott signed a deal with a Canadian grocery retailer, Loblaws, to provide the retailer with its own private-label brand of cola. Priced low, the Loblaws private-label brand, known as President's Choice, was very successful, taking share from both Coke and Pepsi colas.

Emboldened by this success, Cott decided to try to convince other retailers to carry private-label cola. To retailers, the value proposition was simple—unlike its major rivals, Cott spent almost nothing on advertising and promotion. This constituted a major source of cost savings, which it passed on to retailers in the form of lower prices. For their part, the retailers found that they could significantly undercut the price of Coke and Pepsi colas and still make a better profit margin on their private-label brand than on branded colas.

Cott's breakthrough came in 1992, when it signed a deal with Wal-Mart to supply the retailing giant with a private-label cola called Sam's Choice. Wal-Mart proved to be the perfect distribution channel for Cott. The retailer was just starting to get into the grocery business, and consumers went to the stores not to buy branded merchandise, but to get low prices.

As Wal-Mart's grocery business grew, so did Cott's sales. Cott soon added other flavors to its offering, such as a lemon-lime soda that would compete with 7UP and Sprite. Moreover, pressured by Wal-Mart, by the late 1990s other U.S. grocers also started to introduce private-label sodas, often turning to Cott to supply their needs. By 2006, Cott had grown to become a $1.8 billion company. Its volume growth in an otherwise stagnant U.S. market for sodas averaged around 12.5% between 2001 and 2006. Cott captured over 5% of the U.S. soda market in 2005, up from almost nothing a decade earlier, and held onto a 16% share of sodas in grocery stores, its core channel. The losers in this process have been Coca-Cola and PepsiCo, which are now facing the steady erosion of their brand loyalty and market share as consumers have increasingly come to recognize the high quality and low price of private-label sodas.[a]

software applications (e.g., word-processing software, spreadsheet, games) and document files, it is expensive for that person to switch to another computer operating system. To effect the change, this person would have to buy a new set of software applications and convert all existing document files to run with the new system. Faced with such an expenditure of money and time, most people are unwilling to make the switch *unless* the competing operating system offers a *substantial* leap forward in performance. Thus, the higher the switching costs are, the higher is the barrier to entry for a company attempting to promote a new computer operating system.

GOVERNMENT REGULATION Historically, government regulation has constituted a major entry barrier into many industries. For example, until the mid-1990s, U.S. government regulation prohibited providers of long-distance telephone service from competing for local telephone service and vice versa. Other potential providers of telephone service, including cable television service companies such as TimeWarner and Viacom (which could, in theory, use their cables to carry telephone traffic as well as

TV signals), were prohibited from entering the market altogether. These regulatory barriers to entry significantly reduced the level of competition in both the local and the long-distance telephone markets, enabling telephone companies to earn higher profits than might otherwise have been the case. All this changed in 1996, when the government deregulated the industry significantly. In the months that followed this announcement, local, long-distance, and cable TV companies all announced their intention to enter each other's markets, and a host of new players entered the market. The five forces model predicts that falling entry barriers due to government deregulation would result in significant new entry, an increase in the intensity of industry competition, and lower industry profit rates—and indeed, that is what occurred.

In summary, if established companies have built brand loyalty for their products, have an absolute cost advantage with respect to potential competitors, have significant scale economies, are the beneficiaries of high switching costs, or enjoy regulatory protection, the risk of entry by potential competitors is greatly diminished; it is a weak competitive force. Consequently, established companies can charge higher prices, and industry profits are higher. Evidence from academic research suggests that the height of barriers to entry is one of the most important determinants of profit rates in an industry.[5] Clearly, it is in the interest of established companies to pursue strategies consistent with raising entry barriers to secure these profits. By the same token, potential new entrants have to find strategies that allow them to circumvent barriers to entry. Research suggests that the best way to do this is *not* to compete head to head with incumbents, but to look for customers who are poorly served by incumbents, and to go after those customers using new distribution channels and new business models (see the Strategy in Action feature for an example).[6]

Rivalry Among Established Companies

rivalry

The competitive struggle between companies in an industry to gain market share from each other.

fragmented industry

An industry that consists of a large number of small or medium-sized companies, none of which is in a position to determine industry prices.

consolidated industry

An industry dominated by a small number of large companies or, in extreme cases, just one company, which often is in a position to determine industry prices.

The second of Porter's five competitive forces is the intensity of rivalry among established companies within an industry. **Rivalry** refers to the competitive struggle between companies in an industry to gain market share from each other. The competitive struggle can be fought using price, product design, advertising and promotion spending, direct selling efforts, and after-sales service and support. More intense rivalry implies lower prices or more spending on non-price-competitive weapons or both. Because intense rivalry lowers prices and raises costs, it squeezes profits out of an industry. Thus, intense rivalry among established companies constitutes a strong threat to profitability. Alternatively, if rivalry is less intense, companies may have the opportunity to raise prices or reduce spending on non-price-competitive weapons, which leads to a higher level of industry profits. The intensity of rivalry among established companies within an industry is largely a function of four factors: (1) industry competitive structure, (2) demand conditions, (3) cost conditions, and (4) the height of exit barriers in the industry.

INDUSTRY COMPETITIVE STRUCTURE The *competitive structure* of an industry refers to the number and size distribution of companies in it, something that strategic managers determine at the beginning of an industry analysis. Industry structures vary, and different structures have different implications for the intensity of rivalry. A **fragmented industry** consists of a large number of small or medium-sized companies, none of which is in a position to determine industry price. Examples of fragmented industries are agriculture, dry cleaning, video rental, health clubs, real estate brokerage, and tanning parlors. A **consolidated industry** is dominated by a small number of large companies (an oligopoly) or, in extreme cases, just one company (a monopoly), which often is in a position to determine industry prices. Consolidated industries include the aerospace, soft drink, automobile, pharmaceutical, and stockbrokerage industries.

Many fragmented industries are characterized by low entry barriers and commodity-type products that are hard to differentiate. The combination of these traits tends to result in boom-and-bust cycles as industry profits rise and fall. Low entry barriers imply that whenever demand is strong and profits are high, new entrants will flood the market, hoping to profit from the boom. The explosion in the number of video stores, health clubs, and tanning parlors during the 1980s and 1990s exemplifies this situation.

Often the flood of new entrants into a booming fragmented industry creates excess capacity, so companies start to cut prices in order to use their spare capacity. The difficulty companies face when trying to differentiate their products from those of competitors can exacerbate this tendency. The result is a price war, which depresses industry profits, forces some companies out of business, and deters potential new entrants. For example, after a decade of expansion and booming profits, many health clubs are now finding that they have to offer large discounts in order to hold onto their membership. In general, the more commodity-like an industry's product is, the more vicious will be the price war. This bust part of the cycle continues until overall industry capacity is brought into line with demand (through bankruptcies), at which point prices may stabilize again.

A fragmented industry structure, then, constitutes a threat rather than an opportunity. Most booms are relatively short-lived because of the ease of new entry and will be followed by price wars and bankruptcies. Because it is often difficult to differentiate products in these industries, the best strategy for a company is to try to minimize its costs so it will be profitable in a boom and survive any subsequent bust. Alternatively, companies might try to adopt strategies that change the underlying structure of fragmented industries and lead to a consolidated industry structure in which the level of industry profitability is increased. How companies can do this is something we shall consider in later chapters.

In consolidated industries, companies are interdependent, because one company's competitive actions or moves (with regard to price, quality, and so on) directly affect the market share of its rivals, and thus their profitability. When one company makes a move, this generally "forces" a response from its rivals, and the consequence of such competitive interdependence can be a dangerous competitive spiral. Rivalry increases as companies attempt to undercut each other's prices or offer customers more value in their products, pushing industry profits down in the process. The fare wars that have periodically created havoc in the airline industry provide a good illustration of this process.

Companies in consolidated industries sometimes seek to reduce this threat by following the prices set by the dominant company in the industry.[7] However, companies must be careful, for explicit face-to-face price-fixing agreements are illegal (tacit, indirect agreements, arrived at without direct or intentional communication, are legal). Instead, companies set prices by watching, interpreting, anticipating, and responding to each other's behavior.

INDUSTRY DEMAND The level of industry demand is a second determinant of the intensity of rivalry among established companies. Growing demand from new customers or additional purchases by existing customers tend to moderate competition by providing greater scope for companies to compete for customers. Growing demand tends to reduce rivalry because all companies can sell more without taking market share away from other companies. High industry profits are often the result. Conversely, declining demand results in more rivalry as companies fight to maintain market share and revenues. Demand declines when customers are leaving the marketplace or each customer is buying less. Now a company can grow only by taking market share away from other companies. Thus, declining demand constitutes a major threat, for it increases the extent of rivalry between established companies.

COST CONDITIONS The cost structure of firms in an industry is a third determinant of rivalry. In industries where fixed costs are high, profitability tends to be highly leveraged to sales volume and the desire to grow volume can spark intense rivalry. **Fixed costs** refer to the costs that must be borne before the firm makes a single sale. For example, before they can offer service, cable TV companies have to lay cable in the ground—the cost of doing so is a fixed cost. Similarly, in order to offer air express service, a company like FedEx has to invest in planes, package-sorting facilities, and delivery trucks. These all represent fixed costs that require significant capital investments. In industries where the fixed costs of production are high, if sales volume is low firms cannot cover their fixed costs and they will not be profitable. This creates an incentive for firms to cut their prices and/or increase promotion spending in order to drive up sales volume, thereby covering fixed costs. In situations where demand is not growing fast enough and too many companies are engaged in the same actions, cutting prices and/or raising promotion spending in an attempt to cover fixed costs, the result can be intense rivalry and lower profits. Research suggests that it is often the weakest firms in an industry that initiate such actions, precisely because they are the ones struggling to cover their fixed costs.[8]

EXIT BARRIERS **Exit barriers** are economic, strategic, and emotional factors that prevent companies from leaving an industry.[9] If exit barriers are high, companies become locked into an unprofitable industry where overall demand is static or declining. The result is often excess production capacity, which leads to even more intense rivalry and price competition as companies cut prices in the attempt to obtain the customer orders needed to use their idle capacity and cover their fixed costs.[10] Common exit barriers include the following:

- Investments in assets such as specific machines, equipment, and operating facilities that are of little or no value in alternative uses or cannot be sold off. If the company wishes to leave the industry, it has to write off the book value of these assets.

- High fixed costs of exit, such as the severance pay, health benefits, and pensions that have to be paid to workers who are made redundant when a company ceases to operate.

- Emotional attachments to an industry, as when a company's owners or employees are unwilling to exit from an industry for sentimental reasons or because of pride.

- Economic dependence on the industry because a company relies on a single industry for its revenue and profit.

- The need to maintain an expensive collection of assets at or above some minimum level in order to participate effectively in the industry.

- Bankruptcy regulations, particularly in the United States, where Chapter 11 bankruptcy provisions allow insolvent enterprises to continue operating and reorganize themselves under bankruptcy protection. These regulations can keep unprofitable assets in the industry, result in persistent excess capacity, and lengthen the time required to bring industry supply in line with demand.

---

fixed costs

Costs that must be borne before the firm makes a single sale.

---

exit barriers

The economic, strategic, and emotional factors that prevent companies from leaving an industry.

As an example of the effect of exit barriers in practice, consider the express mail and parcel delivery industry. The key players in this industry, such as FedEx and UPS, rely on the delivery business entirely for their revenues and profits. They have to be able to guarantee their customers that they will deliver packages to all major localities in the United States, and much of their investment is specific to this purpose. To meet this guarantee, they need a nationwide network of air routes and ground routes, an asset that is required in order to participate in the industry. If excess capacity develops in this industry, as it does from time to time, FedEx cannot incrementally reduce or minimize its excess capacity by deciding not to fly to and deliver packages in, say, Miami because that proportion of its network is underused. If it did that, it would no longer be able to guarantee to its customers that it would be able to deliver packages to all major locations in the United States, and its customers would switch to some other carrier. Thus, the need to maintain a nationwide network is an exit barrier that can result in persistent excess capacity in the air express industry during periods of weak demand. Finally, both UPS and FedEx managers and employees are emotionally tied to this industry because they were first movers in the ground and air segments of the industry, respectively, and because their employees are also major owners of their companies' stock and are dependent financially on the fortunes of the delivery business.

● **The Bargaining Power of Buyers**

The third of Porter's five competitive forces is the bargaining power of buyers. An industry's buyers may be the individual customers who ultimately consume its products (its end users) or the companies that distribute an industry's products to end users, such as retailers and wholesalers. For example, while soap powder made by Procter & Gamble and Unilever is consumed by end users, the principal buyers of soap powder are supermarket chains and discount stores, which resell the product to end users. The **bargaining power of buyers** refers to the ability of buyers to bargain down prices charged by companies in the industry or to raise the costs of companies in the industry by demanding better product quality and service. By lowering prices and raising costs, powerful buyers can squeeze profits out of an industry. Thus, powerful buyers should be viewed as a threat. Alternatively, when buyers are in a weak bargaining position, companies in an industry can raise prices and perhaps reduce their costs by lowering product quality and service and thus increase the level of industry profits. Buyers are most powerful in the following circumstances:

bargaining power of buyers

The ability of buyers to bargain down prices charged by companies in the industry or to raise the costs of companies in the industry by demanding better product quality and service.

- When the industry that is supplying a particular product or service is composed of many small companies and the buyers are large and few in number. These circumstances allow the buyers to dominate supplying companies.

- When the buyers purchase in large quantities. In such circumstances, buyers can use their purchasing power as leverage to bargain for price reductions.

- When the supplying industry depends on the buyers for a large percentage of its total orders.

- When switching costs are low, so buyers can play off the supplying companies against each other to force down prices.

- When it is economically feasible for buyers to purchase an input from several companies at once, so buyers can play off one company in the industry against another.

- When buyers can threaten to enter the industry and produce the product themselves and thus supply their own needs. This is also a tactic for forcing down industry prices.

The auto component supply industry, whose buyers are large automobile manufacturers such as GM, Ford, and Chrysler, is a good example of an industry in which buyers have strong bargaining power and thus pose a strong competitive threat. Why? The suppliers of auto components are numerous and typically small in scale; their buyers, the auto manufacturers, are large in size and few in number. Chrysler, for example, does business with nearly 2,000 different component suppliers in the United States and normally contracts with a number of different companies to supply the same part. Additionally, to keep component prices down, both Ford and GM have used the threat of manufacturing a component themselves rather than buying it from auto component suppliers. The automakers have used their powerful position to play off suppliers against each other, forcing down the price they have to pay for component parts and demanding better quality. If a component supplier objects, the automaker uses the threat of switching to another supplier or making the part itself as a bargaining tool.

Another issue is that the relative power of buyers and suppliers tends to change in response to changing industry conditions. For example, because of changes now taking place in the pharmaceutical and health care industries, major buyers of pharmaceuticals (hospitals and health maintenance organizations) are gaining power over the suppliers of pharmaceuticals and have been able to demand lower prices. The Running Case discusses how Wal-Mart's buying power has changed over the years as the company has become larger.

The Bargaining Power of Suppliers

bargaining power of suppliers

The ability of suppliers to raise the price of inputs or to raise the costs of the industry in other ways.

The fourth of Porter's five competitive forces is the bargaining power of suppliers—the organizations that provide the industry with inputs such as materials, services, and labor (which may be individuals, organizations such as labor unions, or companies that supply contract labor). The **bargaining power of suppliers** refers to the ability of suppliers to raise input prices or to raise the costs of the industry in other ways—for example, by providing poor-quality inputs or poor service. Powerful suppliers squeeze profits out of an industry by raising the costs of companies in the industry. Thus, powerful suppliers are a threat. Alternatively, if suppliers are weak, companies in the industry have the opportunity to force down input prices and demand higher quality inputs (e.g., more productive labor). As with buyers, the ability of suppliers to make demands on a company depends on their power relative to that of the company. Suppliers are most powerful in these situations:

- The product that a supplier sells has few substitutes and is vital to the companies in an industry.

- The profitability of suppliers is not significantly affected by the purchases of companies in a particular industry—in other words, the industry is not an important customer of the suppliers.

- Companies in an industry would experience significant switching costs if they moved to the product of a different supplier because a particular supplier's products are unique or different. In such cases, the company depends on a particular supplier and cannot play suppliers off against each other to reduce price.

- Suppliers can threaten to enter their customers' industry and use their inputs to produce products that would compete directly with those of companies already in the industry.

- Companies in the industry cannot threaten to enter their suppliers' industry and make their own inputs as a tactic for lowering the price of inputs.

RUNNING CASE

Wal-Mart's Bargaining Power over Suppliers

When Wal-Mart and other discount retailers began in the 1960s, they were small operations with little purchasing power. To generate store traffic, they depended in large part on stocking nationally branded merchandise from well-known companies such as Procter & Gamble and Rubbermaid. Since the discounters did not have high sales volume, the nationally branded companies set the price. This meant that the discounters had to look for other ways to cut costs, which they typically did by emphasizing self-service in stripped-down stores located in the suburbs, where land was cheaper (in the 1960s, the main competitors for discounters were full-service department stores like Sears, which were often located in downtown shopping areas).

Discounters such as Kmart purchased their merchandise through wholesalers, who in turn bought from manufacturers. The wholesaler would come into a store and write an order, and when the merchandise arrived, the wholesaler would come in and stock the shelves, saving the retailer labor costs. However, Wal-Mart was located in Arkansas and placed its stores in small towns. Wholesalers were not particularly interested in serving a company that built its stores in such out-of-the-way places. They would do it only if Wal-Mart paid higher prices.

Wal-Mart's Sam Walton refused to pay higher prices. Instead, he took his fledgling company public and used the capital raised to build a distribution center to stock merchandise. The distribution center would serve all stores within a 300-mile radius, with trucks leaving the distribution center daily to restock the stores. Because the distribution center was serving a collection of stores and thus buying in larger volumes, Walton found that he was able to cut the wholesalers out of the equation and order directly from manufacturers. The cost savings generated by not having to pay profits to wholesalers were then passed on to consumers in the form of lower prices, which helped Wal-Mart continue growing. This growth increased its buying power and thus its ability to demand deeper discounts from manufacturers.

Today Wal-Mart has turned its buying process into an art form. Since 8% of all retail sales in the United States are made in a Wal-Mart store, the company has enormous bargaining power over its suppliers. Suppliers of nationally branded products, such as Procter & Gamble, are no longer in a position to demand high prices. Instead, Wal-Mart is now so important to Procter & Gamble that it is able to demand deep discounts from them. Moreover, Wal-Mart has itself become a brand that is more powerful than the brands of manufacturers. People don't go to Wal-Mart to buy branded goods; they go to Wal-Mart for the low prices. This simple fact has enabled Wal-Mart to bargain down the prices it pays, always passing on cost savings to consumers in the form of lower prices.

Since 1991, Wal-Mart has provided suppliers with real-time information on store sales through the use of individual stock keeping units (SKUs). These have allowed suppliers to optimize their own production processes, matching output to Wal-Mart's demands and avoiding underproduction or overproduction and the need to store inventory. The efficiencies that manufacturers gain from such information are passed on to Wal-Mart in the form of lower prices; Wal-Mart then passes on those cost savings to consumers.[b]

An example of an industry in which companies are dependent on a powerful supplier is the personal computer industry. Personal computer firms are heavily dependent on Intel, the world's largest supplier of microprocessors for PCs. The industry standard for personal computers runs on Intel's microprocessor chips. Intel's competitors, such as Advanced Micro Devices (AMD), must develop and supply chips that are compatible with Intel's standard. Although AMD has developed competing chips, Pentium still accounts for about 85% of the chips used in PCs, primarily because only Intel has the manufacturing capacity required to serve a large share of the market. It is beyond the financial resources of Intel's competitors to match the scale and efficiency of Intel's manufacturing systems. This means that while PC manufacturers can buy some microprocessors from Intel's rivals, most notably

AMD, they still have to turn to Intel for the bulk of their supply. Because Intel is in a powerful bargaining position, it can charge higher prices for its microprocessors than would be the case if its competitors were more numerous and stronger (i.e., if the microprocessor industry were fragmented).

● **Threat of Substitute Products**

substitute products

The products of different businesses or industries that can satisfy similar customer needs.

The final force in Porter's model is the threat of **substitute products,** the products of different businesses or industries that can satisfy similar customer needs. For example, companies in the coffee industry compete indirectly with those in the tea and soft drink industries because all three serve customer needs for nonalcoholic drinks. The existence of close substitutes is a strong competitive threat because it limits the price that companies in one industry can charge for their product and thus industry profitability. If the price of coffee rises too much relative to that of tea or soft drinks, coffee drinkers may switch to those substitutes.

If an industry's products have few close substitutes, so substitutes are a weak competitive force, then, other things being equal, companies in the industry have the opportunity to raise prices and earn additional profits. There is no close substitute for microprocessors, which gives companies like Intel and AMD the ability to charge higher prices than they could if there were a substitute for microprocessors.

● **Summary**

The systematic analysis of forces in the industry environment using the Porter framework is a powerful tool that helps managers to think strategically. It is important to recognize that one competitive force often affects the others, so all forces need to be considered when performing industry analysis. Indeed, industry analysis leads managers to think systematically about the way their strategic choices will both affect and be affected by the five forces of industry competition and change conditions in the industry.

Strategic Groups Within Industries

Companies in an industry often differ significantly from each other with respect to the way they strategically position their products in the market in terms of such factors as the distribution channels they use, the market segments they serve, the quality of their products, technological leadership, customer service, pricing policy, advertising policy, and promotions. As a result of these differences, within most industries it is possible to observe groups of companies in which each company follows a strategy that is similar to that pursued by other companies in the group but *different* from the strategies followed by companies in other groups. These different groups of companies are known as **strategic groups.**[11]

strategic groups

Groups of companies in which each company follows a strategy that is similar to that pursued by other companies in the group but different from the strategies followed by companies in other groups.

Normally, the basic differences between the strategies that companies in different strategic groups use can be captured by a relatively small number of strategic factors. For example, in the pharmaceutical industry, two main strategic groups stand out (see Figure 3.2).[12] One group, which includes such companies as Merck, Eli Lilly, and Pfizer, is characterized by a business model based on heavy R&D spending and a focus on developing new, proprietary, blockbuster drugs. The companies in this *proprietary* strategic group are pursuing a high-risk, high-return strategy. It is a high-risk strategy because basic drug research is difficult and expensive. Bringing a new drug to market can cost up to $800 million in R&D money and require a decade of research and clinical trials. The risks are high because the failure rate in new drug development is very high: only one out of every five drugs entering clinical trials is ultimately approved by the U.S. Food and Drug Administration. However, the

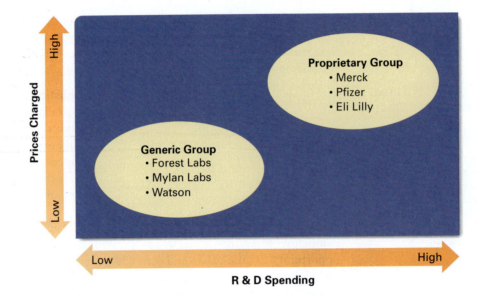

strategy is also a high-return one because a single successful drug can be patented, giving the innovator a twenty-year monopoly on its production and sale. This lets these proprietary companies charge a high price for the patented drug, allowing them to earn millions, if not billions, of dollars over the lifetime of the patent.

The second strategic group might be characterized as the *generic drug* strategic group. This group of companies, which includes Forest Labs, Mylan Labs, and Watson Pharmaceuticals, focuses on the manufacture of generic drugs: low-cost copies of drugs that were developed by companies in the proprietary group whose patents have now expired. Low R&D spending, production efficiency, and an emphasis on low prices characterize the business models of companies in this strategic group. They are pursuing a low-risk, low-return strategy. It is low risk because they are not investing millions of dollars in R&D. It is low return because they cannot charge high prices.

● **Implications of Strategic Groups**

The concept of strategic groups has a number of implications for the identification of opportunities and threats within an industry. First, because all the companies in a strategic group are pursuing a similar business model, customers tend to view the products of such enterprises as *direct substitutes* for each other. Thus, a company's *closest* competitors are those in its strategic group, not those in other strategic groups in the industry. The most immediate threat to a company's profitability comes from rivals within its own strategic group. For example, in the retail industry, there is a group of companies that might be characterized as discounters. Included in this group are Wal-Mart, Kmart, Target, Costco, and Fred Meyer. These companies compete most vigorously with each other, as opposed to with other retailers in different groups, such as Nordstrom or The Gap. Kmart, for example, was driven into bankruptcy in the early 2000s not because Nordstrom or The Gap took business from it, but because Wal-Mart and Target gained share in the discounting group by virtue of their superior strategic execution of the discounting business model.

A second competitive implication is that different strategic groups can have a different standing with respect to each of the competitive forces; thus, *each strategic group may face a different set of opportunities and threats.* The risk of new entry by potential competitors, the degree of rivalry among companies within a group, the bargaining power of buyers, the bargaining power of suppliers, and the competitive force of substitute and complementary products can each be a relatively strong or weak competitive force, depending on the competitive positioning approach adopted by each strategic group in the industry. For example, in the pharmaceutical industry companies in the proprietary group have historically been in a very powerful position in relation to buyers because their products are patented and there are no substitutes. Also, rivalry based on price competition within this group has been low because competition in the industry revolves around being the first to patent a new drug (so-called patent races), not around drug prices. Thus, companies in this group have been able to charge high prices and earn high profits. In contrast, companies in the generic drug group have been in a much weaker position because many are able to produce different versions of the same generic drug after patents expire. In this strategic group, products are close substitutes and rivalry has been high; price competition has led to lower profits for this group compared to companies in the proprietary group.

● The Role of Mobility Barriers

It follows from these two issues that some strategic groups are more desirable than others because the five competitive forces open up greater opportunities and present fewer threats for those groups. Managers, after having analyzed their industry, might identify a strategic group where competitive forces are weaker and higher profits can be made. Sensing an opportunity, they might contemplate changing their business model and move to compete in that strategic group. However, taking advantage of this opportunity may be difficult because of mobility barriers between strategic groups.

mobility barriers

Within-industry factors that inhibit the movement of companies between strategic groups.

Mobility barriers are within-industry factors that inhibit the movement of companies between strategic groups. They include the barriers to entry into a group and the barriers to exit from a company's existing group. For example, Forest Labs would encounter mobility barriers if it attempted to enter the proprietary group in the pharmaceutical industry because it lacks R&D skills and building these skills would be an expensive proposition. Essentially, over time, companies in different groups develop different cost structures and skills and competences that give them different pricing options and choices. A company contemplating entry into another strategic group must evaluate whether it has the ability to imitate, and indeed outperform, its potential competitors in that strategic group. Managers must determine if it is cost-effective to overcome mobility barriers before deciding whether the move is worthwhile.

In summary, an important task of industry analysis is to determine the sources of the similarities and differences among companies in an industry and to work out the broad themes that underlie competition in an industry. This analysis often reveals new opportunities to compete in an industry by developing new kinds of products to meet the needs of customers better. It can also reveal emerging threats that can be countered effectively by changing competitive strategy.

Industry Life Cycle Analysis

An important determinant of the strength of the competitive forces in an industry is the changes that take place in it over time. The strength and nature of each of the competitive forces change as an industry evolves, particularly the two forces of risk of entry by potential competitors and rivalry among existing firms.[13]

Figure 3.3

Stages in the
Industry Life Cycle

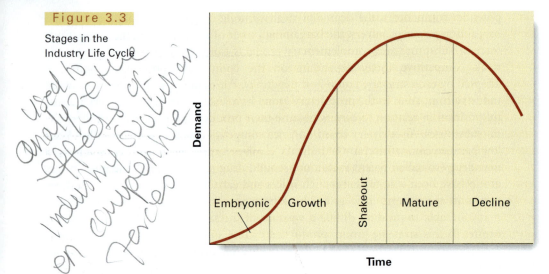

[handwritten note: used to analyze the effects of industry evolution on competitive forces]

A useful tool for analyzing the effects of industry evolution on competitive forces is the industry life cycle model, which identifies five sequential stages in the evolution of an industry that lead to five distinct kinds of industry environments: the embryonic, growth, shakeout, mature, and decline stages (see Figure 3.3). The task facing managers is to *anticipate* how the strength of competitive forces will change as the industry environment evolves and to formulate strategies that take advantage of opportunities as they arise and that counter emerging threats.

● **Embryonic Industries**

embryonic industry

An industry that is just beginning to develop.

An **embryonic industry** is just beginning to develop (for example, personal computers and biotechnology in the 1970s and nanotechnology today). Growth at this stage is slow because of buyers' unfamiliarity with the industry's product, high prices due to the inability of companies to reap any significant scale economies, and poorly developed distribution channels. Barriers to entry tend to be based on access to key technological know-how rather than cost economies or brand loyalty. If the core know-how required to compete in the industry is complex and difficult to grasp, barriers to entry can be quite high, and established companies will be protected from potential competitors. Rivalry in embryonic industries is based not so much on price as on educating customers, opening up distribution channels, and perfecting the design of the product. Such rivalry can be intense, and the company that is the first to solve design problems often has the opportunity to develop a significant market position. An embryonic industry may also be the creation of one company's innovative efforts, as happened with microprocessors (Intel) and photocopiers (Xerox). In such circumstances, the company has a major opportunity to capitalize on the lack of rivalry and build a strong hold on the market.

● **Growth Industries**

growth industry

An industry where demand is expanding as first-time consumers enter the market.

Once demand for the industry's product begins to take off, the industry develops the characteristics of a growth industry. In a **growth industry,** first-time demand is expanding rapidly as many new customers enter the market. An industry grows when customers become familiar with the product, prices fall because experience and scale economies have been attained, and distribution channels develop. The U.S. cellular telephone industry was in the growth stage for most of the 1990s. In 1990, there were only 5 million cellular subscribers in the nation. By 2006, this figure had increased to over 160 million, and overall demand was still expanding.

Normally, the importance of control over technological knowledge as a barrier to entry has diminished by the time an industry enters its growth stage. Because few companies have yet achieved significant scale economies or built brand loyalty, other entry barriers tend to be relatively low as well, particularly early in the growth stage. Thus, the threat from potential competitors generally is highest at this point. Paradoxically, however, high growth usually means that new entrants can be absorbed into an industry without a marked increase in the intensity of rivalry. Thus, rivalry tends to be relatively low. Rapid growth in demand enables companies to expand their revenues and profits without taking market share away from competitors. A strategically aware company takes advantage of the relatively benign environment of the growth stage to prepare itself for the intense competition of the coming industry shakeout.

● **Industry Shakeout**

shakeout stage

The stage of industry evolution in which demand growth goes down, competition intensifies, and weaker competitors exit the industry.

Explosive growth cannot be maintained indefinitely. Sooner or later, the rate of growth slows, and the industry enters the shakeout stage. In the **shakeout stage,** demand approaches saturation levels: most of the demand is limited to replacement because there are few potential first-time buyers left.

As an industry enters the shakeout stage, rivalry between companies becomes intense. Typically, companies that have become accustomed to rapid growth continue to add capacity at rates consistent with past growth. However, demand is no longer growing at historic rates, and the consequence is the emergence of excess production capacity. This condition is illustrated in Figure 3.4, where the solid curve indicates the growth in demand over time and the broken curve indicates the growth in production capacity over time. As you can see, past point t_1, demand growth becomes slower as the industry becomes mature. However, capacity continues to grow until time t_2. The gap between the solid and the broken lines signifies excess capacity. In an attempt to use this capacity, companies often cut prices. The result can be a price war, which drives many of the most inefficient companies into bankruptcy and is enough to deter any new entry.

Figure 3.4

Growth in Demand and Capacity

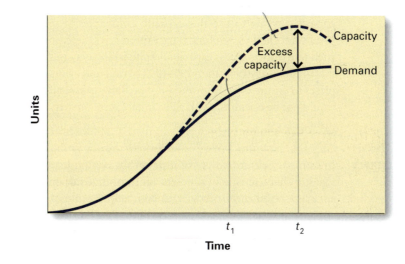

Mature Industries

mature stage

The stage in which the market is saturated, demand is limited to replacement demand, and growth is slow.

The shakeout stage ends when the industry enters its **mature stage:** the market is totally saturated, demand is limited primarily to replacement demand, and growth is low or zero. What growth there is comes from population expansion that brings new customers into the market or an increase in replacement demand.

As an industry enters maturity, barriers to entry increase, and the threat of entry from potential competitors decreases. As growth slows during the shakeout, companies can no longer maintain historic growth rates merely by holding onto their market share. Competition for market share develops, driving down prices. Often the result is a price war, as has happened in the airline industry, for example. To survive the shakeout, companies begin to focus on cost minimization and building brand loyalty. The airlines tried to cut operating costs by hiring nonunion labor and to build brand loyalty by introducing frequent-flyer programs. By the time an industry matures, the surviving companies are those that have brand loyalty and efficient low-cost operations. Because both these factors constitute a significant barrier to entry, the threat of entry by potential competitors is greatly diminished. High entry barriers in mature industries give companies the opportunity to increase prices and profits.

As a result of the shakeout, most industries in the mature stage have consolidated and become oligopolies. In mature industries, companies tend to recognize their interdependence and try to avoid price wars. Stable demand gives them the opportunity to enter into price leadership agreements. The net effect is to reduce the threat of intense rivalry among established companies, thereby allowing greater profitability. Nevertheless, the stability of a mature industry is always threatened by further price wars. A general slump in economic activity can depress industry demand. As companies fight to maintain their revenues in the face of declining demand, price leadership agreements break down, rivalry increases, and prices and profits fall. The periodic price wars that occur in the airline industry seem to follow this pattern.

Declining Industries

decline stage

The stage in which primary demand is declining.

Eventually, most industries enter a **decline stage:** growth becomes negative for a variety of reasons, including technological substitution (for example, air travel for rail travel), social changes (greater health consciousness hitting tobacco sales), demographics (the declining birth rate hurting the market for baby and child products), and international competition (low-cost foreign competition pushing the U.S. steel industry into decline). Within a declining industry, the degree of rivalry among established companies usually increases. Depending on the speed of the decline and the height of exit barriers, competitive pressures can become as fierce as in the shakeout stage.[14] The main problem in a declining industry is that falling demand leads to the emergence of excess capacity. In trying to use this capacity, companies begin to cut prices, thus sparking a price war. The U.S. steel industry experienced these problems because steel companies tried to use their excess capacity despite falling demand. The same problem occurred in the airline industry in the 1990–1992 period and again in 2001–2002, as companies cut prices to ensure that they would not be flying with half-empty planes (that is, that they would not be operating with substantial excess capacity). Exit barriers play a part in adjusting excess capacity. The greater the exit barriers, the harder it is for companies to reduce capacity and the greater is the threat of severe price competition.

Summary

In summary, a third task of industry analysis is to identify the opportunities and threats that are characteristic of different kinds of industry environments in order to develop an effective business model and competitive strategy. Managers have to tailor their strategies to changing industry conditions. And they have to learn to recognize the crucial points in an industry's development so that they can forecast when the shakeout stage of an industry might begin or when an industry might be moving into decline.

This is also true at the level of strategic groups, for new embryonic groups may emerge because of shifts in customer needs and tastes or some groups may grow rapidly because of changes in technology and others decline as their customers defect. Thus, for example, companies in the upscale retail group, such as Macy's, Dillard's, and Nordstrom, are facing declining sales as customers defect to discount retailers like Target and Wal-Mart and online companies like Amazon and Lands' End.

The Macroenvironment

macroenvironment

The broader economic, global, technological, demographic, social, and political context in which an industry is embedded.

Just as the decisions and actions of strategic managers can often change an industry's competitive structure, so too can changing conditions or forces in the wider **macroenvironment**—that is, the broader economic, global, technological, demographic, social, and political context in which companies and industries are embedded (see Figure 3.5). Changes in the forces in the macroenvironment can have a direct impact on any or all of the forces in Porter's model, thereby altering the relative strength of these forces and, with it, the attractiveness of an industry.

● **Macroeconomic Forces**

Macroeconomic forces affect the general health and well-being of a nation or the regional economy of an organization, which in turn affects companies' and industries' ability to earn an adequate rate of return. The four most important factors in the macroeconomic environment are the growth rate of the economy, interest rates, currency exchange rates, and price inflation. Economic growth, because it leads to an expansion in customer expenditures, tends to produce a general easing of competitive pressures within an industry. This gives companies the opportunity to expand their operations and earn higher profits. Because economic decline (a recession)

Figure 3.5

The Role of the Macroenvironment

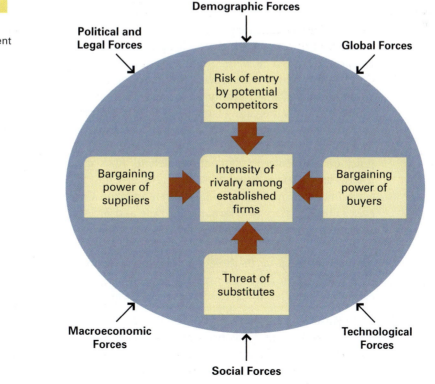

leads to a reduction in customer expenditures, it increases competitive pressures. Economic decline frequently causes price wars in mature industries.

The level of interest rates can determine the demand for a company's products. Interest rates are important whenever customers routinely borrow money to finance their purchase of these products. The most obvious example is the housing market, where mortgage rates directly affect demand. Interest rates also have an impact on the sale of autos, appliances, and capital equipment, to give just a few examples. For companies in such industries, rising interest rates are a threat and falling rates an opportunity.

Currency exchange rates define the value of different national currencies against each other. Movement in currency exchange rates has a direct impact on the competitiveness of a company's products in the global marketplace. For example, when the value of the dollar is low compared with the value of other currencies, products made in the United States are relatively inexpensive and products made overseas are relatively expensive. A low or declining dollar reduces the threat from foreign competitors while creating opportunities for increased sales overseas. Thus, the fall in the dollar against the euro during 2006 and 2007 enabled American companies to export more goods and services to Europe. The fall in the value of the dollar against the Japanese yen that occurred between 1985 and 1995, when the dollar-to-yen exchange rate declined from 240 yen per dollar to 85 yen per dollar, sharply increased the price of imported Japanese cars, giving U.S. car manufacturers some protection against those imports.

Price inflation can destabilize the economy, producing slower economic growth, higher interest rates, and volatile currency movements. If inflation keeps increasing, investment planning becomes hazardous. The key characteristic of inflation is that it makes the future less predictable. In an inflationary environment, it may be impossible to predict with any accuracy the real value of returns that can be earned from a project five years hence. Such uncertainty makes companies less willing to invest. Their holding back in turn depresses economic activity and ultimately pushes the economy into a slump. Thus, high inflation is a threat to companies.

Global Forces

Over the last half-century, there have been enormous changes in the world economic system. We review these changes in detail in Chapter 6 when we discuss global strategy. For now, the important points to note are that barriers to international trade and investment have tumbled, and an increasing number of countries are enjoying sustained economic growth. Economic growth in places like Brazil, China, and India is creating large new markets for the goods and services of companies and gives companies an opportunity to grow their profits faster by entering these nations. Falling barriers to international trade and investment have made it much easier to enter foreign nations. Twenty years ago, it was almost impossible for a Western company to set up operations in China. Today, Western and Japanese companies are investing over $50 billion a year in China. By the same token, however, falling barriers to international trade and investment have made it easier for foreign enterprises to enter the domestic markets of many companies (by lowering barriers to entry), thereby increasing the intensity of competition and lowering profitability. Because of these changes, many formerly isolated domestic markets have now become part of a much larger and more competitive global marketplace, creating a myriad of threats and opportunities for companies.

Technological Forces

Since World War II, the pace of technological change has accelerated.[15] This has unleashed a process that has been called a "perennial gale of creative destruction."[16] Technological change can make established products obsolete overnight and simultaneously create a host of new product possibilities. Thus, technological change is both creative and destructive—both an opportunity and a threat.

One of the most important impacts of technological change is that it can affect the height of barriers to entry and therefore radically reshape industry structure. The Internet, because it is so pervasive, has the potential to change the competitive structure of many industries. It often lowers barriers to entry and reduces customer switching costs, changes that tend to increase the intensity of rivalry in an industry and lower both prices and profits.[17] For example, the Internet has lowered barriers to entry into the news industry. Providers of financial news now have to compete for advertising dollars and customer attention with new Internet-based media organizations that sprang up during the 1990s, such as TheStreet.com, The Motley Fool, and Yahoo!'s Finance. The resulting increase in rivalry has given advertisers more choices, enabling them to bargain down the prices that they must pay to media companies.

● Demographic Forces

Demographic forces are outcomes of changes in the characteristics of a population, such as age, gender, ethnic origin, race, sexual orientation, and social class. Like the other forces in the general environment, demographic forces present managers with opportunities and threats and can have major implications for organizations. Changes in the age distribution of a population are an example of a demographic force that affects managers and organizations. Currently, most industrialized nations are experiencing the aging of their populations as a consequence of falling birth and death rates and the aging of the baby boom generation. In Germany, for example, the percentage of the population over age sixty-five is expected to rise from 15.4% in 1990 to 20.7% in 2010. Comparable figures for Canada are 11.4 and 14.4%; for Japan, 11.7 and 19.5%; and for the United States, 12.6 and 13.5%.[18]

The aging of the population is increasing opportunities for organizations that cater to older people; the home health care and recreation industries, for example, are seeing an upswing in demand for their services. As the baby boom generation (from the late 1950s to the early 1960s) has aged, it has created a host of opportunities and threats. During the 1980s, many baby boomers were getting married and creating an upsurge in demand for the customer appliances normally bought by couples marrying for the first time. Companies such as Whirlpool Corporation and General Electric capitalized on the resulting upsurge in demand for washing machines, dishwashers, dryers, and the like. In the 1990s, many of these same baby boomers were starting to save for retirement, creating an inflow of money into mutual funds and a boom in the mutual fund industry. In the next twenty years, many of these same baby boomers will retire, creating a boom in retirement communities.

● Social Forces

Social forces refer to the way in which changing social mores and values affect an industry. Like other macroenvironmental forces discussed here, social change creates opportunities and threats. One major social movement of recent decades has been the trend toward greater health consciousness. Its impact has been immense, and companies that recognized the opportunities early have often reaped significant gains. Philip Morris, for example, capitalized on the growing health trend when it acquired Miller Brewing Company and then redefined competition in the beer industry with its introduction of low-calorie beer (Miller Lite). Similarly, PepsiCo was able to gain market share from its rival, Coca-Cola, by being the first to introduce diet colas and fruit-based soft drinks. At the same time, the health trend has created a threat for many industries. The tobacco industry, for example, is in decline as a direct result of greater customer awareness of the health implications of smoking.

● Political and Legal Forces

Political and legal forces are outcomes of changes in laws and regulations. They result from political and legal developments within society and significantly affect managers and companies. Political processes shape a society's laws, which constrain the operations of organizations and managers and thus create both opportunities and threats.[19] For example, throughout much of the industrialized world, there has been a strong trend toward deregulation of industries previously controlled by the state and privatization of organizations once owned by the state. In the United States, deregulation of the airline industry in 1979 allowed twenty-nine new airlines to enter the industry between 1979 and 1993. The increase in passenger carrying capacity after deregulation led to excess capacity on many routes, intense competition, and fare wars. To respond to this more competitive task environment, airlines have had to look for ways to reduce operating costs. The development of hub-and-spoke systems, the rise of nonunion airlines, and the introduction of no-frills discount service are all responses to increased competition in the airlines' task environment. Despite these innovations, the airline industry still experiences intense fare wars, which have lowered profits and caused numerous airline company bankruptcies. The global telecommunications service industry is now experiencing the same kind of turmoil, following the deregulation of that industry in the United States and elsewhere.

In most countries, the interplay between political and legal forces, on the one hand, and industry competitive structure, on the other, is a two-way process in which the government sets regulations that influence competitive structure and firms in an industry seek to influence the regulations that governments enact by a number of means. When permitted, they may provide financial support to politicians or political parties that espouse views favorable to the industry and lobby government legislators directly to shape government regulations. For example, in 2002 the United States Steel Industry Association was a prime mover in persuading President Bush to enact a 30% tariff on imports of foreign steel into the United States. The purpose of the tariff was to protect American steel makers from foreign competitors, thereby reducing the intensity of rivalry in the United States steel markets.

Summary of Chapter

1. The main technique used to analyze competition in the industry environment is the five forces model. The five forces are (1) the risk of new entry by potential competitors, (2) the extent of rivalry among established firms, (3) the bargaining power of buyers, (4) the bargaining power of suppliers, and (5) the threat of substitute products. The stronger each force is, the more competitive the industry and the lower the rate of return that can be earned.

2. The risk of entry by potential competitors is a function of the height of barriers to entry. The higher the barriers to entry are, the lower is the risk of entry and the greater are the profits that can be earned in the industry.

3. The extent of rivalry among established companies is a function of an industry's competitive structure, demand conditions, cost conditions, and barriers to exit. Strong demand conditions moderate the competition among established companies and create opportunities for expansion. When demand is weak,

intensive competition can develop, particularly in consolidated industries with high exit barriers.

4. Buyers are most powerful when a company depends on them for business but they themselves are not dependent on the company. In such circumstances, buyers are a threat.

5. Suppliers are most powerful when a company depends on them for business but they themselves are not dependent on the company. In such circumstances, suppliers are a threat.

6. Substitute products are the products of companies serving customer needs similar to the needs served by the industry being analyzed. The more similar the substitute products are to each other, the lower is the price that companies can charge without losing customers to the substitutes.

7. Most industries are composed of strategic groups: groups of companies pursuing the same or a similar strategy. Companies in different strategic groups pursue different strategies.

8. Industries go through a well-defined life cycle: from an embryonic stage through growth, shakeout, and maturity to, eventually, decline. Each stage has different implications for the competitive structure of the industry, and each gives rise to its own set of opportunities and threats.

9. The macroenvironment affects the intensity of rivalry within an industry. Included in the macroenvironment are the macroeconomic environment, the global environment, the technological environment, the demographic and social environment, and the political and legal environment.

Discussion Questions

1. Under what environmental conditions are price wars most likely to occur in an industry? What are the implications of price wars for a company? How should a company try to deal with the threat of a price war?

2. Discuss Porter's five forces model with reference to what you know about the U.S. airline industry. What does the model tell you about the level of competition in this industry?

3. Identify a growth industry, a mature industry, and a declining industry. For each industry, identify the following: (a) the number and size distribution of companies, (b) the nature of barriers to entry, (c) the height of barriers to entry, and (d) the extent of product differentiation. What do these factors tell you about the nature of competition in each industry? What are the implications for the company in terms of opportunities and threats?

4. Assess the impact of macroenvironmental factors on the likely level of enrollment at your university over the next decade. What are the implications of these factors for the job security and salary level of your professors?

Practicing Strategic Management

SMALL-GROUP EXERCISE

Competing with Microsoft

Break up into groups of three to five people, and discuss the following scenario. Appoint one group member as a spokesperson who will communicate your findings to the class when called upon to do so by the instructor.

You are a group of managers and software engineers at a small start-up. You have developed a revolutionary new operating system for personal computers that offers distinct advantages over Microsoft's Windows operating system: it takes up less memory space on the hard drive of a personal computer; it takes full advantage of the power of the personal computer's microprocessor, and in theory can run software applications much faster than Windows; it is much easier to install and use than Windows; and it responds to voice instructions with an accuracy of 99.9% in addition to input from a keyboard or mouse. The operating system is the only product offering that your company has produced.

Complete the following exercises:

1. Analyze the competitive structure of the market for personal computer operating systems. On the basis of this analysis, identify what factors might inhibit adoption of your operating system by customers.

2. Can you think of a strategy that your company might pursue, either alone or in conjunction with other enterprises, in order to "beat Microsoft"? What will it take to execute that strategy successfully?

EXPLORING THE WEB

Visiting Boeing and Airbus

Visit the websites of the Boeing Corporation (**www.boeing.com**) and Airbus Industrie (**www.airbus.com**). Go to the news features of both sites, and read through the press releases issued by the companies. Also look at the annual reports and company profile (or history features) on both sites. With this material as your guide, do the following:

1. Use Porter's five forces model to analyze the nature of competition in the commercial jet aircraft market.

2. Assess the likely outlook for competition over the next ten years in this market. Try to establish whether new entry into this industry is likely, whether demand will grow or shrink, how powerful buyers are likely to become, and

what the implications of all this are for the nature of competition ten years out.

General Task   Search the Web for information that allows you to assess the current state of competition in the market for personal computers. Use that information to perform an analysis of the structure of the market in the United States. (Hint: Try visiting the websites of personal computer companies. Also visit Electronic Business Today at **www.ebtmag.com.**)

CLOSING CASE

The Pharmaceutical Industry

Historically, the pharmaceutical industry has been a profitable one. Between 2002 and 2006, the average rate of return on invested capital (ROIC) for firms in the industry was 16.45%. Put differently, for every dollar of capital invested in the industry, the average pharmaceutical firm generated 16.45 cents of profit. This compares with an average return on invested capital of 12.76% for firms in the computer hardware industry, 8.54% for grocers, and 3.88% for firms in the electronics industry. However, the average level of profitability in the pharmaceutical industry has been declining of late. In 2002, the average ROIC in the industry was 21.6%; by 2006, it had fallen to 14.5%.

The profitability of the pharmaceutical industry can be best understood by looking at several aspects of its underlying economic structure. First, demand for pharmaceuticals has been strong and has grown for decades. Between 1990 and 2003, there was a 12.5% annual increase in spending on prescription drugs in the United States. This growth was driven by favorable demographics. As people grow older, they tend to need and consume more prescription medicines, and the population in most advanced nations has been growing older as the post–World War II baby boom generation ages. Looking forward, projections suggest that spending on prescription drugs will increase between 10 and 11% annually through 2013.

Second, successful new prescription drugs can be extraordinarily profitable. Lipitor, the cholesterol-lowering drug sold by Pfizer, was introduced in 1997, and by 2006 this drug had generated a staggering $12.5 billion in annual sales for Pfizer. The costs of manufacturing, packing, and distributing Lipitor amounted to only about 10% of revenues. Pfizer spent close to $500 million on promoting Lipitor and perhaps as much again on maintaining a sales force to sell the product. That still left

Pfizer with a gross profit of perhaps $10 billion. Since the drug is protected from direct competition by a twenty-year patent, Pfizer has a temporary monopoly and can charge a high price. Once the patent expires, which is scheduled to occur in 2010, other firms will be able to produce "generic" versions of Lipitor and the price will fall—typically by 80% within a year.

Competing firms can produce drugs that are similar (but not identical) to a patent-protected drug. Drug firms patent a specific molecule, and competing firms can patent similar, but not identical, molecules that have a similar pharmacological effect. Thus, Lipitor does have competitors in the market for cholesterol-lowering drugs, such as Zocor, sold by Merck, and Crestor, sold by AstraZeneca. But these competing drugs are also patent protected. Moreover, the high costs and risks associated with developing a new drug and bringing it to market limit new competition. Out of every 5,000 compounds tested in the laboratory by a drug company, only five enter clinical trials, and only one of these will ultimately make it to the market. On average, estimates suggest that it costs some $800 million and takes anywhere from ten to fifteen years to bring a new drug to market. Once on the market, only three out of ten drugs ever recoup their R&D and marketing costs and turn a profit. Thus, the high profitability of the pharmaceutical industry rests on a handful of blockbuster drugs. At Pfizer, the world's largest pharmaceutical company, 55% of revenues were generated from just eight drugs.

To produce a blockbuster, a drug company must spend large amounts of money on research, most of which fails to produce a product. Only very large companies can shoulder the costs and risks of doing this, making it difficult for new companies to enter the industry. Pfizer, for example, spent some $7.44 billion on R&D in 2005 alone, equivalent to 14.5% of its total revenues. In a testament to just how difficult it is to get into the industry, although a large number of companies have been started in the last twenty years in the hope that they might develop new pharmaceuticals, only two of these companies, Amgen and Genentech, were ranked among the top twenty in the industry in terms of sales in 2005. Most have failed to bring a product to market.

In addition to spending on R&D, the incumbent firms in the pharmaceutical industry spend large amounts of money on advertising and sales promotion. While the $500 million a year that Pfizer spends promoting Lipitor is small relative to the drug's revenues, it is a large amount for a new competitor to match, making market entry difficult unless the competitor has a significantly better product.

There are also some big opportunities on the horizon for firms in the industry. New scientific breakthroughs in genomics are holding out the promise that within the next decade pharmaceutical firms might be able to bring to market new drugs that treat some of the most intractable medical conditions, including Alzheimer's, Parkinson's disease, cancer, heart disease, stroke, and AIDS.

However, there are some threats to the long-term dominance and profitability of industry giants like Pfizer. First, as spending on health care rises, politicians are looking for ways to limit health care costs, and one possibility is some form of price control on prescription drugs. Price controls are already in effect in most developed nations, and although they have not yet been introduced in the United States, they could be.

Second, twelve of the thirty-five top-selling drugs in the industry were to lose their patent protection between 2006 and 2009. By one estimate, some 28% of the global drug industry's sales of $307 billion would be exposed to generic challenge in the United States alone, due to drugs going off patent between 2006 and 2012. It is not clear to many industry observers whether the established drug companies have enough new drug prospects in their pipelines to replace revenues from drugs going off patent. Moreover, generic drug companies have been aggressive in challenging the patents of proprietary drug companies and in pricing their generic offerings. As a result, their share of industry sales has been growing. In 2005, they accounted for more than half by volume of all drugs prescribed in the United States, up from one-third in 1990.

Third, the industry has come under renewed scrutiny following studies showing that some FDA-approved prescription drugs, known as COX-2 inhibitors, were associated with a greater risk of heart attacks. Two of these drugs, Vioxx and Bextra, were pulled from the market in 2004.[c]

Case Discussion Questions

1. Drawing on the five forces model, explain why the pharmaceutical industry has historically been a very profitable industry.

2. After 2002, the profitability of the industry, measured by ROIC, started to decline. Why do you think this occurred?

3. What are the prospects for the industry going forward? What are the opportunities, and what are the threats? What must pharmaceutical firms do to exploit the opportunities and counter the threats?

TEST PREPPER

True/False Questions

_____ **1.** An industry can be defined as a group of companies offering products or services that are close substitutes for each other—that is, products or services that satisfy the same basic customer needs.

_____ **2.** The risk of entry by potential competitors is a function of the height of barriers to entry.

_____ **3.** Brand loyalty exists when consumers have a preference for the products of established companies.

_____ **4.** Switching costs arise when it costs a customer time, energy, and money to switch from the products offered by one established company to the products offered by a new entrant.

_____ **5.** A fragmented industry is dominated by a small number of large companies or, in extreme cases, just one company, which is in a position to determine industry prices.

_____ **6.** Fixed costs refer to the costs that must be borne before the firm makes a single sale.

_____ **7.** Social forces are outcomes of changes in the characteristics of a population, such as age, gender, ethnic origin, race, sexual orientation, and social class.

Multiple-Choice Questions

8. Included in the macroenvironment is ____.
   a. risk of entry
   b. the bargaining power of buyers
   c. rivalry among established firms
   d. the global environment
   e. product life cycle

9. ____arise when a company can take advantage of conditions in its environment to formulate and implement strategies that enable it to become more profitable.
   a. Threats
   b. Opportunities
   c. Competitors
   d. Rivalries among competitors
   e. Bargaining powers of buyers

10. ____arise when unit costs fall as a firm expands its output.
    a. Economies of scale
    b. Brand loyalties
    c. Barriers to entry
    d. Absolute cost advantages
    e. none of the above

11. In 1992, ____ signed a deal with Wal-Mart to supply the retailing giant with a private-label cola called Sam's Choice.
    a. Coca-Cola
    b. PepsiCo
    c. RC Cola
    d. Cott Corporation
    e. Seven Up

12. The ____refers to the number and size distribution of companies in an industry, something that strategic managers determine at the beginning of an industry analysis.
    a. competitive structure
    b. consolidated industry
    c. fragmented industry
    d. rivalry
    e. cost condition

13. ____are economic, strategic, and emotional factors that prevent companies from leaving an industry.
    a. Industry demands
    b. Cost conditions
    c. Exit barriers
    d. Bargaining powers of buyers
    e. Substitute products

14. The ____refers to the ability of buyers to bargain down prices charged by companies in the industry or to raise the costs of companies in the industry by demanding better product quality or service.
    a. industry demand
    b. bargaining power of buyers
    c. bargaining power of suppliers
    d. mobility barrier
    e. substitute product

15. ____are within-industry factors that inhibit the movement of companies between strategic groups.
    a. Industry shakeouts
    b. Mobility barriers
    c. First-time demands
    d. Social forces
    e. Technological forces

Chapter 4

Building Competitive Advantage

Learning Objectives

After reading this chapter, you should be able to

1. Discuss the source of competitive advantage

2. Identify and explore the roles of efficiency, quality, innovation, and customer responsiveness in building and maintaining a competitive advantage

3. Discuss the concept of the value chain

4. Explore how functional level strategies can be used to build superior efficiency, quality, innovation, and customer responsiveness

5. Explain the nature of distinctive competences

Chapter Outline

I. Competitive Advantage: Value Creation, Low Cost, and Differentiation
II. The Generic Building Blocks of Competitive Advantage
   a. Efficiency
   b. Quality as Excellence and Reliability
   c. Innovation
   d. Customer Responsiveness
III. The Value Chain
   a. Primary Activities
   b. Support Activities
IV. Functional Strategies and the Generic Building Blocks of Competitive Advantage
   a. Increasing Efficiency
   b. Increasing Quality
   c. Increasing Innovation
   d. Achieving Superior Customer Responsiveness
V. Distinctive Competences and Competitive Advantage
   a. Resources and Capabilities
   b. The Durability of Competitive Advantage

Overview

In Chapter 3, we discussed the elements of the external environment that determine an industry's attractiveness. However, industry structure is not the only force that affects company performance. Within any given industry, some companies are more profitable than others. For example, in the global auto industry, Toyota has consistently outperformed General Motors for most of the last twenty years. In the steel industry, Nucor has consistently outperformed U.S. Steel. And in the U.S. retail industry, Wal-Mart has consistently outperformed Kmart. The question, therefore, is, Why, within a particular industry, do some companies outperform others? What is the basis of their competitive advantage?

As you will see in this chapter, the answer is that companies which outperform their rivals do so because they are more efficient, have higher product quality, are more innovative, or are more responsive to their customers than their rivals. We refer to *efficiency, quality, innovation,* and *customer responsiveness* as the four generic building blocks of competitive advantage. For a company to outperform its rivals, it must have unique strengths, or distinctive competences, in at least one of these building blocks. Wal-Mart, for example, outperforms its rivals in the discount retail industry because it is more efficient and more responsive to its customers.

Competitive Advantage: Value Creation, Low Cost, and Differentiation

As noted in Chapter 1, a company has a *competitive advantage* when its profitability is higher than the average for its industry, and it has a *sustained competitive advantage* when it is able to maintain superior profitability over a number of years. In the United States retail industry, for example, Wal-Mart has had a sustained competitive advantage that has persisted for decades. This has been translated into higher profitability.

Two basic conditions determine a company's profitability: first, the amount of value customers place on the company's goods or services, and second, the company's costs of production. In general, the more value customers place on a company's products, the higher the price the company can charge for those products. Note, however, that the price a company charges for a good or service is typically less than the value placed on that good or service by the average customer. This is because the average customer captures some of that value in the form of what economists call a consumer surplus.[1] The customer is able to do this because the company is competing with other companies for the customer's business, so the company must charge lower prices than it could were it a monopoly supplier. Moreover, it is normally impossible to segment the market to such a degree that the company can charge each customer a price that reflects that individual's assessment of the value of a product—which economists refer to as a customer's reservation price. For these reasons, the price that gets charged tends to be less than the value placed on the product by many customers.

These concepts are illustrated in Figure 4.1. There you can see that the value of a product to a consumer may be V, the price that the company can charge for that product given competitive pressures may be P, and the costs of producing that product are C. The company's profit margin is equal to $P - C$, while the consumer surplus is equal to $V - P$. The company makes a profit so long as $P > C$, and its profit rate will be greater the lower C is *relative* to P. Bear in mind that the difference between V and P is in part determined by the intensity of competitive pressure in the marketplace. The lower the intensity of competitive pressure, the higher the price that can be charged relative to V.[2]

Note also that the value created by a company is measured by the difference between V and C ($V - C$). A company creates value by converting inputs that cost C

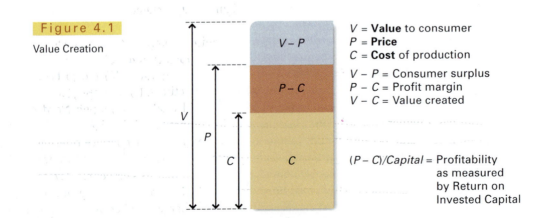

Figure 4.1

Value Creation

V = **Value** to consumer
P = **Price**
C = **Cost** of production

$V - P$ = Consumer surplus
$P - C$ = Profit margin
$V - C$ = Value created

($P - C$)/Capital = Profitability
as measured
by Return on
Invested Capital

Figure 4.2

Comparing Toyota and General Motors

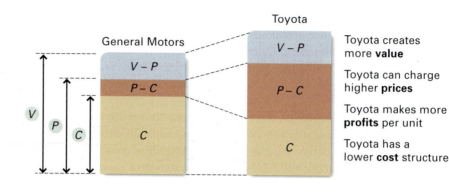

into a product on which consumers place a value of V. A company can create more value for its customers either by lowering C or by making the product more attractive through superior design, functionality, quality, and the like, so that consumers place a greater value on it (V increases) and, consequently, are willing to pay a high price (P increases). This discussion suggests that a company has high profitability, and thus a competitive advantage, when it creates more value for its customers than do rivals. Put differently, *the concept of value creation lies at the heart of competitive advantage.*[3]

For a more concrete example, consider the automobile industry, and compare Toyota with General Motors. According to a study by Harbour & Associates, in 2005 Toyota made $1,200 in profit on every vehicle it manufactured in North America. General Motors, in contrast, lost $2,496 on every vehicle it made.[4] What accounts for the difference? First, Toyota has the best reputation for quality in the industry. According to annual surveys issued by J.D. Power and Associates, Toyota consistently tops the list in terms of quality, while GM cars are at best in the middle of the pack. The higher quality translates into a higher value and allows Toyota to charge 5 to 10% higher prices than General Motors for equivalent cars. Second, Toyota has a lower cost per vehicle than General Motors, in part because of its superior labor productivity. For example, in Toyota's North American plants, it took an average of 29.40 employee hours to build a car, compared to 33.19 at GM plants in North America. That 3.79-hour productivity advantage translates into much lower labor costs for Toyota and, hence, a lower overall cost structure. Therefore, as summarized in Figure 4.2, Toyota's advantage over GM derives from greater value (V), which has allowed the company to charge a higher price (P) for its cars, and from a lower cost structure (C), which taken together imply significantly greater profitability per vehicle ($P - C$).

Superior value creation does not necessarily require a company to have the lowest cost structure in an industry or to create the most valuable product in the eyes of consumers, but it does require that the gap between perceived value (V) and costs of production (C) be greater than the gap attained by competitors. For example, Nordstrom has a strong competitive position among apparel retailers. Although Nordstrom has a higher cost structure than many of its competitors, it has been able to create more value because it successfully differentiated its product/service offering by offering a selection of high-quality merchandise and superior in-store customer service. Indeed, Nordstrom is legendary for the attention that its salespeople devote to individual customers. Thus, consumers assign a higher value (V) to products purchased at Nordstrom, which enables Nordstrom to charge a higher price (P) for the products it sells than many competing full-service department stores. The higher price translates into a greater profit margin ($P - C$) and greater profitability for Nordstrom relative to many of its rivals.

Michael Porter has argued that *low cost* and *differentiation* are two basic strategies for creating value and attaining a competitive advantage in an industry.[5] According to Porter, competitive advantage (and higher profitability) goes to those companies that can create superior value—and the way to create superior value is to drive down the cost structure of the business and/or differentiate the product in some way so that consumers value it more and are prepared to pay a premium price. This is all well and good, but it rather begs the question of exactly how a company can drive down its cost structure and differentiate its product offering from that of competitors so that it can create superior value. In this chapter and the next, we explain just how companies can do these two things. We shall return to Porter's notions of low cost and differentiation strategies in Chapter 5, when we examine his idea in significantly more depth.

The Generic Building Blocks of Competitive Advantage

Four factors build competitive advantage: efficiency, quality, innovation, and customer responsiveness. They are the generic building blocks of competitive advantage that any company can adopt, regardless of its industry or the products or services it produces (Figure 4.3). Although we discuss them separately below, they are interrelated. For example, superior quality can lead to superior efficiency, while innovation can enhance efficiency, quality, and customer responsiveness.

● **Efficiency**

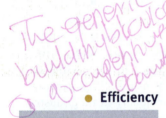

efficiency

The quantity of inputs that it takes to produce a given output (that is, efficiency = outputs/inputs).

In one sense, a business is simply a device for transforming inputs into outputs. Inputs are basic factors of production such as labor, land, capital, management, and technological know-how. Outputs are the goods and services that the business produces. The simplest measure of efficiency is the quantity of inputs that it takes to produce a given output—that is, **efficiency** = outputs/inputs. The more efficient a company is, the fewer the inputs required to produce a given output. For example, if it takes General Motors thirty hours of employee time to assemble

Figure 4.3

Generic Building Blocks of Competitive Advantage

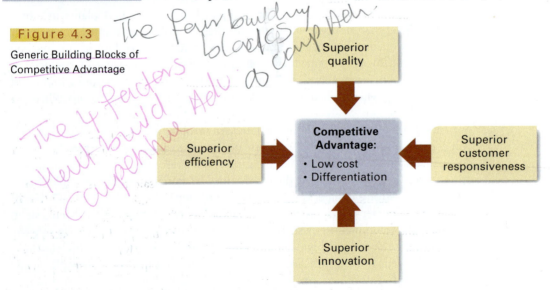

a car and it takes Ford twenty-five hours, we can say that Ford is more efficient than GM. And as long as other things are equal, such as wage rates, we can assume from this information that Ford will have a lower cost structure than GM. Thus, efficiency helps a company attain a competitive advantage through a lower cost structure.

Two of the most important components of efficiency for many companies are employee productivity and capital productivity. **Employee productivity** is usually measured by output per employee and **capital productivity** by output per unit of invested capital. Holding all else constant, the company with the highest labor and capital productivity in an industry will typically have the lowest cost structure and therefore a cost-based competitive advantage. The concept of productivity is not limited to employee and capital productivity. Pharmaceutical companies, for example, often talk about the productivity of their R&D spending, by which they mean how many new drugs they develop from their investment in R&D. Other companies talk about their sales force productivity, which means how many sales they generate from every sales call, and so on. The important point to remember is that high productivity leads to greater efficiency and lower costs.

employee productivity

Output per employee.

capital productivity

Output per unit of invested capital.

● Quality as Excellence and Reliability

A product can be thought of as a bundle of attributes.[6] The attributes of many physical products include the form, features, performance, durability, reliability, style, and design of the product.[7] A product is said to have *superior quality* when customers perceive that the attributes of the product provide them with higher value than attributes of products sold by rivals. For example, a Rolex watch has attributes—such as design, styling, performance, and reliability—that customers perceive as being superior to the same attributes in many other watches. Thus, we can refer to a Rolex as a high-quality product: Rolex has *differentiated* its watches by these attributes.

When customers are evaluating the quality of a product, they commonly measure it against two kinds of attributes; attributes that are related to *quality as excellence* and attributes that are related to *quality as reliability.* From a quality as excellence perspective, the important attributes are things such as a product's design and styling, its aesthetic appeal, its features and functions, the level of service associated with the delivery of the product, and so on. For example, customers can purchase a pair of imitation leather boots for $20 from Wal-Mart, or they can buy a handmade pair of genuine leather boots from Nordstrom for $500. The boots from Nordstrom will have far superior styling, feel more comfortable, and look much better than those from Wal-Mart. The value consumers would get from the Nordstrom boots would in all probability be much greater than the value derived from the Wal-Mart boots, but of course they have to pay far more for them. That is the point, of course; when excellence is built into a product offering, consumers have to pay more to own or consume it.

With regard to *quality as reliability,* a product can be said to be *reliable* when it consistently does the job it was designed for, does it well, and rarely (if ever) breaks down. As with excellence, reliability increases the value a consumer gets from a product, and thus the price the company can charge for that product. Toyota's cars, for example, have the highest reliability ratings in the automobile industry, and as a consequence consumers are prepared to pay more for them than cars that are very similar with regard to their other attributes.

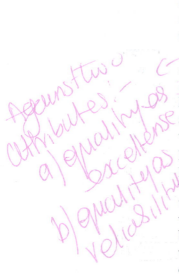

Figure 4.4

A Quality Map for
Automobiles

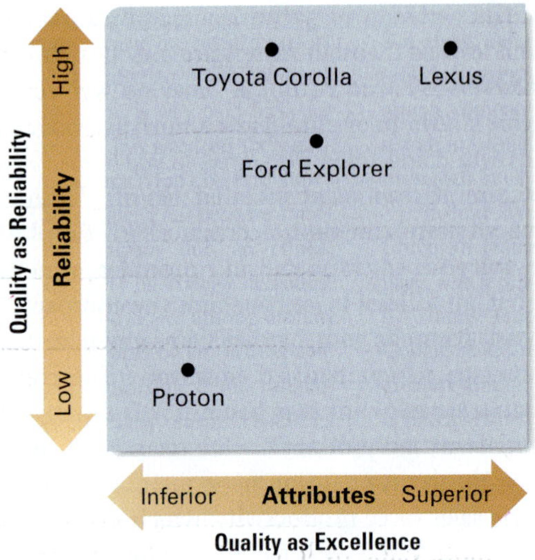

The position of a product against these two dimensions, reliability and other attributes, can be plotted on a figure similar to Figure 4.4. For example, a Lexus has attributes—such as design, styling, performance, and safety features—that customers perceive as demonstrating excellence in quality and are viewed as being superior to those of most other cars. Lexus is also a very reliable car. Thus, the overall level of quality of the Lexus is very high, which means that the car offers consumers significant value, and that gives Toyota the option of charging a premium price for the Lexus. Toyota also produces another very reliable vehicle, the Toyota Corolla, but this model is aimed at less wealthy customers and it lacks many of the superior attributes of the Lexus. Thus, although this is also a high-quality car in the sense of being reliable, it is not as high quality as a Lexus in the sense of being an excellent product. At the other end of the spectrum, we can find poor-quality products that have both low reliability and inferior attributes, such as poor design, performance, and styling. An example is the Proton, which is built by the Malaysian car firm of the same name. The design of the car is over a decade old, and the car has a dismal reputation for styling and safety. Moreover, Proton's reliability record is one of the worst of any car, according J.D. Power.[8]

The concept of quality applies whether we are talking about Toyota automobiles, clothes designed and sold by the Gap, the customer service department of Citibank, or the ability of airlines to arrive on time. Quality is just as relevant to services as it is to goods.[9]

The impact of high product quality on competitive advantage is twofold.[10] First, providing high-quality products increases the value those products provide to customers, which gives the company the option of charging a higher price for them. The second impact of high quality on competitive advantage comes from the greater efficiency and the lower unit costs associated with *reliable* products. When products are reliable, less employee time is wasted making defective products or providing substandard services and less time has to be spent fixing mistakes, which translates into higher employee productivity and lower unit costs. Thus, high product quality not only enables a company to differentiate its product from that of rivals, but also, if the product is reliable, lowers costs.

③ ● **Innovation**

innovation

The creation of new products or processes.

product innovation

The development of products that are new to the world or have attributes superior to those of existing products.

process innovation

The development of a new process for producing products and delivering them to customers.

Innovation refers to the act of creating new products or processes. There are two main types of innovation: product innovation and process innovation. **Product innovation** is the development of products that are new to the world or have attributes superior to those of existing products. Examples are Intel's invention of the microprocessor in the early 1970s, Cisco's development of the router for routing data over the Internet in the mid-1980s, and Palm's development of the PalmPilot, the first commercially successful hand-held computer, in the mid-1990s. **Process innovation** is the development of a new process for producing products and delivering them to customers. An example is Toyota's development of a range of new techniques for making automobiles, collectively known as the Toyota *lean production system,* which includes just-in-time inventory systems, self-managing teams, and reduced setup times for complex equipment.

Product innovation creates value by creating new products, or enhanced versions of existing products, that customers perceive as having more value, thus giving the company the option to charge a higher price. Process innovation often allows a company to create more value by lowering production costs. Toyota's lean production system, for example, helped to boost employee productivity, thus giving Toyota a cost-based competitive advantage.[11]

In the long run, innovation of products and processes is perhaps the most important building block of competitive advantage.[12] Competition can be viewed as a process driven by innovations. Although not all innovations succeed, those that do can be a major source of competitive advantage because, by definition, they give a company something *unique*—something its competitors lack (at least until they imitate the innovation). Uniqueness can allow a company to differentiate itself from its rivals and charge a premium price for its product or, in the case of many process innovations, reduce its unit costs far below those of competitors.

Innovation →

④ ● **Customer Responsiveness**

customer response time

The time that it takes for a good to be delivered or a service to be performed.

To achieve superior customer responsiveness, a company must be able to do a better job than competitors of identifying and satisfying its customers' needs. Customers will then attribute more value to its products, creating a differentiation based on competitive advantage. Improving the quality of a company's product offering is consistent with achieving responsiveness, as is developing new products with features that existing products lack. In other words, achieving superior quality and innovation is integral to achieving superior responsiveness to customers.

Another factor that stands out in any discussion of customer responsiveness is the need to customize goods and services to the unique demands of individual customers or customer groups. For example, the proliferation of soft drinks and beers can be viewed partly as a response to this trend. Similarly, automobile companies have become more adept at customizing cars to the demands of individual customers. For instance, following the lead of Toyota, the Saturn division of General Motors builds cars to order for individual customers, letting them choose from a wide range of colors and options.

An aspect of customer responsiveness that has drawn increasing attention is **customer response time**: the time that it takes for a good to be delivered or a service to be performed.[13] For a manufacturer of machinery, response time is the time that it takes to fill customer orders. For a bank, it is the time that it takes to process a loan or that a customer must stand in line to wait for a free teller. For a supermarket, it is the time that customers must stand in checkout lines. Customer survey after customer survey has shown slow response time to be a major source of customer dissatisfaction.[14]

Other sources of enhanced customer responsiveness include superior design, superior service, and superior after-sales service and support. All of these factors enhance customer responsiveness and allow a company to differentiate itself from its competitors. In turn, differentiation enables a company to build brand loyalty and charge a premium price for its products. Consider how much more people are prepared to pay for next-day delivery of Express Mail, as opposed to delivery in three to four days. In 2007, a two-page letter sent by overnight Express Mail within the United States cost about $14, compared with 41 cents for regular mail. Thus, the price premium for express delivery (reduced response time) was $13.59, or a premium of 3,315% over the regular price.

The Value Chain

In this section, we will take a look at the role played by the different functions of a company—such as production, marketing and sales, R&D, customer service, information systems, materials management, and human resources—in the value creation process. Specifically, we shall review how the different functions of a company can help in the process of driving down costs and increasing the perception of value through differentiation. As a first step toward doing this, consider the concept of the value chain, which is illustrated in Figure 4.5.[15] The term **value chain** refers to the idea that a company is a chain of activities for transforming inputs into outputs customers value. The process of transforming inputs into outputs is composed of a number of primary activities and support activities. Each activity adds value to the product.

value chain

The idea that a company is a chain of activities for transforming inputs into outputs customers value.

● Primary Activities

primary activities

Activities related to the design, creation, and delivery of the product, its marketing, and its support and after-sale service.

Primary activities have to do with the design, creation, and delivery of the product, its marketing, and its support and after-sales service. In the value chain illustrated in Figure 4.5, the primary activities are broken down into four functions: research and development, production, marketing and sales, and customer service.

RESEARCH AND DEVELOPMENT *Research and development (R&D)* is concerned with the design of products and production processes. Although we think of R&D as being associated with the design of physical products and production processes in manufacturing enterprises, many service companies also undertake R&D. For example, banks compete with each other by developing new financial products and new ways

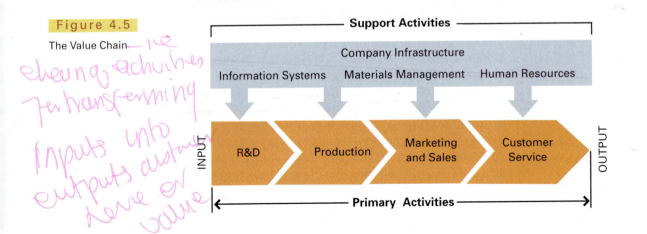

Figure 4.5

The Value Chain

of delivering those products to customers. Online banking and smart debit cards are two recent examples of the fruits of new product development in the banking industry. Earlier examples of innovation in the banking industry were ATM machines, credit cards, and debit cards.

By contributing to superior product design, R&D can increase the functionality of products, which makes them more attractive to customers, thereby adding value. Alternatively, the work of R&D may result in more efficient production processes, thereby lowering production costs. Either way, the R&D function can help to lower costs or raise the value of a product and permit a company to charge higher prices. At Intel, for example, R&D creates value by developing ever more powerful microprocessors and helping to pioneer ever more efficient manufacturing processes (in conjunction with equipment suppliers).

PRODUCTION *Production* is concerned with the creation of a good or service. For physical products, when we talk about production, we generally mean manufacturing. For services such as banking or retail operations, "production" typically takes place when the service is delivered to the customer, as when a bank makes a loan to a customer. By performing its activities efficiently, the production function of a company helps to lower its cost structure. For example, the efficient production operations of Honda and Toyota help those automobile companies achieve higher profitability relative to competitors such as General Motors. The production function can also perform its activities in a way that is consistent with high product quality, which leads to differentiation (and higher value) and lower costs.

MARKETING AND SALES There are several ways in which the *marketing and sales* functions of a company can help to create value. Through brand positioning and advertising, the marketing function can increase the value that customers perceive to be contained in a company's product (and thus the utility they attribute to the product). Insofar as these activities help to create a favorable impression of the company's product in the minds of customers, they increase perceived value. For example, in the 1980s, the French company Perrier persuaded U.S. customers that slightly carbonated bottled water was worth $1.50 per bottle rather than a price closer to the $0.50 that it cost to collect, bottle, and distribute the water. Perrier's marketing function essentially increased the perception of utility that customers ascribed to the product.

Marketing and sales can also create value by discovering customer needs and communicating them back to the R&D function of the company, which can then design products that better match those needs.

CUSTOMER SERVICE The role of the *customer service* function of an enterprise is to provide after-sales service and support. This function can create superior utility by solving customer problems and supporting customers after they have purchased the product. For example, Caterpillar, the U.S.-based manufacturer of heavy earthmoving equipment, can get spare parts to any point in the world within twenty-four hours, thereby minimizing the amount of downtime its customers have to face if their Caterpillar equipment malfunctions. This is an extremely valuable support capability in an industry where downtime is very expensive. It has helped to increase the utility that customers associate with Caterpillar products and thus the price that Caterpillar can charge for its products.

● Support Activities

The **support activities** of the value chain provide inputs that allow the primary activities to take place. These activities are broken down into four functions: materials management (or logistics), human resources, information systems, and company infrastructure (see Figure 4.5).

MATERIALS MANAGEMENT (LOGISTICS)   The *materials management* (or logistics) function controls the transmission of physical materials through the value chain, from procurement through production and into distribution. The efficiency with which this is carried out can significantly lower cost, thereby creating more value. Wal-Mart, for example, has a very efficient materials management setup. By tightly controlling the flow of goods from its suppliers through its stores and into the hands of customers, Wal-Mart has eliminated the need to hold large inventories of goods. Lower inventories mean lower costs and hence greater value creation.

HUMAN RESOURCES   There are a number of ways in which the *human resource* function can help an enterprise to create more value. This function ensures that the company has the right mix of skilled people to perform its value creation activities effectively. It is also the job of the human resource function to ensure that people are adequately trained, motivated, and compensated to perform their value creation tasks. If the human resources are functioning well, employee productivity rises (which lowers costs) and customer service improves (which raises utility), thereby enabling the company to create more value.

INFORMATION SYSTEMS   *Information systems* refer to the largely electronic systems for managing inventory, tracking sales, pricing products, selling products, dealing with customer service inquiries, and so on. Information systems, when coupled with the communications features of the Internet, hold out the promise of being able to improve the efficiency and effectiveness with which a company manages its other value creation activities. As noted in the Running Case, Wal-Mart uses information systems to alter the way it does business. By tracking the sales of individual items very closely, its materials management function has enabled it to optimize its product mix and pricing strategy. Wal-Mart is rarely left with unwanted merchandise on its hands, which saves on costs, and the company is able to provide the right mix of goods to customers, which increases the utility that customers associate with Wal-Mart.

COMPANY INFRASTRUCTURE   **Company infrastructure** is the companywide context within which all the other value creation activities take place: the organization structure, control systems, and company culture. Because top management can exert considerable influence in shaping these aspects of a company, top management should also be viewed as part of the infrastructure of a company. Indeed, through strong leadership, top management can shape the infrastructure of a company and, through that, the performance of all other value creation activities that take place within it.

Functional Strategies and the Generic Building Blocks of Competitive Advantage

Now that we have reviewed the generic building blocks of competitive advantage and discussed how the different functions of a company fit together into the value chain, we can look at some of the functional-level strategies managers pursue to improve the efficiency, quality, innovation, and customer responsiveness of their organization. Since this topic is a vast one, worthy of a book in its own right, we will not attempt an exhaustive review of functional-level strategies. Instead, we shall illustrate the role of functional-level strategies in building competitive advantage by focusing on a limited number of these important strategies.

● Increasing Efficiency

Actions can be taken by functional managers at every step in the value chain to increase the efficiency of a company.

R&D AND EFFICIENCY Managers in the R&D function might look for ways to simplify the design of a product, reducing the number of parts it contains. By doing so, R&D can dramatically decrease the required assembly time, which translates into higher employee productivity, lower costs, and higher profitability. For example, after Texas Instruments redesigned an infrared sighting mechanism that it supplies to the Pentagon, it found that it had reduced the number of parts from 47 to 12, the number of assembly steps from 56 to 13, the time spent fabricating metal from 757 minutes per unit to 219 minutes per unit, and unit assembly time from 129 minutes to 20 minutes. The result was a substantial decline in production costs. Design for manufacturing requires close coordination between the production and R&D functions of the company, of course. Cross-functional teams that contain production and R&D personnel who work jointly on the problem can best achieve this.

PRODUCTION AND EFFICIENCY Managers in the production function of a company might look for ways to increase the productivity of capital and labor. One common strategy is to pursue economies of scale, driving down unit costs by mass-producing output. A major source of economies of scale is the ability to spread fixed costs over a large production volume. *Fixed costs* are costs that must be incurred to produce a product, whatever the level of output. For example, Microsoft spent perhaps $5 billion to develop the latest version of its Windows operating system, Windows Vista. It can realize substantial scale economies by spreading the fixed costs associated with developing the new operating system over the enormous unit sales volume it expects for this system (over 90% of the world's personal computers use a Microsoft operating system). These scale economies are significant because of the trivial incremental (or marginal) cost of producing additional copies of Windows Vista: once the master copy has been produced, additional CDs containing the operating system can be produced for a few cents. The key to Microsoft's efficiency and profitability (and that of other companies with high fixed costs and trivial incremental or marginal costs) is to increase sales rapidly enough that fixed costs can be spread out over a large unit volume and substantial scale economies can be realized.

Another source of scale economies is the ability of companies producing in large volumes to achieve a greater division of labor and specialization. Specialization is said to have a favorable impact on productivity, mainly because it enables employees to become very skilled at performing a particular task. The classic example of such economies is Ford's Model T car. The world's first mass-produced car, the Model T Ford was introduced in 1923. Until then, Ford had made cars using an expensive hand-built craft production method. By introducing mass-production techniques, the company achieved greater division of labor (it split assembly into small, repeatable tasks) and specialization, which boosted employee productivity. Ford was also able to spread the fixed costs of developing a car and setting up production machinery over a large volume of output. As a result of these economies, the cost of manufacturing a car at Ford fell from $3,000 to less than $900 (in 1958 dollars).

learning effects

Cost savings that come
from learning by doing.

In addition to scale effects, production managers might seek to boost efficiency by pursuing strategies that help to maximize learning effects. **Learning effects** are cost savings that come from learning by doing. Labor, for example, learns by repetition how best to carry out a task. Therefore, labor productivity increases over time, and unit costs fall as individuals learn the most efficient way to perform a particular task. Equally important, management in new manufacturing facilities typically learns over time how best to run the new operation. Hence, production costs decline because of increasing labor productivity and management efficiency.

Although learning effects are normally associated with the manufacturing process, there is every reason to believe that they are just as important in service industries. For example, one famous study of learning in the context of the health care industry found that more experienced medical providers posted significantly lower mortality rates for a number of common surgical procedures, suggesting that learning effects are at work in surgery.[16] The authors of this study used the evidence to argue for establishing regional referral centers for the provision of highly specialized medical care. These centers would perform many specific surgical procedures (such as heart surgery), replacing local facilities with lower volumes and presumably higher mortality rates (for another study showing learning effects in surgery, see the Strategy in Action feature). Another recent study found strong evidence of learning effects in a financial institution. The study looked at a newly established document-processing unit with 100 staff and found that over time, documents were processed much more rapidly as the staff learned the process. Overall, the study concluded that unit costs fell every time the cumulative number of documents processed since the unit was established doubled.[17]

**flexible manufacturing
technology,** or **lean
production**

A range of manufacturing
technologies designed to
reduce setup times for
complex equipment,
increase the use of
individual machines
through better scheduling,
and improve quality
control at all stages of the
manufacturing process.

An important source of greater efficiency has been the introduction of flexible manufacturing technology by managers in the production function of an enterprise. The term **flexible manufacturing technology**—or **lean production,** as it is sometimes called—covers a range of manufacturing technologies designed to reduce setup times for complex equipment, increase the use of individual machines through better scheduling, and improve quality control at all stages of the manufacturing process.[18] Flexible manufacturing technologies allow the company to produce a wider variety of end products at a unit cost that at one time could be achieved only through the mass production of a standardized output. Indeed, research suggests that the adoption of flexible manufacturing technologies may increase efficiency and lower unit costs relative to what can be achieved by the mass production of a standardized output, while at the same time enabling the company to customize its product offering to a much greater extent than was once thought possible. The term **mass customization** has been coined to describe the ability of companies to use flexible manufacturing technology to reconcile two goals that were once thought to be incompatible: *low cost* and *differentiation through product customization.*[19]

mass customization

The ability of companies to
use flexible manufacturing
technology to customize
output at costs normally
associated with mass
production.

MARKETING AND EFFICIENCY The marketing strategy that a company adopts can have a major impact on efficiency and cost structure. **Marketing strategy** refers to the position that a company takes with regard to pricing, promotion, advertising, product design, and distribution. Some of the steps leading to greater efficiency are fairly obvious. For example, attaining economies of scale and learning effects can be facilitated by aggressive pricing, promotions, and advertising, all of which build sales volume rapidly and allow for the cost reductions that come from scale and learning effects. Other aspects of marketing strategy have a less obvious but no less important impact on efficiency. For many companies, one important strategy involves reducing customer defection rates.[20]

marketing strategy

The position that a
company takes with regard
to pricing, promotion,
advertising, product
design, and distribution.

Strategy in Action

Learning Effects in Cardiac Surgery

A study carried out by researchers at the Harvard Business School tried to estimate the importance of learning effects in the case of a specific new technology for minimally invasive heart surgery that was approved by federal regulators in 1996. The researchers looked at sixteen hospitals and obtained data on the operations for 660 patients. They examined how the time required to undertake the procedure varied with cumulative experience. Across the sixteen hospitals, they found that average time fell from 280 minutes for the first procedure with the new technology to 220 minutes by the time a hospital had performed fifty procedures (note that not all of the hospitals performed fifty procedures, and the estimates represent an extrapolation based on the data).

Next they looked at differences across hospitals. Here they found evidence of very large differences in learning effects. One hospital, in particular, stood out. This hospital, which they called "Hospital M," reduced its net procedure time from 500 minutes on case 1 to 132 minutes by case 50. Hospital M's 88-minute procedure time advantage over the average hospital at case 50 translated into a cost saving of approximately $2,250 per case and allowed surgeons at the hospital to do one more revenue-generating procedure per day.

The researchers tried to find out why Hospital M was so superior. They noted that all hospitals had similar state-of-the-art operating rooms and used the same set of FDA-approved devices and that all adopting surgeons went through the same training courses and came from highly respected training hospitals. Follow-up interviews, however, suggested that Hospital M differed in how it implemented the new procedure. The team was handpicked by the adopting surgeon to perform the surgery. Members had significant prior experience working together (indeed, that was apparently a key criterion for team members). The team trained together to perform the new surgery. Before undertaking a single procedure, they met with the operating room nurses and anesthesiologists to discuss the procedure. Moreover, the adopting surgeon mandated that the surgical team and surgical procedure be stable in the early cases. The initial team went through fifteen procedures before new members were added or substituted and twenty cases before the procedures were modified. The adopting surgeon also insisted that the team meet prior to each of the first ten cases, and they also met after the first twenty cases to debrief.

The picture that emerges is one of a core team that was selected and managed to maximize the gains from learning. The surgical team at Hospital M learned much faster and ultimately achieved higher productivity than their peers in other institutions, where there was less stability of team members and procedures and where there was not the same attention to briefing, debriefing, and learning. Clearly, differences in the implementation of the new procedure were very important.[a]

customer defection rate

The percentage of a company's customers who defect every year to competitors.

Customer defection rates reflect the percentage of a company's customers who defect every year to competitors. Defection rates are determined by customer loyalty, which in turn is a function of the ability of a company to satisfy its customers. Because acquiring a new customer entails certain one-time fixed costs for advertising, promotions, and the like, there is a direct relationship between defection rates and costs. The longer a company holds onto a customer, the greater the volume of unit sales generated by that customer that can be set against customer acquisition costs. Thus, lowering customer defection rates allows a company to amortize its customer acquisition costs and achieve a lower overall cost structure.

For example, in the wireless telecommunications industry it can cost between $300 and $400 to acquire a customer (this includes the costs of advertising and promotion, providing a customer with a wireless phone, and the cost of service activation). With monthly bills in the United States averaging $50, it can take six to eight months just to recoup the fixed costs of customer acquisition. If customer defection rates are high, costs are driven up by the costs of acquiring customers to replace those who left. In fact, many wireless service providers have customer defection rates as high as 25% per annum, which drives up their costs and reduces their profitability.

To reduce customer defection rates, marketing managers take steps to build brand loyalty and to make it more expensive for customers to defect. In the wireless telecommunications industry, Verizon Wireless has invested heavily in customer service and coverage to try to build brand loyalty. In addition, it has progressively moved customers toward two-year contracts, with penalty clauses attached if customers switch to another service provider within two years. These strategies have been quite successful; at less than 20% per annum, Verizon's customer defection rate is the lowest in the industry.[21]

MATERIALS MANAGEMENT AND EFFICIENCY The contribution of materials management (logistics) to boosting the efficiency of a company can be just as dramatic as the contribution of production and marketing. For a typical manufacturing company, materials and transportation costs account for 50 to 70% of its revenues, so even a small reduction in these costs can have a substantial impact on profitability. According to one estimate, for a company with revenues of $1 million, a return on invested capital of 5%, and materials management costs that amount to 50% of sales revenues (including purchasing costs), increasing total profits by $15,000 would require either a 30% increase in sales revenues or a 3% reduction in materials costs.[22] In a typical competitive market, reducing materials costs by 3% is usually much easier than increasing sales revenues by 30%.

Improving the efficiency of the materials management function often requires the adoption of a just-in-time (JIT) inventory system, designed to economize on inventory holding costs by having components arrive at a manufacturing plant just in time to enter the production process or goods arrive at a retail store only when stock is almost depleted. The major cost saving comes from increasing inventory turnover, which reduces inventory holding costs, such as warehousing and storage costs, and the company's need for working capital.

For example, through efficient logistics Wal-Mart can replenish the stock in its stores at least twice a week; many stores receive daily deliveries if they are needed. Typical competitors replenish their stock every two weeks, so they have to carry a much higher inventory and need more working capital per dollar of sales. Compared to its competitors, Wal-Mart can maintain the same service levels with a lower investment in inventory, a major source of its lower cost structure. Thus, faster inventory turnover has helped Wal-Mart achieve an efficiency-based competitive advantage in the retailing industry.[23]

The drawback of JIT systems is that they leave a company without a buffer stock of inventory. Although buffer stocks are expensive to store, they can help tide a company over during shortages of inputs brought about by disruption among suppliers (for instance, a labor dispute at a key supplier) and help a company respond quickly to increases in demand. However, there are ways around these limitations. For example, to reduce the risks linked to dependence on just one supplier for an important input, a company might decide to source inputs from multiple suppliers.

HUMAN RESOURCE STRATEGY AND EFFICIENCY As noted earlier, employee productivity is one of the key determinants of an enterprise's efficiency, cost structure, and profitability.[24] Many companies well known for their productive employees devote considerable attention to their hiring strategy. Southwest Airlines hires people who have a positive attitude and work well in teams because it believes that people who have a positive attitude will work hard and interact well with customers, thereby helping to create customer loyalty. Nucor hires people who are self-reliant and goal oriented, because its employees work in self-managing teams where they have to be self-

RUNNING CASE

Human Resource Strategy and Productivity at Wal-Mart

Wal-Mart has one of the most productive work forces of any in the retail industry. The roots of Wal-Mart's high productivity go back to the company's early days and the business philosophy of the company's founder, Sam Walton.

Back in 1940, Sam Walton started off his career as a management trainee at JCPenney. There he noticed that all employees were called "associates" and, moreover, that treating them with respect seemed to reap dividends in the form of high employee productivity. Twenty-two years later when he founded Wal-Mart, Walton decided to call all employees "associates" to symbolize their importance to the company. He reinforced this by emphasizing that, at Wal-Mart, "our people make the difference." Unlike many managers who have stated this mantra, Walton believed it and put it into action. He believed that if you treat people well, they will return the favor by working hard, and that if you empower them, ordinary people can work together to achieve extraordinary things. These beliefs formed the basis for a decentralized organization, one that operated with an open door policy and open books—which allowed associates to see just how their store and the company were doing.

Consistent with the open door policy, moreover, Walton continually emphasized that management needed to listen to associates and their ideas. As he noted in his 1992 book, "The folks on the front lines—the ones who actually talk to the customer—are the only ones who really know what's going on out there. You'd better find out what they know. This really is what total quality is all about. To push responsibility down in your organization, and to force good ideas to bubble up within it, you must listen to what your Associates are trying to tell you."

For all of his belief in empowerment, however, Walton was notoriously tight on salaries. Walton opposed unionization, fearing that it would lead to higher pay and restrictive work rules that would sap productivity. The culture of Wal-Mart also encouraged people to work hard. One of Walton's favorite homilies was the "sundown rule," which stated that one should never leave until tomorrow what can be done today. The sundown rule was enforced by senior managers, including Walton, who would drop in unannounced at a store, peppering store managers and employees with questions, but at the same time praising them for a job well done and celebrating the "heroes" who took the sundown rule to heart and did today what could have been done tomorrow.

The key to getting extraordinary effort out of employees, while paying them meager salaries, was to reward them with profit-sharing plans and stock ownership schemes. Long before it became fashionable in American business, Walton was placing a chunk of Wal-Mart's profits into a profit-sharing plan for associates and the company put matching funds into employee stock ownership programs. The idea was simple: reward associates by giving them a stake in the company, and they will work hard for low pay, because they know they will make it up in profit sharing and stock price appreciation.

For years, this formula worked extraordinarily well, but there are now signs that Wal-Mart's very success is creating problems. In 2007, the company had a staggering 1.8 million associates, making it the largest private employer in the world. As the company has grown, it has become increasingly difficult to hire the kinds of people that Wal-Mart has traditionally relied on—those willing to work long hours for low pay based on the promise of advancement and reward through profit sharing and stock ownership. The company has come under attack for paying its associates low wages and pressuring them to work long hours without overtime pay. Labor unions have made a concerted but so far unsuccessful attempt to unionize stores, and the company itself is the target of lawsuits from employees alleging sexual discrimination. Wal-Mart claims that the negative publicity is based on faulty data, and perhaps that is right, but if the company has indeed become too big to put Walton's principles into practice, the glory days may be over.[b]

reliant and goal oriented to perform well. As these examples suggest, it is important to make sure that the hiring strategy of the company is consistent with its own internal organization, culture, and strategic priorities. The people a company hires should have attributes that match the strategic objectives of the company. The Running Case looks at the steps Wal-Mart has taken to boost the productivity of its work force through human resource strategy.

Organizing the work force into self-managing teams is a popular human resource strategy for boosting productivity. In a **self-managing team,** members coordinate their own activities, which might include making their own hiring, training, work, and reward decisions. The typical team comprises five to fifteen employees who produce an entire product or undertake an entire task. Team members learn all team tasks and rotate from job to job. Because a more flexible work force is one result, team members can fill in for absent coworkers and take over managerial duties such as work and vacation scheduling, ordering materials, and hiring new members. The greater responsibility thrust on team members and the empowerment it implies are seen as motivators. People often respond well to being given greater autonomy and responsibility. Performance bonuses linked to team production and quality targets can work as an additional motivator. The effect of introducing self-managing teams is reportedly an increase in productivity of 30% or more and a substantial increase in product quality. Further cost savings arise from eliminating supervisors and creating a flatter organizational hierarchy, which also lowers the cost structure of the company.[25]

Implementing pay-for-performance compensation systems is another common human resource strategy for boosting efficiency. It is hardly surprising that linking pay to performance can help increase employee productivity. However, it is important to define what kind of job performance is to be rewarded and how. Some of the most efficient companies in the world, mindful that cooperation among employees is necessary to realize productivity gains, link pay to group or team (rather than individual) performance. Nucor divides its work force into teams of thirty or so, with bonus pay, which can amount to 30% of base pay, linked to the ability of the team to meet productivity and quality goals. This link creates a strong incentive for individuals to cooperate with each other in pursuit of team goals; that is, it facilitates teamwork.

INFORMATION SYSTEMS AND EFFICIENCY   With the rapid spread of computers, the explosive growth of the Internet and corporate intranets (internal corporate computer networks based on Internet standards), and the spread of high-bandwidth fiber optics and digital wireless technology, the information systems function is moving to center stage in the quest for operating efficiencies and a lower cost structure.[26] The impact of information systems on productivity is wide ranging and potentially affects all other activities of a company. For example, Cisco Systems has been able to realize significant cost savings by moving its ordering and customer service functions online. The company has just 300 service agents handling all of its customer accounts, compared to the 900 it would need if sales were not handled online. The difference represents an annual saving of $20 million a year. Moreover, without automated customer service functions, Cisco calculates that it would need at least 1,000 additional service engineers, which would cost around $75 million.[27]

Like Cisco, many companies are using web-based information systems to reduce the costs of coordination between the company and its customers and the company and its suppliers. By using web-based programs to automate customer and supplier interactions, the number of people required to manage these interfaces can be substantially reduced, thereby reducing costs. This trend extends beyond high-tech companies. Banks and financial service companies are finding that they can substantially reduce costs by moving customer accounts and support functions online. Such a move reduces the need for customer service representatives, bank tellers, stockbrokers, insurance agents, and others. For example, while it costs an average of about $1.07 to execute a transaction such as shifting money from one account to another at a bank, executing the same transaction over the Internet costs $0.01.[28]

INFRASTRUCTURE AND EFFICIENCY A company's infrastructure—that is, its structure, culture, style of strategic leadership, and control system—determines the context within which all other value creation activities take place. It follows that improving infrastructure can help a company increase efficiency and lower its cost structure. Above all, an appropriate infrastructure can help foster a companywide commitment to efficiency and promote cooperation among different functions in pursuit of efficiency goals. These issues are addressed at length in later chapters.

For now, it is important to note that strategic leadership is especially important in building a companywide commitment to efficiency. The leadership task is to articulate a vision that recognizes the need for *all* functions of a company to focus on improving efficiency. It is not enough to improve the efficiency of production or of marketing or of R&D in a piecemeal fashion. Achieving superior efficiency requires a companywide commitment to this goal that must be articulated by general and functional managers. A further leadership task is to facilitate the cross-functional cooperation needed to achieve superior efficiency. For example, designing products that are easy to manufacture requires that production and R&D personnel communicate; integrating JIT systems with production scheduling requires close communication between materials management and production; designing self-managing teams to perform production tasks requires close cooperation between human resources and production; and so on.

SUMMARY: INCREASING EFFICIENCY Table 4.1 summarizes the primary roles that various functions must assume in order to achieve superior efficiency. Bear in mind that achieving superior efficiency is not something that can be tackled on a function-by-

Table 4.1

Primary Roles of Value Creation Functions in Achieving Superior Efficiency

Value Creation Function	Primary Roles
Infrastructure (leadership)	1. Provide companywide commitment to efficiency. 2. Facilitate cooperation among functions.
Production	1. Where appropriate, pursue economies of scale and learning effects. 2. Implement flexible manufacturing systems.
Marketing	1. Where appropriate, adopt aggressive marketing to ride down the experience curve. 2. Limit customer defection rates by building brand loyalty.
Materials management	1. Implement JIT systems. 2. Improve supply chain coordination.
R&D	1. Design products for ease of manufacture. 2. Seek process innovations.
Information systems	1. Use information systems to automate processes. 2. Use information systems to reduce costs of coordination.
Human resources	1. Institute training programs to build skills. 2. Implement self-managing teams. 3. Implement pay for performance.

function basis. It requires an organizationwide commitment and an ability to ensure close cooperation among functions. Top management, by exercising leadership and influencing the infrastructure, plays a major role in this process.

● **Increasing Quality**   Earlier we noted that quality can be thought of in terms of two dimensions: *quality as reliability* and *quality as excellence.* High-quality products are reliable, in the sense that they do the job they were designed for and do it well, and are also perceived by consumers to have superior attributes. Superior quality gives a company two advantages: first, a strong reputation for quality allows a company to *differentiate* its products from those offered by rivals, and second, eliminating defects or errors from the production process reduces waste, increases efficiency, lowers the cost structure of the company, and increases its profitability.

ATTAINING SUPERIOR RELIABILITY   The principal tool that most managers now use to increase the reliability of their product offering is the Six Sigma quality improvement methodology. The Six Sigma methodology is a direct descendent of the total quality management (TQM) philosophy that was widely adopted, first by Japanese companies and then by American companies during the 1980s and early 1990s.[29] The basic philosophy underlying quality improvement methodologies is as follows:

1. Improved quality means that costs decrease because of less rework, fewer mistakes, fewer delays, and better use of time and materials.

2. As a result, productivity improves.

3. Better quality leads to higher market share and allows the company to raise prices.

4. This increases the company's profitability and allows it to stay in business.

Among companies that have successfully adopted quality improvement methodologies, certain imperatives stand out. First, it is important that senior managers buy into a quality improvement program and communicate its importance to the organization. Second, if a quality improvement program is to be successful, individuals must be identified to lead the program. Under the Six Sigma methodology, exceptional employees are identified and put through a "black belt" training course on the Six Sigma methodology. The black belts are taken out of their normal job roles and assigned to work solely on Six Sigma projects for the next two years. In effect, the black belts become internal consultants and project leaders. Because they are dedicated to Six Sigma programs, the black belts are not distracted from the task at hand by day-to-day operating responsibilities. To make a black belt assignment attractive, many companies now use it as a step in a career path. Successful black belts may not return to their prior job after two years, but instead may be promoted and given more responsibility.

Third, quality improvement methodologies preach the need to identify defects that arise from processes, trace them to their source, find out what caused them, and make corrections so that they do not recur. Production and materials management typically have primary responsibility for this task. To uncover defects, quality improvement methodologies rely upon the use of statistical procedures to pinpoint variations in the quality of goods or services. Once variations have been identified, they must be traced to their source and eliminated.

One technique that helps greatly in tracing defects to their source is reducing lot sizes for manufactured products. With short production runs, defects show up immediately. Consequently, they can be quickly traced to the source, and the problem can be addressed. Reducing lot sizes also means that when defective products are produced, their number will not be large, thus decreasing waste. Flexible manufacturing techniques can be used to reduce lot sizes without raising costs. JIT inventory systems also play a part. Under a JIT system, defective parts enter the manufacturing process immediately; they are not warehoused for several months before use. Hence, defective inputs can be quickly spotted. The problem can then be traced to the supply source and corrected before more defective parts are produced. Under a more traditional system, the practice of warehousing parts for months before they are used may mean that large numbers of defects are produced by a supplier before they enter the production process.

Fourth, another key to any quality improvement program is to create a metric that can be used to measure quality. In manufacturing companies, quality can be measured by criteria such as defects per million parts. In service companies, with a little creativity suitable metrics can be devised. For example, one of the metrics Florida Power & Light uses to measure quality is meter-reading errors per month.

Fifth, once a metric has been devised, the next step is to set a challenging quality goal and create incentives for reaching it. Under Six Sigma programs, the goal is 3.4 defects per million units. One way of creating incentives to attain such a goal is to link rewards, like bonus pay and promotional opportunities, to the goal.

Sixth, shop floor employees can be a major source of ideas for improving product quality, so their participation needs to be incorporated into a quality improvement program.

Seventh, a major source of poor-quality finished goods is poor-quality component parts. To decrease product defects, a company has to work with its suppliers to improve the quality of the parts they supply.

Eighth, the more assembly steps a product requires, the more opportunities there are for making mistakes. Thus, designing products with fewer parts is often a major component of any quality improvement program.

Finally, implementing quality improvement methodologies requires organizationwide commitment and substantial cooperation among functions. R&D has to cooperate with production to design products that are easy to manufacture; marketing has to cooperate with production and R&D so that customer problems identified by marketing can be acted on; human resource management has to cooperate with all the other functions of the company in order to devise suitable quality-training programs; and so on.

IMPROVING QUALITY AS EXCELLENCE   As we stated earlier, a product is a bundle of different attributes. In addition to reliability, these attributes include the form, features, performance, durability, and styling of a product. A company can also create quality as excellence by emphasizing attributes of the *service* associated with the product, such as ordering ease, prompt delivery, easy installation, the availability of customer training and consulting, and maintenance services. Singapore Airlines, for example, enjoys an excellent reputation for quality service, largely because passengers perceive their flight attendants as competent, courteous, and responsive to their needs.

For a product to be regarded as high quality on the excellence dimension, its offering must be seen as superior to that of rivals. Achieving a perception of high quality on key attributes requires specific actions by managers. First, it is important for managers to collect marketing intelligence indicating which of these attributes are most important to customers. Second, once the company has identified important attributes, it needs to design its products and the associated services so that those attributes are embodied in the product, and it needs to make sure that personnel in the company are appropriately trained so that the correct attributes are emphasized. This requires close coordination between marketing and product development and the involvement of the human resource management function in employee selection and training.

Third, the company must decide which of the significant attributes to promote and how best to position them in the minds of consumers—that is, how to tailor the marketing message so that it creates a consistent image in the minds of customers.[30] At this point, it is important to recognize that although a product might be differentiated on the basis of six attributes, covering all of those attributes in the company's communication messages may lead to an unfocused message. Many marketing experts advocate promoting only one or two central attributes to customers. For example, Volvo consistently emphasizes the safety and durability of its vehicles in all marketing messages, creating the perception in the minds of consumers (backed by product design) that Volvo cars are safe and durable. Volvo cars are also very reliable and have high performance, but the company does not emphasize these attributes in its marketing messages.

Finally, it must be recognized that competition does not stand still, but instead produces continual improvement in product attributes and often the development of new product attributes. This is obvious in fast-moving high-tech industries, where product features that were considered leading edge just a few years ago are now obsolete, but the same process is also at work in more stable industries. For example, the rapid diffusion of microwave ovens during the 1980s required food companies to build new attributes into their frozen food products: they had to maintain their texture and consistency while being microwaved. A product could not be considered high quality unless it could do that. This speaks to the importance of having a strong R&D function in the company that can work with marketing and manufacturing to continually upgrade the quality of the attributes that are designed into the company's product offerings.

● Increasing Innovation

In many ways, innovation is the most important source of competitive advantage. This is because innovation can result in new products that better satisfy customer needs, can improve the quality (attributes) of existing products, or can reduce the costs of making products that customers want. The ability to develop innovative new products or processes gives a company a major competitive advantage that allows it to (1) *differentiate its products* and charge a premium price and/or (2) *lower its cost structure* below that of its rivals. Competitors, however, attempt to imitate successful innovations and often succeed. Therefore, maintaining a competitive advantage requires a continuing commitment to innovation.

Successful new product launches are major drivers of superior profitability. Robert Cooper looked at more than 200 new product introductions and found that of those classified as successes, some 50% achieve a return on investment in excess of 33%, half have a payback period of two years or less, and half achieve a market share in excess of 35%.[31] Many companies have established a track record for successful innovation, among them Sony, whose successes include the Walkman, the compact disc, and the PlayStation; Nokia, which has been a leader in the development of wireless phones; Pfizer, a drug company that during the 1990s and early 2000s produced eight blockbuster new drugs; 3M, which has applied its core competency in tapes and adhesives to developing a wide range of new products; Intel, which has consistently managed to lead in the development of innovative new microprocessors to run personal computers; and Cisco Systems, whose innovations helped to pave the way for the rapid growth of the Internet.

THE HIGH FAILURE RATE OF INNOVATION Although promoting innovation can be a source of competitive advantage, the failure rate of innovative new products is high. Research evidence suggests that only 10 to 20% of major R&D projects give rise to commercially successful products.[32] Well-publicized product failures include Apple Computer's Newton, a personal digital assistant; Sony's Betamax format in the video player and recorder market; and Sega's Dreamcast videogame console. While many reasons have been advanced to explain why so many new products fail to generate an economic return, five explanations for failure appear on most lists.[33]

First, many new products fail because the demand for innovations is inherently uncertain. It is impossible to know, prior to market introduction, whether the new product has tapped an unmet customer need and if there is sufficient market demand to justify making the product. While good market research can reduce the uncertainty about likely future demand for a new technology, that uncertainty cannot be eradicated, so a certain failure rate is to be expected.

Second, new products often fail because the technology is poorly commercialized. This occurs when there is definite customer demand for a new product, but the product is not well adapted to customer needs because of factors such as poor design and poor quality. For instance, the failure of Apple Computer to establish a market for the Newton, a hand-held personal digital system that Apple introduced in the summer of 1993, can be traced to poor commercialization of a potentially attractive technology. Apple predicted a $1 billion market for the Newton, but sales failed to materialize when it became clear that the Newton's handwriting software, an attribute that Apple chose to emphasize in its marketing promotions, could not adequately recognize messages written on the Newton's message pad.

Third, new products may fail because of poor positioning strategy. **Positioning strategy** is the specific set of options a company adopts for a product on four main dimensions of marketing: price, distribution, promotion and advertising, and product features. Apart from poor product quality, another reason for the failure of the Apple Newton was poor positioning strategy. The Newton was introduced at such a high initial price (close to $1,000) that there would probably have been few buyers even if the technology had been adequately commercialized.

Another reason that many new product introductions fail is that companies often make the mistake of marketing a technology for which there is not enough demand. A company can get blinded by the wizardry of a new technology and fail to examine whether there is customer demand for the product. Finally, companies fail when they are slow to get their products to market. The more time that elapses between initial development and final marketing—the slower the "cycle time"—the more likely it is that someone else will beat the company to market and gain a first-mover advantage.[34] In the car industry, General Motors has suffered from being a slow innovator. Its product development cycle has been about five years, compared with two to three years at Honda, Toyota, and Mazda and three to four years at Ford. Because they are based on five-year-old technology and design concepts, GM cars are already out of date when they reach the market.

REDUCING INNOVATION FAILURES One of the most important things that managers can do to reduce the high failure rate associated with innovation is to make sure that

---

positioning strategy

The specific set of options a company adopts for a product on four main dimensions of marketing: price, distribution, promotion and advertising, and product features.

there is tight integration among R&D, production, and marketing.[35] Tight cross-functional integration can help a company to ensure that

1. Product development projects are driven by customer needs.
2. New products are designed for ease of manufacture.
3. Development costs are kept in check.
4. Time to market is minimized.

A company's customers can be one of its primary sources of new product ideas. The identification of customer needs, and particularly unmet needs, can set the context within which successful product innovation takes place. As the point of contact with customers, the marketing function can provide valuable information. Moreover, integrating R&D and marketing is crucial if a new product is to be properly commercialized. Otherwise, a company runs the risk of developing products for which there is little or no demand.

Integration between R&D and production can help a company to ensure that products are designed with manufacturing requirements in mind. Design for manufacturing lowers manufacturing costs and leaves less room for mistakes and thus can lower costs and increase product quality. Integrating R&D and production can help lower development costs and speed products to market. If a new product is not designed with manufacturing capabilities in mind, it may prove too difficult to build, given existing manufacturing technology. In that case, the product will have to be redesigned, and both overall development costs and time to market may increase significantly. Making design changes during product planning can increase overall development costs by 50% and add 25% to the time it takes to bring the product to market.[36]

One of the best ways to achieve cross-functional integration is to establish cross-functional product development teams, composed of representatives from R&D, marketing, and production. The objective of a team should be to take a product development project from the initial concept development to market introduction. A number of attributes seem to be important in order for a product development team to function effectively and meet all its development milestones.[37]

First, a **heavyweight project manager**—one who has high status within the organization and the power and authority required to get the financial and human resources that the team needs to succeed—should lead the team and be dedicated primarily, if not entirely, to the project. The leader should believe in the project (be a champion) and be skilled at integrating the perspectives of different functions and helping personnel from different functions work together for a common goal. The leader should also be able to act as an advocate of the team to senior management.

Second, the team should be composed of at least one member from each key function. The team members should have a number of attributes, including an ability to contribute functional expertise, high standing within their function, a willingness to share responsibility for team results, and an ability to put functional advocacy aside. It is generally preferable if core team members are 100% dedicated to the project for its duration. This makes sure that their focus is on the project, not on the ongoing work of their function.

Third, the team members should be physically co-located to create a sense of camaraderie and facilitate communication. Fourth, the team should have a clear plan and clear goals, particularly with regard to critical development milestones and development budgets. The team should have incentives to attain those goals—for example, pay bonuses when major development milestones are hit. Fifth, each team needs to develop its own processes for communication and conflict resolution. For example, one product development team at Quantum Corporation, a California-based manufacturer of disk drives for personal computers, instituted a rule that all major decisions would be made and conflicts resolved at meetings that were held every Monday afternoon. This simple rule helped the team to meet its development goals.[38]

● **Achieving Superior Customer Responsiveness**

Customer responsiveness is an important *differentiating* attribute that can help to build brand loyalty. Achieving superior responsiveness means giving customers value for their money. Taking steps to improve the efficiency of a company's production process and the quality of its products is consistent with this aim. Responding to customer needs may also require the development of new products with new features. *In other words, achieving superior efficiency, quality, and innovation is all part of achieving superior responsiveness to customers.* In addition, there are two other prerequisites for attaining this goal; a tight customer focus and an ongoing effort to seek better ways to satisfy those needs.

CUSTOMER FOCUS A company cannot be responsive to its customers' needs unless it knows what those needs are. The first step in building superior responsiveness is to motivate the whole company to focus on the customer. Customer focus must start at the top of the organization. A commitment to superior customer responsiveness brings attitudinal changes throughout a company that ultimately can be built only through strong leadership. A mission statement that puts customers first is one way to send a clear message to employees about the desired focus. Another avenue is top management's own actions. For example, Tom Monaghan, the founder of Domino's Pizza, stayed close to the customer by visiting as many stores as possible every week, running some deliveries himself, insisting that other top managers do the same, and eating Domino's pizza regularly.[39]

Leadership alone is not enough to attain a superior customer focus. All employees must see the customer as the focus of their activity and be trained to focus on the customer, whether their function is marketing, manufacturing, R&D, or accounting. The objective should be to make employees think of themselves as customers—to put themselves in customers' shoes. At that point, employees will be better able to identify ways to improve the quality of a customer's experience with the company.

To reinforce this mindset, incentive systems within the company should reward employees for satisfying customers. For example, senior managers at the Four Seasons hotel chain, who pride themselves on their customer focus, like to tell the story of Roy Dyment, a doorman in Toronto who neglected to load a departing guest's briefcase into his taxi. The doorman called the guest, a lawyer, in Washington, DC, and found that he desperately needed the briefcase for a morning meeting. Dyment hopped on a plane to Washington and returned it—without first securing approval from his boss. Far from punishing Dyment for making a mistake and for not checking with management before going to Washington, the Four Seasons responded by naming Dyment Employee of the Year.[40] This action sent a powerful message to Four Seasons employees about the importance of satisfying customer needs.

SATISFYING CUSTOMER NEEDS Another key to superior responsiveness is to satisfy customer needs that have been identified. As already noted, efficiency, quality, and innovation are crucial competencies that help a company satisfy customer needs.

Beyond that, companies can provide a higher level of satisfaction if they differentiate their products by (1) customizing them, where possible, to the requirements of individual customers and (2) reducing the time it takes to respond to or satisfy customer needs.

customization

Varying the features of a good or service to tailor it to the unique needs or tastes of groups of customers or, in the extreme case, individual customers.

Customization entails varying the features of a good or service to tailor it to the unique needs or tastes of groups of customers or, in the extreme case, individual customers. Although extensive customization can raise costs, the development of flexible manufacturing technologies has made it possible to customize products to a much greater extent than was feasible ten to fifteen years ago, without experiencing a prohibitive rise in cost structure (particularly when flexible manufacturing technologies are linked with web-based information systems). For example, online retailers such as Amazon.com have used web-based technologies to develop a homepage customized for each individual user. When a customer accesses Amazon.com, he or she is offered a list of recommendations for books or music to purchase, based on an analysis of prior buying history—a powerful competency that gives Amazon.com a competitive advantage.

In addition, to gain a competitive advantage a company must often respond to customer demands very quickly, whether the transaction is a furniture manufacturer's delivery of a product once it has been ordered, a bank's processing of a loan application, an automobile manufacturer's delivery of a spare part for a car that has broken down, or a cashier's serving of customers waiting in a supermarket checkout line. We live in a fast-paced society, where time is a valuable commodity. Companies that can satisfy customer demands for rapid response build brand loyalty, differentiate their products, and can charge higher prices for them.

A good example of the value of rapid response time is at Caterpillar, the manufacturer of heavy earthmoving equipment, which can get a spare part to any point in the world within twenty-four hours. Downtime for heavy construction equipment is very costly, so Caterpillar's ability to respond quickly in the event of equipment malfunction is of prime importance to its customers. As a result, many of them have remained loyal to Caterpillar despite aggressive low-price competition from Komatsu of Japan.

In general, reducing response time requires (1) a marketing function that can quickly communicate customer requests to production, (2) production and materials management functions that can quickly adjust production schedules in response to unanticipated customer demands, and (3) information systems that can help production and marketing in this process.

Distinctive Competences and Competitive Advantage

distinctive competence

A unique firm-specific strength that enables a company to better differentiate its products and/or achieve substantially lower costs than its rivals and thus gain a competitive advantage.

If managers are successful in their efforts to improve the efficiency, quality, innovation, and customer responsiveness of their organization, they may lower the cost structure of the company and/or better differentiate its product offering, either of which can be the basis for a competitive advantage. When a company is uniquely skilled at a value chain activity that underlies superior efficiency, quality, innovation, or customer responsiveness relative to its rivals, we say that it has a *distinctive competence* in this activity. A **distinctive competence** is a unique firm-specific strength that allows a company to better *differentiate its products* and/or achieve substantially *lower costs* than its rivals and thus gain a competitive advantage. For example, 3M has a distinctive competence in innovation that has enabled the company to gener-

what are the Resources we have and we name the three different types

ate 30% of its sales from differentiated products introduced within the last five years. Distinctive competences can be viewed as the bedrock of a company's competitive advantage. Distinctive competences arise from two complementary sources: *resources* and *capabilities*.[41]

Resources and Capabilities

Resources are financial, physical, social or human, technological, and organizational factors that allow a company to create value for its customers. Company resources can be divided into two types: tangible and intangible resources. **Tangible resources** are something physical, such as land, buildings, plant, equipment, inventory, and money. **Intangible resources** are nonphysical entities that are the creation of managers and other employees, such as brand names, the reputation of the company, the knowledge that employees have gained through experience, and the intellectual property of the company, including that protected through patents, copyrights, and trademarks.

The more *firm-specific* and *difficult to imitate* a resource is, the more likely a company is to have a distinctive competence. For example, Polaroid's distinctive competence in instant photography was based on a firm-specific and valuable intangible resource: technological know-how in instant film processing that was protected from imitation by a thicket of patents. Once a process can be imitated, as when patents expire, or a superior technology, such as digital photography, comes along, the distinctive competence disappears, as has happened to Polaroid. Another important quality of a resource that leads to a distinctive competence is that it is *valuable*: in some way, it helps to create strong *demand* for the company's products. Thus, Polaroid's technological know-how was valuable while it created strong demand for its photographic products; it became far less valuable when superior digital technology came along.

Capabilities refer to a company's skills at coordinating its resources and putting them to productive use. These skills reside in an organization's rules, routines, and procedures—that is, the style or manner through which a company makes decisions and manages its internal processes to achieve organizational objectives. More generally, a company's capabilities are the product of its organization structure, processes, and control systems. They specify how and where decisions are made within a company, the kind of behaviors the company rewards, and the company's cultural norms and values. (We discuss how organization structure and control systems help a company obtain capabilities in Chapters 9 and 10.) Capabilities are intangible. They reside not so much in individuals as in the way individuals interact, cooperate, and make decisions within the context of an organization.[42]

The distinction between resources and capabilities is critical to understanding what generates a distinctive competence. A company may have firm-specific and valuable resources, but unless it has the capability to use those resources effectively, it may not be able to create a distinctive competence. It is also important to recognize that a company may not need firm-specific and valuable resources to establish a distinctive competence so long as it *does have* capabilities that no competitor possesses. For example, the steel mini-mill operator Nucor is widely acknowledged to be the most cost-efficient steel maker in the United States. Its distinctive competence in low-cost (efficient) steel making does not come from any firm-specific and valuable resources. Nucor has the same resources (plant, equipment, skilled employees, know-how) as many other mini-mill operators. What distinguishes Nucor is its unique capability to manage its resources in a highly productive way. Specifically, Nucor's structure, control systems, and culture promote efficiency at all levels within the company.

resources
Financial, physical, social or human, technological, and organizational factors that allow a company to create value for its customers. Company resources can be divided into two types: tangible and intangible resources.

tangible resources
Physical resources, such as land, buildings, plant, equipment, inventory, and money.

intangible resources
Nonphysical entities that are the creation of managers and other employees, such as brand names, the reputation of the company, the knowledge that employees have gained through experience, and the intellectual property of the company, including that protected through patents, copyrights, and trademarks.

capabilities
A company's skills at coordinating its resources and putting them to productive use.

In sum, for a company to have a distinctive competence it must at a minimum have either (1) a firm-specific and valuable resource and the capabilities (skills) necessary to take advantage of that resource (as illustrated by Polaroid) or (2) a firm-specific capability to manage resources (as exemplified by Nucor). A company's distinctive competence is strongest when it possesses *both* firm-specific and valuable resources and firm-specific capabilities to manage those resources.

Figure 4.6 illustrates the relationship of a company's strategies, resources, distinctive competences, and capabilities. Distinctive competences shape the strategies that the company pursues, which build superior efficiency, quality, innovation, or customer responsiveness. In turn, this leads to competitive advantage and superior profitability. However, it is also very important to realize that the strategies a company adopts can build new resources and capabilities or strengthen the existing resources and capabilities of the company, thereby enhancing the distinctive competences of the enterprise. Thus, the relationship between distinctive competences and strategies is not a linear one; rather, it is a reciprocal one in which distinctive competences shape strategies, and strategies help to build and create distinctive competences.[43]

● **The Durability of Competitive Advantage**

A company with a competitive advantage will have superior profitability. This sends a signal to rivals that the company has some valuable distinctive competence that allows it to create superior value. Competitors will try to identify and imitate that competence, and insofar as they are successful, ultimately the imitators may compete away the company's superior profitability.[44] The speed at which this process occurs depends upon the height of barriers to imitation.

Barriers to imitation are factors that make it difficult for a competitor to copy a company's distinctive competences; the greater the barriers to imitation, the more sustainable is a company's competitive advantage.[45] Barriers to imitation differ depending on whether a competitor is trying to imitate resources or capabilities.

In general, the easiest distinctive competences for prospective rivals to imitate tend to be those based on possession of firm-specific and valuable tangible resources, such as buildings, plant, and equipment. Such resources are visible to competitors and can often be purchased on the open market. For example, if a company's competitive advantage is based on sole possession of efficient-scale manufacturing facilities, competitors may move fairly quickly to establish similar facilities. Although Ford gained a competitive advantage over General Motors in the 1920s by being the first to adopt an assembly line manufacturing technology to produce automobiles, General Motors quickly imitated that innovation, competing away Ford's distinctive competence in the process.

barriers to imitation

Factors that make it difficult for a competitor to copy a company's distinctive competences.

Figure 4.6

Strategy, Resources, Capabilities, and Competences

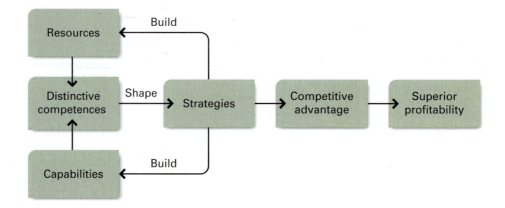

Intangible resources can be more difficult to imitate. This is particularly true of brand names, which are important because they symbolize a company's reputation. In the heavy earthmoving equipment industry, for example, the Caterpillar brand name is synonymous with high quality and superior after-sales service and support. Customers often display a preference for the products of such companies because the brand name is an important guarantee of high quality. Although competitors might like to imitate well-established brand names, the law prohibits them from doing so.

Marketing and technological know-how are also important intangible resources and can be relatively easy to imitate. Successful marketing strategies are relatively easy to imitate because they are so visible to competitors. Thus, Coca-Cola quickly imitated PepsiCo's Diet Pepsi brand with the introduction of its own brand, Diet Coke.

With regard to technological know-how, the patent system in theory should make technological know-how relatively immune to imitation. Patents give the inventor of a new product a twenty-year exclusive production agreement. However, it is often possible to invent around patents—that is, produce a product that is functionally equivalent but does not rely upon the patented technology. One study found that 60% of patented innovations were successfully invented around in four years.[46] This suggests that, in general, distinctive competences based on technological know-how can be relatively short-lived.

Imitating a company's capabilities tends to be more difficult than imitating its tangible and intangible resources, chiefly because capabilities are based on the way in which decisions are made and processes managed deep within a company. It is hard for outsiders to discern them.

On its own, the invisible nature of capabilities would not be enough to halt imitation; competitors could still gain insights into how a company operates by hiring people away from that company. However, a company's capabilities rarely reside in a single individual. Rather, they are the product of how numerous individuals interact within a unique organizational setting.[47] It is possible that no one individual within a company may be familiar with the totality of a company's internal operating routines and procedures. In such cases, hiring people away from a successful company in order to imitate its key capabilities may not be helpful.

In sum, a company's competitive advantage tends to be more secure when it is based upon intangible resources and capabilities, as opposed to tangible resources. Capabilities can be particularly difficult to imitate, since doing so requires the imitator to change its own internal management processes—something that is never easy, owing to organization inertia. Even in such a favorable situation, however, a company is never totally secure. The reason for this is that rather than imitating a company with a competitive advantage, competitors may invent their way around the source of competitive advantage. The decline of once dominant companies like IBM, General Motors, and Sears was due not to imitation of their distinctive competences, but to the fact that rivals such as Dell, Toyota, and Wal-Mart developed new and better ways of competing which nullified the competitive advantage once enjoyed by these enterprises. Herein lies the rationale for the statement popularized by the former CEO of Intel, Andy Grove, that "only the paranoid survive." Even if a company's distinctive competences are protected by high barriers to imitation, it should act as if rivals are continually trying to nullify its source of advantage either by imitation *or* by developing new ways of doing business—for, in reality, that is exactly what they are trying to do.

Summary of Chapter

1. To have superior profitability, a company must lower its costs or differentiate its product (or do both simultaneously) so that it creates more value and can charge a higher price.

2. The four building blocks of competitive advantage are efficiency, quality, innovation, and customer responsiveness. Superior efficiency enables a company to lower its costs; superior quality allows it to charge a higher price and lower its costs; and superior customer service lets it charge a higher price. Superior innovation can lead to higher prices, particularly in the case of product innovations, or lower unit costs, particularly in the case of process innovations.

3. The term *value chain* refers to the idea that a company is a chain of activities for transforming inputs into outputs that customers value. The process of transforming inputs into outputs is composed of a number of primary activities and support activities. Each activity adds value to the product.

4. Actions taken by functional managers at every step in the value chain—functional-level strategies—can increase the efficiency, quality, innovation, and customer responsiveness of a company.

5. Distinctive competences are the firm-specific strengths of a company. Valuable distinctive competences enable a company to generate superior profitability.

6. The distinctive competences of an organization arise from its resources and capabilities.

7. In order to achieve a competitive advantage, a company needs to pursue strategies that build on its existing resources and capabilities and formulate strategies that build additional resources and capabilities (develop new competences).

8. The durability of a company's competitive advantage depends on the height of barriers to imitation.

Discussion Questions

1. What are the main implications of the material discussed in this chapter for strategy formulation?

2. When is a company's competitive advantage most likely to endure over time?

3. It is possible for a company to be the lowest-cost producer in its industry and simultaneously have an output that is the most valued by customers. Discuss this statement.

4. How are the four generic building blocks of competitive advantage related to each other?

5. What role can top management play in helping a company achieve superior efficiency, quality, innovation, and responsiveness to customers?

Practicing Strategic Management

SMALL-GROUP EXERCISE
Analyzing Competitive Advantage

Break up into groups of three to five people, and answer the following questions. Drawing on the concepts introduced in this chapter, analyze the competitive position of your business school in the market for business education.

1. Does your business school have a competitive advantage?

2. If so, on what is this advantage based, and is this advantage sustainable?

3. If your school does not have a competitive advantage in the market for business education, identify the inhibiting factors that are holding it back.

4. How might the Internet change the way in which business education is delivered?

5. Does the Internet pose a threat to the competitive position of your school in the market for business education, or is it the source of an opportunity for your school to enhance its competitive position? (Note that it can be both.)

EXPLORING THE WEB
Visiting Johnson & Johnson

Visit the website of Johnson & Johnson (**www.jnj.com**). Read through the material contained on the site, paying particular at-

tention to the features on company history, Johnson & Johnson's credo, innovations, and company news. On the basis of the information provided there, answer the following questions:

1. Do you think that Johnson & Johnson has a distinctive competence?

2. What is the nature of this competence? How does it help the company to attain a competitive advantage?

3. What are the resources and capabilities that underlie this competence? Where do these resources and capabilities come from?

4. How imitable is Johnson & Johnson's distinctive competence?

General Task   Search the Web for a company site that goes into depth about the history, products, and competitive position of that company. On the basis of the information you collect, answer the following questions:

1. Does the company have a distinctive competence?

2. What is the nature of this competence? How does it help the company to attain a competitive advantage?

3. What are the resources and capabilities that underlie this competence? Where do these resources and capabilities come from?

4. How imitable is the company's distinctive competence?

CLOSING CASE

Starbucks

In 2006, Starbucks, the ubiquitous coffee retailer, closed a decade of astounding financial performance. Sales had increased from $697 million to $7.8 billion and net profits from $36 million to $540 million. In 2006, Starbucks was earning a return on invested capital of 25.5%, which was impressive by any measure, and the company was forecasted to continue growing earnings and main-

tain high profits through the end of the decade. How did this come about?

Thirty years ago, Starbucks was a single store in Seattle's Pike Place Market selling premium roasted coffee. Today it is a global roaster and retailer of coffee with more than 12,000 retail stores, some 3,000 of which are found in forty countries outside the

United States. Starbucks Corporation set out on its current course in the 1980s, when the company's director of marketing, Howard Schultz, came back from a trip to Italy enchanted with the Italian coffeehouse experience. Schultz, who later became CEO, persuaded the company's owners to experiment with the coffeehouse format—and the Starbucks experience was born.

Schultz's basic insight was that people lacked a "third place" between home and work where they could have their own personal time out, meet with friends, relax, and have a sense of gathering. The business model that evolved out of this was to sell the company's own premium roasted coffee, along with freshly brewed espresso-style coffee beverages and a variety of pastries, coffee accessories, teas, and other products, in a coffeehouse setting. The company devoted, and continues to devote, considerable attention to the design of its stores, so as to create a relaxed, informal, and comfortable atmosphere. Underlying this approach was a belief that Starbucks was selling far more than coffee—it was selling an experience. The premium price that Starbucks charged for its coffee reflected this fact.

From the outset, Schultz also focused on providing superior customer service in stores. Reasoning that motivated employees provide the best customer service, Starbucks executives developed employee hiring and training programs that were the best in the restaurant industry. Today, all Starbucks employees are required to attend training classes that teach them not only how to make a good cup of coffee, but also the service-oriented values of the company. Beyond this, Starbucks provided progressive compensation policies that gave even part-time employees stock option grants and medical benefits—a very innovative approach in an industry where most employees are part time, earn minimum wage, and have no benefits.

Unlike many restaurant chains, which expanded very rapidly through franchising arrangements once they had established a basic formula that appeared to work, Schultz believed that Starbucks needed to own its own stores. Although it has experimented with franchising arrangements in some countries and in some situations in the United States such as at airports, the company still prefers to own its own stores whenever possible.

This formula met with spectacular success in the United States, where Starbucks went from obscurity to one of the best known brands in the country in a decade. As it grew, Starbucks found that it was generating an enormous volume of repeat business. Today the average customer comes into a Starbucks store around twenty times a month. The customers themselves are a fairly well heeled group—their average income is about $80,000.

As the company grew, it started to develop a very sophisticated location strategy. Detailed demographic analysis was used to identify the best locations for Starbucks stores. The company expanded rapidly to capture as many premium locations as possible before imitators began to gain ground. Astounding many observers, Starbucks would even sometimes locate stores on opposite corners of the same busy street—so that it could capture traffic going in different directions down the street.

By 1995, with almost 700 stores across the United States, Starbucks began exploring foreign opportunities. First stop was Japan, where Starbucks proved that the basic value proposition could be applied to a different cultural setting (there are now 600 stores in Japan). Next, Starbucks embarked upon a rapid development strategy in Asia and Europe. In 2001, the magazine *Brandchannel* named Starbucks one of the ten most impactful global brands, a position it has held ever since. But this is only the beginning. In late 2006, with 12,000 stores in operation, the company announced that its long-term goal was to have 40,000 stores worldwide. Looking forward, it expects 50% of all new store openings to be outside of the United States.[c]

Case Discussion Questions

1. What functional strategies at Starbucks help the company to achieve superior financial performance?

2. Identify the resources, capabilities, and distinctive competences of Starbucks.

3. How do Starbucks' resources, capabilities, and distinctive competences translate into superior financial performance?

4. Why do you think Starbucks prefers to own its own stores whenever possible?

5. How secure is Starbucks' competitive advantage? What are the barriers to imitation here?

TEST PREPPER

True/False Questions

_____ **1.** A company has a competitive advantage when its profitability is higher than the average for its industry.

_____ **2.** Michael Porter has argued that low cost and differentiation are two basic strategies for creating value and attaining a competitive advantage in an industry.

_____ **3.** The most complicated measure of efficiency is the quantity of inputs that it takes to produce a given output.

_____ **4.** A product can be said to be reliable when it consistently does the job it is designed for, does it well, and rarely (if ever) breaks down.

_____ **5.** Product innovation refers to the act of creating new products or processes.

_____ **6.** The term _value chain_ refers to the idea that a company is a chain of activities for transforming inputs into outputs that customers value.

_____ **7.** Marketing strategy refers to the position that a company takes with regard to pricing, promotion, advertising, product design, and distribution.

Multiple-Choice Questions

8. Which of the following is a primary activity in a firm's value chain?
a. Information systems
b. Human resources
c. Materials management
d. Research and development
e. Company infrastructure

9. Functional-level strategies build _____ by focusing on a limited number of important functions.
a. product innovation
b. competitive advantage
c. customer response time
d. a & b above
e. none of the above

10. The term _____ has been coined to describe the ability of companies to use flexible manufacturing technology to reconcile two goals that were once thought to be incompatible: low cost and differentiation through product customization.
a. marketing strategy
b. lean production
c. mass customization
d. learning effects
e. flexible manufacturing technology

11. In a/an _____, members coordinate their own activities, which might include making their own hiring, training, work, and reward decisions.
a. group work team
b. organizational team
c. self-managing team
d. operating team
e. management team

12. The principal tool that most managers now use to increase the reliability of their product offering is _____.
a. the total quality management philosophy
b. the Six Sigma quality improvement methodology
c. effective human resource training and development
d. information systems efficiency
e. none of the above

13. _____ is the specific set of options a company adopts for a product on four main dimensions of marketing: price, distribution, promotion and advertising, and product features.
a. New product development
b. Time to market strategy
c. Product innovation
d. Positioning strategy
e. Customer focus strategy

14. _____ are something physical, such as land, buildings, plant, equipment, inventory, and money.
   a. Intangible resources
   b. Distinctive competences
   c. Organizational factors
   d. Capabilities
   e. Tangible resources

15. Which of the following is a support activity of the value chain?
   a. Marketing and sales
   b. Customer service
   c. Information systems
   d. Research and development
   e. Production

Chapter 5

Business-Level Strategy and Competitive Positioning

Learning Objectives

After reading this chapter, you should be able to

1. Discuss the nature of competitive positioning in reference to the three main factors that underlie the choice of a successful business-level strategy

2. Differentiate between the principal kinds of generic business-level strategies and appreciate their advantages and disadvantages

3. Appreciate the competitive positioning issues involved in fragmented and growing, mature, and declining industry environments

Chapter Outline

I. The Nature of Competitive Positioning
   a. Customer Needs and Product Differentiation
   b. Customer Groups and Market Segmentation
   c. Distinctive Competences

II. Choosing a Business-Level Strategy
   a. Cost-Leadership Strategy
   b. Differentiation Strategy

   c. Cost Leadership and Differentiation
   d. Focus Strategy
   e. Stuck in the Middle

III. Competitive Positioning in Different Industry Environments
   a. Strategies in Fragmented and Growing Industries
   b. Strategies in Mature Industries
   c. Strategies in Declining Industries

Overview

This chapter examines the various strategies a company can adopt to maximize its competitive advantage and profitability in a business or industry. Chapter 3, on the industry environment, provides concepts for analyzing industry opportunities and threats. Chapter 4 discusses how a company develops functional-level strategies to build distinctive competences to achieve a competitive advantage. In this chapter, we first examine the principal business-level strategies that a company can use to achieve a competitive advantage against rivals in an industry. Second, we discuss a separate but related issue: how to choose appropriate competitive tactics and maneuvers to build a company's competitive advantage over time in different kinds of industry environments. By the end of this chapter, you will be able to identify and distinguish among the business-level strategies and tactics that strategic managers use to give their companies a competitive advantage over their industry rivals.

The Nature of Competitive Positioning

business-level strategy

The plan of action strategic managers adopt to use a company's resources and distinctive competences to gain a competitive advantage.

In order to maximize its competitive advantage, a company must find the best way to position itself against its rivals. It does this by using business-level strategy. **Business-level strategy** is the plan of action that strategic managers adopt to use a company's resources and distinctive competences to gain a competitive advantage over its rivals in a market or industry. In Chapter 2, we discuss how the process of defining a business involves decisions about (1) customer needs, or *what* is to be satisfied; (2) customer groups, or *who* is to be satisfied; and (3) distinctive competences, or *how* customer needs are to be satisfied.[1] These three decisions are the basis of the choice of a business-level strategy because they determine how a company will compete in an industry. Consequently, we need to look at the ways in which a company makes these three decisions in an effort to gain a competitive advantage over its rivals.

● **Customer Needs and Product Differentiation**

customer needs

Desires, wants, or cravings that can be satisfied by means of the characteristics of a product or service.

product differentiation

The process of creating a competitive advantage by designing goods or services to satisfy customer needs.

Customer needs are desires, wants, or cravings that can be satisfied by means of the characteristics of a product or service. For example, a person's craving for something sweet can be satisfied by a carton of Ben & Jerry's ice cream, a Snickers bar, or a spoonful of sugar. **Product differentiation** is the process of creating a competitive advantage by designing products—goods or services—to satisfy customer needs. All companies must differentiate their products to a certain degree in order to attract customers and satisfy some minimal level of need. However, some companies differentiate their products to a much greater degree than others, and this difference can give them a competitive edge.

Some companies offer the customer a low-priced product without engaging in much product differentiation. Others seek to endow their product with some unique attribute(s) so that it will satisfy customers' needs in ways that other products cannot. The uniqueness may be related to the physical characteristics of the product, such as quality or reliability, or it may lie in the product's appeal to customers' psychological needs, such as the need for prestige or status.[2] Thus, a Japanese car may be differentiated by its reputation for reliability, and a Corvette or a Porsche may be differentiated by its ability to satisfy customers' needs for status.

● **Customer Groups and Market Segmentation**

market segmentation

The way a company decides to group customers, based on important differences in their needs or preferences, in order to gain a competitive advantage.

Market segmentation is the way a company decides to group customers, based on important differences in their needs or preferences, in order to gain a competitive advantage.[3] For example, General Motors groups its customers according to the amount of money they want to spend, and can afford to spend, to buy a car, and for each group it builds different cars, which range from the low-priced Chevrolet Aveo to the high-priced Cadillac DTS sedan.

In general, a company can adopt one of three alternative strategies for market segmentation.[4] First, it can choose not to recognize that different groups of customers have different needs and can instead adopt the approach of serving the average customer. Second, a company can choose to segment its market into different constituencies and develop a product to suit the needs of each. For example, Toyota offers over twenty different kinds of vehicles, such as family cars, luxury vehicles, SUVs, and trucks, each targeted at a different market segment. Third, a company can choose to recognize that the market is segmented but concentrate on servicing only one market segment; an example is the luxury-car niche chosen by Mercedes-Benz.

Why would a company want to make complex product/market choices and create a different product tailored to each market segment, rather than creating a single product for the whole market? The answer is that the decision to provide many products for many market niches allows a company to satisfy customers' needs better. As a result, customer demand for a company's products rises and generates more revenue than would be the case if the company offered just one product for the whole market.[5] Sometimes, however, the nature of the product or the nature of the industry does not allow much differentiation; this is the case, for example, with bulk chemicals or cement.[6] In these industries, there is little opportunity to obtain a competitive advantage through product differentiation and market segmentation, because there is little opportunity for serving customers' needs and customer groups in different ways. Instead, price is the main criterion that customers use to evaluate the product, and the competitive advantage lies with the company that has superior efficiency and can provide the lowest priced product.

● **Distinctive Competences**

The third issue in business-level strategy is to decide which distinctive competences to pursue to satisfy customers' needs and customer groups.[7] In Chapter 4, we discuss four ways in which companies can obtain a competitive advantage: superior efficiency, quality, innovation, and responsiveness to customers. The Four Seasons hotel chain, for example, attempts to do all it can to provide its customers with the highest quality accommodations and the best customer service possible. In making business strategy choices, a company must decide how to organize and combine its distinctive competences to gain a competitive advantage.

Choosing a Business-Level Strategy

Companies pursue a business-level strategy to gain a competitive advantage that enables them to outperform rivals and achieve above-average returns. They can choose from three basic generic competitive approaches—cost leadership, differentiation, and focus—although, as we will see, these can be combined in different ways.[8] These strategies are called *generic* because all businesses or industries can pursue them, regardless of whether they are manufacturing, service, or nonprofit enterprises. Each of the generic strategies results from a company's making consistent choices on product, market, and distinctive competences—choices that reinforce each other. Table 5.1 summarizes the choices appropriate for each of the three generic strategies.

● **Cost-Leadership Strategy**

cost-leadership strategy

A strategy of trying to outperform competitors by doing everything possible to produce goods or services at a lower cost than they do.

A company's goal in pursuing a **cost-leadership strategy** is to outperform competitors by doing everything the company can to produce goods or services at a cost lower than those of competitors. Two advantages accrue from a cost-leadership strategy. First, because of its lower costs, the cost leader is able to charge a lower price than its competitors and yet make the same level of profit. If companies in the industry charge similar prices for their products, the cost leader still makes a higher profit than its competitors because of its lower costs. Second, if rivalry within the industry increases and companies start to compete on price, the cost leader will be able to withstand competition better than the other companies because of its lower costs. For both of these reasons, cost leaders are likely to earn above-average profits. How does a company become the cost leader? It achieves this position by means of the product/market/distinctive-competence choices that it makes to gain a low-cost competitive advantage (see Table 5.1).

Table 5.1

Product/Market/Distinctive-Competence Choices and Generic Competitive Strategies

	Cost Leadership	Differentiation	Focus
Product Differentiation	Low (principally by price)	High (principally by uniqueness)	Low to high (price or uniqueness)
Market Segmentation	Low (mass market)	High (many market segments)	Low (one or few segments)
Distinctive Competence	Manufacturing and materials management	Research and development, sales and marketing	Any kind of distinctive competence

STRATEGIC CHOICES The cost leader chooses a low level of product differentiation. Differentiation is expensive; if the company expends resources to make its products unique, then its costs rise.[9] The cost leader aims for a level of differentiation not markedly inferior to that of the differentiator (a company that competes by spending resources on product development), but a level obtainable at low cost.[10] The cost leader does not try to be the industry leader in differentiation; it waits until customers want a feature or service before providing it. For example, a cost leader does not introduce stereo sound in television sets. It adds stereo sound only when consumers clearly want it.

The cost leader also normally ignores the different market segments and positions its product to appeal to the average customer. This is because developing a line of products tailored to the needs of different market segments is an expensive proposition. A cost leader normally engages in only a limited amount of market segmentation. Even though no customer may be totally happy with the product, the fact that the company normally charges a lower price than its competitors attracts customers to its products.

In developing distinctive competences, the overriding goal of the cost leader must be to increase its efficiency and lower its costs compared with its rivals. The development of distinctive competences in manufacturing and materials management is central to achieving this goal. Companies pursuing a low-cost strategy may attempt to ride down the experience curve so that they can lower their manufacturing costs.

Achieving a low-cost position may also require that the company develop skills in flexible manufacturing and adopt efficient materials management techniques. (As you may recall, Table 4.1 outlines the ways in which a company's value creation functions can be used to increase efficiency.) Consequently, the manufacturing and materials management functions are the center of attention for a company pursuing a cost-leadership strategy, and the distinctive competences of other functions are shaped to meet the needs of manufacturing and materials management.[11] For example, the sales function may develop the competence of capturing large, stable sets of customers' orders. This, in turn, allows manufacturing to make longer production runs and so achieve economies of scale and reduce costs. The human resource function may focus on instituting training programs and compensation systems that lower costs by enhancing employees' productivity, and the research and development function may specialize in process improvements to lower the manufacturing costs.

Many cost leaders gear all their strategic choices to the single goal of squeezing out every cent of costs to sustain their competitive advantage. A company such as H. J. Heinz is an excellent example of a cost leader. Because beans and canned vegetables do not permit much of a markup, the profit comes from the large volume of cans sold. Therefore, Heinz goes to extraordinary lengths to reduce costs—by even one-twentieth of a cent per can—because this will lead to large cost savings and thus bigger profits over the long run. The Running Case discusses how Wal-Mart developed its cost-leadership strategy.

RUNNING CASE

How Wal-Mart Became a Cost Leader

As Wal-Mart puts it in its mission statement, "We think of ourselves as buyers for our customers and we apply our considerable strengths to get the best value for you."[a] How does Wal-Mart provide the most value for its customers? By keeping its costs to a minimum so that it can charge lower prices than its competitors. And it achieves this through the fit its managers have achieved between its business- and functional-level strategies. Sam Walton, the company's founder, chose the business-level strategies to increase efficiency and lower costs. One business-level strategy he implemented was to locate his stores outside large cities in small towns, where there were no low-cost competitors; a second was to find ways to manage the value chain to reduce the costs of getting products from manufacturers to customers; and a third was to design and staff store operations to increase efficiency.

From the beginning, Wal-Mart has chosen low product differentiation and minimal advertising, targeting the average customer to attract the mass market. In targeting the average customer, Wal-Mart's managers strive to provide the least number of products that will be desired by the highest number of customers, something at the heart of Wal-Mart's approach to stocking its stores. Similarly, Wal-Mart does not spend hundreds of millions of dollars on store design to create an attractive shopping experience, as chains like Macy's, Dillard's, and Saks Fifth Avenue have done; its stores are bare bones and offer a minimum of customer service.

At the functional level, Wal-Mart has developed distinctive competences in the functions that contribute most to lowering its costs. At Wal-Mart, this is the cost of purchasing products, so the logistics or materials management function is of central importance. Wal-Mart has taken advantage of advances in IT to lower the costs associated with getting goods from manufacturers to customers and is a leader in the development and introduction of cost-lowering IT innovations such as radio frequency tags (RFTs) through which it can track its inventory on a real-time basis. Indeed, given that the use of these RFTs lowers its inventory costs by 5%, Wal-Mart told its suppliers that unless they agreed to use them it would no longer purchase their products.

Today, the task of all functional managers in logistics, materials management, sales, and customer service is to implement specific functional-level strategies that support its low-cost, low-price business strategy. Over time, Wal-Mart has chosen to utilize its cost-cutting skills to develop new kinds of stores, such as superstores, that sell new kinds of products, such as groceries and appliances, and its sales have boomed. It has also chosen to expand abroad and apply its skills in new countries, as we discuss in later chapters.

ADVANTAGES AND DISADVANTAGES The advantages of each generic strategy are best discussed in terms of Porter's five forces model, introduced in Chapter 3.[12] The five forces are the intensity of rivalry among competitors, the bargaining power of suppliers, the bargaining power of buyers, the threat of substitute products, and the risk of entry by potential competitors. The cost leader is protected from *industry competitors* by its cost advantage. Its lower costs also mean that it will be less affected than its competitors by increases in the price of inputs if there are *powerful suppliers* and less affected by a drop in the price it can charge for its products if there are *powerful buyers*. Moreover, because cost leadership usually requires a big market share, the cost leader purchases in relatively large quantities, increasing its bargaining power over suppliers. If *substitute products* start to come into the market, the cost leader can reduce its price to compete with them and retain its market share. Finally, the leader's cost advantage constitutes a *barrier to entry,* because other companies are unable to enter the industry and match the leader's costs or prices. The cost leader is therefore relatively safe as long as it can maintain its cost advantage, and price is the key for a significant number of buyers.

The principal dangers of the cost-leadership approach lurk in competitors' ability to find ways to produce at lower cost and beat the cost leader at its own game. For instance, if technological change makes experience-curve economies obsolete, new companies may apply lower-cost technologies that give them a cost advantage over the cost leader. The steel mini-mills discussed in Chapter 4 gained this advantage. Competitors may also draw a cost advantage from labor-cost savings. Competitors in many Asian countries, for example, have very low labor costs, and U.S. companies now assemble many of their products abroad as part of their low-cost strategy.

Competitors' ability to imitate the cost leader's methods is another threat to the cost-leadership strategy. For example, the ability of IBM-clone manufacturers to produce IBM-compatible products at costs similar to IBM's (but, of course, to sell them at a much lower price) was a major factor contributing to IBM's troubles.

Finally, the cost-leadership strategy carries a risk that the cost leader, in its single-minded desire to reduce costs, may lose sight of changes in customers' tastes. Thus, a company might make decisions that decrease costs but drastically affect demand for the product. For example, Joseph Schlitz Brewing Company lowered the quality of its beer's ingredients, substituting inferior grains to reduce costs. Consumers immediately caught on, and demand for the product dropped dramatically. As mentioned earlier, the cost leader cannot abandon product differentiation, and even low-priced products, such as Timex watches, cannot be too inferior to the more expensive watches made by Seiko if the low-cost, low-price policy is to succeed.

● Differentiation Strategy

differentiation strategy

A strategy of trying to achieve a competitive advantage by creating a product that is perceived by customers as unique in some important way.

The objective of the generic **differentiation strategy** is to achieve a competitive advantage by creating a product that is perceived by customers to be *unique* in some important way. The differentiated product's ability to satisfy a customer's need in a way that its competitors cannot means that the company can charge a *premium price*—a price considerably above the industry average. The ability to increase revenues by charging premium prices (rather than by reducing costs as the cost leader does) allows the differentiator to outperform its competitors and gain above-average profits. The premium price is usually substantially above the price charged by the cost leader, and customers pay it because they believe the product's differentiated qualities are worth the difference. Consequently, the product is priced on the basis of what customers are willing to pay for it.[13]

Cars made by Mercedes-Benz, BMW, and Lexus command premium prices because customers perceive that the luxury and prestige of owning these vehicles are something worth paying for. In watches, the name of Rolex stands out; in jewelry, Tiffany; in airplanes, Learjet. All these products command premium prices because of their differentiated qualities.

STRATEGIC CHOICES   As Table 5.1 shows, a differentiator chooses a high level of product differentiation to gain a competitive advantage. Product differentiation can be achieved in three principal ways, which are discussed in detail in Chapter 4: quality, innovation, and responsiveness to customers. For example, Procter & Gamble claims that its product quality is high and that Ivory soap is 99.44% pure. IBM promotes the quality service provided by its well-trained sales force.

Innovation is very important for high-tech products for which new features are the source of differentiation, and many people pay a premium price for new and innovative products, such as a state-of-the-art computer, stereo, or car.

When differentiation is based on responsiveness to customers, a company offers comprehensive after-sale service and product repair. This is an especially important consideration for complex products such as cars and domestic appliances, which are likely to break down periodically. Companies such as Maytag, Dell, and BMW all excel in responsiveness to customers. In service organizations, quality-of-service attributes are also very important. Why can Neiman Marcus, Nordstrom, and FedEx charge premium prices? They offer an exceptionally high level of service. Similarly, law firms and accounting firms emphasize to clients the service aspects of their operations: their knowledge, professionalism, and reputation.

Finally, a product's appeal to customers' psychological desires can become a source of differentiation. The appeal can be to prestige or status, as it is with BMWs and Rolex watches; to patriotism, as with Chevrolet; to safety of home and family, as with Prudential Insurance; or to value for money, as with Bed, Bath, & Beyond and The Gap. Differentiation can also be tailored to age groups and to socioeconomic groups. Indeed, the bases of differentiation are endless.

A company that pursues a differentiation strategy strives to differentiate itself along as many dimensions as possible. The less it resembles its rivals, the more it is protected from competition and the wider its market appeal. Thus, BMWs do not offer prestige alone. They also offer technological sophistication, luxury, reliability, and good (though very expensive) repair service. All these bases of differentiation help increase sales.

Generally, a differentiator chooses to segment its market into many niches. Now and then, a company may offer a product designed for each market niche and decide to be a **broad differentiator,** but a company may also choose to serve just those niches in which it has a specific differentiation advantage. For example, Sony produces over twenty different kinds of high-definition, flat-screen televisions, filling all the niches from mid-priced to high-priced sets. However, its lowest priced models are always priced hundreds of dollars above those of its competitors, bringing into play the premium-price factor. You have to pay extra for a Sony. Similarly, although Mercedes-Benz has filled niches below its old high-priced models with its S and C series, it has made no attempt to produce a car for every market segment.

Finally, in choosing which distinctive competence to pursue, a differentiated company concentrates on the organizational function that provides the sources of its differentiation advantage. Differentiation on the basis of innovation and technological competence depends on the R&D function, as we noted in Chapter 4. Efforts

broad differentiator

A company that offers a product designed for each market niche.

to improve service to customers depend on the quality of the sales function. A focus on a specific function does not mean, however, that the control of costs is not important for a differentiator. A differentiator does not want to increase costs unnecessarily and tries to keep them somewhere near those of the cost leader. However, because developing the distinctive competence needed to provide a differentiation advantage is often expensive, a differentiator usually has higher costs than the cost leader. Still, it must control all costs that do not contribute to its differentiation advantage so that the price of the product does not exceed what customers are willing to pay. Because bigger profits are earned by controlling costs and by maximizing revenues, it pays to control costs but not to minimize them to the point of losing the source of differentiation.[14]

ADVANTAGES AND DISADVANTAGES Differentiation safeguards a company against competitors to the degree that customers develop *brand loyalty* for its products. Brand loyalty is a very valuable asset that protects the company on all fronts. For example, *powerful suppliers* are rarely a problem because the differentiator's strategy is geared more toward the price it can charge than toward the costs of production. Thus, a differentiator can tolerate moderate increases in the prices of its inputs better than the cost leader can. Differentiators are unlikely to experience problems with *powerful buyers* because the differentiator offers the buyer a unique product. Only it can supply the product, and it commands brand loyalty. Differentiation and brand loyalty also create a *barrier to entry* for other companies seeking to enter the industry. New companies are forced to develop their own distinctive competence to be able to compete, and doing so is very expensive. Finally, the threat of *substitute products* depends on the ability of competitors' products to meet the same customer needs as the differentiator's products and to break the differentiator's customers' brand loyalty. The main problems with a differentiation strategy center on the company's long-term ability to maintain its perceived uniqueness in customers' eyes. We have seen in the last ten years how quickly competitors move to imitate and copy successful differentiators. This has happened in many industries, such as computers, autos, and electronics. Patents and first-mover advantage (the advantage of being the first to market a product or service) last only so long, and as the overall quality of products made by all companies increases, brand loyalty declines.

● **Cost Leadership and Differentiation**

Recently, changes in production techniques—in particular, the development of flexible manufacturing technologies (discussed in Chapter 4)—have made the choice between cost-leadership and differentiation strategies less clear-cut. With technological developments, companies have found it easier to obtain the benefits of both strategies. The reason is that the new flexible technologies allow firms to pursue a differentiation strategy at a low cost; that is, companies can combine these two generic strategies.

Traditionally, differentiation was obtainable only at high cost, because the necessity of producing different models for different market segments meant that firms had to have short production runs, which raised manufacturing costs. In addition, the differentiated firm had to bear higher marketing costs than the cost leader because it was servicing many market segments. As a result, differentiators had higher costs than cost leaders, which produced large batches of standardized products. However, flexible manufacturing may enable a firm pursuing differentiation to manufacture a range of products at a cost comparable to that of the cost leader. The use of flexible manufacturing cells reduces the costs of retooling the production line and the costs associated with small production runs. Indeed, a factor promoting the current trend toward market fragmentation and niche marketing in many consumer goods industries, such as mobile phones, computers, and appliances, is the substantial reduction of the costs of differentiation achieved via flexible manufacturing.

Another way that a differentiated producer may be able to realize significant economies of scale is by standardizing many of the component parts used in its end products. In the 2000s, for example, DaimlerChrysler began to offer more than twenty different models of cars and minivans to different segments of the auto market. However, despite their different appearances, all twenty models are based on only three different platforms. Moreover, most of the cars use many of the same components, including axles, drive units, suspensions, and gear boxes. As a result, DaimlerChrysler has been able to realize significant economies of scale in the manufacture and bulk purchase of standardized component parts.

A company can also reduce both production and marketing costs if it limits the number of models in the product line by offering packages of options rather than letting consumers decide exactly what options they require. It is increasingly common for auto manufacturers, for example, to offer an economy auto package, a luxury package, and a sports package to appeal to their principal market segments. Package offerings substantially lower manufacturing costs because long production runs of the various packages are possible. At the same time, the firm is able to focus its advertising and marketing efforts on particular market segments, so these costs are also decreased. Once again, the firm is reaping gains from differentiation and low cost at the same time.

Taking advantage of new developments in production and marketing, some companies are managing to reap the gains from cost-leadership and differentiation strategies simultaneously. Because they can charge a premium price for their products compared with the price charged by the pure cost leader and because they have lower costs than the pure differentiator, they obtain at least an equal, and probably a higher, level of profit than firms pursuing only one of the generic strategies. Companies have moved quickly to take advantage of new production and marketing techniques because the combined strategy is the most profitable to pursue.

● Focus Strategy

focus strategy

A strategy of serving the needs of one or a few customer groups or segments.

The third generic competitive strategy, the **focus strategy,** differs from the other two chiefly in that it is directed toward serving the needs of a *limited customer group or segment.* A focus strategy concentrates on serving a particular market niche, which can be defined geographically, by type of customer, or by a segment of the product line.[15] For example, a geographic niche can be defined by region or even by locality. Selecting a niche by type of customer might mean serving only the very rich, the very young, or the very adventurous. A company that concentrates on a segment of the product line may focus only on vegetarian foods, on very fast cars, or on designer clothes or sunglasses, for example. In following a focus strategy, a company is *specializing* in some way.

Once it has chosen its market segment, a company pursues a focus strategy through either a differentiation or a low-cost approach. Figure 5.1 shows these two different kinds of focus strategies and compares them with a pure cost-leadership or pure differentiation strategy.

In essence, a focused company is a specialized differentiator *or* a cost leader. If a company uses a focused low-cost approach, it competes against the cost leader in the market segments in which it has no cost disadvantage. For example, in local lumber or cement markets, the focuser has lower transportation costs than the low-cost

Figure 5.1

Types of Business-Level Strategies

national company. The focuser may also have a cost advantage because it is producing complex or custom-built products that do not lend themselves easily to economies of scale in production and, therefore, offer few experience-curve advantages. With a focus strategy, a company concentrates on small-volume custom products, for which it has a cost advantage, and leaves the large-volume standardized market to the cost leader.

If a company uses a focused differentiation approach, then all the means of differentiation that are open to the differentiator are available to the focused company. The point is that the focused company competes with the differentiator in only one or a few segments. For example, Porsche, a focused company, competes against GM in the sports car and luxury SUV segments of the auto market, not in other segments. Focused companies are likely to be able to differentiate their products successfully because of their detailed knowledge of a small customer set (such as sports car buyers) or of a geographic region.

Furthermore, concentration on a small range of products sometimes allows a focuser to develop innovations faster than a large differentiator can. However, the focuser does not attempt to serve all market segments, because doing so would bring it into direct competition with the differentiator. Instead, a focused company concentrates on building market share in one or a few market segments and, if successful, may begin to serve more and more market segments and chip away at the differentiator's competitive advantage over time.

STRATEGIC CHOICES Table 5.1 illustrated the specific product/market/distinctive-competence choices made by a focused company. Differentiation can be high or low because the company can pursue a low-cost or a differentiation approach. As for customer groups, a focused company chooses specific niches in which to compete rather than going for a whole market, as a cost leader does, or filling a large number of niches, as a broad differentiator does. The focused firm can pursue any distinctive competence because it can seek any kind of differentiation or low-cost advantage. Thus, it might find a cost advantage and develop superior efficiency in low-cost manufacturing within a region. Alternatively, a focused firm might develop superior skills in responsiveness to customers, based on its ability to serve the needs of regional customers in ways that a national differentiator would find very expensive.

The many avenues that a focused company can take to develop a competitive advantage explain why there are so many more small companies than large ones. A focused company has enormous opportunity to develop its own niche and compete against larger low-cost and differentiated companies. A focus strategy provides an opportunity for an entrepreneur to find and then take advantage of a gap in the market by developing an innovative product that customers cannot do without.[16] The steel mini-mills discussed in Chapter 4 are a good example of how focused companies specializing in one market can grow so efficient that they become the cost leaders. Many large companies started with a focus strategy, and, of course, one means by which companies can expand is to take over other focused companies.

ADVANTAGES AND DISADVANTAGES A focused company's competitive advantages stem from the source of its distinctive competence: efficiency, quality, innovation, or responsiveness to customers. The firm is protected from *rivals* to the extent that it can provide a good or service that they cannot. This ability also gives the focuser power over its *buyers* because they cannot get the same product from anyone else. With regard to *powerful suppliers,* however, a focused company is at a disadvantage because it buys inputs in small volume and thus is in the suppliers' power. However, as long as it can pass on price increases to loyal customers, this disadvantage may not be a significant problem. *Potential entrants* have to overcome the customer loyalty the focuser has generated, which also reduces the threat from substitute products. This protection from the five forces allows the focuser to earn above-average returns on its investment. A further advantage of the focus strategy is that it permits a company to stay close to its customers and to respond to their changing needs.

Because a focuser produces a small volume, its production costs often exceed those of a low-cost company. Higher costs can also reduce profitability if a focuser is forced to invest heavily in developing a distinctive competence, such as expensive product innovation, in order to compete with a differentiated firm. However, once again, flexible manufacturing systems are opening up new opportunities for focused firms because small production runs become possible at a lower cost. Increasingly, small specialized firms are competing with large companies in specific market segments in which their cost disadvantage is much reduced.

Finally, there is the prospect that differentiators will compete for a focuser's niche by offering a product that can satisfy the demands of the focuser's customers; for example, GM's and Ford's new luxury cars are aimed at Lexus, BMW, and Mercedes-Benz buyers. A focuser is vulnerable to attack and, therefore, has to defend its niche constantly.

● Stuck in the Middle

Each generic strategy requires a company to make consistent product/market/distinctive-competence choices to establish a competitive advantage. Thus, for example, a low-cost company cannot strive for a high level of market segmentation, as a differentiator does, and provide a wide range of products, because doing so would raise production costs too much and the company would lose its low-cost advantage. Similarly, a differentiator with a competence in innovation that tries to reduce its expenditures on research and development, or one with a competence in responsiveness to customers through after-sale service that seeks to economize on its sales force to decrease costs, is asking for trouble because it will lose its competitive advantage as its distinctive competence disappears.

stuck in the middle

The fate of a company whose strategy fails because it has made product/market choices in a way that does not lead to a sustained competitive advantage.

Choosing a business-level strategy successfully means giving serious attention to all elements of the competitive plan. Many companies, through ignorance or error, do not do the planning necessary for success in their chosen strategy. Such companies are said to be **stuck in the middle** because they have made product/market choices in such a way that they have been unable to obtain or sustain a competitive advantage.[17] As a result, they have no consistent business-level strategy, experience below-average performance, and suffer when industry competition intensifies.

Some companies that find themselves stuck in the middle may have started out pursuing one of the three generic strategies but then made poor resource allocation decisions or experienced a hostile, changing environment. It is very easy to lose control of a generic strategy unless strategic managers keep close track of the business and its environment, constantly adjusting product/market choices to suit changing conditions within the industry. There are many paths to getting stuck in the middle. Quite commonly, a focuser gets stuck in the middle when it becomes overconfident and starts to act like a broad differentiator.

People Express, a now defunct airline, exemplified a company in this situation. It started out as a specialized air carrier serving a narrow market niche: low-priced travel on the eastern seaboard. In pursuing this focus strategy based on cost leadership, it was very successful. But when it tried to expand to other geographic regions and began taking over other airlines to gain a larger number of planes, it lost its niche. People Express became just one more carrier in an increasingly competitive market where it had no competitive advantage against other national carriers. The result was financial disaster, and People Express was incorporated into Continental Airlines. By contrast, Southwest Airlines, a focused low-cost company, continues to focus on this strategy and has grown successfully to become a national low-cost leader—as Continental and other national carriers are currently seeking to do.

Differentiators, too, can fail in the market and end up stuck in the middle if competitors attack their markets with more specialized or low-cost products that blunt their competitive edge. This happened to IBM in the mainframe computer market as PCs grew more powerful and became able to do the job of the much more expensive mainframes. The increasing movement toward flexible manufacturing systems aggravates the problems faced by cost leaders and differentiators. Many large firms will become stuck in the middle unless they make the investment needed to pursue both strategies simultaneously. No company is safe in a highly competitive global environment, and each must be constantly on the lookout to take advantage of competitive advantages as they arise and to defend the advantages it already has.

To sum up, successful management of a generic competitive strategy requires that strategic managers attend to two main issues. First, they must ensure that their product/market/distinctive-competence decisions are oriented toward one specific competitive strategy. Second, they need to monitor the environment so that they can keep the firm's sources of competitive advantage in tune with changing opportunities and threats—the issue we turn to now.

Competitive Positioning in Different Industry Environments

If strategic managers succeed in developing a successful generic business-level strategy, they immediately face another crucial issue: how to choose appropriate competitive tactics and maneuvers to position their company to sustain its competitive advantage over time in different kinds of industry environments. In this section, we first focus on how companies in fragmented and growing industries try to develop competitive strategies to support their generic strategies. Second, we consider the challenges of maintaining a competitive advantage in mature industries. Finally, we assess the problems of managing a company's generic competitive strategy in declining industries, in which rivalry between competitors is high because market demand is slowing or falling.

● Strategies in Fragmented and Growing Industries

Many industries are fragmented, which means they are composed of a large number of small and medium-sized companies. The restaurant industry, for example, is fragmented, as are the health club industry and the legal services industry. There are several reasons why an industry may consist of many small companies rather than a few large ones. In some industries there are few economies of scale, so large companies do not have an advantage over smaller ones. Indeed, in some industries there are advantages to staying small, which enables companies to get closer to their customers. Many home buyers, for example, have a preference for dealing with local real estate agents, whom they perceive as having better local knowledge than national chains. Similarly, in the restaurant business, many customers prefer the unique style of a local restaurant. In addition, many industries are fragmented because there are few barriers to entry (such as in the restaurant industry, where a single entrepreneur can often bear the costs of opening a restaurant). High transportation costs, too, can keep an industry fragmented, for regional production may be the only efficient way to satisfy customers' needs, as in the cement business. Finally, an industry may be fragmented because customers' needs are so specialized that only small job lots of products are required, and thus there is no room for a large, mass-production operation to satisfy the market.

For some fragmented industries, these factors dictate the competitive strategy to pursue, and the focus strategy stands out as a principal choice. Companies may specialize by customer group, customer need, or geographic region, so that many small specialty companies operate in local or regional market segments. All kinds of custom-made products—furniture, clothing, hats, boots, and so on—fall into this category, as do all small service operations that cater to particular customers' needs, such as laundries, restaurants, health clubs, and furniture rental stores. Indeed, service companies make up a large proportion of companies in fragmented industries because they provide personalized service to clients and, therefore, need to be responsive to their needs.

Strategic managers, however, are eager to gain the cost advantages of pursuing a low-cost strategy or the revenue-enhancing advantages of differentiation by circumventing the problems of a fragmented industry. Returns from consolidating a fragmented industry are often huge—especially when industry sales and revenues are growing. Thus, over the past decades many companies have developed competitive strategies to consolidate fragmented industries. These companies include large retailers such as Wal-Mart and Target, fast-food chains such as McDonald's and Subway, and chains of health clubs, repair shops, and even lawyers and consultants. To grow and consolidate their industries and to help their companies become dominant within them, strategic managers utilize four main competitive strategies: (1) chaining, (2) franchising, (3) horizontal merger, and (4) using the Internet.

CHAINING Companies such as Wal-Mart and Midas International pursue a chaining strategy to obtain the advantages of cost leadership. They establish networks of linked merchandising outlets that are so interconnected that they function as one large business entity. The amazing buying power that these companies possess through their nationwide store chains enables them to negotiate large price reductions with their suppliers, which in turn promote their competitive advantage. They overcome the barrier of high transportation costs by establishing sophisticated regional distribution centers, which can economize on inventory costs and maximize responsiveness to the needs of stores and customers. (This is Wal-Mart's specialty, as discussed in the Running Case.) Last but not least, they realize economies of scale from sharing managerial skills across the chain and from placing nationwide, rather than local, advertising.

FRANCHISING For differentiated companies in fragmented industries, such as McDonald's and Century 21 Real Estate, the competitive advantage comes from a business strategy that employs franchise agreements. In franchising, the franchisor (parent) grants the franchisee the right to use the parent's name, reputation, and business skills in a particular location or area. If the franchisee also acts as the manager, he or she is strongly motivated to control the business closely and make sure that quality and standards are consistently high so that customer needs are always satisfied. Such motivation is particularly critical in a strategy of differentiation, where it is vital that a company maintain its uniqueness. One reason why industries are fragmented is the difficulty of maintaining control over the many small outlets that they must operate, while at the same time retaining their uniqueness. Franchising solves this problem. In addition, franchising lessens the financial burden of swift expansion and so permits rapid growth of the company. Finally, through franchising a differentiated large company can reap the advantages of large-scale advertising, as well as economies in purchasing, management, and distribution, as McDonald's does very efficiently. Indeed, McDonald's is able to pursue cost leadership and differentiation simultaneously only because franchising allows costs to be controlled locally and differentiation to be achieved by marketing on a national level.

HORIZONTAL MERGER Companies such as Anheuser-Busch, Macy's Inc., and Blockbuster chose a strategy of horizontal merger to consolidate their respective industries. For example, Macy's arranged the merger of many regional store chains in order to form a national company. By pursuing horizontal merger, companies are able to obtain economies of scale or secure a national market for their products. As a result, they are able to pursue a cost-leadership strategy, a differentiation strategy, or both. We discuss merger in more detail in Chapter 7.

USING THE INTERNET The latest way in which companies have been able to consolidate a fragmented industry is by using the Internet. eBay provides a good example of how a company can accomplish this. Before eBay, the auction business was extremely fragmented, with local auctions, fairs, or garage sales in cities being the principal way people could dispose of their antiques and collectibles. Now, by using eBay, sellers can be assured that they are getting global visibility for their collectibles so that they are likely to receive a higher price for their product. Similarly, Amazon.com's success in the online book market led to the closing of thousands of small bookstores that simply could not compete on either price or selection. The trend toward using the Internet seems likely to further consolidate even relatively oligopolistic industries.

The challenge in fragmented and growing industries is to choose the most appropriate means—franchising, chaining, horizontal merger, or the Internet—to consolidate the market and grow sales so that the competitive advantages gained from pursuing generic business-level strategies can be realized. It is difficult to think of any major service activities—from those in consulting and accounting firms to those in businesses satisfying the smallest consumer need, such as beauty parlors and car repair shops—that have not been merged or consolidated by chaining or franchising. In addition, the Internet has brought into being many new industries, such as those that make computer and digital products, and many of these are growing at a rapid pace as Internet broadband service expands.

● Strategies in Mature Industries

As a result of fierce competition in the growth and shakeout stages, an industry becomes consolidated, so a mature industry is often dominated by a small number of large companies. Although a mature industry may also contain many medium-sized companies and a host of small specialized ones, the large companies determine the nature of the industry's competition because they can influence the five competitive forces. Indeed, these are the companies that have developed the most successful generic business-level strategies in the industry.

By the end of the shakeout stage, companies in an industry have learned how important it is to analyze each other's business-level strategies continually. This competitive analysis helps them determine how to modify their competitive positioning to maintain and build their competitive advantage. At the same time, however, they also know that if they move aggressively to change their strategies to attack competitors, this will stimulate a competitive response from rivals threatened by the change in strategy.

For example, a differentiator that starts to lower its prices because it has adopted a more cost-efficient technology threatens other differentiators. It also threatens low-cost companies that see their competitive edge being eroded. All these companies may now change their strategies in response, most likely by reducing their prices too, as is currently occurring in the PC and car industries. Thus, the way one company changes or fine-tunes its business-level strategy over time affects the way the other companies in the industry pursue theirs. Hence, by the time they reach the mature stage of the industry life cycle, companies have learned just how *interdependent* their strategies are.

In fact, the main challenge facing companies in a mature industry is to adopt a competitive strategy that simultaneously allows each individual company to protect its competitive advantage *and* preserves industry profitability. No generic strategy will generate above-average profits if competitive forces in an industry are so strong that companies are at the mercy of each other, of potential entrants, of powerful suppliers, of powerful customers, and so on. As a result, in mature industries, competitive strategy revolves around understanding how large companies try *collectively* to reduce the strength of the five forces of industry competition to preserve both company and industry profitability.

Interdependent companies can help protect their competitive advantage and profitability by adopting competitive moves and tactics to reduce the threat of each competitive force. In the next sections, we examine the various price and nonprice competitive moves and tactics that companies use—first, to deter entry into an industry, and second, to reduce the level of rivalry within an industry.

STRATEGIES TO DETER ENTRY IN MATURE INDUSTRIES Companies can utilize three main methods to deter entry by potential rivals and hence maintain and increase industry profitability. As Figure 5.2 shows, these methods are product proliferation, price cutting, and maintaining excess capacity.

Product Proliferation Companies seldom produce just one product. Most commonly, they produce a range of products aimed at different market segments so that they have broad product lines. Sometimes, to reduce the threat of entry, companies expand the range of products they make to fill a wide variety of niches. This creates a barrier to entry because potential competitors find it harder to break into an industry in which all the niches are filled.[18] This strategy of pursuing a broad product line to deter entry is known as *product proliferation.*

Figure 5.2

Strategies for Deterring
Entry of Rivals

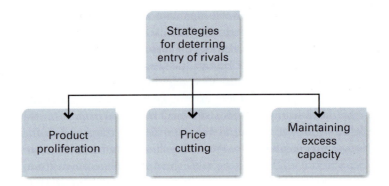

Because the Big Three U.S. carmakers were so slow to fill the small-car niches (they did *not* pursue a product proliferation strategy), they were vulnerable to the entry of the Japanese into these market segments in the United States. U.S. carmakers really had no excuse for this oversight, for in their European operations they had a long history of small-car manufacturing. They should have seen the danger of leaving this market segment open and filled it ten years earlier, but their view was that "small cars mean small profits." In the breakfast cereal industry, on the other hand, competition is based on continually producing new kinds of cereal or improving existing cereals to satisfy consumer desires or create new desires. Thus, the number and kind of breakfast cereals and snacks proliferate, making it very difficult for prospective entrants to find an empty market segment to fill. Filling all the product "spaces" in a particular market creates a barrier to entry and makes it much more difficult for a new company to gain a foothold and differentiate itself.

Price Cutting In some situations, pricing strategies that involve price cutting can be used to deter entry by other companies, thus protecting the profit margins of companies already in an industry. One price-cutting strategy, for example, is initially to charge a high price for a product and seize short-term profits but then to cut prices aggressively in order to build market share *and* deter potential entrants simultaneously.[19] The incumbent companies thus signal to potential entrants that if they enter the industry, the incumbents will use their competitive advantage to drive down prices to a level at which new companies will be unable to cover their costs.[20] This pricing strategy also allows a company to ride down the experience curve and obtain substantial economies of scale. Because costs fall with increasing sales, profit margins can still be maintained.

Still, this strategy is unlikely to deter a strong potential competitor—an established company that is trying to find profitable investment opportunities in other industries. It is difficult, for example, to imagine that IBM or 3M would be afraid to enter an industry because incumbent companies threatened to drive down prices. Companies such as IBM and 3M have the resources to withstand any short-term losses. Hence, it may be in the interests of incumbent companies to accept new entry gracefully, giving up market share gradually to the new entrants to prevent price wars from developing, and thus maintain their profit margins, if this is feasible.

Most evidence suggests that companies first skim the market and charge high prices during the growth stage, maximizing short-run profits.[21] Then they move to increase their market share and charge a lower price to expand the market rapidly; develop a reputation; and obtain economies of scale, driving down costs and barring entry. As competitors do enter, incumbent companies reduce prices to retard entry and give up market share to create a stable industry context—one in which they can use nonprice competitive tactics, such as product differentiation, to maximize long-run profits. At that point, nonprice competition becomes the main basis of industry competition, and prices are quite likely to rise as competition stabilizes. Thus, competitive tactics such as pricing and product differentiation are linked in mature industries; competitive decisions are taken to maximize the returns from a company's generic strategy.

Maintaining Excess Capacity A third competitive technique that allows companies to deter new entrants involves maintaining excess capacity—that is, producing more of a product than customers currently demand. Existing industry companies may deliberately develop some limited amount of excess capacity because it serves to warn potential entrants that if they do enter the industry, existing firms will retaliate by increasing output and forcing down prices, so entry would be unprofitable. However, the threat to increase output has to be *credible;* that is, companies in an industry must collectively be able to raise the level of production quickly if entry appears likely.

STRATEGIES TO MANAGE RIVALRY IN MATURE INDUSTRIES Beyond seeking to deter entry, incumbent companies also need to develop a competitive strategy to manage their competitive interdependence and decrease rivalry. As we noted earlier, unrestricted industry price competition reduces both company and industry profitability. Several competitive tactics and gambits are available to companies to prevent price wars and manage industry relations. The most important are price signaling, price leadership, and nonprice competition.

Price Signaling Most industries start out fragmented, with small companies battling for market share. Then, over time, the leading players emerge, and companies start to interpret each other's competitive moves. Price signaling is the first means by which companies attempt to structure competition within an industry in order to control rivalry.[22] **Price signaling** is the process by which companies increase or decrease product prices to convey their competitive intentions to other companies and so influence the way competitors price their products.[23] There are two ways in which companies can use price signaling to help defend their generic competitive strategies.

First, companies use price signaling to make a clear announcement that they will respond vigorously to hostile competitive moves that threaten them. For example, firms within an industry may signal that if one company starts to cut prices aggressively, they will respond in kind; hence, the term **tit-for-tat strategy** is often used to describe this kind of market signaling. The outcome of a tit-for-tat strategy is that nobody gains and everybody loses. Similarly, as we noted in the last section, companies may signal to potential entrants that if the latter do enter the market, they will fight back by reducing prices so that new entrants may incur significant losses.

A second, and very important, use of price signaling is to allow companies indirectly to coordinate their actions and avoid costly competitive moves that lead to a breakdown in pricing policy within an industry. One company may signal that it intends to lower prices because it wishes to attract customers who are switching to the products of another industry, not because it wishes to stimulate a price war. On the other hand, signaling can be used to improve profitability within an industry. The PC industry is a good example of the power of price signaling. In the 1990s, signals

price signaling

The process by which companies increase or decrease product prices to convey their competitive intentions to other companies.

tit-for-tat strategy

A form of market signaling in which one company starts to cut prices aggressively and then competitors respond in a similar way; when this occurs, nobody gains and everybody loses.

of lower prices set off price wars, but in the 2000s, PC makers have used price signaling to prevent price wars and keep prices steady. In sum, price signaling allows companies to give one another information that enables them to understand each other's competitive product/market strategy and make coordinated competitive moves to protect industry profitability.

price leadership

The process by which one company informally takes the responsibility for setting industry prices.

Price Leadership   **Price leadership**, the process by which one company informally takes the responsibility for setting industry prices, is a second tactic used to enhance the profitability of companies in a mature industry.[24] Formal price leadership, or price setting by companies jointly, is *illegal* under antitrust laws, so the process of price leadership is often very subtle. In the auto industry, for example, vehicle prices are set by imitation. The price set by the weakest company—the one with the highest costs—is often used as the basis for competitors' pricing. Thus, U.S. carmakers set their prices, and Japanese carmakers then set theirs with reference to the U.S. prices. The Japanese are happy to do this because they have lower costs than U.S. companies and are making higher profits than U.S. carmakers without competing with them on price. Pricing is done by market segment. The prices of different vehicles in a company's model range indicate the customer segments that it is aiming for and the price range it believes the market segment can tolerate. Each manufacturer prices a model in the segment with reference to the prices charged by its competitors, not with reference to costs. Price leadership allows differentiators to charge a premium price and also helps low-cost companies by increasing their margins.

Although price leadership can stabilize industry relationships by preventing head-to-head competition and thus raise the level of profitability within an industry, it has its dangers. Price leadership helps companies with high costs, such as GM and Ford, by allowing them to survive without becoming more productive or more efficient. Thus, it may foster complacency; companies may keep extracting profits without reinvesting any to improve their productivity. In the long term, such behavior makes them vulnerable to companies that continually develop new production techniques to lower costs. That is what happened in the U.S. auto industry after the Japanese entered the market. After years of tacit price fixing, with GM as the leader, the carmakers were subjected to growing low-cost Japanese competition. By the 2000s, Japanese carmakers such as Toyota and Honda had become so popular that they were setting the prices. U.S. carmakers were forced to offer incentive price discounts, often around $3,000 to $4,000, to get their cars off the lot, while the Japanese did not drop theirs significantly. Even so, the market share of Japanese carmakers continued to increase, and by 2006 Toyota was selling more cars than Ford in the United States and was expected to become the largest global automaker, overtaking GM by 2008.

Nonprice Competition   A third very important aspect of product/market strategy in mature industries is the use of nonprice competition to manage rivalry within an industry. Using various tactics and maneuvers to try to prevent costly price cutting and price wars does *not* preclude competition by product differentiation. Indeed, in many industries, product differentiation is the principal competitive tactic used to prevent rivals from stealing a company's customers and reducing its market share. In other words, many companies rely on product differentiation to deter potential entrants and manage rivalry within their industry.

Product differentiation allows industry rivals to compete for market share by offering products with *different or superior features* or by utilizing different *marketing*

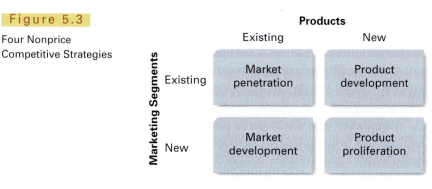

Figure 5.3

Four Nonprice
Competitive Strategies

techniques. In Figure 5.3, product and market segment dimensions are used to identify four nonprice competitive strategies based on product differentiation. (Note that this model applies to new market *segments,* not to new *markets.*)[25]

- When a company concentrates on expanding market share in its existing product markets, it is engaging in a strategy of **market penetration.**[26] Market penetration involves heavy advertising to promote and build product differentiation. In a mature industry, the thrust of advertising is to influence consumers' brand choice and create a brand-name reputation for the company and its products. In this way, a company can increase its market share by attracting the customers of its rivals. Because brand-name products often command premium prices, building market share in this situation is very profitable.

  In some mature industries (for example, soap and detergent, disposable diapers, and brewing), a market-penetration strategy becomes a way of life.[27] In these industries, all companies engage in intensive advertising and battle for market share. Each company fears that by not advertising, it will lose market share to rivals. Consequently, in the soap and detergent industry, for instance, Procter & Gamble spends more than 20% of sales revenues on advertising, with the aim of maintaining and increasing market share. These huge advertising outlays constitute a barrier to entry for prospective entrants.

- **Product development** is the creation of new or improved products to replace existing ones, such as occurs in the fast-food industry.[28] The wet-shaving industry is another industry that depends on product replacement to create successive waves of consumer demand, which then create new sources of revenue for companies in the industry. Gillette, for example, periodically comes out with a new and improved razor, such as the Sensor, the Mach3, and the Fusion shaving system, to boost its market share and profitability. Similarly, each major global carmaker replaces its models every three to five years to encourage customers to trade in their old model and buy a new one that has the latest styling and technology.

  Product development is important for maintaining product differentiation and building market share.[29] For instance, during the past forty years the laundry detergent Tide has gone through more than fifty different changes in formulation to improve its performance. The product is always advertised as Tide, but it is a different product each year. The battle over diet and flavored colas is another interesting example of competitive product differentiation by product development. Royal Crown Cola developed Diet Rite, the first diet cola. However, Coca-Cola and PepsiCo responded quickly with their versions of the diet drink, and by massive advertising they soon achieved dominance. Today, there are dozens of variations of diet colas on the market. Refining and improving products is an important competitive tactic in defending a company's generic competitive strategy in a mature industry. However, this kind of competition can be as vicious as a price war because it is expensive and raises costs dramatically.

- **Market development** involves searching for new market segments, and therefore uses, for a company's products. A company pursuing this strategy wants to capitalize on the brand name it has developed in one market segment by locating new market segments in which to compete. In this way, it can exploit the product differentiation advantages of its brand name. Japanese carmakers provide an interesting example of the use of market development. When they first entered the market, each Japanese manufacturer offered a car, such as the Toyota Corolla and the Honda Accord, aimed at the economy segment of the auto market. However, the Japanese upgraded each car over time, and now each is directed at a more expensive market segment. The Honda Accord and Toyota Camry are the leading contenders in the mid-size car segment, while the Honda Civic and Toyota Corolla compete to lead the small-car segment. By redefining their product offerings, Japanese manufacturers have profitably developed their market segments and successfully attacked their U.S. rivals, continually wresting market share from these companies. Although the Japanese used to compete primarily as low-cost producers, market development has allowed them to become leading differentiators as well. Toyota is an example of a company that has used market development to pursue simultaneously a low-cost and a differentiation strategy; its Lexus brand competes in the luxury segment of the global car market.

- **Product proliferation** can be used to manage rivalry within an industry and to deter entry. The strategy of product proliferation generally means that the leading companies in an industry all have a product in each market segment, or niche, and compete head to head for customers. If a new niche develops (such as SUVs, designer sunglasses, or Internet websites), the leader gets a first-mover advantage, but soon all the other companies catch up, and once again competition is stabilized and rivalry within the industry is reduced. Product proliferation thus allows the development of stable industry competition based on product differentiation, not price—that is, nonprice competition based on the development of new products. The battle is over a product's perceived quality and uniqueness, *not* over its price.

Strategies in Declining Industries

Sooner or later, many industries enter into a decline stage, in which the size of the total market starts to shrink. Examples include the railroad industry, the tobacco industry, and the steel industry. Industries start declining for a number of reasons, including technological change, social trends, and demographic shifts. The railroad and steel industries began to decline when technological changes brought viable substitutes for the products these industries offered. The advent of the internal combustion engine drove the railroad industry into decline, and the steel industry fell into decline with the rise of plastics and composite materials. The decline of the tobacco industry was caused by changing social attitudes toward smoking because of concerns about its deadly health effects.

When the size of the total market is shrinking, competition tends to intensify in a declining industry and profit rates tend to fall. The intensity of competition in a declining industry depends on four critical factors, which are indicated in Figure 5.4.

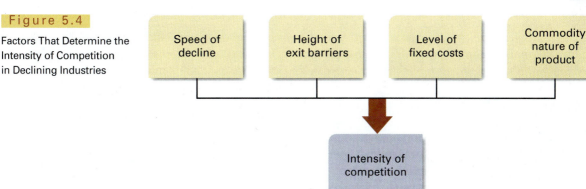

Figure 5.4

Factors That Determine the Intensity of Competition in Declining Industries

First, the intensity of competition is greater in industries where decline is rapid than in industries, such as tobacco, where decline is gradual.

Second, the intensity of competition is greater in declining industries in which exit barriers are high. As discussed in Chapter 3, high exit barriers keep companies locked into an industry even when demand is falling. The result is the emergence of excess productive capacity—and hence an increased probability of fierce price competition.

Third (and related to the previous point), the intensity of competition is greater in declining industries in which fixed costs are high (as in the steel industry). This is because the need to cover fixed costs, such as the costs of maintaining productive capacity, can make companies try to utilize any excess capacity they have by slashing prices, an action that can trigger a price war.

Finally, the intensity of competition is greater in declining industries where the product is perceived as a commodity (as it is in the steel industry) than in industries where differentiation gives rise to significant brand loyalty, as was true until very recently of the declining tobacco industry.

Not all segments of an industry typically decline at the same rate. In some segments demand may remain reasonably strong, despite decline elsewhere. The steel industry illustrates this situation. Although bulk steel products, such as sheet steel, have suffered a general decline, demand has actually risen for specialty steels, such as those used in high-speed machine tools. Vacuum tubes provide another example. Although demand for them collapsed when transistors replaced them as a key component in many electronics products, for years afterward vacuum tubes still had some limited applications in radar equipment. Consequently, demand in this vacuum tube segment remained strong despite the general decline in the demand for vacuum tubes. The point is that there may be pockets in an industry in which demand is declining more slowly than in the industry as a whole or, indeed, is not declining at all. Price competition may be far less intense among the companies serving such pockets of demand than within the industry as a whole.

There are four main strategies that companies can adopt to deal with decline: (1) a **leadership strategy,** by which a company seeks to become the dominant player in a declining industry; (2) a **niche strategy,** which focuses on pockets of demand that are declining more slowly than demand in the industry as a whole; (3) a **harvest strategy,** which optimizes cash flow; and (4) a **divestment strategy,** by which a company sells off the business to others. The choice of strategy depends in part on the

leadership strategy

A strategy through which a company seeks to become the dominant player in a declining industry.

niche strategy

A strategy of focusing on pockets of demand that are declining more slowly than demand in the industry as a whole.

harvest strategy

A strategy that optimizes cash flow.

divestment strategy

A strategy in which a company sells off its business assets and resources to other companies.

Strategy in Action

How to Make Money in the Vacuum Tube Business

At its peak in the early 1950s, the vacuum tube business was a major industry in which companies such as Westinghouse, General Electric, RCA, and Western Electric had a large stake. Then along came the transistor, making most vacuum tubes obsolete, and one by one, all the big companies exited the industry. One company, however, Richardson Electronics, not only stayed in the business but also demonstrated that high returns are possible in a declining industry. Primarily a distributor (although it does have some manufacturing capabilities), Richardson bought the remains of a dozen companies in the United States and Europe as they exited the vacuum tube industry. Richardson now has a warehouse that stocks more than 10,000 different types of vacuum tubes. The company is the world's only supplier of many of them, which helps explain why its gross margin is in the range of 35 to 40%.

Richardson survives and prospers because vacuum tubes are vital parts of some older electronic equipment that would be costly to replace with solid-state equipment. In addition, vacuum tubes still outperform semiconductors in some limited applications, including radar and welding machines. The U.S. government and General Motors are big customers of Richardson.

Speed is the essence of Richardson's business. The company's Illinois warehouse offers overnight delivery to some 40,000 customers, processing 650 orders a day, whose average price is $550.[b] Customers such as GM don't really care whether a vacuum tube costs $250 or $350; what they care about is the $40,000 to $50,000 downtime loss that they face when a key piece of welding equipment isn't working. By responding quickly to the demands of such customers and by being the only major supplier of many types of vacuum tubes, Richardson has placed itself in a position that many companies in growing industries would envy: a monopoly position. In 1997, however, a new company, Westrex, was formed to take advantage of the growing popularity of vacuum tubes in high-end stereo systems, and by 1999 it was competing head to head with Richardson in some market segments. Clearly, competition can be found even in a declining industry.

intensity of the competition. Figure 5.5 provides a framework for guiding choice or strategy on the basis of two factors: (1) the intensity of competition in the declining industry, measured on the vertical axis, and (2) a company's strengths relative to remaining pockets of demand, measured on the horizontal axis.

LEADERSHIP STRATEGY A leadership strategy aims at growing in a declining industry by picking up the market share of companies that are leaving the industry. A leadership strategy makes the most sense (1) when the company has distinctive strengths that enable it to capture market share in a declining industry and (2) when the speed of decline and the intensity of competition in the declining industry are moderate. Philip Morris (now known as the Altria Group) pursued such a strategy in the tobacco industry. By aggressive marketing, Philip Morris increased its market share in a declining industry and earned enormous profits in the process.

The tactical steps companies might use to achieve a leadership position include aggressive pricing and marketing to build market share, acquiring established competitors to consolidate the industry, and raising the stakes for other competitors—for example, by making new investments in productive capacity. Such competitive tactics signal to other competitors that the company is willing and able to stay and compete in the declining industry. These signals may persuade other companies to exit the industry, which would further enhance the competitive position of the industry leader.

Figure 5.5

Strategy Selection in a
Declining Industry

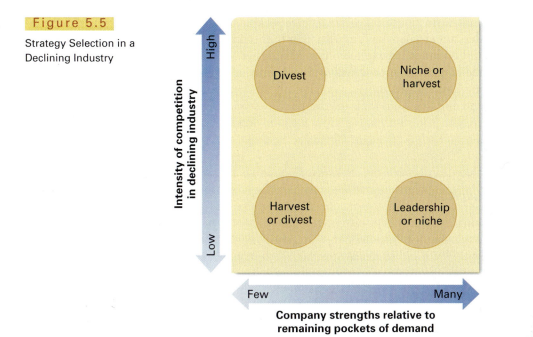

Figure 5.5

Strategy Selection in a
Declining Industry

NICHE STRATEGY A niche strategy focuses on those pockets in the industry in which demand is stable or is declining less rapidly than demand in the industry as a whole. The strategy makes sense when the company has some unique strengths relative to those niches where demand remains relatively strong. As an example, consider Naval, a company that manufactures whaling harpoons and the small guns to fire them and makes money doing so. This might be considered rather odd, given that most whaling has been outlawed by the world community. However, Naval has survived the terminal decline of the harpoon industry by focusing on the one group of people who are still allowed to hunt whales in very limited numbers: the North American Inuit tribe. Inuit are permitted to hunt bowhead whales, provided that they do so only for food and not for commercial purposes. Naval is the sole supplier of small harpoon whaling guns to Eskimo communities, and its monopoly position allows it to earn a healthy return in this small market.[30]

HARVEST STRATEGY A harvest strategy is the best choice when a company wishes to get out of a declining industry and perhaps optimize cash flow in the process. This strategy makes the most sense when the company foresees a steep decline and intense future competition or when it lacks strengths relative to remaining pockets of demand in the industry. A harvest strategy requires the company to cut all new investments in capital equipment, advertising, R&D, and the like. The inevitable result is that the company will lose market share, but because it is no longer investing in this business, initially its positive cash flow will increase. Ultimately, however, cash flows will start to decline, and at this stage it makes sense for the company to liquidate the business.

DIVESTMENT STRATEGY A divestment strategy is based on the idea that a company can maximize its net investment recovery from a business by selling it early, before the industry has entered into a steep decline. This strategy is appropriate when the company has few strengths relative to whatever pockets of demand are likely to remain in the industry and when the competition in the declining industry is likely to be intense. The best option may be to sell out to a company that is pursuing a leadership strategy in the industry. The drawback of the divestment strategy is that its success depends on the ability of the company to notice its industry's decline before it becomes serious and thus to sell out while the company's assets are still valued by others.

Summary of Chapter

1. Companies can use various generic competitive strategies in different industry environments to protect and enhance their competitive advantage. Companies must first develop a successful generic competitive strategy in order to gain a secure position in an industry. Then they must choose industry-appropriate competitive tactics and maneuvers to position their company successfully over time. Companies must always be on the alert for changes in conditions within their industry and in the competitive behavior of their rivals if they are to respond to these changes in a timely manner.

2. Business-level strategy consists of the way strategic managers devise a plan of action to use a company's resources and distinctive competences to gain a competitive advantage over rivals in a market or industry.

3. At the heart of developing a generic business-level strategy are choices concerning customer needs and product differentiation, customer groups and market segmentation, and distinctive competence. The combination of those three choices results in the specific form of generic business-level strategy employed by a company.

4. The three pure generic competitive strategies are cost leadership, differentiation, and focus. Each has advantages and disadvantages. A company must constantly manage its strategy; otherwise, it risks being stuck in the middle.

5. Increasingly, developments in manufacturing technology are allowing firms to pursue both a cost-leadership and a differentiation strategy and thus obtain the economic benefits of both strategies simultaneously. Technical developments also enable small firms to compete with large firms on an equal footing in particular market segments; thus, these developments increase the number of firms pursuing a focus strategy.

6. Companies can also adopt either of two forms of focus strategy: a focused low-cost strategy or a focused differentiation strategy.

7. In fragmented and growing industries composed of a large number of small and medium-sized companies, the principal forms of competitive strategy are chaining, franchising, horizontal merger, and using the Internet.

8. Mature industries are composed of a few large companies whose actions are so highly interdependent that the success of one company's strategy depends on the responses of its rivals.

9. The principal competitive tactics used by companies in mature industries to deter entry are product proliferation, price cutting, and maintaining excess capacity.

10. The principal competitive tactics used by companies in mature industries to manage rivalry are price signaling, price leadership, and nonprice competition.

11. There are four main strategies a company can pursue when demand is falling: leadership, niche, harvest, and divestment strategies. The choice of strategy is determined by the severity of industry decline and the company's strengths relative to the remaining pockets of demand.

Discussion Questions

1. Why does each generic competitive strategy require a different set of product/market/distinctive-competence choices? Give examples of pairs of companies in (a) the computer industry and (b) the auto industry that pursue different competitive strategies.

2. How can companies pursuing a cost-leadership, differentiation, or focus strategy become stuck in the middle? In what ways can they regain their competitive advantage?

3. Why are industries fragmented? What are the main ways in which companies can turn a fragmented industry into a consolidated one?

4. What are the key problems involved in maintaining a competitive advantage in a growing industry environment?

5. Discuss how companies can use (a) product differentiation and (b) nonprice competition to manage rivalry and increase an industry's profitability.

Practicing Strategic Management

SMALL-GROUP EXERCISE

How to Keep the Salsa Hot

Break up into groups of three to five people, and discuss the following scenario. Appoint one group member as a spokesperson for the group who will communicate your findings to the class when called upon to do so by the instructor.

You are the managers of a company that has pioneered a new kind of salsa for chicken that has taken the market by storm. The salsa's differentiated appeal has been based on a unique combination of spices and packaging that has allowed you to charge a premium price. Within the last three years, your salsa has achieved a national reputation, and now major food companies such as Kraft and Nabisco, seeing the potential of this market segment, are beginning to introduce salsas of their own, imitating your product.

1. Describe the generic business-level strategy you are pursuing.

2. Describe the industry environment in which you are competing.

3. What kinds of competitive tactics and maneuvers could you adopt to protect your generic strategy in this kind of environment?

4. What do you think is the best strategy for you to pursue in this situation?

EXPLORING THE WEB

Visiting the Luxury-Car Market

Go to the websites of three luxury-car makers such as Lexus (**www.lexususa.com**), BMW (**www.bmwusa.com**), or Cadillac (**www.cadillac.com**), all of which compete in the same strategic group. Scan the sites to determine the key features of each company's business-level strategy. In what ways are their strategies similar and different? Which of these companies do you think has a competitive advantage over the others? Why?

General Task   Search the Web for a company pursuing a low-cost strategy, a differentiation strategy, or both. What product/market/distinctive-competence choices has the company made to pursue this strategy? How successful has the company been in its industry by using this strategy?

CLOSING CASE

Nike's Business-Level Strategies

Nike, headquartered in Beaverton, Oregon, was founded over thirty years ago by Bill Bowerman, a former University of Oregon track coach, and Phil Knight, an entrepreneur in search of a profitable business opportunity. Bowerman's goal was to dream up a new kind of sneaker tread that would enhance a runner's traction and speed, and he came up with the idea for Nike's "waffle tread" after studying the waffle iron in his home. Bowerman and Knight made their shoe and began by selling it out of the trunk of their car at track meets. From this small beginning, Nike has grown into a company that sold over $12 billion worth of shoes in the $35 billion athletic footwear and apparel industries in 2004.[c]

Nike's amazing growth came from its business model, which has always been based on two original functional strategies: to innovate state-of-the-art athletic shoes and then to publicize the qualities of its shoes through dramatic "guerrilla" marketing. Nike's marketing is designed to persuade customers that its shoes are not only superior but also a high-fashion statement and a necessary part of a lifestyle based on sporting or athletic interests. A turning point came in 1987 when Nike increased its marketing budget from $8 million to $48 million to persuade customers its shoes were the best. A large part of this advertising budget soon went to pay celebrities like Michael Jordan millions of dollars to wear and champion its products. The company has consistently pursued this strategy and many other sporting stars, such as Tiger Woods and Serena Williams, who are part of its charmed circle.

Nike's strategy to emphasize the uniqueness of its product paid off; its market share soared and its revenues hit $9.6 billion in 1998. However, 1998 was also a turning point, for in that year sales began to fall. Nike's $200 Air Jordans no longer sold like they used to, and inventory built up in stores and warehouses. Suddenly it seemed much harder to design new shoes that customers perceived to be significantly better, and Nike's stunning growth in sales was actually reducing its profitability—somehow it had lost control of its business strategy. Phil Knight, who had resigned his management position, was forced to resume the helm and lead the company out of its troubles. He recruited a team of talented top managers from leading consumer products companies to help him improve Nike's business model. As a result, Nike has changed its business strategies in some fundamental ways.

In the past, Nike shunned sports like golf, soccer, and rollerblading and focused most of its efforts on making shoes for the track and basketball market to build its market share in this area. However, when its sales started to fall, it realized that using marketing to increase sales in a particular market segment can grow sales and profits only so far; it needed to start to sell more types of shoes to more segments of the athletic shoe market. So Nike took its design and marketing competences and began to craft new lines of shoes for new market segments. For example, it launched a line of soccer shoes and perfected their design over time, and by 2004 it had won the biggest share of the soccer market from its archrival Adidas.[d] In addition, in 2004 it launched its Total 90 III shoes, which are aimed at the millions of casual soccer players throughout the world who want a shoe they can just "play" in. Once more, Nike's dramatic marketing campaigns aim to make their shoes part of the "soccer lifestyle," to persuade customers that traditional sneakers do not work because soccer shoes are sleeker and fit the foot more snugly.[e]

To take advantage of its competences in design and marketing, Nike then decided to enter new market segments by purchasing other footwear companies that offered shoes that extended or complemented its product lines. For example, it bought Converse, the maker of retro-style sneakers; Hurley International, which makes skateboards and Bauer inline and hockey skates; and Official Starter, a licensor of athletic shoes and apparel whose brands include the low-priced Shaq brand. Allowing Converse to take advantage of Nike's in-house competences has resulted in dramatic increases in the sales of its sneakers, and Converse has made an important contribution to Nike's profitability.[f]

Nike also entered another market segment when it bought Cole Haan, the dress shoemaker, in the 1980s. Now it is searching for other possible acquisitions. It decided to enter the athletic apparel market to use its skills there, and by 2004 sales were over $1 billion. Nike made all these changes to its product line to increase its market share and profitability. Its new focus on developing new and improved products for new market segments is working. Nike's profits have soared from 14% in 2000 to 25% in 2007; it makes over $1 billion profit a year.

Case Discussion Questions

1. What business-level strategies is Nike pursuing?
2. How have Nike's business-level strategies changed the nature of industry competition?

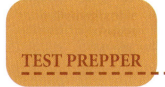

TEST PREPPER

True/False Questions

_____ **1.** A business-level strategy is a strategy of trying to outperform competitors by doing everything possible to produce goods or services at a cost lower than those of competitors.

_____ **2.** Customer needs is the process of creating a competitive advantage by designing products—goods or services—to satisfy customer needs.

_____ **3.** Market segmentation is the way a company decides to group customers, based on important differences in their needs or preferences, in order to gain a competitive advantage.

_____ **4.** Wal-Mart keeps its costs to a minimum so that it can charge lower prices than its competitors, and it does so through the fit its managers have achieved between its business- and functional-level strategies.

_____ **5.** Differentiation strategy is a strategy of trying to achieve a competitive advantage by creating a product that is perceived by customers as unique in some important way.

_____ **6.** In franchising, the franchisee grants the franchisor the right to use the parent's name, reputation, and business skills in a particular location or area.

_____ **7.** Price cutting is the process by which one company informally takes the responsibility for setting industry prices.

Multiple-Choice Questions

8. A very important aspect of product/market strategy in mature industries is the use of _____ to manage rivalry within the industry.
   a. nonprice competition
   b. price leadership
   c. tit-for-tat strategy
   d. price signaling
   e. price cutting

9. _____ is a strategy in which a company concentrates on expanding market share in its existing product markets.
   a. Product development
   b. Market penetration
   c. Product proliferation
   d. Horizontal merger
   e. Franchising

10. _____ involves searching for new market segments, and therefore uses, for a company's products.
   a. Product development
   b. Market development
   c. Niche strategy
   d. Harvest strategy
   e. Divestment strategy

11. The strategy of _____ generally means that the leading companies in an industry all have a product in each market segment, or niche, and compete head to head for customers.
    a. leadership
    b. product proliferation
    c. product development
    d. nonprice competition
    e. price leadership

12. A _____ strategy is the best choice when a company wishes to get out of a declining industry and perhaps optimize cash flow in the process.
    a. divestment
    b. harvest
    c. leadership
    d. niche
    e. none of the above

13. _____ consists of the way strategic managers devise a plan of action to use a company's resources and distinctive competences to gain a competitive advantage over rivals in a market or industry.
    a. Leadership strategy
    b. Cost-leadership strategy
    c. Business-level strategy
    d. Focus strategy
    e. Differentiation strategy

14. The desires, wants, or cravings that can be satisfied by means of the characteristics of a product or service are known as _____.
    a. product differentiation
    b. customer needs
    c. distinctive competences
    d. cost-leadership strategy
    e. generic strategy

15. _____ is the process by which companies increase or decrease product prices to convey their competitive intentions to other companies and so influence the way competitors price their products.
    a. Price leadership
    b. Price signaling
    c. Nonprice competition
    d. Price cutting
    e. Maintaining excess capacity

Chapter 6

Strategy in the Global Environment

Learning Objectives

After reading this chapter, you should be able to

1. Understand the process of globalization and how it impacts a company's strategy

2. Discuss firms' motives for expanding internationally

3. Review the different strategies that companies use to compete in the global marketplace

4. Explain the pros and cons of different modes for entering foreign markets

Chapter Outline

I. The Global Environment

II. Increasing Profitability Through Global Expansion
   a. Expanding the Market: Leveraging Products and Competences
   b. Realizing Economies of Scale
   c. Realizing Location Economies
   d. Leveraging the Skills of Global Subsidiaries

III. Cost Pressures and Pressures for Local Responsiveness
   a. Pressures for Cost Reductions
   b. Pressures for Local Responsiveness

IV. Choosing a Global Strategy
   a. Global Standardization Strategy
   b. Localization Strategy
   c. Transnational Strategy
   d. International Strategy
   e. Changes in Strategy over Time

V. Choices of Entry Mode
   a. Exporting
   b. Licensing
   c. Franchising
   d. Joint Ventures
   e. Wholly Owned Subsidiaries
   f. Choosing an Entry Strategy

Overview

This chapter looks at the process of globalization in the world economy and the strategic response required from companies that compete across national borders. The chapter opens with a discussion of ongoing changes in the global competitive environment and discusses models managers can use for analyzing competition in different national markets. Next, we look at the various ways in which international expansion can increase a company's profitability and profit growth. Then we discuss the different strategies companies can pursue to gain a competitive advantage in the global marketplace and consider the advantages and disadvantages of each. This is followed by a discussion of two related strategic issues: (1) how managers decide which foreign markets to enter, when to enter them, and on what scale and (2) what kind of vehicle or means a company should use to expand globally and enter a foreign country. By the time you have completed this chapter, you will have a good understanding of the various strategic issues that companies face when they decide to expand their operations internationally to achieve competitive advantage and superior profitability.

The Global Environment

Fifty years ago, most national markets were isolated from each other by significant barriers to international trade and investment. In those days, managers could focus on analyzing just those national markets in which their company competed. They did not need to pay much attention to global competitors, for they were few and entry was difficult. Nor did managers need to pay much attention to entering foreign markets, since that was often prohibitively expensive. All of this has now changed. Barriers to international trade and investment have tumbled. Huge global markets for goods and services have been created. Companies from different nations are entering each other's home markets on a hitherto unprecedented scale, increasing the intensity of competition. Rivalry can no longer be understood merely in terms of what happens within the boundaries of a nation; managers now need to consider how globalization is impacting the environment in which their company competes and what strategies their company should adopt to exploit opportunities and counter competitive threats.

Consider barriers to international trade and investment. The average tariff rate on manufactured goods traded between advanced nations has fallen from around 40% to under 4%. Similarly, in nation after nation, regulations prohibiting foreign companies from entering domestic markets and establishing production facilities or acquiring domestic companies have been removed. As a result of these two developments, there has been a surge in both the volume of international trade and the value of foreign direct investment. The volume of world merchandise trade has grown faster than the world economy since 1950.[1] From 1970 to 2005, the volume of world merchandise trade expanded 27-fold, outstripping the expansion of world production, which grew about 7.5 times in real terms. Moreover, between 1992 and 2006, the total flow of foreign direct investment from all countries increased more than sevenfold while world trade by value grew by some 150% and world output by around 45%.[2] These two trends have led to the globalization of production and the globalization of markets.[3]

The globalization of production has been increasing as companies take advantage of lower barriers to international trade and investment to disperse important parts of their production process around the globe. Doing so enables them to take advantage of national differences in the cost and quality of factors of production such as labor, energy, land, and capital, which allows them to lower their cost structures and boost profits. For example, the Boeing Company's commercial jet aircraft the 777 uses 132,500 engineered parts that are produced around the world by 545 suppliers. Eight Japanese suppliers make parts of the fuselage, doors, and wings; a supplier in Singapore makes the doors for the nose landing gear; three suppliers in Italy manufacture wing flaps; and so on. In total, some 30% of the 777, by value, is built by foreign companies. For its most recent jet airliner, the 787, Boeing has pushed this trend even further; some 65% of the total value of the aircraft is scheduled to be outsourced to foreign companies, 35% of which is going to three major Japanese companies.[4] Part of Boeing's rationale for outsourcing so much production to foreign suppliers is that these suppliers are the best in the world at performing their particular activity. Therefore, the result of having foreign suppliers build specific parts is a better final product and higher profitability for Boeing.[5]

As for the globalization of markets, it has been argued that the world's economic system is moving from one in which national markets are distinct entities, isolated from each other by trade barriers and barriers of distance, time, and culture, toward a

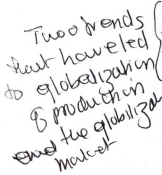

Handwritten margin notes:
Barriers to International trade & Investments.

Two trends that have led to globalization of production and the globalization market

system in which national markets are merging into one huge global marketplace. Increasingly, customers around the world demand and use the same basic product offerings. Consequently, in many industries, it is no longer meaningful to talk about the German market, the U.S. market, or the Japanese market; there is only the global market. Coca-Cola, Citigroup credit cards, blue jeans, the Sony PlayStation and Nintendo Wii, McDonald's hamburgers, the Nokia wireless phone, and Microsoft's Windows operating system are examples of products that have achieved global acceptance.[6]

The trend toward the globalization of production and markets has several important implications for competition within an industry. First, industry boundaries do not stop at national borders. Because many industries are becoming global in scope, actual and potential competitors exist not only in a company's home market but also in other national markets. Managers who analyze only their home market can be caught unprepared by the entry of efficient foreign competitors. The globalization of markets and production implies that companies around the globe are finding their home markets under attack from foreign competitors. For example, in Japan, Merrill Lynch and Citicorp have made inroads against Japanese financial service institutions. In the United States, Finland's Nokia has taken the lead from Motorola in the market for wireless phone handsets.

Second, the shift from national to global markets has intensified competitive rivalry in industry after industry. National markets that once were consolidated oligopolies, dominated by three or four companies and subject to relatively little foreign competition, have been transformed into segments of fragmented global industries where a large number of companies battle each other for market share in country after country. This rivalry has threatened to drive down profitability and made it all the more critical for companies to maximize their efficiency, quality, customer responsiveness, and innovative ability. The painful process of restructuring and downsizing that has been going on at companies such as Motorola and Kodak is as much a response to the increased intensity of global competition as it is to anything else. However, not all global industries are fragmented. Many remain consolidated oligopolies, except that now they are consolidated *global*, rather than *national*, oligopolies. In the video game industry, for example, three companies are battling for global dominance: Microsoft from the United States and Nintendo and Sony from Japan. In the market for wireless handsets, Nokia of Finland does global battle against Motorola of the United States and Samsung of South Korea.

Finally, although globalization has increased both the threat of entry and the intensity of rivalry within many formerly protected national markets, it has also created enormous opportunities for companies based in those markets. The steady decline in barriers to cross-border trade and investment has opened up many once protected markets to companies based outside them. Thus, in recent years, Western European, Japanese, and U.S. companies have accelerated their investments in the nations of Eastern Europe, Latin America, and Southeast Asia, as they try to take advantage of growth opportunities in those areas.

Increasing Profitability Through Global Expansion

There are a number of ways in which expanding globally can enable companies to increase their profitability and grow their profits more rapidly. At the most basic level, global expansion increases the size of the market a company is addressing,

RUNNING CASE

Wal-Mart's Global Expansion

In the early 1990s, managers at Wal-Mart realized that the company's opportunities for growth in the United States were becoming more limited. By 1995, the company would be active in all fifty states. Management calculated that by the early 2000s, domestic growth opportunities would be constrained as a result of market saturation. So the company decided to expand globally. The critics scoffed. Wal-Mart, they said, was "too American a company." While its business model was well suited to America, it would not work in other countries where infrastructure was different, consumer tastes and preferences varied, and established retailers already dominated.

Unperturbed, in 1991 Wal-Mart started to expand internationally with the opening of its first stores in Mexico. The Mexican operation was established as a joint venture with Cifra, the largest local retailer. Initially, Wal-Mart made a number of missteps that seemed to prove the critics right. Wal-Mart had problems replicating its efficient distribution system in Mexico. Poor infrastructure, crowded roads, and a lack of leverage with local suppliers, many of whom could not or would not deliver directly to Wal-Mart's stores or distribution centers, resulted in stocking problems and raised costs and prices. Initially, prices at Wal-Mart in Mexico were some 20% above prices for comparable products in the company's U.S. stores, which limited Wal-Mart's ability to gain market share. There were also problems with merchandise selection. Many of the stores in Mexico carried items that were popular in the United States. These included ice skates, riding lawn mowers, leaf blowers, and fishing tackle. Not surprisingly, these items did not sell well in Mexico, so managers would slash prices to move inventory, only to find that the company's automated information systems would immediately order more inventory to replenish the depleted stock.

By the mid-1990s, however, Wal-Mart had learned from its early mistakes and adapted its operations in Mexico to match the local environment. A partnership with a Mexican trucking company dramatically improved the distribution system, while more careful stocking practices meant that the Mexican stores sold merchandise that appealed more to local tastes and preferences. As Wal-Mart's presence grew, many of Wal-Mart's suppliers built factories close to its Mexican distribution centers so that they could better serve the company, which helped to further drive down inventory and logistics costs. In 1998, Wal-Mart acquired a controlling interest in Cifra. Today, Mexico—where the company is more than twice the size of its nearest rival—is a leading light in Wal-Mart's international operations.

The Mexican experience proved to Wal-Mart that it could compete outside of the United States. It subsequently expanded into fifteen other countries. In Canada, Britain, Germany, Japan, and South Korea, Wal-Mart acquired existing retailers and then transferred its information systems, logistics, and management expertise. In Puerto Rico, Brazil, Argentina, and

[handwritten: Increasing Profitability thro' global expansion can be done by:]

thereby boosting profit growth. Moreover, global expansion offers opportunities for reducing the cost structure of the enterprise or adding value through differentiation, thereby potentially boosting profitability.

① • **Expanding the Market: Leveraging Products and Competences**

A company can increase its growth rate by taking goods or services developed at home and selling them internationally. Indeed, almost all multinationals started out doing just this. Procter & Gamble, for example, developed most of its best-selling products at home and then sold them around the world. Similarly, from its earliest days, Microsoft has always focused on selling its software around the world. Automobile companies like Ford, Volkswagen, and Toyota also grew by developing products at home and then selling them in international markets. The returns from such a strategy are likely to be greater if indigenous competitors lack comparable products. Thus, Toyota has grown its profits by entering the large automobile markets of North America and Europe, offering products that are differentiated from those offered by local rivals (Ford and GM) by their superior quality and reliability.

China, Wal-Mart established its own stores (although it added to its Chinese operations with a major acquisition in 2007). As a result of these moves, by 2008 the company had over 3,000 stores and 600,000 associates outside the United States, generating international revenues of more than $80 billion.

In addition to greater growth, expanding internationally has brought Wal-Mart two other major benefits. First, Wal-Mart has been able to reap significant economies of scale from its global buying power. Many of its key suppliers have long been international companies; for example, GE (appliances), Unilever (food products), and Procter & Gamble (personal care products) are all major Wal-Mart suppliers that have long had their own global operations. By building international reach, Wal-Mart has been able to use its enhanced size to demand deeper discounts from the local operations of its global suppliers, increasing the company's ability to lower prices to consumers, gain market share, and ultimately earn greater profits. Second, Wal-Mart has found that it is benefiting from the flow of ideas across the countries in which it now competes. For example, Wal-Mart's Argentina team worked with its Mexican management to replicate a Wal-Mart store format developed first in Mexico and to adopt the best practices in human resources and real estate that had been developed in Mexico. Other ideas, such as the introduction of wine departments in its stores in Argentina, have now been integrated into layouts worldwide.

Moreover, Wal-Mart realized that if it didn't expand internationally, other global retailers would beat it to the punch. In fact, Wal-Mart does face significant global competition from Carrefour of France, Ahold of Holland, and Tesco of the United Kingdom. Carrefour, the world's second-largest retailer, is perhaps the most global of the lot. The pioneer of the hypermarket concept now operates in twenty-six countries and generates more than 50% of its sales outside France. In comparison, Wal-Mart is a laggard, with just 25% of its sales in 2007 generated from international operations. However, there is still room for significant global expansion. The global retailing market is still very fragmented. The top twenty-five retailers controlled only about a quarter of retail sales in 2007.

Still, for all of its success Wal-Mart has hit some significant speed bumps in its drive for global expansion. In 2006, the company pulled out of two markets—South Korea, where it failed to decode the shopping habits of local customers, and Germany, where it could not beat incumbent discount stores on price. It is also struggling in Japan, where the company does not seem to have grasped the market's cultural nuances. One example is Wal-Mart's decision to sell lower-priced gift fruits at Japanese holidays. It failed because customers felt that spending less would insult the recipient! Interesting, the markets in which Wal-Mart has struggled were all developed markets that it entered through acquisitions, where it faced long-established and efficient local competitors and where shopping habits were very different than in the United States. In contrast, many of the markets in which it has done better have been in developing nations where it lacked strong local competitors and in countries where it has built operations from the ground up (e.g., Mexico, Brazil, and, increasingly, China).[a]

It is important to note that the success of many multinational companies is based not just upon the goods or services that they sell in foreign nations, but also upon the distinctive competences (unique skills) that underlie the production and marketing of those goods or services. Thus, Toyota's success is based upon its distinctive competence in manufacturing automobiles, and expanding internationally can be seen as a way of generating greater returns from this competence. Similarly, Procter & Gamble's global success was based on more than its portfolio of consumer products; it was also based on the company's skills in mass-marketing consumer goods. P&G grew rapidly in international markets between 1950 and 1990 because it was one of the most skilled mass-marketing enterprises in the world and could "out-market" indigenous competitors in the nations it entered. Global expansion was thus a way of generating higher returns from its competence in marketing.

Taking this further, one could say that since distinctive competences are in essence the most valuable aspects of a company's business, successful global expansion by manufacturing companies like Toyota and P&G was based upon their ability to apply their distinctive competences to foreign markets.

The same can be said of companies engaged in the service sectors of an economy, such as financial institutions, retailers, restaurant chains, and hotels. Expanding the market for their services often means replicating their basic business model in foreign nations (albeit with some changes to account for local differences—which we will discuss in more detail shortly). Starbucks, for example, is expanding rapidly outside of the United States by taking the basic business model it developed at home and using that as a blueprint for establishing international operations. As detailed in the Running Case on page 140, Wal-Mart has done the same thing, establishing stores in nine other nations since 1992 by following the blueprint it developed in the United States. Similarly, McDonald's is famous for its international expansion strategy, which has taken the company into more than 120 nations that collectively generate over half of the company's revenues.

● Realizing Economies of Scale

In addition to growing profits more rapidly, by expanding its sales volume through international expansion a company can realize cost savings from economies of scale, thereby boosting profitability. Such scale economies come from several sources. First, by spreading the fixed costs associated with developing a product and setting up production facilities over its global sales volume, a company can lower its average unit cost. Thus, Microsoft can garner significant scale economies by spreading the $5 billion it cost to develop Windows Vista over global demand. Second, by serving a global market, a company can potentially utilize its production facilities more intensively, which leads to higher productivity, lower costs, and greater profitability. For example, if Intel sold microprocessors only in the United States, it might be able to keep its factories open for only one shift, five days a week. But by serving a global market from the same factories, it may be able to utilize those assets for two shifts, seven days a week. In other words, the capital invested in those factories is used more intensively if Intel sells to a global as opposed to a national market, which translates into higher capital productivity and a higher return on invested capital. Third, as global sales increase the size of the enterprise, its bargaining power with suppliers increases, which may allow it to bargain down the cost of key inputs and boost profitability that way. Wal-Mart has been able to use its enormous sales volume as a lever to bargain down the price it pays suppliers for merchandise sold through its stores (see the Running Case).

● Realizing Location Economies

Earlier in this chapter, we discussed how countries differ from each other along a number of dimensions, including the cost and quality of factors of production. These differences imply that some locations are more suited than others to producing certain goods and services.[7] **Location economies** are the economic benefits that arise from performing a value creation activity in the optimal location for that activity, wherever in the world that might be (transportation costs and trade barriers permitting). Locating a value creation activity in the optimal location for that activity can have one of two effects: (1) it can lower the costs of value creation, helping the company achieve a low-cost position, or (2) it can enable a company to differentiate its product offering, which gives it the option of charging a premium price or keeping price low and using differentiation as a means of increasing sales volume. Thus, efforts to realize location economies are consistent with the business-level strategies of low cost and differentiation. In theory, a company that realizes location economies by dispersing each of its value creation activities to the optimal location

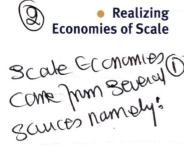

location economies

Economic benefits that arise from performing a value creation activity in the optimal location for that activity, wherever in the world that might be (transportation costs and trade barriers permitting).

for that activity should have a competitive advantage over a company that bases all of its value creation activities at a single location; it should be able to differentiate its product offering better and lower its cost structure more than its single-location competitor. In a world where competitive pressures are increasing, such a strategy may well become an imperative for survival.

As an illustration, consider IBM's ThinkPad X31 laptop computer (this business was acquired by China's Lenovo in 2005).[8] The ThinkPad was designed in the United States by IBM engineers because IBM believed that the United States was the best location in the world to do the basic design work. The case, keyboard, and hard drive were made in Thailand; the display screen and memory were made in South Korea; the built-in wireless card was made in Malaysia; and the microprocessor was manufactured in the United States. In each case, these components were manufactured in the optimal location, given managers' assessment of the relative costs of performing each activity at different locations. These components were then shipped to an IBM operation in Mexico, where the product was assembled before being shipped to the United States for final sale. IBM assembled the ThinkPad in Mexico because IBM's managers calculated that, because of low labor costs, the costs of assembly could be minimized there. The marketing and sales strategy for North America was developed by IBM personnel in the United States, primarily because IBM believed that their marketing efforts would add more value to the product, given their knowledge of the local marketplace.

● Leveraging the Skills of Global Subsidiaries

Many multinational companies initially develop the valuable competences and skills that underpin their business in their home nation and then expand internationally, primarily by selling products and services based on those competences. Thus, Wal-Mart honed its retailing skills in the United States before transferring them to foreign locations. However, for more mature multinational enterprises that have already established a network of subsidiary operations in foreign markets, the development of valuable skills can just as well occur in foreign subsidiaries.[9] Skills can be created anywhere within a multinational's global network of operations, wherever people have the opportunity and incentive to try new ways of doing things. The creation of skills that help to lower the costs of production or to enhance perceived value and support higher product pricing is not the monopoly of the corporate center.

Leveraging the skills created within subsidiaries and applying them to other operations within a firm's global network may create value. For example, McDonald's increasingly is finding that its foreign franchisees are a source of valuable new ideas. Faced with slow growth in France, its local franchisees have begun to experiment not only with the menu, but also with the layout and theme of restaurants. Gone are the ubiquitous Golden Arches; gone too are many of the utilitarian chairs and tables and other plastic features of the fast-food giant. Many McDonald's restaurants in France now have hardwood floors, exposed brick walls, and even armchairs. Half of the 930 or so outlets in France have been upgraded to a level that would make them unrecognizable to an American. The menu, too, has been changed to include premier sandwiches such as chicken on focaccia bread, priced some 30% higher than the average hamburger. In France, at least, the strategy seems to be working. Following the change, increases in same-store sales rose from 1% annually to 3.4%. Impressed with the impact, McDonald's executives are now considering adopting similar changes at other McDonald's restaurants in markets where same-store sales growth is sluggish, including the United States.[10]

Cost Pressures and Pressures for Local Responsiveness

[handwritten: Two types of competitive pressures in the global market]

Companies that compete in the global marketplace typically face two types of competitive pressures: *pressures for cost reductions* and *pressures to be locally responsive* (see Figure 6.1).[11] These competitive pressures place conflicting demands on a company. Responding to pressures for cost reductions requires that a company try to minimize its unit costs. To attain this goal, it may have to base its production activities at the most favorable low-cost location, wherever in the world that might be. It may also have to offer a standardized product to the global marketplace in order to realize the cost savings that come from economies of scale and learning effects. On the other hand, responding to pressures to be locally responsive requires that a company differentiate its product offering and marketing strategy from country to country in an effort to accommodate the diverse demands arising from national differences in consumer tastes and preferences, business practices, distribution channels, competitive conditions, and government policies. Because differentiation across countries can involve significant duplication and a lack of product standardization, it may raise costs.

While some companies, such as Company A in Figure 6.1, face high pressures for cost reductions and low pressures for local responsiveness and others, such as Company B, face low pressures for cost reductions and high pressures for local responsiveness, many companies are in the position of Company C. They face high pressures for *both* cost reductions and local responsiveness. Dealing with these conflicting and contradictory pressures is a difficult strategic challenge, primarily because being locally responsive tends to raise costs.

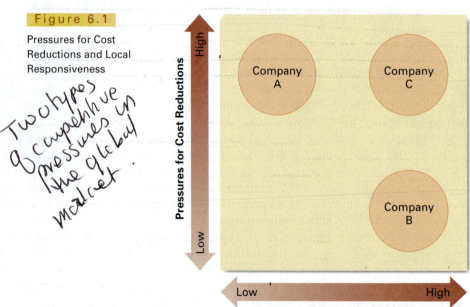

Figure 6.1

Pressures for Cost Reductions and Local Responsiveness

[handwritten: Two types of competitive pressures in the global market.]

● Pressures for Cost Reductions

In competitive global markets, international businesses often face pressures for cost reductions. Responding to pressures for cost reductions requires a firm to try to lower the costs of value creation. A manufacturer, for example, might mass-produce a standardized product at the optimal location in the world, wherever that might be, to realize scale economies and location economies. Alternatively, it might outsource certain functions to low-cost foreign suppliers in an attempt to reduce costs. Thus, many computer companies have outsourced their telephone-based customer service functions to India, where qualified technicians who speak English can be hired for a lower wage rate than in the United States. In the same vein, a retailer like Wal-Mart might push its suppliers (who are manufacturers) to do the same. (In fact, the pressure that Wal-Mart has placed on its suppliers to reduce prices has been cited as a major cause of the trend among North American manufacturers to shift production to China.[12]) A service business, such as a bank, might move some back-office functions, such as information processing, to developing nations where wage rates are lower.

Cost reduction pressures can be particularly intense in industries producing commodity-type products, where meaningful differentiation on nonprice factors is difficult and price is the main competitive weapon. This tends to be the case for products that serve universal needs. **Universal needs** exist when the tastes and preferences of consumers in different nations are similar if not identical. This is the case for conventional commodity products such as bulk chemicals, petroleum, steel, sugar, and the like. It also tends to be the case for many industrial and consumer products—for example, handheld calculators, semiconductor chips, personal computers, and liquid crystal display screens. Pressures for cost reductions are also intense in industries where major competitors are based in low-cost locations, where there is persistent excess capacity, and where consumers are powerful and face low switching costs. Many commentators have argued that the liberalization of the world trade and investment environment in recent decades, by facilitating greater international competition, has generally increased cost pressures.[13]

universal needs

Needs arising from the similar, if not identical, tastes and preferences of consumers in different nations.

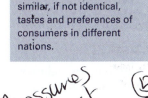

● Pressures for Local Responsiveness

Pressures for local responsiveness arise from differences in consumer tastes and preferences, infrastructure and traditional practices, distribution channels, and host government demands. Recall that responding to pressures to be locally responsive requires that a company differentiate its products and marketing strategy from country to country to accommodate these factors, all of which tend to raise a company's cost structure.

DIFFERENCES IN CUSTOMER TASTES AND PREFERENCES Strong pressures for local responsiveness emerge when customer tastes and preferences differ significantly between countries, as they may for historical or cultural reasons. In such cases, a multinational company's products and marketing message have to be customized to appeal to the tastes and preferences of local customers. This typically creates pressures for the delegation of production and marketing responsibilities and functions to a company's overseas subsidiaries.

For example, the automobile industry in the 1980s and early 1990s moved toward the creation of "world cars." The idea was that global companies such as General Motors, Ford, and Toyota would be able to sell the same basic vehicle the world over, sourcing it from centralized production locations. If successful, the strategy would have enabled automobile companies to reap significant gains from global scale economies. However, this strategy frequently ran aground upon the hard rocks of consumer reality. Consumers in different automobile markets seem to have different tastes and preferences, and these require different types of vehicles. North American consumers show a strong demand for pickup trucks. This is particularly true in the South and West, where many families have a pickup truck as a second or third car. But in European countries, pickup trucks are seen purely as utility vehicles and are purchased primarily by firms rather than individuals. As a consequence, the product mix and marketing message need to be tailored to take into account the different nature of demand in North America and Europe.

DIFFERENCES IN INFRASTRUCTURE AND TRADITIONAL PRACTICES   Pressures for local responsiveness arise from differences in infrastructure or traditional practices among countries, creating a need to customize products accordingly. Fulfilling this need may require the delegation of manufacturing and production functions to foreign subsidiaries. For example, in North America consumer electrical systems are based on 110 volts, whereas in some European countries 240-volt systems are standard. Thus, domestic electrical appliances have to be customized to take this difference in infrastructure into account. Traditional practices also often vary across nations. For example, in Britain people drive on the left-hand side of the road, creating a demand for right-hand-drive cars, whereas in France (and the rest of Europe) people drive on the right-hand side of the road and therefore want left-hand-drive cars. Obviously, automobiles have to be customized to take this difference in traditional practices into account.

Although many of the country differences in infrastructure are rooted in history, some are quite recent. For example, in the wireless telecommunications industry, different technical standards are found in different parts of the world. A technical standard known as GSM is common in Europe, and an alternative standard, CDMA, is more common in the United States and parts of Asia. The significance of these different standards is that equipment designed for GSM will not work on a CDMA network, and vice versa. Thus, companies like Nokia, Motorola, and Ericsson, which manufacture wireless handsets and infrastructure such as switches, need to customize their product offerings according to the technical standard prevailing in a given country.

DIFFERENCES IN DISTRIBUTION CHANNELS   A company's marketing strategies may have to be responsive to differences in distribution channels among countries, which may necessitate the delegation of marketing functions to national subsidiaries. In the pharmaceutical industry, for example, the British and Japanese distribution system is radically different from the U.S. system. British and Japanese doctors would not accept or respond favorably to a U.S.-style high-pressure sales force. Thus, pharmaceutical companies have to adopt different marketing practices in Britain and Japan that are softer than the hard sell used in the United States.

HOST GOVERNMENT DEMANDS   Economic and political demands imposed by host country governments may require local responsiveness. For example, pharmaceutical companies are subject to local clinical testing, registration procedures, and pricing restrictions, all of which make it necessary that the manufacturing and marketing of a drug meet local requirements. Moreover, because governments control a significant proportion of the health care budget in most countries, they are in a powerful position to demand a high level of local responsiveness.

More generally, threats of protectionism, economic nationalism, and local content rules (which require that a certain percentage of a product be manufactured locally) dictate that international businesses manufacture locally. As an example, consider Bombardier, the Canada-based manufacturer of railcars, aircraft, jet boats, and snowmobiles. Bombardier has twelve railcar factories across Europe. Critics of the company argue that the resulting duplication of manufacturing facilities leads to high costs and helps explain why Bombardier has lower profit margins on its railcar operations than on its other business lines. In reply, managers at Bombardier argue that in Europe informal rules with regard to local content favor people who use local workers. To sell railcars in Germany, they claim, you must manufacture in Germany. The same goes for Belgium, Austria, and France. To try to address its cost structure in Europe, Bombardier has centralized its engineering and purchasing functions, but it has no plans to centralize manufacturing.[14]

Choosing a Global Strategy

Pressures for local responsiveness imply that it may not be possible for a firm to realize the full benefits from scale economies and location economies. It may not be possible to serve the global marketplace from a single low-cost location, producing a globally standardized product and marketing it worldwide to achieve economies of scale. In practice, the need to customize the product offering for local conditions may work against the implementation of such a strategy. For example, automobile firms have found that Japanese, American, and European consumers demand different kinds of cars, and this necessitates producing products that are customized for local markets. In response, firms like Honda, Ford, and Toyota are pursuing a strategy of establishing top-to-bottom design and production facilities in each of these regions so that they can better serve local demands. Although such customization brings benefits, it also limits the ability of a firm to realize significant scale economies and location economies.

In addition, pressures for local responsiveness imply that it may not be possible to take skills and products associated with a firm's distinctive competences and leverage them wholesale from one nation to another. Concessions often have to be made to local conditions. Despite being depicted as a "poster child" for the proliferation of standardized global products, even McDonald's has found that it has to customize its product offerings (i.e., its menu) in order to account for national differences in tastes and preferences.

Given the need to balance the cost and differentiation (value) sides of a company's business, how do differences between the strength of pressures for cost reductions and those for local responsiveness affect the choice of a company's strategy? Companies typical make a choice among four main strategic postures when competing internationally: a global standardization strategy, a localization strategy, a transnational strategy, and an international strategy.[15] The appropriateness of each strategy varies with the extent of pressures for cost reductions and local responsiveness. Figure 6.2 illustrates the conditions under which each of these strategies is most appropriate.

Figure 6.2

Four Basic Strategies

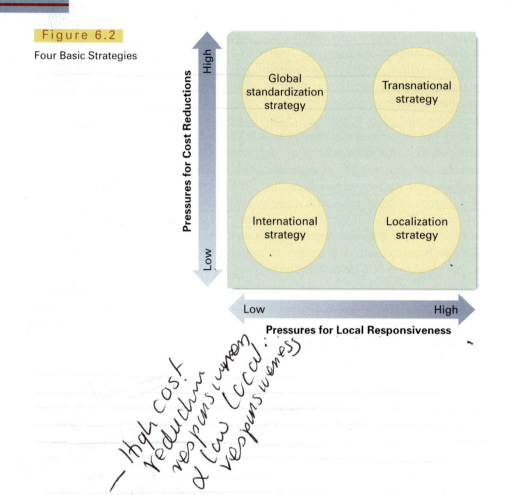

Companies that pursue a **global standardization strategy** focus on increasing profitability by reaping the cost reductions that come from scale economies and location economies; that is, their strategy is to pursue a low-cost strategy on a global scale. The production, marketing, and R&D activities of companies pursuing a global strategy are concentrated in a few favorable locations. Companies pursuing a global standardization strategy try not to customize their product offering and marketing strategy to local conditions because customization, which involves shorter production runs and the duplication of functions, can raise costs. Instead, they prefer to market a standardized product worldwide so that they can reap the maximum benefits from economies of scale. They also tend to use their cost advantage to support aggressive pricing in world markets.

This strategy makes most sense when there are strong pressures for cost reductions and demand for local responsiveness is minimal. Increasingly, these conditions are prevailing in many industrial goods industries, whose products often serve universal needs. In the semiconductor industry, for example, global standards have emerged, creating enormous demand for standardized global products. Accordingly, companies such as Intel, Texas Instruments, and Motorola all pursue a global strategy. These conditions are not always found in consumer goods markets, where demand for local responsiveness often remains high. However, even some consumer goods companies are moving toward a global standardization strategy in an attempt to drive down their costs. Procter & Gamble, which is featured in the Strategy in Action, is one example of such a company.

● Global Standardization Strategy

global standardization strategy

A strategy that focuses on increasing profitability by reaping the cost reductions derived from scale economies and location economies.

Strategy in Action

The Evolution of Strategy at Procter & Gamble

Founded in 1837, Cincinnati-based Procter & Gamble has long been one of the world's most international of companies. Today, P&G is a global colossus in the consumer products business, with annual sales in excess of $50 billion, some 54% of which are generated outside of the United States. P&G sells more than 300 brands—including Ivory, Tide, Pampers, IAMS, Crisco, and Folgers—to consumers in 160 countries. Historically, the strategy at P&G was to develop new products in Cincinnati and then rely on semiautonomous foreign subsidiaries to manufacture, market, and distribute those products in different nations. In many cases, foreign subsidiaries had their own production facilities and tailored the packaging, brand name, and marketing message to local tastes and preferences. For years, this strategy delivered a steady stream of new products and reliable growth in sales and profits. By the 1990s, however, profit growth at P&G was slowing.

The essence of the problem was simple: P&G's costs were too high because of extensive duplication of manufacturing, marketing, and administrative facilities in different national subsidiaries. The duplication of assets made sense in the world of the 1960s, when national markets were separated by barriers to cross-border trade. Products produced in Great Britain, for example, could not be sold economically in Germany because of high tariff duties levied on imports into Germany. By the 1980s, however, barriers to cross-border trade were falling rapidly worldwide and fragmented national markets were merging into larger regional or global markets. Also, the retailers through which P&G distributed its products, such as Wal-Mart, Tesco of the United Kingdom, and Carrefour of France,

were growing larger and more global. These emerging global retailers were demanding price discounts from P&G.

In the 1990s, P&G embarked on a major reorganization in an attempt to control its cost structure and recognize the new reality of emerging global markets. The company shut down thirty manufacturing plants around the globe, laid off 13,000 employees, and concentrated production in fewer plants that could better realize economies of scale and serve regional markets. It wasn't enough. Profit growth remained sluggish, so in 1999 P&G launched a second reorganization. The goal was to transform P&G into a truly global company. The company tore up its old organization, which was based on countries and regions, and replaced it with one based on seven self-contained global business units, ranging from baby care to food products. Each business unit was given complete responsibility for generating profits from its products and for manufacturing, marketing, and product development. Each business unit was told to rationalize production, concentrating it in fewer larger facilities; to build global brands wherever possible, thereby eliminating marketing differences between countries; and to accelerate the development and launch of new products. P&G announced that as a result of this initiative, it would close another ten factories and lay off 15,000 employees, mostly in Europe, where there was still extensive duplication of assets. The annual cost savings were estimated to be about $800 million. P&G planned to use the savings to cut prices and increase marketing spending in an effort to gain market share and thus further lower costs through the attainment of scale economies. This time, the strategy seems to be working. Between 2003 and 2007, P&G reported strong growth in both sales and profits. Significantly, during the same time period P&G's global competitors, such as Unilever, Kimberly-Clark, and Colgate-Palmolive, were struggling.[b]

● **Localization Strategy**

localization strategy

A strategy that focuses on increasing profitability by customizing the company's goods or services so that they provide a good match to tastes and preferences in different national markets.

A **localization strategy** focuses on increasing profitability by customizing the company's goods or services so that they provide a good match to tastes and preferences in different national markets. Localization is most appropriate where there are substantial differences across nations with regard to consumer tastes and preferences and where cost pressures are not too intense. By customizing the product offering to local demands, the company increases the value of that product in the local market. On the downside, because it involves some duplication of functions and smaller production runs, customization limits the ability of the company to capture the cost reductions associated with mass-producing a standardized product for global consumption. The strategy may make sense, however, if the added value associated with local customization supports higher pricing, which enables the company to recoup its higher costs, or if it leads to substantially greater local demand, enabling the company to reduce costs through the attainment of some scale economies in the local market.

MTV is a good example of a company that has had to pursue a localization strategy. MTV has varied its programming to match the demands of viewers in different nations. If it had not done this, it would have lost market share to local competitors, its advertising revenues would have fallen, and its profitability would have declined. Thus, even though it raised costs, localization became a strategic imperative at MTV.

At the same time, it is important to realize that companies like MTV still have to keep a close eye on costs. Companies pursuing a localization strategy still need to be efficient, and, whenever possible, to capture some scale economies from their global reach. As noted earlier, many automobile companies have found that they have to customize some of their product offerings to local market demands—for example, producing large pickup trucks for U.S. consumers and small fuel-efficient cars for European and Japanese consumers. At the same time, these companies try to get some scale economies from their global volume by using common vehicle platforms and components across many different models and manufacturing those platforms and components at efficiently scaled factories that are optimally located. By designing their products in this way, these companies have been able to localize their product offerings, yet simultaneously capture some scale economies.

● Transnational Strategy

Both strong cost pressure and strong local responsiveness

We have argued that a global standardization strategy makes most sense when cost pressures are intense and demands for local responsiveness limited. Conversely, a localization strategy makes most sense when demands for local responsiveness are high but cost pressures are moderate or low. What happens, however, when the company simultaneously faces both strong cost pressures and strong pressures for local responsiveness? How can managers balance the competing and inconsistent demands that such divergent pressures place on the company? According to some researchers, the answer is to pursue what has been called a transnational strategy.

According to some, in today's global environment competitive conditions are so intense that, to survive, companies must do all they can to respond to pressures for cost reductions and local responsiveness. They must try to realize location economies and scale economies from global volume, transfer distinctive competences and skills within the company, and simultaneously pay attention to pressures for local responsiveness.[16] Moreover, in the modern multinational enterprise, distinctive competences and skills do not reside just in the home country but can develop in any of the company's worldwide operations. Thus, the flow of skills and product offerings should not be all one way, from home company to foreign subsidiary. Rather, the flow should also be from foreign subsidiary to home country and from foreign subsidiary to foreign subsidiary. Transnational companies, in other words, must also focus on leveraging subsidiary skills.

In essence, companies that pursue a **transnational strategy** are trying to simultaneously achieve low costs, differentiate the product offering across geographic markets, and foster a flow of skills among different subsidiaries in their global network of operations. As attractive as this may sound, the strategy is not an easy one to pursue since it places conflicting demands on the company. Differentiating the product to respond to local demands in different geographic markets raises costs, which runs counter to the goal of reducing costs. Companies like Ford and ABB (one of the world's largest engineering conglomerates) have tried to embrace a transnational strategy and found it difficult to implement in practice.

transnational strategy

A strategy in which firms try to simultaneously achieve low costs, differentiate the product offering across geographic markets, and foster a flow of skills among different subsidiaries in their global network of operations.

● International Strategy

Sometimes it is possible to identify multinational companies that find themselves in the fortunate position of being confronted with low cost pressures and low pressures for local responsiveness. Typically, these enterprises are selling a product that serves universal needs, but they do not face significant competitors and thus are not confronted with pressures to reduce their cost structure. Xerox found itself in this position in the 1960s, after its invention of the photocopier. The technology underlying the photocopier was protected by strong patents, so for several years Xerox did not face competitors—it had a monopoly. The product was highly valued in most developed nations, so Xerox was able to sell the same basic product the world over and charge a relatively high price for that product. Because it did not face direct competitors, the company did not have to deal with strong pressures to minimize its costs.

Historically, companies in this position have followed a developmental pattern similar to that of Xerox as they built their international operations. Companies pursuing an **international strategy** tend to centralize product development functions such as R&D at home. However, they also tend to establish manufacturing and marketing functions in each major country or geographic region in which they do business. Although they may undertake some local customization of product offering and marketing strategy, it tends to be rather limited in scope. Ultimately, in most international companies, the head office retains tight control over marketing and product strategy.

Other companies that have pursued this strategy include Procter & Gamble, which historically always developed innovative new products in Cincinnati and then transferred them wholesale to local markets (see the Strategy in Action feature). Another company that has followed a similar strategy is Microsoft. The bulk of Microsoft's product development work takes place in Redmond, Washington, where the company is headquartered. Although some localization work is undertaken elsewhere, it is limited to producing foreign-language versions of popular Microsoft programs such as Office.

international strategy

A strategy in which firms try to centralize product development functions such as R&D at home but establish manufacturing and marketing functions in each major country or geographic region in which they do business.

● Changes in Strategy over Time

The Achilles' heel of international strategy is that, over time, competitors inevitably emerge, and if managers do not take proactive steps to reduce their cost structure, their company may be rapidly outflanked by efficient global competitors. This is exactly what happened to Xerox. Japanese companies such as Canon ultimately invented their way around Xerox's patents, produced their own photocopiers in very efficient manufacturing plants, priced them below Xerox's products, and rapidly took global market share from Xerox. Xerox's fall was not due to the emergence of competitors, for ultimately that was bound to occur, but due to its failure to proactively reduce its cost structure in advance of the emergence of efficient global competitors. The message in this story is that an international strategy may not be viable in the long term, so, to survive, companies need to shift toward a global standardization strategy, or perhaps a transnational strategy, in advance of competitors (see Figure 6.3).

The same can be said about a localization strategy. Localization may give a company a competitive edge, but if it is simultaneously facing aggressive competitors, the company will also have to reduce its cost structure, and the only way to do that may be to adopt more of a transnational strategy. Thus, as competition intensifies, international and localization strategies tend to become less viable, and managers need to orient their companies toward either a global standardization strategy or a transnational strategy. Procter & Gamble, for example, has moved from a localization strategy to more of a transnational strategy in recent years (see the Strategy in Action feature).

Figure 6.3

Changes over Time

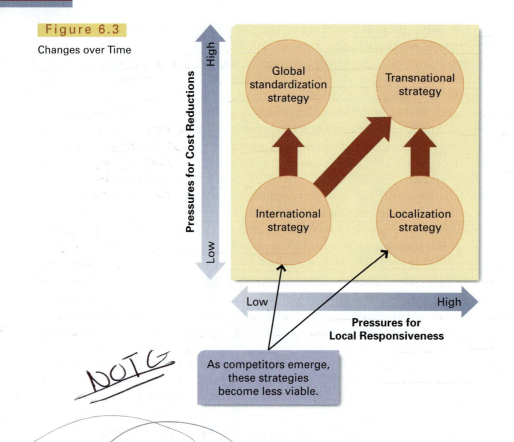

As competitors emerge, these strategies become less viable.

NOTE

Choices of Entry Mode

There are five main choices of entry mode

Another key strategic issue confronting managers in a multinational enterprise is deciding upon the best strategy for entering a market. There are five main choices of entry mode: exporting, licensing, franchising, entering into a joint venture with a host country company, and setting up a wholly owned subsidiary in the host country. Each mode has its advantages and disadvantages, and managers must weigh these carefully when deciding which mode to use.[17]

① ● Exporting

Adv

Most manufacturing companies begin their global expansion as exporters and only later switch to one of the other modes for serving a foreign market. Exporting has two distinct advantages: it avoids the costs of establishing manufacturing operations in the host country, which are often substantial, and it may be consistent with scale economies and location economies. By manufacturing the product in a centralized location and then exporting it to other national markets, a company may be able to realize substantial scale economies from its global sales volume. That is how Sony came to dominate the global television market, how Matsushita came to dominate the VCR market, and how many Japanese auto companies originally made inroads into the U.S. auto market.

Disadv

There are also a number of drawbacks to exporting. First, exporting from a company's home base may not be appropriate if there are lower-cost locations for manufacturing the product abroad (that is, if the company can realize location economies by moving production elsewhere). Thus, particularly in the case of a company pursuing a global standardization or transnational strategy, it may pay to manufacture in a location where conditions are most favorable from a value creation perspective and then export from that location to the rest of the globe. This is not so much an argument against exporting as an argument against exporting from the company's home country. For example, many U.S. electronics companies have moved some of their manufacturing to Asia because low-cost but highly skilled labor is available there. They export from that location to the rest of the globe, including the United States.

Another drawback is that high transport costs can make exporting uneconomical, particularly in the case of bulk products. One way of getting around this problem is to manufacture bulk products on a regional basis, realizing some economies from large-scale production while limiting transport costs. Many multinational chemical companies manufacture their products on a regional basis, serving several countries in a region from one facility.

Tariff barriers, too, can make exporting uneconomical, and a government's threat to impose tariff barriers can make the strategy very risky. Indeed, the implicit threat from the U.S. Congress to impose tariffs on Japanese cars imported into the United States led directly to the decision by many Japanese auto companies to set up manufacturing plants in the United States.

Finally, a common practice among companies that are just beginning to export also poses risks. A company may delegate marketing activities to a local agent in each country in which it does business, but there is no guarantee that the agent will act in the company's best interest. Often foreign agents also carry the products of competing companies and thus have divided loyalties. Consequently, they may not do as good a job as the company would if it managed marketing itself. One way to solve this problem is to set up a wholly owned subsidiary in the host country to handle local marketing. In this way, the company can reap the cost advantages that arise from manufacturing the product in a single location and exercise tight control over marketing strategy in the host country.

Licensing

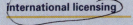

international licensing

An arrangement whereby a foreign licensee buys the rights to produce a company's product in the licensee's country for a negotiated fee.

International licensing is an arrangement whereby a foreign licensee buys the rights to produce a company's product in the licensee's country for a negotiated fee (normally, royalty payments on the number of units sold). The licensee then puts up most of the capital necessary to get the overseas operation going.[18] The advantage of licensing is that the company does not have to bear the development costs and risks associated with opening up a foreign market. Licensing therefore can be a very attractive option for companies that lack the capital to develop operations overseas. It can also be an attractive option for companies that are unwilling to commit substantial financial resources to an unfamiliar or politically volatile foreign market where political risks are particularly high.

Licensing has three serious drawbacks, however. First, it does not give a company the tight control over manufacturing, marketing, and strategic functions in foreign countries that it needs to have in order to realize scale economies and location economies, as companies pursuing both global standardization and transnational strategies try to do. Typically, each licensee sets up its own manufacturing operations. Hence, the company stands little chance of realizing scale economies and location economies by manufacturing its product in a centralized location. When these economies are likely to be important, licensing may not be the best way of expanding overseas.

Second, competing in a global marketplace may make it necessary for a company to coordinate strategic moves across countries so that the profits earned in one country can be used to support competitive attacks in another. Licensing, by its very nature, severely limits a company's ability to coordinate strategy in this way. A licensee is unlikely to let a multinational company take its profits (beyond those due in the form of royalty payments) and use them to support an entirely different licensee operating in another country.

Disadv 3°

A third problem with licensing is the risk associated with licensing technological know-how to foreign companies. For many multinational companies, technological know-how forms the basis of their competitive advantage, and they need to maintain control over its use. By licensing its technology, a company can quickly lose control over it. RCA, for instance, once licensed its color television technology to a number of Japanese companies. The Japanese companies quickly assimilated RCA's technology and then used it to enter the U.S. market. Now the Japanese have a bigger share of the U.S. market than the RCA brand does.

③ ● **Franchising**

 franchising

A specialized form of licensing in which the franchiser sells the franchisee intangible property (normally a trademark) and insists that the franchisee agree to abide by strict rules about how it does business.

Franchising is similar to licensing, although franchising tends to involve longer-term commitments than licensing. **Franchising** is basically a specialized form of licensing in which the franchiser not only sells to the franchisee intangible property (normally a trademark), but also insists that the franchisee agree to abide by strict rules as to how it does business. The franchiser will also often assist the franchisee in running the business on an ongoing basis. As with licensing, the franchiser typically receives a royalty payment, which amounts to some percentage of the franchisee's revenues.

Whereas licensing is a strategy pursued primarily by manufacturing companies, franchising, which resembles licensing in some respects, is a strategy employed chiefly by service companies. McDonald's provides a good example of a firm that has grown by using a franchising strategy. McDonald's has set down strict rules as to how franchisees should operate a restaurant. These rules extend to control over the menu, cooking methods, staffing policies, and restaurant design and location. McDonald's also organizes the supply chain for its franchisees and provides management training and financial assistance. [19]

Adv The advantages of franchising are similar to those of licensing. Specifically, the franchiser does not have to bear the development costs and risks of opening up a foreign market on its own, for the franchisee typically assumes those costs and risks. Thus, using a franchising strategy, a service company can build up a global presence quickly and at a low cost.

Disadv The disadvantages are less pronounced than in the case of licensing. Because franchising is a strategy used by service companies, a franchiser does not have to consider the need to coordinate manufacturing in order to achieve scale economies and location economies. Nevertheless, franchising may inhibit a company's ability to achieve global strategic coordination.

Disadv A more significant disadvantage of franchising is the lack of quality control. The foundation of franchising arrangements is the notion that the company's brand name conveys a message to consumers about the quality of the company's product. Thus, a traveler booking a room at a Hilton International hotel in Hong Kong can reasonably expect the same quality of room, food, and service as she would receive in New York; the Hilton brand name is a guarantee of the consistency of product quality. However, foreign franchisees may not be as concerned about quality as they should be, and poor quality may mean not only lost sales in the foreign market but also a decline in the company's worldwide reputation. For example, if the traveler has a bad experience at the Hilton in Hong Kong, she may never go to another Hilton hotel and steer her colleagues away as well. The geographic distance separating it from its foreign franchisees and the sheer number of individual franchisees—

tens of thousands in the case of McDonald's—can make it difficult for the franchiser to detect poor quality. Consequently, quality problems may persist.

To reduce this problem, a company can set up a subsidiary in each country or region in which it is expanding. The subsidiary, which might be wholly owned by the company or a joint venture with a foreign company, then assumes the right and obligation to establish franchisees throughout that particular country or region. The combination of proximity and the limited number of independent franchisees that have to be monitored reduces the quality control problem. Besides, since the subsidiary is at least partly owned by the company, the company can place its own managers in the subsidiary to ensure the kind of quality monitoring it wants. This organizational arrangement has proved very popular in practice. It has been used by McDonald's, KFC, and Hilton Hotels Corporation to expand their international operations, to name just three examples.

Joint Ventures

joint venture

A separate corporate entity in which two or more companies have an ownership stake.

Establishing a joint venture with a foreign company has long been a favored mode for entering a new market. A **joint venture** is a separate corporate entity in which two or more companies have an ownership stake. One of the most famous long-term joint ventures is the Fuji-Xerox joint venture to produce photocopiers for the Japanese market. The most typical form of joint venture is a fifty-fifty venture, in which each party takes a 50% ownership stake and operating control is shared by a team of managers from both parent companies. Some companies have sought joint ventures in which they have a majority shareholding (for example, a 51 to 49% ownership split), which permits tighter control by the dominant partner.[20]

Joint ventures have a number of advantages. First, a company may feel that it can benefit from a local partner's knowledge of a host country's competitive conditions, culture, language, political systems, and business systems. Second, when the development costs and risks of opening up a foreign market are high, a company might gain by sharing these costs and risks with a local partner. Third, in some countries, political considerations make joint ventures the only feasible entry mode.[21] For example, historically many U.S. companies found it much easier to get permission to set up operations in Japan if they went in with a Japanese partner than if they tried to enter on their own. This is why Xerox originally teamed up with Fuji to sell photocopiers in Japan.

Despite these advantages, joint ventures can be difficult to establish and run because of two main drawbacks. First, as in the case of licensing, a company that enters into a joint venture risks losing control over its technology to its venture partner. To minimize this risk, it can seek a majority ownership stake in the joint venture, for as the dominant partner it would be able to exercise greater control over its technology. The trouble with this strategy is that it may be difficult to find a foreign partner willing to accept a minority ownership position.

The second disadvantage is that a joint venture does not give a company the tight control over its subsidiaries that it might need in order to realize scale economies or location economies—as both global standardization and transnational companies try to do—or to engage in coordinated global attacks against its global rivals.

Wholly Owned Subsidiaries

wholly owned subsidiary

A subsidiary in which the parent company owns 100% of the stock.

A **wholly owned subsidiary** is one in which 100% of the subsidiary's stock is owned by the parent company. To establish a wholly owned subsidiary in a foreign market, a company can either set up a completely new operation in that country or acquire an established host country company and use it to promote its products in the host market.

Setting up a wholly owned subsidiary offers three advantages. First, when a company's competitive advantage is based on its control of a technological competence, a wholly owned subsidiary will normally be the preferred entry mode, since it reduces the company's risk of losing this control. Consequently, many high-tech companies prefer wholly owned subsidiaries to joint ventures or licensing arrangements. Wholly owned subsidiaries tend to be the favored entry mode in the semiconductor, computer, electronics, and pharmaceutical industries. Second, a wholly owned subsidiary gives a company the kind of tight control over operations in different countries that it needs if it is going to engage in global strategic coordination—taking profits from one country to support competitive attacks in another.

Third, a wholly owned subsidiary may be the best choice if a company wants to realize the location economies and scale economies that flow from producing a standardized output from a single plant or a limited number of manufacturing plants. When pressures on costs are intense, it may pay a company to configure its value chain in such a way that the value added at each stage is maximized. Thus, a national subsidiary may specialize in manufacturing only part of the product line or certain components of the end product, exchanging parts and products with other subsidiaries in the company's global system. Establishing such a global production system requires a high degree of control over the operations of national affiliates. Different national operations have to be prepared to accept centrally determined decisions as to how they should produce, how much they should produce, and how their output should be priced for transfer between operations. A wholly owned subsidiary would have to comply with these mandates, whereas licensees or joint venture partners would most likely shun such a subservient role.

On the other hand, establishing a wholly owned subsidiary is generally the most costly method of serving a foreign market. The parent company must bear all the costs and risks of setting up overseas operations—in contrast to joint ventures, where the costs and risks are shared, or licensing, where the licensee bears most of the costs and risks. But the risks of learning to do business in a new culture diminish if the company acquires an established enterprise in the host country. Acquisitions, though, raise a whole set of additional problems, such as trying to marry divergent corporate cultures, and these problems may more than offset the benefits.

Choosing an Entry Strategy

The advantages and disadvantages of the various entry modes are summarized in Table 6.1. Inevitably, there are tradeoffs in choosing one entry mode over another. For example, when considering entry into an unfamiliar country with a track record of nationalizing foreign-owned enterprises, a company might favor a joint venture with a local enterprise. Its rationale might be that the local partner will help it establish operations in an unfamiliar environment and speak out against nationalization should the possibility arise. But if the company's distinctive competence is based on proprietary technology, entering into a joint venture might mean risking loss of control over that technology to the joint venture partner, which would make this strategy unattractive. Despite such hazards, some generalizations can be offered about the optimal choice of entry mode.

DISTINCTIVE COMPETENCES AND ENTRY MODE When companies expand internationally to earn greater returns from their differentiated product offerings, entering markets where indigenous competitors lack comparable products, the companies are pursuing an international strategy. The optimal entry mode for such companies depends to some degree on the nature of their distinctive competence. In particular, we need to distinguish between companies with a distinctive competence in technological know-how and those with a distinctive competence in management know-how.

If a company's competitive advantage—its distinctive competence—derives from its control of proprietary technological know-how, licensing and joint venture

Table 6.1

The Advantages and Disadvantages of Different Entry Modes

Entry Mode	Advantages	Disadvantages
Exporting	• Ability to realize location and scale economies	• High transport costs • Trade barriers • Problems with local marketing agents
Licensing	• Low development costs and risks	• Inability to realize location and scale economies • Inability to engage in global strategic coordination • Lack of control over technology
Franchising	• Low development costs and risks	• Inability to engage in global strategic coordination • Lack of control over quality
Joint ventures	• Access to local partner's knowledge • Shared development costs and risks • Political dependency	• Inability to engage in global strategic coordination • Inability to realize location and scale economies • Lack of control over technology
Wholly owned subsidiaries	• Protection of technology • Ability to engage in global strategic coordination • Ability to realize location and scale economies	• High costs and risks

arrangements should be avoided if possible, in order to minimize the risk of losing control of that technology. Thus, if a high-tech company is considering setting up operations in a foreign country in order to profit from a distinctive competence in technological know-how, it should probably do so through a wholly owned subsidiary.

However, this rule should not be viewed as a hard and fast one. For instance, a licensing or joint venture arrangement might be structured in such a way as to reduce the risks that a company's technological know-how will be expropriated by licensees or joint venture partners. We consider this kind of arrangement in more detail in Chapter 8, when we discuss the issue of structuring strategic alliances. In another exception to the rule, a company may perceive its technological advantage as being only transitory and expect rapid imitation of its core technology by competitors. In this situation, the company might want to license its technology as quickly as possible to foreign companies in order to gain global acceptance of its technology before imitation occurs.[22] Such a strategy has some advantages. By licensing its technology to competitors, the company may deter them from developing their own, possibly superior, technology. It also may be able to establish its technology as the dominant design in the industry (as Matsushita did with its VHS format for VCRs), ensuring a steady stream of royalty payments. Such situations apart, however, the attractions of licensing are probably outweighed by the risks of losing control of technology, and therefore licensing should be avoided.

The competitive advantage of many service companies, such as McDonald's or Hilton Hotels, is based on management know-how. For such companies, the risk of losing control of their management skills to franchisees or joint venture partners is not that great. The reason is that the valuable asset of such companies is their brand name, and brand names are generally well protected by international laws pertaining to trademarks. Given this fact, many of the issues that arise in the case of technological know-how do not arise in the case of management know-how. As a result, many service companies favor a combination of franchising and subsidiaries to control franchisees within a particular country or region. The subsidiary may be wholly owned or a joint venture. In most cases, however, service companies have found that entering into a joint venture with a local partner in order to set up a controlling subsidiary in a country or region works best because a joint venture is often politically more acceptable and brings a degree of local knowledge to the subsidiary.

PRESSURES FOR COST REDUCTION AND ENTRY MODE   The greater the pressures for cost reductions are, the more likely it is that a company will want to pursue some combination of exporting and wholly owned subsidiaries. By manufacturing in the locations where factor conditions are optimal and then exporting to the rest of the world, a company may be able to realize substantial location economies and substantial scale economies. The company might then want to export the finished product to marketing subsidiaries based in various countries. Typically, these subsidiaries would be wholly owned and have the responsibility for overseeing distribution in a particular country. Setting up wholly owned marketing subsidiaries is preferable to a joint venture arrangement or using a foreign marketing agent because it gives the company the tight control over marketing that might be required to coordinate a globally dispersed value chain. In addition, tight control over a local operation enables the company to use the profits generated in one market to improve its competitive position in another market. Hence companies pursuing global or transnational strategies prefer to establish wholly owned subsidiaries.

Summary of Chapter

1. For some companies, international expansion represents a way of earning greater returns by transferring the skills and product offerings derived from their distinctive competences to markets where indigenous competitors lack those skills.

2. Because of national differences, it pays a company to base each value creation activity it performs at the location where factor conditions are most conducive to the performance of that activity. This strategy focuses on the attainment of location economies.

3. By building sales volume more rapidly, international expansion can assist a company in the process of gaining a cost advantage through the realization of scale economies and learning effects.

4. The best strategy for a company to pursue may depend on the kind of pressures it must cope with: pressures for cost reductions or for local responsiveness. Pressures for cost reductions are greatest in industries producing commodity-type products, where price is the main competitive weapon. Pressures for local responsiveness arise from differences in consumer tastes and preferences, as well as from national infrastructure and traditional practices, distribution channels, and host government demands.

5. Companies pursuing a global standardization strategy focus on reaping the cost reductions that come from scale economies and location economies.

6. Companies pursuing a localization strategy customize their product offering, marketing strategy, and business strategy to national conditions.

7. Many industries are now so competitive that companies must adopt a transnational strategy. This involves a simultaneous focus on reducing costs, transferring skills and products, and local responsiveness. Implementing such a strategy may not be easy.

8. Companies pursuing an international strategy transfer the skills and products derived from distinctive competences to foreign markets, while undertaking some limited local customization.

9. There are five different ways of entering a foreign market: exporting, licensing, franchising, entering into a joint venture, and setting up a wholly owned subsidiary. The optimal choice among entry modes depends on the company's strategy.

Discussion Questions

1. Plot the positions of the following companies on Figure 6.3: Procter & Gamble, IBM, Coca-Cola, Dow Chemical, Pfizer, and McDonald's. In each case, justify your answer.

2. Are the following global industries or are they characterized by local responsiveness: bulk chemicals, pharmaceuticals, branded food products, moviemaking, television manufacture, personal computers, airline travel, and cell phones?

3. Discuss how the need for control over foreign operations varies with the strategy and distinctive competences of a company. What are the implications of this relationship for the choice of entry mode?

4. Discuss this statement: Licensing proprietary technology to foreign competitors is the best way to give up a company's competitive advantage.

Practicing Strategic Management

SMALL-GROUP EXERCISE
Developing a Global Strategy

Break into groups of three to five people, and discuss the following scenario. Appoint one group member as a spokesperson who will communicate your findings to the class when called upon to do so by the instructor.

You work for a company in the soft drink industry that has developed a line of carbonated fruit-based drinks. You have already established a significant presence in your home market, and now you are planning the global strategy development of the company in the soft drink industry. You need to make a decision about the following:

1. What overall strategy to pursue—a global standardization strategy, localization strategy, international strategy, or transnational strategy

2. Which markets to enter first

3. What entry strategy to pursue—exporting, licensing, franchising, joint venture, or wholly owned subsidiary

What information do you need in order to make this kind of decision? On the basis of what you do know, what strategy would you recommend?

EXPLORING THE WEB
Visiting IBM

IBM stands for International Business Machines. Using the significant resources located at IBM's corporate website (**www.ibm.com**), including annual reports and company history, explain what the word *international* means in IBM. Specifically, in how many countries is IBM active? How does IBM create value by expanding into foreign markets? What entry mode does IBM adopt in most markets? Can you find any exceptions to this? How would you characterize IBM's strategy for competing in the global marketplace? Is IBM pursuing a transnational, global, international, or localization strategy?

General Task   Search the Web for a company site where there is a good description of that company's international operations. On the basis of this information, try to establish how the company enters foreign markets and what overall strategy it is pursuing (global, international, localization, transnational).

CLOSING CASE

IKEA—The Global Retailer

IKEA may be the world's most successful global retailer. Established by Ingvar Kamprad in Sweden in 1943 when he was just seventeen years old, the home furnishing superstore has grown into a global cult brand, with 230 stores in 33 countries that host 410 million shoppers a year and generate sales of €15 billion ($23 billion). Kamprad himself, who still owns the private company, is rumored to be the world's richest man.

IKEA's target market is members of the global middle class who are looking for low-priced but attractively designed furniture and household items. The company applies the same basic formula worldwide: Open large warehouse stores, festooned in the blue and yellow colors of the Swedish flag, that offer 8,000 to 10,000 items from kitchen cabinets to candlesticks. Use wacky promotions to drive traffic into the stores. Configure the interiors of the stores so that customers have to pass through each department to get to the checkout. Add restaurants and child care facilities so that shoppers stay as long as possible. Price the items as low as possible. Make sure that product design reflects the simple, clean Swedish lines that have become IKEA's trademark. And then watch the results—customers who enter the store planning to buy a $40 coffee table and end up spending $500 on everything from storage units to kitchenware.

IKEA aims to reduce the price of its offerings by 2 to 3% per year, which requires relentless attention to cost cutting. With a network of 1,300 suppliers in fifty-three countries, IKEA devotes considerable attention to finding the right manufacturer for each item. Consider the company's best-selling Klippan loveseat. Designed in 1980, the Klippan, with its clean lines, bright colors, simple legs, and compact size, has sold some 1.5 million units since its introduction. After originally manufacturing it in Sweden, IKEA soon transferred production to lower-cost suppliers in Poland. As demand for the Klippan grew, IKEA decided that it made more sense to work with suppliers in each of the company's big markets to avoid the costs associated with shipping the product all over the world. Today, there are five suppliers of the frames in Europe, plus three in the United States and two in China. To reduce the cost of the cotton slipcovers, production has been concentrated in four core suppliers in China and Europe. The resulting efficiencies from these global sourcing decisions enabled IKEA to reduce the price of the Klippan by some 40% between 1999 and 2006.

Despite its standard formula, however, IKEA has found that global success requires that it adapt its offerings to the tastes and preferences of consumers in different nations. IKEA first discovered this in the early 1990s, when it entered the United States. The company soon found that its European-style offerings didn't always resonate with American consumers. Beds were measured in centimeters, not the king, queen, and twin sizes that Americans are familiar with. Sofas weren't big enough, wardrobe drawers were not deep enough, glasses were too small, curtains were too short, and kitchens didn't fit U.S.-size appliances. Since then, IKEA has redesigned its offerings in the United States to appeal to American consumers and has been rewarded with stronger store sales. The same process is now unfolding in China, where the company plans to have ten stores by 2010. The store layout in China reflects the layout of many Chinese apartments: since many Chinese apartments have balconies, IKEA's Chinese stores include a balcony section. IKEA has had to adapt its locations in China, where car ownership is still not widespread. In the West IKEA stores are generally located in suburban areas and have lots of parking space, but in China they are located near public transportation and IKEA offers delivery services so that Chinese customers can get their purchases home.[c]

Case Discussion Questions

1. How is IKEA profiting from global expansion? What is the essence of its strategy for creating value by expanding internationally?

2. How would you characterize IKEA's original strategic posture in foreign markets? What were the strengths of this posture? What were its weaknesses?

3. How has the strategic posture of IKEA changed as a result of its experiences in the United States? Why did it change its strategy?

4. How would you characterize the strategy of IKEA today?

TEST PREPPER

True/False Questions

___I___ **1.** The average tariff rate on manufactured goods traded between advanced nations has fallen from around 40% to under 4%.

___F___ **2.** The success of many multinational companies is based solely on the goods or services that are sold in foreign nations.

___I___ **3.** Location economies are the economic benefits that arise from performing a value creation activity in the optimal location for that activity, wherever in the world that might be.

___I___ **4.** Universal needs exist when the tastes and preferences of consumers in different nations are similar if not identical.

___I___ **5.** Companies that pursue a global standardization strategy focus on increasing profitability by reaping the cost reductions that come from scale economies and location economies.

___F___ **6.** Companies that pursue a transnational strategy tend to centralize product development functions such as R&D at home.

___I___ **7.** The greater the pressures for cost reductions are, the more likely it is that a company will want to pursue some combination of exporting and wholly owned subsidiaries.

Multiple-Choice Questions

8. Low pressure for local responsiveness combined with low pressure for cost reductions suggests a/an _____ strategy?
  a. universal
  b. global standardization
  c. localization
  d. transnational
  e. international

9. Among strategies for entering into international operations, _____ offers the lowest level of control.
  a. exporting
  b. licensing
  c. a joint venture
  d. franchising
  e. a wholly owned subsidiary

10. Creating pressure for local responsiveness are all of the following *except* _____.
  a. differences in customer tastes
  b. differences in customer preferences
  c. differences in infrastructure
  d. differences in distributions channels
  e. differences in localization strategy

11. The four main strategic postures that companies choose when competing internationally include all of the following *except* _____.
  a. global standardization strategy
  b. localization strategy
  c. international licensing strategy
  d. transnational strategy
  e. international strategy

12. _____ avoids the costs of establishing manufacturing operations in the host country, which are often substantial, and may be consistent with scale economies and location economies.
  a. Licensing
  b. Exporting
  c. Franchising
  d. A joint venture
  e. A wholly owned subsidiary

13. The disadvantages of licensing as an entry mode include all of the following *except* _____.
  a. the inability to realize location and scale economies
  b. the lack of control over quality
  c. the ability to engage in global strategic coordination
  d. the lack of control over technology
  e. none of the above

14. A _____ is a business in which a parent company owns 100% of the stock.
  a. joint venture
  b. wholly owned subsidiary
  c. strategic alliance
  d. franchising operation
  e. licensing operation

15. All of the following are advantages of a joint venture *except* _____.
  a. having complete control of the operation of the entity
  b. benefiting from local partners' knowledge about the foreign market
  c. sharing development costs with a local partner
  d. sharing the risks of opening up a foreign market with a local partner
  e. gaining access to markets that are often closed to foreign investors

Chapter 7

Corporate-Level Strategy and Long-Run Profitability

Learning Objectives

After reading this chapter, you should be able to

1. Discuss the arguments for and against concentrating a company's resources and competing in just one industry

2. Explain the conditions under which a company is likely to pursue vertical integration as a means to strengthen its position in its core industry

3. Appreciate the conditions under which a company can create more value through diversification and why there is a limit to successful diversification

4. Understand why restructuring a company is often necessary and discuss the pros and cons of the strategies a company can adopt to exit businesses and industries

Chapter Outline

I. Concentration on a Single Industry
   a. Horizontal Integration
   b. Benefits and Costs of Horizontal Integration
   c. Outsourcing Functional Activities
II. Vertical Integration
   a. Arguments for Vertical Integration
   b. Arguments Against Vertical Integration
   c. Vertical Integration and Outsourcing
III. Entering New Industries Through Diversification
   a. Creating Value Through Diversification
   b. Related versus Unrelated Diversification
IV. Restructuring and Downsizing
   a. Why Restructure?
   b. Exit Strategies

Overview

The principal concern of corporate-level strategy is to identify the industry or industries a company should participate in to maximize its long-run profitability. A company has several options when choosing which industries to compete in. First, a company can concentrate on only one industry and focus its activities on developing business-level strategies to improve its competitive position in that industry (see Chapter 5). Second, a company may decide to enter new industries in adjacent stages of the industry value chain by pursuing a strategy of *vertical integration*, which means

162

Supplier
Distribution
③

it begins to make its own inputs and/or sell its own products. Third, a company can choose to enter new industries that may or may not be connected to its existing industry by pursuing a strategy of *diversification*. Finally, a company may choose to exit businesses and industries to increase its long-run profitability and to shrink the boundaries of the organization by restructuring and downsizing its activities.

In this chapter, we explore these different alternatives and discuss the pros and cons of each as a method of increasing a company's profitability over time. The chapter repeatedly stresses that if corporate-level strategy is to increase long-run profitability, it must enable a company, or its different business units, to perform one or more value creation functions at a *lower cost* and/or in a way that leads to increased *differentiation* (and thus a premium price). Thus, successful corporate-level strategy works to build a company's distinctive competences and increase its competitive advantage over industry rivals. There is, therefore, a very important link between corporate-level strategy and creating competitive advantage at the business level.

Concentration on a Single Industry

concentration on a single industry

The strategy a company adopts when it focuses its resources and capabilities on competing successfully within a particular product market.

For many companies, the appropriate choice of corporate-level strategy entails **concentration on a single industry**, whereby a company focuses its resources and capabilities on competing successfully within the confines of a particular product market. Examples of companies that currently pursue such a strategy include McDonald's with its focus on the fast-food restaurant market, Starbucks with its focus on the premium coffee shop business, and Neiman Marcus with its focus on luxury department store retailing. These companies have chosen to stay in one industry because there are several advantages to concentrating on the needs of customers in just one product market (and the different segments within it).

A major advantage of concentrating on a single industry is that doing so enables a company to focus all its managerial, financial, technological, and functional resources and capabilities on developing strategies to strengthen its competitive position in just one business. This strategy is important in fast-growing industries that make heavy demands on a company's resources and capabilities but also offer the prospect of substantial long-term profits if a company can sustain its competitive advantage. For example, it would make little sense for a company such as Starbucks to enter new industries such as supermarkets or specialty doughnuts when the coffee shop industry is still in a period of rapid growth and when finding new ways to compete successfully would impose significant demands on Starbucks' managerial, marketing, and financial resources and capabilities. In fact, companies that spread their resources too thin, in order to compete in several different product markets, run the risk of starving their fast-growing core business of the resources needed to expand rapidly. The result is loss of competitive advantage in the core business and—often—failure.

Nor is it just rapidly growing companies that benefit from focusing their resources and capabilities on one business, market, or industry. Many mature companies that expand over time into too many different businesses and markets find out later that they have stretched their scarce resources too far and that their performance declines as a result. For example, Sears found that its decision to enter into financial services and real estate diverted top management's attention from its core retailing business at a time when competition from Wal-Mart and Target was increasing. The result was a major decline in profitability. Concentrating on a single business allows a company to "stick to the knitting"—that is, to focus on doing what it knows best and avoid entering new businesses it knows little about and where it can create little value.[1] This prevents companies from becoming involved in businesses that their managers do not understand and where their poor, uninformed decision making can result in huge losses.

On the other hand, concentrating on just one market or industry can result in disadvantages emerging over time. As we discuss later in the chapter, a certain amount of vertical integration may be necessary to strengthen a company's competitive advantage within its core industry. Moreover, companies that concentrate on just one industry may miss out on opportunities to create more value and increase their profitability by using their resources and capabilities to make and sell products in *other* markets or industries.

Horizontal Integration

horizontal integration

Acquiring or merging with industry competitors to achieve the competitive advantages that come with large size.

acquisition

A company's use of capital resources, such as stock, debt, or cash, to purchase another company.

merger

An agreement between two companies to pool their operations and create a new business entity.

For many companies, as we have just noted, profitable growth and expansion often entail concentrating on competing successfully within a single industry. One tactic or tool that has been widely used at the corporate level to help managers position their companies to compete better in an industry is horizontal integration, which we discussed briefly in Chapter 5. **Horizontal integration** is the process of acquiring or merging with industry competitors in an effort to achieve the competitive advantages that come with large size or scale. An **acquisition** occurs when one company uses its capital resources (such as stock, debt, or cash) to purchase another company, and a **merger** is an agreement between two companies to pool their resources in a combined operation. For example, Rupert Murdoch, CEO of News Corp, made scores of acquisitions in the newspaper industry so that all his newspapers could reduce costs by taking advantage of the news and stories written by News Corp journalists anywhere in the world.

In industry after industry, there have been thousands of mergers and acquisitions over the past decades. In the auto industry, GM acquired Saab and Daewoo; in the aerospace industry, Boeing merged with McDonnell Douglas to create the world's largest aerospace company; in the pharmaceutical industry, Pfizer acquired Warner-Lambert to become the largest pharmaceutical firm; in the computer hardware industry, Compaq acquired Digital Equipment and then was itself acquired by HP; and in the Internet industry, Yahoo!, Google, and AOL have taken over hundreds of small Internet companies to better position themselves in segments such as streaming video, music downloading, and digital photography.

The result of wave upon wave of global mergers and acquisitions has been to increase the level of concentration in most industries. Twenty years ago, cable television was dominated by a patchwork of thousands of small family-owned businesses, but by the 2000s three companies controlled over two-thirds of the market. In 1990, the three main publishers of college textbooks accounted for 35% of the market; by 2008, they accounted for over 75%. In semiconductor chips, mergers and acquisitions among the industry leaders resulted in the four largest firms controlling 85% of the global market in 2007, up from 45% in 1997. Why is this happening? An answer can be found by examining the ways in which horizontal integration can improve the competitive position and profitability of companies that decide to stay within one industry.

Benefits and Costs of Horizontal Integration

Managers who pursue horizontal integration have decided that the best way to increase their company's profitability is to invest its capital to purchase the resources and assets of industry competitors. Profitability increases when horizontal integration lowers operating costs, increases product differentiation, reduces rivalry within an industry, and/or increases a company's bargaining power over suppliers and buyers.

LOWER OPERATING COSTS Horizontal integration lowers a company's operating costs when it results in increasing economies of scale. Suppose there are five major competitors, each of which owns a manufacturing plant in every region of the United States, but none of these plants is operating at full capacity (so costs are relatively high). If one competitor buys up another and shuts down that competitor's plant, it can then operate its own plant at full capacity and so reduce manufacturing costs.

Achieving economies of scale is very important in industries that have high fixed costs, because large-scale production allows a company to spread its fixed costs over a large volume, which drives down average operating costs. In the telecommunications industry, for example, the fixed costs of building a fiber-optic or wireless network are very high, so to make such an investment pay off, a company needs a large volume of customers. Thus, companies such as AT&T and Verizon acquired many large telecommunications companies in order to obtain those companies' customers, who were then "switched" to their network. This drives up network utilization and drives down the cost of serving each customer on the network. Similarly, mergers and acquisitions in the pharmaceutical industry are often driven by the need to realize scale economies in sales and marketing. The fixed costs of building a nationwide pharmaceutical sales force are very high, and pharmaceutical companies need to have a large number of drugs to sell if they are to use their sales force effectively. For example, Pfizer acquired Warner-Lambert because its combined sales force would have many more products to sell when salespeople visited physicians, an advantage that would increase their productivity.

A company can also lower its operating costs when horizontal integration eliminates the need for two sets of corporate head offices, two separate sales forces, and so on, such that the costs of operating the combined company fall. One thing that HP considered when making its decision to acquire rival computer maker Compaq was that the combined company would save $2.5 billion in R&D and marketing costs, which would enable it to better compete with Dell. This had proved correct by 2007, when HP announced record sales and profits based on its new low-cost capabilities.

INCREASED PRODUCT DIFFERENTIATION Horizontal integration may also boost profitability when it increases product differentiation, by, for example, allowing a company to combine the product lines of merged companies in order to offer customers a wider range of products that can be bundled together. **Product bundling** involves offering customers the opportunity to buy a complete range of products they need at a single, combined price. This increases the value that customers see in a company's product line, because (1) they often obtain a price discount by purchasing products as a set and (2) they get used to dealing with just one company. For this reason, a company may obtain a competitive advantage from increased product differentiation.

An early example of the value of product bundling is provided by Microsoft Office, which is a bundle of different software programs, including a word processor, spreadsheet, and presentation program. At the beginning of the 1990s, Microsoft was number 2 or 3 in each of these product categories, behind companies such as WordPerfect (which led in the word-processing category), Lotus (which had the best-selling spreadsheet), and Harvard Graphics (which had the best-selling presentation software). When it offered all three programs in a single-price package, however, Microsoft presented consumers with a superior value proposition. Its product bundle quickly gained market share, ultimately accounting for more than 90% of all sales of word-processing, spreadsheet, and presentation software.

product bundling

The strategy of offering customers the opportunity to buy a complete range of products at a single, combined price.

③

REDUCED INDUSTRY RIVALRY Horizontal integration can help to reduce industry rivalry in two ways. First, acquiring or merging with a competitor helps to eliminate excess capacity in an industry, which, as we saw in Chapter 5, often triggers price wars. By taking excess capacity out of an industry, horizontal integration creates a more benign environment in which prices might stabilize or even increase.

In addition, by reducing the number of competitors in an industry, horizontal integration often makes it easier to use tacit price coordination among rivals. (Tacit coordination is coordination reached without communication; explicit communication to fix prices is illegal.) In general, the larger the number of competitors in an industry, the more difficult it is to establish an informal pricing agreement, such as price leadership by a dominant firm, which reduces the chances that a price war will erupt. Horizontal integration makes it easier for rivals to coordinate their actions because it increases industry concentration and creates an oligopoly.

Both of these motives seem to have been behind HP's acquisition of Compaq. The PC industry was suffering from significant excess capacity, and a serious price war was raging, triggered by Dell's desire to dominate the market. HP knew that by acquiring Compaq it could remove excess capacity from the industry and reduce the number of competitors so that some pricing discipline (and price increases) would emerge in the industry. By 2005, this happened when Dell, the market leader, increased the price of many of its PCs by 10% or more, signaling to HP that it would not start a new price war unless HP did. Since 2005, the companies have begun to compete more on the basis of the features of their PCs, especially the size, screen quality, and multimedia capabilities of their laptops.

④

INCREASED BARGAINING POWER A final reason for a company to use horizontal integration is to achieve more bargaining power over suppliers or buyers, which strengthens its competitive position and increases its profitability at their expense. By using horizontal integration to consolidate its industry, a company becomes a much larger buyer of a supplier's product; it can use this buying power as leverage to bargain down the price it pays for inputs, and this also lowers its costs. Similarly, a company that acquires its competitors controls a greater percentage of an industry's final product or output, and so buyers become more dependent on it. Other things being equal, the company now has more power to raise prices and profits, because customers have less choice of suppliers from whom to buy. When a company has greater ability to raise prices to buyers or to bargain down the price it pays for inputs, it has increased market power.

Although horizontal integration can clearly strengthen a company's competitive position in several ways, this strategy does have some problems and limitations. As we discuss in detail in Chapter 8, the gains that are anticipated from mergers and acquisitions often are not realized for a number of reasons. These include problems associated with merging very different company cultures, high management turnover in the acquired company when the acquisition was a hostile one, and a tendency for managers to overestimate the benefits to be had from a merger or acquisition and to underestimate the problems involved in merging their operations. For example, there was considerable opposition to the merger between HP and Compaq because critics believed that HP's former CEO, Carly Fiorina, was glossing over the difficulties and costs associated with merging the operations of these two companies, which had very different cultures. As it turned out, she was right and the merger went smoothly; however, it took longer than she expected and she was removed as CEO before the benefits of her strategy were apparent.

Another problem with horizontal integration is that when a company uses it to become a dominant industry competitor, an attempt to keep using the strategy to grow even larger brings the company into conflict with the Federal Trade Commission (FTC), the government agency responsible for enforcing antitrust laws. Antitrust authorities are concerned about the potential for abuse of market power; they believe that more competition is better for consumers than less competition. They worry that large companies that dominate their industry are in a position to abuse their market power and raise prices above the level that would exist in a more competitive environment. The FTC also believes that dominant companies may use their market power to crush potential competitors by, for example, cutting prices whenever new competitors enter a market and so forcing them out of business and then raising prices again once the threat has been eliminated. Because of these concerns, the antitrust authorities may block any merger or acquisition that they perceive as creating too much consolidation and the potential for future abuse of market power.

● Outsourcing Functional Activities

A second tactic that a company may deploy to improve its competitive position in an industry is to outsource one or more of its own value creation functions and contract with another company to perform that activity on its behalf. In recent years, the amount of outsourcing of functional activities, especially manufacturing and information technology (IT) activities, has grown enormously.[2] The expansion of global outsourcing has become one of the most significant trends in modern strategic management, as companies seek not only to improve their competitive advantage at home but also to compete more effectively in today's cutthroat global environment.

We discussed this trend in Chapter 6 and noted that the outsourcing of functions begins with a company identifying those value chain activities that form the basis of its competitive advantage—that give it its distinctive competences. A company's goal is to nurture and protect these vital functions and competences by performing them internally. The remaining noncore functional activities are then reviewed to see whether they can be performed more efficiently and effectively by specialist companies either at home or abroad. If they can, these activities are outsourced to specialists in manufacturing, distribution, IT, and so on. The relationships between the company and its subcontractors are then structured by a competitive bidding process; subcontractors compete for a company's business for a specified price and length of time. The term **virtual corporation** has been coined to describe companies that outsource most of their functional activities and focus on one or a few core value chain functions.[3]

virtual corporation

A company that outsources most of its functional activities and focuses on one or a few core value chain functions.

Xerox is one company that has significantly increased its use of outsourcing in recent years. It decided that its distinctive competences are in the design and manufacture of photocopying systems. Accordingly, to reduce costs Xerox outsourced the responsibility for performing its noncore value chain activities, such as its IT, to other companies. For example, Xerox has a $3.2 billion contract with Electronic Data Systems (EDS), a global IT consulting company, to manage and maintain all Xerox's internal computer and telecommunications networks. As part of this relationship, 1,700 Xerox employees were transferred to EDS.[4] As another example, Nike, the world's largest maker of athletic shoes, has outsourced all its manufacturing operations to Asian partners, while keeping its core product design and marketing capabilities in-house.

ADVANTAGES AND DISADVANTAGES OF OUTSOURCING There are several advantages to outsourcing functional activities.[5] First, outsourcing a particular noncore activity to a specialist company that is more efficient at performing that activity than the company itself lowers a company's operating costs. Second, a specialist often has a distinctive competence in a particular functional activity, so the specialist can help the company better differentiate its products. For example, Convergys, formerly a division of phone company Cincinnati Bell, developed a distinctive competence in the customer care function, which includes activating accounts, billing customers, and dealing with customer inquiries. To take advantage of this competence, other phone companies, and more recently other large companies such as Ann Taylor, Nortel Networks, and Wachovia, have decided to outsource their customer care function to Convergys; they recognize that it can provide better customer care service than they can. Thus, Convergys helps its client companies to better differentiate their service offerings.

A third advantage of outsourcing is that it enables a company to concentrate scarce human, financial, and physical resources on further strengthening its core competences. Thus, Nortel and Wachovia can devote their energies to building wireless networks and providing insurance, secure in the knowledge that Convergys is providing first-class customer care.

On the other hand, there are some disadvantages associated with outsourcing functions. A company that outsources an activity loses both the ability to learn from that activity and the opportunity to transform that activity into one of its distinctive competences. Thus, although outsourcing customer care activities to Convergys may make sense right now for Nortel, a potential problem is that it will not be building its own internal competence in customer care, which may become crucial in the future. A second drawback of outsourcing is that in its enthusiasm for outsourcing, a company may go too far and outsource value creation activities that are central to the maintenance of its competitive advantage. As a result, the company may lose control over the future development of a competence, and its performance may start to decline as a result. Finally, over time a company may become too dependent on a particular subcontractor. This may hurt the company if the performance of that supplier starts to deteriorate or if the supplier starts to use its power to demand higher prices from the company. These problems do not mean that strategic outsourcing should not be pursued, but they do suggest that managers should carefully weigh the pros and cons of the strategy before pursuing it and should negotiate contracts that prevent some of these problems.

In sum, the corporate strategy of concentrating on one industry may enable a company to significantly strengthen its competitive position in that industry, because such concentration may help it either to lower costs or to better differentiate its products. Both horizontal integration and outsourcing functional activities are powerful tools that help a company make better use of its resources and capabilities and build its competitive advantage over time. To the extent that a company becomes the dominant industry competitor, it also gains increasing market power that helps it to increase its long-run profitability.

Vertical Integration

Vertical integration is a corporate-level strategy that involves a company's entering new industries to increase its long-run profitability. Once again, the justification for pursuing vertical integration is that a company is able to enter new industries that *add value* to the core products it makes and sells because entry into these new industries increases the core products' differentiated appeal or reduces the costs of making them.

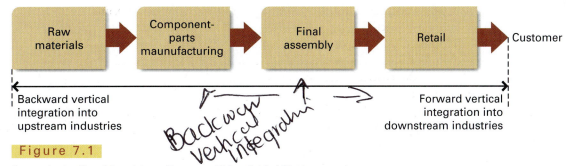

Figure 7.1

Stages in the Raw-Materials-to-Customer Value-Added Chain

vertical integration

A strategy in which a company expands its operations either backward into industries that produce inputs for its core products *(backward vertical integration)* or forward into industries that use, distribute, or sell its products *(forward vertical integration).*

When a company pursues a strategy of **vertical integration**, it expands its operations either backward into industries that produce inputs for its core products *(backward vertical integration)* or forward into industries that use, distribute, or sell its products *(forward vertical integration)*. To enter a new industry, a company may establish its own operations and create the set of value chain functions it needs to compete effectively in this industry. Alternatively, it may acquire or merge with a company that is already in the industry. A steel company that establishes the value chain operations necessary to supply its iron ore needs from company-owned iron ore mines exemplifies backward integration. A PC maker that sells its laptops through a nationwide chain of company-owned retail outlets illustrates forward integration. For example, Apple Computer entered the retail industry when it decided to set up the value chain functions necessary to sell its computers and iPods through Apple Stores. IBM is a highly vertically integrated company. It integrated backward and entered the microprocessor and disk drive industries to produce the major components that go into its computers. It also integrated forward and established the value chain functions necessary to compete in the computer software and IT consulting services industries.

Figure 7.1 illustrates four *main* stages in a typical raw-materials-to-customer value-added chain. For a company based in the final assembly stage, backward integration means moving into component-parts manufacturing and raw materials production. Forward integration means moving into distribution and sales. At each stage in the chain, *value is added* to the product, which means that a company at that stage takes the product produced in the previous stage and transforms it in some way so that it is worth more to the company at the next stage in the chain and, ultimately, to the customer.

It is important to note that each stage of the value-added chain is a *separate industry or industries* in which many different companies may be competing. And within each industry, every company has a value chain composed of the functions we discussed in Chapter 4: R&D, manufacturing, marketing, customer service, and so on. In other words, we can think of a value chain that runs *across* industries, and embedded within that are the value chains of companies *within* each industry.

As an example of the value-added concept, consider the production chain involved in the PC industry illustrated in Figure 7.2. Companies in the raw materials stage of the PC value chain include the manufacturers of specialty ceramics, chemicals, and metals, such as Kyocera of Japan, which makes the ceramic substrate for semiconductors. Raw materials companies sell their output to the manufacturers of intermediate or component products. Intermediate manufacturers, which include companies such

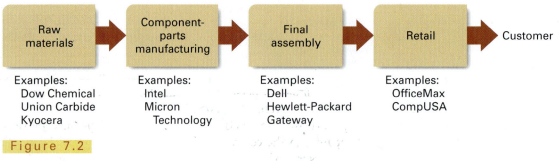

Figure 7.2

The Raw-Materials-to-Customer Value-Added Chain in the Personal Computer Industry

as Intel, Seagate, and Samsung, transform the ceramics, chemicals, and metals they purchase into computer components such as microprocessors, disk drives, and flash memory chips. In doing so, they *add value* to the raw materials they purchase.

In turn, at the final assembly stage, these components are sold to companies such as Apple, Dell, and HP, which take these components and transform them into PCs—that is, they add value to the components they purchase. Many of the completed PCs are then sold to distributors such as Wal-Mart, OfficeMax, and Staples, which in turn sell them to final customers. The distributors also add value to the product by making it accessible to customers and by providing PC service and support. Thus, value is added by companies at each stage in the raw-materials-to-customer chain.

As a corporate-level strategy, vertical integration gives companies a choice about which industries in the raw-materials-to-consumer chain they should compete in to maximize long-run profitability. In the PC industry, most companies have not entered industries in adjacent stages because of the many advantages of specialization and concentration on one industry. However, there are exceptions, such as IBM and HP, which are involved in several different industries.

● Arguments for Vertical Integration

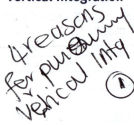

A company pursues vertical integration to strengthen its competitive position in its original or core business.[6] There are four main reasons for pursuing a vertical integration strategy: (1) it enables the company to build barriers to new competition, (2) it facilitates investments in efficiency-enhancing specialized assets, (3) it protects product quality, and (4) it results in improved scheduling.

BUILDING BARRIERS TO ENTRY   By vertically integrating backward to gain control over the source of critical inputs or by vertically integrating forward to gain control over distribution channels, a company can build barriers to new entry into its industry. To the extent that this strategy is effective, it limits competition in the company's industry, thereby enabling the company to charge a higher price and make greater profits than it could otherwise.[7] To grasp this argument, consider a famous example of this strategy from the 1930s.

At that time, the commercial smelting of aluminum was pioneered by companies such as Alcoa and Alcan. Aluminum is derived from smelting bauxite. Although bauxite is a common mineral, the percentage of aluminum in bauxite is usually so low that it is not economical to mine and smelt. During the 1930s, only one large-scale deposit of bauxite had been discovered where the percentage of aluminum in the mineral made smelting economical. This deposit was on the Caribbean island of

Jamaica. Alcoa and Alcan vertically integrated backward and acquired ownership of this deposit. This action created a barrier to entry into the aluminum industry. Potential competitors were deterred from entry because they could not get access to high-grade bauxite; it was all owned by Alcoa and Alcan. Because they had to use lower-grade bauxite, those that did enter the industry found themselves at a cost disadvantage. This situation persisted until the 1950s, when new high-grade deposits were discovered in Australia and Indonesia.

During the 1970s and 1980s, a similar strategy was pursued by vertically integrated companies in the computer industry, such as IBM and Digital Equipment. These companies manufactured the main components of computers (such as microprocessors and memory chips), designed and assembled the computers, produced the software that ran the computers, and sold the final product directly to end users. The original rationale behind this strategy was that many of the key components and software used in computers contained proprietary elements. These companies reasoned that by producing the proprietary technology in-house, they could limit rivals' access to it, thereby building barriers to entry. Thus, when IBM introduced its PS/2 PC system in the mid-1980s, it announced that certain component parts incorporating proprietary technology would be manufactured in-house by IBM.

This strategy worked well from the 1960s until the early 1980s, but it has been failing since then, particularly in the PC and server segments of the industry. In the early 1990s, the worst performers in the computer industry were precisely the companies that had pursued the vertical integration strategy: IBM and Digital Equipment. Why? The shift to open standards in computer hardware and software nullified the advantages to computer companies of extensive vertical integration. In addition, new PC companies such as Dell took advantage of open standards to search out the world's lowest-cost producer of every PC component in order to drive down costs, effectively circumventing this barrier to entry. In 2005, IBM sold its loss-making PC unit to a Chinese company, and what was left of Digital was swallowed up by Compaq, which, as we noted earlier, was then integrated into HP.

specialized asset

A value creation tool that is designed to perform a specific set of activities and whose value creation potential is significantly lower in its next-best use.

FACILITATING INVESTMENTS IN SPECIALIZED ASSETS A **specialized asset** is a value creation tool that is designed to perform a specific set of activities and whose value creation potential is *significantly* lower in its next-best use.[8] A specialized asset may be a piece of equipment used to make only one kind of product, or it may be the know-how or skills that a person or company has acquired through training and experience. Companies invest in specialized assets because these assets allow them to lower the costs of value creation and/or to better differentiate their products from those of competitors—which permits premium pricing.

A company might invest in specialized equipment because that equipment enables it to lower its manufacturing costs and increase its quality, or it might invest in developing highly specialized technological knowledge because doing so allows it to develop better products than its rivals. Thus, specialization can be the basis for achieving a competitive advantage at the business level.

Why does a company have to vertically integrate and invest in the specialized assets itself? Why can't another company perform this function? Because it may be very difficult to persuade other companies in adjacent stages in the raw-materials-to-customer value-added chain to undertake investments in specialized assets. To realize the economic gains associated with specialized assets, the company may have to vertically integrate into such adjacent stages and make the investments itself.

As an illustration, imagine that Ford has developed a new high-performance, high-quality, uniquely designed fuel injector. The injector will increase fuel efficiency, which in turn will help differentiate Ford's cars from those of its rivals and give it a competitive advantage. Ford has to decide whether to make the injector in-house (vertical integration) or contract its manufacture out to an independent supplier. Manufacturing these fuel injectors requires substantial investments in equipment that can be used only for this purpose. Because of its unique design, the equipment cannot be used to manufacture any other type of injector for Ford or any other carmaker. Thus, the investment in this equipment constitutes an investment in specialized assets.

First consider this situation from the perspective of an independent supplier that has been asked by Ford to make this investment. The supplier might reason that once it has made the investment, it will be dependent on Ford for business because Ford is the only possible customer for this equipment. The supplier perceives this as putting Ford in a strong bargaining position and worries that the carmaker might use this position to force down the price it pays for the injectors. Given this risk, the supplier declines to invest in the specialized equipment.

Now consider Ford's position. Ford might reason that if it contracts out production of these fuel injectors to an independent supplier, it might become too dependent on that supplier for a vital input. Because specialized equipment is needed to produce the injector, Ford cannot easily switch its orders to other suppliers that lack the equipment. Ford perceives this as increasing the bargaining power of the supplier and worries that the supplier might use its bargaining strength to demand higher prices.

The situation of *mutual dependence* that would be created by this investment in specialized assets makes Ford hesitant to contract out and makes any potential suppliers hesitant to undertake the investments in specialized assets required to produce the fuel injectors. The real problem here is a lack of trust: neither Ford nor the supplier trusts the other to play fair in this situation. The lack of trust arises from the risk of *holdup*—that is, the risk of being taken advantage of by a trading partner after the investment in specialized assets has been made.[9] Because of this risk, Ford might reason that the only safe way to get the new fuel injectors is to manufacture them itself.

To generalize from this example, consider that, when achieving a competitive advantage requires one company to make investments in specialized assets in order to trade with another, the risk of holdup may serve as a deterrent, and the investment may not take place. Consequently, the potential gains from lower costs or increased differentiation will not be realized. To obtain these gains, companies must vertically integrate into adjacent stages in the value chain. This consideration has driven automobile companies to vertically integrate backward into the production of component parts, steel companies to vertically integrate backward into the production of iron, computer companies to vertically integrate backward into chip production, and aluminum companies to vertically integrate backward into bauxite mining.

PROTECTING PRODUCT QUALITY By protecting product quality, vertical integration enables a company to become a differentiated player in its core business. The banana industry illustrates this situation. Historically, a problem facing food companies that import bananas was the variable quality of delivered bananas, which often arrived on the shelves of American stores either too ripe or not ripe enough. To correct this problem, major U.S. food companies such as General Foods have integrated backward to gain control over supply sources. Consequently, they have been able to distribute bananas of a standard quality at the optimal time for consumption. Knowing they can rely on the quality of these brands, consumers are willing to pay more for them. Thus, by vertically integrating backward into plantation ownership, the banana companies have built consumer confidence, which enables them to charge a premium price for their product. Similarly, when McDonald's decided to open up its first restaurant in Moscow, it found, much to its initial dismay, that in order to serve food and drink indistinguishable from that served in McDonald's restaurants elsewhere, it had to vertically integrate backward and supply its own needs. The quality of Russian-grown potatoes and meat was simply too poor. Thus, to protect the quality of its product, McDonald's set up its own dairy farms, cattle ranches, vegetable plots, and food-processing plant within Russia.

The same kinds of considerations can result in forward integration. Ownership of distribution outlets may be necessary if the required standards of after-sale service for complex products are to be maintained. For example, in the 1920s Kodak owned retail outlets for distributing photographic equipment. The company felt that few established retail outlets had the skills necessary to sell and service its photographic equipment. By the 1930s, however, Kodak had decided that it no longer needed to own its retail outlets, because other retailers had begun to provide satisfactory distribution and service for Kodak products. The company then withdrew from retailing. Now, in the 2000s, Kodak has a chain of digital photo-processing booths that it has established to attract people to use its paper, digital cameras, and other products.

● Arguments Against Vertical Integration

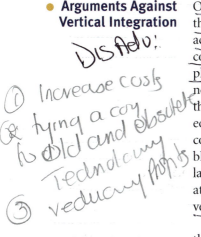

Over time, however, vertical integration can result in some major disadvantages. Even though it is often undertaken to reduce production costs, vertical integration may actually increase costs when a company has to purchase high-cost inputs from company-owned suppliers despite the existence of low-cost external sources of supply. For example, during the early 1990s General Motors made 68% of the component parts for its vehicles in-house, more than any other major automaker (at Chrysler the figure was 30%, and at Toyota 28%). This high level of vertical integration resulted in GM being the highest-cost global carmaker, and despite its attempts to reduce costs, such as spinning off its Delco components division, GM was still in deep trouble in 2006.[10] Indeed, Delco was forced to declare bankruptcy in 2005 to try to reduce labor costs, and GM has been working hard with the UAW to find ways to cut operating costs in order to survive in the battle against efficient Japanese carmakers. Thus, vertical integration can be a major disadvantage when operating costs increase.

Frequently, the operating costs of company-owned suppliers become higher than those of independent suppliers because managers know that they can always sell their components to their company's assembly divisions—which are captive buyers. For example, GM's glass-making division knows it can sell its products to GM's car-making divisions. Because they do not have to compete for orders, company suppliers have less incentive to be efficient and find ways to reduce operating costs. Indeed, the managers of the supply divisions may be tempted to pass on any cost increases to other company divisions in the form of higher prices for components, rather than looking for ways to lower costs! This problem is far less serious, however, when the company pursues taper, rather than full, integration (see Figure 7.3).

A company pursues full integration when it produces *all* of a particular input needed for its processes or when it disposes of *all* of its output through its own operations. Taper integration occurs when a company buys some components from independent suppliers and some from company-owned suppliers, or when it sells some of its output through independent retailers and some through company-owned outlets. When a company pursues taper integration, as most companies do today, company-owned suppliers have to compete with independent suppliers. This

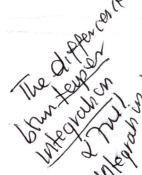

Figure 7.3

Full Integration and
Taper Integration

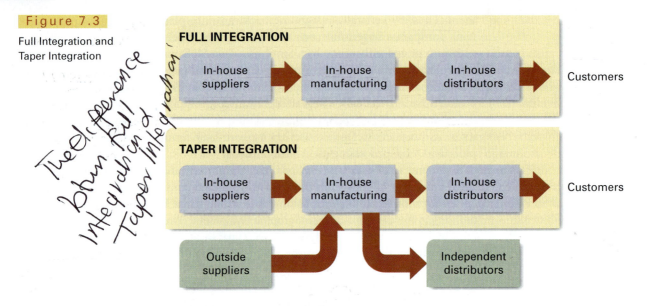

[handwritten note: The difference btwn Full Integration and Taper Integration]

gives managers a strong incentive to reduce costs; if they do not do so, a company might close down or sell off its component operations, which is what GM did when it spun off its Delco components division.

Another problem is that when technology is changing rapidly, a strategy of vertical integration often ties a company to old, obsolescent, high-cost technology.[11] In general, because a company has to develop value chain functions in each industry stage in which it operates, any significant changes in the environment of each industry, such as major changes in technology, can put its investment at risk. The more industries in which a company operates, the more risk it incurs.

On the one hand, vertical integration may create value and increase profitability when it lowers operating costs or increases differentiation. On the other hand, it can reduce profitability if a lack of cost-cutting incentive on the part of company-owned suppliers increases operating costs, or if the inability to change its technology quickly results in lower quality and reduced differentiation. How much vertical differentiation, then, should a company pursue? In general, a company should pursue vertical integration only if the extra value created by entering a new industry in the value chain exceeds the extra costs involved in managing its new operations when it decides to perform additional upstream or downstream value creation activities. Not all vertical integration opportunities have the same potential for value creation. Therefore, strategic managers will first vertically integrate into those industry stages that will realize the *most* value at the *least* cost. Then, when the extra value created by entering each new industry falls and the costs of managing exchanges along the industry value chain increase, managers stop the vertical integration process. Indeed (as we saw in the case of GM), if operating costs rise faster, over time, than the value being created in a particular industry, companies will *vertically disintegrate* and exit the industries that are now unprofitable. Clearly, there is a limit to how much a strategy of vertical integration can increase a company's long-run profitability.[12]

● Vertical Integration and Outsourcing

Can the advantages associated with vertical integration be obtained if a company makes agreements with specialized suppliers to perform specific upstream or downstream activities on its behalf? Under certain circumstances, companies can realize the advantages of vertical integration, without experiencing problems due to low in-

cooperative outsourcing relationship

centive to contain costs or due to changing technology, by entering into *cooperative outsourcing relationships* with suppliers or distributors. The advantages and disadvantages of outsourcing were discussed earlier in this chapter.

In general, research suggests that outsourcing promotes a company's competitive advantage when the company enters into long-term relationships or strategic alliances with its partners, because trust and goodwill build up between them over time. However, if a company enters into only short-term or "once and for all" contracts with suppliers or distributors, it is often unable to realize the gains associated with vertical integration through outsourcing. This is because its outsourcing partners have no incentive to take the long view and find ways to help the company reduce costs or improve product features or quality. For this reason, carmakers such as GM and DaimlerChrysler are increasingly forming long-term relationships with companies at different stages in the value chain.

Indeed, in 2005 Chrysler announced plans to outsource the assembly of some of its car bodies and transmissions to external suppliers—something that traditionally has been the task of a carmaker! However, Chrysler believes it can create more value by focusing on car engineering and design and leaving manufacturing to specialists. The popularity of vertical integration seems to be falling in an age when advanced IT and flexible manufacturing enable specialist manufacturers to achieve a competitive advantage over large "generalist" companies.

Entering New Industries Through Diversification

diversification

The process of entering one or more industries that are distinct or different from a company's core or original industry to find ways to use the company's distinctive competences to increase the value to customers of products it offers in those industries.

diversified company

A company that operates in two or more industries to find ways to increase long-run profitability.

● **Creating Value Through Diversification**

Diversification creates value in 3 ways

① ②

High-performing companies first choose corporate-level strategies that allow them to achieve the best competitive position in their core business or market. Then they may vertically integrate to strengthen their competitive advantage in that industry. Still later, they may decide to vertically disintegrate, exit the industry, and use outsourcing instead. At this point, strategic managers must make another decision about how to invest their company's growing resources and capital to maximize its long-run profitability: They must decide whether to pursue the corporate-level strategy of diversification.

Diversification is the process of entering one or more industries that are distinct or different from a company's core or original industry in order to find ways to use its distinctive competences to increase the value to customers of products in those industries. A **diversified company** is one that operates in two or more industries to find ways to increase its long-run profitability. In each industry a company enters, it establishes an operating division or business unit, which is essentially a *self-contained company* that performs a complete set of the value chain functions needed to make and sell products for that particular market. Once again, to increase profitability, a diversification strategy should enable the company, or its individual business units, to perform one or more of the value chain functions either at a *lower cost* or in a way that results in *higher differentiation* and premium prices.

Most companies first consider diversification when they are generating financial resources in excess of those necessary to maintain a competitive advantage in their original business or industry.[13] The question strategic managers must tackle is how to invest a company's excess resources in such a way that they will create the most value and profitability in the long run. Diversification can help a company create greater value in three main ways: (1) by permitting superior internal governance, (2) by transferring competences among businesses, and (3) by realizing economies of scope.

what is Internal governance

note

SUPERIOR INTERNAL GOVERNANCE The term *internal governance* refers to the manner in which the top executives of a company manage (or "govern") its business units, divisions, and functions. In a diversified company, effective or superior governance revolves around how well top managers can develop strategies that improve the competitive positioning of its business units in the industries where the units compete. Diversification creates value when top managers operate the company's different business units so effectively that they perform better than they would if they were *separate and independent companies.*[14]

It is important to recognize that this is *not* an easy thing to do. In fact, it is one of the most difficult tasks facing top managers—and the reason why some CEOs and other top executives are paid tens of millions of dollars a year. Certain senior executives develop superior skills in managing and overseeing the operation of many business units and pushing the managers in charge of these business units to achieve high performance. Examples include Jeffrey Immelt at General Electric, Bill Gates and Steve Ballmer at Microsoft, and Michael Dell at Dell.

Research suggests that the top, or corporate, managers who are successful at creating value through superior internal governance seem to make a number of similar kinds of strategic decisions. First, they organize the different business units of the company into self-contained divisions. For example, GE has over 300 self-contained divisions, including light bulbs, turbines, NBC, and so on. Second, these divisions tend to be managed by corporate executives in a highly decentralized fashion. Corporate executives do not get involved in the day-to-day operations of each division. Instead, they set challenging financial goals for each division, probe the general managers of each division about their strategy for attaining these goals, monitor divisional performance, and hold divisional managers accountable for that performance. Third, corporate managers are careful to link their internal monitoring and control mechanisms to incentive pay systems that reward divisional personnel for attaining, and especially for surpassing, performance goals. Although this may sound easy to do, in practice it requires highly skilled corporate executives to pull it off.

An extension of this approach is an **acquisition and restructuring strategy**, which involves corporate managers acquiring inefficient and poorly managed enterprises and then creating value by installing their superior internal governance in these acquired companies and restructuring their operations systems to improve their performance. This strategy can be considered diversification because the acquired company does not have to be in the same industry as the acquiring company.

The performance of an acquired company can be improved in various ways. First, the acquiring company usually replaces the top management team of the acquired company with a more aggressive top management team—one often drawn from its own ranks of executives who understand the ways to achieve superior governance. Then the new top management team in charge looks for ways to reduce operating costs: for example, selling off unproductive assets such as executive jets and very expensive corporate headquarters buildings and finding ways to reduce the number of managers and employees (badly managed companies frequently let their labor forces grow out of control).

The top management team put in place by the acquiring company then focuses on how the acquired businesses were managed previously and seeks ways to improve the business unit's efficiency, quality, innovativeness, and responsiveness to customers. In addition, the acquiring company often establishes for the acquired company performance goals that cannot be met without significant improvements in operating efficiency. It also makes the new top management aware that failure to

acquisition and restructuring strategy

A strategy in which a company acquires inefficient and poorly managed enterprises and creates value by putting a superior internal governance structure in place in these acquired companies and restructuring their operations systems to improve their performance.

achieve performance improvements consistent with these goals within a given amount of time will probably result in their losing their jobs. Finally, to motivate the new top management team and the other managers of the acquired unit to undertake such demanding and stressful activities, the acquiring company directly links performance improvements in the acquired unit to pay incentives.

This system of rewards and punishments established by the corporate executives of the acquiring company gives the new managers of the acquired business unit every incentive to look for ways of improving the efficiency of the unit under their charge. GE, Textron, UTC, and IBM are good examples of companies that operate in this way.

TRANSFERRING COMPETENCES A second way for a company to create value from diversification is to transfer its existing distinctive competences in one or more value creation functions (for example, manufacturing, marketing, materials management, and R&D) to other industries. Top managers seek out companies in new industries where they believe they can apply these competences to create value and increase profitability. For example, they may use the superior skills in one or more of their company's value creation functions to improve the competitive position of the new business unit. Alternatively, corporate managers may decide to acquire a company in a different industry because they believe the acquired company possesses superior skills that can improve the efficiency of their existing value creation activities.

If successful, such competence transfers can lower the costs of value creation in one or more of a company's diversified businesses or enable one or more of these businesses to perform their value creation functions in a way that leads to differentiation and a premium price. The transfer of Philip Morris's existing marketing skills to Miller Brewing is one of the classic examples of how value can be created by competence transfers. Drawing on its marketing and competitive positioning skills, Philip Morris pioneered the introduction of Miller Lite, a product that redefined the brewing industry and moved Miller from number 6 to number 2 in the market (see Figure 7.4).

For such a strategy to work, the competences being transferred must allow the acquired company to establish a competitive advantage in its industry; that is, they must confer a competitive advantage on the acquired company. All too often,

Figure 7.4

Transfer of Competences at Philip Morris

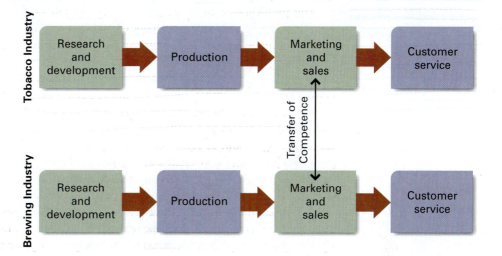

Strategy in Action

Diversification at 3M: Leveraging Technology

3M is a 100-year-old industrial colossus that in 2007 generated over $17 billion in revenues and $1.5 billion in profits from a portfolio of more than 50,000 individual products ranging from sandpaper and sticky tape to medical devices, office supplies, and electronic components. The company has consistently created new businesses by leveraging its scientific knowledge to find new applications for its proprietary technology. Today, the company is composed of more than forty discrete business units grouped into six major sectors: transportation, health care, industrial, consumer and office, electronics and communications, and specialty materials. The company has consistently generated 30% of sales from products introduced within the prior five years and currently operates with the goal of producing 40% of sales revenues from products introduced within the previous four years.

The process of leveraging technology to create new businesses at 3M can be illustrated by the following quotation from William Coyne, head of R&D at 3M:

> It began with sandpaper: mineral and glue on a substrate. After years as an abrasives company, it created a tape business. A researcher left off the mineral, and adapted the glue and substrate to create the first sticky tape. After creating many varieties of sticky tape—consumer, electrical, medical—researchers created the world's first audiotapes and videotapes. In their search to create better tape backings, other researchers happened on multilayer films that, surprise, have remarkable light management qualities. This multiplayer film technology is being used in brightness enhancement films, which are incorporated in the displays of virtually all laptops and palm computers.[a]

How does 3M do it? First, the company is a science-based enterprise with a strong tradition of innovation and risk taking. Risk taking is encouraged, and failure is not punished but seen as a natural part of the process of creating new products and business. Second, 3M's management is relentlessly focused on the company's customers and the problems they face. Many of 3M's products have arisen from efforts to help solve difficult problems. Third, managers set "stretch goals" that require the company to create new products and businesses at a rapid pace (an example is the current goal that 40% of sales should come from products introduced within the last four years). Fourth, employees are given considerable autonomy to pursue their own ideas. An employee can spend 15% of his or her time working on a project of his or her own choosing without management approval. Many products have resulted from this autonomy, including the ubiquitous Post-it Notes.

Fifth, although products belong to business units and it is business units that are responsible for generating profits, the technologies belong to every unit within the company. Anyone at 3M is free to try to develop new applications for a technology developed by its business units. Sixth, 3M has implemented an IT system that promotes the sharing of technological knowledge between business units so that new opportunities can be identified. Also, it hosts many in-house conferences where researchers from different business units are brought together to share the results of their work. Finally, 3M uses numerous mechanisms to recognize and reward those who develop new technologies, products, and businesses, including peer-nominated award programs, a corporate hall of fame, and, of course, monetary rewards.

however, corporate executives incorrectly assess the advantages that will result from the competence transfer and overestimate the benefits that will accrue from it. The acquisition of Hughes Aircraft by GM, for example, took place because GM's managers believed cars and car manufacturing were "going electronic" and Hughes was an electronics concern. The acquisition failed to realize any of the anticipated gains for GM, which finally sold the company off in 2005. On the other hand, Yahoo! has taken over many companies in the electronics, media, video, and entertainment industries because it recognized the need to strengthen its competitive position as a Web portal. 3M has done the same, as the Strategy in Action feature recounts.

ECONOMIES OF SCOPE   The phrase "two can live more cheaply than one" expresses the idea behind economies of scope. When two or more business units can share resources such as manufacturing facilities, distribution channels, advertising campaigns, and R&D costs, total operating costs fall because of economies of scope. Each business unit that shares a common resource has to pay less to operate a particular functional activity.[15] Procter & Gamble's disposable diaper and paper towel businesses offer one of the best examples of the successful realization of economies of scope. These businesses share the costs of procuring certain raw materials (such as paper) and of developing the technology for new products and processes. In addition, a joint sales force sells both products to supermarkets, and both products are shipped via the same distribution system (see Figure 7.5). This resource sharing has given both business units a cost advantage that has enabled them to undercut the prices of their less diversified competitors.[16]

Similarly, one of the motives behind the merger of Citicorp and Travelers to form Citigroup was that the merger would allow Travelers to sell its insurance products and financial services through Citicorp's retail banking network. To put it differently, the merger was intended to allow the expanded group to better utilize a major existing common resource: its retail banking network. This merger failed, however, when it turned out that customers had little interest in buying insurance from a bank. In 2005, Citigroup sold Travelers to MetLife because the merger had not created value. Diversification, like all corporate strategies, is complex, and it is hard to pursue it successfully all the time.

Like competence transfers, diversification to realize economies of scope is possible only if there is a real opportunity for sharing the skills and services of one or more of the value creation functions between a company's existing and new business units. Diversification for this reason should be pursued only when sharing is likely to generate a *significant* competitive advantage in one or more of a company's business units. Moreover, managers need to be aware that the costs of managing and coordinating the activities of the newly linked business units to achieve economies of scope are substantial and may outweigh the value that can be created by such a strategy. This is apparently what happened at Citigroup.[15]

Thus, just as in the case of vertical integration, the costs of managing and coordinating the skill and resource exchanges between business units increase

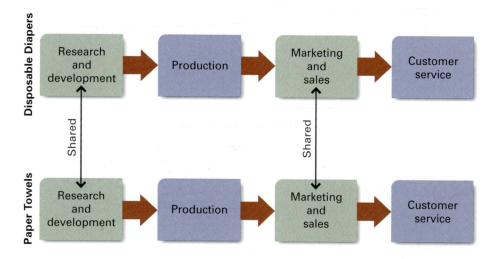

Figure 7.5

Sharing Resources at
Procter & Gamble

substantially as the number and diversity of the business units increase. This places a limit on the amount of diversification that can profitably be pursued. It makes sense for a company to diversify only as long as the extra value created by such a strategy exceeds the increased costs associated with incorporating additional business units into a company. Many companies diversify past this point, acquiring too many new companies, and their performance declines. To solve this problem, a company must reduce the scope of the enterprise through divestments—that is, through the selling of business units and exiting industries, which is discussed at the end of this chapter.

● **Related versus Unrelated Diversification**

One issue that a diversifying company must resolve is whether to diversify into totally new businesses and industries or into those that are related to its existing business because their value chains share something in common. The choices it makes determine whether a company pursues related diversification and/or unrelated diversification.

Related diversification is the strategy of operating a business unit in a new industry that is related to a company's existing business units by some form of linkage or connection between one or more components of each business unit's value chain. Normally, these linkages are based on manufacturing, marketing, or technological connections or similarities. The diversification of Philip Morris into the brewing industry with the acquisition of Miller Brewing is an example of related diversification, because there are marketing similarities between the brewing and tobacco businesses (both are consumer product businesses in which competitive success depends on competitive positioning skills).

Unrelated diversification is diversification into a new business or industry that has *no* obvious value chain connection with any of the businesses or industries in which a company is currently operating. A company pursuing unrelated diversification is often called a *conglomerate,* a term that implies the company is made up of a number of diverse businesses.

By definition, a related company can create value by resource sharing and by transferring competences between businesses. It can also carry out some restructuring. In contrast, because there are no connections or similarities between the value chains of unrelated businesses, an unrelated company cannot create value by sharing resources or transferring competences. Unrelated diversifiers can create value *only by pursuing an acquisition and restructuring strategy.*

Related diversification can create value in more ways than unrelated diversification, so one might expect related diversification to be the preferred strategy. In addition, related diversification is normally perceived as involving fewer risks, because the company is moving into businesses and industries about which top management has some knowledge. Probably because of those considerations, most diversified companies display a preference for related diversification.[16] Indeed, in the last decade, many companies pursuing unrelated diversification have decided to split themselves up into totally self-contained companies to increase the value they can create. In 2007, for example, the conglomerate Tyco split into three separate public companies focusing on the electronics, health care, and security and fire protection businesses for this reason.

However, United Technology Corporation (UTC), a conglomerate pursuing unrelated diversification, provides an excellent example of a company that has created a lot of value using this strategy. UTC's CEO George David uses all the kinds of superior governance skills that we have discussed to improve the profitability of his company's business units. The closing case describes how UTC has pursued unrelated diversification successfully and why it is one of the highest performing of the *Fortune* 500 companies.

related diversification

The strategy of operating a business unit in a new industry that is related to a company's existing business units through some commonality in their value chains.

unrelated diversification

The strategy of operating a business unit in a new industry that has no value chain connection with a company's existing business units.

Restructuring and Downsizing

So far, we have focused on strategies for expanding the scope of a company and entering into new business areas. We turn now to their opposite: strategies for reducing the scope of the company by *exiting* business areas. In recent years, reducing the scope of a company through restructuring and downsizing has become an increasingly popular strategy, particularly among the companies that diversified their activities during the 1980s and 1990s. In most cases, companies that are engaged in restructuring are divesting themselves of diversified activities and downsizing in order to concentrate on fewer businesses.[17] For example, in 1996 AT&T spun off its telecommunications equipment business (Lucent); then, after acquiring two large cable TV companies in the late 1990s, AT&T sold its cable unit to rival cable TV provider Comcast for $72 billion in 2002. Finally, in 2005 a downsized AT&T became a takeover target for SBC Communications, which acquired AT&T to strengthen its position in the core telephone business. By 2007, SBC, renamed AT&T, had once again become the largest U.S. and global communications company.

The first question that must be asked is why so many companies are restructuring during this period. After answering it, we examine the different strategies that companies adopt for exiting from business areas.

Why Restructure?

diversification discount

The phenomenon that shares of stock in highly diversified companies are often assigned a lower market valuation than shares of stock in less diversified companies.

A prime reason why extensively diversified companies restructure is that in recent years the stock market has assigned a diversification discount to the stock of such enterprises.[18] **Diversification discount** is the term used to refer to the empirical fact that the stock of highly diversified companies is often assigned a lower valuation relative to their earnings than the stock of less diversified enterprises. Investors apparently see highly diversified companies as less attractive investments than more focused enterprises. There are two reasons for this. First, investors are often put off by the complexity and lack of transparency in the consolidated financial statements of highly diversified enterprises, which are harder to interpret and may not give them a good picture of how the individual parts of the company are performing. In other words, they perceive diversified companies as riskier investments than more focused companies. In such cases, restructuring tends to be an attempt to boost the returns to shareholders by splitting the company into a number of parts.

A second reason for the diversification discount is that many investors have learned from experience that managers often have a tendency to pursue too much diversification or to diversify for the wrong reasons, such as the pursuit of growth for its own sake, rather than the pursuit of greater profitability.[19] Some senior managers tend to expand the scope of their company beyond that point where the bureaucratic costs of managing extensive diversification exceed the additional value that can be created, and the performance of the company begins to decline. Restructuring in such cases is often a response to declining financial performance.

Restructuring can also be a response to failed acquisitions. This is true whether the acquisitions were made to support a horizontal integration, vertical integration, or diversification strategy. We noted earlier in the chapter that many acquisitions fail to deliver the anticipated gains. When this is the case, corporate managers often respond by cutting their losses and exiting from the acquired business.

A final factor of some importance in restructuring trends is that innovations in management processes and strategy have diminished the advantages of vertical integration and those of diversification. In response, companies have reduced the scope of their activities through restructuring and divestments. For example, ten years ago there was little understanding that long-term cooperative relationships between a company and its suppliers could be a viable alternative to vertical integration. Most companies considered only two alternatives for managing the supply chain: vertical integration or competitive bidding. However, if conditions are right, a third alternative for managing the supply chain, *long-term contracting,* can be a better strategy than either vertical integration or competitive bidding. Like vertical integration, long-term contracting facilitates investments in specialization. But unlike vertical integration, it does not involve high bureaucratic costs, nor does it dispense with market discipline. As this strategic innovation has spread throughout the business world, the relative advantages of vertical integration have declined.

● **Exit Strategies**

Companies can choose from three main strategies for exiting business areas: divestment, harvest, and liquidation. Of the three strategies, divestment is usually favored. It represents the best way for a company to recoup as much of its initial investment in a business unit as possible.

DIVESTMENT   **Divestment** involves selling a business unit to the highest bidder. Three types of buyers are independent investors, other companies, and the management of the unit to be divested. Selling off a business unit to another company or to independent investors is normally referred to as a **spinoff.** A spinoff makes good sense when the unit to be sold is profitable and when the stock market has an appetite for new stock issues (which is normal during market upswings, but *not* during market downswings). However, spinoffs do not work if the unit to be spun off is unprofitable and unattractive to independent investors or if the stock market is slumping and unresponsive to new issues.

Selling off a unit to another company is a strategy frequently pursued when the unit can be sold to a company in the same line of business as the unit. In such cases, the purchaser is often prepared to pay a considerable amount of money for the opportunity to substantially increase the size of its business virtually overnight. For example, as we noted earlier, in 2002 AT&T sold off its cable TV business to Comcast for a hefty $72 billion; SBC then bought AT&T for $16 billion in 2005.

Selling off a unit to its management is normally referred to as a **management buyout (MBO).** In an MBO, the unit is sold to its management, which often finances the purchase through the sale of high-yield bonds to investors. The bond issue is normally arranged by a buyout specialist, which, along with management, will typically hold a sizable proportion of the shares in the MBO. MBOs often take place when financially troubled units have only two other options: a harvest strategy or liquidation.

An MBO can be very risky for the management team involved, because its members may have to sign personal guarantees to back up the bond issue and may lose everything if the MBO ultimately fails. On the other hand, if the management team succeeds in turning around the troubled unit, its reward can be a significant increase in personal wealth. Thus, an MBO strategy can be characterized as a *high-risk/high-return* strategy for the management team involved. Faced with the possible liquidation of their business unit, many management teams are willing to take the risk. However, the viability of this option depends not only on a willing management team but also on there being enough buyers of high-yield/high-risk bonds (so-called junk bonds) to be able to finance the MBO. In recent years, the general slump in the junk bond market has made the MBO strategy a more difficult one for companies to follow.

divestment

The sale of a business unit to the highest bidder.

spinoff

The sale of a business unit to another company or to independent investors.

management buyout (MBO)

The sale of a business unit to its current management.

harvest strategy

The halting of investment in a business unit to maximize short- to medium-term cash flow from that unit.

HARVEST STRATEGY   A **harvest strategy** involves halting investment in a unit in order to maximize short- to medium-term cash flow from that unit. Although this strategy seems fine in theory, it is often a poor one to apply in practice. Once it becomes apparent that the unit is pursuing a harvest strategy, the morale of the unit's employees, as well as the confidence of the unit's customers and suppliers in its continuing operation, can sink very quickly. If this occurs, as it often does, the rapid decline in the unit's revenues can make the strategy untenable.

liquidation strategy

The shutting down of the operations of a business unit and the sale of its assets.

LIQUIDATION STRATEGY   A **liquidation strategy** involves shutting down the operations of a business unit and selling its assets. A pure liquidation strategy is the least attractive of all to pursue, because it requires that the company write off its investment in a business unit, often at considerable cost. However, for a poorly performing business unit where a selloff or spinoff is unlikely and where an MBO cannot be arranged, it may be the only viable alternative.

Summary of Chapter

1. There are different corporate-level strategies that companies pursue in order to increase their long-run profitability; they may choose to remain in the same industry, to enter new industries, or even to leave businesses and industries in order to prosper over time.

2. Corporate strategies should add value to a corporation, enabling it or one or more of its business units to perform one or more of the value creation functions at a lower cost and/or in a way that allows for differentiation and thus a premium price.

3. Concentrating on a single industry allows a company to focus its total managerial, financial, technological, and physical resources and competences on competing successfully in just one area. It also ensures that the company sticks to doing what it knows best.

4. The strategic outsourcing of noncore value creation activities may allow a company to lower its costs, better differentiate its product offering, and make better use of scarce resources, while also enabling it to respond rapidly to changing market conditions. However, strategic outsourcing may have a detrimental effect if the company outsources important value creation activities or if it becomes too dependent on key suppliers of those activities.

5. The company that concentrates on a single business may be missing out on the opportunity to create value through vertical integration and/or diversification.

6. Vertical integration can enable a company to achieve a competitive advantage by helping build barriers to entry, facilitating investments in specialized assets, safeguarding product quality, and improving scheduling.

7. The disadvantages of vertical integration include cost disadvantages, if a company's internal source of supply is a high-cost one, and lack of strategic flexibility, if technology and the environment are changing rapidly.

8. Entering into cooperative long-term outsourcing agreements can enable a company to realize many of the benefits associated with vertical integration without having to contend with the problems.

9. Diversification can create value through the application of superior governance skills, including a restructuring strategy, competence transfers, and the realization of economies of scope.

10. Related diversification is often preferred to unrelated diversification because it enables a company to engage in more value creation activities and is less risky.

11. Restructuring is often a response to excessive diversification, failed acquisitions, and innovations in the management process that have reduced the advantages of vertical integration and diversification.

12. Exit strategies include divestment, harvest, and liquidation. The choice of exit strategy is governed by the characteristics of the business unit involved.

Discussion Questions

1. Why was it profitable for General Motors and Ford to integrate backward into component-parts manufacturing in the past, and why are both companies now trying to buy more of their parts from outside suppliers?

2. Under what conditions might concentration on a single business be inconsistent with the goal of maximizing stockholder wealth? Why?

3. GM integrated vertically in the 1920s, diversified in the 1930s, and expanded overseas in the 1950s. Explain these developments with reference to the prof-

itability of pursuing each strategy. Why do you think vertical integration is normally the first strategy to be pursued after concentration on a single business?

4. What value creation activities should a company outsource to independent suppliers? What are the risks involved in outsourcing these activities?

5. When is a company likely to choose related diversification, and when is it likely to choose unrelated diversification? Discuss your answers with reference to an electronics manufacturer.

Practicing Strategic Management

SMALL-GROUP EXERCISE
Comparing Vertical Integration Strategies

Break up into groups of three to five people. Appoint one group member as a spokesperson who will communicate your findings to the class when called upon to do so by the instructor. Then read the following description of the activities of Seagate Technologies and Quantum Corporation, both of which manufacture computer disk drives. On the basis of this description, outline the pros and cons of a vertical integration strategy. Which strategy do you think makes most sense in the context of the computer disk drive industry?

Quantum Corporation and Seagate Technologies are both major producers of disk drives for PCs and workstations. The disk drive industry is characterized by sharp fluctuations in the level of demand, intense price competition, rapid technological change, and product life cycles of no more than twelve to eighteen months. In recent years, Quantum and Seagate have pursued very different vertical integration strategies. Seagate is a vertically integrated manufacturer of disk drives, both designing and manufacturing the bulk of its own disk drives. Quantum specializes in design, while outsourcing most of its manufacturing to a number of independent suppliers; its most important supplier is Matsushita Kotobuki Electronics (MKE) of Japan. Quantum makes only its newest and most expensive products in-house. Once a new drive is perfected and ready for large-scale manufacturing, Quantum turns over manufactur-

ing to MKE. MKE and Quantum have cemented their partnership over eight years. At each stage in designing a new product, Quantum's engineers send the newest drawings to a production team at MKE. MKE examines the drawings and is continually proposing changes that make the new disk drives easier to manufacture. When the product is ready for manufacture, eight to ten Quantum engineers travel to MKE's plant in Japan for at least a month to work on production ramp-up.

EXPLORING THE WEB
Visiting Motorola

Visit the website of Motorola (**www.motorola.com**), and review the various business activities of Motorola. Using this information, answer the following questions:

1. To what extent is Motorola vertically integrated?

2. Does vertical integration help Motorola establish a competitive advantage, or does it put the company at a competitive disadvantage?

3. How diversified is Motorola? Does Motorola pursue a related or an unrelated diversification strategy?

4. How, if at all, does Motorola's diversification strategy create value for the company's stockholders?

General Task Search the Web for an example of a company that has pursued a diversification strategy. Describe that strategy and assess whether the strategy creates or dissipates value for the company.

CLOSING CASE

United Technologies Has an ACE in Its Pocket

United Technologies Corporation (UTC), based in Hartford, Connecticut, is a *conglomerate*, a company that owns a wide variety of other companies that operate in different businesses and industries. Some of the companies in UTC's portfolio are more well known than UTC itself, such as Sikorsky Aircraft Corporation; Pratt & Whitney, the aircraft engine and component maker; Otis Elevator Company; Carrier air conditioning; and Chubb, the lock maker and security business that UTC acquired in 2003. Today, investors frown upon companies like UTC that own and operate companies in widely different industries. There is a growing perception that managers can better manage a company's business model when the company operates as an independent or stand-alone entity. How can UTC justify holding all these companies together in a conglomerate? Why would this lead to a greater increase in their long-term profitability than if they operated as separate companies? In the last decade, the boards of directors and CEOs of many conglomerates, such as Dial, ITT Industries, and Textron, have realized that by holding diverse companies together they were reducing, not increasing, the profitability of their companies. As a result, many conglomerates have been broken up and their companies spun off as separate, independent entities.

UTC's CEO George David claims that he has created a unique and sophisticated multibusiness model that adds value across UTC's diverse businesses. David joined Otis Elevator as an assistant to its CEO in 1975, but within one year Otis was acquired by UTC, during a decade when "bigger is better" ruled corporate America and mergers and acquisitions, of whatever kind, were seen as the best way to grow profits. UTC sent David to manage its South American operations and later gave him responsibility for its Japanese operations. Otis had formed an alliance with Matsushita to develop an elevator for the Japanese market, and the resulting "Elevonic 401," after being installed widely in Japanese buildings, proved to be a disaster. It broke down much more often than elevators made by other Japanese companies, and customers were concerned about its reliability and safety.

Matsushita was extremely embarrassed about the elevator's failure and assigned one of its leading total quality management (TQM) experts, Yuzuru Ito, to head a team of Otis engineers to find out why it performed so poorly. Under Ito's direction all the employees—managers, designers, and production workers—who had produced the elevator analyzed why the elevators were malfunctioning. This intensive study led to a total redesign of the elevator, and when their new and improved elevator was launched worldwide, it met with great success. Otis's share of the global elevator market increased dramatically, and one result was that David was named president of UTC in 1992. He was given the responsibility to cut costs across the entire corporation, including its important Pratt & Whitney division; his success in reducing UTC's cost structure and increasing its ROIC led to his appointment as CEO in 1994.

Now responsible for all of UTC's diverse companies, David decided that the best way to increase UTC's profitability, which had been falling, was to find ways to improve efficiency and quality in all its constituent companies. He convinced Ito to move to Hartford and take responsibility for championing the kinds of improvements that had by now transformed the Otis division, and Ito began to develop UTC's TQM system, which is known as Achieving Competitive Excellence, or ACE.

ACE is a set of tasks and procedures that are used by employees from the shop floor to top managers to analyze all aspects of the way a product is made. The goal is to find ways to improve *quality and reliability,* to lower the *costs* of making the product, and especially to find ways to make the next generation of a particular product perform better—in other words, to encourage *technological innovation.* David makes every employee in every function and at every level take responsibility for achieving the incremental, step-by-step gains that can result in innovative and efficient products that enable a company to dominate its industry—to push back the value creation frontier.

David calls these techniques "process disciplines," and he has used them to increase the performance of all UTC companies. Through these techniques, he has created the extra value for UTC that justifies its owning and operating such a diverse set of businesses. David's success can be seen in his company's performance in the decade since he took control: he has quadrupled UTC's earnings per share, and in the first six months of 1994 profit grew by 25%, to $1.4 billion, while sales increased by 26%, to $18.3 billion. UTC has been in the top three performers of the companies that make up the Dow Jones industrial average for the last three years, and the company has consistently outperformed GE, another huge conglomerate, in its returns to investors.

David and his managers believe that the gains that can be achieved from UTC's process disciplines are never-ending because its own R&D—in which it invests over $2.5 billion a year—is constantly producing product innovations that can help all its businesses. Indeed, recognizing that its skills in creating process improvements are specific to manufacturing companies, UTC's strategy is to acquire only companies that make products that can benefit from the use of its ACE program—hence its Chubb acquisition. At the same time, David invests only in companies that have the potential to remain leading companies in their industries and so can charge above-average prices. His acquisitions strengthen the competences of UTC's existing businesses. For example, he acquired a company called Sundstrand, a leading aerospace and industrial systems company, and combined it with UTC's Hamilton aerospace division

to create Hamilton Sundstrand, which is now a major supplier to Boeing and makes products that command premium prices.

Case Discussion Questions

1. In what ways does UTC's corporate-level strategy of unrelated diversification create value?

2. What are the dangers and disadvantages of this strategy?

3. Collect some recent information on UTC from sources like Yahoo! Finance. How successful has it been in pursuing its strategy?

TEST PREPPER

True/False Questions

_T_ **1.** The principal concern of corporate-level strategy is to identify the industry or industries a company should participate in to maximize its long-run profitability.

_T_ **2.** Horizontal integration is the process of acquiring or merging with industry competitors in an effort to achieve the competitive advantages that come with large size or scale.

_T_ **3.** Product bundling is a strategy of offering customers the opportunity to buy a complete range of products at a single, combined price.

_F_ **4.** A virtual corporation outsources all of its functional activities.

_F_ **5.** Vertical integration is a corporate-level strategy that involves a company's entering new industries to increase its short-run profitability.

_T_ **6.** A specialized asset is a value creation tool that is designed to perform a specific set of activities and whose value creation potential is significantly lower in its next-best use.

_T_ **7.** A diversified company is one that operates in two or more industries to find ways to increase its long-run profitability.

Multiple-Choice Questions

8. Creating value through diversification includes all of the following *except* _____.
    a. permitting superior internal governance
    b. transferring competences among businesses
    c. realizing economies of scope
    d. vertical integration
    e. none of the above

9. The choices that a company has for exiting a business area include all of the following *except* _____.
    a. divestment
    b. harvest
    c. liquidation
    d. diversification discount
    e. none of the above

10. _____ involves halting investment in a unit in order to maximize short- to medium-term cash flow from that unit.
    a. Harvest strategy
    b. Liquidation strategy
    c. Spinoff strategy
    d. Management buyout strategy
    e. Divestment strategy

11. _____ involves shutting down the operations of a business unit.
    a. Liquidation
    b. Harvest
    c. Management buyout
    d. Divestment
    e. Spinoff

12. A divestment _____.
    a. entails selling a unit to another company, a group of independent investors, or the management of that unit
    b. is the least attractive exit strategy
    c. is the same as a spinoff
    d. is not an effective restructuring strategy
    e. usually happens right after an acquisition

13. The major disadvantages of vertical integration include all of the following _except_ _____.
    a. increasing costs
    b. tying a company to old, obsolescent, high-cost technology
    c. reducing profits
    d. mutual dependence   + can adv.
    e. all of the above

14. _____ refers to the manner in which the top executives of a company manage its business units, divisions, and functions.
    a. Management by objective
    b. Management by walking around
    c. Internal governance
    d. Restructuring strategy
    e. Related diversification

15. _____ is _not_ one of the options a company has when choosing which industry to compete in.
    a. Developing the portfolio of businesses that creates the highest level of returns and growth opportunities
    b. Concentrating on only one industry
    c. Entering new industries in adjacent stages of the industry value chain
    d. Entering new industries that may or may not be connected to its existing industry
    e. Exiting businesses and industries to increase its long-run profitability

Chapter 8

Strategic Change: Implementing Strategies to Build and Develop a Company

Learning Objectives

After reading this chapter, you should be able to

1. Understand the main steps involved in the strategic change process

2. Appreciate the need to analyze a company's set of businesses from a portfolio of competences perspective

3. Review the advantages and risks of implementing strategy through internal new ventures, acquisitions, and strategic alliances

4. Discuss how to limit the risks associated with internal new ventures, acquisitions, and strategic alliances

5. Appreciate the special issues associated with using a joint venture to structure a strategic alliance

Chapter Outline

I. Strategic Change
  a. Types of Strategic Change
  b. A Model of the Change Process
II. Analyzing a Company as a Portfolio of Core Competences
  a. Fill in the Blanks
  b. Premier Plus 10
  c. White Spaces
  d. Mega-Opportunities
III. Implementing Strategy Through Internal New Ventures
  a. Pitfalls with Internal New Ventures

  b. Guidelines for Successful Internal New Venturing
IV. Implementing Strategy Through Acquisitions
  a. Pitfalls with Acquisitions
  b. Guidelines for Successful Acquisition
V. Implementing Strategy Through Strategic Alliances
  a. Advantages of Strategic Alliances
  b. Disadvantages of Strategic Alliances
  c. Making Strategic Alliances Work

> How are we going to change our strategy?

Overview

In Chapter 7, we examined the different corporate-level strategies that managers can pursue to increase a company's long-run profitability. All these choices of strategy have important implications for a company's future prosperity, and it is vital that managers understand the issues and problems involved in implementing these

[handwritten margin note: How are we going to change our Strategy?]

strategies if the strategies are to be successful. We begin this chapter by examining the nature of strategic change and the obstacles that may hinder managers' attempts to change a company's strategy and structure to improve its future performance. We then focus on the steps managers can take to overcome these obstacles and make their efforts to change a company successful.

Second, we tackle a crucial question: How do managers determine which businesses or industries a company should continue to participate in or exit from, and how do they determine whether a company should enter one or more new businesses? Obviously, managers need to have a vision of where their company should be in the future—that is, a vision of its desired future state—and we discuss an important technique, the portfolio of competences approach, that helps them accomplish this.

[handwritten margin note: Is it to implement g Corporate level Strategy thro 1) Internal new ventures 2) acquisitions 3) Strategic alliances]

Third, we turn our attention to the different methods that managers can use to enter new businesses or industries in order to build and develop their company and improve its performance over time. The choice here is whether to implement a corporate-level strategy through *internal new ventures, acquisitions,* or *strategic alliances* (including joint ventures). Finally, we examine the pros and cons of these different ways of implementing strategy, given the goal of increasing a company's competitive advantage and long-run profitability.

Strategic Change — *The nature* *Barrier to change*

[handwritten margin note: 3 level 1) Simpl 2) policie 3) value]

Strategic change is the movement of a company away from its present state toward some desired future state to increase its competitive advantage and profitability.[1] In the last decade, most large *Fortune* 500 companies have gone through some kind of strategic change as their managers have tried to strengthen their existing core competences and build new ones to compete more effectively. Often, because of drastic unexpected changes in the environment, such as the emergence of aggressive new competitors or technological breakthroughs, strategic managers need to develop a new strategy and structure to raise the level of their business's performance.[2]

[handwritten note: one way to change el Company's strategy]

One way of changing a company to enable it to operate more effectively is by **reengineering,** a process in which managers focus not on a company's functional activities but on the business processes underlying the value creation process.[3] A **business process** is any activity (such as order processing, inventory control, or product design) that is vital to delivering goods and services to customers quickly or that promotes high quality or low costs.[4] Business processes are not the responsibility of any one function but cut across functions.

● Types of Strategic Change

Hallmark Cards, for example, reengineered its card design process with great success. Before the reengineering effort, artists, writers, and editors worked in different functions to produce all kinds of cards. After reengineering, these same artists, writers, and editors were organized into cross-functional teams, each of which now works on a specific type of card (such as birthday, Christmas, or Mother's Day). The result was that the time it took to bring a new card to market dropped from years to months, and Hallmark's performance improved dramatically.

Reengineering and total quality management (TQM, discussed in Chapter 4) are highly interrelated and complementary.[5] After reengineering has taken place and the question "What is the best way to provide customers with the goods or service they require?" has been answered, TQM takes over and addresses the question "How can we now continue to improve and refine the new process and find better ways of

business process

Any business activity, such as order processing, inventory control, or product design, that is vital to delivering goods and services to customers quickly or that promotes high quality or low costs.

managing task and role relationships?" Successful companies examine both questions together, and managers continuously work to identify new and better processes for meeting the goals of increased efficiency, quality, and responsiveness to customer needs. Thus, managers are always working to improve their vision of their company's desired future state.

Recall from Chapter 7 that *restructuring* is the process through which managers simplify organization structure by eliminating divisions, departments, or levels in the hierarchy and downsize by terminating employees, thereby lowering operating costs. Restructuring may also involve *outsourcing*, the process whereby one company contracts with other companies to perform a functional activity such as manufacturing, marketing, or customer service. Restructuring is a second form of strategic change that managers can implement to improve performance. As we noted, there are many reasons why it can become necessary for an organization to streamline, simplify, and downsize its operations. Sometimes a change in the business environment occurs that could not have been foreseen; perhaps a shift in technology renders a company's products obsolete or a worldwide recession reduces the demand for its products. Sometimes an organization has excess capacity because customers no longer want the goods and services it provides, perhaps because they are outdated or offer poor value for the money. Sometimes organizations downsize because they have grown too tall and bureaucratic and operating costs have become excessive. And sometimes they restructure even when they are in a strong position, simply to build and improve their competitive advantage and stay on top.

All too often, however, companies are forced to downsize and lay off employees because managers have *not* continuously monitored the way they operate their basic business processes and have not made the incremental changes to their strategies that would allow them to contain costs and adjust to changing conditions. Paradoxically, because they have not paid attention to the need to reengineer themselves, they are forced into a position where restructuring is the only way they can survive and compete in an increasingly competitive environment.

● **A Model of the Change Process**

In order to understand the issues involved in implementing strategic change, it is useful to focus on the series of distinct steps that strategic managers must follow if the change process is to succeed.[6] These steps are listed in Figure 8.1.

DETERMINING THE NEED FOR CHANGE The first step in the change process is for strategic managers to recognize the need for change. Sometimes this need is obvious, as when divisions are fighting or when competitors introduce a product that is clearly superior to anything the company has in production. More often, however, managers have trouble determining that something is going wrong in the organization. Problems may develop gradually, and organizational performance may slip for a number of years before the decline becomes obvious. Thus, the first step in the change process occurs when strategic managers or others in a position to take action, such as directors or takeover specialists, recognize that there is a gap between desired

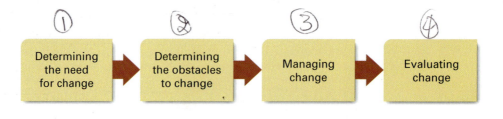

Figure 8.1

Stages in the Change Process

company performance and actual performance. Using measures such as a decline in profitability, return on investment (ROI), stock price, or market share as indicators that change is needed, managers can start looking for the source of the problem. To discover it, they conduct a strengths, weaknesses, opportunities, and threats (SWOT) analysis.

Strategic managers examine the company's *strengths* and *weaknesses,* for example, when they conduct a strategic audit of all functions and divisions and assess their contribution to profitability over time. Perhaps some divisions have become relatively unprofitable as innovation has slowed, without management's realizing it. Perhaps sales and marketing have failed to keep pace with changes in the competitive environment. Perhaps the company's product is simply outdated. Strategic managers also analyze the company's level of differentiation and integration to make sure that it is appropriate for its strategy. Perhaps a company does not have the integrating mechanisms in place to achieve gains from synergy, or perhaps the structure has become so tall and inflexible that bureaucratic costs have escalated.

Strategic managers then examine environmental *opportunities* and *threats* that might explain the problem, using all the concepts developed in Chapter 3 of this book. For instance, intense competition may have arisen unexpectedly from substitute products or a shift in technology or consumers' tastes may have caught the company unawares.

Once the source of the problem has been identified via SWOT analysis, strategic managers must determine the desired future state of the company—that is, how it should change its strategy and structure to achieve the new goals they have set for it. In the next section, we discuss one important tool managers can use to work out the best future mission and strategy for maximizing company profitability—analyzing a company as a portfolio of core competences. Of course, the choices they make are specific to each individual company, because each company has a unique set of skills and competences. The challenge for managers is that there is no way they can determine in advance, or even reliably estimate, the accuracy of their assumptions about the future. Strategic change always involves considerable uncertainty and risks that must be borne if above-average returns are to be achieved.

DETERMINING THE OBSTACLES TO CHANGE Strategic change is frequently resisted by people and groups inside an organization. Often, for example, the decision to reengineer and restructure a company requires the establishment of a new set of role and authority relationships among managers in different functions and divisions. Because this change may threaten the status and rewards of some managers, they resist the changes being implemented. Many efforts at change take a long time, and many fail because of the high level of resistance to change at all levels in the organization. Thus, the second step in implementing strategic change is to determine what obstacles to change exist in a company. Obstacles to change can be found at four levels in the organization: corporate, divisional, functional, and individual.

At the corporate level, changing strategy even in seemingly trivial ways may significantly affect a company's behavior. For example, suppose that to reduce costs, a company decides to centralize all divisional purchasing and sales activities at the corporate level. Such consolidation could severely damage each division's ability to develop a unique strategy for its own individual market. Alternatively, suppose that in response to low-cost foreign competition, a company decides to pursue a strategy of increased differentiation. This action would change the balance of power among functions and could lead to problems as functions start fighting to retain their status in the organization. A company's present strategies constitute a powerful obstacle to change. They generate a massive amount of resistance that has to be overcome before change can take place. This is why strategic change is usually a slow process.

Similar factors operate at the divisional level. Change is difficult at the divisional level if divisions are highly interrelated, because a shift in one division's operations affects other divisions. Furthermore, changes in strategy affect different divisions in different ways, because change generally favors the interests of some divisions over those of others. Managers in the different divisions may thus have different attitudes toward change, and some will be less supportive than others. Existing divisions may resist establishing new product divisions, for example, because they will lose resources and their status in the organization will diminish.

The same obstacles to change exist at the functional level. Just like divisions, different functions have different strategic orientations and goals and react differently to the changes management proposes. For example, manufacturing generally has a short-term, cost-directed efficiency orientation; research and development is oriented toward long-term, technical goals; and the sales function is oriented toward satisfying customers' needs. Thus, production may see the solution to a problem as one of reducing costs; sales, as one of increasing demand; and research and development, as product innovation. Differences in functional orientation make it hard to formulate and implement a new strategy and may significantly slow a company's response to changes in the competitive environment.

At the individual level, too, people are notoriously resistant to change because change implies uncertainty, which breeds insecurity and fear of the unknown. Because managers are people, this individual resistance reinforces the tendency of each function and division to oppose changes that may have uncertain effects on them. Restructuring and reengineering efforts can be particularly stressful for managers at all levels of the organization. All these obstacles make it difficult to change strategy or structure quickly. That is why U.S. carmakers and companies such as IBM, Kodak, and Motorola were so slow to respond to fierce global competition, first from Japan and then from China and other Asian countries.

Paradoxically, companies that experience the greatest uncertainty may become best able to respond to it. When companies have been forced to change frequently, managers often develop the ability to handle change easily. Strategic managers must identify potential obstacles to change as they design and implement new strategies. The larger and more complex the organization, the harder it is to implement change, because inertia is likely to be more pervasive.

Managing and Evaluating Change The processes of managing and evaluating change raise several questions. For instance, who should actually carry out the change: internal managers or external consultants? Although internal managers may have the most experience or knowledge about a company's operations, they may lack perspective because they are too close to the situation and "can't see the forest for the trees." They also run the risk of appearing to be politically motivated and of having a personal stake in the changes they recommend. This is why companies often turn to external consultants, who can view a situation more objectively. Outside consultants, however, have to spend a lot of time learning about the company and its problems before they can propose a plan of action. It is for both of these reasons that many companies (such as Quaker, Gap, and IBM) bring in new CEOs from outside the company, and even from outside its industry, to spearhead their change efforts. In this way, companies can get the benefits of both inside information and external perspective.

Generally, a company can take one of two main approaches to implementing and managing change: top-down change or bottom-up change.[7] With top-down change, a strong CEO or top management team analyzes what strategies need to be pursued, recommends a course of action, and then moves quickly to restructure and implement change in the organization. The emphasis is on speed of response and prompt management of problems as they occur. Bottom-up change is much more gradual. Top management consults with managers at all levels in the organization. Then, over time, it develops a detailed plan for change, with a timetable of events and stages that the company will go through. The emphasis in bottom-up change is on participation and on keeping people informed about the situation so that uncertainty is minimized.

The advantage of bottom-up change is that it removes some of the obstacles to change by including them in the strategic plan. Furthermore, the purpose of consulting with managers at all levels is to reveal potential problems. The disadvantage of bottom-up change is its slow pace. On the other hand, in the case of the much speedier top-down change, problems may emerge later and may be difficult to resolve. Giants such as GM and Kodak often must apply top-down change because managers are so unaccustomed to and threatened by change that only a radical restructuring effort provides enough momentum to overcome organizational inertia.

The last step in the change process is to evaluate the effects of the changes in strategy on organizational performance. A company must compare the way it operates after implementing change with the way it operated before. Managers use indexes such as changes in stock market price, increases in market share, and higher revenues from increased product differentiation. They also can benchmark their company's performance against market leaders to see how much they have improved and how much more they need to improve to catch the market leader.

Analyzing a Company as a Portfolio of Core Competences

Earlier, we noted that managers must have access to tools that help them determine their companies' desired future state—specifically, the businesses and industries that they should compete in to increase long-run competitive advantage. One conceptual technique, developed by Gary Hamel and C. K. Prahalad, that helps them do this is to analyze a company as a portfolio of core competences, as opposed to a portfolio of actual businesses.[8] Recall from Chapter 1 the importance of adopting a customer-oriented, rather than a product-oriented, business definition; now the core competence becomes the key competitive variable.

According to Hamel and Prahalad, a core competence is a central value creation capability of a company—that is, a core skill. They argue, for example, that Canon, the Japanese concern best known for its cameras and photocopiers, has core competences in precision mechanics, fine optics, microelectronics, and electronic imaging. Corporate development is oriented toward maintaining existing competences, building new competences, and leveraging competences by applying them to new business opportunities. For example, Hamel and Prahalad argue that the success of a company such as 3M in creating new business has come from its ability to apply its core competence in adhesives to a wide range of businesses opportunities, from Scotch Tape to Post-it Notes.

Hamel and Prahalad maintain that identifying current core competences is the first step a company should take in deciding which business opportunities to pursue.

Figure 8.2

Establishing a
Competence Agenda

Industry

Existing   New

<table>
<tr><td></td><td></td><td colspan="2">**Industry**</td></tr>
<tr><td></td><td></td><td>Existing</td><td>New</td></tr>
<tr><td rowspan="2">**Competence**</td><td>New</td><td>**Premier plus 10**
What new competences will we need to build to protect and extend our franchise in current industries?</td><td>**Mega-opportunities**
What new competences will we need to build to participate in the most exciting industries of the future?</td></tr>
<tr><td>Existing</td><td>**Fill in the blanks**
What is the opportunity to improve our position in existing industries and better leverage our existing competences?</td><td>**White spaces**
What new products or services could we create by creatively redeploying or recombining our current competences?</td></tr>
</table>

Once a company has identified its core competences, they advocate using a matrix similar to that illustrated in Figure 8.2 to establish an agenda for building and leveraging core competences to create new business opportunities. This matrix distinguishes between existing and new competences, and between existing and new industries. Each quadrant in the matrix has a title; the strategic implications of these quadrants and their titles are discussed below.

● **Fill in the Blanks**   The lower-left quadrant represents the company's existing portfolio of competences and products. Twenty years ago, for example, Canon had competences in precision mechanics, fine optics, and microelectronics and was active in two basic businesses, producing cameras and photocopiers. The competences in precision mechanics and fine optics were used in the production of basic mechanical cameras. These two competences, plus an additional competence in microelectronics, were needed to produce plain paper copiers. The title for this quadrant of the matrix, *Fill in the blanks,* refers to the opportunity to improve the company's competitive position in existing markets by leveraging existing core competences. For example, Canon was able to improve the position of its camera business by leveraging microelectronics skills from its copier business to support the development of cameras with electronic features, such as autofocus capabilities.

● **Premier Plus 10**   The upper-left quadrant is referred to as *Premier plus 10,* to suggest an important question: What new core competences must be built today to ensure that the company remains a premier provider of its existing products in ten years' time? Canon, for example, decided that in order to maintain a competitive edge in its copier business, it was going to have to build a new competence in digital imaging. This new competence subsequently helped Canon to extend its product range to include laser copiers, color copiers, and digital cameras.

● **White Spaces**   The lower-right quadrant is titled *White spaces.* The question to be addressed here is how best to fill the "white space," or gaps between traditional markets, by creatively redeploying or recombining current core competences. In Canon's case, the company has been able to recombine its established core competences in precision mechanics, fine optics, and microelectronics with its more recently acquired competence in digital imaging to enter the market for computer printers and scanners.

● Mega-Opportunities

Mega-opportunities, represented by the upper-right quadrant of Figure 8.2, are those opportunities that do not overlap with the company's current market position or with its current endowment of competences. Nevertheless, a company may choose to pursue such opportunities if they are particularly attractive, significant, or relevant to the company's existing business opportunities. For example, back in 1979 Monsanto was primarily a manufacturer of chemicals, including fertilizers. However, the company saw that there were enormous opportunities in the emerging field of biotechnology. Specifically, senior research scientists at Monsanto believed it might be possible to produce genetically engineered crop seeds that would produce their own "organic" pesticides. The company embarked upon a massive investment that ultimately amounted to over a billion dollars to build a world-class competence in biotechnology. This investment was funded by cash flows generated from Monsanto's core chemical operations. The investment began to bear fruit in the mid-1990s, when Monsanto introduced a series of genetically engineered crop seeds, among which were Bollgard, a cotton seed that is resistant to many common pests including the bollworm, and Roundup-resistant soybean seeds (Roundup is an herbicide produced by Monsanto).[9]

The framework proposed by Hamel and Prahalad helps a company identify business opportunities, and it has clear implications for resource allocation (as exemplified by the Monsanto case). However, the great advantage of Hamel and Prahalad's framework is that it focuses explicitly on how a company can create value by building new competences or by recombining existing competences to enter new business areas (as Canon did with fax machines and bubble jet printers). Whereas traditional portfolio tools treat businesses as independent, Hamel and Prahalad's framework recognizes the interdependencies among businesses and focuses on opportunities to create value by building and leveraging competences. In this sense, their framework is a useful tool to help strategic managers reconceptualize their company's core competences, activities, and businesses to determine its desired future state—and so reduce the uncertainty surrounding the investment of its scarce resources.

Having reviewed the different businesses in the company's portfolio, corporate managers might decide to enter a new business area or industry to create more value and profit—something Monsanto did when it decided to enter the biotechnology industry. In the next three sections, we discuss the three main vehicles that companies can use to enter new businesses or industries: internal new ventures, acquisitions, and strategic alliances (including joint ventures).

Implementing Strategy Through Internal New Ventures

internal new venture

A company's creation of the value chain functions necessary to start a new business from scratch.

Internal new ventures involve creating the value chain functions necessary to start a new business from scratch. Internal new venturing is typically used to execute corporate-level strategy when a company possesses a set of valuable competences (resources and capabilities) in its existing businesses that can be leveraged or recombined to enter the new business area. As a rule, science-based companies that use their technology to create market opportunities in related areas tend to favor internal new venturing as an entry strategy. 3M, for example, has a near-legendary knack for shaping new markets from internally generated ideas. HP started out making test and measurement instruments and later moved into computers and then printers through an internal new-venture strategy. Microsoft started out making software for PCs, but it developed the Xbox video game business by leveraging its software skills and applying them to this new industry.

Even if it lacks the competences required to compete in a new business, a company may pursue internal new venturing if the industry it is entering is an emerging or embryonic industry. In such an industry, there are no established companies that possess the competences required to compete in that industry. Thus, a company is at no competitive disadvantage if it starts a new venture. Also, the option of acquiring an established enterprise that possesses those competences is not available, so a company may have no choice but to enter via an internal new venture.

This was the position in which Monsanto found itself back in 1979, when it contemplated entering the biotechnology field to produce herbicide and seeds yielding pest-resistant crops. The biotechnology field was young at that time, and there were no incumbent companies focused on applying biotechnology to agricultural products. Accordingly, Monsanto established an internal new venture to enter the business, even though at the time it lacked the required competences. Indeed, Monsanto's whole venturing strategy was built around the notion that it had the ability to build competences ahead of potential competitors and so gain a strong competitive lead in this newly emerging field.

● **Pitfalls with Internal New Ventures**

Despite the popularity of the internal new-venture strategy, the failure rate of internal new ventures is reportedly very high. Although precise figures are hard to come by, some commentators argue that the failure rate may be as high as 90%.[10] Three reasons are typically given to explain this relatively high failure rate: (1) market entry on too small a scale, (2) poor commercialization of the new-venture product, and (3) poor corporate management of the new-venture process.[11]

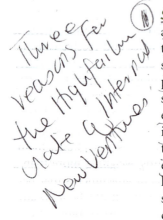

Three reasons for the high failure rate of Internal New Ventures

SMALL-SCALE MARKET ENTRY Research suggests that, on average, large-scale entry into a new business is often a critical precondition of success with a new venture. Although in the short run large-scale entry means significant development costs and substantial losses, in the long run (which can be as long as five to twelve years, depending on the industry) it brings greater returns than small-scale entry.[12] The reasons for this include the ability of large-scale entrants to more rapidly realize scale economies, build brand loyalty, and gain access to distribution channels, all of which increase the probability of a new venture's succeeding. In contrast, small-scale entrants may find themselves handicapped by high costs due to a dearth of scale economies and by a lack of market presence that limits their ability to build brand loyalties and gain access to distribution channels. These scale effects are particularly significant when a company is entering an established industry where incumbent companies do have the benefit of scale economies and have established brand loyalties—and the new entrant has to match these in order to succeed.

Figure 8.3 plots the relationships among scale of entry, profitability, and cash flow over time for successful small-scale and large-scale ventures. The slope of the curve shows how cash flow goes up and down over time. The figure illustrates that successful small-scale entry initially results in smaller negative cash flow and losses, but in the long run large-scale entry generates greater cash flows and profits. However, perhaps because of the costs of large-scale entry and the potential losses if the venture fails, many companies prefer a small-scale entry strategy. Acting on this preference can be a mistake, for the company fails to build up the market share necessary for long-term success.

POOR COMMERCIALIZATION Many internal new ventures are high-technology operations. To be commercially successful, science-based innovations must be developed with market requirements in mind. Many internal new ventures fail when a com-

Figure 8.3

Scale of Entry and Profitability

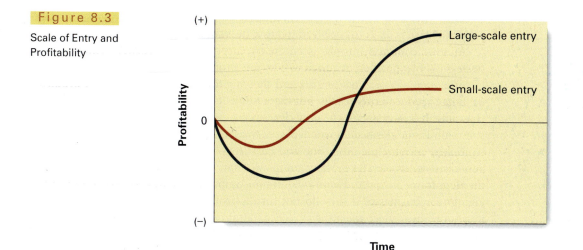

pany ignores the basic needs of the market. A company can be blinded by the technological possibilities of a new product and fail to analyze market opportunities properly. Thus, a new venture may fail because of a lack of commercialization or because it is marketing a technology for which there is no demand. One of the most dramatic new-venture failures in recent years, the Iridium satellite communications system developed by Motorola, illustrates this well. The Iridium project was breathtaking in its scope. It called for sixty-six communications satellites to be placed in an orbital network. In theory, this network of flying telecommunications switches would enable anyone with an Iridium satellite phone to place and receive calls, no matter where they were on the planet. Motorola's CEO, Christopher Galvin, called the project the eighth wonder of the world. Five billion dollars later, Iridium went live on November 1, 1998; nine months later, Iridium declared bankruptcy.

To its critics, the Iridium project was a classic case of a company being so blinded by the promise of a technology that it ignored market realities. Several serious shortcomings of the Iridium project limited its market acceptance. First, the phones themselves were large and heavy by current cell phone standards, weighing more than a pound. They were difficult to use and came with all sorts of attachments that perplexed many customers. Call clarity was poor, and despite the "it can be used anywhere" marketing theme, the phones could not be used inside cars or buildings—a major inconvenience for the busy globe-trotting executives at whom the service was aimed. Second, the service was expensive. The phones themselves cost $3,000 each, and airtime ranged from $4 to $9 per minute, placing the service way out of the reach of a mass market! Finally, the wide acceptance of much cheaper and more convenient cell phones limited the need for the Iridium phone. Why would a customer who had a cheaper, more convenient alternative pay $3,000 for the privilege of owning a phone the size and weight of a brick that would not work in places where cell phones do? Few customers chose Iridium, and the project collapsed.[13]

POOR CORPORATE MANAGEMENT Managing the new-venture process raises difficult organizational issues.[14] The shotgun approach of supporting many different internal new-venture projects can be a major error.[15] It places great demands on a company's cash flow and can result in the best ventures being starved of the cash they need for success.

In addition, if a company has too many internal new ventures in progress, management attention is likely to be spread too thin over these ventures, inviting disaster.

Another common mistake is failure by corporate management to establish the strategic context within which new-venture projects should be developed. Simply taking a team of research scientists and allowing them to do research in their favorite field may produce novel results, but these results may have little strategic or commercial value. It is necessary to be very clear about the strategic objectives of the venture and to understand exactly how it will seek to establish a competitive advantage.

Failure to anticipate the time and costs involved in the new-venture process is another common mistake. Many companies have unrealistic expectations regarding the time frame involved. Reportedly, some companies operate with a philosophy of killing new businesses if they do not turn a profit by the end of the third year—a most unrealistic view, given the evidence that it can take five to twelve years before a new venture generates substantial profits.

● Guidelines for Successful Internal New Venturing

To avoid the pitfalls just discussed, a company should adopt a structured approach to managing internal new venturing.[16] New venturing typically begins with R&D. To make effective use of its R&D capacity, a company must first spell out its strategic objectives and then communicate them to its scientists and engineers. Research, after all, makes sense only when it is undertaken in areas relevant to strategic goals.[17]

To increase the probability of commercial success, a company should foster close links between R&D and marketing personnel, for this is the best way to ensure that research projects address the needs of the market. The company should also foster close links between R&D and manufacturing personnel to ensure that the company has the capability to manufacture any proposed new products.

Many companies successfully integrate different functions by setting up project teams. Such teams comprise representatives of the various functional areas; their task is to oversee the development of new products. Another advantage of such teams is that they can significantly reduce the time it takes to develop a new product. Thus, while R&D personnel are working on the design, manufacturing personnel can be setting up facilities and marketing can be developing its plans. Because of such integration, Compaq needed only six months to take the first portable PC from an idea on the drawing board to a marketable product.

To use resources to the best effect, a company must also devise a selection process for choosing only the ventures that are most likely to meet with commercial success. Picking future winners is a tricky business; by their very definition, new ventures have an uncertain future. One study found the uncertainty surrounding new ventures to be so great that it usually took a company four to five years after launching the venture to reasonably estimate the venture's future profitability.[18] Nevertheless, a selection process is necessary if a company is to avoid spreading its resources over too many projects.

Once a project has been selected, management needs to monitor the progress of the venture closely. Evidence suggests that the most important criterion for evaluating a venture during its first four to five years is growth in market share, rather than cash flow or profitability. In the long run, the most successful ventures are those that increase their market share. A company should have clearly defined market share objectives for an internal new venture and should decide whether to retain or kill it in its early years on the basis of its ability to achieve market share goals. Only in the medium term should profitability and cash flow begin to take on greater importance.

Finally, the association of large-scale entry with greater long-term profitability suggests that a company can increase the probability of success for an internal new venture by "thinking big." Thinking big means the construction of efficient-scale production facilities before demand has fully materialized, large marketing expenditures to build a market presence and brand loyalty, and a commitment by corporate management to accept initial losses as long as market share is expanding. Note that it is not just high-tech companies that utilize internal new venturing—any company can use its existing skills and distinctive competences to develop new ways to gain access to customers, as the experience of Wal-Mart in the Running Case suggests.

RUNNING CASE

Wal-Mart Internally Ventures a New Kind of Retail Store

Wal-Mart has long recognized that its huge supercenters and discount stores do not serve the needs of customers who want a quick and convenient shopping experience—for example, when they want to pick up food for an evening meal. It also recognized that places like neighborhood supermarkets, drugstores, and convenience stores are a very lucrative segment of the food retailing market and customers spend billions of dollars shopping in these locations. So, in the early 2000s it decided to explore the concept of internally venturing a chain of what it calls Neighborhood Market supermarkets. These supermarkets are around 40,000 square feet, about a quarter the size of its superstores, and stock 20,000 to 30,000 items, as opposed to the over 100,000 items available in its larger stores. These stores are positioned to compete directly with supermarkets like Kroger and Albertsons and are open twenty-four hours a day. Moreover, they have a pharmacy and film-processing unit to draw trade from drugstores, which don't sell food that customers can shop for while they wait for their prescriptions to be filled. In addition, they have a large health and beauty products section (a high-profit-margin business), which encourages impulse buying.

Of course, Wal-Mart's main concern was that these new stores make a profitable return on its investment, and so it wanted to experiment by opening stores slowly in good locations to see if its cost-leadership model would work on this small a scale of operations. After all, margins are small in the supermarket business—often between 1 and 2%, which is lower than Wal-Mart is accustomed to. To keep costs low, it located its new stores in areas where it had a very efficient warehouse food preparation and delivery system. Its plan was to prepare items like bakery goods and meat and deli items in a central location and then ship them to the supermarkets in prepackaged containers. Each Neighborhood Market store is also tied in by satellite to Wal-Mart's retail link network, so food service managers know what kind of food is selling and what is not. They can then adjust the food each store sells by changing the mix that is trucked fresh to each store each day. Also, because no butcher or baker is present in each store, labor costs are reduced by 10%.

The effect of Wal-Mart's ability to apply its low-cost skills to this new kind of store is that the 100-plus stores that had been opened across the United States by 2007 are able to undercut the prices that supermarkets such as Publix, Kroger, and Albertsons charge by 10%. A typical Neighborhood Market generates around $20 million a year in sales, has a staff of ninety, and has a 2.3% profit margin, which is significantly higher than average in the supermarket industry.

Wal-Mart has been opening stores in widely different locations, such as Manhattan, Dallas, Salt Lake City, Tampa, and Ogden, apparently in an attempt to see if its business model for the new store will work in different kinds of urban settings. If it does, then the company plans to roll out 60 to 100 new stores each year and so build the Neighborhood Market chain in the way it has built others.

Implementing Strategy Through Acquisitions

acquisition

The purchase of one company by another.

An **acquisition** involves one company's purchasing another company. A company may use acquisitions in two ways: to strengthen its competitive position in an existing business by purchasing a competitor (horizontal integration) or to enter a new business or industry. Companies may use acquisitions to enter a new business when they lack the distinctive competences (resources and capabilities) required to compete in that area but can purchase, at a reasonable price, an incumbent company that *does* have those competences.

Companies also have a preference for acquisitions as an entry mode when they feel the need to *move fast*. As we noted earlier, building a new business through internal venturing can be a relatively slow process. Acquisition is a much quicker way to establish a significant market presence, create value, and increase profitability. A company can purchase a market leader in a strong cash position overnight, rather than spending years building up a market-leadership position through internal development, for example. Thus, when speed is important, acquisition is the favored entry mode.

Acquisitions are also often perceived as somewhat *less risky* than internal new ventures, primarily because they involve less uncertainty about the outcome. It is in the very nature of internal new ventures that large uncertainties are associated with projecting future profitability, revenues, and cash flows. In contrast, when one company acquires another, it knows the profitability, revenues, and market share of the acquired company, so there is considerably less uncertainty. In short, acquisition enables a company to buy an established business with a track record, and for this reason many companies favor an acquisition strategy.

Finally, acquisitions may be the preferred entry mode when the industry to be entered is well established and incumbent companies enjoy significant protection from barriers to entry. As we discussed in Chapter 3, barriers to entry arise from factors associated with product differentiation (brand loyalty), absolute cost advantages, and economies of scale, among others. When such barriers are substantial, a company finds entering an industry through internal new venturing difficult. To enter, a company may have to construct an efficient-scale manufacturing plant, undertake massive advertising to break down established brand loyalties, and quickly build up distribution outlets—all challenging goals likely to involve substantial expenditures.

In contrast, by acquiring an established enterprise, a company can circumvent most entry barriers. It can purchase a market leader that already benefits from substantial scale economies and brand loyalty. Thus, the greater the barriers to entry, the more likely it is that acquisition will be the favored entry mode. (We should note, however, that the attractiveness of acquisition is based on the assumption that an incumbent company can be acquired for less than it would cost to enter the same industry through internal new venturing. As we discuss in the next section, the validity of this assumption is often questionable.)

- **Pitfalls with Acquisitions**

For the reasons just noted, acquisitions have long been a popular vehicle for expanding the scope of the organization into new business areas. However, despite their popularity, there is ample evidence that many acquisitions fail to add value for the acquiring company and, indeed, often end up dissipating value. For example, a study by Mercer Management Consulting of 150 acquisitions worth more than $500 million concluded that 50% of these acquisitions ended up reducing shareholder value, often substantially, and another 33% generated only marginal returns.[19] Only 17% of these acquisitions were judged to be successful.

In fact, a wealth of evidence from academic research suggests that many acquisitions fail to realize their anticipated benefits.[20] Not only do profits and market share often decline following acquisition, but a substantial subset of acquired companies experience traumatic difficulties that ultimately lead to their being sold off by the acquiring company.[21] Thus, many acquisitions dilute value rather than create it.[22]

Why do so many acquisitions fail to create value? There appear to be four major reasons: (1) companies often experience difficulties when trying to integrate divergent corporate cultures, (2) companies overestimate the potential economic benefits from an acquisition, (3) acquisitions tend to be very expensive, and (4) companies often do not adequately screen their acquisition targets.

DIFFICULTIES WITH POSTACQUISITION INTEGRATION Having made an acquisition, the acquiring company has to integrate the acquired business into its own organization structure. Integration can entail the adoption of common management and financial control systems, the joining together of operations from the acquired and the acquiring company, or the establishment of linkages to share information and personnel. When integration is attempted, many unexpected problems can occur. Often, these problems stem from differences in corporate cultures. After an acquisition, many acquired companies experience high management turnover, possibly because their employees do not like the acquiring company's way of doing things.[23] Research evidence suggests that the loss of management talent and expertise, to say nothing of the damage from constant tension between different business units, can harm the performance of the acquired unit.[24]

OVERESTIMATING ECONOMIC BENEFITS Even when companies achieve integration, they often overestimate the potential for creating value by marrying different businesses. They overestimate the strategic advantages that can be derived from the acquisition and thus pay more for the target company than it is probably worth. Why? Top managers typically overestimate their ability to create value from an acquisition, primarily because rising to the top of a corporation gives them an exaggerated sense of their own capabilities.[25] The overestimation of economic benefits seems to have been a factor in the acquisitions of AOL by Time Warner and CBS by Paramount, for example.

THE EXPENSE OF ACQUISITIONS Acquisitions of companies whose stock is publicly traded tend to be very expensive, as Time Warner found out. When a company moves to acquire the stock of another company, the stock price frequently gets bid up in the acquisition process. In such cases, the acquiring company must often pay a significant premium over the current market value of the target. Often these premiums are 40 to 50% above the stock value of the target company before the acquisition was announced. Such a situation is particularly likely to occur in the case of contested bids, where two or more companies simultaneously bid for control of a single target company. For example, in 2005 Verizon and Qwest entered into a bidding war for another phone company, MCI Communications. Verizon initially bid $7.5 billion, but Qwest raised the bid to $9.75 billion, forcing Verizon to respond with an $8.5 billion bid, which MCI accepted (MCI accepted Verizon's bid, even though it was lower than Qwest's, because Verizon was in better financial shape).[26]

The debt taken on in order to finance expensive acquisitions can later become a noose around the acquiring company's neck, particularly if interest rates rise. Moreover, if the market value of the target company prior to an acquisition was a true reflection of that company's worth under its management at that time, a premium of 50% over this value means that the acquiring company has to improve the performance of the acquired unit by just as much if it is to reap a positive return on its investment. Such performance gains can be very difficult to achieve.

INADEQUATE PREACQUISITION SCREENING One common reason for the failure of acquisitions is management's inadequate attention to preacquisition screening.[27] Many companies decide to acquire other firms without thoroughly analyzing the potential benefits and costs. After the acquisition has been completed, many acquiring companies discover that instead of buying a well-run business, they have purchased a troubled organization. That was the experience of the insurance company Conseco when it purchased subprime lender Green Tree Financial. Once the acquisition was complete, Conseco discovered that there were serious financial problems at Green Tree, which had understated its bad loans by a wide margin. Ultimately, Green Tree's problems became so serious that Conseco was forced into bankruptcy. Even when the acquiring company believes that it has done its due diligence and thoroughly screened the target company, problems may be overlooked, as the target company has an incentive to hide negative information that might lead to a lower bid, just as Green Tree hid information about its bad loans from Conseco.

• Guidelines for Successful Acquisition

To avoid pitfalls and make successful acquisitions, companies need to take a structured approach with three main components: (1) target identification and preacquisition screening, (2) bidding strategy, and (3) integration.[28]

TARGET IDENTIFICATION AND SCREENING Thorough preacquisition screening increases a company's knowledge about potential takeover targets, leads to a more realistic assessment of the problems involved in executing an acquisition and integrating the new business into the company's organization structure, and lessens the risk of purchasing a problem business. The screening should begin with a detailed assessment of the strategic rationale for making the acquisition and with identification of the kind of enterprise that would make an ideal acquisition candidate.

Next, the company should scan a target population of potential acquisition candidates, evaluating each in terms of a detailed set of criteria, focusing on (1) financial position, (2) product market position, (3) competitive environment, (4) management capabilities, and (5) corporate culture. Such an evaluation should enable the company to identify the strengths and weaknesses of each candidate, the extent of potential economies of scope between the acquiring and the acquired companies, potential integration problems, and the compatibility of the corporate cultures of the acquiring and the acquired companies.

The company should then reduce the list of candidates to the most promising ones and evaluate them further. At this stage, it should sound out third parties such as investment bankers, whose opinions may be important and who may be able to offer valuable insights into the efficiency of target companies. The company that heads the list after this process should be the acquisition target.

BIDDING STRATEGY The objective of bidding strategy is to reduce the price that a company must pay for an acquisition candidate. The essential element of a good bidding strategy is timing. For example, Hanson PLC, one of the all-time most successful companies specializing in growth through takeovers, always looked for essentially sound businesses that were suffering from short-term problems due to cyclical in-

Strategy in Action

News Corp's Successful Acquisition Strategy

News Corporation is a company that has engineered scores of acquisitions to become one of the four largest and most powerful entertainment media companies in the world. What kinds of strategies has its CEO, Rupert Murdoch, used to create his media empire?

Rupert Murdoch was born into a newspaper family; his father owned and ran the *Adelaide News,* an Australian regional newspaper. When his father died in 1952, Murdoch gained control of the newspaper. He quickly set his sights on enlarging his customer base—after all, more profit is earned when more customers buy your products—and so he used his financial acumen to acquire more and more Australian newspapers. One of these, the *Daily Mirror* (which is quite similar to the *National Enquirer*), had connections to a major British "pulp" newspaper called *The Sun,* and Murdoch acquired *The Sun* and established it as a leading British tabloid.

His growing reputation as an entrepreneur enabled him to borrow more and more money from investors, who saw that he could create a much higher return from the assets he controlled than competitors could. Murdoch continued buying well-known newspapers, such as the British *Sunday Telegraph* and his first U.S. newspaper, the *San Antonio Express.* Then he launched the *National Star.* His growing profits allowed him to continue to borrow money, and he acquired the *New York Post, The Times,* and *The Sunday Times.*

Pursuing this strategy of horizontal integration through acquisitions to create one of the world's biggest newspaper empires was just one part of Murdoch's corporate strategy, however. He realized that industries in the entertainment and media sector can be divided into those that provide media content, or "software," such as books, movies, and television programming, and those that provide or supply the media channels or "hardware" necessary to get media software to customers, such as movie theaters, TV networks, and cable and satellite broadcasters. Murdoch realized he could create the most profit by getting involved in both the media software *and* the media hardware industries, which are essentially adjacent stages in the value chain of the entertainment and media sector. So Murdoch went all out to pursue a strategy of vertical integration and went on a buying spree to purchase global media companies in both the software and the hardware stages of the entertainment sector. He paid $1.5 billion for Metromedia, which owned seven stations that reached over 20% of households in the United States. He scored another major coup when he bought Twentieth Century Fox movie studios, a premium content provider. Now he had Fox's huge film library and the creative talents the studio possessed to make new films and TV programming. Murdock decided to create the Fox Broadcasting Company and buy or create its own U.S. network of Fox affiliates that would show programming developed by its own Fox movie studios. After a slow start, the Fox network gained popularity with shows like *The Simpsons*, which became Fox's first blockbuster program. Murdoch also engineered another coup when Fox purchased the sole rights to broadcast all NFL games for over $1 billion, shutting out NBC and making Fox the "fourth network." The Fox network has never looked back; it was one of the first to get into "reality" programming. News Corp has acquired a host of companies in the entertainment value chain that fit well with its newspaper, TV station, movie, and broadcasting companies to strengthen its competitive position in these industries.

dustry factors or from problems localized in one division. Such companies are typically undervalued by the stock market and thus can be picked up without payment of the standard 40 or 50% premium over current stock prices. With good timing, a company can make a bargain purchase.

③ **INTEGRATION** Despite good screening and bidding, an acquisition will fail unless positive steps are taken to integrate the acquired company into the organization structure of the acquiring firm. Integration should center on the source of the potential strategic advantages of the acquisition—for instance, opportunities to share marketing, manufacturing, procurement, R&D, financial, or management resources.

Integration should also be accompanied by steps to eliminate any duplication of facilities or functions. In addition, any unwanted divisions of the acquired company should be sold. Finally, if the different business activities are closely related, they will require a high degree of integration. In the case of a company pursuing unrelated diversification, the level of integration may be a minimal problem. But with a strategy of related diversification, the problem of integrating the two companies' operations is much greater. One company that has succeeded well in its acquisition strategy is News Corporation, discussed in the Strategy in Action feature.

Implementing Strategy Through Strategic Alliances

strategic alliance

A cooperative agreement between two or more companies to work together and share resources to achieve a common business objective.

joint venture

A formal type of strategic alliance in which two companies jointly create a new, separate company to enter a new product market or industry.

Strategic alliances are cooperative agreements between two or more companies to work together and share resources to achieve a common business objective. A **joint venture** is a formal type of strategic alliance in which two companies jointly create a new, separate company to enter a new business area.

A company may prefer internal new venturing to acquisition as an entry strategy into new business areas and yet hesitate to commit itself to an internal new venture because of the risks and costs of building a new operation "from the ground up." Such a situation is likely when a company sees the advantages of establishing a new business in an embryonic or growth industry, but the risks and costs associated with the business are more than it is willing to assume on its own. In this case, a company may decide to form some kind of strategic alliance with another company.

As noted earlier, strategic alliances are cooperative agreements between companies. The parties to an alliance may be actual or potential competitors, they may be situated at different stages in an industry's value chain, or they may be in different businesses but have a joint interest in working together to develop distinctive competences in R&D or marketing that are useful to both parties or decide to cooperate on a particular problem, such as developing a new product or technology.

Strategic alliances run the gamut from informal agreements and short-term contracts, where companies agree to share know-how, to formal contractual agreements, such as long-term outsourcing agreements and joint ventures in which both companies establish and assume ownership of a new company. Thus, some strategic alliances are meant to be temporary, but others may be a prelude to a permanent relationship. For example, sometimes long-term agreements result in the establishment of a joint venture (they may even lead to a merger through acquisition). Strategic alliances of all kinds are often used as a vehicle that enables companies to share the risks and costs of developing a new business. In any event, strategic alliances are a valuable strategic tool that helps companies maximize their business opportunities, especially in today's competitive global environment.

• Advantages of Strategic Alliances

Companies enter into strategic alliances with competitors to achieve a number of strategic objectives.[29] First, strategic alliances may be a way of facilitating entry into a market. For example, Motorola initially found it very difficult to gain access to the Japanese cellular telephone market because of formal and informal Japanese trade barriers. The turning point for Motorola came when it formed an alliance with Toshiba to build microprocessors. As part of the deal, Toshiba provided Motorola with marketing help, including some of its best managers. This helped Motorola win government approval to enter the Japanese market.[30]

Second, many companies enter into strategic alliances to share the fixed costs and associated risks that arise from the development of new products or processes. Motorola's alliance with Toshiba was partly motivated by a desire to share the high fixed costs associated with setting up the capital-intensive operation that manufacturing microprocessors entailed (it cost Motorola and Toshiba close to $1 billion to set up their facility). Few companies can afford the costs and risks of going it alone on such a venture. Similarly, an alliance between Boeing and a number of Japanese companies to build Boeing's latest commercial jetliner, the 787, was motivated by Boeing's desire to share the burden of the estimated $8 billion investment required to develop the aircraft.

Third, many alliances can be seen as a way of bringing together complementary skills and assets that neither company could easily develop on its own. For example, Microsoft and Toshiba established an alliance aimed at developing embedded microprocessors (essentially, tiny computers) that can perform a variety of entertainment functions in an automobile (for example, they can run a backseat DVD player or a wireless Internet connection). The processors will run a version of Microsoft's Windows CE operating system. Microsoft brings its software engineering skills to the alliance, and Toshiba brings its skills in developing microprocessors.[31]

● Disadvantages of Strategic Alliances

Strategic alliances have many significant advantages, but there are also several disadvantages that may arise. First, strategic alliances may provide a company's competitors with access to valuable low-cost manufacturing knowledge and a route to gain new technology and market access.[32] For example, some commentators have argued that many strategic alliances between U.S. and Japanese firms facilitated an implicit Japanese strategy to keep higher-paying, higher-value-added jobs in Japan while gaining the project engineering and production process skills that underlie the competitive success of many U.S. companies.[33] These observers maintain that Japanese success in the machine tool and semiconductor industries was the result of knowledge acquired through strategic alliances with U.S. companies. And they contend that U.S. managers aided the Japanese by entering into alliances that channeled new inventions to Japan and provided a convenient sales and distribution network for the resulting Japanese products sent back for sale in the United States. Although such agreements may generate short-term profits, in the long run the result is to "hollow out" U.S. firms, leaving them with no competitive advantage in the global marketplace.

Consider, for example, the situation in a joint venture, a formal strategic alliance in which two companies team up and establish a separate company to pool their complementary skills and assets. Such an arrangement enables a company to share the substantial risks and costs involved in developing a new business opportunity and may increase the probability of success in the new business. But there are three main drawbacks to joint-venture arrangements.

First, just as a joint venture allows a company to share the risks and costs of developing a new business, it also requires the sharing of profits if the new business succeeds. Second, a company that enters into a joint venture always runs the risk of giving critical know-how away to its joint-venture partner, which might use that know-how to compete directly with the company in the future. Third, the venture partners must share control. If the partners have different business philosophies, time horizons, or investment preferences, substantial problems can arise. Conflicts over how to run the joint venture can tear it apart and result in business failure.

Thus, the critics of strategic alliances have a point: alliances do have risks, and the more formal or extensive the alliance, the greater the possibility that a company may give away more than it gets in return. Nevertheless, there are so many examples of apparently successful alliances between companies, including alliances between U.S. and Japanese companies, that it seems that long-term strategic alliances can and often do have more advantages than disadvantages. The next section suggests why, and under what conditions, companies can gain these advantages.

● Making Strategic Alliances Work

The failure rate for strategic alliances is quite high. For example, one study of forty-nine global strategic alliances found that two-thirds ran into serious managerial and financial troubles within two years of their formation. The same study suggests that although many of these problems are ultimately resolved, 33% of strategic alliances are ultimately rated as failures by the parties involved.[34] The success of a strategic alliance seems to be a function of three main factors: partner selection, alliance structure, and the manner in which the alliance is managed.

PARTNER SELECTION One of the keys to making a strategic alliance work is to select the right kind of partner. A good partner has three principal characteristics. First, a good partner helps the company achieve strategic goals, such as gaining market access, sharing the costs and risks of new-product development, or gaining access to critical core competences. In other words, the partner must have capabilities that the company lacks and that it values. Second, a good partner shares the firm's vision for the purpose of the alliance. If two companies approach an alliance with radically different agendas, the chances are great that the relationship will not be harmonious and will end in divorce. Third, a good partner is unlikely to try to exploit the alliance opportunistically for its own ends—that is, to expropriate or even steal the company's technological know-how while giving little in return. In this respect, firms with reputations for fair play to maintain probably make the best partners. For example, IBM is involved in so many strategic alliances that it would not pay the company to cheat on individual alliance partners (in 2003, IBM reportedly had more than 150 major strategic alliances, and the number has increased since then).[35] Doing so would tarnish IBM's reputation as a good ally and make it difficult for IBM to attract alliance partners in the future. Because IBM attaches great importance to its alliances, it is unlikely to engage in the kind of underhanded behavior that critics highlight. Similarly, their reputations make it less likely (though by no means impossible) that such Japanese firms as Sony, Toshiba, and Fuji, which have histories of alliances with non-Japanese firms, would exploit an alliance partner.

To find and select a partner with these three characteristics, a company needs to thoroughly investigate potential alliance candidates. To increase the probability of selecting a good partner, the company should collect as much relevant publicly available information about potential allies as possible; collect data from informed third parties, including companies that have had alliances with the potential partners, investment bankers who have had dealings with them, and some of their former employees; and get to know potential partners as well as possible before committing to an alliance. This last step should include face-to-face meetings between senior managers to ensure that the "chemistry" is right.

ALLIANCE STRUCTURE Once a partner has been selected, the alliance should be structured so that the company's risk of giving too much away to the partner is reduced to an acceptable level. Figure 8.4 depicts the four safeguards against opportunism or

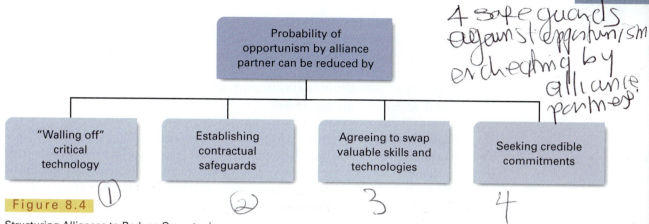

4 safeguards against opportunism or cheating by alliance partners

Figure 8.4
Structuring Alliances to Reduce Opportunism

(1)

cheating by alliance partners, discussed below. First, alliances can be designed to make it difficult or impossible to transfer technology meant to be kept secret and proprietary. Specifically, the design, development, and servicing of a product manufactured by an alliance can be structured so as to "wall off" and thus protect sensitive technologies from partners. In the alliance between GE and Snecma to build commercial aircraft engines, for example, GE reduced the risk of "excess transfer" by walling off certain sections of the production process. This effectively cut off the transfer of what GE regarded as key competitive technology, while permitting Snecma access to final assembly. Similarly, in the alliance between Boeing and the Japanese to build the 767, Boeing walled off research, design, and marketing functions considered central to its competitive position, while allowing the Japanese to share in production technology. Boeing also walled off new technologies not required for 767 production.[36]

Second, contractual safeguards can be written into an alliance agreement to guard against the risk of being exploited by a partner. For example, TRW Systems, an auto-parts supplier now part of Honeywell, had strategic alliances with large Japanese car component suppliers to produce seat belts, engine valves, and steering gears for sale to Japanese-owned car assembly plants in the United States. TRW ensured that clauses in each of its alliance contracts barred the Japanese firms from competing with TRW to supply U.S.-owned auto companies with component parts. So TRW protected itself against the possibility that the Japanese companies entered the alliances only as a way of gaining access to the U.S. market to compete with TRW on its home turf.

Third, both parties to an alliance can promise in advance to swap important proprietary skills and technologies, thereby ensuring the opportunity for equitable gain. Cross-licensing agreements are one way to achieve this goal. For example, in an alliance between Motorola and Toshiba, Motorola licensed some of its microprocessor technology to Toshiba and in return Toshiba licensed some of its memory-chip technology to Motorola.

Fourth, the risk of deceitful behavior by an alliance partner can be reduced if the less powerful firm extracts a significant *credible commitment* from its partner in advance. The purpose of a credible commitment is to send a signal that the company making the commitment will do its best to ensure that the alliance works. Such credible commitments often come in the form of capital investments. For example, in 2004 the small British biotechnology firm Cambridge Antibody Technology entered into a five-year alliance with the large pharmaceutical company AstraZeneca to develop new treatments for inflammatory disorders. As part of the deal, AstraZeneca agreed to invest $140 million, a 20% equity stake in the smaller company. This investment increases the probability that AstraZeneca will do its best to ensure that the alliance achieves its strategic goals.[37]

MANAGING THE ALLIANCE Once a partner has been selected and an appropriate alliance structure agreed on, the task facing the company is to maximize the benefits from the alliance. One important ingredient of success appears to be sensitivity to cultural differences. Many differences in management style are attributable to cultural differences, and managers need to make allowances for these in dealing with their partner. Beyond this, maximizing the benefits from an alliance seems to involve building trust between partners and learning from partners.[38]

Managing an alliance successfully requires building interpersonal relationships between the firms' managers, or what is sometimes referred to as *relational capital*.[39] This is one lesson that can be learned from the successful strategic alliance between Ford and Mazda. Ford and Mazda set up a framework of meetings within which their managers not only discuss matters pertaining to the alliance but also have time to get to know each other better. The belief is that the resulting friendships help build trust and facilitate harmonious relations between the two firms. Personal relationships also foster an informal management network between the firms. This network can then be used to help solve problems arising in more formal contexts (such as in joint committee meetings between personnel from the two firms). When entering an alliance, a company must take some measures to ensure that it learns from its alliance partner and then puts that knowledge to good use within its own organization.

In sum, although strategic alliances often have a distinct advantage over internal new venturing or acquisitions as a means of establishing a new business operation, they also have certain drawbacks. When deciding whether to go it alone, acquire, or cooperate with another company in a strategic alliance, managers need to assess carefully the pros and cons of the alternatives.

Summary of Chapter

1. Strategic change is the movement of a company from its present state to some desired future state to increase its competitive advantage. Two main types of strategic change are reengineering and restructuring.

2. Strategic change is implemented through a series of stages. The first stage in the change process is determining the need for change. Strategic managers use a SWOT analysis to determine the company's present state and then characterize its desired future state. The second stage in the change process is identifying the obstacles to change at all levels in the organization. The last two stages are managing change and evaluating change.

3. An important technique used to identify a company's desired future state is to analyze it as a portfolio of core competences—as opposed to a portfolio of businesses. In this approach, strategic change is oriented toward maintaining existing competences, building new competences, and leveraging competences by applying them to new business opportunities.

4. There are three vehicles that companies use to enter new business areas: internal ventures, acquisitions, and strategic alliances (including joint ventures).

5. Internal new venturing is used as an entry strategy when a company possesses a set of valuable competences in its existing businesses that can be leveraged or recombined to enter the new business area.

6. Many internal ventures fail because of entry on too small a scale, poor commercialization, and/or poor corporate management of the internal venture process. Guarding against failure involves a structured approach to project selection and management, integration of R&D and marketing to improve commercialization of a venture idea, monitoring by management, and entry on a significant scale.

7. Acquisitions are often favored as an entry strategy when the company lacks important competences (resources and capabilities) required to compete in an area but can purchase, at a reasonable price, an incumbent company that has those competences. Acquisitions also tend to be favored when the barriers to entry into the target industry are high and when the company is unwilling to accept the time frame, development costs, and risks of internal new venturing.

8. Many acquisitions fail because of poor postacquisition integration, overestimation of the value that can be created from an acquisition, the high cost of acquisition, and poor preacquisition screening. Guarding against acquisition failure requires structured screening, good bidding strategies, and positive attempts to integrate the acquired company into the organization of the acquiring firm.

9. Strategic alliances may be the preferred entry strategy when (1) the risks and costs associated with setting up a new business unit are more than the company is willing to assume on its own and (2) the company can increase the probability of successfully establishing a new business by teaming up with another company that has skills and assets complementing its own.

10. Strategic alliances range from short-term informal to long-term formal cooperative agreements between companies. Alliances can facilitate entry into markets, enable partners to share the fixed costs and risks associated with new products and processes, and facilitate the transfer of complementary skills and assets between companies.

11. The drawbacks of formal strategic alliances, particularly joint ventures, include the risk that a company may give away technological know-how and market access to its alliance partner without getting much in return.

12. The disadvantages associated with alliances can be reduced if the company selects partners carefully, paying close attention to their reputation, and structures the alliance in such a way as to avoid unintended transfers of know-how. Once the alliance structure has been agreed on, being sensitive to cultural differences and building relational capital can help to maximize the benefits from the alliance.

Discussion Questions

1. Outline the issues and problems involved in identifying a company's desired future state.

2. How should a company manage the change process to ensure that it reaches its desired future state?

3. Under what circumstances might it be best to enter a new business area by acquisition? Under what circumstances might internal new venturing be the preferred mode of entry?

4. If IBM decides to diversify into the wireless telecommunications business, what entry strategy would you recommend that the company pursue? Why?

5. Under what circumstances might a long-term strategic alliance with a key supplier enable a company to capture most of the benefits associated with vertical integration, without bearing the associated risks and costs?

Practicing Strategic Management

SMALL-GROUP EXERCISE

Identifying News Corp's Strategies

Break up into groups of three to five people, and discuss the following questions. Appoint one group member as a spokesperson who will communicate your findings to the class when called upon to do so by the instructor.

1. What kind of corporate-level strategies did News Corp pursue to build its multibusiness model?

2. What are the advantages and disadvantages associated with these strategies?

EXPLORING THE WEB

Visiting UTC

Visit the website of United Technologies, or UTC (**www.utc.com**). Using the information contained on that website, answer the following questions.

1. In what major businesses is UTC involved? Does this portfolio make sense from a value creation perspective? Why?

2. What (if any) changes would you make to UTC's portfolio of businesses? Why would you make these changes?

3. What (if any) core competences do you think UTC's major business units share? Is there any evidence that UTC creates new businesses by leveraging its core competences?

4. How did UTC enter new business areas—through acquisitions, internal new ventures, or some combination of the two? Historically, which entry mode has been the most important for UTC?

5. Is UTC an example of a successful acquirer? Justify your answer.

General Task   By searching through information sources on the Web, find an example of a company that has recently made a major acquisition. Identify and evaluate the strategic rationale behind this acquisition. Does it make sense?

CLOSING CASE

Oracle's Growing Portfolio of Businesses

Oracle Corporation, based in Redwood City, California, is the world's largest maker of database software and the third-largest global software company in terms of sales, after Microsoft and IBM. This commanding position is not enough for Oracle, however, which has set its sights on becoming the global leader in the corporate applications software market. Here, Germany's SAP, which has 45% of the market, is the acknowledged leader, and Oracle, with only 19%, is a distant second.[a] Corporate applications is a fast growing and highly profitable market, however, and Oracle has been snapping up leading companies in this segment at a fast pace. Its goal is to quickly build the distinctive competences it needs to expand the range of products that it can offer to its existing customers and to attract new customers to compete with SAP. Beginning in 2005, Oracle's CEO, Larry Ellison, spent $19 billion to acquire fourteen leading suppliers of corporate software, including two of the top

five companies: PeopleSoft, a leading human resource management (HRM) software supplier, which it bought for $10 billion, and Siebel Systems, a leader in customer relationship management (CRM) software, which cost Oracle $5.8 billion.

Oracle expects several competitive advantages to result from its use of acquisitions to pursue the corporate strategy of horizontal integration. First, it is now able to meld or bundle the best software applications of these acquired companies with Oracle's own first-class set of corporate and database software programs to create a new integrated suite of software that will allow corporations to manage all their functional activities, such as accounting, marketing, sales, HRM, CRM, and supply-chain management. Second, through these acquisitions Oracle obtained access to thousands of new customers—all the companies that currently use the software of the companies it acquired. These companies now become potential new customers for all of Oracle's other database and corporate software offerings. Third, beyond increasing the range of its products and number of its customers, Oracle's acquisitions have consolidated the corporate software industry. By taking over some of its largest rivals, Oracle has become the second largest supplier of corporate software, and so it is better positioned to compete with leader SAP.

Achieving the advantages of its new strategy may not be easy, however. The person in charge of assembling Oracle's new unified software package and selling it to customers is John Wookey, Oracle's senior vice president in charge of applications, who jokingly says that his "head is the one on the chopping block if this doesn't work." In the past, CEO Ellison, who expects a lot from his top executives, has been quick to fire executives who don't perform well. To grow Oracle's market share and profits, Wookey must draw on the best of the technology Oracle has obtained from each of the companies it acquired to build its new suite of state-of-the-art corporate software applications. He also has to persuade customers not to switch software vendors—for example, jump ship to SAP—while Oracle builds its package and then to gradually adopt more and more of Oracle's software offerings to run their functional activities.

Wookey is well placed to implement Oracle's new strategy: he is known as a consensus builder and product champion both inside the company and outside, when interacting with Oracle's customers. He spends his working day sharing information with the top managers of Oracle's various businesses and meeting with his team of fourteen senior staff members to work out how the whole package should be put together and what it should include. He also regularly visits major customers, especially those that came with its acquisitions, to gain their input into how and what kind of software package Oracle should build. Wookey even formed an advisory council of leading customers to help make sure the final package meets their needs. One of Wookey's notable achievements was retaining the top-rate software engineers Oracle obtained from its acquired rivals. These people could have easily found high-paying jobs elsewhere, but most of the top engineers Oracle wanted stayed to help it achieve its new goals.

Nevertheless, by the end of 2006 there were signs that all was not going well with Oracle's new strategy. SAP is a powerful competitor, and its popular software is fast becoming the industry standard, so unseating SAP in the $23.4 billion corporate software market will not be easy. Moreover, SAP is still the leader in more advanced functional applications incorporating the latest technologies, and its proprietary technology is all homegrown so it doesn't face the huge implementation issue of bringing together the applications from many different acquisitions. Preventing customers from switching to SAP may not be easy now that their loyalty to their old software supplier has been broken because of its acquisition by Oracle. Analysts also say that Oracle runs the risk of stretching itself too thin if it continues to purchase too many companies too quickly, because high-tech acquisitions are the most difficult to pull off in terms of management and execution.[b]

Larry Ellison is under pressure to accelerate sales growth and surpass investors' expectations, and only if Oracle can put out corporate application software sales numbers that beat expectations will analysts regard its strategy as a success. Still, Oracle's stock gained 47% in 2006 compared to SAP's 15%, and in 2007 Oracle announced record revenues and profits. Its stock price jumped, as investors now believe Ellison and Wookey have the ability to make its acquisitions pay. In 2008, Oracle announced yet another major acquisition—software supplier BEA Systems. Will it be able to continue its track record of success?

Case Discussion Questions

1. In what ways is Oracle seeking to create value from its acquisitions?

2. Based upon the ways it is seeking to increase the value it creates, what is its corporate-level strategy?

TEST PREPPER

True/False Questions

___ **1.** Strategic change is the movement of a company away from its present state toward some desired future state to increase its competitive advantage and profitability.

___ **2.** Business processes are the responsibility of one specific function in the organization.

___ **3.** The second step in implementing strategic change is for strategic managers to recognize the need for change—to see that there is a gap between desired company performance and actual performance.

___ **4.** The larger and more complex the organization, the harder it is to implement change, because inertia is likely to be more pervasive.

___ **5.** The advantage of bottom-up change is that it removes some of the obstacles to change by including them in the strategic plan.

___ **6.** A joint venture is a formal type of strategic alliance in which two companies jointly create a new, separate company to enter a new business area.

___ **7.** According to Hamel and Prahalad, a core competence is a central value creation capability of a company—that is, a core skill.

Multiple-Choice Questions

8. ___ is a process whereby, in their effort to boost company performance, managers focus not on the company's functional activities but on the business processes underlying its value creation operations.
   a. A business process
   b. Restructuring
   c. Reengineering
   d. Outsourcing
   e. A change process

9. When a company is analyzed as a portfolio of core competences, corporate development is oriented toward all of the following except ___.
   a. maintaining existing competences
   b. building new competences
   c. decreasing obstacles to change

   d. leveraging competences by applying them to new business opportunities
   e. all of the above

10. Safeguards against opportunism or cheating by alliance partners include all of the following except ___.
   a. walling off and protecting sensitive technologies from partners
   b. establishing contractual safeguards to guard against being exploited
   c. promising in advance to swap important proprietary skills
   d. reengineering the organization
   e. extracting a significant credible commitment from the partner in advance

11. Obstacles to change can be found at four levels in the organization: ___.
   a. divisional, corporate, functional, research and development
   b. divisional, functional, corporate, human resource management
   c. individual, organizational, divisional, corporate
   d. marketing, service support, corporate, divisional
   e. none of the above

12. The success of a strategic alliance includes all of the following except ___.
   a. a supply partner with valuable low-cost manufacturing knowledge
   b. partner selection
   c. alliance structure
   d. alliance management
   e. all of the above

13. Microsoft and Toshiba pooled resources to develop embedded microprocessors that can perform a variety of entertainment functions in an automobile. This is an example of ___.
   a. joint diversification
   b. divestment
   c. a strategic alliance
   d. global integration
   e. restructuring

14. The main drawbacks to joint-venture arrangements include all of the following *except* _____ .
a. selecting partners carefully
b. sharing profits
c. the risk of giving critical know-how away
d. sharing control
e. none of the above

15. Means of guarding against the failure of an internal venture include all of the following *except* _____ .
a. strategic alliances
b. a structured approach to project selection
c. a structured approach to management
d. integration of R&D and marketing to improve commercialization
e. entry on a significant scale

Chapter 9

Implementing Strategy Through Organizational Design

Learning Objectives

After reading this chapter, you should be able to

1. Discuss how organizational strategy is implemented through organization structure

2. Explain the building blocks of organization structure

3. Distinguish between vertical and horizontal differentiation

4. Discuss the importance of integration and the relationship between differentiation and integration

5. Explain the nature and functions of strategic control systems

Chapter Outline

I. The Role of Organization Structure
  a. Building Blocks of Organization Structure
II. Vertical Differentiation
  a. Problems with Tall Structures
  b. Centralization or Decentralization?
III. Horizontal Differentiation
  a. Functional Structure
  b. Product Structure
  c. Product-Team Structure
  d. Geographic Structure
  e. Multidivisional Structure

IV. Integration and Organizational Control
  a. Forms of Integrating Mechanisms
  b. Differentiation and Integration
V. The Nature of Organizational Control
  a. Strategic Controls
  b. Financial Controls
  c. Output Controls
  d. Behavior Controls

Overview

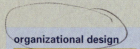

organizational design

The process through which managers select the combination of organization structure and control systems that they believe will enable the company to create and sustain a competitive advantage.

In this chapter, we examine how a company should organize its activities to create the most value. In Chapter 1, we defined *strategy implementation* as the way a company creates the organizational arrangements that enable it to pursue its strategy most effectively. Strategy is implemented through organizational design.

Organizational design means selecting the combination of organization structure and control systems that allows a company to pursue its strategy most effectively—that lets it *create and sustain a competitive advantage*. Good organizational design increases profits in two ways. First, it economizes on operating costs and lowers the costs of value creation activities. Second, it enhances the ability of a company's value creation functions to achieve superior efficiency, quality, innovativeness, and customer responsiveness and to obtain a differentiation advantage.

The primary role of organization structure and control is twofold: (1) to *coordinate* the activities of employees in such a way that they work together effectively to implement a strategy that increases competitive advantage and (2) to *motivate* em-

[handwritten note in margin: strategy based on the environment, integration, control and structure]

ployees and provide them with incentives to achieve superior efficiency, quality, innovation, or customer responsiveness. Microsoft's strategy, for example, is to speed decision making and new-product development, and it constantly works to keep its structure as flexible as possible to allow its teams of programmers to respond quickly to the ever-changing nature of competition in the software industry.

Organization structure and control shape the way people behave and determine how they will act in the organizational setting. If a new CEO wants to know why it takes a long time for people to make decisions in a company, why there is a lack of cooperation between sales and manufacturing, or why product innovations are few and far between, he or she needs to look at the design of the organization structure and control system and analyze how it coordinates and motivates employees' behavior. An analysis of how structure and control work makes it possible to change them to improve both coordination and motivation. Good organizational design allows an organization to improve its ability to create value and obtain a competitive advantage.

In this chapter, we first examine the organization structures available to strategic managers to coordinate and motivate employees. Then we consider the strategic control systems that companies use in conjunction with their organization structures to monitor and motivate managers and employees at all levels and encourage them to be responsive to changes in the competitive environment.

The Role of Organization Structure

After formulating a company's strategies, management must make designing organization structure its next priority, for strategy is also implemented through organization structure. The value creation activities of organizational members are meaningless unless some type of structure is used to assign people to tasks and link the activities of different people and functions.[1] As we saw in Chapter 4, each organizational function needs to develop a distinctive competence in a value creation activity in order to increase efficiency, quality, innovation, or customer responsiveness. Thus, each function needs a structure designed to allow it to develop its skills and become more specialized and productive. As functions become increasingly specialized, however, employees often begin to pursue their own function's goals exclusively and lose sight of the need to communicate and coordinate with other functions. The goals of R&D, for example, center on innovation and product design, whereas the goals of manufacturing often revolve around increasing efficiency. Left to themselves, people associated with the various functions may have little to say to one another, and value creation opportunities will be lost.

The role of organization structure is to provide the vehicle through which managers can coordinate the activities of a company's various functions, divisions, and business units to take advantage of skills and competences. To pursue a cost-leadership strategy, for example, a company must design a structure that facilitates close coordination between the activities of manufacturing and those of R&D to ensure that innovative products can be produced reliably and cost-effectively. To achieve gains from economies of scope and resource sharing between divisions, management must design mechanisms that motivate and encourage divisional managers to communicate and share their skills and knowledge. In pursuing a global or transnational strategy, managers must create the right kind of organization structure for managing the flow of resources and capabilities between domestic and overseas divisions. Next, we examine the basic building blocks of organization structure to understand how it shapes the behavior of people, functions, and divisions.

● Building Blocks of Organization Structure

differentiation

The way in which a company allocates people and resources to organizational tasks and divides them into functions and divisions so as to create value.

vertical differentiation

The process by which strategic managers choose how to distribute decision-making authority to best control value creation activities in an organization.

horizontal differentiation

The process by which strategic managers choose how to divide people and tasks into functions and divisions to increase their ability to create value.

integration

The means a company uses to coordinate people, functions, and divisions to accomplish organizational tasks.

The basic building blocks of organization structure are differentiation and integration. **Differentiation** is the way in which a company allocates people and resources to organizational tasks in order to create value.[2] Generally, the greater the number of different functions or divisions in an organization and the more skilled and specialized they are, the higher is the level of differentiation. For example, a company such as General Motors, with more than 300 different divisions and a multitude of different sales, research and development, and design departments, has a much higher level of differentiation than a local manufacturing company or restaurant. In deciding how to differentiate the organization to create value, strategic managers face two choices.

First, strategic managers must choose how to distribute *decision-making authority* in the organization to best control value creation activities; these are **vertical differentiation** choices.[3] For example, corporate managers must decide how much authority to delegate to managers at the divisional or functional level. Second, corporate managers must choose how to divide people and tasks into functions and divisions to increase their ability to create value; these are **horizontal differentiation** choices. Should there be separate sales and marketing departments, for example, or should the two be combined? What is the best way to divide the sales force to maximize its ability to serve customers' needs—by type of customer or by region in which customers are located?

Integration is the means by which a company seeks to coordinate people, functions, and divisions to accomplish organizational tasks.[4] As we have just noted, when separate and distinct value creation functions exist, people tend to pursue their own function's goals and objectives. An organization has to create a structure that encourages the different functions and divisions to coordinate their activities. An organization uses integrating mechanisms and control systems to promote coordination and cooperation between functions and divisions. For instance, to speed innovation and product development, Microsoft established teams so that employees could work together to exchange information and ideas effectively. Similarly, establishing organizational norms, shared values, and a common culture that supports innovation promotes integration.

In short, differentiation consists of the way a company divides itself into parts (functions and divisions), and integration consists of the way those parts are then combined. Together, the two processes determine how an organization structure will operate and how successfully strategic managers will be able to create value through their chosen strategies. Consequently, it is necessary to understand the principles behind organizational design. We start by looking at differentiation.

Vertical Differentiation

The aim of vertical differentiation is to specify the reporting relationships that link people, tasks, and functions at all levels of a company. Fundamentally, this means that management chooses the appropriate number of hierarchical levels and the correct span of control for implementing a company's strategy most effectively.

Figure 9.1

Tall and Flat Structures

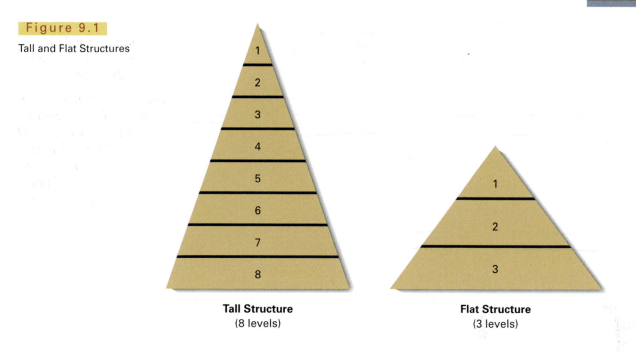

Tall Structure
(8 levels)

Flat Structure
(3 levels)

span of control

The number of subordinates a manager directly manages.

flat structure

A structure with few hierarchical levels and a relatively wide span of control.

tall structure

A structure with many hierarchical levels and a relatively narrow span of control.

The organizational hierarchy establishes the authority structure from the top to the bottom of the organization. The **span of control** is defined as the number of subordinates a manager directly manages.[5] The basic choice is whether to aim for a **flat structure**, with few hierarchical levels and thus a relatively wide span of control, or a **tall structure**, with many levels and thus a relatively narrow span of control (see Figure 9.1). Tall structures have many hierarchical levels relative to their size, and flat structures have relatively few.[6] For example, research suggests that the average number of hierarchical levels for a company employing 3,000 people is seven. Thus, such an organization having nine levels would be called tall, and one having four would be called flat. With its 30,000 employees and five hierarchical levels, Microsoft has a relatively flat structure.

Companies choose the number of levels they need on the basis of their strategy and the functional tasks necessary to achieve this strategy.[7] High-tech companies, for example, often pursue a strategy of differentiation based on service and quality. Consequently, these companies usually have flat structures, giving employees wide discretion to meet customers' demands without having to continuously consult with supervisors.[8] The crux of the matter is that the allocation of authority and responsibility in a company must match the needs of its corporate-, business-, and functional-level strategies.[9]

● **Problems with Tall Structures**

As a company grows and diversifies, the number of levels in its hierarchy of authority increases to allow it to monitor and coordinate employee activities efficiently. Research shows that the number of hierarchical levels is predictable based on company size (see Figure 9.2).[10]

Companies with approximately 1,000 employees usually have four levels in the hierarchy: chief executive officer, departmental vice presidents, first-line supervisors, and shop-floor employees. Those with 3,000 employees tend to have increased their level of vertical differentiation by raising the number of levels to eight. Something interesting happens to those with more than 3,000 employees, however. Even when

Figure 9.2

Relationship Between
Company Size and
Number of Hierarchical
Levels

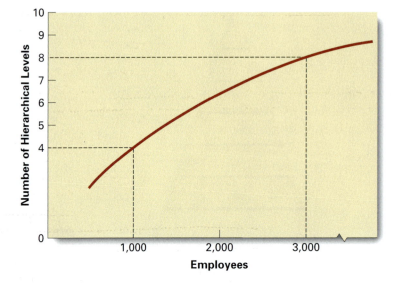

**principle of the minimum
chain of command**

The principle that
managers should choose
a hierarchy with the
minimum number of
levels of authority
necessary to achieve
the company's strategy.

companies grow to 10,000 employees or more, the number of hierarchical levels rarely increases beyond nine or ten. As organizations grow, managers apparently try to limit the number of hierarchical levels.

Managers try to keep the organization as flat as possible and follow what is known as the **principle of the minimum chain of command**, which states that an organization should choose a hierarchy with the minimum number of levels of authority necessary to achieve its strategy. Managers try to keep the hierarchy as flat as possible, because when companies become too tall, several problems arise that make strategy more difficult to implement.[11]

COORDINATION PROBLEMS Having too many hierarchical levels impedes communication and coordination between employees and functions and also raises costs. Communication between the top and the bottom of the hierarchy takes much longer as the chain of command lengthens. This leads to inflexibility, and valuable time is lost in bringing a new product to market or in keeping up with technological developments.[12] For FedEx, rapid communication and coordination is vital, so the company allows a maximum of only five layers of management between employees and the CEO.[13] In contrast, Procter & Gamble had a tall hierarchy, and the company needed twice as much time as its competitors to introduce new products. To improve coordination and reduce costs, the company moved to streamline its structure and reduce its number of hierarchical levels.[14] Other companies have also taken measures to flatten their structures in order to speed communication and decision making.

INFORMATION DISTORTION More subtle, but just as important, are the problems of information distortion that occur as the hierarchy of authority lengthens. Going down the hierarchy, managers at different levels (for example, divisional or corporate managers) may misinterpret information, either through accidental garbling of messages or on purpose to suit their own interests. In either case, information from the top may not reach its destination intact. For instance, a request to share divisional knowledge to achieve gains from synergy may be overlooked or ignored by divisional managers who perceive it as a threat to their autonomy and power. Information transmitted upward in the hierarchy may also be distorted. Subordinates may transmit to their superiors only information that enhances their own standing in the organization. The greater the number of hierarchical levels, the more scope subordinates have to distort facts, and as a consequence the costs of managing the hierarchy increase.

MOTIVATIONAL PROBLEMS As the number of levels in the hierarchy increases, the amount of authority possessed by managers at each hierarchical level diminishes. For example, consider the situation of two organizations of identical size, one of which has three levels in its hierarchy and the other seven. Managers in the flat structure have much more authority, and greater authority increases their motivation to perform effectively and take responsibility for the organization's performance. Besides, when there are fewer managers, their performance is more visible, so they can expect greater rewards when the business does well.

By contrast, the ability of managers in a tall structure to exercise authority is limited, and their decisions are constantly scrutinized by their superiors. As a result, managers tend to pass the buck and refuse to take the risks that are often necessary when new strategies are pursued. This increases the costs of coordination because more managerial time must be spent coordinating task activities. Thus, the shape of the organization structure strongly affects the motivation of people within it and the way strategy is implemented.[15]

TOO MANY MIDDLE MANAGERS Another drawback of tall structures is that having many hierarchical levels implies having many middle managers, and employing managers is expensive. As noted earlier, managerial salaries, benefits, offices, and secretaries are a huge expense for an organization. If the average middle manager costs a company a total of $200,000 a year, then employing 100 "surplus" managers costs $20 million a year. Most large U.S. companies have recognized this fact, and in the 2000s companies such as IBM, GM, HP, and P&G have moved to downsize their hierarchies, terminating thousands of managers to reduce operating costs. Also, when companies grow and are successful, they often hire personnel and create new positions without much regard for the effect of these actions on the organizational hierarchy. Later, when managers review the structure, they frequently act to reduce the number of levels because of the disadvantages we have noted.

In sum, when companies become too tall and the chain of command becomes too long, strategic managers tend to lose control over the hierarchy, which means that they lose control over their strategies. Disaster often follows, because a tall organization structure decreases, rather than promotes, motivation and coordination between employees and functions, and operating costs escalate as a result. One way to address such problems and lower costs is to decentralize authority—that is, to vest authority in the hierarchy's lower levels as well as at the top.

● **Centralization or Decentralization?**   Authority is centralized when managers at the upper levels of the organizational hierarchy retain the authority to make the most important decisions. When authority is decentralized, it is delegated to divisions, functions, and managers and workers at lower levels in the organization. By delegating authority in this fashion, managers can avoid communication and coordination problems because information does not have to be continually sent to the top of the organization for decisions to be made (as discussed in the Strategy in Action feature). Decentralization has three main advantages:

1. When strategic managers delegate operational decision-making responsibility to middle and first-level managers, they reduce information overload, leaving

themselves more time to spend on strategic decision making. Consequently, they can make more effective decisions.

2. When managers at the bottom layers of the organization become responsible for adapting the organization to local conditions, their motivation and accountability increase. The result is that decentralization promotes organizational flexibility because lower-level managers are authorized to make on-the-spot decisions. This can often provide a company with a significant competitive advantage. Companies such as IBM and Dell empower their employees by allowing them to make significant decisions so that they can respond quickly to customers' needs and so ensure superior service.

3. When lower-level employees are given the right to make important decisions, fewer managers are needed to oversee their activities and tell them what to do. And fewer managers means lower costs.

Strategy in Action

How to Flatten and Decentralize Structure

Tall hierarchies cause such severe coordination and communication problems that many companies have been striving to shrink their hierarchies. For example, General Electric CEO Jack Welch flattened the GE hierarchy from nine levels to four to bring him closer to his divisional managers and reduce the time it took them to make decisions. At Alcoa, planning and decision making at the divisional level once were scrutinized by five levels of corporate management before divisional managers were allowed to proceed with their plans. Chairman Paul O'Neill wiped out these layers so that divisional managers would report directly to him. At both companies, these changes have brought top management closer to customers and provided divisional managers with the autonomy to be innovative and responsive to customers' needs. Moreover, flattening the hierarchy has saved these companies billions of dollars in managerial salaries and significantly reduced costs. Flattening their structures has clearly paid off for GE and Alcoa.

In 1998, Union Pacific, one of the biggest rail freight carriers in the United States, was experiencing a crisis. The U.S. economic boom was causing a record increase in the amount of freight that the railroad had to transport, but at the same time

the railroad was experiencing record delays in moving the freight. Union Pacific's customers were irate and were complaining bitterly about the problem, and the delays had cost the company millions of dollars in penalty payments—$150 million, to be precise!

Why was there a problem? Because Union Pacific, in its attempt to cut costs, had developed a very centralized management approach. All the scheduling and route planning was handled at company headquarters in an effort to promote operating efficiency. The job of regional managers was largely to ensure the smooth flow of freight through their regions. Now, recognizing that efficiency had to be balanced by the need to be responsive to customers, Union Pacific's CEO Dick Davidson announced a sweeping reorganization. Henceforth, regional managers were to be given the authority to make operational decisions at the level at which it was most important—field operations. Regional managers could now alter scheduling and routing to accommodate customer requests, even if doing so raised costs. The goal of the organization was to "return to excellent performance by simplifying our processes and becoming easier to deal with." In making this decision, the company was following the lead of its competitors, most of which had already moved to decentralize their operations, recognizing the many advantages of decentralization.[a]

If decentralization is so effective, why don't all companies decentralize decision making and avoid the problems of tall hierarchies? The answer is that centralization has its advantages, too. First, centralized decision making facilitates coordination of the organizational activities needed to pursue a company's strategy. If managers at all levels can make their own decisions, overall planning becomes extremely difficult, and the company may lose control of its decision making. Second, centralization also means that decisions fit broad organizational objectives. When its branch operations were getting out of hand, for example, Merrill Lynch increased centralization by installing more information systems to give corporate managers greater control over branch activities. Similarly, HP centralized R&D responsibility at the corporate level to provide a more directed corporate strategy.

Horizontal Differentiation

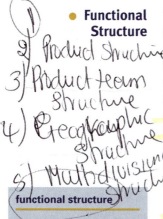

Managing the strategy-structure relationship when the number of hierarchical levels becomes too great is difficult and expensive. Depending on a company's situation, the problems of tall hierarchies can be reduced by decentralization. As company size increases, however, decentralization may become less effective. How, then, as firms grow and diversify, can they operate effectively without becoming too tall or decentralized? How can a firm such as Exxon control 300,000 employees without becoming too bureaucratic and inflexible? There must be alternative ways of creating organizational arrangements to achieve corporate objectives.

The first of these ways is to choose the appropriate form of *horizontal differentiation*—that is, to decide how best to group organizational tasks and activities to meet the objectives of a company's strategies.[16] The kinds of structures that companies can choose among are discussed next.

● **Functional Structure**

The issue facing a company is to find the best way to invest its resources to create an infrastructure that allows it to build the distinctive competences that increase the amount of value the company can create. As a company grows, two things begin to happen. First, the range of tasks that must be performed expands. For example, it suddenly becomes apparent that a professional accountant, production manager, or marketing expert is needed to perform specialized tasks. Second, no one person can successfully perform more than one organizational task without becoming overloaded. The company's founder, for example, can no longer simultaneously make and sell the product. The question that arises is "What grouping of activities—what form of horizontal differentiation—can most efficiently handle the needs of the growing company at least cost?" The answer for most companies is a functional structure.

functional structure

A structure in which people are grouped on the basis of their common expertise and experience or because they use the same resources.

Functional structures arrange and group people on the basis of their common expertise and experience or because they use the same resources.[17] For example, engineers are grouped in a function because they perform the same tasks and use the same skills or equipment. Figure 9.3 shows a typical functional structure. Each of the rectangles represents a different functional specialization (research and development, sales and marketing, manufacturing, and so on), and each function concentrates on its own specialized task.

ADVANTAGES OF A FUNCTIONAL STRUCTURE Functional structures have several advantages. First, if people who perform similar tasks are grouped together, they can learn from one another and become better—more specialized and productive—at what they do.

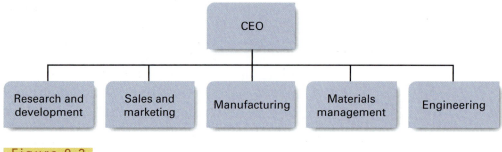

Figure 9.3

Functional Structure

Second, they can monitor each other to make sure that all are performing their tasks effectively and not shirking their responsibilities. As a result, the work process becomes more efficient, reducing manufacturing costs and increasing operational flexibility.

A third important advantage of functional structures is that they give managers greater control of organizational activities. As already noted, many difficulties arise when the number of levels in the hierarchy increases. However, if people are grouped into different functions, each with their own managers, then *several different hierarchies are created* and the company can avoid becoming too tall. There will be one hierarchy in manufacturing, for example, and another in accounting and finance. Managing the business is much easier when different groups specialize in different organizational tasks and are managed separately.

DISADVANTAGES OF A FUNCTIONAL STRUCTURE   In adopting a functional structure, a company increases its level of horizontal differentiation to handle more complex tasks. The structure enables it to keep control of its activities as it grows. This structure serves the company well until it starts to grow and diversify. If the company becomes geographically diverse and begins operating in many locations or if it starts producing a wide range of products, control and coordination problems arise that undermine the company's ability to coordinate its activities and reduce costs.[18] Control and coordination problems may arise in the areas of communication, measurement, location, and strategy.

Communication Problems   As separate functional hierarchies evolve, functions grow more remote from one another. As a result, it becomes increasingly difficult to communicate across functions and to coordinate their activities. This communication problem arises because with greater differentiation, the various functions develop different orientations toward the problems and issues facing the organization. Different functions have different time or goal orientations, for example. Some, such as manufacturing, see things in a short time frame and concentrate on achieving short-run goals, such as reducing manufacturing costs. Others, such as research and development, see things from a long-term point of view, and their goals (innovation and product development) may have a time horizon of several years. These factors may cause each function to develop a different view of the strategic issues facing the company. Manufacturing, for example, may see the strategic issue as the need to reduce costs, sales may see it as the need to increase customer responsiveness, and research and development may see it as the need to create new products. In such cases, functions have trouble coordinating with one another, and costs increase.

Measurement Problems As the number of its products grows, a company may find it difficult to measure the contribution of one or a few products to its overall profitability. Consequently, the company may turn out some unprofitable products without realizing it and so make poor resource allocation decisions. This means that the company's measurement systems are not complex enough to serve its needs. Dell Computer's explosive growth in the early 1990s, for example, caused it to lose control of its inventory management systems; it could not accurately project supply and demand for the components that go into its personal computers. Problems with its organization structure plagued Dell, reducing efficiency and quality. As one manager commented, designing its structure to keep pace with its growth was like building a high-performance car while going around the race track. Dell succeeded, however, and today it enjoys a 20% cost advantage over competitors such as HP and Gateway, in part because of its innovative organizational design.

Location Problems Location factors may also hamper coordination and control. If a company makes and sells in many different regions, then the centralized system of control provided by the functional structure no longer suits it because managers in the various regions must have the flexibility to respond to the needs of their customers. Thus, the functional structure is not complex enough to handle regional diversity.

Strategic Problems Sometimes the combined effect of all these factors is that long-term strategic considerations are ignored because management is preoccupied with solving communication and coordination problems. As a result, a company may lose direction and fail to take advantage of new opportunities while costs escalate.

Experiencing these problems is a sign that the company does not have an appropriate form of differentiation to achieve its objectives. A company must change its mix of vertical and horizontal differentiation if it is to perform effectively the organizational tasks that will enhance its competitive advantage. Essentially, these problems indicate that the company has outgrown its structure. It needs to invest resources in developing a more complex structure, one that can meet the needs of its competitive strategy. Once again, this is expensive, but as long as the value a company can create is greater than the costs of operating the structure, it makes sense to adopt a more complex structure. To this end, many companies reorganize, adopting a product, geographic, or product-team structure depending on the source of the coordination problem.

Product Structure

In a product structure, activities are grouped by product line. The manufacturing function is broken down into different product lines, based on the similarities and differences among the products. Figure 9.4 presents a product structure typical of an imaging company. In this company, products are classified as consumer, health, or commercial imaging products. Inside each product group, many kinds of similar products are being manufactured.

Because three different product groupings now exist, the degree of horizontal differentiation in this structure is higher than that in the functional structure. The specialized support functions, such as accounting and sales, are centralized at the top of the organization, but each support function is divided in such a way that personnel tend to specialize in one of the different product categories to avoid communication problems. Thus, there may be three groups of accountants, one for each of the three product categories. In sales, separate sales forces dealing with the different product lines may emerge, but because maintaining a single sales function brings

Figure 9.4

Product Structure

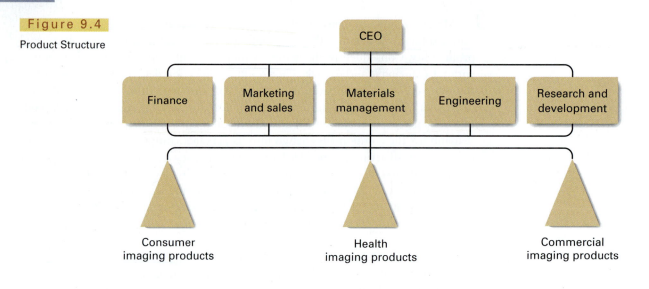

economies of scale to selling and distribution, these groups will coordinate their activities. Dell, for example, moved to a product structure based on serving the product needs of different customer groups; the commercial and public sectors are two such groups. Dell's salespeople specialize in one customer group, but all groups coordinate their sales activities to ensure good communication and the transfer of knowledge among product lines.

The use of a product structure reduces the problems of control and coordination associated with the functional structure. It pushes aside barriers among functions because the product line, rather than each individual function, becomes the focus of attention. In addition, the profit contribution of each product line can be clearly identified, and resources can be allocated more efficiently. Note that the product structure has one more level in the hierarchy than the functional structure—that of the product line manager. This increase in vertical differentiation allows managers at the level of the production line to concentrate on day-to-day operations and gives top managers more time to develop the company's competitive advantage. Although operating costs are higher, that expense is warranted by the extra coordination and control the structure provides.

Another example of a company that adopted a product structure to manage its product lines is Maytag. Initially, when it manufactured only washers and dryers, Maytag used a functional structure. In trying to increase its market share, however, Maytag bought two other appliance manufacturers: Jenn-Air, known for its electric ranges, and Hardwick, which made gas ranges. Maytag moved to a product structure in which each company operated as a separate product line, but major specialized support functions were centralized to reduce costs (this is similar to the structure of the imaging company shown in Figure 9.4). Maytag continued to diversify, however, and, as we discuss in the next section, it then needed to move to a multidivisional structure to manage its strategy more effectively.

Product-Team Structure

A major structural innovation in recent years has been the product-team structure. In today's competitive environment, many companies have been forced to find better ways of coordinating their support functions in order to bring their products to

Figure 9.5

Product-Team Structure

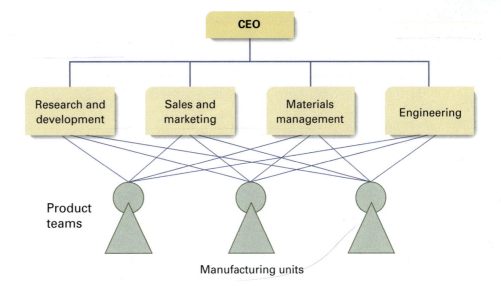

Product teams

Manufacturing units

market more rapidly and protect their competitive advantage. One way to do this is to use cross-functional teams and develop a product-team structure (see Figure 9.5).

In the product-team structure, as in the product structure, task activities are divided along product lines to reduce costs and increase management's ability to monitor and control the manufacturing process. However, specialists are taken from the various support functions and assigned to work on a product or project, where they are combined into cross-functional teams to serve the needs of the product. These teams are formed right at the beginning of the product development process so that any problems that arise can be ironed out early, before they lead to major redesign problems. When all functions have direct input from the beginning, design costs and subsequent manufacturing costs can be kept low. Moreover, the use of cross-functional teams can speed innovation and responsiveness to customers, because when authority is decentralized to the team level, decisions can be made more quickly.

Geographic Structure

When a company is organized geographically, geographic regions become the basis for the grouping of organizational activities. For example, a company may divide up its manufacturing operations and establish manufacturing plants in different regions of the country. This allows it to be responsive to the needs of regional customers and reduces transportation costs. Similarly, service organizations such as store chains and banks may organize their sales and marketing activities on a regional, rather than national, level to get closer to their customers. Like a product structure, a geographic structure provides more control than a functional structure because several regional hierarchies carry out the work previously performed by a single centralized hierarchy. A company like FedEx clearly needs a geographic structure to fulfill its corporate goal: next-day delivery. Large merchandising organizations, such as Neiman Marcus, Dillard's, and Wal-Mart, also moved to a geographic structure soon after they started building stores across the country. With a geographic structure, different regional clothing needs—sun wear in the West, down coats in the East—can be handled as required. At the same time, because the purchasing function remains centralized, one central organization can buy for all regions. Thus a company both achieves economies of scale in buying and distribution and reduces coordination and communication problems. For example,

Figure 9.6

Geographic Structure

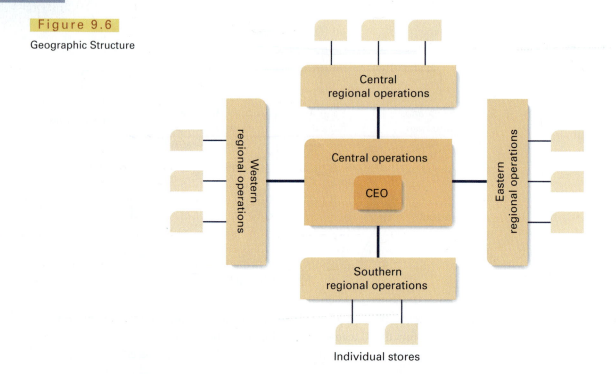

Neiman Marcus developed a geographic structure similar to the one shown on Figure 9.6 to manage its nationwide store chain.

Neiman Marcus established four teams of regional buyers to respond to the needs of customers in the western, central, eastern, and southern regions. The regional buyers feed their information to the central buyers at corporate headquarters, who coordinate their demands in order to obtain purchasing economies and to ensure that Neiman Marcus's high-quality standards, on which its differentiation advantage depends, are maintained nationally. Today, it is the most profitable luxury department store chain.

Once again, however, the usefulness of the product or geographic structure depends on the size of the company and its range of products and regions. If a company starts to diversify into unrelated products or to integrate vertically into new industries, the product structure will not be capable of handling the increased diversity because it does not allow managers to coordinate the company's value creation activities effectively; it is not complex enough to deal with the needs of the large multibusiness company. At this point in its development, the company would normally adopt the multidivisional structure.

Multidivisional Structure

The multidivisional structure possesses two main advantages over a functional structure, innovations that let a company grow and diversify yet overcome problems that stem from loss of control. First, each distinct product line or business unit is placed in its own *self-contained unit or division,* with all support functions. For example, PepsiCo has two major divisions—soft drinks and snack foods—and each has its own functions, such as marketing and research and development. The result is a higher level of horizontal differentiation.

Second, the office of *corporate headquarters staff* is created to monitor divisional activities and exercise financial control over each of the divisions.[19] This staff con-

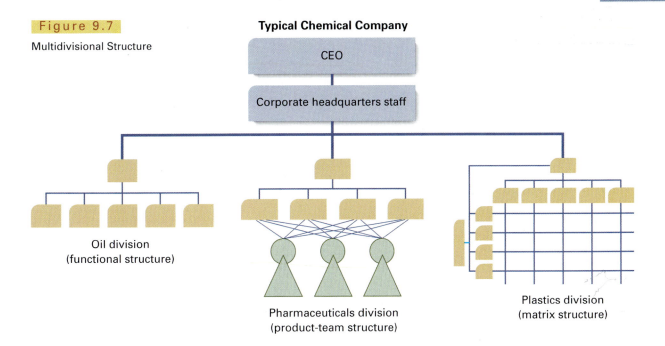

Figure 9.7

Multidivisional Structure

Typical Chemical Company

tains corporate managers who oversee the activities of divisional and functional managers, and it constitutes an additional level in the organizational hierarchy. Hence, there is a higher level of vertical differentiation in a multidivisional structure than in a functional structure.

Figure 9.7 presents a typical multidivisional structure found in a large chemical company such as DuPont. Although this company might easily have seventy operating divisions, only three—the oil, pharmaceuticals, and plastics divisions—are represented here. As a self-contained business unit, each division possesses a full array of support services. For example, each has self-contained accounting, sales, and personnel departments. Each division functions as a profit center, which makes it much easier for corporate headquarters staff to monitor and evaluate each division's activities.[20]

The costs of operating a multidivisional structure are very high compared with the costs of a functional structure. The size of the corporate staff is a major expense; thousands of managers remain on the corporate staffs of such companies as GM and IBM, even after their massive downsizing. Similarly, the use of product divisions, each with its own specialist support functions such as research and development and marketing, is a major expense. Here again, however, if higher operating costs are offset by a higher level of value creation, it makes sense to move to a more complex structure. For example, GM operates the whole corporation through a multidivisional structure, but each car division is part of a different product division based on the kind of car it makes, as this allows it to operate more efficiently. Each division is also able to adopt the structure that best suits its needs. Figure 9.7 shows that the oil division has a functional structure because its activities are standardized; the pharmaceuticals division has a product-team structure; and the plastics division has a matrix structure. In a **matrix structure,** functional managers work with project managers in temporary teams to develop a new product. But once the product is completed and ready

matrix structure

A structure in which functional managers work with project managers in temporary teams to develop new products.

operating responsibility

In the multidivisional structure, the responsibility of divisional managers for the day-to-day operations of their divisions.

strategic responsibility

In the multidivisional structure, the responsibility of managers at corporate headquarters for overseeing long-term plans and providing guidance for divisional managers.

for customers, both functional and project managers move to new teams where they can apply their skills to develop a string of new products. In the multidivisional structure, day-to-day operations of a division are the responsibility of divisional management; that is, divisional management has **operating responsibility**. Corporate headquarters staff, however, which includes members of the board of directors as well as top executives, is responsible for overseeing long-term plans and providing the guidance for interdivisional projects. This staff has **strategic responsibility**. Such a combination of self-contained divisions with a centralized corporate management represents a high level of both vertical and horizontal differentiation.

These two innovations provide the extra control necessary to coordinate growth and diversification. Because this structure, despite its high costs, has now been adopted by more than 90% of all large U.S. corporations, we need to consider its advantages and disadvantages in more detail.

ADVANTAGES OF A MULTIDIVISIONAL STRUCTURE When managed effectively at both the corporate level and the divisional level, a multidivisional structure offers several advantages. Together, they can raise corporate profitability to a new high because they enable the organization to operate more complex kinds of corporate-level strategies.

Enhanced Corporate Financial Control The profitability of different business divisions is clearly visible in the multidivisional structure.[21] Because each division is its own profit center, financial controls can be applied to each business on the basis of profit criteria. Typically, these controls cover establishing targets, monitoring performance on a regular basis, and selectively intervening when problems arise. Corporate headquarters is also in a better position to allocate corporate financial resources among competing divisions. The visibility of divisional performance means that corporate headquarters can identify the divisions in which investment of funds will yield the greatest long-term returns. In a sense, the corporate office is in a position to act as the investor or the banker in an internal capital market, channeling funds to high-yield uses.

Enhanced Strategic Control The multidivisional structure frees corporate staff from operating responsibilities. The staff thus gains time for contemplating wider strategic issues and for developing responses to environmental changes. The multidivisional structure also enables corporate headquarters to obtain the information it needs to perform strategic planning functions. For example, separating individual businesses is a necessary prerequisite to portfolio planning.

Growth The multidivisional structure lets the company overcome an organizational limit on its growth. By reducing information overload at the center, it allows corporate managers to handle a greater number of businesses. They can consider opportunities for further growth and diversification. Communication problems are reduced because the same set of standardized accounting and financial control techniques can be used for all divisions. Corporate managers are also able to implement a policy of management by exception, which means that they intervene only when problems arise.

Stronger Pursuit of Internal Efficiency Within a functional structure, the interdependence of functional departments means that the *individual* performance of each function inside a company cannot be measured by objective criteria. For example, the profitability of the finance function, marketing function, or manufacturing function cannot be assessed in isolation, because these functions are only part of the whole. This means that within the functional structure, considerable degrees of organizational slack—that is, functional resources that are being used unproductively—can go undetected. For example, in order to reduce work pressure within the department and achieve higher personal status, the head of the finance function might employ a larger staff than necessary, resulting in relatively inefficient operation.

In a multidivisional structure, however, the individual efficiency of each autonomous division can be directly observed and measured in terms of the profit it generates. Autonomy makes divisional managers accountable; they have no alibis for poor performance. The corporate office is thus in a better position to identify inefficiencies.

DISADVANTAGES OF A MULTIDIVISIONAL STRUCTURE   Because multidivisional structure has a number of powerful advantages, it seems to be the preferred choice of most large, diversified enterprises today. Indeed, research suggests that large companies that adopt this structure outperform those that retain a functional structure.[22] A multidivisional structure has its disadvantages as well, however. Good management can eliminate some of them, but others are inherent in the way the structure operates and require constant managerial attention.

Balancing Divisional and Corporate Authority   The multidivisional structure introduces a new level in the hierarchy, the corporate level. The problem lies in deciding how much authority and control to assign to the operating divisions and how much authority to retain at corporate headquarters.

This problem was first noted by Alfred Sloan, who introduced the multidivisional structure at General Motors, which became the first company to adopt it, and created GM's original five automobile divisions: Chevrolet, Pontiac, Oldsmobile, Buick, and Cadillac.[23] What Sloan found was that when headquarters retained too much power and authority, the operating divisions lacked sufficient autonomy to develop the business strategy that might best meet the needs of the division. On the other hand, when too much power was delegated to the divisions, they pursued divisional objectives, paying little heed to the needs of the whole corporation. As a result, not all of the potential gains from synergy could be achieved, for example.

Thus, the central issue in managing the multidivisional structure is how much authority should be *centralized* at corporate headquarters and how much should be *decentralized* to the divisions. This issue must be decided by each company, taking into account the nature of its business-level and corporate-level strategies. There are no easy answers, and over time, as the environment changes or the company alters its strategies, the balance between corporate and divisional control will also change.

Distortion of Information   If corporate headquarters puts too much emphasis on divisional return on investment—by setting very high and stringent return-on-investment targets, for instance—divisional managers may choose to distort the information they supply to top management and paint a rosy picture of the present situation at the expense of future profits. That is, divisions may maximize short-run profits, perhaps by cutting product development or new investments or marketing expenditures, and this may cost the company dearly in the future. In recent years, GM has suffered from this problem, which stems from too tight financial control, as declining performance prompted divisional managers to try to make their divisions look good to corporate headquarters. Managing the corporate-divisional interface requires coping with subtle power issues.

Competition for Resources A third problem in managing a multidivisional structure is that the divisions themselves may compete for resources, and this rivalry prevents synergy gains or economies of scope from emerging. For example, the amount of money that corporate personnel have to distribute to the divisions is fixed. Generally, the divisions that can demonstrate the highest return on investment will get the lion's share of the money. Because that large share strengthens them in the next time period, the strong divisions grow stronger. Consequently, divisions may actively compete for resources and, by doing so, reduce interdivisional coordination.

transfer pricing

Establishment of the prices at which the products produced by one business unit are sold to other company-owned business units.

Transfer Pricing Divisional competition may also lead to battles over **transfer pricing**. One of the main challenges that vertical integration or related diversification imposes is the need to set the prices at which products are transferred between divisions. Rivalry among divisions increases the problem of setting fair prices. Each supplying division tries to set the highest price for its outputs to maximize its own profitability. Such competition can completely undermine the corporate culture and make the company a battleground. Many companies have a history of competition among divisions. Some, of course, may encourage competition if managers believe that it leads to maximum performance.

Focus on Short-Term Research and Development If extremely high profitability targets are set by corporate headquarters, the danger arises that the divisions will cut back on research and development expenditures to improve the financial performance of the division. Although this inflates divisional performance in the short term, it reduces a division's ability to develop new products and leads to a fall in the stream of long-term profits. Hence, corporate headquarters personnel must carefully control their interactions with the divisions to ensure that both the short-term and the long-term goals of the business are being achieved.

High Operating Costs As noted earlier, because each division possesses its own specialized functions, such as finance and R&D, multidivisional structures are expensive to run and manage. R&D is especially costly, so some companies centralize such functions at the corporate level to serve all divisions. The duplication of specialist services is not a problem if the gains from having separate specialist functions outweigh the costs. Again, strategic managers must decide whether duplication is financially justified. Activities (particularly advisory services and planning functions) are often centralized in times of downturn or recession; divisions, however, are retained as profit centers.

The advantages of divisional structures must be balanced against their disadvantages, but the disadvantages can be managed by an observant, professional management team that is aware of the issues involved. Today, the multidivisional structure is the dominant one, a fact that clearly supports its usefulness as a means of managing the multibusiness corporation.

Integration and Organizational Control

As we have seen, an organization must choose the appropriate form of differentiation to match its strategy. Greater diversification, for example, requires that a company move from a functional structure to a multidivisional structure. Choosing a type of differentiation, however, is only the first organizational design decision to be made. The second decision concerns the level and type of integration and control necessary to make an organization structure work effectively.

● **Forms of Integrating Mechanisms**

As noted earlier, a company's level of *integration* is the extent to which it seeks to co-ordinate its value creation activities and make them interdependent. The design issue can be summed up simply: The higher a company's level of differentiation, the higher the level of integration needed to make organization structure work effectively.[24] Thus, if a company adopts a more complex form of differentiation, it requires a more complex form of integration to accomplish its goals. FedEx, for example, needs a tremendous amount of integration to fulfill its promise of next-day package delivery. It is renowned for its innovative use of integrating mechanisms, such as customer liaison personnel, to coordinate its activities quickly and efficiently.

As its level of differentiation increases, a company can use a series of integrating mechanisms to increase its level of integration.[25] Some of these mechanisms—on a continuum from simple to complex—are diagrammed in Figure 9.8. Like increasing the level of differentiation, however, increasing the level of integration is expensive. There are high costs associated with using managers to coordinate value creation activities. Hence, a company uses more complex integrating mechanisms to coordinate its activities only to the extent necessary to implement its strategy effectively.

DIRECT CONTACT The aim behind establishing direct contact among managers is to set up a context within which managers from different divisions or functions can work together to solve mutual problems. Managers from different functions have different goals and interests but equal authority, so they may tend to compete rather than co-operate when conflicts arise. In a typical functional structure, for example, the heads of each of the functions have equal authority; the nearest common point of authority is the CEO. Consequently, when disputes arise, no mechanism—except the authority of the boss—exists to resolve the conflicts.

In fact, one sign of conflict in organizations is the number of problems sent up the hierarchy for upper-level managers to solve. This wastes management time and effort, retards strategic decision making, and makes it difficult to create a cooperative culture in the company. For this reason, companies generally choose more complex integrating mechanisms to coordinate interfunctional and divisional activities.

INTERDEPARTMENTAL LIAISON ROLES A company can improve its interfunctional coordination through the interdepartmental liaison role. When the volume of contacts between two departments or functions increases, one of the ways of improving coordination is to give one manager in *each* division or function the responsibility for coordinating with the other function. These managers may meet daily, weekly, monthly, or as needed. Figure 9.8a depicts the nature of the liaison role; the small dot represents the manager inside the functional department who has responsibility for coordinating with the other function. The responsibility for coordination is part of a manager's full-time job, but through these roles a permanent relationship forms between the managers involved, greatly easing strains between departments. Furthermore, liaison roles offer a way of transferring information across the organization, which is important in large, anonymous organizations whose employees may not know anyone outside their immediate department.

Figure 9.8

Types of Integrating
Mechanisms

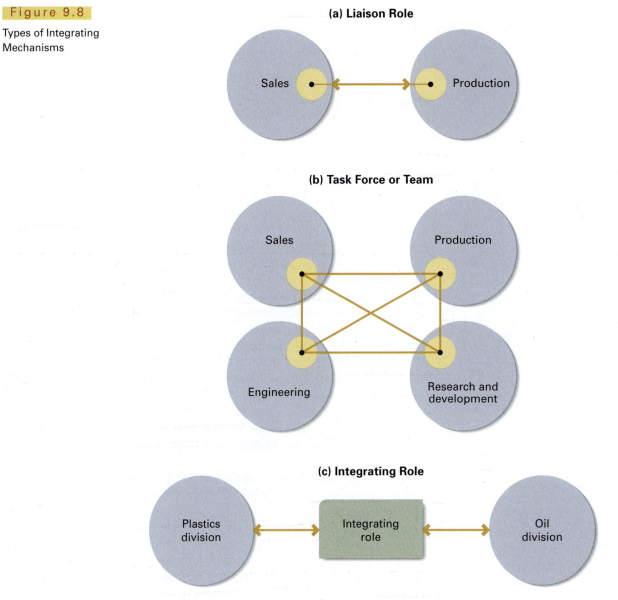

(a) Liaison Role

Sales ⟷ Production

(b) Task Force or Team

Sales   Production

Engineering   Research and
development

(c) Integrating Role

Plastics
division ⟷ Integrating
role ⟷ Oil
division

● Indicates manager with responsibility for integration

TEMPORARY TASK FORCES When more than two functions or divisions share common problems, direct contact and liaison roles are of limited value because they do not provide enough coordination. The solution is to adopt a more complex integrating mechanism called a task force. The nature of the task force is represented diagrammatically in Figure 9.8b. One member of each function or division is assigned to a task force created to solve a specific problem. Essentially, task forces are *ad hoc committees,* and members are responsible for reporting to their departments on the issues addressed and the solutions recommended. Task forces are temporary because once the problem has been solved, members return to their normal roles in their own departments or are assigned to other task forces. Task force members also perform many of their normal duties while serving on the task force.

PERMANENT TEAMS In many cases, the issues addressed by a task force recur. To deal with these issues effectively, an organization must establish a permanent integrating mechanism, such as a permanent team. An example of a permanent team is a new-product development committee, which is responsible for the choice, design, and marketing of new products. Such an activity obviously requires a great deal of integration among functions if new products are to be successfully introduced, and establishing a permanent integrating mechanism accomplishes this. Intel, for instance, emphasizes teamwork. It devised a council system based on approximately ninety cross-functional groups, which meet regularly to set functional strategy in areas such as engineering and marketing and to develop business-level strategy.

The importance of teams in the management of the organization structure cannot be overemphasized. Essentially, permanent teams are the organization's *standing committees,* and much of the strategic direction of the organization is formulated in their meetings. Henry Mintzberg, in a study of how the managers of corporations spend their time, discovered that they spend more than 60% of their time in these committees.[26] The reason is not bureaucracy but rather that integration is possible only in intensive, face-to-face sessions, in which managers can understand others' viewpoints and develop a cohesive organizational strategy. The more complex the company, the more important these teams become. Microsoft, for example, has established a whole new task force and team system to promote integration among divisions and improve corporate performance. As we noted earlier, the product-team structure is based on the use of cross-functional teams to speed products to market. These teams assume the responsibility for all aspects of product development; their goal is to increase coordination and integration among functions.

INTEGRATING ROLES The only function of the integrating role is to prompt integration among divisions or departments; it is a full-time job. As Figure 9.8c indicates, this role is independent of the subunits or divisions being integrated. It is staffed by an independent expert, who is normally a senior manager with a great deal of experience in the joint needs of the two departments. The job is to coordinate the decision process among departments or divisions in order to reap synergetic gains from cooperation. One study found that DuPont had created 160 integrating roles to provide coordination among the different divisions of the company and improve corporate performance.[27] Once again, the more differentiated the company, the more common are these roles. Often people in these roles take the responsibility for chairing task forces and teams, and this provides additional integration. Sometimes the number of integrating roles becomes so high that a permanent integrating department is established at corporate headquarters. Normally, this occurs only in large, diversified corporations that see the need for integration among divisions.

● **Differentiation and Integration**

Clearly, firms have a large number of options available to them when they increase their level of differentiation as a result of increased growth or diversification. For managers, the implementation issue is to match differentiation with the level of integration necessary to meet organizational objectives. Note that just as too much differentiation and not enough integration lead to a failure of implementation, the converse is also true. The combination of low differentiation and high integration leads to an overcontrolled, bureaucratized organization in which flexibility and speed of response are reduced rather than enhanced by the level of integration. Besides, too much integration is expensive for the company because it raises costs. For these reasons, the goal is to decide on the optimum amount of integration necessary for meeting organizational goals and objectives. A company needs to operate the simplest structure consistent with implementing its strategy effectively.

In practice, integrating mechanisms are only the first means through which a company seeks to increase its ability to coordinate its activities. Control systems are the second means.

The Nature of Organizational Control

organizational control

The process by which managers monitor the ongoing activities of an organization and its members to evaluate whether activities are being performed efficiently and effectively and to take corrective action to improve performance if they are not.

Organizational control is the process by which managers monitor the ongoing activities of an organization and its members to evaluate whether activities are being performed efficiently and effectively and to take corrective action to improve performance if they are not. First, strategic managers choose the organizational strategy and structure they hope will allow the organization to use its resources most effectively to create value for its customers. Second, strategic managers create control systems to monitor and evaluate whether, in fact, their organization's strategy and structure are working as managers intended, how they could be improved, and how they should be changed if they are not working.

Organizational control does not just mean reacting to events *after* they have occurred; it also means keeping an organization on track, anticipating events that might occur, and responding swiftly to new opportunities that present themselves. For this reason, control is a strategic process. Companies develop *strategic control systems* that establish ambitious goals and targets for all managers and employees, and then they develop *performance measures* that stretch and encourage managers and employees to excel in their quest to raise performance. Thus, control is not just about monitoring how well an organization and its members are achieving current goals or how well the firm is utilizing its existing resources. It is also about keeping employees motivated, focused on the important problems confronting an organization now and in the future, and working together to find ways to change a company so that it will perform better over time.[28]

● Strategic Controls

strategic control systems

The formal target-setting, measurement, and feedback systems that enable strategic managers to evaluate a company's achievement and whether the company is implementing its strategy successfully.

Strategic control systems are developed to measure performance at four levels in an organization: the corporate, divisional, functional, and individual levels. Managers at all levels must develop the most appropriate set of measures to evaluate corporate-, business-, and functional-level performance. These measures should be tied as closely as possible to the goals of achieving superior efficiency, quality, innovativeness, and responsiveness to customers. Care must be taken, however, to ensure that the standards used at each level do not cause problems at the other levels. Rather, the controls at each level should provide a platform on which managers at the levels below can base their control systems.

Strategic control systems are the formal target-setting, measurement, and feedback systems that allow strategic managers to evaluate whether a company is achieving superior efficiency, quality, innovation, and customer responsiveness and is implementing its strategy successfully. An effective control system should have three

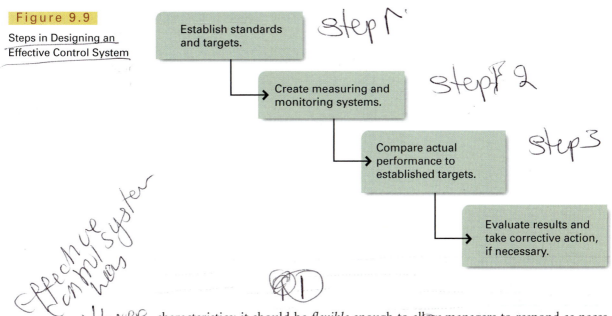

Figure 9.9

Steps in Designing an Effective Control System

(handwritten annotations: step 1, step 2, step 3, effective control system, three)

characteristics: it should be *flexible* enough to allow managers to respond as necessary to unexpected events; it should provide *accurate information*, giving a true picture of organizational performance; and it should supply managers with the information in a *timely manner*, because making decisions on the basis of outdated information is a recipe for failure.[29] As Figure 9.9 shows, designing an effective strategic control system requires four steps.

1. *Establish the standards and targets against which performance is to be evaluated.* The standards and targets that managers select are the ways in which a company chooses to evaluate its performance. General performance standards often derive from the goal of achieving superior efficiency, quality, innovation, or responsiveness to customers. Specific performance targets are derived from the strategy pursued by the company. For example, if a company is pursuing a low-cost strategy, then reducing costs by 7% a year might be a target. If the company is a service organization such as McDonald's, then its standards might include time targets for serving customers or guidelines for food quality.

2. *Create the measuring and monitoring systems that indicate whether the standards and targets are being reached.* The company establishes procedures for assessing whether work goals at all levels in the organization are being achieved. In some cases, measuring performance is fairly straightforward. For example, managers can measure quite easily how many customers their employees serve by counting the number of receipts from the cash register. In many cases, however, measuring performance is difficult because the organization is engaged in many complex activities. How can managers judge how well their research and development department is doing when it may take five years for products to be developed? How can they measure the company's performance when the company is entering new markets and serving new customers? How can they evaluate how well divisions are integrating their activities? The answer is that managers need to use various types of control systems, which we discuss later in this chapter.

3. *Compare actual performance to established targets.* Managers evaluate whether and to what extent performance deviates from the standards and targets developed in step 1. If performance is higher, management may decide that it has set

the standards too low and may raise them for the next time period. The Japanese are renowned for the way they use targets on the production line to control costs; they are continually trying to raise performance, and they raise the standards to provide a goal for managers to work toward. On the other hand, if performance is too low, managers must decide whether to take remedial action. This decision is easy when the reasons for poor performance can be identified—for instance, high labor costs. More often, however, the reasons for poor performance are hard to uncover. They may stem from external factors, such as a recession. Alternatively, the cause may be internal. For instance, the research and development laboratory may have underestimated the problems it would encounter or the extra costs of doing unforeseen research.

4. *Initiate corrective action when it is determined that the standards and targets are not being achieved.* The final stage in the control process is to take the corrective action that will allow the organization to meet its goals. Such corrective action may mean changing any aspect of strategy or structure discussed in this book. For example, managers may invest more resources in improving R&D, diversify, or even decide to change their organization structure. The goal is to continuously enhance the organization's competitive advantage.

Table 9.1 shows the various types of strategic control systems that managers can use to monitor and coordinate organizational activities. Each of these types of control, along with its use at the corporate, divisional, functional, and individual levels, is discussed next.

Financial Controls

The measures most commonly used by managers and other stakeholders to monitor and evaluate a company's performance are financial controls. Typically, strategic managers select financial goals they wish their company to achieve (such as goals related to growth, profitability, and/or return to shareholders), and then they measure whether these goals have been achieved. One reason for the popularity of financial performance measures is that they are objective. The performance of one company can be compared with that of another in terms of stock market price, return on investment, market share, or even cash flow so that strategic managers and other stakeholders, particularly shareholders, have some way of judging their company's performance relative to that of other companies.

Stock price, for example, is a useful measure of a company's performance, primarily because the price of the stock is determined competitively by the number of

Table 9.1

Types of Control Systems

Financial Controls	Output Controls	Behavior Controls
Stock price	Divisional goals	Operating budgets
ROI	Functional goals	Standardization
	Individual goals	Rules and procedures
		Organizational culture

buyers and sellers in the market. The stock's value is an indication of the market's *expectations* for the firm's future performance. Thus, movements in the price of a stock provide shareholders with feedback on a company's and its managers' performance. Stock market price acts as an important measure of performance because top managers watch it closely and are sensitive to its rise and fall—particularly its fall! When Ford's stock price plunged in the 2000s, for example, its then CEO Bill Ford and present CEO Alan Mulally heeded its shareholders' complaint that Ford's operating costs were too high. In response, they both took radical steps, such as laying off thousands of employees and closing many plants to reduce costs in order to boost the company's profitability and stock price. Finally, because stock price reflects the long-term future return from the stock, it can be regarded as an indicator of the company's long-run potential.

Return on investment (ROI), a measure of profitability determined by dividing net income by invested capital, is another popular kind of financial control. At the corporate level, the performance of the whole company can be evaluated *against* that of other companies to assess its relative performance. Top managers, for example, can assess how well their strategies have worked by comparing their company's performance to that of similar companies. In the PC industry, companies such as Dell, HP, Acer, and Apple use ROI to gauge their performance relative to that of their competitors. A declining ROI signals a potential problem with a company's strategy or structure. When HP's ROI fell in relation to Dell's in the early 2000s because HP could not match the efficiency of Dell's inventory management systems, this signaled to its managers the need to find new and improved materials management strategies. By 2007, they had succeeded, and HP overtook Dell to become the largest global PC maker.

ROI can also be used inside the company at the divisional level to judge the performance of an operating division by comparing it to that of a similar free-standing business or other internal division. Indeed, one reason for selecting a multidivisional structure is that each division can be evaluated as a self-contained profit center. Consequently, management can directly measure the performance of one division against that of another. GM moved to a divisional structure partly because it gave corporate managers information about the relative costs of the various divisions, allowing them to base capital allocations on the divisions' relative performance.

Similarly, manufacturing companies often establish production facilities at different locations, domestically and globally, so that they can measure the performance of one against the other. For example, Xerox was able to identify the relative inefficiency of its U.S. division by comparing its profitability with that of its Japanese counterpart. ROI is a powerful form of control at the divisional level, especially if divisional managers are rewarded on the basis of their performance vis-à-vis other divisions. The most successful divisional managers are promoted to become the next generation of corporate executives.

Failure to meet stock price or ROI targets also indicates that corrective action is necessary. It signals the need for corporate reorganization in order to meet corporate objectives, and such reorganization can involve a change in structure or the liquidation and divestiture of businesses. It can also indicate the need for new strategic leadership. In recent years, the CEOs of HP, Ford, and Motorola have all been ousted by disgruntled boards of directors, dismayed at the declining performance of their companies relative to that of competitors.

Output Controls

output control

A system of control in which strategic managers estimate or forecast appropriate performance goals for each division, department, and employee and then measure actual performance relative to these goals.

Financial goals and controls are important, but it is also necessary to develop goals and controls that tell managers how well their strategies are creating a competitive advantage and building distinctive competences and capabilities that will lead to future success. When strategic managers establish goals and measures to evaluate efficiency, quality, innovation, and responsiveness to customers, they are using output control. In **output control**, strategic managers estimate or forecast appropriate performance goals for each division, department, and employee and then measure actual performance relative to these goals. Often a company's reward system is linked to performance on these goals, so that output control also provides an incentive structure for motivating employees at all levels in the organization.

DIVISIONAL GOALS Divisional goals state corporate managers' expectations for each division's performance on such dimensions as efficiency, quality, innovation, and responsiveness to customers. Generally, corporate managers set challenging divisional goals to encourage divisional managers to create more effective strategies and structures in the future. At GE, for example, CEO Jeffrey Immelt sets clear performance goals for GE's more than 150 divisions. He expects each division to be number 1 or number 2 in its industry in terms of market share. Divisional managers are given considerable autonomy to formulate a strategy to meet this goal (to find ways to increase efficiency, innovation, and so on), and the divisions that fail are divested.

FUNCTIONAL AND INDIVIDUAL GOALS Output control at the functional and individual levels is a continuation of control at the divisional level. Divisional managers set goals for functional managers that will allow the division to achieve *its* goals. As at the divisional level, functional goals are established to encourage development of competences that give the company a competitive advantage. The same four building blocks of competitive advantage (efficiency, quality, innovation, and customer responsiveness) act as the standards against which functional performance is evaluated. In the sales function, for example, goals related to efficiency (such as cost of sales), quality (such as number of returns), and customer responsiveness (such as the time needed to respond to customer needs) can be established for the entire function.

Finally, functional managers establish goals that individual employees are expected to achieve to allow the function to achieve its goals. Sales personnel, for example, can be given specific goals (related to functional goals) that they, in turn, are required to achieve. Functions and individuals are then evaluated on the basis of whether they achieve their goals—and in sales, compensation is commonly pegged to achievement. The achievement of these goals is a sign that the company's strategy is working and it is meeting organizational objectives.

Behavior Controls

behavior control

A system of control based on the establishment of a comprehensive system of rules and procedures to direct the actions or behavior of divisions, functions, and individuals.

The first step in strategy implementation is for managers to design the right kind of organization structure. To make the structure work, however, employees must learn the kinds of behaviors they are expected to perform. Using managers to tell employees what to do lengthens the organizational hierarchy, is expensive, and raises costs; consequently, strategic managers rely on behavior controls. **Behavior control** is control through the establishment of a comprehensive system of rules and procedures to direct the actions or behavior of divisions, functions, and individuals.[30]

The objective of using behavior controls is not to specify the goals but to standardize the way of reaching them. Rules standardize behavior and make outcomes predictable. If employees follow the rules, then actions are performed and decisions handled the same way, time and time again. The result is predictability and accuracy, the aim of all control systems. The main kinds of behavior controls are operating budgets, standardization, rules and procedures, and organizational culture.

OPERATING BUDGETS Once managers at each level have been given a goal to achieve, operating budgets that regulate how managers and workers are to attain those goals are established. An **operating budget** is a blueprint that shows how managers intend to use organizational resources to achieve organizational goals most efficiently. Most often, managers at one level allocate to managers at a lower level a specific amount of resources to use to produce goods and services.

operating budget

A blueprint that shows how managers intend to use organizational resources to achieve organizational goals most efficiently.

Once they have been given a budget, managers must decide how they will allocate certain amounts of money for different organizational activities. These lower-level managers are then evaluated on the basis of their ability to stay inside the budget and make the best use of it. For example, if managers at GE's washing machine division have a budget of $50 million to develop and sell a new line of washing machines, they have to decide how much money to allocate to R&D, engineering, sales, and the other functions so that the division will generate the most revenue and hence make the biggest profit possible. Most commonly, large organizations treat each division as a stand-alone profit center, and corporate managers evaluate each division's performance by its relative contribution to corporate profitability.

STANDARDIZATION **Standardization** is the degree to which a company specifies how decisions are to be made so that employees' behavior becomes predictable.[31] In practice, there are three things an organization can standardize: *inputs, conversion activities,* and *outputs*. An organization can control the behavior of both people and resources by standardizing inputs into the organization. This means that managers screen inputs according to preestablished criteria or standards and then decide which inputs to allow into the organization. If employees are the input in question, one way of standardizing them is to specify which qualities and skills they must possess and then to select only those applicants who possess them. If the inputs in question are raw materials or component parts, the same considerations apply. The Japanese are renowned for the high quality and precise tolerances they demand from component parts to minimize problems with the product at the manufacturing stage. Just-in-time inventory systems help standardize the flow of inputs.

standardization

The degree to which a company specifies how decisions are to be made so that employees' behavior becomes predictable.

The aim of standardizing conversion activities is to program work activities so that they are done the same way time and time again. The goal is predictability. Behavior controls, such as rules and procedures, are among the chief means by which companies can standardize throughputs. Fast-food restaurants such as McDonald's and Burger King, for example, standardize all aspects of their restaurant operations; the result is standardized fast food.

The goal of standardizing outputs is to specify what the performance characteristics of the final product or service should be—what dimensions or tolerances the product should conform to, for example. To ensure that their products are standardized, companies apply quality control and use various criteria to measure this standardization. One criterion might be the number of goods returned from customers or the number of customers' complaints. On production lines, periodic sampling of products can indicate whether they are meeting performance standards.

RULES AND PROCEDURES As with other kinds of controls, the use of behavior control is accompanied by potential pitfalls that must be managed if the organization is to avoid strategic problems. Top management must be careful to monitor and evaluate the usefulness of behavior controls over time. Rules constrain people and lead to standardized, predictable behavior. However, rules are always easier to establish than to get rid of, and over time the number of rules an organization uses tends to increase. As new developments lead to additional rules, often the old rules are not discarded and the company becomes overly bureaucratized. Consequently, the organization and the people in it become inflexible and are slow to react to changing or unusual circumstances. Such inflexibility can reduce a company's competitive advantage by slowing the pace of innovation and reducing responsiveness to customers.

Similarly, inside the organization, integration and coordination may fall apart as rules impede communication between functions. Managers must therefore be constantly on the alert for opportunities to reduce the number of rules and procedures necessary to manage the business, and they should always prefer to discard a rule rather than add a new one. Reducing the number of rules and procedures to the essential minimum is important. Strategic managers frequently neglect this task, however, and often only a change in strategic leadership brings the company back on course.

ORGANIZATIONAL CULTURE One important kind of behavior control that serves the dual function of keeping organizational members goal-directed yet open to new opportunities to use their skills to create value is organizational culture. **Organizational culture** is the specific collection of values and norms that are shared by people and groups in an organization and that control the way they interact with each other and with stakeholders outside the organization.[32] **Organizational values** are beliefs and ideas about what kinds of goals members of an organization *should* pursue and what kinds or standards of behavior employees *should* use to achieve these goals. Bill Gates of Microsoft is famous for the set of organizational values that he created for his company, which include entrepreneurship, ownership, honesty, frankness, and open communication. Gates stressed entrepreneurship and ownership because he wanted Microsoft to operate less like a big bureaucracy and more like a collection of smaller and very adaptive companies. Gates also emphasized giving lower-level managers considerable decision-making autonomy and encouraged them to take risks—that is, to behave more like entrepreneurs and less like corporate bureaucrats. The emphasis Gates and Microsoft's current top managers place on values such as honesty, frankness, and open communication reflects their belief that an open internal dialogue is necessary for Microsoft's competitive success.

From organizational values develop **organizational norms**, the unwritten guidelines or expectations that *prescribe* appropriate kinds of behavior by employees in particular situations and control the behavior of organizational members toward one another. The norms of behavior for software programmers at Microsoft include working long hours and weekends, wearing whatever clothing is comfortable (but never a suit and tie), consuming junk food, and communicating with other employees via electronic mail and the company's state-of-the-art intranet.

Organizational culture functions as a form of control in that strategic managers can influence the values and norms that develop in an organization—values and norms that specify appropriate and inappropriate behaviors and that shape the way its members behave.[33] Strategic managers such as Gates and Michael Dell, for example, deliberately cultivate values that encourage subordinates to perform their roles in innovative, creative ways. They establish and support norms dictating that, to be

---

organizational culture

The specific collection of values and norms that are shared by people and groups in an organization and that control the way they interact with each other and with stakeholders outside the organization.

organizational values

Beliefs and ideas about what kinds of goals members of an organization should pursue and what kinds or standards of behavior they should use to achieve these goals.

organizational norms

Unwritten guidelines or expectations that prescribe the kinds of behavior employees should adopt in particular situations and regulate the way they behave toward each other.

innovative and entrepreneurial, employees should feel free to experiment and go out on a limb even if there is a significant chance of failure.

Managers of other companies, however, might cultivate values that encourage employees always to be conservative and cautious in their dealings with others, to consult their superiors before they make important decisions, and to record their actions in writing so that they can be held accountable for what happens. Managers of organizations such as chemical and oil companies, financial institutions, and insurance companies—indeed, any organization in which caution is needed—may encourage such an approach to making decisions.[34] In a bank or mutual fund, the risk of losing all your investors' money makes a cautious approach to investing highly appropriate. Thus, we might expect that managers of different kinds of organizations would deliberately try to cultivate and develop the organizational values and norms that are best suited to their strategy and structure.

CULTURE AND STRATEGIC LEADERSHIP Because both an organization's structure (the design of its task and reporting relationships) and its culture shape employees' behavior, it is crucial to match organization structure and culture to implement strategy successfully. How do managers design and create their cultures? In general, organizational culture is the product of *strategic leadership* provided by an organization's founder and top managers. The organization's founder is particularly important in determining culture, because the founder imprints his or her values and management style on the organization. Walt Disney's conservative influence on the company he established continued until well after his death, for example. Managers were afraid to experiment with new forms of entertainment because they were afraid Walt Disney wouldn't have liked it.

The leadership style established by the founder is transmitted to the company's managers, and as the company grows, it typically attracts new managers and employees who share the same values. Moreover, members of the organization typically recruit and select only those who share their values. Thus, a company's culture becomes more and more distinct as its members become more similar.

The virtue of these shared values and common culture is that they *increase integration and improve coordination among organizational members.* For example, the common language that typically emerges in an organization because people share the same beliefs and values facilitates cooperation among managers. Similarly, rules and procedures and direct supervision are less important when shared norms and values regulate behavior and motivate employees. When organizational members subscribe to the organization's cultural norms and values, this bonds them to the organization and increases their commitment to find new ways to help it succeed. That is, such employees are more likely to commit themselves to organizational goals and work actively to develop new skills and competences to help achieve those goals. Strategic managers need to establish the values and norms that will help them bring their organizations into the future.

Finally, organization structure contributes to the implementation process by providing a framework of tasks and roles that reduces transaction difficulties and allows employees to think and behave in ways that enable a company to achieve superior performance. As discussed in the Running Case, the way in which the frugal Sam Walton (who drove a thirty-year-old pickup truck and lived in a very modest home) used all the kinds of control systems just discussed to implement Wal-Mart's cost-leadership strategy is very instructive.

RUNNING CASE

Sam Walton's Approach to Implementing Wal-Mart's Strategy

Wal-Mart, headquartered in Bentonville, Arkansas, is the largest retailer in the world, with sales of over $350 billion in 2007. Its success rests on the way that its founder, the late Sam Walton, decided to implement the company's low-cost business strategy. Walton wanted all his managers and workers to have a hands-on approach to their jobs and to be totally committed to Wal-Mart's main goal, which he defined as total customer satisfaction. To motivate his employees, Walton created a sophisticated control system and a culture that gave employees at all levels continuous feedback about their and the company's performance.

First, Walton developed a financial control system that provided managers with day-to-day feedback about the performance of all aspects of the business. Through a sophisticated companywide satellite system, corporate managers at its Bentonville headquarters can evaluate the performance of each store, and even of each department in each store. Information about store profits and the rate of turnover of goods is provided to store managers daily, and store managers in turn communicate this information to Wal-Mart's 1.2 million U.S. employees (who are called associates). By sharing such information, Walton's method encourages all associates to learn the fundamentals of the retailing business so that they can work to improve it.

If any store seems to be underperforming, managers and associates meet to probe the reasons and to find solutions to help raise performance. Wal-Mart's top managers routinely visit stores having problems to lend their expertise, and each month top managers use the company's aircraft to fly to various Wal-Mart stores so that they can keep their fingers on the pulse of the business. It is also customary for Wal-Mart's top managers to spend their Saturdays meeting together to discuss the week's financial results and their implications for the future.

Walton insisted on linking performance to rewards. Each manager's individual performance, measured by his or her ability to meet specific goals or output targets, is reflected in pay raises and chances for promotion (promotion to bigger stores in the company's 4,000-store empire and even to corporate headquarters, because Wal-Mart routinely promotes from within the company rather than hire managers from other companies). While top managers receive large stock options linked to the company's performance targets and stock price, even ordinary associates receive stock in the company. An associate who started with Walton in the 1970s would by now have accumulated more than $500,000 in stock because of the appreciation of Wal-Mart's stock over time.

Walton instituted an elaborate system of controls, such as rules and budgets, to shape employees' behavior. Each store performs the same activities in the same way, and all employees receive the same kind of training so that they know how to behave toward customers. In this way, Wal-Mart is able to standardize its operations, which leads to major cost savings and allows managers to make storewide changes easily.

Finally, Walton was not content just to use output and behavior controls and monetary rewards to motivate his associates. To involve associates in the business and encourage them to develop work behaviors focused on providing quality customer service, he established strong cultural values and norms for his company. Some norms that associates are expected to follow include the ten-foot attitude that developed when Walton, during his visits to the stores, encouraged associates to "promise that whenever you come within 10 feet of a customer you will look him in the eye, greet him, and ask him if you can help him"; the sundown rule, which states that employees should strive to answer customers' requests by sundown on the day they receive them; and the Wal-Mart cheer ("Give me a W, give me an A," and so on), which is used in all its stores.

The strong customer-oriented values that Walton created are exemplified in the stories its members tell one another about the company's concern for its customers. They include stories such as the one about Sheila, who risked her own safety when she jumped in front of a car to prevent a little boy from being struck; about Phyllis, who administered CPR to a customer who had suffered a heart attack in her store; and about Annette, who gave up the Power Ranger she had on layaway for her own son so a customer's son could have his birthday wish. The strong Wal-Mart culture also helps to control and motivate its employees and helps associates to achieve the stringent output and financial targets the company has set for itself.

Summary of Chapter

1. Implementing a strategy successfully depends on selecting an organization structure and control system appropriate to the company's strategy.

2. The basic tool of strategy implementation is organizational design. Good organizational design increases profits in two ways. First, it economizes on operating costs and lowers the costs of value creation activities. Second, it enhances the ability of a company's value creation functions to achieve a differentiation advantage through superior efficiency, quality, innovativeness, and responsiveness to customers.

3. Differentiation and integration are the two design concepts that govern how a structure will work. Differentiation has two aspects: vertical differentiation reflects how a company chooses to allocate its decision-making authority, and horizontal differentiation reflects the way a company groups organizational activities into functions and divisions.

4. Tall hierarchies have a number of disadvantages, such as problems with communication and coordination, information transfer, motivation, and costs. Decentralization, or delegation of authority, can solve some of these problems.

5. Most companies first choose a functional structure. Then, as a company grows and diversifies, it adopts a multidivisional structure. Although a multidivisional structure has higher costs than a functional structure, it overcomes the control problems associated with a functional structure and gives a company the capability to handle its value creation activities effectively.

6. Other kinds of structures include the product, product-team, and geographic structures. Each has a specialized use and, to be effective, must match the needs of the organization.

7. The more complex the company and the higher its level of differentiation, the higher the level of integration needed to manage its structure. The kinds of integrating mechanisms available to a company range from direct contact to integrating roles. The more complex the mechanism, the greater the costs of using it. A company should take care to match these mechanisms to its strategic needs.

8. Strategic control is the process of setting standards and targets, monitoring and evaluating organizational performance, and taking corrective action, if necessary. Managers should develop strategic control systems that measure all important aspects of their organization's performance.

9. Control takes place at all levels in the organization: corporate, divisional, functional, and individual. Effective control systems are flexible, accurate, and able to provide quick feedback to strategic planners.

10. Control systems range from those directed at measuring financial and managerial performance to those that measure behaviors or actions. Exercising financial controls involves selecting financial goals for the company and then measuring whether they have been achieved. Output controls establish goals for divisions, functions, and individuals. They can be used only when outputs can be objectively measured and are often linked to a "management by objectives" system. Behavior controls are achieved through budgets, standardization, rules and procedures, and organizational culture, which is the collection of norms and values that govern the way people behave inside the organization.

Discussion Questions

1. What is the difference between vertical differentiation and horizontal differentiation? Rank the various structures discussed in this chapter along these two dimensions.

2. What kind of structure best describes the way your business school or university operates? Why is that structure appropriate? Would another structure fit better?

3. When would a company decide to change from a functional to a multidivisional structure?

4. What are the relationships among differentiation, integration, and strategic control systems? Why are these relationships important?

5. For each of the structures discussed in this chapter, outline the most suitable control system.

6. What kinds of control systems would likely be found in (a) a small manufacturing company, (b) a chain store, (c) a high-tech company, and (d) a Big Five accounting firm?

Practicing Strategic Management

SMALL-GROUP EXERCISE
Speeding Up Product Development

Break up into groups of three to five people, and discuss the following scenario. Appoint one group member as a spokesperson who will communicate your findings to the class when called upon to do so by the instructor.

You are the top functional manager of a small greeting card company whose new lines of humorous cards for every occasion are selling out as fast as they are reaching the stores. Currently, your employees are organized into different functions such as card designers, artists, and joke writers, as well as functions such as marketing and manufacturing. Each function works on a wide range of different kinds of cards (birthday, Christmas, Hanukkah, Thanksgiving, and so on). Sometimes the design department comes up with the initial idea for a new card and sends the idea to the artists, who draw and color the picture. Then the card is sent to the joke writers, who write the joke to suit the card. At other times the process starts with writing the joke, which is then sent to the design department to find the best use for the idea.

The problem you are experiencing is that your current functional structure does not allow you to produce new cards fast enough to satisfy customers' demands. It typically takes a new card one year to reach the market, and you want to shorten this time by half in order to protect and expand your market niche.

1. Discuss ways in which you can improve the way your current functional structure operates to speed up the product development process.

2. Discuss the pros and cons of moving to a multidivisional or product-team structure to reduce card development time.

3. Which of these structures do you think is more appropriate? Why?

EXPLORING THE WEB
Visiting Google's Control System

Go to Google's website and look at the section on its corporate culture and operating philosophy.

1. How would you characterize Google's approach to strategic control?

2. How does its control system help it to implement its strategies?

General Task   Explore the Web to find a website that displays a company's organizational chart or that talks about a company's method of managing and controlling its structure. (For example, does it use a centralized or a decentralized approach?) What kind of structure and what control systems does the company use to manage its activities? Why?

CLOSING CASE

Ford Has a New CEO and a New Global Structure

Designing a global business organization to operate across countries is a very critical issue for multinational companies. Ford is a good example of a company that has experienced structural problems. Early on, Ford realized there was a major opportunity to increase profitability by taking its skills in car making abroad. Over time, it established car-making business units in different countries in Europe, Asia, and Australia. Decision-making authority was decentralized to each of these units, which controlled its own activities and developed cars suited to its local market. The result was that each unit came to operate independently from Ford in the United States. Ford of Europe, for example, became the largest and most profitable carmaker in Europe.

Ford remained a highly profitable enterprise until Japanese carmakers began to flood the world with their small, reliable, low-priced cars in the 1980s. When car buyers began to flock to these imports, Ford tried to draw upon the skills of its European unit to help build smaller, more fuel-efficient cars for the U.S. market. But it had never before tried to get its U.S. and European design and manufacturing units to cooperate and this proved very difficult to achieve because of the nature of its global organization structure. In the 1990s, Ford embarked on a massive project to create a new global matrix structure for the company that would solve the decentralized task and authority problems that were preventing it from utilizing its resources effectively. In its Ford 2000 plan, for example, it laid out a timetable for how all its global car-making units would learn to cooperate with one set of global support functions, such as design, purchasing, and so on. However, huge political problems arose with its new structure, the redesign went through one iteration after another, and by the mid-2000s Ford was still operating as a collection of different "empires" and its North American, European, and Asia Pacific and Africa units were operating almost autonomously.

So Ford decided to restructure itself. It moved to a "world structure" in which one set of managers was given authority over the whole of a specific global operation such as manufacturing or car design. Then it began to design cars for the global market. Its new structure never worked, however, to quicken car design and production; it constantly changed global lines of authority and the locations in which it operated to increase profitability. Ford went through multiple reorganizations to try to meet the Japanese challenge, but nothing worked, and by 2006 it was in deep trouble. In September 2006, after losing billions of dollars, Ford announced a revamped "Way Forward" plan to turn around its U.S. and global operations, a plan that called for cutting 44,000 jobs, closing sixteen plants, and freshening 70% of the company's Ford, Mercury, and Lincoln car lineup.

In October 2006, Ford also appointed a new CEO, Alan Mulally, an expert in organizational design, to help it turn around its operations. Mulally, a former Boeing executive, had led that company's global reorganization effort. Now he began to work out how to change Ford's global structure to reduce costs and speed product development. In the structure Mulally inherited, Ford's Americas unit reported to the CEO, while its other global and functional operations reported to the next two most senior executives: Mark Fields, president of Ford's Americas operation, and Mark Schulz, president of international operations. Mulally decided that Ford's downsizing should be accompanied by a major reorganization of its hierarchy. He decided to flatten Ford's structure and recentralize control, but at the same time he put the focus on teamwork and adopted a cross-functional approach to handling the enormous value chain challenges that still confronted the organization.

The position of president of international operations has been eliminated. Mark Fields continues to report to Mulally but so, too, do the heads of the other two world regions—Lewis Booth, head of Ford of Europe, and John Parker, head of Ford of Asia Pacific and Africa and Mazda. So two levels in the hierarchy are gone, and Mulally's new organizational design clearly defines each global executive's role in the company's hierarchy so that Ford can begin acting like one company instead of separate global units, each with its own interests.[b] Mulally's goal is to provide a centralized focus on using the company's global functional strength to better support its car-making business units.[c]

Mulally's goal is to force on all his top managers a cross-functional approach—one that he will personally oversee—so as to standardize Ford's global car making and allow functional units to continuously improve quality, productivity, and the speed at which new products can be introduced. All Ford executives understand that the company's very survival is at stake and that they must work together to accelerate efforts to reduce costs and catch up with more efficient competitors such as Toyota. If Mulally's new global design cannot achieve this, it is likely that Ford will be taken over by a competitor in the next decade.

Case Discussion Questions

1. How did Mulally change Ford's organization structure—for example, the form of its vertical and horizontal differentiation and integration?

2. In what ways does he hope to increase performance by making these organizational design changes?

TEST PREPPER

True/False Questions

F 1. Control systems range from those directed at measuring outputs to those that measure behaviors or actions.

T 2. The basic tool of strategy implementation is organizational design.

T 3. Differentiation and integration are the two design concepts that govern how a structure will work.

F 4. Transfer pricing establishes the prices at which the products produced by one business unit are then sold to the end user—the customer.

T 5. Organizational design is the process through which managers select the combination of organization structure and control systems that they believe will enable the company to create and sustain a competitive advantage

T 6. The span of control is defined as the number of subordinates a manager directly manages.

T 7. A company's level of integration is the extent to which it seeks to coordinate its value creation activities and make them interdependent.

Multiple-Choice Questions

8. _____ are based on the establishment of a comprehensive system of rules and procedures to direct the actions or behavior of divisions.
   a. Values
   b. Functional goals
   c. Behavior controls
   d. Financial controls
   e. Strategic controls

9. Organizational culture includes all of the following except _____.
   a. stock price
   b. values
   c. norms
   d. socialization
   e. all of the above

10. Return on investment (ROI), a measure of profitability determined by dividing net income by invested capital, is a tool used for _____.
   a. financial control
   b. informational control
   c. behavior control
   d. implicit control
   e. functional control

11. The characteristics of an effective control system include all of the following except _____.
   a. flexibility
   b. formal target setting
   c. accurate information
   d. supplying managers with information in a timely manner
   e. all of the above

12. Designing an effective control system includes all of the following except _____.
   a. establishing standards and targets against which performance is to be measured
   b. selecting financial controls that are objective
   c. creating measuring and monitoring systems that indicate whether the standards and targets are being reached
   d. comparing actual performance against established targets
   e. initiating corrective action when it is determined that the standards and targets are not being achieved

13. Output controls include all of the following except _____.
   a. divisional goals   b. budget goals
   c. functional goals   d. individual goals
   e. all of the above

14. Beliefs and ideas about what kinds of goals members of an organization should pursue and what kinds or standards of behavior employees should use to achieve these goals constitute _____.
   a. organizational culture
   b. organizational rules
   c. organizational values
   d. organizational procedures
   e. organizational development

15. Organizational culture is the product of _____ provided by an organization's founder and top managers.
   a. strategic coordination
   b. organizational norms
   c. strategic leadership
   d. behavior controls
   e. functional goals

Boeing Commercial Aircraft: Comeback?

This case was prepared by Charles W. L. Hill, the University of Washington.

It looked as if 2006 would be the year that Boeing could boast of a comeback in its three-decades-long duel with Airbus Industries. Long the dominant player in the commercial aerospace industry, Boeing has been steadily losing market share to Airbus from the mid-1990s onwards (represented in Exhibit 1). In 1999, for the first time in its history, Airbus garnered more orders for new commercial jet aircraft than Boeing. The European upstart repeated this achievement regularly between 2001 and 2005.

By mid-2006, however, the tide seemed to be shifting in Boeing's favor. Underlying this were strong sales of Boeing's newest jet, the super-efficient wide-bodied 787, along with surging sales of its well-established 737 and 777 jets. For the first six months of 2006, Boeing took orders for 487 aircraft; Airbus took just 117. While Boeing seemed to be leaving a decade of production problems and ethics scandals behind it, Airbus was mired in problems of its own. Its largest jet to date, the A380 super jumbo, had been delayed from entering service while the company struggled with production problems. Orders for the A380 had stalled at 159 for almost a year, and analysts were beginning to question whether the aircraft would be a commercial success. Moreover, Airbus's contender to the Boeing 787, the A350, had to be scrapped before it even left the drawing board

due to negative customer feedback. The challenge facing Boeing's management was to translate this revival in fortunes for the company into a sustainable competitive advantage. It was off to a good start, but what else needed to be done?

The Competitive Environment

By the 2000s, the market for large commercial jet aircraft was dominated by just two companies, Boeing and Airbus. A third player in the industry, McDonnell Douglas, had been significant historically but had lost share during the 1980s and 1990s. In 1997, Boeing acquired McDonnell Douglas, primarily for its strong military business. Since the mid-1990s, Airbus had been gaining orders at Boeing's expense. By the mid-2000s, the two companies were splitting the market.

Both Boeing and Airbus now have a full range of aircraft. Boeing offers five aircraft "families" that range in size from 100 to over 500 seats. They are the narrow-bodied 737 and the wide-bodied 747, 767, 777, and 787 families. Each family comes in various forms. For example, there are currently four main variants of the 737 aircraft. They vary in size from 110 to 215 seats and in range capability from 2,000 to over 5,000 miles. List prices vary from $47 million for the smallest member of the 737 family, the 737-600, to $282 million for the largest Boeing aircraft, the 747-8. The newest member of the Boeing family, the 787, lists for between $138 million and $188 million, depending on the model.[1]

Similarly, Airbus offers four families: the narrow-bodied A320 family and the wide-bodied A300/310,

A330/340, and A380 families. These aircraft vary in size from 100 to 550 seats. The range of list prices is similar to Boeing's. The A380 super jumbo lists for between $282 million and $302 million, while the smaller A320 lists for between $62 million and $66.5 million.[2] Both companies also offer freighter versions of their wide-bodied aircraft.

Airbus was a relatively recent entrant into the market. Airbus began its life as a consortium between a French and a Germany company in 1970. Later a British and a Spanish company joined the consortium. Initially, few people gave Airbus much chance for success, but the consortium gained ground by innovating. It was the first aircraft maker to build planes that "flew by wire," made extensive use of composites, flew with only two flight crew members (most flew with three), and used a common cockpit layout across models. It also gained sales by being the first company to offer a wide-bodied twin engine jet, the A300, that was positioned between smaller single-aisle planes like the 737 and large aircraft such as the Boeing 747.

In 2001, Airbus became a fully integrated company. The European Defense and Space Company (EADS), formed by a merger between French, German, and Spanish interests, acquired 80% of the shares in Airbus, and BAE Systems, a British company, took a 20% stake.

Development and Production

The economics of development and production in the industry are characterized by a number of facts. First, the R&D and tooling costs associated with developing a new airliner are very high. Boeing spent some $5 billion to develop the 777. Its latest aircraft, the 787, is expected to cost $8 billion to develop. Development costs for Airbus's latest aircraft, the A380 super jumbo, could run as high as $15 billion.

Second, given the high upfront costs, to break even a company has to capture a significant share of projected world demand. The breakeven point for the Airbus super jumbo, for example, is estimated to be between 250 and 270 aircraft. Estimates of the total potential market for this aircraft vary widely. Boeing suggests that the total world market will be no more than 320 aircraft over the next twenty years. Airbus believes that demand for this size aircraft will be more like 1,250 jets. In any event, it may take five to ten years of production before Airbus breaks even on the A380—and that's on top of years of negative cash flow during development.[3]

Third, there are significant learning effects in aircraft production.[4] On average, unit costs fall by about 20% each time *cumulative* output of a specific model is doubled. The phenomenon occurs because managers and shop floor workers learn over time how to assemble a particular model of plane more efficiently, reducing assembly time, boosting productivity, and lowering the marginal costs of producing subsequent aircraft.

Fourth, the assembly of aircraft is an enormously complex process. Modern planes have over 1 million component parts that have to be designed to fit with each other, and then produced and brought together at the right time to assemble the engine. At several times in the history of the industry, problems with the supply of critical components have held up production schedules and resulted in losses. In 1997, Boeing took a charge of $1.6 billion against earnings when it had to halt the production of its 737 and 747 models due to a lack of component parts.

Historically, airline manufacturers tried to manage the supply process through vertical integration, making many of the component parts that went into an aircraft (engines were long the exception to this). Over the last two decades, however, there has been a trend to contract out production of components and even entire subassemblies to independent suppliers. On the 777, for example, Boeing outsourced about 65 percent of the aircraft production, by value, excluding the engines.[5] While helping to reduce costs, contracting out has placed an enormous onus on airline manufacturers to work closely with their suppliers to coordinate the entire production process.

Finally, all new aircraft are now designed digitally and assembled virtually before a single component is produced. Boeing was the first to do this with its 777 in the early 1990s and its new version of the 737 in the late 1990s.

Customers

Demand for commercial jet aircraft is very volatile and tends to reflect the financial health of the commercial airline industry, which is prone to boom and bust cycles (see Exhibits 1 and 2). After a moderate boom during the 1990s, the airline industry went through a particularly nasty downturn during 2001–2005. The downturn started in early 2001 due to a slowdown in business travel after the boom of the 1990s. It was compounded by a dramatic slump in airline travel after the terrorist attacks on the United States on September 11, 2001. Between 2001

Exhibit 1

Commercial Aircraft Orders 1990–2005

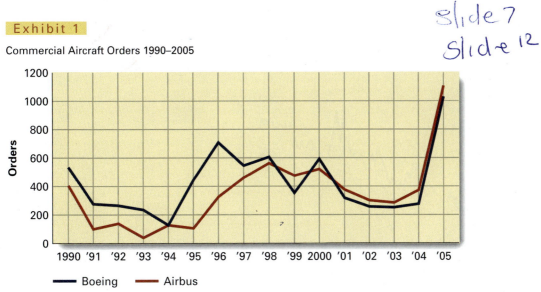

Sources: http://www.boeing.com, accessed September 2006; and http://www.airbus.com/en, accessed September 2006.

and 2005, the entire global airline industry lost some $40 billion, more money than it had made since its inception.[6]

For 2006, the industry was forecasted to lose $1.7 billion, which represents an incremental improvement over the $3.2 billion lost in 2005. The industry would have been profitable in both 2005 and 2006 were it not for surging jet fuel prices after January 2004 (prices for jet fuel more than doubled between 2004 and 2006—see Exhibit 3). The International Air Travel Association estimates that the fuel bill for all airlines in 2006 was around $115 billion. This would represent over 25% of the industry's total operating costs in 2006, compared to less than 10% in 2001.[7]

Exhibit 2

World Airline Industry Revenues

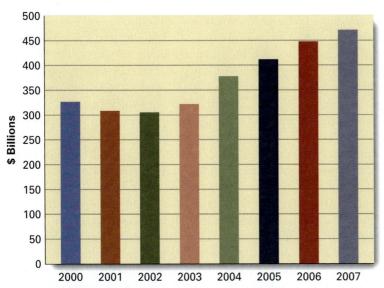

Source: IATA data (figures for 2006 and 2007 are forecasts), http://www.iata.org/whatwedo/economics/fuel_monitor/price_development.htm, accessed February 12, 2007.

Jet Fuel and Crude Oil Prices

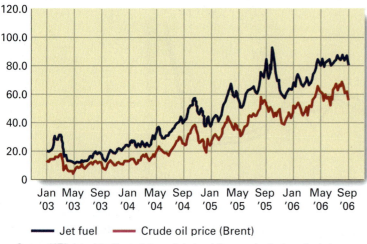

Source: IATA data, http://www.iata.org/whatwedo/economics/fuel monitor/price_development.htm, accessed February 12, 2007.

Losses were particularly severe among the big six airlines in the world's largest market, the United States (American Airlines, United, Delta, Continental, US Airways, and Northwest). Three of these airlines (United, Delta, and Northwest) were forced to seek chapter 11 bankruptcy protections. Even though demand and profits plummeted at the big six airlines, some carriers continued to make profits during 2001–2005, most notably the budget airline Southwest. In addition, other newer budget airlines, including AirTran and Jet Blue (which was started in 2000), gained market share during this period. Indeed, between 2000 and 2003, the budget airlines in the United States expanded capacity by 44%, even as the majors slashed their carrying capacities and parked unused planes in the desert. In 1998, the budget airlines held a 16% share of the U.S. market; by mid-2004, their share had risen to 29%.[8]

The key to the success of the budget airlines is a strategy that gives them a 30 to 50% cost advantage over traditional airlines. The budget airlines all follow the same basic script: They purchase just one type of aircraft (some standardize on Boeing 737s, others on Airbus 320s). They hire nonunion labor and cross-train employees to perform multiple jobs (to help meet turnaround times, for example, pilots might help check tickets at the gate). As a result of flexible work rules, Southwest needs only 80 employ-ees to support and fly an aircraft, compared to 115 at the big six airlines. The budget airlines also favor flying "point to point" rather than through hubs, and often use less costly secondary airports rather than major ones. They focus on large markets with lots of traffic (up and down the East Coast, for example). There are no frills on the flights (passengers receive no in-flight food or complementary drinks, for example). And prices are set low to fill the seats.

In contrast, major airlines base their operations on the network, or "hub and spoke," system. Network airlines route their flights through major hubs; one airline often dominates a single hub (United dominates Chicago's O'Hare airport, for example). This system was developed for good reason: It efficiently uses airline capacity when there isn't enough demand to fill a plane flying point to point. By using a hub and spoke system, major network airlines are able to serve some 38,000 city pairs, some of which generate fewer than fifty passengers per day. By focusing on a few hundred city pairs, where there is sufficient demand to fill their planes, and flying directly between them (point to point), the budget airlines seem to have found a way around this constraint. The network carriers also suffer from a higher cost structure due to their legacy of a unionized workforce. In addition, their costs are pushed higher by their superior in-flight service. In good times, the network carriers can recoup their costs by charging higher prices than the discount airlines, particularly for business travelers, who pay more to book late and to fly business or first class. In the competitive environment of the early 2000s, however, this was no longer the case.

Due to the effect of increased competition, the real yield that U.S. airlines get from passengers has fallen from 8.70 cents per mile in 1980 to 6.37 cents per mile in 1990, 5.12 cents per mile in 2000, and 4.00 cents per mile in 2005 (these figures are expressed in constant 1978 cents).[9] Real yields are also declining elsewhere. With real yields declining, the only way that airlines can become profitable is to reduce their operating costs.

Outside of the United States, competition has intensified as deregulation has allowed low-cost airlines to enter local markets and capture share from long-established national airlines that have used the hub and spoke model. In Europe, for example, Ryan Air and Easy Jet have adopted the business model of Southwest and used it to grow aggressively.

By the mid-2000s, large airlines in the United States were starting to improve their operating efficiency, helped by growing traffic volumes, higher load factors, and reductions in operating costs, particularly labor costs. Load factor refers to the percentage of a plane that is full on average, which hit a record 86% in 2006 in the United States and 81% in international markets. Total losses for the U.S. industry were projected to be $4.5 billion in 2006, primarily due to one-time accounting charges. European airlines were projected to make profits of $1.8 billion in 2006, and Asian airlines profits of $1.7 billion. For 2007, the U.S. airlines were projected to break even, and the global industry was projected to earn around $2 billion.[10]

Demand Projections

Both Boeing and Airbus issue annual projections of likely future demand for commercial jet aircraft. These projections are based on assumptions about future global economic growth, the resulting growth in demand for air travel, and the financial health of the world's airlines.

In its 2006 report, Boeing assumed that the world economy would grow by 3.1% per annum over the next twenty years, which should generate growth in passenger traffic of 4.8% per annum and growth in cargo traffic of 6.1% per year. On this basis, Boeing

forecast demand for some 27,210 new aircraft valued at $2.6 trillion over the next twenty years (1,360 deliveries per year). Of this, some 9,580 aircraft will be replacements for aircraft retired from service, with the balance being aircraft to satisfy an expanded market. In 2025, Boeing estimates that the total global fleet of aircraft will be 35,970, up from 17,330 in 2005. Boeing believes that North America will account for 28% of all new orders, Asia Pacific for 36%, and Europe for 24%. Passenger traffic is projected to grow at 6.4% per annum in Asia versus 3.6% in North America and 3.4% in Europe.[11]

Regarding the mix of orders, Boeing believes that the majority will be for aircraft between regional jets (which have fewer than 100 seats) and the Boeing 747 (see Exhibit 4). Aircraft in the 747 range (including the Airbus A380) will account for some 3% of deliveries and 10% of value between 2006 and 2025, according to Boeing.

The latest Airbus forecast covers 2004–2023. Over that period, Airbus forecasts world passenger traffic to grow by 5.3% per annum and predicts demand for 17,328 new aircraft worth $1.9 trillion. (Note that Airbus excludes regional jets from its forecasts; Boeing's forecasts include some 3,450 regional jet deliveries.) Airbus believes that demand for very large aircraft will be robust, amounting to 1,648 large passenger aircraft and freighters in the 747 range and above, or 22% of the total value of aircraft delivered.[12]

The differences in the mix of orders projected by Boeing and Airbus reflect different views of how future demand will evolve. Airbus believes that hubs will continue to play an important role in airline travel, particularly international travel, and that very large jets will be required to transport people between hubs. Airbus bases this assumption partly on an analysis of data over the last twenty years, which shows that traffic between major airline hubs has grown faster than traffic between other city pairs. Airbus also assumes that urban concentrations will continue to grow, with fifteen cities having populations of more than 20 million by 2023, up from five in 2004. Airbus states that demand is simply a function of where people want to go, and most people want to travel between major urban centers. The company notes, for example, that 90% of travelers going from the United States to China travel to three major cities. Fifty other cities make up the remaining 10%, and Airbus believes that very few of these cities

Exhibit 4

Projected New Airplane Deliveries, 2006–2025

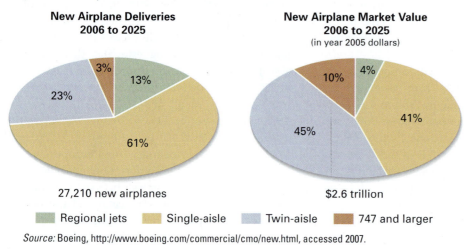

| Regional jets | Single-aisle | Twin-aisle | 747 and larger |

Source: Boeing, http://www.boeing.com/commercial/cmo/new.html, accessed 2007.

will have demand large enough to justify a nonstop service from North America or Europe. Based on this assumption, Airbus sees robust demand for very large aircraft, particularly its A380 offering.

Boeing has a different view of the future. The company theorizes that hubs will become increasingly congested and that many travelers will seek to avoid them. Boeing thinks that passengers prefer frequent nonstop service between the cities they wish to visit. It also sees growth in travel between city pairs as being large enough to support an increasing number of direct long-haul flights. The company notes that continued liberalization of regulations governing airline routes around the world will allow for the establishment of more direct flights between city pairs. As in the United States, the company believes that long-haul, low-cost airlines will emerge that serve city pairs worldwide and avoid hubs.

In sum, Boeing believes that airline travelers will demand more frequent nonstop flights, not larger aircraft.[13] To support this, the company has data showing that all of the growth in airline travel since 1995 has been met by the introduction of new non-stop flights between city pairs and by an increased frequency of flights between city pairs, not by an increase in airplane size. For example, Boeing notes that following the introduction of the 767, airlines introduced more flights between city pairs in North America and Europe and more frequent departures. In 1984, 63% of all flights across the North Atlantic were in the 747. By 2004, the figure had declined to

13%, with smaller wide-bodied aircraft such as the 767 and 777 dominating traffic. Following the introduction of the 777, which can fly nonstop across the Pacific and is smaller than the 747, the same process occurred in the North Pacific. In 2006, there were seventy-two daily flights serving twenty-six city pairs in North America and Asia.

Boeing's History[14]

William Boeing established the Boeing Company in 1916 in Seattle. In the early 1950s, Boeing took an enormous gamble when it decided to build a large jet aircraft that could be sold both to the military as a tanker and to commercial airlines as a passenger plane. Known as the Dash 80, the plane had swept-back wings and four jet engines. Boeing invested $16 million to develop the Dash 80, two-thirds of the company's entire profits during the postwar years. The Dash 80 was the basis for two aircraft, the KC-135 Air Force tanker and the Boeing 707. Introduced into service in 1957, the 707 was the world's first commercially successful passenger jet aircraft. Boeing went on to sell some 856 Boeing 707s, along with 820 KC-135s. The final 707, a freighter, rolled off the production line in 1994 (production of passenger planes ended in 1978). The closest rival to the 707 was the Douglas DC 8, of which some 556 were ultimately sold.

The 707 was followed by a number of successful jet liners, including the 727, which entered service in 1962; the 737, which entered service in 1967; and the 747, which entered service in 1970. The single-aisle 737 went on to become the workhorse of many airlines. In the 2000s, a completely redesigned version of the 737 that could seat between 110 and 180 passengers was still selling strong. Cumulative sales of the 737 totaled 6,500 by mid-2006, making it by far the most popular commercial jet aircraft ever sold.

It was the 747 "jumbo jet," however, that probably best defined Boeing. In 1966, when Boeing's board decided to develop the 747, they were widely viewed as betting the company on the jet. The 747 was born out of the desire of Pan Am, then America's largest airline, for a 400-seat passenger aircraft that could fly 5,000 miles. Pan Am believed that the aircraft would be ideal for the growing volume of transcontinental traffic. However, beyond Pan Am, which committed to purchasing 25 aircraft, demand was very uncertain. Moreover, the estimated $400 million in development and tooling costs placed a heavy burden on Boeing's financial resources. To make a return on its investment, the company estimated it would have to sell close to 400 aircraft. To complicate matters further, Boeing's principal competitors, Lockheed and McDonnell Douglas, were each developing 250-seat jumbo jets.

Boeing's big bet turned out to be auspicious. Pan Am's competitors feared being left behind, and by the end of 1970, almost 200 orders for the aircraft had been placed. Successive models of the 747 extended the range of the aircraft. The 747-400, introduced in 1989, had a range of 8,000 miles and a maximum seating capacity of 550 (although most configurations seated around 400 passengers). By this time, both Douglas and Lockheed had exited the market, giving Boeing a lucrative monopoly in the very large commercial jet category. By 2005, the company had sold some 1,430 747s and was actively selling its latest version of the 747 family, the 747-8, which was scheduled to enter service in 2008.

By the mid-1970s, Boeing was past the breakeven point on all of its models (707, 727, 737, and 747). The positive cash flow helped to fund investment in two new aircraft, the narrow-bodied 757 and the wide-bodied 767. The 757 was designed as a replacement to the aging 727, while the 767 was a response to a similar aircraft from Airbus. These were the first Boeing aircraft to be designed with two-person cockpits, rather than three. Indeed, the cockpit lay-out was identical, allowing the crew to shift from one aircraft to the other. The 767 was also the first aircraft for which Boeing subcontracted a significant amount of work to a trio of Japanese manufacturers—Mitsubishi, Kawasaki, and Fuji—which supplied about 15% of the airframe. Introduced in 1981, both aircraft were successful. Some 1,049 757s were sold during the life of the program, which ended in 2003. Over 950 767s had been sold by 2006, and the program is still going.

The next Boeing plane was the 777. A two-engine, wide-bodied aircraft with seating capacity of up to 400 and a range of almost 8,000 miles, the 777 program was initiated in 1990. The 777 was seen as a response to Airbus's successful A330 and A340 wide-bodied aircraft. Development costs were estimated at some $5 billion. The 777 was the first wide-bodied, long-haul jet to have only two engines. It was also the first to be designed entirely on computer. To develop the 777, for the first time Boeing used cross-functional teams composed of engineering and production employees. It also brought major suppliers and customers into the development process. As with the 767, a significant amount of work was outsourced to foreign manufacturers, including the Japanese trio of Mitsubishi, Kawasaki, and Fuji, which supplied 20% of the 777 airframe. In total, some 60% of parts for the 777 were outsourced. The 777 proved to be another successful venture. By mid-2006, 850 777s had been ordered, far more than the 200 or so required to break even.

In December 1996, Boeing stunned the aerospace industry by announcing it would merge with long-time rival McDonnell Douglas in a deal estimated to be worth $13.3 billion. The merger was driven by Boeing's desire to strengthen its presence in the defense and space side of the aerospace business, where McDonnell Douglas was traditionally strong. On the commercial side of the aerospace business, Douglas had been losing market share since the 1970s. By 1996, Douglas accounted for less than 10% of production in the large commercial jet aircraft market and only 3% of new orders placed that year. The dearth of new orders meant the long-term outlook for Douglas's commercial business was increasingly murky. With or without the merger, many analysts felt that it was only a matter of time before McDonnell Douglas would be forced to exit from the commercial jet aircraft business. In their view, the merger with Boeing merely accelerated that process.

The merger transformed Boeing into a broad-based aerospace business within which commercial aerospace accounted for 40 to 60% of total revenue, depending on the stage of the commercial production cycle. In 2001, for example, the commercial aircraft group accounted for $35 billion in revenues out of a corporate total of $58 billion, or 60%. In 2005, with the delivery cycle at a low point (but the order cycle rebounding), the commercial airplane group accounted for $22.7 billion out of a total of $54.8 billion, or 41%. The balance of revenue was made up by a wide range of military aircraft, weapons and defense systems, and space systems.

In the early 2000s, in a highly symbolic act, Boeing moved its corporate headquarters from Seattle to Chicago. The move was an attempt to put some distance between top corporate officers and the commercial aerospace business, the headquarters of which remained in Seattle. The move was also intended to signal to the investment community that Boeing was far more than its commercial businesses.

To some extent, the move to Chicago may have been driven by a number of production missteps in the late 1990s that hit the company at a time when it should have been enjoying financial success. During the mid-1990s, orders boomed as Boeing cut prices in an aggressive move to gain share from Airbus. However, delivering these aircraft meant that Boeing had to more than double its production schedule between 1996 and 1997. As it attempted to do this, the company ran into some severe production bottlenecks.[15] The company scrambled to hire and train some 41,000 workers, recruiting many from suppliers, a move it came to regret when many of the suppliers could not meet Boeing's demands and shipments of parts were delayed. In the fall of 1997, things got so bad that Boeing shut down its 747 and 737 production lines so that workers could catch up with out-of-sequence work and wait for back-ordered parts to arrive. Ultimately, the company had to take a $1.6 billion charge against earnings to account for higher costs and penalties paid to airlines for the late delivery of jets. As a result, Boeing made very little money out of its mid-1990s' order boom. The head of Boeing's commercial aerospace business was fired, and the company committed itself to a major acceleration of its attempt to overhaul its production system, elements of which dated back half a century.

Boeing in the 2000s

In the 2000s, three things dominated the development of Boeing Commercial Aerospace. First, the company accelerated a decade-long project aimed at improving the company's production methods by adopting the lean production systems initially developed by Toyota and applying them to the manufacture of large jet aircraft. Second, the company considered and then rejected the idea of building a successor to the 747. Third, Boeing decided to develop a new wide-bodied, long-haul jetliner, the 787.

Lean Production at Boeing

Boeing's attempt to revolutionize the way planes are built dates back to the early 1990s. Beginning in 1990, the company started to send teams of executives to Japan to study the production systems of Japan's leading manufacturers, particularly Toyota. Toyota had pioneered a new way of assembling automobiles known as *lean production* (in contrast to conventional *mass production*).

Toyota's lean production system was developed by one of the company's engineers, Ohno Taiichi.[16] After working at Toyota for five years and visiting Ford's U.S. plants, Ohno became convinced that the mass-production philosophy for making cars was flawed. He saw numerous problems, including three major drawbacks. First, long production runs created massive inventories, which had to be stored in large warehouses. This was expensive because of the cost of warehousing and because inventories tied up capital in unproductive uses. Second, if the initial machine settings were wrong, long production runs resulted in the production of a large number of defects (that is, waste). And third, the mass-production system was unable to accommodate consumer preferences for product diversity.

In looking for ways to make shorter production runs economical, Ohno developed a number of techniques designed to reduce setup times for production equipment, a major source of fixed costs. By using a system of levers and pulleys, he was able to reduce the time required to change dies on stamping equipment from a full day in 1950 to three minutes by 1971. This advance made small production runs economical, which allowed Toyota to respond more efficiently to consumer demands for product diversity. Small production runs also eliminated the need to hold large inventories, thereby reducing warehousing costs. Furthermore, small product runs and the lack of inventory meant that defective parts were produced only in small numbers and entered the assembly process immediately. This reduced waste made it easier to trace defects to their source and fix the problem. In sum, Ohno's innovations enabled Toyota to produce a more diverse range of products at a lower unit cost than was possible with conventional mass production.

Impressed with what Toyota had done, in the mid-1990s Boeing started to experiment with applying Toyota-like lean production methods to the production of aircraft. Production at Boeing used to be all about producing parts in high volumes and then storing them in warehouses until they were ready to be used in the assembly process. After visiting Toyota, engineers realized that Boeing was drowning in inventory. A huge amount of space and capital was tied up in things that didn't add value. Moreover, expensive specialized machines often took up a lot of space and were frequently idle for long stretches of time.

Like Ohno at Toyota, company engineers started to think about how they could modify equipment and processes at Boeing to reduce waste. Boeing set aside space and time for teams of creative plant employees—design engineers, maintenance technicians, electricians, machinists, and operators—to start experimenting with machinery. They called these teams moonshiners. The term *moonshine* was coined by Japanese executives who visited the United States after World War II. They were impressed by two things in the United States—supermarkets and the stills built by people in the Appalachian hills. They noticed that people built these stills with no money. They would use salvaged parts to make small stills that produced alcohol that they sold for money. The Japanese took this philosophy back home with them and applied it to industrial machinery, which is where Boeing executives saw the concept in operation in the 1990s. With the help of Japanese consultants, they decided to apply the moonshine creative philosophy at Boeing to produce new low-cost, "right-sized" machines that could be used to increase profits.

The moonshine teams were trained in lean production techniques, given a small budget, and then set loose. Initially, many of the moonshine teams focused on redesigning equipment to produce parts. Underlying this choice was a Boeing study that showed that more than 80% of the parts manufactured for aircraft were less than 12 inches long, and yet the metal-working machinery was huge and inflexible and could economically produce parts only in large lots.[17]

Soon, empowered moonshine teams were designing their own equipment—small-scale machines that took up little space and used wheels to allow the machines to move around the plant. One team, for example, replaced a large stamping machine that cost six figures and was used to produce L-shaped metal parts in batches of 1,000 with a miniature stamping machine powered by a small hydraulic motor that could be wheeled around the plant. With the small machine, which cost a couple of thousand dollars, parts could be produced very quickly in small lots, eliminating the need for inventory. They also made a sanding machine and a parts cleaner of equal size. Now the entire process—from stamping the raw material to the finished part—was completed in minutes (instead of hours or days) just by configuring these machines into a small cell and having them serviced by a single person. The small scale and quick turnaround now made it possible to produce these parts just in time, eliminating the need to produce and store inventory.[18]

Another example of a moonshine innovation concerned the process for loading seats onto a plane during assembly. Historically, this was a cumbersome process. After the seats arrived at Boeing from a supplier, wheels were attached to each seat, and then the seats were delivered to the factory floor in a large container. An overhead crane lifted the container up to the level of the aircraft door. Then the seats were unloaded and rolled into the aircraft, before being installed. The process was repeated until all of the seats had been loaded. For a single-aisle plane, this could take twelve hours. For a wide-bodied jet, it would take much longer. A moonshine team adapted a hay elevator to perform the same job (see Exhibit 5). It cost a lot less, delivered seats quickly through the passenger door, and took just two hours, while eliminating the need for cranes.[19]

Multiply the examples given here, and soon you have a very significant impact on production costs: A drill machine was built for 5% of the cost of a full-scale machine from Ingersoll-Rand. Portable routers were built for 0.2% of the cost of a large fixed router. One process that took 2,000 minutes for a 100-part order (20 minutes per part because of setup, machining, and transit) now takes 100 minutes (1 minute per part). Employees building 737 floor

Exhibit 5

The Converted Hay Loader at Work

beams reduced labor hours by 74%, increased inventory turns from two to eighteen per year, and reduced manufacturing space by 50%. Employees building the 777 tail cut lead time by 70% and reduced space and work in progress by 50%. Production of parts for landing gear support used to take thirty-two moves from machine to machine and required ten months; production now takes three moves and twenty-five days.[20]

In general, Boeing found that it was able to produce smaller lots of parts economically, often from machines that it built itself, which were smaller and cost less than the machines available from outside vendors. In turn, these innovations enabled Boeing to switch to just-in-time inventory systems and reduce waste. Boeing was also able to save on space. By eliminating large production machinery at its Auburn facility, replacing much of it with smaller, more flexible machines, Boeing was able to free up 1.3 million square feet of space and sold seven buildings.[21]

In addition to moonshine teams, Boeing adopted other process improvement methodologies, using

them when deemed appropriate. Six Sigma quality improvement processes are widely used within Boeing. The most wide-reaching process change, however, was the decision to switch from a static assembly line to a moving line. In traditional aircraft manufacture, planes are docked in angled stalls. Ramps surround each plane, and workers go in and out to find parts and install them. Moving a plane to the next workstation is a complex process. The aircraft has to be down-jacked from its workstation, a powered cart brought in, and the aircraft towed to the next station, where it is then jacked up. This can take two shifts. A lot of time is wasted bringing parts to a stall and moving a plane from one stall to the next.

In 2001, Boeing introduced a moving assembly line into its Renton plant near Seattle, which manufactures the 737 (see Exhibit 6). With a moving line, each aircraft is attached to a "sled" that rides a magnetic strip embedded in the factory floor, pulling the aircraft at a rate of 2 inches per minute, moving past a series of stations where tools and parts arrive at the moment needed, allowing workers to install the proper assemblies. The setup eliminates wandering for tools and parts, as well as expensive tug pulls or crane lifts (just having tools delivered to workstations, rather than having workers fetch them, was found to save twenty to forty-five minutes on every shift). Preassembly tasks are performed on feeder lines. For example, inboard and outboard flaps are assembled on the wing before it arrives for joining to the fuselage.[22]

Like a Toyota assembly line, the moving line can be stopped if a problem arises. Lights are used to indicate the state of the line. A green light indicates a normal work flow; the first sign of a stoppage brings a yellow warning light; and, if the problem isn't solved within fifteen minutes, a purple light indicates that the line has stopped. Each work area and feeder line has its own lights, so there is no doubt where the problem is.[23]

The cumulative effects of these process innovations have been significant. By 2005, assembly time for the 737 had been cut from twenty-two days to just eleven days. In addition, work-in-progress in-

ventory had been reduced by 55 percent and stored inventory by 59 percent.[24] By 2006, all of Boeing's production lines except that for the 747 had shifted from static bays to moving lines. The 747 was expected to shift to moving line when Boeing started production of the 747-8.

The Super-Jumbo Decisions

In the early 1990s, Boeing and Airbus started to contemplate new aircraft to replace Boeing's aging 747. The success of the 747 had given Boeing a monopoly in the market for very large jet aircraft, making the plane one of the most profitable in the jet age. But the basic design dated back to the 1960s, and some believed there might be sufficient demand for a super-jumbo aircraft with as many as 900 seats.

Initially, the two companies considered establishing a joint venture to share the costs and risks associated with developing a super-jumbo aircraft, but Boeing withdrew in 1995, citing costs and uncertain demand prospects. Airbus subsequently concluded that Boeing was never serious about the joint venture,

Exhibit 6

The Moving Line

Source: Copyright © Boeing. All rights reserved.

and the discussions were nothing more than a ploy to keep Airbus from developing its own plane.[25]

After Boeing withdrew, Airbus started to talk about offering a competitor to the 747 in 1995. The plane, then dubbed the A3XX, was to be a super jumbo with capacity for over 500 passengers. Indeed, Airbus stated that some versions of the plane might carry as many as 900 passengers. Airbus initially estimated that there would be demand for some 1,400 planes of this size over twenty years, and that development costs would total around $9 billion (estimates ultimately increased to some $15 billion). Boeing's latest 747 offering—the 747-400—could carry around 416 passengers in three classes.

Boeing responded by drafting plans to develop new versions of the 747 family—the 747-500X and the 747-600X. The 747-600X was to have a new (larger) wing and a fuselage almost 50 feet longer than that of the 747-400, carry 550 passengers in three classes, and have a range of 7,700 miles. The smaller 747-500X would carry 460 passengers in three classes and have a range of 8,700 miles.

After taking a close look at the market for a super-jumbo replacement to the 747, in early 1997 Boeing announced that it would not proceed with the program. The reasons given for this decision included the limited market and high development costs, which at the time were estimated to be $7 billion. There were also fears that the wider wing span of the new planes would mean that airports would have to redesign some of their gates to take the aircraft. Boeing, McDonnell Douglas (prior to the merger with Boeing), and the major manufacturers of jet engines all forecast demand for about 500 to 750 such aircraft over the next twenty years. Airbus alone forecast demand as high as 1,400 aircraft. Boeing stated that the fragmentation of the market due to the rise of "point-to-point" flights across oceans would limit demand for a super jumbo. Instead of focusing on the super-jumbo category, Boeing stated that it would develop new versions of the 767 and 777 aircraft that could fly up to 9,000 miles and carry as many as 400 passengers.

Airbus, however, continued to push forward with plans to develop the A3XX. In December 2000, with more than fifty orders in hand, the board of EADS, Airbus's parent company, approved development of the plane, which was now dubbed the A380. Development costs at this point were pegged at $12 billion, and the plane was forecast to enter service in

2006 with Singapore Airlines. The A380 was to have two passenger decks, more space per seat, and wider aisles. It would carry 555 passengers in great comfort, something that passengers would appreciate on long transoceanic flights. According to Airbus, the plane would carry up to 35% more passengers than the most popular 747-400 configuration, yet cost per seat would be 15 to 20% lower due to operating efficiencies. Concerns were raised about turnaround time at airport gates for such a large plane, but Airbus stated that dual-boarding bridges and wider aisles meant that turnaround times would be no more than those for the 747-400.

Airbus also stated that the A380 was designed to operate on existing runways and within existing gates. However, London's Heathrow airport found that it had to spend some $450 million to accommodate the A380, widening taxiways and building a baggage reclaim area for the plane. Similarly, eighteen U.S. airports had reportedly spent some $1 billion just to accommodate the A380.[26]

The 787

While Airbus pushed forward with the A380, in March 2001 Boeing announced the development of a radically new aircraft. Dubbed the *Sonic Cruiser,* the plane would carry 250 passengers 9,000 miles and fly just below the speed of sound, cutting one hour off transatlantic flights and three hours off transpacific flights. To keep down operating costs, the sonic cruiser would be built out of low-weight carbon fiber "composites." Although the announcement created considerable interest in the aviation community, in the wake of the recession that hit the airline industry after September 11, 2001, both Boeing and the airlines became considerably less enthusiastic. In March 2002, the program was canceled. Instead, Boeing said that it would develop a more conventional aircraft using composite technology. The plane was initially known as the 7E7, with the *E* standing for *efficient* (the plane was renamed the 787 in early 2005).

In April 2004, the 7E7 program was formally launched with an order for fifty aircraft worth $6 billion from All Nippon Airlines of Japan. It was the largest launch order in Boeing's history. The 7E7 was a twin-aisle, wide-bodied, two-engine plane designed to carry 200 to 300 passengers up to 8,500 miles, making the 7E7 well suited for long-haul, point-to-point flights. The range exceeded that of all but the longest range plane in the 777 family, and the 7E7 could fly 750 miles more than Airbus's closest competitor, the mid-sized A330-200. With a fuselage built entirely out of composites, the aircraft was lighter and would use 20% less fuel than existing aircraft of comparable size.

The plane was also designed with passenger comfort in mind. The seats would be wider, as would the aisles, and the windows were larger than in existing aircraft. The plane would be pressurized at an altitude of 6,000 feet, as opposed to 8,000 feet, which is standard industry practice. Airline cabin humidity was typically kept at 10% to avoid moisture buildup and corrosion, but composites don't corrode, so humidity would be closer to 20 to 30%.[27]

Initial estimates suggested that the jet would cost some $7 to $8 billion to develop and enter service in 2008. Boeing decided to outsource more work for the 787 than on any other aircraft to date. Some 35% of the plane's fuselage and wing structure would be built by Boeing. The trio of Japanese companies that worked on the 767 and 777—Mitsubishi Heavy Industries, Kawasaki Heavy Industries, and Fuji Heavy Industries—would build another 35%, and some 26% would be built by Italian companies, particularly Alenia.[28] For the first time, Boeing asked its major suppliers to bear some of the development costs for the aircraft.

The plane was to be assembled at Boeing's wide-bodied plant in Everett, Washington. Large subassemblies were to be built by major suppliers and then shipped to Everett for final assembly. The idea was to "snap together" the parts in Everett in three days, cutting down on total assembly time. To speed up transportation, Boeing would adopt air freight as its major transportation method for many components.

Airbus's initial response was to dismiss Boeing's claims of cost savings as inconsequential. They pointed out that even if the 787 used less fuel than the A330, that was equivalent to just 4% of total operating costs.[29] However, even by Airbus's calculations, as fuel prices started to accelerate, the magnitude of the savings rose. Moreover, Boeing quickly started to snag some significant orders for the 787. In 2004, Boeing booked 56 orders for the 787, and in 2005, some 232 orders. Another 85 orders were booked in the first nine months of 2006 for a running total of 373—well beyond the breakeven point.

In December 2004, Airbus announced that it would develop a new model, the A350, to compete directly with the 787. The planes were to be long-haul, twin-aisle jets, seating 200 to 300 passengers, and constructed of composites. The order flow, however, was slow, with airlines complaining that the A350 did not match the Boeing 787 on operating efficiency, range, or passenger comfort. Airbus went back to the drawing board and, in mid-2006, announced a new version of the A350, the A350 XWB (for "extra-wide body"). Airbus estimates that the A350 XWB will cost $10 billion to develop and enter service in 2012, several years behind the 787. The two-engine A350 XWB will carry between 250 and 375 passengers and fly up to 8,500 miles. The largest versions of the A350 XWB will be competing directly with the Boeing 777, not the 787. Like the 787, the A350 XWB will be built primarily of composite materials. The extra-wide body is designed to enhance passenger comfort. To finance the A350 XWB, Airbus stated that it would probably seek launch aid from Germany, France, Spain, and the United Kingdom, all countries where major parts of Airbus are based.[30]

Trade Tensions

It is impossible to discuss the global aerospace industry without touching on trade issues. Over the last three decades, both Boeing and Airbus have charged that their competitor benefited unfairly from government subsidies. Until 2001, Airbus functioned as a consortium of four European aircraft manufacturers: one British (20.0% ownership stake), one French (37.9% ownership), one German (37.9% ownership), and one Spanish (4.2% ownership). In the 1980s and early 1990s, Boeing maintained that subsidies from these nations allowed Airbus to set unrealistically low prices, to offer concessions and attractive financing terms to airlines, to write off development costs, and to use state-owned airlines to obtain orders. According to a study by the U.S. Department of Commerce, Airbus received more than $13.5 billion in government subsidies between 1970 and 1990 ($25.9 billion if commercial interest rates are applied). Most of these subsidies were in the form of loans at below-market interest rates and tax breaks. The subsidies financed research and development and provided attractive financing terms for Airbus's customers. Airbus responded by pointing out that Boeing had benefited for years from hidden U.S. government subsidies, particularly Pentagon R&D grants.

In 1992, the two sides appeared to reach an agreement that put to rest their long-standing trade dispute. The 1992 pact, which was negotiated by the European Union (EU) on behalf of the four member states, limited direct government subsidies to 33% of the total costs of developing a new aircraft and specified that such subsidies had to be repaid with interest within seventeen years. The agreement also limited indirect subsidies, such as government-supported military research that has applications to commercial aircraft, to 3% of a country's annual total commercial aerospace revenues or 4% of commercial aircraft revenues of any single company in that country. Although Airbus officials stated that the controversy had now been resolved, Boeing officials argued that they would still be competing for years against subsidized products.

The trade dispute heated up again in 2004 when Airbus announced the first version of the A350 to compete against Boeing's 787. What raised a red flag for the U.S. government was a sign from Airbus that it would apply for $1.7 billion in launch aid to help fund the development of the A350. As far as the United States was concerned, this was too much. In late 2004, U.S. Trade Representative Robert Zoellick issued a statement formally renouncing the 1992 agreement and calling for an end to launch subsidies. According to Zoellick,

> Since its creation 35 years ago, some Europeans have justified subsidies to Airbus as necessary to support an infant industry. If that rationalization were ever valid, its time has long passed. Airbus now sells more large civil aircraft than Boeing.

Zoellick went on to claim that Airbus has received some $3.7 billion in launch aid for the A380 plus another $2.8 billion in indirect subsidies, including $1.7 billion in taxpayer-funded infrastructure improvements, for a total of $6.5 billion.

Airbus shot back that Boeing too continued to enjoy lavish subsidies and that the company had received some $12 billion from NASA to develop technology, much of which had found its way into commercial jet aircraft. The Europeans also contended that Boeing would receive as much as $3.2 billion in tax breaks from Washington State, where the 787 is to be assembled, and more than $1 billion in loans from the Japanese government to three Japanese suppliers, who will build over one-third of the 787.

Moreover, Airbus was quick to point out that a trade war would not benefit either side and that Airbus purchased some $6 billion a year in supplies from companies in the United States.

In January 2005, both the United States and the EU agreed to freeze direct subsidies to the two aircraft makers while talks continued. However, in May 2005 news reports suggested, and Airbus confirmed, that the jet maker had applied to four EU governments for launch aid for the A350 and that the British government would announce some $700 million in aid at the Paris Air Show in mid-2005. Simultaneously, the EU offered to cut launch aid for the A350 by 30%. Dissatisfied, the U.S. side decided that the talks were going nowhere, and on May 31 the United States formally filed a request with the World Trade Organization (WTO) for the establishment of a dispute resolution panel to resolve the issues. The EU quickly responded, filing a countersuit with the WTO claiming that U.S. aid to Boeing exceeded the terms set out in the 1992 agreement. The dispute is currently before the WTO.[31]

Although the decision to scrap the original design of the A350 took some of the heat out of the dispute, Airbus is expected to ask for launch aid for the redesigned A350 XWB.

The Next Chapter

Huge financial bets have been placed on very different visions of the future of airline travel: Airbus with the A380 and Boeing with the 787. Airbus has hedged its bets by announcing the A350 XWB, but will this be too little too late? Moreover, there are signs of production turmoil at Airbus. Orders for the A380 have stalled. In mid-2006, the company announced that deliveries for the aircraft would be delayed by six months while the company dealt with "production issues" arising from problems installing the wiring bundles in the A380. Estimates suggest that the delay would cost Airbus some $2.6 billion over the next four years.[32] Within months, Airbus had revised the expected delay to eighteen months and stated that the number of A380s it now needed to sell to break even had increased from 250 to 420 aircraft. The company also stated that due to production problems, it would be able to deliver only 84 A380 planes by 2010, compared to an original estimate of 420.[33] In response, several significant launch customers for the A380 were said to be reconsidering their purchase decisions. United Parcel Service, which has 10 A380 cargo planes on order, was reportedly considering switching to the Boeing 747-8, Boeing's latest offering in the venerable 747 family.

Boeing quietly launched the 747-8 program in November 2005. This plane will be a completely redesigned version of the 747 and will incorporate many of the technological advances developed for the 787, including significant use of composites. It will be offered in both a freighter and an intercontinental passenger configuration that will carry 467 passengers in a three-seat configuration and have a range of 8,000 miles (the 747-400 can carry 416 passengers). The 747-8 will also use the fuel-efficient engines developed for the 787 and will have the same cockpit configuration as the 737, 777, and 787. Development costs are estimated to be around $4 billion. By October 2006, Boeing had orders for forty-four 787-8 freighters, but none for passenger planes. However, some analysts speculated that with the A380 mired in delays, the 747-8 passenger configuration might begin to garner more orders.

Not all is smooth sailing at Boeing. The company experienced some problems with suppliers for the 787, who have fallen behind schedule designing some components for the project. As of late 2006, Boeing was insisting that the 787 was still on schedule. Some analysts, however, are concerned that this might be a sign of things to come and that the complexity associated with coordinating a diverse base of suppliers might lead to delays in the 787.

Complicating issues, both Airbus and Boeing have been through some changes in key management over the last few years. At Boeing, CEO Phil Condit resigned in late 2003, after it was revealed that the company's CFO, Mike Sears, had hired a key Department of Defense procurement officer in return for her backing of a huge order for air force tankers based on the 767. Sears was subsequently prosecuted and sent to jail. The Sears scandal was only the latest in a number that Boeing executives had become embroiled in during the early 2000s. Condit's resignation was widely taken to indicate that the board felt that a new CEO was needed to clean house. Condit was replaced by Harry Stonecipher, who was CEO of McDonnell Douglas when it was acquired by Boeing and later president of Boeing. Stonecipher resigned fifteen months later, when it was revealed that he had had an affair with a subordinate and communicated with her using the company's email service. Stoneci-

pher was replaced by Jim McNerney, who moved to Boeing from the CEO position at 3M. Prior to joining 3M, McNerney had run the aircraft engine business at General Electric. McNerney was widely viewed as a skilled manager who had brought the operating discipline that GE is famous for to 3M. He was expected to do the same at Boeing, pushing the company to continue to pursue various productivity initiatives, such as lean production, Six Sigma processes, and global sourcing.

At Airbus, following the announcement of the delay in A380 production, there was pressure on Noel Forgeard, the CEO of EADS, Airbus's parent company, to resign. Forgeard refused, although Gustav Humbert, the CEO of Airbus, did offer to step down. After a three-week crisis, the board of EADS took matters into its own hands and fired both Forgeard and Humbert. They were replaced by Louis Gallois, a Frenchman who once ran an aerospace company that was acquired by EADS, and Christian Streiff, the former number 2 at Saint Gobain, the French glassmaker.

With new management in place at both companies, the focus is on the unfolding competitive battle. Can Airbus make money on the A380, and, if it does, will it gain a monopoly that rivals Boeing's 747 dynasty? Will the 787 live up to its promise and become the right plane for a new era of global travel? Can Airbus come back at Boeing with its new version of the A350, the A350 XWB? And what of the ongoing trade dispute? How will this impact on the long-running dog fight between the two companies?

ENDNOTES

1. http://www.boeing.com, accessed September 2006.
2. http://www.airbus.com/en, accessed September 2006.
3. J. Palmer, "Big Bird," *Barron's* (December 19, 2005): 25–29; http://www.yeald.com/Yeald/a/33941/both_a380_and_787_have_bright_futures.html.
4. G. J. Steven, "The Learning Curve: from Aircraft to Spacecraft," *Management Accounting* (May 1999): 64–66.
5. D. Gates, "Boeing 7E7 Watch: Familiar Suppliers Make Short List," *Seattle Times.*
6. The figures are from the International Airline Travelers Association (IATA).
7. IATA, "2006 Loss Forecast Drops to US$1.7 Billion," Press Release, August 31, 2006.
8. "Turbulent Skies: Low Cost Airlines," *Economist* (July 10, 2004): 68–72; "Silver Linings, Darkening Clouds," *Economist* (March 27, 2004): 90–92.
9. Data from the Air Transport Association at www.airlines.org.
10. IATA, "2006 Loss Forecast Drops to US$1.7 Billion."
11. Boeing, Current Market Outlook, 2006, http://www.boeing.com.
12. http://www.airbus.com/en/myairbus/global_market_forecast.html.

13. Presentation by Randy Baseler, vice president of Boeing Commercial Airplanes, given at the Farnborough Air Show, July 2006, http://www.boeing.com/nosearch/exec_pres/CMO.pdf.

14. This material is drawn from an earlier version of the Boeing case written by Charles W. L. Hill. See C. W. L. Hill, "The Boeing Corporation: Commercial Aircraft Operations," in C. W. L. Hill and G. R. Jones, *Strategic Management,* 3rd ed. (Boston: Houghton Mifflin, 1995). Much of Boeing's history is described in R. J. Sterling, *Legend and Legacy* (New York: St. Martin's Press, 1992).

15. S. Browder, "A Fierce Downdraft at Boeing," *Business Week* (January 26, 1988): 34.

16. M. A. Cusumano, *The Japanese Automobile Industry* (Cambridge, MA: Harvard University Press, 1989); Ohno Taiichi, *Toyota Production System* (Cambridge, MA: Productivity Press, 1990); J. P. Womack, D. T. Jones, and D. Roos, *The Machine That Changed the World* (New York: Rawson Associates, 1990).

17. J. Gillie, "Lean Manufacturing Could Save Boeing's Auburn Washington Plant," *Knight Ridder Tribune Business News,* May 6, 2002, p. 1.

18. P. V. Arnold, "Boeing Knows Lean," *MRO Today* (February 2002).

19. Boeing, "Converted Farm Machine Improves Production Process," Press Release, July 1, 2003.

20. Arnold, "Boeing Knows Lean"; Also see Boeing, "Build in Lean: Manufacturing for the Future," http://www.boeing.com/aboutus/environment/create_build.htm; and Gillie, "Lean Manufacturing Could Save Boeing's Auburn Washington Plant."

21. Gillie, "Lean Manufacturing Could Save Boeing's Auburn Washington Plant."

22. Arnold, "Boeing Knows Lean."

23. M. Mecham, "The Lean, Green Line," *Aviation Week* (July 19, 2004): 144–148.

24. Boeing, "Boeing Reduces 737 Airplane's Final Assembly Time by 50 Percent," Press Release, January 27, 2005.

25. "A Phony War," *Economist* (May 5, 2001): 56–57.

26. J. D. Boyd, "Building Room for Growth," *Traffic World* (August 7, 2006): 1.

27. W. Sweetman, "Boeing, Boeing, Gone," *Popular Science* (June 2004): 97.

28. "Who Will Supply the Parts?" *Seattle Times,* June 15, 2003.

29. Sweetman, "Boeing, Boeing, Gone."

30. D. Michaels and J. L. Lunsford, "Airbus Chief Reveals Plans for New Family of Jetliners," *Wall Street Journal,* July 18, 2006, p. A3.

31. J. Reppert-Bismarck and W. Echikson, "EU Countersues over U.S. Aid to Boeing," *Wall Street Journal,* June 1, 2005, p. A2; "United States Takes Next Steps in Airbus WTO Litigation," United States Trade Representative Press Release, May 30, 2005.

32. "Airbus Agonistes," *Wall Street Journal,* September 6, 2006, p. A20.

33. "Forecast Dimmer for Profit on Airbus' A380," *Seattle Times,* October 20, 2006.

Apple Computer

This case was prepared by Charles W. L. Hill, the University of Washington.

Back in 1997, Apple Computer was in deep trouble. The company that had pioneered the personal computer market with its easy-to-use Apple II in 1978 and had introduced the first graphical user interface with the Macintosh in 1984 was bleeding red ink. Apple's worldwide market share, which had been fluctuating between 7 and 9% since 1984, had sunk to 4%. Sales were declining. Apple was on track to lose $378 million on revenues of $7 billion, and that on top of a $740 million loss in 1996. In July 1997, the co-founder of the company, Steve Jobs, who had been fired from Apple back in 1985, returned as CEO. At an investor conference, Michael Dell, CEO of Dell Computer, was asked what Jobs should do as head of Apple. Dell quipped, "I'd shut it down and give the money back to shareholders."[1]

By 2006, the situation looked very different. Apple was on track to book record sales of over $19 billion and net profits of close to $1.9 billion. The stock price, which had traded as low as $6 a share in 2003, was in the mid-70s, and the market capitalization, at $63 billion, surpassed that of Dell Computer, which was around $48 billion. Driving the transformation were strong sales of Apple's iPod music player and music downloads from the iTunes store. In addition, strong sales of Apple's MacBook laptop computers had lifted Apple's market share in the U.S. PC business to 4.8%, up from a low of under 3% in 2004.[2] Moreover, analysts were predicting that the halo ef-

fect of the iPod, together with Apple's recent adoption of Intel's microprocessor architecture, would drive strong sales going forward.

For the first time in twenty years, it looked as if Apple, the perennial also-ran, might be seizing the initiative. But serious questions remained. Could the company continue to build on its momentum? Would sales of Apple's computers really benefit from the iPod? Could the company break out of its niche and become a mainstream player? And how sustainable was the iPod-driven sales boom? With new competitors coming along, could Apple hold onto its leadership position in the market for digital music players?

Apple 1976–1997

The Early Years

Apple's genesis is the stuff of computer industry legend.[3] On April Fools' Day, 1976, two young electronics enthusiasts, Steve Jobs and Steve Wozniak, started a company to sell a primitive personal computer (PC) that Wozniak had designed. Steve Jobs was just twenty; Wozniak, or Woz, as he was commonly called, was five years older. They had known each other for several years, having been introduced by a mutual friend who realized that they shared an interest in consumer electronics. Woz had designed the computer just for the fun of it. That's what people did in 1976. The idea that somebody would actually want to purchase his machine had not occurred to Woz, but it did to Jobs. Jobs persuaded a reluctant Woz to form a company and sell the machine. The location of the company was Steve Jobs's garage. Jobs suggested they call the company Apple and their first machine the Apple I. They sold around two hundred of them at $666 each. The price point was picked as something of a prank.

The Apple I had several limitations—no case, keyboard, or power supply being obvious ones. It also required several hours of laborious assembly by hand. By late 1976, Woz was working on a replacement to the Apple I, the Apple II.[4] In October 1976, with the Apple II under development, Jobs and Woz were introduced to Mike Markkula. Only thirty-four, Markkula was already a retired millionaire, having made a small fortune at Fairchild and Intel. Markkula had no plans to get back into business anytime soon, but a visit to Jobs's garage changed all that. He committed to investing $92,000 for one-third of the company and promised that his ultimate investment would be $250,000. Stunned, Jobs and Woz agreed to let him join as a partner. It was a fateful decision. The combination of Woz's technical skills, Jobs's entrepreneurial zeal and vision, and Markkula's business savvy and connections was a powerful one. Markkula told Jobs and Woz that neither of them had the experience to run a company and persuaded them to hire a president, Michael Scott, who had worked for Markkula at Fairchild.

The Apple II was introduced in 1977 at a price of $1,200 (see Exhibit 1). The first version was an integrated computer with a Motorola microprocessor and included a keyboard, power supply, monitor, and the BASIC programming software. It was Jobs who pushed Woz to design an integrated machine—he wanted something that was easy to use and not just a toy for geeks. Jobs also insisted that the Apple II look good. It had an attractive case and no visible screws or bolts. This differentiated it from most PCs at the time, which looked as if they had been assembled by hobbyists at home (as many had).

In 1978, Apple started to sell a version of the Apple II that incorporated something new—a disk drive. The disk drive turned out to be a critical innovation, for it enabled third-party developers to write software programs for the Apple II that could be loaded via floppy disks. Soon programs started to appear, among them EasyWriter, a basic word-processing program, and VisiCalc, a spreadsheet. VisiCalc was an instant hit and pulled in a new customer set, business types who could use VisiCalc for financial planning and accounting. Since VisiCalc was available only for the Apple II, it helped to drive demand for the machine.

Exhibit 1

The Apple II Computer

Source: Courtesy of Apple Inc.

By the end of 1980, Apple had sold over 100,000 Apple IIs, making the company the leader in the embryonic PC industry. The company had successfully executed an IPO, was generating over $200 million in annual sales, and was profitable. With the Apple II series selling well, particularly in the education market, Apple introduced its next product, the Apple III, in the fall of 1980. It was a failure. The computer was filled with bugs and crashed constantly. The Apple III had been rushed to market too quickly. Apple reintroduced a reengineered Apple III in 1981, but it continued to be outsold by Apple II. Indeed, successive versions of the Apple II family, each an improvement on the preceding version, continued to be produced by the company until 1993. In total, over 2 million Apple II computers were sold. The series became a standard in American classrooms, where it was valued for its intuitive ease of use. Moreover, the Apple II was the mainstay of the company until the late 1980s, when an improved version of the Macintosh started to garner significant sales.

The IBM PC and Its Aftermath

Apple's success galvanized the world's largest computer company, IBM, to speed up development of its entry into the PC market. IBM had a huge and very profitable mainframe computer business, but it had so far failed to develop a PC, despite two attempts. To get to market quickly with this, its third PC project, IBM broke with its established practice of using its own proprietary technology to build the PC. Instead, IBM adopted an "open architecture," purchasing the components required to make the IBM PC from other manufacturers. These components included a 16-bit microprocessor from Intel and an operating system, MS-DOS, which was licensed from a small Washington State company, Microsoft.

Microsoft had been in the industry from its inception, writing a version of the BASIC software programming language for the MITS Atari in 1977, the first PC ever produced. IBM's desire to license BASIC brought its representatives to Redmond to talk with the company's CEO, Bill Gates. Gates, still in his early twenties, persuaded IBM to adopt a 16-bit processor (originally IBM had been considering a less powerful 8-bit processor). He was also instrumental in pushing IBM to adopt an open architecture, arguing that IBM would benefit from the software and peripherals that other companies could then make.

Initially, IBM was intent on licensing the CP/M operating system, produced by Digital Research, for the IBM PC. However, the current version of CP/M was designed to work on an 8-bit processor, and Gates had persuaded IBM that it needed a 16-bit processor. In a series of quick moves, Gates purchased a 16-bit operating system from a local company, Seattle Computer, for $50,000. Gates then hired the designer of the operating system, Tim Paterson, renamed the system MS-DOS, and offered to license it to IBM. In what turned out to be a master stroke, Gates persuaded IBM to accept a nonexclusive license for MS-DOS (which IBM called PC-DOS).

To stoke sales, IBM offered a number of applications for the IBM PC that were sold separately, including a version of VisiCalc, EasyWriter, and a well-known series of business programs from Peachtree Software.

Introduced in 1981, the IBM PC was an instant success. Over the next two years, IBM would sell more than 500,000 PCs, seizing market leadership from Apple. IBM had what Apple lacked, an ability to sell to corporate America. As sales of the IBM PC mounted, two things happened. First, independent software developers started to write programs to run on the IBM PC. These included two applications that drove adoptions of the IBM PC: a word-processing program (WordPerfect) and a spreadsheet (Lotus 1-2-3). Second, the success of IBM gave birth to clone manufacturers who made IBM-compatible PCs that also utilized an Intel microprocessor and Microsoft's MS-DOS operating system. The first and most successful of the clone makers was Compaq, which in 1983 introduced its first PC, a twenty-eight-pound "portable" PC. In its first year, Compaq booked $111 million in sales, which at the time was a record for first-year sales of a company. Before long, a profusion of IBM clone makers entered the market, including Tandy, Zenith, Leading Edge, and Dell. The last was established in 1984 by Michael Dell, then a student at the University of Texas, who initially ran the company out of his dorm room.

The Birth of the Macintosh

By 1980, two other important projects were under way at Apple: Lisa and the Macintosh. Lisa was originally conceived as a high-end business machine, and the Macintosh as a low-end portable machine (see Exhibit 2).

Exhibit 2

The Macintosh

Source: Courtesy of Apple Inc.

The development of the Lisa and, ultimately, the Macintosh was influenced by two visits Steve Jobs paid to Xerox's fabled Palo Alto Research Center (PARC) in November and December 1979. Funded out of Xerox's successful copier business, PARC had been set up to do advanced research on office technology. Engineers at PARC had developed a number of technologies that were later to become central to PCs, including a graphical user interface (GUI), software programs that were made tangible through on-screen icons, a computer mouse that let a user click on and drag screen objects, and a laser printer. Jobs was astounded by what he saw at PARC and decided on the spot that these innovations had to be incorporated into Apple's machines.

Jobs initially pushed the Lisa team to implement PARC's innovations, but he was reportedly driving people on the project nuts with his demands, so President Mike Scott pulled him off the project. Jobs reacted by essentially hijacking the Macintosh project and transforming it into a skunk works that would put his vision into effect. By one account:

He hounded the people on the Macintosh project to do their best work. He sang their praises, bullied them unmercifully, and told them "they weren't making a computer, they were making history." He promoted the Mac passionately,

making people believe that he was talking about much more than a piece of office equipment.[5]

It was during this period that Bud Tribble, a software engineer on the Mac project, quipped that Jobs could create a "reality distortion field." Jobs insisted that the Mac would ship by early 1982. Tribble knew that the schedule was unattainable, and, when asked why he didn't point this out to Jobs, he replied:

Steve insists that we're shipping in early 1982 and won't accept answers to the contrary. The best way to describe the situation is a term from *Star Trek*. Steve has a reality distortion field. . . . In his presence, reality is malleable. He can convince anyone of practically anything. It wears off when he's not around, but it makes it hard to have realistic schedules.[6]

Andy Hertzfeld, another engineer on the Macintosh project, thought Tribble was exaggerating

. . . until I observed Steve in action over the next few weeks. The reality distortion field was a confounding mélange of a charismatic rhetorical style, an indomitable will, and an eagerness to bend any fact to fit the purpose at hand. If one line of argument failed to persuade, he would deftly switch to another. Sometimes, he would throw you off balance by suddenly adopting your position as his own, without acknowledging that he ever thought differently.[7]

Back at Apple, things were changing too. Mike Scott had left the company after clashes with other executives, including Markkula, who had become chairman. Jobs persuaded John Sculley to join Apple as CEO. Sculley was the former vice president of marketing at Pepsi, where he had become famous for launching the Pepsi Challenge. Jobs had reportedly asked Sculley, "Do you want to sell sugar water for the rest of your life, or do you want to change the world?" Sculley opted for changing the world. A Wharton MBA, Sculley had been hired for his marketing savvy, not his technical skills.

While the Lisa project suffered several delays, Jobs pushed the Macintosh team to finish the project and beat the Lisa team to market with a better product. Introduced in 1984, the Macintosh certainly captured attention for its stylish design and its use of a GUI, icons, and a mouse, all of which made the machine easy to use and were not found on any other PC at the time. Jobs, ever the perfectionist, again insisted that not a single screw should be visible on the case. He reportedly fired a designer who presented a mockup that had a screw that could be seen by lifting a handle.

Early sales were strong; then they faltered. For all of its appeal, the Macintosh lacked some important features—it had no hard disk drive, only one floppy drive, and insufficient computer memory. Moreover, there were few applications available to run on the machine, and the Mac proved to be a more difficult machine to develop applications for than the IBM PC and its clones. Jobs, however, seemed oblivious to the problems and continued to talk about outsized sales projections, even when it was obvious to all around him that they were unattainable.

In early 1985, Apple posted its first loss. Aware that the drastic action necessary could not be taken while Jobs was running the Macintosh division, Sculley got backing from the board of directors to strip Jobs of his management role and oversight of the Macintosh division. In late 1985, an embittered Jobs resigned from Apple, sold all of his stock, and left to start another computer company, aptly named NeXT.

The Golden Years

With Jobs gone, Sculley shut down the Lisa line, which had done poorly in the market due to a very high price point of $10,000, and pushed developers to fix the problems with the Macintosh. In January 1986, a new version of the Macintosh, the Mac Plus, was introduced. This machine fixed the shortcomings of the original Mac, and sales started to grow again.

What also drove sales higher was Apple's domination of the desktop publishing market. Several events came together to make this happen. Researchers from Xerox PARC formed a company, Adobe, to develop and commercialize the PostScript page description language. PostScript enabled the visual display and printing of high-quality page layouts loaded with graphics such as colored charts, line drawings, and photos. Apple licensed PostScript and used it as the output for its Apple LaserWriter, which was introduced in 1985. Shortly afterwards, a Seattle company, Aldus, introduced a program called PageMaker for the Mac. PageMaker used Adobe's PostScript page description language for output. Although Aldus introduced a version of PageMaker for MS-DOS in 1986, Apple already had a lead, and with the Mac's GUI appealing to graphic artists, Apple tightened its hold on the desktop publishing segment. Apple's position in desktop publishing was further strengthened by the release of Adobe Illustrator in 1987 (a freehand drawing program) and Adobe Photoshop in 1990.

The years between 1986 and 1991 were in many ways golden ones for Apple. Since it made both hardware and software, Apple was able to control all aspects of its computers, offering a complete desktop solution that allowed customers to "plug and play." With the Apple II series still selling well in the education market, and the Mac dominating desktop publishing, Apple was able to charge a premium price for its products. Gross margins on the Mac line got as high as 55%. In 1990, Apple sales reached $5.6 billion; its global market share, which had fallen rapidly as the IBM-compatible PC market had grown, stabilized at 8%; the company had a strong balance sheet; and Apple was the most profitable PC manufacturer in the world.

During this period, executives at Apple actively debated the merits of licensing the Mac operating system to other computer manufacturers, allowing them to make Mac clones. Sculley was in favor of this move. So was Microsoft's Bill Gates, who wrote two memos to Sculley laying out the argument for licensing the Mac OS. Gates argued that the closed architecture of the Macintosh prevented independent investment in the standard by third parties and put Apple at a disadvantage next to the IBM PC standard. However, some senior executives at Apple were against the licensing strategy, arguing that once Apple licensed its intellectual property, it would be difficult to protect it. In one version of events, senior executives debated the decision at a meeting and took a vote on whether to license. Given the controversial nature of the decision, it was decided that the vote in favor had to be unanimous. It wasn't—a single executive voted against the licensing decision, and it was never pursued.[8] In another version of events, Jean-Louis Gassée, head of R&D at Apple, vigorously opposed Sculley's plans to clone, and Sculley backed down.[9] Gassée was deeply distrustful of Microsoft and Bill Gates and believed that Gates probably had an ulterior motive, given how his company had benefited from the IBM standard.

Ironically, in 1985 Apple had licensed its "visual displays" to Microsoft. Reportedly Gates had strongarmed Sculley, threatening that Microsoft would stop developing crucial applications for the Mac unless Apple granted Microsoft the license. At the time, Microsoft had launched development of its own GUI. Called Windows, it mimicked the look and feel of the Mac operating system, and Microsoft didn't want to be stopped by a lawsuit from Apple. Several years later, when Apple did file a lawsuit against Microsoft, arguing that Windows 3.1 imitated the "look and feel" of the Mac, Microsoft was able to point to the 1985 license agreement to defend its right to develop Windows—a position that the judge in the case agreed with.

1990–1997

By the early 1990s, the prices of IBM-compatible PCs were declining rapidly. So long as Apple was the only company to sell machines that used a GUI, its differential appeal gave it an advantage over MS-DOS-based PCs with their clunky text-based interfaces, and the premium price could be justified. However, in 1990 Microsoft introduced Windows 3.1, its own GUI that sat on top of MS-DOS, and Apple's differential appeal began to erode. Moreover, the dramatic growth of the PC market had turned Apple into a niche player. Faced with the choice of writing software to work with an MS-DOS/Windows operating system and an Intel microprocessor, now the dominant standard found on 90% of all PCs, or the Mac OS and a Motorola processor, developers

logically opted for the dominant standard (desktop publishing remained an exception to this rule). Reflecting on this logic, Dan Eilers, then vice president of strategic planning at Apple, reportedly stated that "the company was on a glide path to history."[10]

Sculley, too, thought that the company was in trouble. Apple seemed boxed in its niche. Apple had a high cost structure. It spent significantly more on R&D as a percentage of sales than its rivals (in 1990, Apple spent 8% of sales on R&D, Compaq around 4%). Its microprocessor supplier, Motorola, lacked the scale of Intel, which translated into higher costs for Apple. Moreover, Apple's small market share made it difficult to recoup the spiraling cost of developing a new operating system, which by 1990 amounted to at least $500 million.

Sculley's game plan to deal with these problems involved a number of steps. First, he appointed himself chief technology officer in addition to CEO, a move that raised some eyebrows, given Sculley's marketing background. Second, he committed the company to bringing out a low-cost version of the Macintosh to compete with IBM clones. The result was the Mac Classic, introduced in October 1990 and priced at $999. He also cut prices for the Macs and Apple IIs by 30%. The reward was a 60% increase in sales volume, but lower gross margins. So third, he cut costs. The workforce at Apple was reduced by 10%, the salaries of top managers (including Sculley's) were cut by as much as 15%, and Apple shifted much of its manufacturing to subcontractors (for example, the PowerBook was built in Japan, a first for Apple). Fourth, he called for the company to maintain its technological lead by bringing out hit products every six to twelve months. The results included the first Apple portable, the PowerBook notebook, which was shipped in late 1991 and garnered very favorable reviews, and the Apple Newton handheld computer, which bombed. Fifth, Apple entered into an alliance with IBM, which realized that it had lost its hold on the PC market to companies like Intel, Microsoft, and Compaq.

The IBM alliance had several elements. One was the decision to adopt IBM's Power PC microprocessor architecture, which IBM would also use in its offerings. A second was the establishment of two joint ventures—Taligent, which had the goal of creating a new operating system, and Kaleida, to develop multimedia applications. A third was a project to help IBM and Apple machines work better together.

While Sculley's game plan helped to boost the top line, the bottom line shrunk in 1993 due to a combination of low gross margins and continuing high costs. In 1994, Sculley left Apple. He was replaced by Michael Spindler, a German engineer who had gained prominence as head of Apple Europe.

It was Spindler who in 1994 finally took the step that had been long debated in the company—he decided to license the Mac OS to a handful of companies, allowing them to make Mac clones. The Mac OS would be licensed for $40 a copy. It was too little too late—the industry was now waiting for the introduction of Microsoft's Windows 95. When it came, it was clear that Apple was in serious trouble. Windows 95 was a big improvement over Windows 3.1, and it closed the gap between Windows and the Mac. While many commentators criticized Apple for not licensing the Mac OS in the 1980s, when it still had a big lead over Microsoft, ironically Bill Gates disagreed. In a 1996 interview with *Fortune*, Gates noted:

> As Apple has declined, the basic criticism seems to be that Apple's strategy of doing a unique hardware/software combination was doomed to fail. I disagree. Like all strategies, this one fails if you execute poorly. But the strategy can work, if Apple picks its markets and renews the innovation in the Macintosh.[12]

Spindler responded to Windows 95 by committing Apple to develop a next-generation operating system for the Macintosh, something that raised questions about the Taligent alliance with IBM. At the end of 1995, IBM and Apple parted ways, ending Taligent, which after $500 million in investments had produced little.

By then, Spindler had other issues on his mind. The latter half of 1995 proved to be a disaster for Apple. The company seemed unable to predict demand for its products. It overestimated demand for its low-end Macintosh Performa computers and was left with excess inventory, while underestimating demand for its high-end machines. To compound matters, its new PowerBooks had to be recalled after batteries started to catch fire, and a price war in Japan cut margins in one of its best markets. As a consequence, in the last quarter of 1995, gross margins slumped to 15%, down from 29% in 1994, and Apple lost $68 million. Spindler responded in January 1996 by announcing 1,300 layoffs. He suggested that up to 4,000 might ultimately go—some 23% of the workforce.[13] That was his last significant act. He was replaced in February by Gilbert Amelio.

Amelio, who joined Apple from National Semiconductor where he had gained a reputation for his turnaround skills, lasted just seventeen months. He followed through on Spindler's plans to cut the head count and stated that Apple would return to its differentiation strategy. His hope was that the new Mac operating system would help, but work on that was in total disarray. He made the decision to scrap the project after an investment of over $500 million. Instead, Apple purchased NeXT, the computer company founded by none other than Steve Jobs, for $425 million. The NeXT machines had received strong reviews, but had gained no market traction due to a lack of supporting applications. Amelio felt that the NeXT OS could be adapted to run on the Mac. He also hired Steve Jobs as a consultant, but Jobs was rarely seen at Apple; he was too busy running Pixar, his computer animation company that was riding a wave of success after a huge hit with the animated movie *Toy Story*.[14]

Amelio's moves did nothing to stop the slide in Apple's fortunes. By mid-1997, market share had slumped to 3%, down from 9% when Amelio took the helm. The company booked a loss of $742 million in 1996 and was on track to lose another $400 million in 1997. It was too much for the board. In July 1997, Amelio was fired. With market share falling, third-party developers and distributors were rethinking their commitments to Apple. Without them, the company would be dead.

The Return of Steve Jobs

Following Amelio's departure, Steve Jobs was appointed interim CEO. In April 1998, he took the position on a permanent basis, while staying on at Pixar as CEO. Jobs moved quickly to fix the bleeding. His first act was to visit Bill Gates and strike a deal with Microsoft. Microsoft agreed to invest $150 million in Apple and to continue producing Office for the Mac until at least 2002. Then Jobs ended the licensing deals with the clone makers, spending over $100 million to acquire the assets of the leading Mac clone maker, Power Computing, including its license. Jobs killed slow-selling products, most notably the Apple Newton hand-held computer, and reduced the number of product lines from sixty to just four. He also pushed the company into online

Exhibit 3

(a) The iMac

(b) The iBook

Source: Courtesy of Apple Inc.

distribution, imitating Dell Computer's direct-selling model. While these fixes bought the company time and caused a favorable reaction from the stock market, they were not recipes for growth.

New Computer Offerings

Almost immediately, Jobs started to think about a new product that would embody the spirit of Apple. What emerged in May 1998 was the iMac (see Exhibit 3a). The differentiator for the iMac was not its software, or its power, or its monitor—it was the design of the machine itself. A self-contained unit that combined the monitor and central processing unit in translucent teal and with curved lines, the iMac was a bold departure in a world dominated by putty-colored PC boxes.

To develop the iMac, Jobs gave a team of designers, headed by Jonathan Ive, an unprecedented say in the development project. Ive's team worked closely with engineers, manufacturers, marketers, and Jobs himself. To understand how to make a plastic shell look exciting rather than cheap, the designers visited a candy factory to study the finer points of making jelly beans. They spent months working with Asian partners, designing a sophisticated process capable of producing millions of iMacs a year. The designers also pushed for the internal electronics to be redesigned, to make sure that they looked good through the thick shell. Apple may have spent as

much as $65 a machine on the casing, compared with perhaps $20 for the average PC.[15]

Sales of the iMac, priced at $1,299, were strong, with orders placed for 100,000 units even before the machine was available. Moreover, one-third of iMac purchases were by first-time buyers, according to Apple's own research.[16] The iMac line was continually updated, with faster processors, more memory, and bigger hard drives. The product was also soon available in many different colors. In 1999, Apple followed up the iMac with introduction of the iBook portable (see Exhibit 3b). Aimed at consumers and students, the iBook had the same design theme as the iMac and was priced aggressively at $1,599.

Sales of the iMac and iBook helped push Apple back into profitability. In 1999, the company earned $420 million on sales of $6.1 billion. In 2000, it made $611 million on sales of almost $8 billion.

To keep sales growing, Apple continued to invest in development of a new operating system, based on the technology acquired from NeXT. After three years of work by nearly one thousand software engineers, and a cost of around $1 billion, the first version of Apple's new operating system was introduced in 2001. Known as OS X, it garnered rave reviews from analysts who saw the UNIX-based program as offering superior stability and faster speed than the old Mac OS. OS X also had an enhanced ability to run multiple programs at once to support multiple users, connected easily to other devices such as digital camcorders, and was easier for developers to write applications for. In typical Apple fashion, OS X also sported a well-designed and intuitively appealing interface. Since 2001, new versions of OS X have been introduced almost once a year. The most recent version, OS X Tiger, was introduced in 2005 and retailed for $129.

To get the installed base of Mac users, who at the time numbered 25 million, to upgrade to OS X, Apple had to offer applications. The deal with Microsoft ensured that its popular Office program would be available for the OS X. Steve Jobs had assumed that the vote of confidence by Microsoft would encourage other third-party developers to write programs for OS X, but it didn't always happen. Most significantly, in 1998 Adobe Systems refused to develop a Mac version of their consumer video-editing program, which was already available for Windows PCs.

Shocked, Jobs directed Apple to start working on its own applications. The first fruits of this effort were two video-editing programs, Final Cut Pro for professionals and iMovie for consumers. Next was iLife, a bundle of multimedia programs now prein-stalled on every Mac, which includes iMovie, iDVD, iPhoto, Garage Band, and the iTunes digital jukebox. Apple also developed its own web browser, Safari.

Meanwhile, Apple continued to update its computer lines with eye-catching offerings. In 2001, Apple introduced its Titanium PowerBook G4 notebooks. Cased in titanium, these ultralight and fast notebooks featured a clean postindustrial look that marked a distinct shift from the whimsical look of the iMac and iBook. As with the iMac, Jonathan Ive's design team played a central part in the product's development. A core team of designers set up a design studio in a San Francisco warehouse, far away from Apple's main campus. They worked for six weeks on the basic design and then headed to Asia to negotiate for widescreen flat-panel displays and to work with tool makers.[17]

The titanium notebooks were followed by a redesigned desktop line that appealed to the company's graphic design customers and included an offering of elegantly designed widescreen cinema displays. In 2004, Ive's design team came out with yet another elegant offering, the iMac G5 computer, which *PC Magazine* described as a "simple, stunning all-in-one design" (see Exhibit 4).[18]

Exhibit 4

The iMac G5

Source: Courtesy of Apple Inc.

Exhibit 5

Worldwide Market Share and Units Sold, 2005

Company	Market Share (%)	Units Sold (millions)
Dell Computer	18.1%	37.76
Hewlett-Packard	15.6%	32.54
Lenovo	6.2%	12.93
Acer	4.70%	9.80
Fujistu-Siemens	4.10%	8.55
Apple	2.20%	4.59
Other	49.1%	102.42
Total	100%	208.6

Source: Standard & Poor's Industry Surveys, Computers: Hardware, December 8, 2005.

For all of Apple's undisputed design excellence and the loyalty of its core user base—graphic artists and students—Apple's market share remained anemic, trailing far behind industry leaders Dell, Hewlett-Packard, and IBM/Lenovo (see Exhibit 5). Weak demand, combined with its low market share, translated into another loss for Apple in 2001, leading some to question the permanence of Steve Jobs's turnaround. While Apple's worldwide market share fell to as low as 1.9% in 2004, it started to pick up again in 2005 and throughout 2006. Momentum was particularly strong in the United States, where Apple had shipped 1.3 million computers in the year through to July 2006, giving it a 12% year-over-year growth rate and a 4.8% share of the U.S. market. Driving growth, according to many analysts, was the surging popularity of Apple's iPod music player, which had raised Apple's profile among younger consumers and was having a spillover effect on Mac sales.[19]

Intel Inside, Windows on the Desktop

Since the company's inception, Apple had not used Intel microprocessors, which had become the industry standard for microprocessors since the introduction of the IBM PC in 1981. In June 2005, Apple announced that it would start to do so. Driving the transition was growing frustration with the performance of the PowerPC chip line made by IBM that Apple had been using for over a decade. The PowerPC had failed to keep up with the Intel chips, which both were faster and had lower power con-

sumption—something that was very important in the portable computer market, where Apple had a respectable market share.

The transition created significant risks for Apple. Old applications and OS X had to be rewritten to run on Intel processors. By the spring of 2006, Apple had produced Intel-compatible versions of OS X and its own applications, but many other applications had not been rewritten for Intel chips. To make the transition easier, Apple provided a free software program, known as Rosetta, that enabled users to run older applications on Intel-based Macs. Moreover, Apple went a step further by issuing a utility program, known as Boot Camp, which enabled Mac owners to run Windows XP on their machines. (Boot Camp was included as a part of the next version of OS X, OS X Leopard, which came out in 2007.)

Reviews of Apple's Intel-based machines were generally favorable, with many reviewers noting the improvement in speed over the older PowerPC Macs—although the speed improvement tended to evaporate if the Rosetta program had to be used to run an application.[20]

In the fall of 2006, Apple reported that its transition to an Intel-based architecture was complete, some six months ahead of schedule. Although sales of Macs had been slow during late 2005 and early 2006, this seems to have been the result of consumers' putting off purchases while waiting for the new machines. The company's sales of the new Macs exhibited healthy growth in the second and third

Exhibit 6

An Apple Store

Source: Courtesy of Apple Inc.

quarters of the year. Sales of portable MacBooks were particularly strong.

The move to Intel architecture may have helped Apple to close the price differential that had long existed between Windows-based PCs and Apple's offerings. According to one analysis, by September 2006 Apple's products were selling at a *discount* to comparable product offerings from Dell and Hewlett-Packard.[21]

Moving into Retail

In 2001, Apple made another important strategic shift—the company opened its first retail store. In an industry that had long relied on third-party retailers or direct sales, as in the case of Dell, this shift seemed risky. One concern was that Apple might encounter a backlash from its long-standing retail partners. Another was that Apple would never be able to generate the sales volume required to justify expensive retail space; the product line seemed too thin. However, Apple clearly believed that it had been hurt by a lack of retail presence. Many computer retailers didn't carry Apple machines, and some of those that did often buried Mac displays deep in the store.

From the start, Apple's stores exhibited the same stylish design that characterized its products, with clean lines, attractive displays, and a postindustrial feel (see Exhibit 6). Steve Jobs himself was intimately involved in the design process. Indeed, he is one of the named inventors on a patent Apple secured for the design of the signature glass staircase found in many stores, and he was apparently personally involved in the design of a glass cube atop a store on New York's Fifth Avenue that opened in 2006. In an interview, Jobs noted that "we spent a lot of time designing the store, and it deserves to be built perfectly."[22]

Customers and analysts were immediately impressed by the product fluency that the employees in Apple stores exhibited. They also liked the highlight of many stores—a "genius bar," where technical experts help customers fix problems with their Apple products. The wide-open interior space, however, did nothing to allay the fears of critics that Apple's product portfolio was just too narrow to generate the traffic required to support premium space. The critics couldn't have been more wrong. Spurred on by booming sales of the iPod, Apple's stores did exceptionally well. By 2005, Apple had 137 stores in upscale locations that generated $2.3 billion in sales and $140 million in profits. Sales per square foot during 2005 were an almost unprecedented $4,000, making Apple the envy of other retailers.[23]

The iPod Revolution

In the late 1990s and early 2000s, the music industry was grappling with the implications of two new technologies. The first was the development of inexpensive portable MP3 players that could store and play digital music files, such as Diamond Media's Rio, which was introduced in 1997 and could hold two hours of music. The second was the rise of peer-to-peer computer networks, such as Napster, Kazaa, Grokster, and Morpheus, that enabled individuals to efficiently swap digital files over the Internet. By the early 2000s, millions of individuals were downloading music files over the Internet without the permission of the copyright holders, the music publishing companies. For the music industry, this development was devastating. After years of steady growth, global sales of music peaked in 1999 at $38.5 billion, falling to $32 billion in 2003. Despite the fall in sales, the International Federation of the Phonographic Industry (IFPI) claimed that demand for music was higher than ever, but that the decline in sales reflected the fact that "the commercial value of music is being widely devalued by mass copying and piracy."[24]

The music industry had tried to counter piracy over the Internet by taking legal action to shut down the peer-to-peer networks, such as Napster, and filing lawsuits against individuals who made large numbers of music files available over the Internet. Its success was limited, in part because these peer-to-peer networks offered tremendous utility to consumers. They were fast and immediate and enabled consumers to unbundle albums, downloading just the tracks they wanted while ignoring junk filler tracks. And, of course, they were free.

The music industry was desperate for a legal alternative to illegal downloading. Its own initiatives, introduced in 2002, had gained little traction. MusicNet, which offered songs from Warner Music, BMG, and EMI, had a single subscription plan—$9.85 a month for one hundred streams and one hundred downloads. After thirty days, downloads expired and couldn't be played. Pressplay, which offered music from Sony, Universal, and EMI, had four subscription plans, from $9.95 to $24.95 a month, for up to one thousand streams and one hundred downloads. The higher subscription fee service from Pressplay let users burn up to twenty songs a month onto CDs that would not expire, but no more than two songs could be burned from any one artist.[25]

Then along came the iPod and iTunes. These products were born out of an oversight. In the late 1990s, when consumers were starting to burn their favorite CDs, Macs did not have CD burners or software to manage users' digital music collections. Realizing the mistake, CEO Steven Jobs ordered Apple's software developers to create the iTunes program to help Mac users manage their growing digital music collections. The first iTunes program led to the concept of the iPod. If people were going to maintain the bulk of their music collection on a computer, they needed a portable MP3 player to take music with them—a Sony Walkman for the digital age. While there were such devices on the market already, they could hold only a few dozen songs each.

To run the iPod, Apple licensed software from PortalPlayer. Apple also learned that Toshiba was building a tiny 1.8-inch hard drive that could hold over one thousand songs. Apple quickly cut a deal with Toshiba, giving it exclusive rights to the drive for eighteen months. Meanwhile, Apple focused on designing the user interface, the exterior styling, and the synchronization software to make it work with the Mac. As with so many product offerings unveiled since Jobs returned to the helm, the design team led by Jonathan Ive played a pivotal role in giving birth to the iPod. Ive's team worked in secrecy in San Francisco. The members, all paid extremely well by industry standards, worked together in a large open studio with little personal space. The team was able to figure out how to put a layer of clear plastic over the white and black core of an iPod, giving it tremendous depth of texture. The finish was superior to that of other MP3 players, with no visible screws or obvious joints between parts. The serial number of the iPod was not on a sticker, as with most products; it was elegantly etched onto the back of the device. This attention to detail and design elegance, although not without cost implications, was to turn the iPod into a fashion accessory.[26]

The iPod was unveiled in October 2001 to mixed reviews. The price of $399 was significantly above that of competing devices, and since the iPod worked only with Apple computers, it seemed destined to be a niche product. However, initial sales were strong. It turned out that consumers were willing to pay a premium price for the iPod's huge storage capacity. Moreover, Jobs made the call to develop a version of the iPod that would be compatible with Windows; after it was introduced in mid-2002, sales took off.

By this time, Jobs was dealing with a bigger strategic issue—how to persuade the music companies to make their music available for legal downloads. It was here that Steve Job's legendary selling ability came into play. With a prototype for an online iTunes store in hand, Jobs met with executives from the major labels. He persuaded them that it was in their best interests to support a legal music download business as an alternative to widespread illegal downloading of music over peer-to-peer networks, which, despite its best efforts, the music industry had not been able to shut down. People would pay to download music over the Internet, he argued. Although all of the labels were setting up their own online businesses, Jobs felt that since they were limited to selling music owned by the parent companies, demand would be limited too. What was needed was a reputable independent online music retailer, and Apple fit the bill. If it was going to work, however, all of the labels needed to get on board. Under Jobs's scheme, iTunes files would be downloaded for 99 cents each. The only portable digital player that the files could be stored and played on was an iPod. Jobs's argument was that this closed world made it easier to protect copyrighted material from unauthorized distribution.

Jobs also meet with twenty of the world's top recording artists, including U2's Bono, Sheryl Crow, and Mick Jagger. His pitch to them was this—digital distribution is going to happen, and the best way to protect your interests is to support a legal online music distribution business. Wooed by Jobs, these powerful stakeholders encouraged the music recording companies to take Apple's proposal seriously.[27]

By early 2003, Jobs had all of the major labels on board. Launched in April 2003, within days the iTunes store was clearly a major hit. A million songs were sold in the first week. In mid-2004, iTunes passed the 100 million download mark, and sales kept accelerating, hitting the 150 million download mark in October 2004. At that point, customers were downloading over 4 million songs per week, which represented a run rate of more than 200 million a year. While Steve Jobs admitted that Apple does not make much money from iTunes downloads—probably only 10 cents a song— it does make good margins on sales of the iPod, and sales of the iPod ballooned in 2005 (see Exhibit 7).

Helped by new models, which as always were elegantly designed, iPod sales continued to boom in the

Sales of Apple's Main Product Lines (millions)

	2003	2004	2005
Computers	$4,491	$4,923	$6,275
iPod	$345	$1,306	$4,540
iTunes	$36	$278	$899
Software	$644	$821	$1,091
Peripherals	$691	$951	$1,126

Source: Apple Computer 10-K Reports, 2006.

first half of Apple's fiscal 2006 (the last three months of 2005 and the first three months of 2006). In this six-month period, Apple sold 22.5 million iPods and generated $4.26 billion in sales, surpassing computer sales for the first time, which stood at $3.29 billion for the six-month period. iTunes kicked in another $976 million.

As the installed base of iPods expanded, an ecosystem of companies selling iPod accessories started to emerge. The accessories include speakers, head phones, and add-on peripherals that allow iPod users to record their voices, charge their iPods on the go, play their tunes over the radio, or use their iPods wirelessly with a remote. There are also cases, neck straps, belt clips, and so on. By 2006, it was estimated that there were over one hundred companies in this system. Collectively, they may have sold as much as $1 billion of merchandise during the last three months of 2005. Apple collects an unspecified royalty from companies whose products access the iPod's ports and thus benefits indirectly from the preference of buyers for the iPod over competing products that lack the same accessories.[28]

Success such as this attracts competitors, and soon there were plenty. RealNetworks, Yahoo!, and Napster all set up legal downloading services to compete with iTunes. Even Wal-Mart got into the act, offering music downloads for 89 cents a track. However, iTunes continued to outsell its rivals by a wide margin. In mid-2006, iTunes was accounting for about 80% of all legal music downloads.[29] iTunes was also the fourth largest music retailer in the United States; the other three all had physical stores.

The iPod also had plenty of competition. Many of the competing devices were priced aggressively and had as much storage capacity as the iPod. Few, however, managed to gain share against the iPod, which by mid-2006 still accounted for 77% of annual sales in the U.S. market. The most successful rival to date has been SanDisk, which captured almost 10% of the market with its family of music players.

One reason for the failure of competitors to garner more market share has been hardware and software problems that arise when consumers try to download songs sold by one company to a machine made by another. In contrast, iTunes and iPod have always worked seamlessly together.

In an effort to counter this, Microsoft announced the release of its own digital music player in 2006, Zune. Zune is designed to work with Microsoft's own online music store. Similarly, RealNetworks announced a deal with SanDisk to make a digital music device that's specifically designed to work with Real-Networks' online music store, Rhapsody.[30] Both products were expected to debut in late 2007.

However, Apple was not standing still. New, even smaller versions of the iPod, such as the iPod Shuffle and iPod Nano, were keeping sales strong. The latest iPods, introduced in September 2006, had longer battery lives, bigger hard drives (enabling some models to store up to 15,000 songs or 150 hours of video), and brighter displays. They were priced aggressively, while still maintaining the thin, elegant look that characterized the line.

At the same time, Apple announced that the iTunes store would start to sell movie downloads. Initially, the movies were limited to offerings from Disney (where Steve Jobs had become the largest shareholder after Disney had acquired Pixar in 2005), but Apple expected to add other movie studios in the near future. Downloaded movies would have near DVD quality and could be played on TVs, computers, or iPods. In addition, Apple announced that it would be introducing a small "box," which would connect to a TV, cable set top box, or stereo and pull digital files (videos, music, and photos) wirelessly from any iTunes-enabled PC (Windows or Mac).

The Personal Computer Industry in the 2000s

While Apple dominated the music downloading and portable music player businesses with iTunes and the iPod, it remained a niche player in the computer industry. After years of growth, sales of PCs had fallen for the first time ever in 2001, but the growth path had soon been resumed. According to IDC, a market research firm, total PC shipments were expected to hit 287 million units in 2008, up from 179 million units in 2004 (see Exhibit 8). The U.S. market would remain the world's largest, with 82 million units being sold in 2008, up from 58 million in 2004, representing a growth rate in the high single digits. Sales

Exhibit 8

Unit Shipments in the PC Industry

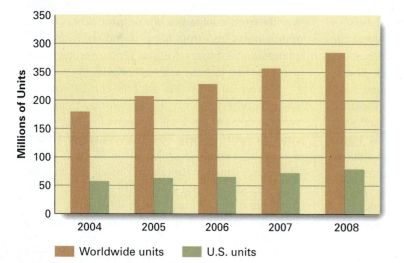

Source: Data from IDC. Data for years 2007 and 2008 are forecasts.

to consumers accounted for about 88.5 million of the 230 million PCs sold in 2006.[31]

The industry is characterized by a handful of players who collectively account for about half the market, and a long tail of small enterprises that produce unbranded or locally branded "white box" computers, often selling their machines at a significant discount to globally branded products (see the "Other" row in Exhibit 5).

Among the larger players, consolidation has been a theme for several years. In 2002, Hewlett-Packard acquired Compaq Computer; Gateway and eMachines merged in 2004; and in 2005, the Chinese firm Lenovo acquired the PC business of IBM. The large PC firms compete aggressively by offering ever more powerful machines, producing them as efficiently as possible, and lowering prices to sell more volume. The average selling price of a PC has fallen from around $1,700 in 1999 to under $1,000 in 2006, and projections indicate that it may continue to fall, fueled in part by aggressive competition between Dell Computer and Hewlett-Packard.[32]

All of these players focus on the design, assembly, and sales of PCs, while purchasing the vast majority of component parts from independent companies. In recent years, the top PC companies have reduced their R&D spending as a percentage of sales, as the industry has transitioned toward a commodity business.

The existence of the long tail of white box makers is made possible by the open architecture of the dominant PC standard, based on Intel-compatible microprocessors and a Microsoft operating system, as well as the low-tech nature of the assembly process. The components for these boxes, which are themselves commodities, can be purchased cheaply off the shelf. White box makers have strong positions in many developing nations. In Mexico, for example, domestic brands accounted for 60% of all sales in 2005, up from 44% in 2000. In Latin America as a whole, 70% of personal computers are produced locally. White box makers have much weaker positions in the United States, western Europe, and Japan, where consumers display a stronger preference for branded products that incorporate leading-edge technology. In contrast, in the developing world, consumers are willing to accept older components if it saves a few hundred dollars.[33]

During the 1990s and early 2000s, Dell grew rapidly to capture the market lead. Dell's success was based on the inventory management efficiencies associated with its direct-selling model (the company could build machines to order, which reduced its need to hold inventory). Dell was also helped by the problems Hewlett-Packard faced when it merged with Compaq Computer. By 2005, however, a resurgent Hewlett-Packard had lowered its costs, could price more aggressively, and was starting to gain ground against Dell. Apple Computer continued to be the odd man out in this industry and was the only major manufacturer that did not adhere to the Windows architecture.

Strategic Issues

As 2006 drew to a close, Apple was in an enviable position. The iPod business was continuing to exhibit rapid growth, and sales of Apple computers, particularly portables, were strong. Still, there were questions surrounding the company. Apple had always been good at innovating, but never good at profiting from innovation. Would it be different this time? Forecasts called for 2006 and 2007 to be strong years for Apple, with record sales and profits, but much of this was due to the iPod boom, and there were questions about how sustainable that might be. In the PC business, Apple was still a niche player, albeit one with renewed growth prospects. The company had very limited presence in the large business market. Could this be changed? Would Apple be able to capitalize on the strong iPod business to expand its share of computer sales? And what were the implications for Apple's long-term competitive position?

ENDNOTES

1. Quoted in Pete Burrows, "Steve Jobs' Magic Kingdom," *Business Week* (February 6, 2006): 62–68.
2. N. Wingfield, "Apple Unveils New Computers," *Wall Street Journal,* August 8, 2006, p. B3.
3. Much of this section is drawn from P. Freiberger and M. Swaine, *Fire in the Valley* (New York: McGraw-Hill, 2000).
4. For a detailed history of the development of the Apple II, see Steve Weyhrich, "Apple II History," http://apple2history.org/history/ah01.html.
5. Freiberger and Swaine, *Fire in the Valley,* p. 357.
6. Andy Hertzfeld, "Reality Distortion Field," http://www.folklore.org/ProjectView.py?project=Macintosh.
7. Hertzfeld, "Reality Distortion Field."
8. This version of events was told to the author by a senior executive who was present in the room at the time.
9. Jim Carlton, "Playing Catch Up—Apple Finally Gives in and Attempts Cloning," *Wall Street Journal,* October 17, 1994, p. A1.
10. D. B. Yoffie, "Apple Computer 1992," Harvard Business School Case 792–081.
11. Andrew Kupfer, "Apple's Plan to Survive and Grow," *Fortune* (May 4, 1992): 68–71; B. R. Schlender, "Yet Another Strategy for Apple," Fortune (October 22, 1990): 81–85.

12. B. Schlender, "Paradise Lost: Apple's Quest for Life After Death," *Fortune* (February 1996): 64–72.

13. Jim Carlton, "Apple's Losses to Stretch into 2nd Period," *Wall Street Journal,* January 18, 1996, p. B7.

14. Peter Burrows, "Dangerous Limbo," *Business Week* (July 21, 1997): 32.

15. Peter Burrows, "The Man Behind Apple's Design Magic," *Business Week* (September 2005): 27–34.

16. A. Reinhardt, "Can Steve Jobs Keep His Mojo Working?" *Business Week* (August 2, 1999): 32.

17. Burrows, "The Man Behind Apple's Design Magic."

18. "Apple iMac G5 Review," *PC Magazine,* http://www.pcmag.com/article2/0,1759,1648796,00.asp.

19. Standard & Poor's Industry Surveys, Computers: Hardware, "Global Demand for PCs Accelerates," December 8, 2005; Mark Veverka, "Barron's Insight: Apple's Horizon Brightens," *Wall Street Journal,* July 23, 2006, p. A4.

20. Peter Lewis, "Apple's New Core," *Fortune* (March 29, 2006): 182–184.

21. Citigroup Global Markets, "Apple Computer: New Products Position Apple Well for Holidays," September 13, 2006.

22. N. Wingfield, "How Apple's Store Strategy Beat the Odds," *Wall Street Journal,* May 17, 2006, p. B1.

23. M. Frazier, "The Bigger Apple," *Advertising Age* (February 13, 2006): 4–6.

24. IFPI, "Global Music Sales Down 5% in 2001," Press Release, http://www.ifpi.org.

25. W. S. Mossberg, "Record Labels Launch Two Feeble Services to Replace Napster," *Wall Street Journal,* February 7, 2002, p. B1.

26. Burrows, "The Man Behind Apple's Design Magic."

27. N. Wingfield and E. Smith. "U2's Gig: Help Apple Sell iPods," *Wall Street Journal,* October 20, 2004, p. D5; Apple Computer, "iTunes Music Store Downloads Top 150 Million Songs," Press Release, October 14, 2004.

28. Paul Taylor, "iPod Ecosystem Offers Rich Pickings," FT.com, January 24, 2006, p. 1.

29. T. Braithwaite and K. Allison, "Crunch Time for Apple's Music Icon," *Financial Times,* June 14, 2006, p. 27.

30. N. Wingfield and R. A. Guth, "iPod, They Pod: Rivals Imitate Apple's Success," *Wall Street Journal,* September 18, 2006, p. B1.

31. IDC, "Long-Term PC Outlook Improves," Press Release, September 14, 2006.

32. Standard & Poor's Industry Surveys, Computers: Hardware, "Global Demand for PCs Accelerates."

33. M. Dickerson, "Plain PCs Sitting Pretty," *Los Angeles Times,* December 11, 2005, p. C1.

Case 3

Amazon.com

This case was prepared by Gareth R. Jones, Texas A&M University.

In just over a decade, Amazon.com has grown from an online bookseller to a virtual retail supercenter, selling products as diverse as books, toys, food, and electronics. Today, its mission is to be "Earth's most customer-centric company, where customers can find and discover virtually anything they might want to buy online." In many ways, the last decade has been a wild ride for Amazon, as its revenues, profits, and stock price have soared and plunged as a result of the dot-com boom and then bust of the early 2000s. It has also been a wild ride for Amazon's founder, Jeff Bezos, who through it all has consistently championed his company and claimed investors have to look long term to measure the success of Amazon's business model. Indeed, he originally said he did not expect his company to become profitable for several years, and his forecast turned out to be correct.

By the early 2000s, however, Amazon had become profitable, and its business model seemed to be working. But then, around the mid-2000s, its future prospects started to look bleak again, as its revenue growth seemed to stall when its new retail ventures seemed not to be succeeding. In 2007, the problem facing Amazon was to find new strategies to keep its revenues growing at a fast pace and to keep its costs under control, not easy when competition was increasing in Internet commerce.

Amazon's Beginnings: The Online Bookstore Business

In 1994, Jeffrey Bezos, a computer science and electrical engineering graduate from Princeton University, was growing weary of working for a Wall Street investment bank. Seeking to take advantage of his computer science background, he saw an entrepreneurial opportunity in the fact that usage of the Internet was growing enormously, as every year tens of millions of new users were becoming aware of its potential uses. Bezos decided the bookselling market offered an excellent opportunity for him to take advantage of his IT skills in the new electronic, virtual marketplace. His vision was an online bookstore that could offer millions more books to millions more customers than a typical bricks and mortar (B&M) bookstore. To act on his vision, he packed up his belongings and headed for the West Coast to found his new dot-com start-up. On route, he had a hunch that Seattle, the hometown of Microsoft and Starbucks, was a place where first-rate software developers could be easily found. His trip ended there, and he began to flesh out the business model for his new venture.

What was his vision for his new venture? To build an online bookstore that would be customer-friendly, be easy to navigate, provide buying advice, and offer the broadest possible selection of books at low prices. Bezos's original mission was to use the Internet to offer books "that would educate, inform and inspire." And from the beginning, Bezos realized that compared to a physical B&M bookstore, an online bookstore could offer customers a much larger and more diverse selection of books. Indeed, there are about 1.5 million books in print, but most B&M bookstores stock only around 10,000 books; the largest stores in major cities might stock 40,000 to

60,000. Moreover, online customers would be able to search easily for any book in print using computerized catalogs. There was also scope for an online company to find ways to tempt customers to browse books in different subject areas, read reviews of books, and even ask other shoppers for online recommendations—all of which would encourage people to buy more books. A popular feature of Amazon is the ability of users to submit product reviews on its website. As part of their reviews, users rate the products on a scale from one to five stars and then provide detailed information that helps other users decide whether to purchase the products. In turn, the users of these ratings can then rate the usefulness of the reviews so the best reviews are those that rise to the top and are read first in the future!

Operating from his garage in Seattle with a handful of employees, Bezos launched his online venture in 1995 with $7 million in borrowed capital. Because Amazon was one of the first major Internet, or dot-com, retailers, it received a huge amount of free national publicity, and the new venture quickly attracted more and more book buyers. Book sales quickly picked up as satisfied Internet customers spread the good word and Amazon became a model for other dot-com retailers to follow. Within weeks, Bezos was forced to relocate to larger premises, a 2,000-square-foot warehouse, and hire new employees to receive books from book publishers and fill and mail customer orders as book sales soared. Within six months, he was once again searching for additional capital to fund his growing venture; he raised another $7 million from venture capitalists, which he used to move to a 17,000-square-foot warehouse that was now required to handle increasing book sales. As book sales continued to soar month by month over the next two years, Bezos decided that the best way to raise more capital would be to take his company public and issue stock. This, of course, would reward him as the founder and the venture capitalists who had funded Amazon because they would all receive significant percentages of the company's stock. On May 1997, Amazon.com's stock began trading on the NASDAQ stock exchange.

Building Up Amazon's Value Chain

Amazon's rapid growth continued to put enormous pressure on the company's physical warehousing and distribution capabilities. The costs of operating an online website—for example, continuously developing the website's software and maintaining and hosting the computer hardware and Internet bandwidth connections necessary to serve customers—are relatively low, given the hundreds of millions of visits to the website and the millions of sales that are completed. However, Bezos soon found out that the costs of developing and maintaining the physical infrastructure necessary to obtain supplies of books from book publishers and then to stock, package, and ship the books to customers were much higher than he had anticipated, as was the cost of the employees required to perform these activities.

Developing and maintaining the physical side of Amazon's value chain is the source of the greatest proportion of its operating costs, and these high costs were draining its profitability, given the low prices at which it was selling its books. And price competition was also heating up because of new competition from B&M booksellers, such as Barnes & Noble and Borders, that had also opened online bookstores to compete in this market segment. In fact, in 1997, as it passed the 1-million-different-customers-served point, Amazon was forced to open up a new 200,000-square-foot warehouse and distribution center and expand its old one to keep pace with demand.

On the employee front, Bezos sought ways to increase the motivation of his employees across the company. Working to fill customer orders quickly is vital to an online company; minimizing the wait time for a product like a book to arrive is a key success factor in building customer loyalty. On the other hand, motivating Amazon's rapidly expanding army of software engineers to develop innovative software, such as its patented 1-Click[SM] Internet ordering and payment software, was also a vital issue. To ensure good responsiveness to customers, Bezos implemented a policy of decentralizing significant decision-making authority to employees and empowering them to find ways of meeting customer needs quickly. Because Amazon.com employed a relatively small number of people—about 2,500 worldwide in 2000—Bezos also empowered employees to recruit and train new employees so that they could quickly get up to speed in their new jobs. And to motivate employees, Bezos decided to give all employees stock in the company. Amazon employees own over 10% of their company, a factor behind Amazon.com's rapid growth.

In fact, Jeff Bezos is a firm believer in the power of using teams of employees to spur innovation. At Amazon, teams are given considerable autonomy to develop their ideas and experiment without interference from managers. Teams are kept deliberately small, and, according to Bezos, no team should need more than "two pizzas to feed its members"; if more pizza is needed, the team is too large. Amazon's "pizza teams," which usually have no more than five to seven members, have come up with many of the innovations that have made its site so user-friendly. For example, one team developed the "Gold Box" icon that customers can click on to receive special offers that expire within an hour of opening the treasure chest; another developed "Bottom of the Page Deals," low-priced offers for products such as batteries and power bars; and yet another team developed the "Search Inside!" feature, discussed later. These teams have helped Amazon expand into many different retail storefronts and provide the wide range of IT services it does today. Indeed, Bezos and his top managers believe that Amazon is a *technology company* first and foremost, and its mission is to use and develop its technological expertise to sell more and more goods and services in ways that satisfy customers and so keep its profit growing.

Since the beginning, Bezos has personally played a very important part in energizing his employees and representing his company to customers. He is a hands-on, articulate, forward-looking executive who puts in long hours and works closely with employees to find innovative and cost-saving solutions to problems. Moreover, Bezos has consistently acted as a figurehead for his company and has become well recognized in the national media as he works to further Amazon's visibility with customers. He spends a great deal of time flying around the world to publicize his company and its activities, and he has succeeded because Amazon has one of the best recognized names of any dot-com company.

An important strategy that Amazon created in 1996 to attract new customers to its website and grow sales is its Amazon Associates program. Any person or small business that operates a website can become affiliated with Amazon by putting an official Amazon hyperlink to Amazon's website on its own website. If a referral results in a sale, the associate receives a commission from Amazon. Today, about 40% of Amazon's sales come from referrals from its associates, who have received over $1 billion in sales commissions. By 2004, Amazon had signed up over 1 million associates, and its Associates program has been copied by many other Internet companies.

By 1998, Amazon could claim that 45% of its business was repeat business, which translated into lower marketing and sales expenses and higher profit margins. By using all his energies to act on the online bookselling opportunity, Bezos gave his company a first-mover advantage over rivals, and this has been an important contributor to its strong position in the marketplace. Nevertheless, Amazon still had to make a profit, just as Bezos had predicted.

The Bookselling Industry Environment

The book distribution and bookselling industry was changed forever in July 1995 when Jeff Bezos brought virtual bookseller Amazon.com online. His new company changed the whole nature of the environment. Previously, book publishers had sold their books indirectly to book wholesalers that supplied small bookstores and directly to large book chains like Barnes & Noble or Borders or book-of-the-month clubs. There were so many book publishers and so many individual booksellers that the industry was relatively stable, with both large and small bookstores enjoying a comfortable, nonprice competitive niche in the market. In this stable environment, competition was relatively low, and all companies enjoyed good revenues and profits.

Amazon.com's electronic approach to both buying and selling books changed all this. First, since it was able to offer customers quick access to all of the over 1.5 million books in print and it discounted the prices of its books, a higher level of industry competition developed. Second, since it also negotiated directly with the large book publishers over price and supply because it wanted to get books quickly to its customers, the industry value chain changed: All players—book publishers, wholesalers, stores, and customers—became more closely linked. Third, as a result of these factors and continuing changes in information technology, the bookselling business began to change rapidly as the sources of competitive advantage changed, and price and service became important.

By being the first to enter the online bookselling business, Amazon was able to capture customers' attention and establish a first-mover advantage. Its entry into the bookselling industry using its new IT posed a major threat for B&M bookstores; Barnes & Noble, the largest U.S. bookseller, and Borders, the second largest, realized that with its competitive prices, Amazon would be able to siphon off a significant percentage of industry revenues. So these B&M bookstores decided to launch their own online ventures to meet Amazon's challenge and to convince book buyers that they, not Amazon, were still the best places to shop for books. However, being first to market with a new way to deliver books to customers resulted in satisfied Amazon customers who became loyal customers. And once a customer had signed up as an Amazon customer, it was often difficult to get that person to register again at a competing website.

Amazon's early success also made it difficult for new "unknown" competitors to enter the industry because they faced the major hurdle of attracting customers to their websites rather than to Amazon.com's. Even well-known competitors such as Barnes & Noble and Borders, which had imitated Amazon's online business model, faced major problems in attracting away Amazon's customer base and securing their positions. If large B&M bookstores had problems attracting customers, small specialized B&M bookstores were in desperate trouble. Their competitive advantage had been based on providing customers with hard-to-find books, a convenient location, and good customer service. Now they were faced with competition from an online bookstore that could offer customers all 1.5 million books in print at 10% lower prices, with delivery to anywhere in a few days.

Thousands of small specialized B&M bookstores closed their doors nationwide, and even the large B&M bookstores struggled to compete. Its strong competitive position, combined with Internet investors' "irrational exuberance," led Amazon's stock price to soar in the dot-com bubble of the late 1990s. By 1998, its market capitalization was $6.8 billion, almost twice that of its two biggest rivals, Barnes & Noble and Borders, whose combined sales at this time were many times that of Amazon!

Competition increased in 1999, as large B&M bookstores began a price war with Amazon that resulted in falling book prices; this squeezed Amazon's profit margins and put more pressure on it to contain its increasing operating costs. In the spring of 1999, for example, Amazon and its largest competi-

tors, Barnes & Noble and Borders, announced a 50% discount off the price of new best-selling books to defend their market shares; they were locked in a fierce battle to see which company would dominate the bookselling industry in the new millennium.

From Online Bookstore to Internet Retailer

While Bezos initially chose to focus on selling books, he soon realized that Amazon's IT could be used to sell other kinds of products, but he was cautious because he also now understood how high the value-chain costs involved in delivering a wide range of products to customers were. However, Amazon's slow growth in the late 1990s led many of its stockholders to complain that the company was not on track to becoming profitable fast enough, so Bezos began to search for other products that could be sold profitably over the Internet. One growing online business was music CDs, and he realized CDs were a good fit with books, so in 1999 Amazon announced its intention to become "Earth's biggest book and music store." The company used its IT competences to widen its product line by selling music CDs on its retail website. The strategy of selling CDs also seemed like a good move because the leading Internet music retailers at this time, such as CD Now, were struggling because they, too, had discovered the high physical costs associated with delivering products bought online to customers. Amazon now had built up its skills in this area, and its online retail competences were working to its advantage; for example, its IT now allowed it to constantly alter the mix of products it offered in its virtual store to keep up-to-date with changing customer needs.

Amazon took many more steps to increase the usefulness of its retail sites to attract more customers and get its established customers to spend more. For example, to entice customers to send books and CDs as presents at important celebration and holiday shopping times such as birthdays, Christmas, and New Year's, Amazon opened a holiday gift store. Customers could take advantage of a gift-wrapping service as well as use a free greeting card email service to announce the arrival of the Amazon gift. Amazon also began to explore other kinds of online retail ventures. For example, recognizing the growing popularity of online auctions pioneered by eBay, Bezos moved into this market by purchasing

Livebid.com, the Internet's only provider of live on-line auctions at that time. Also in 1999, Amazon entered into an agreement with Sotheby's, the famous auction house, to enter the high end of the online auction business.

Nevertheless, starting in 2000, Amazon's stock price fell sharply, as investors came to believe that intense competition from Barnes & Noble and other retailers might keep its operating margins low into the foreseeable future. Despite his company's moves into CDs and the auction business, Bezos was increasingly criticized for being much too slow to take advantage of Amazon's brand name and core skills and to use them to sell other kinds of products on-line—much as a general B&M retailer sells many different kinds of products. Bezos responded that he had to make sure his company's business model would work successfully in book retailing before he could commit his company to a widespread expansion into new kinds of retail ventures. However, Amazon's plunging stock price forced him into action, and from 2000 on, Bezos expanded Amazon's storefronts and began to sell a wider and wider range of electronic and digital products, such as cameras, DVD players, and MP3 players. To achieve a competitive advantage in these new product categories, Amazon used its IT to provide customers with more in-depth information about the nature of the products they were buying and to offer users better ways to review, rank, and comment on the products they bought on its website. Customers were increasingly seeing the utility of Amazon's service.

Bezos had pushed Amazon's "pizza teams" to find new ways to use the company's core skills to expand into different kinds of retail segments. By 2003, they had developed twenty-three different storefronts. By 2006, Amazon had thirty-five storefronts selling products as varied as books, CDs, DVDs, software, consumer electronics, kitchen items, tools, lawn and garden items, toys and games, baby products, apparel, sporting goods, gourmet food, jewelry, watches, health and personal-care items, beauty products, musical instruments, and industrial and scientific supplies. Increasingly consumers came to see Amazon as the low-price retailer for many products. Customers began to visit B&M retail stores to view the physical product, but then they would go online to buy from Amazon. One advantage Amazon has is that customers avoid paying state sales tax when they buy online, and for high-ticket items, this is an important savings, even though shipping costs must be paid.

New Problems

As time went on, however, customers increasingly began to compare the prices charged by different online retail websites to locate the lowest priced product, and many dot-coms, desperate to survive in a highly competitive online retail environment, undercut Amazon's prices and so put more pressure on its profit margins. To strengthen Amazon's competitive position and make it the preferred online retailer, Bezos moved aggressively to find ways to attract customers, such as by offering them free shipping or "deals of the day." To make its service more convenient, Amazon also began to forge alliances with B&M companies like Toys "R" Us, Office Depot, Circuit City, Target, and many others. Now, customers could buy products online at Amazon's website, but if they wanted their purchases immediately, they could pick them up from these retailers' local B&M stores. Amazon had to share its profits with these retailers, but it avoided high product-stocking and distribution costs. These alliances also helped Bezos quickly transform his company from "online bookseller" to "leading Internet product provider." His goal was for Amazon to become the leading online retailer across many market segments, driving out the weaker online competitors in those segments and so consolidating many segments of the online retail industry.

Bezos was helped because new online retailers had quickly discovered the high costs of operating the value-chain functions necessary to deliver products to customers. In the bookselling market, for example, with the exception of Barnes & Noble, which still has an Internet business unit, other booksellers, such as Borders.com, Borders.co.uk, and Waldenbooks.com, could not compete with Amazon. They closed down their online operations and became Amazon Associates, directing Internet traffic from their websites to Amazon's in return for sales commissions. Amazon's competitive advantage also strengthened in 2001 when the Internet bubble burst, the stock price of dot-com companies plunged, and thousands of cut-price online retailers went out of business. Even though its own stock price plunged, too, Amazon was now the strongest dot-com in the most important retail segments, and losers like CD Now, Virginmega.com, and online toy and electronics retailers also redirected traffic to Amazon's website for a fee, as they shut down their operations.

Many B&M retailers that had established virtual storefronts found they could not make their online storefronts profitable in the 2000s because of high operating costs. Those that did succeed, like Lands' End, already had well-developed catalog sales operations. Their failure was another opportunity for Amazon; for example, when Toys "R" Us found its virtual site too expensive to operate, it also reached an agreement to redirect customers to Amazon's Toys and Games storefront, although at first customers could still pick up their toys from Toys "R" Us stores, if they chose. Many other established B&M companies that found online retailing too complex and expensive also formed agreements with Amazon to operate their online stores. Indeed, Amazon seized this opportunity to get into the new business of using its proprietary IT to design, operate, and host other companies' online storefronts for them for a fee. It had become an IT services company as well, and this helped its revenues grow. Amazon formed agreements to operate retail websites for Target, the NBA, Sears Canada, and Bombay Company, for example.

Branching off into all these new retail market segments also allowed Amazon to more fully utilize its expensive warehouse and distribution system; faster sales across product categories increased inventory turnover and reduced costs. Moreover, its alliances with retailers allowed it to reduce the quantity of expensive merchandise it had to purchase and warehouse until sold, which helped its profit margins. In addition, by offering many different kinds of products for sale, Amazon allowed its customers to "mix" purchases, adding a book or CD to their electronic product order, which led to economies of scale for Amazon. By giving customers more and more reasons to visit its site, Amazon hoped to drive business and sales across all its product categories, using its 1-Click system to make the transactions as easy as possible for consumers. However, to keep its operating costs low from the beginning, Amazon adopted a low-key approach to providing customer service; it did not reveal a customer service telephone number anywhere on its U.S. website. However, as the complexity of its business grew, it recognized the need to provide some level of service, and in 2006 Amazon added to its website an email link.

Using this link, customers provide their phone numbers, which Amazon customer service reps then call to provide whatever help is needed—for example, with parcel tracking information. Customer service for North American customers is now handled by centers in Washington State, North Dakota, and West Virginia, as well as a number of outsource centers.

After its failure in the online auction market, in 2001 Amazon added a new retail service that turned out to be highly profitable and important to maintaining its online leadership position in retailing. Amazon launched zShops, a fixed-price retail marketplace that became the foundation of the current and very successful Amazon Marketplace Service. This retail service allows customers to sell their used books, CDs, DVDs, and other products alongside the identical brand-new products that Amazon offers on the product pages of its retail website. This has significantly added to its sales revenues. eBay bought a company called half.com to compete with Amazon Marketplace and is Amazon's main rival today, as both companies compete to provide a profitable fee-based service to sellers of used products.

In the 2000s, as Amazon became the acknowledged leader in Internet retailing, it decided to offer a consulting service to other virtual retailers (it had already provided this service to B&M retailers) to create for them a unique, customer-friendly storefront using Amazon's proprietary IT. Moreover, to protect the competitive advantage its proprietary IT gives it, Amazon also started lawsuits against other virtual or B&M companies that, it claimed, implemented checkout systems similar to 1-Click by imitating and infringing on its proprietary software that is protected by patents. This consulting service has proved to be a very profitable business activity, and in the process of designing storefronts for other companies, Amazon has also found opportunities to improve its own IT systems by learning from its "leading customers."

Global Expansion

Since IT is not limited to any one country or world region, a virtual company can use the Internet and World Wide Web to sell to customers around the world—providing, of course, that the products it sells can be customized to meet the needs of overseas consumers. Bezos was quick to realize that Amazon's IT could be profitably transferred to other countries to sell books. However, the ability to enter new overseas markets was limited by one major factor: Amazon.com offered its customers the biggest selection of books written in the *English* language, so overseas customers had to be able to read English. Where could these customers be found?

An obvious first choice was the United Kingdom (UK), followed by other English-speaking nations such as Australia, New Zealand, India, and Germany (Germany has one of the highest proportions of English-as-a-second-language speakers in the world because English is taught in all its schools). To speed entry into overseas markets, Amazon searched for overseas Internet companies that had gained a strong foothold in local domestic markets and then acquired them. In the United Kingdom, Amazon bought Bookpages.com in 1996, installed its proprietary IT, replicated its value creation functions, and renamed it Amazon.co.uk. In Germany, it acquired a new online venture, ABC Bücherdienst/Telebuch.de, and created Amazon.de in 1998. Amazon continued its path of global expansion, and by 2006 it also operated retail websites in Canada, France, China, and Japan and shipped its English language books to customers anywhere in the world.

To facilitate the growth of its global IT and distribution systems, Amazon also has product development centers in England, Scotland, India, Germany, and France. Just as Amazon expanded the range of products it sold on its U.S. website, it also increased the range of products it sold abroad, as its warehouse and distribution systems became strong enough to sustain expansion and its local managers decided on the mix of products best suited to the needs of local customers.

New Developments

After Amazon's stock price reached a low of around $6 a share in late 2001 after the Internet bubble burst and many dot-coms went out of business, Amazon continued to persevere. When it finally turned its first profit in the fourth quarter of 2002—a meager $5 million, just 1 cent per share on revenues of over $1 billion—this was an important signal to investors. It seemed to confirm that Amazon's business model was working, it would survive, and its stock price would increase. In fact, Amazon's stock price began to soar in the early 2000s, as investors now believed it would become a highly profitable online retail

leader; its stock price increased to $20 by the end of 2002 and to almost $60 by the end of 2003. Amazon's net profits also increased to $35 million in 2003 and to $588 million in 2004. Revenue kept growing because of the company's entry into many different retail segments and global markets, from $3.9 billion in 2002, to $5.3 billion in 2003, and $6.9 billion in 2004. Amazon's future looked bright indeed as it became the largest Internet retailer and achieved a dominant position in many market segments.

New Acquisitions and Business Opportunities

To make better use of its resources and capabilities and to maintain its profit growth, Amazon began to acquire many small companies in the late 1990s. One of its goals was to acquire small IT companies that would allow it to strengthen its distinctive competences in IT and to develop more kinds of web-based IT commercial services that it could sell to both B&M and online companies. As mentioned earlier, Bezos has always preached that Amazon is first and foremost a *technology company* and that its core skills drive its retail mission. Another goal in buying small companies was to find new opportunities to increase sales of existing retail storefronts and to allow Amazon to establish new storefronts in new segments of the retail market. Some acquisitions have been successful and some have not.

In 1998, for example, Amazon bought Internet Movie Database (www.IMDb.com), a company that hosted a comprehensive listing of all movies in existence. Formerly a free service, Amazon transformed it into a commercial venture whose function is to help customers easily find and identify DVDs to purchase and to make related suggestions to encourage additional purchases. As with Amazon's regular site, IMDb users are allowed to review and make detailed comments on movies and may even start a message board. In 1999, Amazon acquired Exchange.com, which specialized in hard-to-find book titles at its Bibliofind.com website and hard-to-find music titles and memorabilia at MusicFile.com. The acquisition also helped Amazon develop user-friendly search engines to help customers identify and buy its products, once again using its 1-Click system.

In 1998, Amazon bought PlanetAll.com, which operated a web-based address book, calendar, and reminder service that had over 1 million registered users, and Junglee.com, an XML-based data-mining start-up that had technology for searching for and tracking Internet users' website visits based on their personal interests. In 2000, after Amazon had absorbed these companies' technology, it shut them down, making their employees Amazon employees and relocating them to Amazon's Seattle headquarters. For example, PlanetAll's "relationship-building" software applications were folded into Amazon's Friends and Favorites area. Within Friends and Favorites, Amazon customers are able to set up wish lists and view those of friends, view product critiques from specific reviewers, and create and view homepages from Amazon's website. Amazon's new employees also went on to build community-focused features for Amazon's website, including the unsuccessful Amazon.com Auctions and successful Amazon.com Marketplace and Amazon.com Purchase Circles. Amazon became driven by the need to find and use the most successful new web-based techniques for attracting and keeping Internet customers as rivalry with companies like Yahoo!, eBay, and then Google started to increase as these companies began to enter each other's businesses.

In pursuit of this goal, in 1999 Amazon bought Alexa Internet, which had developed software that works in conjunction with Internet Explorer to track and monitor the way people search the Internet. Amazon hoped to use this technology to help it improve its ability to track its customers as they moved around the Internet and so provide them with a personalized browsing experience—for example, making product suggestions based on the specific nature of their site visits—similar to Google's offering customized advertising specific to the webpage a user was visiting. In 2003, Amazon launched a separately controlled subsidiary called A9.com, Inc. to take control of all its search engine research and build innovative technologies to improve users' search experiences and so increase the utility of its e-commerce applications.

A9.com's search engine, which searches both Amazon.com and other websites, used to be powered by Google's search engine. Today, it is powered by Microsoft's Live Search technology, because Google has emerged as the leader in this area. The differentiating feature of Amazon's A9.com search technology was meant to be that users would log into the service, and then A9 would continually record every page they searched for. By creating a personalized memory of users' visits, A9 could provide them with a highly customized search service that could take

them quickly to already visited sites but that would also be able to suggest relevant new sites based on all the personal data collected by the engine. In this way, Amazon hoped it could drive more traffic to its constantly increasing storefronts.

The search engine did not prove popular with Internet users, however, because many believed the engine was highly invasive of their privacy, creating as it does a permanent record of their website visits. Instead, in the 2000s, Google's search engine has become the search engine of choice, both because it is technologically the most advanced and because users can opt out of creating a personalized search history if they choose to disable its advanced features. Thus, Google struck the right balance between usefulness and privacy and thwarted Amazon's attempts to become the leader in the crucial search engine market. In 2006, Amazon announced its A9 site would no longer ask users to log in or accumulate such personal data. Instead, it would focus on improving the usefulness of the search results users obtained on Amazon's own storefronts. For example, one of the technologies A9.com had developed was a "mini" search engine feature called "Search Inside!" mentioned earlier, that allows users to search within the text of books as well as searching for text on the Web. "Search Inside!" is a feature that makes it possible for customers to search for keywords in the full text of many of the books in its catalog to identify books that may be of interest to them. There are currently about 250,000 books in the program, and Amazon has cooperated with around 130 publishers to allow users to perform these searches. To avoid copyright violations, Amazon.com does not return computer-readable text of the book but rather a picture of the page containing the relevant text, disables printing of the pages, and puts limits on the number of pages in a book a single user can access. In 2005, A9 also developed an interactive wiki feature that allows any Amazon customer who has purchased at least one product from the company to add to or edit the relevant product descriptions or wikis, such as for books.

Thus, although Amazon has used these acquisitions to steadily improve its customers' ability to search and use its own storefronts, its attempt to gain a leading position in providing generalized web-based search services to Internet users failed. Today, its A9.com generates only 0.1% of all searches, compared to over 60% claimed by the leader Google. Amazon also has failed in other areas; another search technology A9.com developed was the "Find It on the Block" feature that allowed users not just to find the phone number, address, map, and directions for a business but also to see a picture of it, as well as all the businesses and shops on that same street. However, in 2006, Amazon announced it was ending this service because most users preferred the mapping services offered by Google and Yahoo!. Many of Amazon's failures can be explained by the fact that established Internet companies already had a first-mover advantage in specific industries in the Internet sector. For example, Amazon.com's Auctions could not compete successfully against eBay, which, with its 30 million registered sellers and buyers, dominated the online auction industry.

In an effort to keep its customers loyal, Amazon began providing a range of new customer services. In January 2006, it launched Amazon Prime, a $79-per-year service that allows users to get unlimited free two-day shipping and upgraded overnight shipping for $3.99 on eligible items bought from its storefronts. Also in January, Amazon established a partnership with travel meta-search company Side-Step and used its service to power searches in Amazon's travel store. In March, it launched an online storage service called Amazon S3 that allows users to store an unlimited number of data objects ranging in size from 1 byte to 5 gigabytes for a storage service charge of 15 cents per gigabyte per month and data transfer fees of 20 cents per gigabyte each when users distribute their data (for example, advertisements or catalog mailing lists) using HTTP or Bit Torrent services provided by Amazon.

In July 2006, Amazon entered the grocery delivery business when its website officially launched Amazon Grocery, a new storefront that sells a wide variety of nonperishable food and household items that, once ordered, can be reordered or modified easily using Amazon's shopping-list software. To ensure competitive pricing with B&M grocery stores, customers receive free shipping on purchases of canned and packed food products over $25.

In September 2006, Amazon Business Solutions group, which serves the needs of business customers, also extended the range of its services by launching Fulfillment by Amazon and WebStore by Amazon. These services give small and medium-sized businesses access to Amazon's order fulfillment, customer service, customer shipping offers, and under-

lying website technology to improve the retail experience they can offer customers on their own websites. For example, Fulfillment by Amazon allows small businesses to use Amazon's own order fulfillment and after-order customer services and gives their customers the right to receive the benefit of Amazon.com shipping offers. Fulfillment by Amazon performs the value-chain activities that free online small businesses from the time and costs required to store, pick, pack, ship, and provide customer service for the products they sell online. After paying Amazon's service fee, small businesses ship their products to an Amazon fulfillment center, which stores and sends those products to customers who order them on the small business's or Amazon's storefront. Amazon will also manage post-order customer service, such as customer returns and refunds, for businesses that use Fulfillment by Amazon. Amazon.com customers can also use services such as Amazon Prime and Free Super Saver Shipping when buying products that have the Fulfilled by Amazon icon. Small businesses benefit from the cost savings that result when Amazon's service fees are lower than the costs of performing the value-chain service themselves.

WebStore by Amazon allows businesses to create their own privately branded e-commerce websites using Amazon's technology. Businesses can choose from a variety of website layout options and can customize their sites using their own photos and branding. For example, Seattle Gift Shop now has its own WebStore at http://www.seattlesgifts.com. WebStore by Amazon users pay a commission of 7% (price includes credit card processing fees and fraud protection) for each product purchased through their site and a monthly fee of $59.95. As one business owner commented, "Not only has WebStore increased my sales dramatically, but also its easy-to-use tools give me complete control of the look and feel of my site." WebStore allows small businesses to build their brand name while using Amazon's easy-to-use flexible "back-end" technology—including Amazon's 1-Click checkout system—and allows them to refer customers through the Amazon Associates program if they choose.

Jeff Bezos and his top management team seem committed to leveraging Amazon's core competences in whatever ways they can to find ways to realize the value of the company's assets. The range of possible services Amazon can offer seems endless. For example, Amazon established a wholly owned subsidiary, CustomFlix, Inc., to provide first a DVD and then a CD on Demand Service. The DVD and CD on Demand Services allow independent musicians, artists, labels, and other video and music content owners an inventory-free way to reach a worldwide audience and make their videos and audio CDs available to Amazon's customers. Customers can preview a DVD or CD on the CustomFlix website and then decide whether to make a purchase, much as customers in record stores listen to tracks before making a purchase decision. Once again, because CustomFlix can burn the DVD/CD on demand, there are no inventory costs for musicians to bear, so the service offers an easy, attractive, and low-cost way for musicians, artists, and labels to profitably connect to customers. It also expands Amazon's content offerings, making it even more unique compared to other DVD/CD retailers. If they attract a following, successful musicians and artists can then set up their own customizable CustomFlix E-Store so that they can personalize the products they offer to customers. CustomFlix on Demand provides high-quality DVD and CD media with full-color hub-printed faces; full-color, double-sided tray cards; and four-page, full-color inserts in overwrapped clear jewel cases.

In another bold venture, in September 2006, Amazon launched an eagerly awaited digital download video service. Called Amazon Unbox, the new download service offered customers thousands of television shows, movies, and other video content from more than thirty studio and network partners from Hollywood and around the world. Unbox claimed to be the only video download service to offer a DVD-quality picture that could be downloaded from one PC (such as an office computer) and then transferred to another PC (such as a home computer). At no additional charge, Unbox automatically included a second file optimized for playback on any Windows Media-compatible portable device. Also, Unbox used progressive downloading, which eliminated the need to wait for the entire video to download before watching. A broadband customer could start watching a downloaded Unbox video or movie within five minutes of ordering.

However, within weeks, this important new download service—one that Amazon investors had eagerly awaited—generated many negative comments from users. The number of movies downloaded was disappointingly few because the service's poor software caused many glitches and very slow—hours-long—download time. Amazon quickly updated the movie player to fix the bugs, but many complaints remained: long download time, poor resolution, and restrictions on when and where movies could be played. Amazon continues to improve this service and in January 2007 announced an agreement with TiVo, the set-box DVD recording company, to develop a joint program to allow TiVo's millions of customers easy access to Amazon's download service. Amazon is currently searching for more partners, but one development that may seriously impair its progress in this area is Wal-Mart's February 2007 agreement with the six major movie studios to offer movie downloads through its online store. Wal-Mart is the leading seller of DVDs with over 40% of the market, and its ability to negotiate this deal, rather than Amazon, might be a major setback.

Amazon's Future Prospects

Today, Amazon is the leading Internet retailer. It has over 12,000 employees and in 2006 earned $700 million on $10.7 billion in revenues. This was a significant increase in profit from the year before, and its stock price rose significantly as investors became more optimistic about its future prospects. Nevertheless, its stock price is still lower than it was in 2004 because investors have realized many of its new ventures, such as its attempt to dominate the search engine segment, have not worked out, and because the future success of ventures such as movie downloads is not clear. Moreover, all its expenditures to develop the new IT platforms necessary to launch complex digital storefronts have been increasing its operating costs, which rose from 6.1% of revenue in 2005 to 7.8% in the second quarter of 2006. These increased operating costs have reduced its profit margins. Once again, Amazon's operating costs are rising, now not because of the development of the physical infrastructure necessary to support its retail sales, but because of the investment in the IT infrastructure necessary to launch new digital products. Some analysts are concerned that in its attempts to grow profits, Amazon is losing its knack of creating the customer-friendly retail technology that made it a leading dot-com company. And they are watching the growing success of Google as it enters new businesses, including retail Internet segments, with its

Froogle product-search service and its new online payment system that is a challenge to Amazon's 1-Click system. So investors are watching to see how operating costs will affect operating margins and net profits in the next few years and how Amazon will fend off increasing competition from companies like Wal-Mart that are building up their own online presence and are willing to charge low prices to build their market share. What new strategies can Bezos pursue to take Amazon to the next level, analysts wonder? Are any new mergers and acquisitions on the horizon?

SOURCES

Amazon.com Annual and 10-K Reports, 1997–2007, http://www.amazon.com, accessed 2007.

Daisey, Mike. *21 Dog Years.* New York: The Free Press: 2002.

Deutschman, A. "Inside the Mind of Jeff Bezos," *Fast Company* (August 2004): 50–58.

Spector, Robert. *Amazon.com—Get Big Fast: Inside the Revolutionary Business Model That Changed the World.* New York: HarperCollins Publishers: 2001.

Blockbuster's Challenges in the Video Rental Industry

This case was prepared by Gareth R. Jones, Texas A&M University.

In January 2007, John Antioco, Blockbuster Inc.'s CEO, was reflecting on the challenges facing the company in the year ahead. The pace of change was quickening as Netflix's online video rental business model was proving very robust. And there was a growing movement to directly download or stream videos using the Internet, which would bypass Blockbuster's store. With its nearly 9,000 global stores, 6,000 in the United States alone, Blockbuster had an enviable brand name and enormous marketing clout. But how could it best use its resources to maintain its number 1 place in the movie-rental market and keep its revenues and profits growing? What strategies needed to be developed to strengthen Blockbuster's business model?

Blockbuster's History

David Cook, the founder of Blockbuster, formed David P. Cook & Associates, Inc., in 1978 to offer consulting and computer services to the petroleum and real estate industries. He created programs to analyze and evaluate oil and gas properties and to compute oil and gas reserves. When oil prices began to decline in 1983 due to the breakdown of the OPEC cartel, his business started to decline, and

Cook began evaluating alternative businesses in which he could apply his skills. He decided to exit his current business by selling his company and to enter the video-rental business based on a concept for a "video superstore." He opened his first superstore, called Blockbuster Video, in October 1985 in Dallas.

Cook developed his idea for a video superstore by analyzing the trends in the video industry that were occurring at that time. During the 1980s, the number of households that owned VCRs was increasing rapidly and, consequently, so was the number of video-rental stores set up to serve their needs. In 1983, 7,000 video-rental stores were in operation; by 1985, there were 19,000; and by 1986, there were over 25,000, of which 13,000 were individually owned. These "mom-and-pop" video stores generally operated for only a limited number of hours, offered customers only a limited selection of videos, and were often located in out-of-the-way strip-mall shopping centers. These small stores often charged a membership fee in addition to the tape rental charge, and generally customers brought an empty box to the video-store clerk, who would exchange it for a tape if it was available—a procedure that was often time-consuming, particularly at peak times such as evenings and weekends.

Cook realized that as VCRs became more widespread and the number of film titles available steadily increased, customers would begin to demand a larger and more varied selection of titles from video stores. Moreover, they would demand more convenient store locations and quicker in-store service than mom-and-pop stores could offer. He realized that the time was right for the development of the next generation of video stores, and he used this opportunity to implement his video superstore concept, which is still the center of Blockbuster's strategy.

The Video Superstore Concept

Cook's superstore concept was based on several components. First, Cook decided that in order to give his video superstores a unique identity that would appeal to customers, the stores should be highly visible stand-alone structures, rather than part of a shopping center. In addition, his superstores were to be large—between 3,800 and 10,000 square feet—well lit, and brightly colored (for example, each store has a bright blue sign with "Blockbuster Video" displayed in huge yellow letters). Each store would have ample parking and would be located in the vicinity of a large urban population to maximize potential exposure to customers.

Second, each superstore was to offer a wide variety of tapes, such as adventure, children's, instructional, and videogame titles. Believing that movie preferences differ in different locations, Cook decided to have each store offer a different selection of between 7,000 and 13,000 film titles, organized alphabetically in over thirty categories. New releases were arranged alphabetically against the back wall of each store to make it easier for customers to make their selections.

Third, believing that many customers, particularly those with children, wanted to keep tapes for longer than a one-day period, he created the concept of a three-day rental period for $3. (In 1991, a two-evening rental program was implemented, making new releases only $2.50 for two evenings during the first three weeks after release; after this period, the usual $3 for three evenings would apply.) If the tape was available, it could be found behind the cover box. The customer would take the tape to the checkout line and hand the cassette and his or her membership card to the clerk, who would scan the bar codes on both the tape and the card. The customer was then handed the tape and told that it was due back by midnight two days later. For example, if the tape were rented Thursday afternoon, it would be due back Saturday at midnight.

Fourth, Cook's superstores targeted the largest market segments, adults in the eighteen- to forty-nine-year-old group and children in the six- to twelve-year-old group. Cook believed that if his stores could attract children, then the rest of the family probably would follow. Blockbuster carried no X-rated movies, and its goal was to be "America's Family Video Store." New releases were carefully chosen based on reviews and box-office success to maximize their appeal to families.

Finally, believing that customers wanted to choose a movie and get out of the store quickly, Cook decided that his superstores would offer customers the convenience of quick service and long operating hours, generally from 10:00 A.M. to midnight, seven days a week. Members received a plastic identification card that was read by the point-of-sale equipment developed by the company. This system used a laser bar-code scanner to read important information from both the rental cassette and the ID card. The rental amount was computed by the system and due at the time of rental. Movie returns were scanned by laser, and any late or rewind fees were recorded on the account and automatically recalled the next time the member rented a tape. This system reduced customer checkout time and increased convenience. In addition, it provided Blockbuster with data on customer demographics, cassette rental patterns, and the number of times each cassette had been rented, all of which resulted in a database that increased in value over time as it grew bigger.

These five elements of Blockbuster's approach were successful, and customers responded well. Wherever a new Blockbuster store opened, the local mom-and-pop stores usually closed down, unable to compete with the number of titles and the quality of service that a Blockbuster store could provide. By 1986, Blockbuster owned eight stores and had franchised eleven more to interested investors who could see the potential of this new approach to video rental. Initially, the company opened stores in markets with a minimum population of 100,000; franchises were located in Atlanta, Chicago, Detroit, Houston, San Antonio, and Phoenix. New stores, which cost about $500,000 to $700,000 to equip, grossed an average of $70,000 to $80,000 a month.

Early Growth and Expansion

John Melk, an executive at Waste Management Corp. who had invested in a Blockbuster franchise in

Chicago, was to change the history of the company. In February 1987, he contacted H. "Wayne" Huizinga, a former Waste Management colleague, to tell him of the enormous revenue and profits his franchise was making. Huizinga had experience in growing small companies in fragmented industries. In 1955, he had quit college to manage a three-truck trash-hauling operation; in 1962, he bought his own operation, Southern Sanitation. In 1968, Southern Sanitation merged with Ace Partnership, Acme Disposal, and Atlas Refuse Service to form Waste Management. In succeeding years, Huizinga borrowed against Waste Management stock to buy over 100 small companies that provided such services as auto-parts cleaning, dry cleaning, lawn care, and portable-toilet rentals. He used their cash flows to purchase yet more firms. By the time Huizinga, the vice chairman, resigned in 1984, Waste Management was a $6 billion *Fortune* 500 company and Huizinga was a wealthy man.

Although Huizinga had a low opinion of video retailers, he agreed to visit a Blockbuster store. Expecting a dingy store renting X-rated films, he was pleasantly surprised to find a brightly lit family video supermarket. Detecting the opportunity to take Cook's superstore concept national, Huizinga, Melk, and Donald Flynn (another Waste Management executive) agreed to purchase 33% of Blockbuster from Cook for $18.6 million in 1986; they became directors at this time. In 1987, CEO David Cook decided to take his money and leave Blockbuster to pursue another venture at Amtech Corp. With the departure of the founder, Huizinga took over as CEO in April 1987 with the goal of making Blockbuster a national company and the industry leader in the video-rental market.

Blockbuster's Explosive Growth

Huizinga and his new top management team mapped out Blockbuster's growth strategy, the elements of which follow.

Location

Store location is a critical issue to a video-rental store, and Huizinga moved quickly with Luigi Salvaneschi, a marketing guru renowned for selecting retail locations for maximum profits, to obtain the best store locations in each geographic area that Blockbuster had identified. They developed a "cluster strategy" whereby they targeted a particular geographic market, such as Dallas, Boston, or Los Angeles, and then opened up new stores one at a time until they had saturated the market. Thus, within a few years, the local mom-and-pop stores found themselves surrounded, and many, unable to compete with Blockbuster, closed down. Video superstores were always located near busy, well-traveled routes to establish a broad customer base. The cluster strategy eventually brought Blockbuster into 133 television markets (the geographic area that television reaches), where it reached 75 to 85% of the U.S. population.

Marketing

On the marketing side, Blockbuster's chief marketing officer, Tom Gruber, applied his knowledge of McDonald's family-oriented advertising strategy to strengthen Cook's original vision of the video retail business. In 1988, he introduced "Blockbuster Kids" to strengthen the company's position as a family video store. This promotion, aimed at the six- to twelve-year-old age group, introduced four characters and a dog to appeal to Blockbuster's young customers. To further demonstrate commitment to families, each store stocked forty titles recommended for children and a kids' clubhouse with televisions and toys so that children could amuse themselves while their parents browsed for videos. In addition, Blockbuster allowed its members to specify what rating category of tapes (such as PG or R) could be rented through their account. A policy called "Youth-Restricted Viewing" forbade R-rated tape rentals to children under seventeen. Blockbuster also implemented the free "Kidprint Program," through which a child's name, address, and height were recorded on a videotape that was given to parents and local police for identification purposes. In addition, Blockbuster started a program called "America's Most Important Videos Are Free," which offered free rental of public-service tapes about topics such as fire safety and parenting. Finally, to attract customers and to build brand recognition, Gruber initiated joint promotions between Blockbuster and companies like Domino's Pizza, McDonald's, and Pepsi-Cola, something it continues to do today.

Operations

Blockbuster also made great progress on the operations side of the business. As discussed earlier, the operation of a Blockbuster superstore is designed to provide fast checkout and effective inventory management. The company designed its point-of-sale computer system to make rental and return transactions easy; this system is available only to company-owned and franchised stores.

Rapid expansion strains a company's operating systems. To support its stores, Blockbuster opened a 25,000-square-foot distribution center in 1986 in Dallas. The distribution center had the capacity to store 200,000 videotapes, which were removed from the original containers and labeled with security devices affixed to the cassettes. Each videotape was then bar-coded and placed into a hard plastic rental case. The facility could process the initial inventory requirement of about 10,000 tapes for up to three superstores per day. In addition, Blockbuster supplied the equipment and fixtures needed to operate new stores, such as computer software and hardware, shelving, signs, and cash registers. In 1987, the physical facilities of the distribution center were expanded to double capacity to 400,000 videocassettes.

Blockbuster's growing buying power also gave it another operations advantage. As the then largest single purchaser of prerecorded videotapes in the U.S. market, it was able to negotiate discounts off retail price. Cassettes were bought at an average of $40 per tape and rented three nights for $3. Thus, the cash investment on "hit" videotapes was recovered in forty-five to sixty days, and the investment on non-hit titles was regained in two-and-a-half to three months. In its early days, Blockbuster was also able to use its efficient distribution system to distribute extra copies of films declining in popularity to new stores where demand was increasing. This ability to transfer tapes to where they were most demanded was very important because customers wanted new tapes on the shelves when they came out. It also allowed the company to use its inventory to best advantage and to receive the maximum benefit from each videotape.

Management and Structure

For Blockbuster, as for any company, rapid growth posed the risk of losing control over daily operations and allowing costs to escalate. Recognizing this, Blockbuster established three operating divisions to manage the functional activities necessary to retain effective control over its operations as it grew. Blockbuster Distribution Corp. was created to handle the area licensing and franchising of new stores and to service their start-up and operation—offering assistance with the selection, acquisition, assembling, packaging, inventorying, and distribution of videocassettes, supplies, and computer equipment. Blockbuster Management Corp. was established to assist with the training of new store management, facility location and acquisition, and employee training. Finally, Blockbuster Computer Systems Inc. was formed to install, maintain, and support the software programs for the inventory and point-of-sale equipment. Together, these three divisions provided all the support services necessary to manage store expansion.

Rapid growth also led Blockbuster to oversee store operations through a regional and district level organizational structure. In 1988, responsibility for store development and operations was decentralized to the regional level. However, corporate headquarters was kept fully informed of developments in each regional area, and even in each store, through its computerized inventory and sales system. For example, Blockbuster's corporate inventory and point-of-sale computer systems tracked sales and inventory in each store and each region. The role of regional management was to oversee the stores in their regions, providing advice and monitoring stores' performance to make sure that they kept up Blockbuster's high standards of operation as its chain of superstores grew.

New-Store Expansion

With Blockbuster's functional-level competences in place, the next step for Huizinga was to begin a rapid program of growth and expansion. Huizinga believed that expanding rapidly to increase revenue and market share was crucial for success in the video-rental industry. Under his leadership, Blockbuster opened new stores quickly, developed a franchising program, and began to acquire competitors to increase the number of its stores.

To facilitate rapid expansion, Blockbuster used its skills in determining store locations, streamlining distribution, and making sales. At first, Blockbuster focused on large markets, preferring to enter a market with a potential capacity for 500 stores—

normally, a large city. Later, Blockbuster decided to enter smaller market segments, like towns with a minimum of 20,000 people within driving distance. All stores were built and operated using the super-store concept described earlier. Using the services of its three divisions, Blockbuster steadily increased its number of new-store openings until, by 1993, it owned over 2,500 video stores.

Blockbuster's rapid growth was also attributable to Huizinga's skills in making acquisitions. In 1986, the company began to acquire many smaller regional video chains to gain a significant market presence in a city or region. In 1987, for example, the twenty-nine video stores of Movies To Go were acquired to expand Blockbuster's presence in the Midwest. Block-buster then used this acquisition as a jumping-off point for opening many more stores in the region. Similarly, in 1989 it acquired 175 video stores from Major Video Corp. and Video Library to develop a presence in southern California. In 1991, it took over 209 Erol's Inc. stores to obtain the stronghold that Erol's previously held in the Mid-Atlantic states. All acquired stores were made to conform to Block-buster's standards, and any store that could not con-form was closed down. Most acquisitions were fi-nanced by existing cash flow or by issuing new shares of stock rather than taking on new debt. These deals reflect Huizinga's reluctance to borrow money.

Licensing and Franchising

Recognizing the need to build market share rapidly and develop a national brand name, Huizinga also recruited top management to put in place his ambi-tious franchise program. Franchising, in which the franchisee is solely responsible for all financial com-mitments connected with opening a new store, al-lowed Blockbuster to expand rapidly without incur-ring debt. The downside of franchising was that Blockbuster had to share profits with the franchise owners. When franchising, it is important to main-tain consistency in stores. Thus, the franchisees were required to operate their stores in the same way as company-owned stores and to follow the same store format for rental selection and the use of proprietary point-of-sale equipment.

Franchising facilitated the rapid expansion of Blockbuster Video. By 1992, the company had over 1,000 franchised stores, as compared to 2,000 company-owned stores. However, by the end of 1992, despite its rapid growth, Blockbuster still controlled only about 15% of the market—its 27,000 smaller rivals shared the rest. Consequently, in 1993 Blockbuster announced plans for a new round of store openings and acquisitions that would give it a 25 to 30% market share within two or three years. Recognizing the long-term profit advantages of own-ing its own stores, Blockbuster began to repurchase attractive territories from franchisees. In 1993, the company spent $248 million to buy the 400 stores of its two largest franchisees, and, with a new store opening every day, by the end of 1993 it owned over 2,500 stores.

The Home-Video Industry

By 1990, revenues from video rentals exceeded the revenues obtained in movie theaters. For example, video-rental revenues rose to $11 billion in 1991, compared to movie theaters' $4.8 billion. The huge growth in industry revenues led to increased compe-tition for customers.

Blockbuster's rapid growth had put it in a com-manding position. In 1990, it had no national com-petitor and was the only company operating beyond a regional level. The next largest competitor, West Coast Video, had only $120 million in 1991 rev-enues, while Blockbuster had revenues of $868 mil-lion. However, Blockbuster faced many competitors at the local and regional levels.

Mature Market

As just discussed, as the video-rental market ma-tured, the level of competition in the industry changed. During the 1980s, video rentals grew rapidly due to the proliferation of VCRs. By 1990, however, 70% of households had VCRs, compared to 2% in 1980, and industry growth had dropped from the previous double digits to 7%. The slow growth in VCR ownership and rentals made competition more severe. To a large degree, competition in the video-rental industry was fierce because new competitors could enter the market with relative ease; the only purchase necessary was videotapes. However, unlike small video-rental companies, Blockbuster was able to negotiate discounts with tape suppliers because it bought new releases in such huge volumes.

New Technology

One growing problem facing Blockbuster by the early 1990s was the variety of new ways in which customers could view movies and other kinds of entertainment. Blockbuster had always felt competition both from other sources of movies—such as cable TV and movie theaters—and from other forms of entertainment—such as bowling, baseball games, and outdoor activities. In the 1990s, technology began to give customers more ways to watch movies. New technological threats included pay-per-view (PPV) or video-on-demand (VOD) systems, digital compression, and direct broadcast satellites.

Pay-per-view movies became a major competitive threat to video-rental stores. With PPV systems, cable customers can call their local cable company and pay a fee to have a scheduled movie, concert, or sporting event aired on their television set. In the future, perhaps cable customers would be able to call up their local "video company" and choose any movie to be aired on their television for a fee; the cable company would make the movie available when customers wanted it. Increasingly, telephone companies were becoming interested in the potential for pay-for-view because the networks of fiber-optic cable they installed throughout the country in the 1990s can be used to transmit movies as well. Huizinga claimed Blockbuster was not overly concerned about PPV systems because only one-third of U.S. households had access to PPV, and fiber optics were expensive. Also, he claimed home-video rental was cheaper than PPV, and new releases are attained thirty to forty-five days before PPV.

Video-on-demand takes the PPV concept further. Bellcore, the research branch of the regional Bell companies, invented VOD. With this system (still in the development stage for many companies), a customer will use an interactive box to select a movie from a list of thousands, and the choice will be transmitted to an "information warehouse" that stores thousands of tapes in digital formats. The selected video is then routed back to the customer's house through either fiber-optic cable or phone lines. This bypasses the local video-rental store because the movies are stored digitally on tape at the cable company's headquarters.

Movie companies or video stores like Blockbuster could function as the information warehouse from which the video selections are made. Blockbuster actively tried to canvass movie studios to become the warehouse so that it could control the VOD market; however, it could not put any deal together. The linking of phone companies with other entertainment companies could also become a direct threat, but Huizinga believed the local Blockbuster store would eventually become the hub of the VOD network. He felt that phone companies would prefer to deal with Blockbuster over companies like Time Warner or Paramount, which lacked both Blockbuster's skills in video retailing and its established customer base—the 30 million customers who make 600 million trips per year to the local store.

Blockbuster's Emerging Strategies

In the 1990s, 70% of the world's VCRs were in countries outside the United States, and foreign countries accounted for half of total world video-rental revenues. In 1991, the United States was the largest video market with revenues of $11 billion, Japan was second with $2.6 billion, followed by the United Kingdom with $1.4 billion and Canada with $1.2 billion. Blockbuster began to expand into international markets in 1989, when it saw the opportunity to exploit its marketing expertise, superstore concept, operating knowledge, financial strength, and ability to attract franchisees abroad.

Just as in the United States, Blockbuster started a program both to build new video superstores and to acquire foreign competitors abroad. Planning to be a leader in home entertainment around the world, Blockbuster's objective was to obtain a 25% share of international revenue by 1995 and to have 2,000 stores in international markets by 1996. In 1989, stores were opened in Canada and the UK. In 1990, Blockbuster opened its first store in Puerto Rico. It continued its expansion into the UK, Canada, the Virgin Islands, Venezuela, and Spain. Franchise agreements were also signed in Japan, Australia, and Mexico.

To expand in the UK in 1992, Blockbuster purchased Cityvision PLC, the UK's largest video retailer, for $81 million cash and 3.9 million shares of stock. At this time, Cityvision ran 875 stores in Britain and Austria under the name Ritz. Blockbuster transformed the Ritz outlets into Blockbuster stores and used the chain as a start for further expansion into Europe, just as it had taken over large video chains in the United States on its way to becoming the national leader. Joint ventures were also negotiated in France, Germany, and Italy. Blockbuster increased the number of franchise stores in Mexico, Chile, Venezuela, and Spain. By 1995, the company had over 2,000 stores in nine foreign countries.

Blockbuster created an international home-video division to oversee and manage its expansion into foreign markets. Besides having expertise in international operations, marketing, merchandising, product purchasing, distribution, franchising, real estate, and field support, this division is proficient at dealing with differences in entertainment, language, and business culture between different countries and is successfully implementing Blockbuster's domestic strategy in its foreign operations.

Blockbuster became a national video-rental chain because of the way it positioned itself in the market as a family-oriented store with a wide selection of videos, convenient hours and locations, and fast checkout. Blockbuster began to expand its entertainment concept into several new markets or industries such as film entertainment programming and music retailing. Also, to increase its revenue, Blockbuster made deals to broaden its range of product offerings.

To enter entertainment programming, Blockbuster invested in Spelling Entertainment Group and Republic Pictures. Both of these companies have large film libraries—a source of inexpensive movies for Blockbuster's retail operations. Blockbuster also chose the music retail business as an area into which it could expand its entertainment concept. Blockbuster saw a fit between selling records, cassettes, and compact discs and renting or selling videos, so it decided to employ the same strategy it had used in the video-rental market: opening new stores and acquiring chains of music stores using the revenues from its video superstores. Blockbuster agreed to buy Sound Warehouse and Music Plus, two record-store chains, for $185 million. At the time, Sound Warehouse was the seventh largest music retailer and Music Plus was the twelfth largest. These two retail chains had a total of 236 stores in thirty-five states, primarily in California and the South. This acquisition made Blockbuster the seventh largest music chain.

Huizinga Sells Blockbuster to Viacom

Although Blockbuster, with its rapid growth and large positive cash flow, seemed poised to become an entertainment powerhouse, Huizinga knew there

were clouds ahead. The rapid advance in digital technology, including broadband Internet, meant VOD was increasingly likely to become a reality. Some analysts were suggesting even that Blockbuster was a "dinosaur." At the same time, Huizinga was finding out that the music retailing industry was highly competitive and had many more experienced competitors than the video-rental industry. Major competitors like Sam Goody's and Tower Records also had plans to accelerate the development of their own music megastores, and profit margins in music retailing were low. Moreover, Wal-Mart began a major push to lower the prices of CDs and then VHS tapes, and price wars were developing. Even in the video-rental business, entrepreneurs who had watched Blockbuster's rapid growth still believed there were opportunities for entry. Chains such as Hollywood Video began to expand rapidly, and increased competition seemed imminent here too.

Huizinga decided that the time was ripe to sell the Blockbuster chain, just as he had sold other chains before. His opportunity came when Sumner Redstone, chairman of Viacom, became involved in an aggressive bidding war to buy Paramount Studios, the movie company. Redstone recognized the value of Blockbuster's huge cash flow in helping to fund the debt needed to take over Paramount. Ignoring the risks involved in taking over Blockbuster, in 1994 Viacom acquired the company for $8.4 billion in stock, and Huizinga cashed in his huge stockholdings.

Just the next year, in 1995, a tidal wave of problems hit the Blockbuster chain. First, a brutal price war hit the video-rental industry as new video chain start-ups fought to find a niche in major markets to get some of the lucrative industry revenues. Second, movie studios started to lower the price of tapes, realizing they could make more money by selling them directly to customers rather than letting companies like Blockbuster make the money through tape rentals. Third, as Blockbuster's video and music operations both expanded, it became obvious that the company did not have in hand the materials management and distribution systems needed to manage the complex flow of products to its stores. Overhead costs started to soar, accompanied by declines in revenues, and the company turned from making a profit to losing money. Blockbuster's cash flow was much less useful to Redstone now, burdened as he was by the huge debt for Paramount. Blockbuster's declining performance led to Viacom's stock price dropping sharply, and Redstone reacted by firing its top managers and searching for an experienced executive to turn the Blockbuster division around.

Blockbuster, 1996–1998

To control Blockbuster's soaring overhead costs, Redstone looked for an executive with experience in low-cost merchandising. In 1996, he pulled off a coup by hiring William Fields, the heir apparent to David Glass, Wal-Mart's CEO, and an information systems and logistics expert. Fields began planning a huge state-of-the-art distribution facility that would serve all Blockbuster's U.S. stores, replacing its outdated facility. He also started the development of a new state-of-the-art point-of-sale merchandising information system that would give Blockbuster real-time feedback on which videos were generating the most money and when they should be transferred to stores in other regions to make the most use of Blockbuster's stock of videos—its most important physical resource. Third, Fields added more retail merchandise to Blockbuster's product mix, such as candy, comics, and audio books. The results of these efforts would take a couple of years to bear fruit, however.

Some analysts believe that by 1997 Redstone, recognizing the negative impact of Blockbuster's operations on Viacom's stock price, was trying to cut costs to boost short-term profits and "harvest" the company so that he could spin off Blockbuster—sensing that the troubled division was not going to be fixed quickly. Apparently, Fields and Redstone came into conflict over what Blockbuster's future was to be in the Viacom empire. With Blockbuster's performance continuing to decline in the first quarter of 1997 with a drop in profit of 20%, Fields resigned in April 1997, only thirteen months after taking over at Blockbuster. Viacom's stock fell to a three-year low. Redstone argued that this was absurd because Blockbuster had generated $3 billion in revenue and $800 in cash flow for Viacom in 1996. However, the specter of video-on-demand and increased price competition in the music and video business made analysts wonder if Blockbuster was going to recover. Furthermore, Fields was the expert in distribution and logistics.

Once again, Redstone looked around for an executive who could help turn Blockbuster around, and in the news was John Antioco, the chief of PepsiCo's Taco Bell restaurants. In just eight months, Antioco, by introducing a new menu, new pricing, and a new store setup, had engineered a 180-degree turnaround in Taco Bell's performance, turning a mounting loss into rising profit. Antioco seemed the perfect choice as Blockbuster's CEO.

After Antioco took the helm, he started to assess the situation. The video-rental market was still flat; sales of movie videos were soaring as their prices came down in outlets such as Wal-Mart. Fields's strategy of enlarging the entertainment product lines carried in Blockbuster stores, while it had seemed like a logical move, had failed as costs continued to rise and products had short shelf lives because changing fads and fashions made the value of Blockbuster's inventory unpredictable. What should be Blockbuster's merchandising mix? And how should Antioco manage the purchase and distribution of Blockbuster's biggest ongoing expense—videotapes—to create a value chain that would lead to increased profitability?

Antioco realized he needed to focus on how to reorganize Blockbuster's value chain to simultaneously reduce costs and generate more revenues. Blockbuster's biggest expense and asset was its inventory of videos, so this was the logical place to start. Antioco and Redstone examined the way Blockbuster obtained its movies. It was presently purchasing tapes from the big studios—MGM, Disney, and so on—at the high price of $65. Because it had to pay this high price, it could not purchase enough copies of a particular hit movie to satisfy customer demand when the movie was released. As a result, customers left stores unsatisfied and revenues were lost. Perhaps there was a better way of managing the process for both the movie studios and Blockbuster to raise revenues from movie tape rental.

Antioco and Redstone proposed that Blockbuster and the movie studios enter into a revenue-sharing agreement, whereby the movie studios would supply Blockbuster with tapes at cost, around $8, which would allow it to purchase 800% more copies of a single title; Blockbuster would then split rental revenues with the studios 50/50. The result, they hoped, would be that they could "grow the market" for rental tapes by 20 to 30% a year; thus both Blockbuster's and the movie studios' revenues would grow. This would also counter the threat from satellite programming, which was taking away all their revenues; 6 million households were now subscribing to direct satellite services. While this deal was being negotiated in 1997, video rentals at Blockbuster dropped 4% more, and the studios that had been hesitating to enter into this radically different kind of sales agreement came on board. This came at a crucial point for Blockbuster too, since its cash flow continued to drop as it faced higher write-off costs for outdated tapes. With the new revenue-sharing agreement signed, however, the profitability of its new business model would increase dramatically. (Blockbuster's market share increased from something less than 30% to over 40% in the next five years, and after a few years, the division returned to profitability.) The movie studios also benefited, as their stream of income increased enormously.

Antioco's second major change in strategy was to abandon the attempt to transform Blockbuster's stores into more general entertainment outlets and refocus on its core movie-rental business. He also abandoned the idea of expanding its music chain; in October 1998, the company sold its 378 Blockbuster music chains to Wherehouse Entertainment for $115 million.

Nevertheless, all these changes hurt Blockbuster's performance in the short term. In 1998, Viacom announced it would record a $437 million charge in the second quarter to write down the value of its Blockbuster tape inventory, since it now had to revise the accounting method it had adopted when it entered into the new revenue-sharing agreement for tapes from Hollywood studios. These charges wiped out Viacom's profits, and Redstone once again announced that a spinoff or initial public offering of Blockbuster was likely because the unit was punishing Viacom's stock price and threatening Viacom's future profitability.

On the plus side, however, the revenue-sharing agreement was yielding a sharp increase in revenues; same-store video rentals increased by 13% in 1998. Since rental tapes would now be amortized over only a three-month period—the time of greatest rental sales—and not the old six to twenty-six months, the new business model seemed poised to finally increase cash flows. One good year for Blockbuster would allow Redstone, who had been increasingly criticized for his purchase of Blockbuster, to go forward with his desire to pursue an "IPO carve out" whereby Viacom would sell between 10 and 20% of the Blockbuster stock to the public in an IPO to cre-

ate a public market for the stock and make an eventual spinoff possible.

By the end of 1998, there were continuing signs of recovery. The move to a revenue-sharing agreement had allowed Blockbuster's managers to develop strategies to increase responsiveness to customers that allowed them to pursue the business model in a profitable way. With the huge increase in the supply of new tapes made possible by the revenue-sharing agreement, Blockbuster was now able to offer the Blockbuster Promise to its customers that their chosen title would be in stock or "next time, it's free." Also, lower prices could now be charged for older video titles to generate additional revenues without threatening profitability. It turned out that the real threat to Blockbuster in the 1990s was not from new technology like video-on-demand, but from a lack of the right strategies to keep customers happy—like having the products they wanted in stock—and a failure to understand the important dynamics behind the value chain, such as revenue sharing, that would grow the market.

Outside the United States, Blockbuster had been increasing the scope of its international operations. In 1994, it opened its first stores in Italy and New Zealand; in 1995, it entered Israel, Brazil, Peru, Colombia, and Thailand; in 1996, it opened stores in Ecuador, Portugal, El Salvador, Panama, and Scandinavia, where it purchased Christianshavn Video in Denmark. In 1996, it went into Taiwan and Uruguay; in 1998, it acquired Video Flick's stores in Australia; in 1999, it entered Hong Kong as a gateway to China and opened its two-hundredth store in Mexico; and in 2000, it expanded its operations in Central America to Costa Rica and Guatemala. By 2002, it operated almost 2,600 stores outside the United States. The main advantage of its global operations is that it can continuously distribute copies of tapes that are less in demand in the United States to countries overseas, where they appear as new releases and customers are willing to pay the highest rental prices for them. The tapes then trickle down to still other countries, so that even though revenues might be less, operations will still be profitable since the cost of the tape has already been amortized. Blockbuster can also identify foreign-made movies that might attract a large U.S. viewing audience.

In 1998, Blockbuster finally opened its 820,000-square-foot distribution center in Kinney, Texas; now it was in a real position to reduce costs and speed delivery of tapes to locations where they were most in demand, and to move them when demand dropped. Also in 1998, Blockbuster began to offer "neighborhood favorites," a program in which each store stocked tapes customized to local tastes. In keeping with this differentiation approach, Blockbuster Rewards, its frequent renters program, was developed. It is a rewards program designed to keep customers returning regularly to its stores and seeing the changes it has made, with a coupon for a free video every month.

Antioco Transforms Blockbuster, 1999–2002

A major turning point for Blockbuster occurred in 1999. After reestablishing Blockbuster's business model, Antioco orchestrated a successful initial public stock offering in August 1999. It turned out that 1999 was the first of four consecutive years of same-store sales increases, as Antioco set about to change the entertainment mix in stores to increase revenues, getting rid of music, candy, and comics. A new opportunity arose in 1999 with the introduction of DVDs, whose high quality suggested that they would soon become the next entertainment medium of choice. DVDs were a natural product-line extension for Blockbuster. In 1999, Blockbuster introduced DVDs into 3,000 of its stores to assess their promise; customer reaction was favorable, as sales of DVD players and other digital media were soaring.

It was here that Antioco apparently made a major error. Given the success of the video revenue-sharing deal with movie studios, it seemed likely that the same kind of deal could be negotiated for DVDs. Reportedly, Warner Brothers started the ball rolling by offering Blockbuster a DVD revenue-sharing deal. Antioco turned down the offer, however; one reason seems to have been Antioco's belief that the high price of DVDs would deter rental customers from buying them. He believed that Blockbuster would reap more returns from buying the DVDs themselves and then renting them. Another reason was that Blockbuster was about to face a lawsuit from independent video retailers, who claimed that the company had gained an unfair competitive advantage from the agreement; signing a new DVD revenue-sharing agreement might therefore generate more potential lawsuits.

In any event, to test the popularity of DVD rentals, in 2000 Blockbuster increased the number of DVD titles it carried because they had much higher profit margins than VHS tapes—DVDs rented for a couple of dollars more. The result was dramatic: revenues soared and the pace of change speeded up. In 2001, Blockbuster abandoned attempts to customize tape offerings to local markets and eliminated 25% of the company's less productive VHS tapes in order to focus on the booming market for DVD rentals. Once again, it took a charge to amortize these tapes, but then shipped them to its stores overseas to capitalize on growing global demand for its products. The result was that by the end of 2001 the company had achieved record revenues, strong cash flow, and increased profitability, while it lowered its debt by more than $430 million. Since 1997, Antioco had grown Blockbuster's revenues from $3.3 billion to over $5 billion and turned free cash flow from a negative position to over $250 million for 2001. Its stock rose, as investors realized that the company now had a business model that generated cash.

By 2002, it had become clear the future was in DVDs. Blockbuster announced that it was phasing out even more of its VHS tapes and switching even more quickly to high-margin DVDs and that DVDs would account for 40% of the chain's rental inventory. This percentage has increased sharply ever since. DVDs swept away VHS tapes much as CDs swept away vinyl records. DVD rentals increased 115%, and in the spring of 2002 Blockbuster made $66 million in net income.

The Growing Videogame Market

Antioco searched for more ways to broaden Blockbuster's product line to keep revenues increasing and ward off possible future declines from rental revenues. One answer came at the end of 2001 when Microsoft introduced its Xbox videogame console to compete with the Sony PlayStation 2 and the Nintendo GameCube and the robust nature of sales in the videogame market became clear—it was a $15-billion-a-year revenue market. Blockbuster decided to carry a full lineup of GameCube, Xbox, and PlayStation software and hardware for rental and to rent and sell videogames in its stores. It also began to try to work exclusive deals with game makers for old gaming systems and software, since there is a huge installed base of older-generation videogames. The attraction of these products to customers is that they can try any game they want before they are forced to pay the high price of buying a game that they may not like. Videogames seemed to be a natural complementary product line, and in May 2002, Blockbuster announced that it wanted to become "gamers' most comprehensive rental and retail resource."

Blockbuster's new product line was a success, and it pushed to double its videogame rentals by 2003. To help achieve this goal, in the summer of 2002 Blockbuster began to offer $19.95 monthly rental service for unlimited videogame rentals. This fit well with Blockbuster's family profile since parents could come into a store to rent a DVD while their children picked up a videogame.

The company tested a new concept of a videogame store-in-store called Game Rush in 2003, and its success at attracting new customers, who also paid a monthly fee for unlimited videogame rental, led to its fast decision to roll the game program out to half its stores by 2004. However, marketing all its new initiatives cost between $80 and $100 million, and this, together with the high capital costs of maintaining its stores, caused its net income to fall, despite growing revenues.

A Blockbuster Performance?

In June 2003, Blockbuster went to court to confront independent video retailers who claimed that Blockbuster's VHS revenue-sharing agreement, which had saved the company in 1999, violated antitrust laws by discriminating against them since they did not obtain preferential price treatment. Independents argued that before the revenue-sharing deals were negotiated, Blockbuster had only 24% of the market while they had 55%, but by 2003 Blockbuster's share had grown to 40%. The court ruled that the independents had had a similar opportunity to negotiate such revenue-sharing agreements and dismissed the suit against Blockbuster. Once the case was over, and as DVD rentals soared, Antioco tried to establish a new revenue-sharing agreement for DVDs with movie studios. Antioco argued that raising wholesale prices and developing a sharing agreement would generate the highest long-term returns for both movie studios and Blockbuster—but it was too late.

The main reason was that by 2002 the movie studios had begun to sell DVDs directly to the general public, and they decided to set the wholesale price of DVDs relatively low to generate sales. Sales took off, and there was an unexpectedly strong customer demand to own DVDs and develop a home-movie library. The movie studios were generating billions of dollars in DVD sales, and they no longer saw the need for a middleman like Blockbuster to take a major share of DVD sales revenues.

This came as a major blow to Blockbuster, but Antioco tried to make the best of it by becoming a major player in the DVD retail market, hoping it could generate high DVD sales revenues, in addition to increasing DVD rental revenues. However, he was in for a shock because the movie studios were obtaining such high revenues from DVD sales that they were willing to reduce their wholesale prices for major low-cost retailers like Wal-Mart and Best Buy, which could sell millions of copies in their stores. Wal-Mart, in particular, began to aggressively discount DVDs and sell at prices well below Blockbuster's; the result was that Blockbuster gained a much smaller share of the DVD retail market than expected. And, because customers were not going to Blockbuster stores to buy DVDs, it also did not enjoy any spillover from increased DVD rentals.

In fact, the boom in DVD sales that started in 2002 caused a major shift, as by 2003 customers were spending significantly more on purchasing movies on DVDs and tapes than on renting them. Thus, while Blockbuster's retail sales of movies rose 19% to $12.3 billion, movie rentals slipped 3% to $9.9 billion; the result was that same-store sales at Blockbuster stores open for one year fell by 6%—a very disappointing result. Although Blockbuster could claim record revenues and profits because of its decision in 2002 and 2003 to switch to DVD rentals, revenues also had increased because it had opened over 550 new stores in 2003—so this was growth without profitability. Moreover, things were not so rosy as they might appear because a large part of these extra profits had come from aggressive cost-cutting efforts in its stores throughout this period and from a substantial reduction in local and national advertising to reduce operating costs—once and for all gains that could not be repeated.

Blockbuster had to find new ways to increase rental revenues and do it quickly. To reduce customers' incentive to buy DVDs and build up their own movie libraries, Blockbuster tested a new marketing strategy, a monthly fee of $24.99 for unlimited DVD rentals, in some of its stores. The program was successful, and in 2004 Blockbuster began to roll it out nationally and experiment with variations in pricing and number of rentals per visit. As mentioned earlier, it already had a similar program in videogame rentals that was performing well.

In another major move, it announced the end to late fees in 2004, as it became clear this was a major motivation of customers to buy DVDs and not to rent them; also, other forms of movie delivery such as pay-per-view were becoming more common, and these had no late fees. This was a significant decision because late fees were a significant contributor to Blockbuster's revenues and profits; indeed, it was estimated that late fees accounted for over 35% of Blockbuster's profit! The company hoped no late fees would translate into more rentals, but this did not happen and put a damper on revenue growth in 2004 and 2005.

The Split from Viacom

Recall that Viacom had decided to take Blockbuster public in August 1999 at $15 a share, but it maintained an 82% stake in the company. Blockbuster stock traded as high as $30 a share in May 2000, and although Viacom had originally planned to sell the rest of Blockbuster to the public soon after the 1999 stock offering, the company decided to retain its stake—in part because of the business's steady cash flow and because Viacom became distracted by integrating CBS, which it had acquired in 2001, into its operations.

Through its aggressive cost cutting, particularly in marketing, Blockbuster continued to perform well financially into 2003, when it generated 22.5% of Viacom's $19.1 billion in revenue and 12% of its $4.4 billion in cash flow. But Blockbuster's 8% revenue growth was anemic, and with most of the cost cuts already made and the continuing high fixed costs of running its stores, it was clear that future revenue growth and stock appreciation was going to be challenging. Also, the uncertainty concerning how quickly home-video and videogame rentals might fall in the future because of the growth in broadband technology once again began to worry Viacom. So throughout 2003, Redstone tried, but failed, to find a buyer for Viacom's Blockbuster shares while they were on the rise.

In January 2004 (well before it announced the end to late fees), Blockbuster's stock hit a high of $20. Believing that the two companies' business models were now diverging too fast, Viacom announced that it would totally spin off its Blockbuster unit by allowing holders of Viacom shares to swap them for shares in Blockbuster. To sweeten the deal, shareholders would also receive a substantial once-and-for-all dividend for swapping their Viacom stock for Blockbuster stock. Enough shareholders took advantage of the offer for Viacom to unload its 82% stake, and Blockbuster was spun off as a fully independent company. Antioco now had to find a way to increase Blockbuster's revenues and free cash flow, but there were still many challenges confronting the company.

The Growing Use of Broadband

Since the 1990s, the new technology of PPV or VOD, the direct download or streaming of movies to customers over cable, satellite, phone lines, or other forms of broadband connection, had been seen as a growing threat to Blockbuster's business model. Essentially, this technology would bypass the need for a bricks-and-mortar store, and the potential threat of this new technology had depressed Blockbuster's stock for years.

In 2000, recognizing the growing importance of satellite programming in PPV delivery, Blockbuster formed an alliance with DIRECTTV to provide a co-branded PPV service on DIRECTTV. Blockbuster also became a new distribution channel for DIRECTTV; under their deal, Blockbuster received a fee for each dish sold, a share of future monthly payments, and a share of revenues from DIRECTTV customers' future orders of PPV movies, which would provide a higher net profit than Blockbuster made from each in-store rental and so lessen its dependence on video rentals. Antioco hoped this alliance would boost Blockbuster's ambition to be the major player in PPV and, at the very least, add 5% to Blockbuster's revenues, enough to make a substantial impact on its bottom line.

In an attempt to maintain its dominant position in the movie-rental marketplace and gain more control of the content or "entertainment software" end of the business, in 2000 Blockbuster announced an agreement with MGM to digitally stream and download recent theatrical releases, films, and television programming from the MGM library to Blockbuster's website for PPV consumption. It started to roll out its "Blockbuster on Demand" PPV, arguing that video rentals and PPV could exist side by side. Initial testing of the program started at the end of 2000, and Blockbuster announced it would try to form similar agreements with other movie studios. It even signed a deal with TiVo, a maker of set-top digital recorders, to offer a VOD service through broadband using TiVo's recorders. TiVo agreed to put demonstration kiosks in over 4,000 Blockbuster stores for its 65 million customers. However, all these moves failed to establish Blockbuster as a major player in the PPV delivery market.

The push toward VOD steadily increased in the mid-2000s, as new technologies were improved to ensure its fast delivery to customers over broadband connections. In August 2005, for example, five major movie studios—Sony, Time Warner, Universal, MGM, and Paramount—announced a plan to bypass powerful middlemen like Blockbuster and HBO and offer their own PPV service directly to customers, although this service was still not up and running by 2006. In addition, Disney and Twentieth-Century Fox were planning their own PPV services, and in 2006 Disney announced its intention of being the hub of the future PPV service, thereby making Blockbuster redundant with its new PPV technology that it reportedly was going to roll out in 2007. Also in 2006, Amazon.com launched a form of PPV service whereby its customers could download a wide range of movie content. Its PPV ran into technology glitches, including long download times (which it has since improved), but it is not clear it has made much of an impression in the industry. Also in 2006, Apple made a big push into the VOD market with its new video iPods; by 2007, Apple had formed two major agreements with large media companies Disney and Paramount to allow its customers to download both TV shows and movies. Analysts believe Apple clearly intends to try to establish itself as the primary PPV video wholesaler, just as it has become the main wholesaler in the music download business.

PPV buy rates are still relatively low and below expectations, however, because cable TV companies and phone companies or satellite operators simply do not have the Internet bandwidth necessary for fast downloads, especially at peak periods such as in the evening or on weekends. Also, VOD was conceived as a more convenient way to watch movies at home; rather than fighting traffic and risking late fees, customers could watch new video releases without leaving their couches—and without waiting. But the process of selecting and downloading a movie is still not easy. Movie studios, too, have a policy of not releasing films for PPV/VOD for at least thirty days after they are first released to protect DVD rentals at video stores; this generates billions more in revenue than home PPV services.

Nevertheless, by 2007, the threat of new easy-to-use digital technology had become an emerging reality as movie studios and distributors like Amazon and Apple fought to become the hub of choice. It was clear by now that although Antioco's goal, just as Huizinga's before him, was that Blockbuster should provide this pivotal role, it obviously had no special technological competences in the digital PPV media arena—no more than movie studios, cable operators, satellite providers, and so on. Moreover, in the future, all movies could be licensed to any VOD on a nonexclusive basis, so each studio would control the pricing and availability of its films. Now, as PCs, TVs, and even MP3 players like iPod began to converge, the potentially huge VOD market would annihilate Blockbuster's niche. By 2006, Blockbuster's stock had dropped to a low of $5.

The Netflix Battle

Although the way future broadband PPV service will unfold will have major consequences for Blockbuster's business model, in the last few years Blockbuster has also had to deal with the growing threat from online DVD rental services, such as that offered by Netflix, which has cut into its rental business. The emergence of Netflix in 2003, with its business model of using the combination of the Internet and regular mail service to rent and deliver DVDs to customers, was revolutionary in the movie-rental industry. The big appeal of Netflix's new plan was the promise of multiple movie rentals for a single monthly price. With Netflix's most popular plan, subscribers can rent an unlimited number of movies for $17.99 a month, keeping as many as three DVDs at a time. Once they send the movies back, by popping them into a postage-paid envelope and dropping them in a mailbox, they can immediately get more. The services don't limit the number of DVDs that can be ordered in any one month.

Obviously, using the Internet to deliver DVDs to customers is a far less expensive way of renting DVDs than owning a chain of bricks-and-mortar video stores. Apparently, Blockbuster was offered the chance to buy Netflix in the early 2000s for $100 million, but Antioco refused; he did not consider this market segment big enough to be profitable, given that most movie rentals tend to be spur of the moment decisions. He believed few customers would sit down and work out in advance which movies to watch. Netflix, however, went to work to attract customers, and through massive online advertising and mailing campaigns it began to attract increasing numbers of customers and became a real threat. By 2004, Netflix claimed to have over 1.4 million customers, and the proven success of its business model showed Antioco he had made a mistake.

In 2004, Blockbuster announced it would also launch an online DVD rental service, although Antioco still commented that he thought this segment would only ever reach about 3 million customers. Blockbuster claimed its new program would be better than Netflix's because customers who ordered DVDs online could then return them to Blockbuster stores if they chose. Antioco argued Blockbuster's business model was the best because it was the only company able to provide a simultaneous online *and* bricks-and-mortar service that would give customers more options and better service. For example, if Blockbuster customers returned DVDs to their local store, as part of Blockbuster's "Total Service" plan, they would then receive a coupon for a free in-store rental. The point, of course, was that by getting customers into its stores, Blockbuster could potentially generate more rental, sales, and other kinds of revenues. Also, Blockbuster's hybrid service overcame one of the big disadvantages of Netflix for rental customers—the inability to get a movie instantly if you suddenly decide Saturday night you want to rent something. Blockbuster's program allowed for advance planning *and* spontaneous rental.

Given that Blockbuster has 48 million members, an online DVD service may prove a useful way of increasing future revenues, but in the short run the problem for Blockbuster was that the new service required a major financial investment to set up the online infrastructure and national marketing campaign. This helped drain Blockbuster's profits, and its stock price fell from $20 a share at the beginning of 2004 to just $10 share at the beginning of 2005, as investors became concerned it could not provide the online service in a cost-effective way. Analysts also wondered if Netflix had gained the first-mover advantage and so would be hard to compete with. To make things worse, Wal-Mart, which already sold low-priced DVDs to attract customers, started a similar online rental program.

However, in 2006, Antioco announced that the company, after a shaky start, had achieved its year-end goal of 2 million subscribers to Total Access. Moreover, significant subscriber growth was achieved without any broadcast media advertising, except in a handful of test markets; in-store and online marketing had been the key to Blockbuster's success. Nevertheless, Netflix and Blockbuster were now locked in a vicious battle for subscribers, and both companies were paying heavily for online ads on major websites such as eBay and Yahoo!. Once again, Antioco argued, because customers would no longer have to choose between renting online or renting in-store, they would never need to be without a movie, and this would make Blockbuster.com the fastest growing online DVD rental service in 2007.

And, of course, cable TV operators, and then movie studios, started PPV services that allowed consumers to order a movie over the TV or computer to watch immediately for $3 or $4. These offerings have all the convenience of a video because movies can be paused, rewound, or fast-forwarded for as long as twenty-four hours after the initial rental and they have no late fees.

Global Problems

Blockbuster has over 3,000 stores globally, but it has faced challenging problems in recent years in managing problems that have arisen in different countries. For example, in the UK it has maintained steady expansion into both DVDs and videogame rentals, and its video store chain is profitable. But in Germany it shut down its operations in 2006, because in the German rental market there is no profit without sex and violence; Blockbuster's policy is to stock only family entertainment and movie classics. Similarly, it closed all twenty-four of its Hong Kong stores in 2005 because of intense competition from pirated DVDs available for sale throughout China for a dollar each! Blockbuster had planned to use Hong Kong as a gateway to the huge market in mainland China, but the availability of pirated low-cost movies for sale in China made this impossible. Nevertheless, Blockbuster continues to operate in a number of markets where video piracy is a big problem, including Taiwan, Thailand, and Mexico.

The Future

The year 2007 may be a pivotal year in Blockbuster's history as the company tries to position itself for success in the quickly changing movie DVD sales and rental business. In January 2007, Blockbuster's stock rose when it announced that it would sell its Rhino videogame chain, which has ninety-four stores, and use the capital to pay down debt and fund its expansion into online movie rental. Its stock then rose sharply a few days later when Antioco announced that Blockbuster was contemplating reducing the size of its DVD inventory in its stores to focus more of its resources on its online business to attract more customers there.

However, a few days later Netflix, responding to criticism that it was allowing Blockbuster to catch up and take its customers, announced a major new instant movie streaming service to its users' PCs over the Internet, which is being offered at no additional charge. Netflix expected to introduce the instant viewing system to about 250,000 more subscribers each week through June 2007 to ensure its computers could cope with the increased demand. The allotted viewing time will be tied to how much customers already pay for their DVD rentals. Under Netflix's most popular $17.99 monthly package, subscribers will receive eighteen hours of Internet viewing time. A major drawback of the instant viewing system is that it works only on PCs and laptops equipped with a high-speed Internet connection and Windows; movies can't be watched on cell phones, TVs, or video iPods or on Apple's operating system.

Also, new technology has emerged that allows for DVDs obtained through the mail or downloaded online to "self-destruct" within some defined time period, preventing the threat of video piracy. This technology is also available for physical DVDs, which also self-destruct when the rental time period has expired. This is likely to be important because of the growth in the number of DVD rental kiosks that have appeared in supermarkets and fast-food restaurants, which allow users to quickly rent a just-released movie. Currently, these kiosks charge expensive late fees, but with self-destruct technology they could be seen as a convenient way to rent new movies in the future.

What future strategies Blockbuster would take was unclear in early 2007. Will Blockbuster contemplate closing more and more of its stores if its online business model proves more profitable? And if so, what will be its mix of mail versus Internet movie delivery, and what kind of PPV technology will it adopt? Certainly, a virtual business would be a more appropriate hub for a complete VOD operation with a recognized brand name, but what then would happen to its physical stores? Is the combination of bricks-and-mortar and online retailing still the ideal mix in this market for movie and videogame rentals and sales? How quickly movie and video storefronts like Apple's, Amazon.com's, and Disney's become popular is likely to determine this. Is there a potential buyer for the company on the horizon? Could Blockbuster stores become Apple stores?

Finally, a new dilemma emerged for the company in 2007 when on January 25 Netflix announced it ended the fourth quarter with about 6.31 million subscribers, compared with a total of 4.18 million at the end of 2005. The total represented 12% growth over the third-quarter total of 5.66 million, and its revenue had climbed to $277.2 million, from $193 million a year earlier. Now, its stock shot up and Blockbuster's plunged. Clearly, Netflix remains a major competitor, the fight to dominate the movie-rental market and movie and TV program instant streaming video service in the future is open, and who will win remains to be seen.

SOURCES

Apar, Bruce. "Ruminations on Burstyn, Bezos & Blockbuster," *Video Store* (January 14–January 20, 2001): 6.

Arnold, Thomas K. "Broadbuster," *Video Store* (August 6–August 12, 2000): 1, 38.

Blockbuster 10-Ks and Annual Reports, 1988–2001, http://www.blockbuster.com.

"Citibank Reaches Pact to Install Its ATMs in Blockbuster Stores," *Wall Street Journal,* May 28, 1998, p. A11.

Clarkin, Greg. "Fast Forward," *Marketing and Media Decisions* (March 1990): 57–59.

DeGeorge, Gail. *Business Week* (January 22, 1990): 47–48.

DeGeorge, Gail, Jonathan Levine, and Robert Neff, "They Don't Call It Blockbuster for Nothing," *Business Week* (October 19, 1992): 113–114.

Desjardins, Doug. "Blockbuster Scores with Games, DVDs," *DSN Retailing Today* (May 6, 2002): 5.

Fabrikant, Geraldine. "Blockbuster President Resigns: Video Chain Revamps to Adapt to New Units," *New York Times,* January 5, 1993, p. D6.

Frankel, Daniel. "Blockbuster Revamps Play Areas," *Video Business* (May 27, 2002): 38.

Gaudiosi, John. "Blockbuster Pushes PS2," *Video Store* (December 2–December 8, 2001): 1, 38.

"Global Notes: Focus 1-Blockbuster Entertainment Corp. (BV)," *Research Highlights* (October 26, 1990): 9.

Grossman, Laurie, and Gabriella Stern, "Blockbuster to Buy Controlling Stake in Spelling in Swap," *Wall Street Journal,* March 9, 1993, p. B9.

Heller, Laura. "Radio Shack, Blockbuster Put Synergies to the Test," *DSN Retailing Today* (June 4, 2001): 5.

Hume, Scott. "Blockbuster Means More than Video," *Advertising Age* (June 1, 1992): 4.

Kadlec, Daniel. "How Blockbuster Changed the Rules," *New York Times,* August 3, 1998, pp. 48–49.

Kirkwood, Kyra. "Blockbuster Moves into Used DVDs," *Video Store* (March 25, 2000): 1.

McCarthy, M. *Wall Street Journal,* March 22, 1991, pp. A1, A6.

Orwall, Bruce. "Five Studios Join Venture for Video on Demand," *Wall Street Journal,* August 17, 2001, p. A3.

QRP Merrill Lynch Extended Company Comment, November 16, 1990.

Roberts, Johnnie. "Blockbuster Officials Envision Superstores for Music Business," *Wall Street Journal,* October 28, 1992, p. B10.

Rosenblum, Trudi M. "Blockbuster to Add Audiobooks," *Publishers Weekly* (June 19, 2000): 14.

Sandomir, S. *New York Times,* June 19, 1991, pp. S22–S25.

Savitz, Eric. "An End to Fast Forward?" *Barron's* (December 11, 1989): 13, 43–46.

Shapiro, Eben. "Heard on the Street: Chief Redstone Tries to Convince Wall Street There's Life Beyond Blockbuster at Viacom," *Wall Street Journal,* April 24, 1997, p. C2.

Shapiro, Eben. "Movies: Blockbuster Seeks a New Deal With Hollywood," *Wall Street Journal,* March 25, 1998, p. B1.

Shapiro, Eben. "Viacom Net Drops 70% as Cash Flow Slips on Weakness at Blockbuster Unit," *Wall Street Journal,* October 30, 1997, p. B8.

Shapiro, Eben. "Viacom Sets Major Charge Tied to Blockbuster," *Wall Street Journal,* July 23, 1998, p. A3.

Shapiro, Eben. "Viacom Trims Blockbuster's Expansion, Igniting Speculation of Eventual Spinoff," *Wall Street Journal,* March 28, 1997, p. B5.

Shapiro, Eben, and Nikhil Deogun, "Antioco Takes Top Job at Troubled Blockbuster," *Wall Street Journal,* June 4, 1997, p. A3.

Shapiro, Eben, and Susan Pulliam, "Heard on the Street: Viacom to Name Wal-Mart's Heir Apparent, William Fields, to Head Blockbuster Video," *Wall Street Journal,* March 29, 1996, p. C2.

Sweeting, Paul. "Big Blue Trimming Tapes," *Video Business* (September 17, 2001): 1.

Tarr, Greg. "DirecTV Teams with Blockbuster," *Twice* (May 15, 2000): 1.

Tedesco, Richard. "MGM, Blockbuster to Stream TV, Films," *Broadcasting & Cable* (January 24, 2000): 128.

"TiVo, Blockbuster Ink Cross-Promo Deal," *Twice* (January 17, 2000): 24.

"Video Stocks Stumbled," *Video Business* (September 3, 2001): 4.

Villa, Joan. "Blockbuster Game Exclusive," *Video Store* (January 20–January 26, 2002): 1, 40.

Warren, Audrey, and Martin Peers, "Video Retailers Have Day in Court—Plaintiffs Say Supply Deals Between Blockbuster Inc. and Studios Violate Laws," *Wall Street Journal,* June 13, 2002, p. B10.

Whole Foods Market: Will There Be Enough Organic Food to Satisfy the Growing Demand?

This case was prepared by Patricia Harasta and Alan N. Hoffman, Bentley College.

Reflecting back over his three decades of experience in the grocery business, John Mackey smiled to himself over his previous successes. His entrepreneurial history began with a single store, which he has now grown to the nation's leading natural food chain. While proud of the past, John had concerns about the future direction in which the Whole Foods Market® chain should head. Whole Foods Market was an early entrant into the organic food market, and it has used its early-mover advantage to solidify its position and continue its steady growth.

With the changing economy and a more competitive industry landscape, John Mackey is uncertain about how to meet the company's aggressive growth targets. Whole Foods Market's objective is to reach $10 billion in revenue with 300+ stores by 2010 without sacrificing quality and its current reputation. This is not an easy task, and John is unsure of the best way to proceed.

Company Background

Whole Foods carries both natural and organic food, offering customers a wide variety of products. "Natural" refers to food that is free of growth hormones or antibiotics, whereas "certified organic" food conforms to the standards defined by the U.S. Department of Agriculture in October 2002.[1] Whole Foods Market is the world's leading retailer of natural and organic foods, with 172 stores in North America and the United Kingdom. John Mackey, current president and cofounder of Whole Foods, opened the Safer Way natural grocery store in 1978. The store had limited success, as it was a small location allowing only for a limited selection, focusing entirely on vegetarian foods.[2] John joined forces with Craig Weller and Mark Skiles, founders of Clarksville Natural Grocery (founded in 1979), to create Whole Foods Market.[3] This joint venture took place in Austin, Texas, in 1980, resulting in a new company, a single natural food market with a staff of nineteen.

In addition to the supermarkets, Whole Foods owns and operates several subsidiaries. Allegro Coffee Company, formed in 1977 and purchased by Whole Foods Market in 1997, now acts as its coffee roasting and distribution center. Pigeon Cove, which was founded in 1985 in Gloucester, Massachusetts, and known as M & S Seafood until 1990, is Whole Foods' seafood-processing facility. Whole Foods purchased Pigeon Cove in 1996. The company is now the only supermarket to own and operate a waterfront seafood facility.[4] The last two subsidiaries are Produce Field Inspection Office and Select Fish, which is Whole Foods' West Coast seafood-processing facility, acquired in 2003.[5] In addition to the above, the company has eight distribution centers, seven regional bake houses, and four commissaries.[6] According to the company's website,

> Whole Foods Market remains uniquely mission driven: The company is highly selective about what they sell, dedicated to stringent quality standards, and committed to sustainable agriculture. They believe in a virtuous circle entwining the food chain, human beings and Mother Earth: each is reliant upon the others through a beautiful and delicate symbiosis.[7]

The messages of preservation and sustainability are followed, while providing high-quality goods to customers and high profits to investors.

Whole Foods has grown over the years through mergers, acquisitions, and several new store openings.[8] Today, Whole Foods Market is the largest natural food supermarket in the United States.[9] The company consists of 32,000 employees operating 172 stores in the United States, Canada, and United Kingdom, with an average store size of 32,000 square feet.[10] While the majority of Whole Foods locations are in the United States, the company has made acquisitions expanding its presence in the UK. European expansion provides enormous potential growth due to the large population, and it represents "a more sophisticated organic-foods market than the U.S. in terms of suppliers and acceptance by the public."[11] Whole Foods targets its locations specifically by an area's demographics. The company targets locations where 40% or more of the residents have a college degree, as they are more likely to be aware of nutritional issues.[12]

Whole Foods Market's Philosophy

Its corporate website defines the company philosophy as follows:

> Whole Foods Market's vision of a sustainable future means our children and grandchildren will be living in a world that values human creativity, diversity, and individual choice. Businesses will harness human and material resources without devaluing the integrity of the individual or the planet's ecosystems. Companies, governments, and institutions will be held accountable for their actions. People will better understand that all actions have repercussions and that planning and foresight coupled with hard work and flexibility can overcome almost any problem encountered. It will be a world that values education and a free exchange of ideas by an informed citizenry; where people are encouraged to discover, nurture, and share their life's passions.[13]

While Whole Foods recognizes it is only a supermarket, it is working toward fulfilling its vision within the context of its industry. In addition to leading by example, it strives to conduct business in a manner consistent with its mission and vision. By offering minimally processed, high-quality food, engaging in ethical business practices, and providing a motivational, respectful work environment, the company believes it is on the path to a sustainable future.[14]

Whole Foods incorporates the best practices of each location back into the chain.[15] This can be seen in the company's store product expansion from dry goods to perishable produce, including meats, fish, and prepared foods. The lessons learned at one location are absorbed by all, enabling the chain to maximize effectiveness and efficiency while offering a product line customers love. Whole Foods carries only natural and organic products. The best tasting and most nutritious food available is found in its purest state—unadulterated by artificial additives, sweeteners, colorings, and preservatives.[16]

Whole Foods continually improves customer offerings, catering to its specific locations. Unlike business models for traditional grocery stores, Whole Foods products differ by geographic regions and local farm specialties.

Employee and Customer Relations

Whole Foods encourages a team-based environment, allowing each store to make independent decisions regarding its operations. Teams consist of up to eleven employees and a team leader. The team leaders typically head up one department or another. Each store employs anywhere from 72 to 391 team members.[17] The manager is referred to as the "store team leader." The "store team leader" is compensated by an Economic Value Added (EVA) bonus and is also eligible to receive stock options.[18]

Whole Foods tries to instill a sense of purpose among its employees and has been named one of the "100 Best Companies to Work For in America" by *Fortune* magazine for the past six years. In employee surveys, 90% of its team members stated that they always or frequently enjoy their job.[19]

The company strives to take care of its customers, realizing they are the "lifeblood of our business" and the two are "interdependent on each other."[20] Whole Foods' primary objective goes beyond 100% customer satisfaction with the goal to "delight" customers in every interaction.

Competitive Environment

American shoppers spent nearly $45.8 billion on natural and organic products in 2004, according to research published in the "24th Annual Market Overview" in the June issue of *The Natural Foods Merchandiser*. In 2004, natural products sales increased 6.9% across all sales channels, including supermarkets, mass marketers, direct marketers, and the Internet. Sales of organic products rose 14.6% in natural products stores. As interest in low-carb diets waned, sales of organic baked goods rose 35%. Other fast-growing organic categories included meat, poultry, and seafood, up 120%; coffee and cocoa, up 64%; and cookies, up 63%.

At the time of Whole Foods' inception, there was almost no competition, with fewer than six other natural food stores in the United States. Today, the organic foods industry is growing, and Whole Foods finds itself competing hard to maintain its elite presence. As the population has become increasingly concerned about their eating habits, natural foods stores, such as Whole Foods, are flourishing. Other successful natural foods grocery chains today include Trader Joe's Co. and Wild Oats Market[21] (see Exhibit 1).

Trader Joe's, originally known as Pronto Markets, was founded in 1958 in Los Angeles by Joe Coulombe. By expanding its presence and product offerings while maintaining high quality at low prices, the company has found its competitive niche.[22] The company has 215 stores, primarily on the west and east coasts of the United States. The company "offers upscale grocery fare such as health foods, prepared meals, organic produce and nutritional supplements."[23] A low cost structure allows Trader Joe's to offer competitive prices while still maintaining its margins. Trader Joe's stores have no service department and average just 10,000 square feet in store size. A privately held company, Trader Joe's enjoyed sales of $2.5 million in 2003, a 13.6% increase from 2002.[24]

Wild Oats was founded in 1987, in Boulder, Colorado. Its founders had no experience in the natural foods market, relying heavily on their employees to learn the industry. Acknowledging the increased competition within the industry, Wild Oats is committed to strengthening and streamlining its opera-

Sales

	Sales (in millions)						
Company	2000	2001	% Growth	2002	% Growth	2003	% Growth
Whole Foods Market[a]	$1,838.60	$2,272.20	23.60%	$2,690.50	18.40%	$3,148.60	17.00%
Trader Joe's Company[b]	$1,670.00	$1,900.00	13.80%	$2,200.00	15.80%	$2,500.00	13.60%
Wild Oats Market[c]	$838.10	$893.20	6.60%	$919.10	2.90%	$969.20	5.50%

[a] Hoovers Online, http://www.hoovers.com/whole-foods/--ID_10952--/free-co-factsheet.xhtml, December 1, 2004.

[b] Hoovers Online, http://www.hoovers.com/trader-joe's-co/--ID-47619--/free-co-factsheet.xhtml, December 1, 2004.

[c] Hoovers Online, http://www.hoovers.com/wild-oats-markets/--ID_41717--/free-co-factsheet.xhtml, December 1, 2004.

tions in an effort to continue to build the company.[25] Its product offerings range from organic foods to traditional grocery merchandise. Wild Oats, a publicly owned company on NASDAQ, is traded under the ticker symbol of OATS and "is the third largest natural foods supermarket chain in the United States in terms of sales." Although it falls behind Whole Foods and Trader Joe's, the company enjoyed $1,048,164 in sales in 2004, a 7.5% increase over 2003. Wild Oats operates 100 full-service stores in twenty-four states and Canada.[26]

Additional competition has arisen from grocery stores such as Stop & Shop and Shaw's, which now incorporate natural foods sections in their conventional stores, placing them in direct competition with Whole Foods. Because larger grocery chains have more flexibility in their product offerings, they are more likely to promote products through sales, a strategy Whole Foods rarely practices.

Despite being in a highly competitive industry, Whole Foods maintains its reputation as "the world's #1 natural foods chain."[27] As the demand for natural and organic food continues to grow, pressures on suppliers will rise. Only 3% of U.S. farmland is organic, so there is limited output.[28] The increased demand for these products may further elevate prices or result in goods being out of stock, with possible price wars looming.

The Changing Grocery Industry

Before the emergence of the supermarket, the public was largely dependent upon specialty shops or street vendors for dairy products, meats, produce, and other household items. In the 1920s, chain stores began to threaten independent retailers by offering convenience and lower prices by procuring larger quantities of products. David Appel explains that the emergence of the supermarkets in the 1930s was a result of three major changes in society:

1. The shift in population from rural to urban areas

2. An increase in disposable income

3. Increased mobility through ownership of automobiles.[29]

Perhaps the earliest example of the supermarket as we know it today is King Kullen, "America's first supermarket," which was founded by Michael Cullen in 1930. "The essential key to his plan was volume, and he attained this through heavy advertising of low prices on nationally advertised merchandise." As the success of Cullen's strategy became evident, others such as Safeway, A&P, and Kroger adopted it as well. By the time the United States entered World War II, 9,000 supermarkets accounted for 25% of industry sales.[30]

Low prices and convenience continue to be the dominant factors driving consumers to supermarkets today. The industry is characterized by low margins and continuous downward pressure on prices, made evident by coupons, weekly specials, and rewards cards. Over the years, firms have introduced subtle changes to the business model by providing additional conveniences, such as the inclusion of bakeries, banks, pharmacies, and even coffeehouses co-located within the supermarket. Throughout their existence, supermarkets have also tried to cater to the changing tastes and preferences of society such as healthier diets, the Atkins diet, and low-carbohydrate foods. The moderate changes to strategy within supermarkets have been imitated by competitors, which are returning the industry to a state of price competition. Supermarkets themselves now face additional competition from wholesalers such as Costco, BJ's, and Sam's Club.

A Different Shopping Experience

The setup of the organic grocery store is a key component of Whole Foods' success. The store's setup and its products are carefully researched to ensure that they are meeting the demands of the local community. Locations are primarily in cities and are chosen for their large space and heavy foot traffic. According to Whole Foods' 10-K, "approximately 88% of our existing stores are located in the top 50 statistical metropolitan areas."[31] The company uses a specific formula to choose its store sites that is based upon several metrics, which include but are not limited to income levels, education, and population density.

Upon entering a Whole Foods supermarket, it becomes clear that the company is attempting to sell the consumer on the entire experience. Team members (employees) are well trained, and the stores themselves are immaculate. There are in-store chefs to help with recipes, wine tasting, and food sampling. There are "Take Action food centers,"[32] where customers can access information on the issues that affect their food such as legislation and environmental factors. Some stores offer extra services such as home delivery, cooking classes, massages, and valet parking.[33] Whole Foods goes out of its way to appeal to the above-average income earner.

Whole Foods uses price as a marketing tool in a few select areas, as demonstrated by the 365 Whole Foods brand name products, priced less than similar organic products that are carried within the store. However, the company does not use price to differentiate itself from competitors.[34] Rather, Whole Foods focuses on quality and service as a means of standing out from the competition.

Whole Foods spent only 0.5% of its total sales from the fiscal year 2004 on advertising; it relies on other means to promote its stores.[35] The company relies heavily on word-of-mouth advertising from its customers to help market itself in the local community. It is also promoted in several health-conscious magazines, and each store budgets for in-store advertising each fiscal year.

Whole Foods also gains recognition via its charitable contributions and the awareness that it brings to the treatment of animals. The company donates 5% of its after-tax profits to charities.[35] The company is also very active in establishing systems to make sure that the animals used in its products are treated humanely.

The Aging Baby Boomers

The aging of the Baby Boomer generation will expand the senior demographic over the next decade, as their children grow up and leave the nest. Urban singles are another group who have extra disposable income due to their lack of dependents. These two groups present an opportunity for growth for Whole Foods. Americans spent 7.2% of their total expenditures on food in 2001, making it the seventh highest category on which consumers spend their money.[36] Additionally, U.S. households with income of more than $100,000 per annum represent 22% of aggregate income today, compared with 18% a decade ago.[37]

This shift in demographics has created an expansion in the luxury-store group, while slowing growth in the discount retail market.[38] To that end, there is a gap in supermarket retailing between consumers who can only afford to shop at low-cost providers, like Wal-Mart, and the population of consumers who prefer gourmet food and are willing to pay a premium for perceived higher quality.[39] "'The Baby Boomers are driving demand for organic food in general because they're health-conscious and can afford to pay higher prices,' says Professor Steven G. Sapp, a sociologist at Iowa State University who studies consumer food behavior."[40]

The perception that imported, delicatessen, exotic, and organic foods are of higher quality, and therefore command higher prices, continues to bode well for Whole Foods Market. As John Mackey explains, "We're changing the [grocery-shopping] experience so that people enjoy it. . . . It's a richer, [more fun], more enjoyable experience. People don't shop our stores because we have low prices."[41] The consumer focus on a healthy diet is not limited to food. More new diet plans emerged in America in the last half of the twentieth century than in any other country. This trend has also increased the demand for nutritional supplements and vitamins.[42]

In recent years, consumers have made a gradual move toward the use of fresher, healthier foods in their everyday diets. Consumption of fresh fruits and vegetables, pasta, and other grain-based products has increased.[43] This is evidenced by the aggressive expansion by consumer products companies into healthy food and natural and organic products.[44] "Natural and organic products have crossed the chasm to mainstream America."[45] The growing market can be attributed to the acceptance and widespread expansion of organic product offerings, beyond milk and dairy.[46] Mainstream acceptance of the Whole Foods offering can be attributed to this shift in consumer food preferences as consumers continue to cite taste as the number one motivator for purchasing organic foods.[47]

With a growing percentage of women working out of the home, the traditional role of home-cooked meals, prepared from scratch, has waned. As fewer women have the time to devote to cooking, consumers are giving way to the trend of convenience through prepared foods. Sales of ready-to-eat meals have grown significantly. "The result is that grocers are starting to specialize in quasi-restaurant food."[48] Just as women entering the work force has propelled the sale of prepared foods, it has also increased consumer awareness of the need for the one-stop shopping experience. Hypermarkets such as Wal-Mart, which offer nonfood items and more mainstream product lines, allow consumers to conduct more shopping in one place rather than moving from store to store.

The growth in sales of natural foods is expected to continue at the rate of 8 to 10% annually, according to the National Nutritional Foods Association. The sale of organic food has largely outpaced that of traditional grocery products due to consumer perception that organic food is healthier.[49] The purchase of organic food is perceived to be beneficial to consumer health by 61% of consumers, according to a Food Marketing Institute (FMI)/*Prevention* magazine study. Americans believe organic food can help improve fitness and increase longevity.[50] Much of this perception has grown out of fear of how nonorganic foods are treated with pesticides for growth and then preserved for sale. Therefore, an opportunity exists for Whole Foods to contribute to consumer awareness by funding nonprofit organizations that focus on educating the public on the benefits of organic lifestyles.

Operations

Whole Foods purchases most of its products from regional and national suppliers. This allows the company to leverage its size in order to receive deep discounts and favorable terms with its vendors. The company still permits stores to purchase from local producers to keep the stores aligned with local food trends and seen as supporting the community. The company owns two procurement centers and handles the majority of procurement and distribution itself. Whole Foods also owns several regional bake houses, which distribute products to its stores. The largest independent vendor is United Natural Foods, which accounted for 20% of Whole Foods total purchases for fiscal year 2004.[51] Product categories at Whole Foods include, but are not limited to,

- Produce
- Seafood
- Grocery
- Meat and Poultry
- Bakery
- Prepared Foods and Catering
- Specialty (beer, wine, and cheese)
- Whole body (nutritional supplements, vitamins, body care and educational products such as books)
- Floral
- Pet Products
- Household Products[52]

While Whole Foods carries all the items that one would expect to find in a grocery store (and plenty that one would not), its "heavy emphasis on perishable foods is designed to appeal to both natural foods and gourmet shoppers."[53] Perishable foods accounted for 67% of its retail sales in 2004 and are the core of Whole Foods' success.[54] This is demonstrated by its own statement that "We believe it is our strength of execution in perishables that has attracted many of our most loyal shoppers."[55]

Whole Foods also provides fully cooked frozen meal options through its private label Whole Kitchen, to satisfy the demands of working families. For example, the Whole Foods Market located in Woodland Hills, California, has redesigned its prepared foods section more than three times[56] in response to a 40% growth in prepared foods sales.[57]

Whole Foods doesn't take just any product and put it on its shelves. In order to make it into the Whole Foods grocery store, products have to undergo a strict test to determine if they are "Whole Foods material." The quality standards that all potential Whole Foods products must meet include

- Food that is free of preservatives and other additives
- Food that is fresh, wholesome, and safe to eat
- Standards that promote organically grown foods
- Food that supports health and well-being[58]

Meat and poultry products must adhere to a higher standard:

- No antibiotics or added growth hormones
- An affidavit from each producer that outlines the whole process of production and how the animals are treated
- An annual inspection of all producers by Whole Foods Market
- Successful completion of a third party audit to attest to these findings[59]

Also, due to the lack of available nutritional brands with a national identity, Whole Foods decided to enter into the private-label product business. It currently has three private-label products and a fourth program called Authentic Food Artisan, which promotes distinctive products that are certified organic. The three private-label products are 365 Everyday Value, a well-recognized and trusted brand that meets the standards of Whole Foods and is less expensive than the regular product lines; Whole Kids Organic, healthy items that are directed at children; and 365 Organic Everyday Value, all the benefits of organic food at reduced prices.[60]

When opening a new store, Whole Foods stocks it with almost $700,000 worth of initial inventory, which its vendors partially finance.[61] Like most conventional grocery stores, Whole Foods turns over the majority of its inventory fairly quickly; this is especially true of produce. Fresh organic produce is central to Whole Foods' existence and turns over on a faster basis than other products.

Financial Operations

Whole Foods Market focuses on earning a profit while providing job security to its workforce to lay the foundation for future growth. The company is determined not to let profits deter the company from providing excellent service to its customers and a quality work environment for its staff. Its mission statement defines its recipe for financial success:

> Our motto—Whole Foods, Whole People, Whole Planet—emphasizes that our vision reaches far beyond just being a food retailer. Our success in fulfilling our vision is measured by customer satisfaction, Team Member excellence and happiness, return on capital investment, improvement in the state of the environment, and local and larger community support.[62]

Whole Foods also caps the salaries of its executives at no more than fourteen times the average annual salary of a Whole Foods worker; this includes wages and incentive bonuses as well. The company also donates 5% of its after-tax profits to nonprofit organizations.[63]

Over a five-year period from 2000 through 2004, the company experienced an 87% growth in sales, with sales reaching $3.86 billion in 2004. Annual sales increases during that period were equally dramatic: 24% in 2001, 18% in 2002, 17% in 2003, and 23% in 2004.[64] (See Exhibit 2.) This growth is perhaps more impressive given the relatively negative economic environment and recession in the United States.

Whole Foods' strategy of expansion and acquisition has fueled growth in net income since the company's inception. This is particularly evident when looking at the net income growth in 2002 (24.47%), 2003 (22.72%) and 2004 (27.94%).[65]

The ticker symbol for Whole Foods, Inc. is WFMI. A review of the performance history of Whole Foods stock since its IPO reveals a mostly upward trend. The ten-year price trend shows the company increasing from under $10 per share to a high of over $100 per share, reflecting an increase of over 1,000%.[66] For the past year, the stock has been somewhat volatile, but with a mostly upward trend. The current price of $136, with 65.3 million shares outstanding, gives the company a market valuation of $8.8 billion (Aug. 2005).[67]

The Code of Conduct

From its inception, the company has sought to be different from conventional grocery stores, with a

Exhibit 2

Whole Foods Annual Sales

Annual Income (values in 000's)				
Company	2001	2002	2003	2004
Sales	$2,272,231	$2,690,475	$3,148,593	$3,864,950
%	23.58%	18.04%	17.03%	22.75%
Net Income	$67,880	$84,491	$103,687	$132,657
%		24.47%	22.72%	27.94%
Increase from 2000–2004 = 87%				

heavy focus on ethics. Besides an emphasis on organic foods, the company has also established a contract of animal rights, which states that the company will do business only with companies that treat their animals humanely. While it realizes that animal products are vital to its business, it opposes animal cruelty.[68]

The company has a unique fourteen-page Code of Conduct document that addresses the expected and desired behavior for its employees. The code is broken down into the following four sections:

- Potential conflicts of interest
- Transactions or situations that should never occur
- Situations where you may need the authorization of the Ethics committee before proceeding
- Times when certain actions must be taken by executives of the company or team leaders of individual stores[69]

This Code of Conduct covers, in detail, the most likely scenarios a manager of a store might encounter. It includes several checklists that are to be filled out on a regular, or at least an annual, basis by team leaders and store managers. After completion, the checklists must be signed and submitted to corporate headquarters and copies retained on file in the store.[70] They ensure that the ethics of Whole Foods are being followed by everyone. The ethical efforts of Whole Foods don't go unrecognized; the company was ranked number 70 out of the "100 Best Corporate Citizens."[71]

Possible Scarce Resources: Prime Locations and the Supply of Organic Foods

Prime store locations and the supply of organic foods are potential scarce resources and could be problematic for Whole Foods Market in the future.

Whole Foods likes to establish a presence in highly affluent cities, where its target market resides. The majority of Whole Foods customers are well educated, thereby earning high salaries enabling them to afford the company's higher prices. Whole Foods is particular when deciding on new locations, as location is extremely important for top and bottom line growth. However, there are a limited number of communities where 40% of the residents have college degrees.

Organic food is another possible scarce resource. Organic crops yield a lower quantity of output and are rarer, accounting for only 3% of U.S. farmland usage.[72] Strict government requirements must be satisfied; these are incredibly time consuming, more effort intensive, and more costly to adhere to. With increased demand from mainstream supermarkets also carrying organics, the demand for such products could outreach the limited supply. The market for organic foods grew from $2.9 billion in 2001 to $5.3 billion in 2004, an 80.5% increase in the three-year period.[73]

Whole Foods recognizes that the increased demand for organic foods may adversely affect its earnings and so informs its investors:

Changes in the availability of quality natural and organic products could impact our business. There is no assurance that quality natural and organic products will be available to meet our future needs. If conventional supermarkets increase their natural and organic product offerings or if new laws require the reformulation of certain products to meet tougher standards, the supply of these products may be constrained. Any significant disruption in the supply of quality natural and organic products could have a material impact on our overall sales and cost of goods.[74]

ENDNOTES

1. http://www.organicconsumers.org/organic/most071904.cfm.
2. Julia Boorstin, "No Preservatives, No Unions, Lots of Dough," *Fortune* 148:5 (September 15, 2003): 127.
3. http://www.wholefoods.com/company/timeline.html, November 4, 2004.
4. Boorstin, "No Preservatives, No Unions, Lots of Dough."
5. http://www.wholefoods.com/company/facts.html, November 5, 2004.
6. http://www.wholefoods.com/issues/org_commentsstandards0498.html, November 5, 2004.
7. http://www.wholefoods.com/company/index.html, November 5, 2004.
8. http://www.wholefoods.com/company/history.html, November 5, 2004.
9. "The Natural: Whole Foods Founder John Mackey Builds an Empire on Organic Eating," *Time* (2002).
10. http://www.wholefoods.com/company/facts.html, November 11, 2004.
11. Robert Elder, Jr., "Whole Foods Buying Chain of Stores Based in London: $38 Million Deal Marks U.S. Health-Food Retailer's Initial Thrust into Overseas Market," January 17, 2004.
12. Jeanne Lang Jones, "Whole Foods Is Bagging Locations," *Puget Sound Business Journal* 25:15 (August 13, 2004): 1.
13. http://www.wholefoodsmarket.com/company/sustainablefuture.html, November 5, 2004.

14. http://www.wholefoodsmarket.com/company/sustainablefuture .html, November 5, 2004.

15. Boorstin, "No Preservatives, No Unions, Lots of Dough."

16. http://www.wholefoodsmarket.com/products/index.html, July 25, 2005.

17. Whole Foods 10K-Q, 2003, p. 7, http://www.wholefoodsmarket.com/ investor/10K-Q/2003_10K.pdf, November 11, 2004.

18. Whole Foods10K-Q, 2003, p. 7.

19. Whole Foods 10K-Q, 2004, p. 10, http://www.wholefoodsmarket .com/investor/10K-Q/2004_10KA.pdf, August 15, 2005.

20. http://www.wholefoodsmarket.com/company/declaration.html, July 29, 2005.

21. http://www.hoovers.com/whole-foods/--ID_10952--/free-co- factsheet.xhtml, November 8, 2004.

22. www.traderjoes.com, November 8, 2004.

23. http://www.hoovers.com/trader-joe's-co/--ID-47619--/free-co- factsheet.xht, November 8, 2004.

24. http://www.hoovers.com/trader-joe's-co/--ID-47619--/free-co- factsheet.xht, November 8, 2004.

25. www.wildoats.com, November 8, 2004.

26. http://www.hoovers.com/wild-oats-markets/--ID_41717--/free- co-factsheet.xhtml, November 8, 2004.

27. http://www.hoovers.com/whole-foods/--ID_10952--/free-co- factsheet.xhtml, November 8, 2004.

28. Paul Grimaldi, "Providence, RI, Grocery Targets New Approach to Pricing," *Knight-Ridder Tribune Business News,* September 28, 2004, p. 1.

29. David Appel, "The Supermarket: Early Development of an Insti- tutional Innovation," *Journal of Retailing* 48:1 (Spring 1972): 40.

30. Appel, "The Supermarket."

31. Whole Foods 10K-Q, 2003, p. 8,

32. Whole Foods 10K-Q, 2003, p. 8.

33. Whole Foods 10K-Q, 2003, p. 8.

34. Whole Foods 10K-Q, 2003, p. 10.

35. Whole Foods 10K-Q, 2004, p. 10.

36. Whole Foods 10K-Q, 2003, p. 9.

37. Euromonitor, "Consumer Lifestyles in the United States: 12.2 Expenditure on Food," May 2003, accessed November 1, 2004.

38. John Gapper, "Organic Food Stores Are on a Natural High," *The Financial Times,* September 2004.

39. Gapper, "Organic Food Stores Are on a Natural High."

40. Gapper, "Organic Food Stores Are on a Natural High."

41. Richard Murphy McGill, "Truth or Scare," *American Demograph- ics* 26:2 (March 2004): 26.

42. Bob Sechler, "Whole Foods Picks Up the Pace of Its Expansion," *Wall Street Journal,* September 29, 2004, p. 1.

43. Euromonitor, "Consumer Lifestyles in the United States: 12.7 What Americans Eat," May 2003, accessed November 1, 2004.

44. Euromonitor, "Consumer Lifestyles in the United States: 12.4 Popular Foods," May 2003, accessed November 1, 2004.

45. "Profile in B2B Strategy: Supermarket News Sidles into Natural, Organic Trend with New Quarterly," *Business CustomerWire,* Re- gional Business News (October 25, 2004).

46. "Profile in B2B Strategy."

47. Euromonitor, "The World Market for Dairy Products: 4.5 Or- ganic Foods; 4.5.1 Global Market Trends in Organic Foods," Jan- uary 2004, accessed November 1, 2004.

48. Euromonitor, "The World Market for Dairy Products."

49. "Supermarkets' Prepared Meals Save Families Time," *Knight- Ridder Tribune Business News,* September 13, 2004.

50. Euromonitor, "Packaged Food in the United States: 3.4 Organic Food," January 2004, accessed November 1, 2004.

51. Euromonitor, "Packaged Food in the United States."

52. Whole Foods 10K-Q, 2004, p. 10.

53. Whole Foods 10K-Q, 2003, p. 6.

54. Whole Foods 10K-Q, 2003, p. 5.

55. Whole Foods 10K-Q, 2004, p. 14.

56. Whole Foods 10K-Q, 2003, p. 6.

57. "Supermarkets' Prepared Meals Save Families Time."

58. "Supermarkets' Prepared Meals Save Families Time."

59. Whole Foods 10K-Q, 2003, p. 5.

60. Whole Foods 10K-Q, 2003, p. 6.

61. Whole Foods 10K-Q, 2003, p. 7.

62. Whole Foods 10K-Q, 2003, p. 8.

63. http://www.WholeFoodsmarket.com/company/declaration.html, November 7, 2004.

64. http://www.WholeFoodsmarket.com/company/declaration.html.

65. Whole Foods 10K-Q, 2003.

66. Whole Foods 10K-Q, 2003.

67. http://quotes.nasdaq.com/quote.dll?page=charting&mode= basics&intraday=off&timeframe=10y&charttype=ohlc&splits= off&earnings=off&movingaverage=None&lowerstudy= volume&comparison=off&index=&drilldown=off&symbol= WFMI&selected=WFM, November 11, 2004.

68. http://quotes.nasdaq.comQuote.dll?mode=stock&symbol= wfmi&symbol=&symbol=&symbol=&symbol=&symbol= &symbol=&symbol=&symbol=&symbol=&multi.x= 31&multi.y=6, November 11, 2004.

69. Whole Foods 10K-Q, 2003, p. 6.

70. Whole Foods Code of Conduct, http://www.wholefoodsmarket .com/investor/codeofconduct.pdf, November 11, 2004.

71. Whole Foods Code of Conduct, p. 11.

72. "Business Ethics 100 Best Companies to Work For," http://www .business-ethics.com/100best.htm, November 12, 2004.

73. Grimaldi, "Providence, RI, Grocery Targets New Approach to Pricing."

74. http://www.preparedfoods.com/PF/FILES/HTML/Mintel_ Reports/Mintel_PDF/Summaries/sum-OrganicFoodBeverages- Aug2004.pdf.

75. Whole Foods 10K–Q, 2004, p. 14.

Case 6

3M in 2006

This case was prepared by Charles W. L. Hill, the University of Washington.

Established in 1902, by 2006 3M was one of the largest technology-driven enterprises in the United States with annual sales of $23 billion, 61% of which were outside the United States. Throughout its history, 3M's researchers had driven much of the company's growth. In 2006, the company sold some 50,000 products, including Post-it Notes, Flex Circuits, Scotch tape, abrasives, specialty chemicals, Thinsulate insulation products, Nexcare bandages, optical films, fiber-optic connectors, drug delivery systems, and much more. Around 6,500 of the company's 69,000 employees were technical employees. 3M's annual R&D budget exceeded $1.25 billion. The company had garnered over 7,000 patents since 1990, with 487 new patents awarded in 2005 alone. 3M was organized into thirty-five different business units in a wide range of sectors, including consumer and office products; display and graphics; electronics and telecommunications; health care; industrial; safety, security, and protection services; and transportation (see Exhibit 1 for more details).

The company's 100-year anniversary was a time for celebration, but also one for strategic reflection. During the prior decade, 3M had grown profits and sales by between 6 and 7% per annum, a respectable figure but one that lagged behind the growth rates achieved by some other technology-based enterprises and diversified industrial enterprises like General Electric. In 2001, 3M took a step away from its

past when the company hired the first outsider to become CEO, James McNerney Jr. McNerney, who joined 3M after heading up GE's fast-growing medical equipment business (and losing out in the race to replace legendary GE CEO Jack Welch), was quick to signal that he wanted 3M to accelerate its growth rate. McNerney set an ambitious target for 3M—to grow sales by 11% per annum and profits by 12% per annum. Many wondered if McNerney could achieve this without damaging the innovation engine that had propelled 3M to its current stature. The question remained unanswered, as McNerney left to run the Boeing Co. in 2005. His successor, George Buckley, however, seemed committed to continuing on the course McNerney had set for the company.

The History of 3M: Building Innovative Capabilities

The story of 3M goes back to 1902, when five Minnesota businessmen established the Minnesota Mining and Manufacturing Co. to mine a mineral that they thought was corundum, which is ideal for making sandpaper. The mineral, however, turned out to be low-grade anorthosite, nowhere near as suitable for making sandpaper, and the company nearly failed. To try to salvage the business, 3M turned to making the sandpaper itself, using materials purchased from another source.

In 1907, 3M hired a twenty-year-old business student, William McKnight, as assistant bookkeeper. This turned out to be a pivotal move in the history of the company. The hardworking McKnight soon made his mark. By 1929, he was CEO of the company, and in 1949, he became chairman of 3M's board of directors, a position that he held until 1966.

Exhibit 1

3M Financial Facts—Year-End 2005[a]

Sales		
Worldwide	$21.167 billion	
International	$12.900 billion	
	61% of company's total	

Organization

- More than 35 business units, organized into 6 businesses: Consumer and Office; Display and Graphics; Electro and Communications; Health Care; Industrial and Transportation; Safety, Security and Protection Services
- Operations in more than 60 countries—29 international companies with manufacturing operations, 35 with laboratories
- In the United States, operations in 22 states

Net Income

Net income	$3.199 billion
Percent to sales	15.1%
Earnings per share—diluted	$4.12

Taxes

Income tax expense	$1.694 billion

Dividends (paid every quarter since 1916)

Cash dividends per share	$1.68
One original share, if held, is now . . .	3,072 shares

Contributions

Cash and gifts-in-kind (3M and 3M Foundation)	Nearly $39 million

R&D and Related Expenditures

For 2005	$1.242 billion
Total for last five years	$5.814 billion

Patents

U.S. patents awarded	487

Capital Spending

For 2005	$943 million
Total for last five years	$4.3 billion

Employees

Worldwide	69,315
United States	33,033
International	36,282

3M Values

- Provide investors an attractive return through sustained, quality growth.
- Satisfy customers with superior quality, value, and service.
- Respect our social and physical environment.
- Be a company employees are proud to be part of.

[a] 3M is one of thirty companies in the Dow Jones Industrial Average and also is a component of the Standard & Poor's 500 Index.

Source: 3M website, http://www.3m.com. Reprinted by permission.

From Sandpaper to Post-it Notes

It was McKnight, then 3M's president, who hired the company's first scientist, Richard Carlton, in 1921. Around the same time, McKnight's interest had been piqued by an odd request from a Philadelphian printer by the name of Francis Okie for samples of every sandpaper grit size that 3M made. McKnight dispatched 3M's East Coast sales manager to find out what Okie was up to. The sales manager discovered that Okie had invented a new kind of sandpaper that he had patented. It was waterproof sandpaper that could be used with water or oil to reduce dust and decrease the friction that marred auto finishes. In addition, the lack of dust reduced the poisoning associated with inhaling the dust of paint that had a high lead content. Okie had a problem, though; he had no financial backers to commercialize the sand-

paper. 3M quickly stepped into the breach, purchasing the rights to Okie's Wetordry waterproof sandpaper and hiring the young printer to come and join Richard Carlton in 3M's lab. Wet and dry sandpaper went on to revolutionize the sandpaper industry and was the driver of significant growth at 3M.

Another key player in the company's history, Richard Drew, also joined 3M in 1921. Hired straight out of the University of Minnesota, Drew would round out the trio of scientists, Carlton, Okie, and Drew, who under McKnight's leadership would do much to shape 3M's innovative organization.

McKnight charged the newly hired Drew with developing a stronger adhesive to better bind the grit for sandpaper to paper backing. While experimenting with adhesives, Drew accidentally developed a weak adhesive that had an interesting quality—if placed on the back of a strip of paper and stuck to a surface, the strip of paper could be peeled off the surface it was adhered to without leaving any adhesive residue on that surface. This discovery gave Drew an epiphany. He had been visiting auto-body paint shops to see how 3M's wet and dry sandpaper was used, and he noticed that there was a problem with paint running. His epiphany was to cover the back of a strip of paper with his weak adhesive and use it as "masking tape" to cover parts of the auto body that were not to be painted. An excited Drew took his idea to McKnight and explained how masking tape might create an entirely new business for 3M. McKnight reminded Drew that he had been hired to fix a specific problem and pointedly suggested that he concentrate on doing just that.

Chastised, Drew went back to his lab, but he could not get the idea out of his mind, so he continued to work on it at night, long after everyone else had gone home. Drew succeeded in perfecting the masking tape product and then went to visit several auto-body shops to show them his innovation. He quickly received several commitments for orders. Drew then went to see McKnight again. He told him that he had continued to work on the masking tape idea on his own time, had perfected the product, and now had several customers interested in purchasing it. This time it was McKnight's turn to be chastised. Realizing that he had almost killed a good business idea, McKnight reversed his original position and gave Drew the go-ahead to pursue the idea.[1]

Introduced into the market in 1925, Drew's invention of masking tape represented the first significant product diversification at 3M. Company legend has it that this incident was also the genesis for 3M's famous 15% rule. Reflecting on Drew's work, both McKnight and Carlton agreed that technical people could disagree with management and should be allowed to go and do some experimentation on their own. The company then established a norm that technical people could spend up to 15% of their own workweeks on projects that might benefit the consumer, without having to justify the project to their managers.

Drew himself was not finished. In the late 1920s, he was working with cellophane, a product that had been invented by Du Pont, when lightning struck for a second time. Why, Drew wondered, couldn't cellophane be coated with an adhesive and used as a sealing tape? The result was Scotch Cellophane Tape.

The first batch was delivered to a customer in September 1930, and Scotch Tape went on to become one of 3M's best-selling products. Years later, Drew noted, "Would there have been any masking or cellophane tape if it hadn't been for earlier 3M research on adhesive binders for 3M™ Wetordry™ Abrasive Paper? Probably not!"[2]

Over the years, other scientists followed in Drew's footsteps at 3M, creating a wide range of innovative products by leveraging existing technology and applying it to new areas. Two famous examples illustrate how many of these innovations occurred— the invention of Scotch Guard and the development of the ubiquitous Post-it Notes.

The genesis of Scotch Guard was in 1953, when a 3M scientist named Patsy Sherman was working on a new kind of rubber for jet aircraft fuel lines. Some of the latex mixture splashed onto a pair of canvas tennis shoes. Over time, the spot stayed clean while the rest of the canvas got soiled. Sherman enlisted the help of fellow chemist Sam Smith. Together they began to investigate polymers, and it didn't take long for them to realize that they were onto something. They discovered an oil- and water-repellent substance, based on the fluorocarbon fluid used in air conditioners, with enormous potential for protecting fabrics from stains. It took several years before the team perfected a means to apply the treatment using water as the carrier, thereby making it economically feasible for use as a finish in textile plants.

Three years after the accidental spill, the first rain and stain repellent for use on wool was announced. Experience and time revealed that one product could not, however, effectively protect all fabrics, so 3M continued working, producing a wide range of Scotch Guard products that could be used to protect all kinds of fabrics.[3]

The story of Post-it Notes began with Spencer Silver, a senior scientist studying adhesives.[4] In 1968, Silver had developed an adhesive with properties like no other; it was a pressure-sensitive adhesive that would adhere to a surface, but it was weak enough to easily peel off the surface and leave no residue. Silver spent several years shopping his adhesive around 3M, to no avail. It was a classic case of a technology in search of a product. Then one day in 1973, Art Fry, a new product development researcher who had attended one of Silver's seminars, was singing in his church choir. He was frustrated that his bookmarks kept falling out of his hymn book, when he had a Eureka moment. Fry realized that Silver's adhesive could be used to make a wonderfully reliable bookmark.

Fry went to work the next day and, using 15% time, started to develop the bookmark. When he started using samples to write notes to his boss, Fry suddenly realized that he had stumbled on a much bigger potential use for the product. Before the product could be commercialized, however, Fry had to solve a host of technical and manufacturing problems. With the support of his boss, Fry persisted, and after eighteen months, the product development effort moved from 15% time to a formal development effort funded by 3M's own seed capital.

The first Post-it Notes were test marketed in 1977 in four major cities, but customers were lukewarm at best. This did not gel with the experience within 3M, where people in Fry's division were using samples all the time to write messages to each other. Further research revealed that the test-marketing effort, which focused on ads and brochures, didn't resonate well with consumers, who didn't seem to value Post-it Notes until they had the actual product in their hands. In 1978, 3M tried again, this time descending on Boise, Idaho, and handing out samples. Follow-up research revealed that 90% of consumers who tried the product said they would buy it. Armed with this knowledge, 3M rolled out the national launch of Post-it Notes in 1980. The product went on to become a bestseller.

Institutionalizing Innovation

Early on, McKnight set an ambitious target for 3M—a 10% annual increase in sales and 25% profit target. He also indicated how he thought that should be achieved—with a commitment to plow 5% of sales back into R&D every year. The question, though, was how to ensure that 3M would continue to produce new products.

The answer was not apparent all at once, but rather evolved over the years from experience. A prime example was the 15% rule, which came out of McKnight's experience with Drew. In addition to the 15% rule and the continued commitment to push money back into R&D, a number of other mechanisms evolved at 3M to spur innovation.

Initially, research took place in the business units that made and sold products, but by the 1930s, 3M had already diversified into several different fields, thanks in large part to the efforts of Drew and others. McKnight and Carlton realized that there was a need for a central research function. In 1937, they established a central research laboratory that was charged with supplementing the work of product divisions and undertaking long-run basic research. From the outset, the researchers at the lab were multidisciplinary, with people from different scientific disciplines often working next to each other on research benches.

As the company continued to grow, it became clear that there was a need for some mechanism to knit together the company's increasingly diverse business operations. This led to the establishment of the 3M Technical Forum in 1951. The goal of the Technical Forum was to foster idea sharing, discussion, and problem solving among technical employees located in different divisions and the central research laboratory. The Technical Forum sponsored "problem-solving sessions" at which businesses would present their most recent technical nightmares in the hope that somebody might be able to suggest a solution—and that often was the case. The forum also established an annual event in which each division put up a booth to show off its latest technologies. Chapters were also created to focus on specific disciplines, such as polymer chemistry or coating processes.

During the 1970s, the Technical Forum cloned itself, establishing forums in Australia and England. By 2001, the forum had grown to 9,500 members in eight U.S. locations and nineteen other countries, becoming an international network of researchers who could share ideas, solve problems, and leverage technology.

According to Marlyee Paulson, who coordinated the Technical Forum from 1979 to 1992, the great virtue of the Technical Forum is to cross-pollinate ideas:

> 3M has lots of polymer chemists. They may be in tape; they may be medical or several other divisions. The forum pulls them across 3M to share what they know. It's a simple but amazingly effective way to bring like minds together.[5]

In 1999, 3M created another unit within the company, 3M Innovative Properties (3M IPC), to leverage technical know-how. 3M IPC is explicitly charged with protecting and leveraging 3M's intellectual property around the world. At 3M, there has been a long tradition that while divisions "own" their

Exhibit 2

Recent Examples of Leveraging Technology at 3M

Richard Miller, a corporate scientist in 3M Pharmaceuticals, began experimental development of an antiherpes medicinal cream in 1982. After several years of development, his research team found that the interferon-based materials they were working with could be applied to any skin-based virus. The innovative cream was applied topically and was more effective than other compounds on the market. They found that the cream was particularly effective to interfering with the growth mechanism of genital warts. Competitive materials on the market at the time were caustic and tended to be painful. Miller's team obtained FDA approval for its Aldara (imiquimod) line of topical patient-applied creams in 1997.

Miller then applied the same Aldara-based chemical mechanism to basal cell carcinomas and found that, here too, it was particularly effective to restricting the growth of the skin cancer. "The patient benefit is quite remarkable," says Miller. New results in efficacy have been presented for treating skin cancers. His team recently completed phase III clinical testing and expects to apply later this year for FDA approval for this disease preventative. This material is already FDA-approved for use in the treatment of genital warts. Doctors are free to use it to treat those patients with skin cancers.

Andrew Ouderkirk is a corporate scientist in 3M's Film & Light Management Technology Center. 3M has been working in light management materials applied to polymer-based films since the 1930s, according to Ouderkirk. Every decade since then, 3M has introduced some unique thin film structure for a specific customer application, from high-performance safety reflectors for street signs to polarized lighting products. And every decade, 3M's technology base has become more specialized and more sophisticated. Its technology has now reached the point where 3M can produce multiple-layer interference films to 100-nm thicknesses each and hold the tolerances on each layer to within ±3 nm. "Our laminated films are now starting to compete with vacuum-coated films in some applications," says Ouderkirk.

Rick Weiss is technical director of 3M's Microreplication Technology Center, one of 3M's twelve core technology centers. The basic microreplication technology was discovered in the early 1960s, when 3M researchers were developing the fresnel lenses for overhead projectors. 3M scientists have expanded on this technology to a wide variety of applications, including optical reflectors for solar collectors and adhesive coatings with air bleed ribs that allow large area films to be applied without having the characteristic "bubbles" appear. Weiss is currently working on development of dimensionally precise barrier ribs that can be applied to separate the individual "gas" cells on the new high-resolution large-screen commercial plasma displays. Other applications include fluid management, where capillary action can be used in biological testing systems to split a drop of blood into a large number of parts.

Source: Tim Studt, "3M—Where Innovation Rules," *R&D Magazine* 45 (April 2003): 20–24. Reprinted by permission.

products, the company as a whole "owns" the underlying technology, or intellectual property. One task of 3M IPC is to find ways in which 3M technology can be applied across business units to produce unique marketable products. Historically, the company has been remarkably successful at leveraging company technology to produce new product ideas (see Exhibit 2 for some recent examples).

Another key to institutionalizing innovation at 3M has been the principle of "patient money." The basic idea is that producing revolutionary new products requires substantial long-term investments, and often repeated failures, before a major payoff occurs. The principle can be traced back to 3M's early days. It took the company twelve years before its initial sandpaper business started to show a profit, a fact that drove home the importance of taking the long view. Throughout the company's history, similar examples can be found. Scotchlite reflective sheeting, now widely used on road signs, didn't show much profit for ten years. The same was true of fluorochemicals and duplicating products. Patient money doesn't mean substantial funding for long periods of time, however. Rather, it might imply that a small group of five researchers is supported for ten years while they work on a technology.

More generally, if a researcher creates a new technology or idea, he or she can begin working on it using 15% time. If the idea shows promise, the researcher may request seed capital from his or her business unit managers to develop it further. If that funding is denied, which can occur, the researcher is free to take the idea to any other 3M business unit. Unlike the case in many other companies, requests for seed capital do not require that researchers draft detailed business plans that are reviewed by top management. That comes later in the process. As one former senior technology manager noted:

> In the early stages of a new product or technology, it shouldn't be overly managed. If we start asking for business plans too early and insist on tight financial evaluations, we'll kill an idea or surely slow it down.[6]

Explaining the patient money philosophy, Ron Baukol, a former executive vice president of 3M's international operations and a manager who started as a researcher, noted:

> You just know that some things are going to be worth working on, and that requires technological patience. . . . [Y]ou don't put too much money into the investigation, but you keep one to five people working on it for twenty years if you have to. You do that because you know that, once you have cracked the code, it's going to be big.[7]

An internal review of 3M's innovation process in the early 1980s concluded that despite the liberal process for funding new product ideas, some promising ideas did not receive funding from business units or the central research budget. This led to the establishment in 1985 of Genesis Grants, which provide up to $100,000 in seed capital to fund projects that do not get funded through 3M's regular channels. About a dozen of these grants are given every year. One of the recipients of these grants, a project that focused on creating a multilayered reflective film, subsequently produced a breakthough reflective technology that may have applications in a wide range of businesses, from better reflective strips on road signs to computer displays and the reflective linings in light fixtures. Company estimates in 2002 suggested that the commercialization of this technology might ultimately generate $1 billion in sales for 3M.

Underlying the patient money philosophy is recognition that innovation is a very risky business. 3M has long acknowledged that failure is an accepted and essential part of the new product development process. As former 3M CEO Lew Lehr once noted:

> We estimate that 60% of our formal new product development programs never make it. When this happens, the important thing is to not punish the people involved.[8]

In an effort to reduce the probability of failure, in the 1960s, 3M started to establish a process for auditing the product development efforts ongoing in the company's business units. The idea has been to provide a peer review, or technical audit, of major development projects taking place in the company. A typical technical audit team is composed of ten to fifteen business and technical people, including technical directors and senior scientists from other divisions. The audit team looks at the strengths and weaknesses of a development program and its probability of success, from both a technical standpoint and a business standpoint. The team then makes nonbinding recommendations, but they are normally taken very seriously by the managers of a project. For example, if an audit team concludes that a project has enormous potential but is terribly underfunded, managers of the unit often increase the funding level. Of course, the converse can also happen, and in many instances the audit team can provide useful feedback and technical ideas that can help a development team to improve its project's chance of success.

By the 1990s, the continuing growth of 3M had produced a company that was simultaneously pursuing a vast array of new product ideas. This was a natural outcome of 3M's decentralized and bottom-up approach to innovation, but it was problematic in one crucial respect: The company's R&D resources were being spread too thinly over a wide range of opportunities, resulting in potentially major projects being underfunded. To try to channel R&D resources into projects that had blockbuster potential, in 1994 3M introduced what was known as the Pacing Plus Program.

The program asked businesses to select a small number of projects that would receive priority funding, but 3M's senior executives made the final decision on which projects were to be selected for the Pacing Plus Program. An earlier attempt to do this in 1990 had met with limited success because each sector in 3M submitted as many as two hundred programs. The Pacing Plus Program narrowed the list down to twenty-five key programs that by 1996 were receiving some 20% of 3M's entire R&D funds (by the early 2000s, the number of projects funded under the Pacing Plus Program had grown to sixty). The focus was on "leapfrog technologies," revolutionary ideas that might change the basis of competition and lead to entirely new technology platforms that might, in typical 3M fashion, spawn an entire range of new products.

To further foster a culture of entrepreneurial innovation and risk taking, over the years 3M established a number of reward and recognition programs to honor employees who make significant contributions to the company. These include the Carlton Society award, which honors employees for outstanding career scientific achievements, and the Circle of Technical Excellence and Innovation Award, which recognizes people who have made exceptional contributions to 3M's technical capabilities.

Another key component of 3M's innovative culture has been an emphasis on dual career tracks. Right from its early days, many of the key players in 3M's history, people like Richard Drew, chose to stay in research, turning down opportunities to go into the management side of the business. Over the years, this became formalized in a dual career path. Today, technical employees can choose to follow a technical career path or a management career path, with equal advancement opportunities. The idea is to let researchers develop their technical professional interests without being penalized financially for not going into management.

Although 3M's innovative culture emphasizes the role of technical employees in producing innovations, the company also has a strong tradition of emphasizing that new product ideas often come from watching customers at work. Richard Drew's original idea for masking tape, for example, came from watching workers use 3M wet and dry sandpaper in auto-body shops. As with much else at 3M, the tone was set by McKnight, who insisted that salespeople needed to "get behind the smokestacks" of 3M customers, going onto the factory floor, talking to workers, and finding out what their problems were. Over the years, this theme has become ingrained in 3M's culture, with salespeople often requesting time to watch customers work and then bringing their insights about customer problems back into their organization.

By the mid-1990s, McKnight's notion of getting behind the smokestacks had evolved into the idea that 3M could learn a tremendous amount from what were termed "lead users," who were customers working in very demanding conditions. Over the years, 3M had observed that in many cases customers themselves can be innovators, developing new products to solve problems that they face in their work settings. This is most likely to occur for customers working in very demanding conditions. To take advantage of this process, 3M has instituted a lead user process in the company in which cross-functional teams from a business unit observe how customers work in demanding situations.

For example, 3M has a $100 million business selling surgical drapes, which are drapes backed with adhesives that are used to cover parts of a body during surgery and help prevent infection. As an aid to new product development, 3M's surgical drapes business formed a cross-functional team that went to observe surgeons at work in very demanding situations—including on the battlefield, in hospitals in developing nations, and in vets' offices. The result was a new set of product ideas, including low-cost surgical drapes that were affordable in developing nations and devices for coating a patient's skin and surgical instruments with antimicrobial substances that would reduce the chance of infection during surgery.[9]

Driving the entire innovation machine at 3M has been a series of stretch goals set by top managers. The goals date back to 3M's early days and McKnight's ambitious growth targets. In 1977, the company established "Challenge 81," which called for 25% of sales to come from products that had been on the market for less than five years by 1981. By the 1990s, the goal had been raised to the requirement that 30% of sales should come from products that had been on the market less than four years.

The flip side of these goals was that, over the years, many products and businesses that had been 3M staples were phased out. More than twenty of the businesses that were 3M mainstays in 1980, for example, had been phased out by 2000. Analysts estimate that sales from mature products at 3M generally fall by 3 to 4% per annum. The company has a long history of inventing businesses, leading the market for long periods of time, and then shutting those businesses down or selling them off when they can no longer meet 3M's own demanding growth targets. Notable examples include the duplicating business, a business 3M invented with Thermo-Fax copiers (which were ultimately made obsolete by Xerox's patented technology), and the video and audio magnetic tape business. The former division was sold off in 1985, and the latter in 1995. In both cases, the company exited these areas because they had become low-growth commodity businesses that could not generate the kind of top-line growth that 3M was looking for.

Still, 3M was by no means invulnerable in the realm of innovation and on occasion squandered huge opportunities. A case in point was the document copying business. 3M invented this business in 1951, when it introduced the world's first commercially successful Thermo-Fax copier (which used specially coated 3M paper to copy original typed documents). 3M dominated the world copier business until 1970, when Xerox overtook the company with its revolutionary xerographic technology that used plain paper to make copies. 3M saw Xerox coming, but rather than try to develop its own plain paper copier, the company invested funds in trying to improve its (increasingly obsolete) copying technology. It wasn't until 1975 that 3M introduced its own plain paper copier, and by then it was too late. Ironically, 3M had turned down the chance to acquire Xerox's technology twenty years earlier, when the company's founders had approached 3M.

Building the Organization

McKnight, a strong believer in decentralization, organized the company into product divisions in 1948, making 3M one of the early adopters of this organizational form. Each division was set up as an individual profit center that had the power, autonomy, and resources to run independently. At the same time, certain functions remained centralized, including significant R&D, human resources, and finance.

McKnight wanted to keep the divisions small enough that people had a chance to be entrepreneurial and retained their focus on the customer. A key philosophy of McKnight's was "divide and grow." Put simply, when a division became too big, some of its embryonic businesses were spun off into a new division. Not only did this new division then typically attain higher growth rates, but the original division had to find new drivers of growth to make up for the contribution of the businesses that had gained independence. This drove the search for further innovations.

At 3M, the process of organic diversification by splitting divisions became known as "renewal." The examples of renewal within 3M are legion. A copying machine project for Thermo-Fax copiers grew to become the Office Products Division. When Magnetic Recording Materials was spun off from the Electrical Products division, it grew to become its own division and then in turn spawned a spate of divisions.

However, this organic process was not without its downside. By the early 1990s, some of 3M's key customers were frustrated that they had to do business with a large number of different 3M divisions. In some cases, there could be representatives from ten to twenty 3M divisions calling on the same customer. To cope with this problem, in 1992, 3M started to assign key account representatives to sell 3M products directly to major customers. These representatives typically worked across divisional lines. Implementing the strategy required many of 3M's general managers to give up some of their autonomy and power, but the solution seemed to work well, particularly for 3M's consumer and office divisions.

Underpinning the organization that McKnight put in place was his own management philosophy. As explained in a 1948 document, his basic management philosophy consisted of the following values:

> As our business grows, it becomes increasingly necessary to delegate responsibility and to encourage men and women to exercise their initiative. This requires considerable tolerance. Those men and women to whom we delegate authority and responsibility, if they are good people, are going to want to do their jobs in their own way.
>
> Mistakes will be made. But if a person is essentially right, the mistakes he or she makes are not as serious in the long run as the mistakes management will make if it undertakes to tell those in authority exactly how they must do their jobs.
>
> Management that is destructively critical when mistakes are made kills initiative. And it's essential that we have many people with initiative if we are to continue to grow.[10]

At just 3% per annum, the employee turnover rate at 3M has long been among the lowest in corporate America, a fact that is often attributed to the tolerant, empowering, and family-like corporate culture that McKnight helped to establish. Reinforcing this culture has been a progressive approach toward employee compensation and retention. In the depths of the Great Depression, 3M was able to avoid laying off employees while many other employers did because the company's innovation engine was able to keep building new businesses even through the worst of times.

In many ways, 3M was ahead of its time in management philosophy and human resource practices. The company introduced its first profit-sharing plan in 1916, and McKnight instituted a pension plan in 1930 and an employee stock purchase plan in 1950. McKnight himself was convinced that people would be much more likely to be loyal to a company if they had a stake in it. 3M also developed a policy of promoting from within and of giving its employees a plethora of career opportunities within the company.

Going International

The first steps abroad occurred in the 1920s. There were some limited sales of wet and dry sandpaper in Europe during the early 1920s. These increased after 1929 when 3M joined the Durex Corp., a joint venture for international abrasive product sales in which 3M was involved along with eight other U.S. companies. In 1950, however, the Department of Justice alleged that the Durex Corp. was a mechanism for achieving collusion among U.S. abrasive manufacturers, and a judge ordered that the corporation be broken up. After the Durex Corp. was dissolved in 1951, 3M was left with a sandpaper factory in Britain, a small plant in France, a sales office in Germany, and a tape factory in Brazil. International sales at this point amounted to no more than 5% of 3M's total revenues.

Although 3M opposed the dissolution of the Durex Corp., in retrospect it turned out to be one of the most important events in the company's history, for it forced the corporation to build its own international operations. By 2002, international sales amounted to 55% of total revenues.

In 1952, Clarence Sampair was put in charge of 3M's international operations and charged with getting them off the ground. He was given considerable strategic and operational independence. Sampair and his successor, Maynard Patterson, worked hard to protect the international operations from getting caught up in the red tape of a major corporation. For example, Patterson recounts:

> I asked Em Monteiro to start a small company in Colombia. I told him to pick a key person he wanted to take with him. "Go start a company," I said, "and no one from St. Paul is going to visit you unless you ask for them. We'll stay out of your way, and if someone sticks his nose in your business you call me."[11]

The international businesses were grouped into an International Division that Sampair headed. From the get-go, the company insisted that foreign ventures pay their own way. In addition, 3M's international companies were expected to pay a 5 to 10% royalty to the corporate head office. Starved of working capital, 3M's International Division relied heavily on local borrowing to fund local operations, a fact that forced those operations to quickly pay their own way.

The international growth at 3M typically occurred in stages. The company would start by exporting to a country and working through sales subsidiaries. In that way, it began to understand the country, the local marketplace, and the local business environment. Next 3M established warehouses in each nation and stocked them with goods paid for in local currency. The next phase involved converting products to the sizes and packaging forms that the local market conditions, customs, and culture dictated. 3M would ship jumbo rolls of products from the United States, which were then broken up and repackaged for each country. The next stage was designing and building plants, buying machinery, and getting the plants up and running. Over the years, R&D functions were often added, and by the 1980s, considerable R&D was being done outside of the United States.

Both Sampair and Patterson set an innovative, entrepreneurial framework that, according to the company, still guides 3M's international operations today. The philosophy can be reduced to several key and simple commitments:

1. Get in early (within the company, the strategy is known as FIDO—"First in Defeats Others").

2. Hire talented and motivated local people.

3. Become a good corporate citizen of the country.

4. Grow with the local economy.

5. American products are not one-size-fits-all around the world; tailor products to fit local needs.

6. Enforce patents in local countries.

As 3M stepped into the international market vacuum, foreign sales surged from less than 5% in 1951 to 42% by 1979. By the end of the 1970s, 3M was beginning to understand how important it was to integrate the international operations more closely with the U.S. operations and to build innovative capabilities overseas. It expanded the company's international R&D presence (there are now more than 2,200 technical employees outside the United States), built closer ties between the U.S. and foreign research organizations, and started to transfer more managerial and technical employees between businesses in different countries.

In 1978, the company started the Pathfinder Program to encourage new product and new business initiatives born outside the United States. By 1983, products developed under the initiative were generating sales of over $150 million a year. 3M Brazil invented a low-cost, hot-melt adhesive from local raw materials, 3M Germany teamed up with Sumitomo 3M of Japan (a joint venture with Sumitomo) to develop electronic connectors with new features for the worldwide electronics industry, 3M Philippines developed a Scotch-Brite cleaning pad shaped like a foot after learning that Filipinos polished floors with their feet, and so on. On the back of such developments, in 1992 international operations exceeded 50% for the first time in the company's history.

By the 1990s, 3M started to shift away from a country-by-country management structure to more regional management. Drivers behind this development included the fall of trade barriers, the rise of trading blocks such as the European Union and NAFTA, and the need to drive down costs in the face of intense global competition. The first European Business Center (EBC) was created in 1991 to manage 3M's chemical business across Europe. The EBC was charged with product development, manufacturing, sales, and marketing for Europe, but also with paying attention to local country requirements. Other EBCs soon followed, such as EBCs for Disposable Products and Pharmaceuticals.

As the millennium ended, 3M seemed set on transforming the company into a transnational organization characterized by an integrated network of businesses that spanned the globe. The goal was to get the right mix, achieving global scale to deal with competitive pressures while at the same time maintaining 3M's traditional focus on local market differences and decentralized R&D capabilities.

The New Era

The DeSimone Years

In 1991, Desi DeSimone became CEO of 3M. A long-time 3M employee, the Canadian-born DeSimone was the epitome of a twenty-first-century manager—he had made his name by building 3M's Brazilian business and spoke five languages fluently. Unlike most prior 3M CEOs, DeSimone came from the manufacturing side of the business rather than the technical side. He soon received praise for managing 3M through the recession of the early 1990s. By the late 1990s, however, his leadership had come under fire from both inside and outside the company.

In 1998 and 1999, the company missed its earnings targets, and the stock price fell as disappointed investors sold. Sales were flat, profit margins fell, and earnings slumped by 50%. The stock had underperformed the widely tracked S&P 500 stock index for most of the 1980s and 1990s.

One cause of the earnings slump in the late 1990s was 3M's sluggish response to the 1997 Asian crisis. During the Asian crisis, the value of several Asian currencies fell by as much as 80% against the U.S. dollar in a matter of months. 3M generated a quarter of its sales from Asia, but it was slow to cut costs there in the face of slumping demand following the collapse of currency values. At the same time, a flood of cheap Asian products cut into 3M's market share in the United States and Europe as lower currency values made Asian products much cheaper.

Another problem was that for all of its vaunted innovative capabilities, 3M had not produced a new blockbuster product since Post-it Notes. Most of the new products produced during the 1990s were just improvements over existing products, not truly new products.

DeSimone was also blamed for not pushing 3M hard enough earlier in the decade to reduce costs. An example was the company's supply-chain excellence program. Back in 1995, 3M's inventory was turning over just 3.5 times a year, subpar for manufacturing. An internal study suggested that every half-point increase in inventory turnover could reduce 3M's working capital needs by $700 million and boost its return on invested capital. But by 1998, 3M had made no progress on this front.[12]

By 1998, there was also evidence of internal concerns. Anonymous letters from 3M employees were sent to the board of directors, claiming that DeSimone was not as committed to research as he should have been. Some letters complained that DeSimone was not funding important projects for future growth, others that he had not moved boldly enough to cut costs, and still others that the company's dual career track was not being implemented well and that technical people were underpaid. Critics argued that he was a slow and cautious decision maker in a time that required decisive strategic decisions. For example, in August 1998, DeSimone announced a restructuring plan that included a commitment to cut 4,500 jobs, but reports suggest that other senior managers wanted 10,000 job cuts and DeSimone had watered down the proposals.[13]

Despite the criticism, 3M's board, which included four previous 3M CEOs among its members, stood behind DeSimone until he retired in 2001. However, the board began a search for a new top executive in February 2000 and signaled that it was looking for an outsider. In December 2000, the company announced that it had found the person it wanted: Jim McNerney, a fifty-one-year-old General Electric veteran who ran GE's medical equipment businesses and, before that, GE's Asian operations. McNerney was one of the front runners in the race to succeed Jack Welsh as CEO of GE, but lost out to Jeffrey Immelt. One week after that announcement, 3M hired him.

McNerney's Plan for 3M

In his first public statement days after being appointed, McNerney said that his focus would be on getting to know 3M's people and culture and its diverse lines of business:

> I think getting to know some of those businesses and bringing some of GE here to overlay on top of 3M's strong culture of innovation will be particularly important.[14]

It soon became apparent that McNerney's game plan was exactly that: to bring the GE playbook to 3M and use it to try to boost 3M's results, while simultaneously not destroying the innovative culture that had produced the company's portfolio of 50,000 products.

The first move came in April 2001, when 3M announced that the company would cut 5,000 jobs, or about 7% of the workforce, in a restructuring effort that would zero in on struggling businesses. To cover severance and other costs of restructuring, 3M announced that it would take a $600 million charge against earnings. The job cuts were expected to save $500 million a year. In another effort to save costs, the company streamlined its purchasing processes— for example, by reducing the number of packaging suppliers on a global basis from fifty to five—saving another $100 million a year in the process.

Next, McNerney introduced the Six Sigma process, a rigorous statistically based quality control process that was one of the drivers of process improvement and cost savings at GE. At heart, Six Sigma is a management philosophy, accompanied by a set of tools, that is rooted in identifying and prioritizing customers and their needs, reducing variation in all business processes, and selecting and grading all projects based on their impact on financial results. Six Sigma breaks every task (process) in an organization down into increments to be measured against a perfect model.

McNerney called for Six Sigma to be rolled out across 3M's global operations. He also introduced a GE-like performance evaluation system at 3M, under which managers were asked to rank every single employee who reported to them.

In addition to boosting performance from existing business, McNerney quickly signaled that he wanted to play a more active role in allocating resources between new business opportunities. At any given time, 3M had around 1,500 products in the development pipeline. McNerney believed that was too many and indicated that he wanted to funnel more cash to the most promising ideas, those with a potential market of $100 million a year or more, while cutting funding to weaker looking development projects.

In the same vein, he signaled that he wanted to play a more active role in resource allocation than had traditionally been the case for a 3M CEO, using cash from mature businesses to fund growth opportunities elsewhere. He scrapped the requirement that each division get 30% of its sales from products introduced in the past four years, noting that

> To make that number, some managers were resorting to some rather dubious innovations, such as pink Post-it Notes. It became a game, what could you do to get a new SKU?[15]

Some long-time 3M watchers, however, worried that by changing resource allocation practices, McNerney might harm 3M's innovative culture. If the company's history proved anything, they said, it's that it is hard to tell which of today's tiny products will become tomorrow's home runs. No one predicted that Scotch Guard or Post-it Notes would earn millions. They began as little experiments that evolved without planning into big hits. McNerney's innovations all sound fine in theory, they said, but there is a risk that he will transform 3M into "3E" and lose what is valuable in 3M in the process.

Exhibit 3

Selected Financial Data, 1996–2006

	1996	1997	1998	1999	2000	2001	2002	2003	2004	2005	2006
Sales (billion)	$14.2	$15.1	$15.0	$15.7	$16.7	$16.1	$16.3	$18.2	$20.0	$21.0	$22.9
Operating margin	23.7%	23.5%	22.6%	24.7%	23.3%	20.3%	24.5%	26.5%	30.6%	31.1%	31.0%
ROIC	21.7%	23.9%	20.7%	22.5%	25.2%	19.4%	25.1%	25.5%	27.3%	28.5%	28.0%
EPS	$1.82	$1.94	$1.87	$2.11	$2.32	$1.79	$2.50	$3.02	$3.75	$4.12	$4.55

Source: 3M Company, *Value Line Investment Survey,* November 17, 2006.

In general, though, securities analysts greeted McNerney's moves favorably. One noted that "McNerney is all about speed" and that there will be "no more Tower of Babel—everyone speaks one language." This "one company" vision was meant to replace the program under which 3M systematically spun off successful new products into new business centers. The problem with this approach, according to the analyst, was that there was no leveraging of best practices across businesses.[16]

McNerney also signaled that he would reform 3M's regional management structure, replacing it with a global business unit structure that would be defined by either products or markets.

At a meeting for investment analysts, held on September 30, 2003, McNerney summarized a number of achievements.[17] At the time, the indications seemed to suggest that McNerney was helping to revitalize 3M. Profitability, measured by return on invested capital, had risen from 19.4% in 2001 and was projected to hit 25.5% in 2003 (see Exhibit 3 for details). 3M's stock price had risen from $42 just before McNerney was hired to $73 in October 2003.

Like his former boss, Jack Welsh at GE, McNerney seemed to place significant value on internal executive education programs as a way of shifting to a performance-oriented culture. McNerney noted that some 20,000 employees had been through Six Sigma training by the third quarter of 2003. Almost 400 higher level managers had been through an Advanced Leadership Development Program set up by McNerney and offered by 3M's own internal executive education institute. Some 40% of participants had been promoted on graduating. All of the company's top managers had graduated from an Executive Leadership Program offered by 3M.

McNerney also emphasized the value of five initiatives that he had put in place at 3M: indirect cost control, global sourcing, e-productivity, Six Sigma, and the 3M Acceleration program. With regard to indirect cost control, some $800 million had been taken out of 3M's cost structure since 2001, primarily by reducing employee numbers, introducing more efficient processes to boost productivity, benchmarking operations internally, and leveraging best practices. According to McNerney, internal benchmarking highlighted another $200 to $400 million in potential cost savings over the next few years.

On global sourcing, McNerney noted that more than $500 million had been saved since 2000 by consolidating purchasing, reducing the number of suppliers, switching to lower cost suppliers in developing nations, and introducing dual sourcing policies to keep price increases under control.

The e-productivity program at 3M embraces the entire organization and all functions. It involves the digitalization of a wide range of processes, from customer ordering and payment, through supply-chain management and inventory control, to managing employee process. The central goal is to boost productivity by using information technology to more effectively manage information within the company and between the company and its customers and suppliers. McNerney cited some $100 million in annual cost savings from this process.

The Six Sigma program overlays the entire organization and focuses on improving processes to boost cash flow, lower costs (through productivity

Exhibit 4

The New Product Development Process at 3M

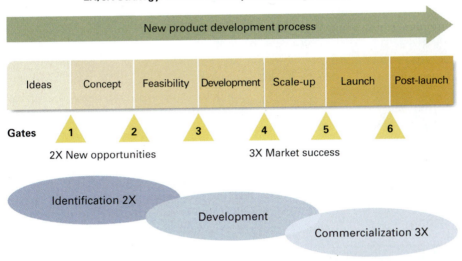

2X/3X Strategy: 2X Idea Velocity/3X Winning Products Out

New product development process

| Ideas | Concept | Feasibility | Development | Scale-up | Launch | Post-launch |

Gates   1   2   3   4   5   6

2X New opportunities   3X Market success

Identification 2X

Development

Commercialization 3X

Source: Adapted from a presentation by Jay Inlenfeld, 3M Investor Meeting, September 30, 2003, archived at http://www.corporate-ir.net/ireye/ir_site.zhtml?ticker=MMM&script=2100.

enhancements), and boost growth rates. By late 2003, there were some 7,000 Six Sigma projects in process at 3M. By using working capital more efficiently, Six Sigma programs had helped to generate some $800 million in cash, with the total expected to rise to $1.5 billion by the end of 2004. 3M has applied the Six Sigma process to the company's R&D process, enabling researchers to engage customer information in the initial stages of a design discussion. According to Jay Inlenfeld, the vice president of R&D, Six Sigma tools "allow us to be more closely connected to the market and give us a much higher probability of success in our new product designs."[18]

Finally, the 3M Acceleration program is aimed at boosting the growth rate from new products through better resource allocation, particularly by shifting resources from slower growing to faster growing markets. As McNerney noted:

> 3M has always had extremely strong competitive positions, but not in markets that are growing fast enough. The issue has been to shift emphasis into markets that are growing faster.[19]

Part of this program is a tool termed 2X/3X. 2X is an objective for two times the number of new products that were introduced in the past, and 3X is a business objective for three times as many winning products as there were in the past (see Exhibit 4). 2X focuses on generating more "major" product initiatives, and 3X on improving the commercialization of those initiatives. The process illustrated in Exhibit 4 is 3M's "stage gate" process, where each gate represents a major decision point in the development of a new product, from idea generation to postlaunch.

Other initiatives aimed at boosting 3M's organization growth rate through innovation include the Six Sigma process, leadership development programs, and technology leadership (see Exhibit 5). The purpose of these initiatives was to help implement the 2X/3X strategy.

As a further step in the Acceleration program, 3M decided to centralize its corporate R&D effort. Prior to the arrival of McNerney, there were twelve technology centers, staffed by 900 scientists, that focused on core technology development. The company is replacing these with one central research lab, staffed by 500 scientists, some 120 of whom will be located outside the United States. The remaining 400 scientists will be relocated to R&D centers in the business units. The goal of this new corporate research lab is to focus on developing new technology that might fill high-growth "white spaces," which are

Exhibit 5

R&D's Role in Organic Growth

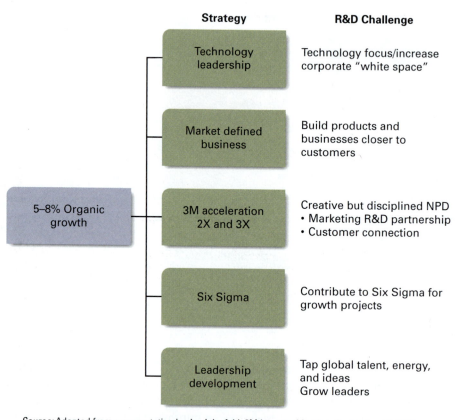

Source: Adapted from a presentation by Jay Inlenfeld, 3M Investor Meeting, September 30, 2003, archived at http://www.corporate-ir.net/ireye/ir_site.zhtml?ticker=MMM&script=2100.

areas where the company currently has no presence but where the long-term market potential is great. An example is research on fuel cells, which is currently a big project within 3M.

Responding to critics' charges that changes such as these might impact on 3M's innovative culture, vice president of R&D Inlenfeld noted:

> We are not going to change the basic culture of innovation at 3M. There is a lot of culture in 3M, but we are going to introduce more systematic, more productive tools that allow our researchers to be more successful.[20]

For example, Inlenfeld repeatedly emphasized that the company remains committed to basic 3M principles, such as the 15% rule and leveraging technology across businesses.

By late 2003, McNerney noted that some 600 new product ideas were under development and that, col-

lectively, they were expected to reach the market and generate some $5 billion in new revenues between 2003 and 2006, up from $3.5 billion eighteen months earlier. Some $1 billion of these gains were expected to come in 2003.

The Acceleration program was helping to increase 3M's organic growth rate in earnings per share, which hit an annual rate of 3.6% in the first half of 2003, up from 1% a year earlier and a decline in 2001. To complement internally generated growth, McNerney signaled that he would make selected acquisitions in businesses that 3M already had a presence in.

George Buckley Takes Over

In mid-2005, McNerney announced that he would leave 3M to become CEO and chairman of Boeing, a company on whose board he had served for some time. He was replaced in late 2005 by another outsider, George Buckley, the highly regarded CEO of Brunswick Industries. Over the next year, in several presentations Buckley outlined his strategy for 3M, and it soon became apparent that he was essentially sticking to the general course laid out by McNerney, albeit with some minor corrections.[21]

Buckley does not see 3M as an enterprise that needs radical change. He sees 3M as a company with impressive internal strengths, but one that has been too cautious about pursuing growth opportunities.[22] Buckley's overall strategic vision for 3M is that the company must solve customer needs through the provision of innovative and differentiated products that increase the efficiency and competitiveness of customers. Consistent with long-term 3M strategy, he sees this as being achieved by taking 3M's multiple technology platforms and applying them to different market opportunities.

Controlling costs and boosting productivity through Six Sigma continue to be a major thrust under Buckley. This was hardly a surprise, since Buckley had pushed Six Sigma at Brunswick. By late 2006, some 55,000 3M employees had been trained in Six Sigma methodology, 20,000 projects had been completed, and some 15,000 were still under way. 3M was also adding techniques gleaned from Toyota's lean production methodology to its Six Sigma tool kit. As a result of Six Sigma and other cost control methods, between 2001 and 2005 productivity measured by sales per employee increased from $234 to $311, and some $750 million were taken out of overhead costs.

In addition to productivity initiatives, Buckley has stressed the need for 3M to more aggressively pursue growth opportunities. He wants the company to use its differentiated brands and technology to continue to develop core businesses and extend those core businesses into adjacent areas. In addition, like McNerney, Buckley wants the company to focus R&D resources on emerging business opportunities, and he too seems to be prepared to play a more proactive role in this process. Areas of focus include filtration systems, track and trace information technology, energy and mineral extraction, and food safety. 3M made a number of acquisitions during 2005 and 2006 to achieve scale and acquire technology and other assets in these areas. In addition, it increased its own investment in technologies related to these growth opportunities, particularly nanotechnology.

In addition to focusing on growth opportunities, 3M under Buckley has made selective divestitures of businesses not seen as core. Most notably, in November 2006, 3M reached an agreement to sell its pharmaceutical business for $2.1 billion. 3M took this step after deciding that slow growth combined with high regulatory and technological risk made the sector an unattractive one that would dampen the company's growth rate.

Finally, Buckley is committed to continuing internationalization at 3M. The goal is to increase foreign sales to 70% of total revenues by 2011, up from 61% in 2006. 3M plans to double its capital investment in the fast-growing markets of China, India, Brazil, Russia, and Poland by 2009. All of these markets are seen as expanding two to three times as fast as the U.S. market.

Judged by the company's financial results between 2001 and 2006, the McNerney and Buckley eras do seem to have improved 3M's financial performance. Most notably, return on invested capital increased from 19.4% to 28%, earnings per share from $1.79 to $4.55, operating margins from 20.3% to 31%, and sales from $16 billion to $23 billion. Despite this improvement, the company's stock price has remained mired in the $70 to $80 range since 2003, raising the question of what Buckley needs to do to deliver value to shareholders.

ENDNOTES

1. M. Dickson, "Back to the Future," *Financial Times*, May 30, 1994, p. 7, http://www.3m.com/profile/looking/mcknight.jhtml.
2. http://www.3m.com/about3M/pioneers/drew2.jhtml.
3. http://www.3m.com/about3M/innovation/scotchgard50/index.jhtml.
4. 3M, "A Century of Innovation, the 3M Story," 2002, http://www.3m.com/about3m/century/index.jhtml.
5. 3M, "A Century of Innovation, the 3M Story," p. 33.
6. 3M, "A Century of Innovation, the 3M Story," p. 78.
7. 3M, "A Century of Innovation, the 3M Story," p. 78.
8. 3M, "A Century of Innovation, the 3M Story," p. 42.
9. Eric Von Hippel et al., "Creating Breakthroughs at 3M," *Harvard Business Review* (September–October 1999).
10. http://www.3m.com/about3M/history/mcknight.jhtml.
11. 3M, "A Century of Innovation, the 3M Story," pp. 143–144.
12. Michelle Conlin, "Too Much Doodle?" *Forbes* (October 19, 1998): 54–56.
13. De'Ann Weimer, "3M: The Heat Is on the Boss," *Business Week* (March 15, 1999): 82–83.
14. Joseph Hallinan, "3M's Next Chief Plans to Fortify Results with Discipline He Learned at GE Unit," *Wall Street Journal*, December 6, 2000, p. B17.
15. Jerry Useem, "(Tape) + (Light Bulb) = ?" *Fortune* (August 12, 2002): 127–131.

16. Rick Mullin, "Analysts Rate 3M's New Culture," *Chemical Week* (September 26, 2001): 39–40.

17. 3M Investor Meeting, September 30, 2003, http://www.corporte-it.net/ireye/ir-site.zhtml?ticker=MMM&script=2100.

18. Tim Studt, "3M—Where Innovation Rules," *R&D Magazine* (April 2003): 22.

19. 3M Investor Meeting, September 30, 2003.

20. Studt, "3M—Where Innovation Rules."

21. Material here drawn from George Buckley's presentation for Prudential's investor conference on "Inside Our Best Ideas," September 28, 2006. This and other relevant presentations are archived at http://investor.3m.com/ireye/ir_site.zhml?ticker=MMM&script=1200.

22. Jeffery Sprague, "MMM: Searching for Growth with New CEO Leading," *Citigroup Global Markets,* May 2, 2006.

Philips versus Matsushita: A New Century, a New Round

This case was prepared by Christopher A. Bartlett, Harvard Business School

Throughout their long histories, N.V. Philips (Netherlands) and Matsushita Electric (Japan) had followed very different strategies and emerged with very different organizational capabilities. Philips built its success on a worldwide portfolio of responsive national organizations, while Matsushita based its global competitiveness on its centralized, highly efficient operations in Japan.

During the 1990s, both companies experienced major challenges to their historic competitive positions and organizational models, and at the end of the decade, both companies were struggling to reestablish their competitiveness. At the start of the new millennium, new CEOs at both companies were implementing yet another round of strategic initiatives and organizational restructurings. Observers wondered how the changes would affect their long-running competitive battle.

Philips: Background

In 1892, Gerard Philips and his father opened a small light-bulb factory in Eindhoven, Holland. When their venture almost failed, they recruited Gerard's brother, Anton, an excellent salesman and manager. By 1900, Philips was the third largest light-bulb producer in Europe.

From its founding, Philips developed a tradition of caring for workers. In Eindhoven it built company houses, bolstered education, and paid its employees so well that other local employers complained. When Philips incorporated in 1912, it set aside 10% of profits for employees.

Technological Competence and Geographic Expansion

While larger electrical products companies were racing to diversify, Philips made only light bulbs. This one-product focus and Gerard's technological prowess enabled the company to create significant innovations. Company policy was to scrap old plants and use new machines or factories whenever advances were made in new production technology. Anton wrote down assets rapidly and set aside substantial reserves for replacing outdated equipment. Philips also became a leader in industrial research, creating physics and chemistry labs to address production problems as well as more abstract scientific

Philips core competence was R/O

ones. The labs developed a tungsten metal filament bulb that was a great commercial success and gave Philips the financial strength to compete against its giant rivals.

Holland's small size soon forced Philips to look beyond its Dutch borders for enough volume to mass produce. In 1899, Anton hired the company's first export manager, and soon the company was selling in such diverse markets as Japan, Australia, Canada, Brazil, and Russia. In 1912, as the electric lamp industry began to show signs of overcapacity, Philips started building sales organizations in the United States, Canada, and France. All other functions remained highly centralized in Eindhoven. In many foreign countries Philips created local joint ventures to gain market acceptance.

In 1919, Philips entered into the Principal Agreement with General Electric, giving each company the use of the other's patents. The agreement also divided the world into "three spheres of influence": General Electric would control North America; Philips would control Holland; but both companies agreed to compete freely in the rest of the world. (General Electric also took a 20% stake in Philips.) After this time, Philips began evolving from a highly centralized company, whose sales were conducted through third parties, to a decentralized sales organization with autonomous marketing companies in fourteen European countries, China, Brazil, and Australia.

During this period, the company also broadened its product line significantly. In 1918, it began producing electronic vacuum tubes; eight years later, its first radios appeared, capturing a 20% world market share within a decade; and during the 1930s, Philips began producing X-ray tubes. The Great Depression brought with it trade barriers and high tariffs, and Philips was forced to build local production facilities to protect its foreign sales of these products.

Philips: Organizational Development

One of the earliest traditions at Philips was a shared but competitive leadership by the commercial and technical functions. Gerard, an engineer, and Anton, a businessman, began a subtle competition where Gerard would try to produce more than Anton could sell and vice versa. Nevertheless, the two agreed that strong research was vital to Philips' survival.

During the late 1930s, in anticipation of the impending war, Philips transferred its overseas assets to two trusts, British Philips and the North American Philips Corporation; it also moved most of its vital research laboratories to Redhill in Surrey, England, and its top management to the United States. Supported by the assets and resources transferred abroad, and isolated from their parent, the individual country organizations became more independent during the war.

Because waves of Allied and German bombing had pummeled most of Philips' industrial plants in the Netherlands, the management board decided to build the postwar organization on the strengths of the national organizations (NOs). Their greatly increased self-sufficiency during the war had allowed most to become adept at responding to country-specific market conditions—a capability that became a valuable asset in the postwar era. For example, when international wrangling precluded any agreement on three competing television transmission standards (PAL, SECAM, and NTSC), each nation decided which to adopt. Furthermore, consumer preferences and economic conditions varied: in some countries, rich, furniture-encased TV sets were the norm; in others, sleek, contemporary models dominated the market. In the United Kingdom, the only way to penetrate the market was to establish a rental business; in richer countries, a major marketing challenge was overcoming elitist prejudice against television. In this environment, the independent NOs had a great advantage in being able to sense and respond to the differences.

Eventually, responsiveness extended beyond adaptive marketing. As NOs built their own technical capabilities, product development often became a function of local market conditions. For example, Philips of Canada created the company's first color TV; Philips of Australia created the first stereo TV; and Philips of the United Kingdom created the first TVs with teletext.

While NOs took major responsibility for financial, legal, and administrative matters, fourteen product divisions (PDs), located in Eindhoven, were formally responsible for development, production, and global distribution. (In reality, the NOs' control of assets and the PDs' distance from the operations often undercut this formal role.) The research function remained independent and, with continued strong funding, set up eight separate laboratories in Europe and the United States.

While the formal corporate-level structure was represented as a type of geographic/product matrix, it was clear that NOs had the real power. NOs reported directly to the management board, which Philips enlarged from four members to ten to ensure that top management remained in contact with and control of the highly autonomous NOs. Each NO also regularly sent envoys to Eindhoven to represent its interests. Top management, most of whom had careers that included multiple foreign tours of duty, made frequent overseas visits to the NOs. In 1954, the board established the International Concern Council to formalize regular meetings with the heads of all major NOs.

Within the NOs, the management structure mimicked the legendary joint technical and commercial leadership of the two Philips brothers. Most were led by a technical manager and a commercial manager. In some locations, a finance manager filled out the top management triad that typically reached key decisions collectively. This cross-functional coordination capability was reflected down through the NOs in front-line product teams, product-group-level management teams, and at the senior management committee of the NOs' top commercial, technical, and financial managers.

The overwhelming importance of foreign operations to Philips, the commensurate status of the NOs within the corporate hierarchy, and even the cosmopolitan appeal of many of the offshore subsidiaries' locations encouraged many Philips managers to take extended foreign tours of duty, working in a series of two- or three-year posts. This elite group of expatriate managers identified strongly with each other and with the NOs as a group and had no difficulty representing their strong, country-oriented views to corporate management.

Philips: Attempts at Reorganization

In the late 1960s, the creation of the Common Market eroded trade barriers within Europe and diluted the rationale for maintaining independent, country-level subsidiaries. New transistor- and printed circuit-based technologies demanded larger production runs than most national plants could justify, and many of Philips' competitors were moving production of electronics to new facilities in low-wage areas in East Asia and Central and South America. Despite its many technological innovations, Philips' ability to bring products to market began to falter. In the 1960s, the company invented the audiocassette and the microwave oven but let its Japanese competitors capture the mass market for both products. A decade later, its R&D group developed the V2000 videocassette format—superior technically to Sony's Beta or Matsushita's VHS—but was forced to abandon it when North American Philips decided to outsource, brand, and sell a VHS product which it manufactured under license from Matsushita.

In the following pages, we will see how over three decades, seven chairmen experimented with reorganizing the company to deal with its growing problems. Yet, entering the new millennium, Philips' financial performance remained poor and its global competitiveness was still in question. (See Exhibits 1 and 2.)

Van Reimsdijk and Rodenburg Reorganizations, 1970s

Concerned about what one magazine described as "continued profitless progress," newly appointed CEO Hendrick van Riemsdijk created an organization committee to prepare a policy paper on the division of responsibilities between the PDs and the NOs. Their report, dubbed the "Yellow Booklet," outlined the disadvantages of Philips' matrix organization in 1971:

> Without an agreement [defining the relationship between national organizations and product divisions], it is impossible to determine in any given situation which of the two parties is responsible. . . . As operations become increasingly complex, an organizational form of this type will only lower the speed of reaction of an enterprise.

On the basis of this report, van Reimsdijk proposed rebalancing the managerial relationships between PDs and NOs—"tilting the matrix towards the PDs" in his words—to allow Philips to decrease the number of products marketed, build scale by concentrating production, and increase the flow of goods among national organizations. He proposed closing the least efficient local plants and converting the best into International Production Centers (IPCs), each supplying many NOs. In so doing, van Reimsdijk hoped that PD managers would gain control over manufacturing operations. Due to the political and organizational difficulty of closing local plants, however, implementation was slow.

Exhibit 1

Philips Group—Summary Financial Detail, 1970–2000 (millions of guilders, unless otherwise stated)

	2000	1995	1990	1985	1980	1975	1970
Net sales	ƒ83,437	ƒ64,462	ƒ55,764	ƒ60,045	ƒ36,536	ƒ27,115	ƒ15,070
Income from operations (excluding restructuring)	NA	4,090	2,260	3,075	1,577	1,201	1,280
Income from operations (including restructuring)	9,434	4,044	−2,389	NA	NA	NA	NA
As a percentage of net sales	11.3%	6.3%	−4.3%	5.1%	4.3%	4.5%	8.5%
Income after taxes	ƒ12,559	ƒ2,889	ƒ−4,447	ƒ1,025	ƒ532	ƒ341	ƒ446
Net income from normal business operations	NA	2,684	−4,526	NA	328	347	435
Stockholders' equity (common)	49,473	14,055	11,165	16,151	12,996	10,047	6,324
Return on stockholders' equity	42.8%	20.2%	−30.2%	5.6%	2.7%	3.6%	7.3%
Distribution per common share, par value ƒ10 (in guilders)	ƒ2.64	ƒ1.60	ƒ0.0	ƒ2.00	ƒ1.80	ƒ1.40	ƒ1.70
Total assets	86,114	54,683	51,595	52,833	39,647	30,040	19,088
Inventories as a percentage of net sales	13.9%	18.2%	20.7%	23.2%	32.8%	32.9%	35.2%
Outstanding trade receivables in month's sales	1.5	1.6	1.6	2.0	3.0	3.0	2.8
Current ratio	1.2		1.4	1.6	1.7	1.8	1.7
Employees at year-end (in thousands)	219	265	273	346	373	397	359
Wages, salaries and other related costs	NA	NA	ƒ17,582	ƒ21,491	ƒ15,339	ƒ11,212	ƒ5,890
Exchange rate (period end; guilder/$)	2.34	1.60	1.69	2.75	2.15	2.69	3.62
Selected data in millions of dollars:							
Sales	$35,253	$40,039	$33,018	$21,802	$16,993	$10,098	$4,163
Operating profit	3,986	2,512	1,247	988	734	464	NA
Pretax income	5,837	2,083	−23,80	658	364	256	NA
Net income	5,306	1,667	−2,510	334	153	95	120
Total assets	35,885	32,651	30,547	19,202	18,440	11,186	5,273
Shareholders' equity (common)	20,238	8,784	6,611	5,864	6,044	3,741	1,747

Source: Annual reports; Standard & Poors' *Compustat;* Moody's Industrial and International Manuals.
Note: Exchange rate 12/31/00 was 1 guilder: 0.42751 U.S. dollar.

Exhibit 2

Philips Group—Sales by Product and Geographic Segment, 1985–2000 (millions of guilders)

	2000		1995		1990		1985	
Net sales by product segment:								
Lighting	ƒ11,133	13%	ƒ8,353	13%	ƒ7,026	13%	ƒ7,976	12%
Consumer electronics	32,357	39	22,027	34	25,400	46	16,906	26
Domestic appliances	4,643	6	—				6,644	10
Professional products/Systems	—	—	11,562	18	13,059	23	17,850	28
Components/Semiconductors	23,009	28	10,714	17	8,161	15	11,620	18
Software/Services	—	—	9,425	15	—	—	—	—
Medical systems	6,679	8	—	—	—	—	—	—
Origin	1,580	2	—	—	—	—	—	—
Miscellaneous	4,035	5	2,381	4	2,118	4	3,272	5
Total	ƒ83,437	100%	ƒ64,462	100%	ƒ55,764	100%	ƒ64,266	100%
Operating income by sector:								
Lighting	ƒ1,472	16%	ƒ983	24%	ƒ419	18%	ƒ910	30%
Consumer electronics	824	9	167	4	1,499	66	34	1
Domestic appliances	632	7	—	—	—	—	397	13
Professional products/Systems	—	—	157	4	189	8	1,484	48
Components/Semiconductors	4,220	45	2,233	55	−43	−2	44	1
Software/Services	—	—	886	22	—	—	—	—
Medical systems	372	4	—	—	—	—	—	—
Origin	2,343	25	—	—	—	—	—	—
Miscellaneous	−249	−3	423	10	218	10	220	7
Increase not attributable to a sector	−181	−2	(805)	(20)	−22	−1	6	0
Total	ƒ9,434	100%	ƒ4,044	100%	ƒ2,260	100%	ƒ3,075	100%

Source: Annual reports.
Notes:
Conversion rate (12/31/00): 1 guilder: 0.42751 U.S. dollar
Totals may not add due to rounding.
Product sector sales after 1988 are external sales only; therefore, no eliminations are made. Sector sales before 1988 include sales to other sectors; therefore, eliminations are made.
Data are not comparable to consolidated financial summary due to restating.

In the late 1970s, his successor CEO, Dr. Rodenburg, continued this thrust. Several IPCs were established, but the NOs seemed as powerful and independent as ever. He furthered matrix simplification by replacing the dual commercial and technical leadership with single management at both the corporate and the national organizational levels. Yet the power struggles continued.

Wisse Dekker Reorganization, 1982

Unsatisfied with the company's slow response and concerned by its slumping financial performance, upon becoming CEO in 1982, Wisse Dekker outlined a new initiative. Aware of the cost advantage of Philips' Japanese counterparts, he closed inefficient operations—particularly in Europe where 40 of the company's more than 200 plants were shut. He focused on core operations by selling some businesses (for example, welding, energy cables, and furniture) while acquiring an interest in Grundig and Westinghouse's North American lamp activities. Dekker also supported technology-sharing agreements and entered alliances in offshore manufacturing.

To deal with the slow-moving bureaucracy, he continued his predecessor's initiative to replace dual leadership with single general managers. He also continued to "tilt the matrix" by giving PDs formal product management responsibility, but leaving NOs responsible for local profits. And, he energized the management board by reducing its size, bringing on directors with strong operating experience, and creating subcommittees to deal with difficult issues. Finally, Dekker redefined the product planning process, incorporating input from the NOs, but giving global PDs the final decision on long-range direction. Still sales declined and profits stagnated.

Van der Klugt Reorganization, 1987

When Cor van der Klugt succeeded Dekker as chairman in 1987, Philips had lost its long-held consumer electronics leadership position to Matsushita and was one of only two non-Japanese companies in the world's top ten. Its net profit margins of 1 to 2% lagged behind not only General Electric's 9%, but even its highly aggressive Japanese competitors' slim 4%. Van der Klugt set a profit objective of 3 to 4% and made beating the Japanese companies a top priority.

As van der Klugt reviewed Philips' strategy, he designated various businesses as core (those that shared related technologies, had strategic impor-

tance, or were technical leaders) and noncore (standalone businesses that were not targets for world leadership and could eventually be sold if required). Of the four businesses defined as core, three were strategically linked: components, consumer electronics, and telecommunications and data systems. The fourth, lighting, was regarded as strategically vital because its cash flow funded development. The noncore businesses included domestic appliances and medical systems, which van der Klugt spun off into joint ventures with Whirlpool and GE, respectively.

In continuing efforts to strengthen the PDs relative to the NOs, van der Klugt restructured Philips around the four core global divisions rather than the former fourteen PDs. This allowed him to trim the management board, appointing the displaced board members to a new policy-making Group Management Committee. Consisting primarily of PD heads and functional chiefs, this body replaced the old NO-dominated International Concern Council. Finally, he sharply reduced the 3,000-strong headquarters staff, reallocating many of them to the PDs.

To link PDs more directly to markets, van der Klugt dispatched many experienced product-line managers to Philips' most competitive markets. For example, management of the digital audio tape and electric-shaver product lines were relocated to Japan, while the medical technology and domestic appliances lines were moved to the United States.

Such moves, along with continued efforts at globalizing product development and production efforts, required that the parent company gain firmer control over NOs, especially the giant North American Philips Corp. (NAPC). Although Philips had obtained a majority equity interest after World War II, it was not always able to make the U.S. company respond to directives from the center, as the V2000 VCR incident showed. To prevent replays of such experiences, in 1987 van der Klugt repurchased publicly owned NAPC shares for $700 million.

Reflecting the growing sentiment among some managers that R&D was not market oriented enough, van der Klugt halved spending on basic research to about 10% of total R&D. To manage what he described as "R&D's tendency to ponder the fundamental laws of nature," he made the R&D budget the direct responsibility of the businesses being supported by the research. This required that each research lab become focused on specific business areas (see Exhibit 3).

Exhibit 3

Philips Research Labs by Location and Specialty, 1987

Location	Size (Staff)	Specialty
Eindhoven, The Netherlands	2,000	Basic research, electronics, manufacturing technology
Redhill, Surrey, England	450	Microelectronics, television, defense
Hamburg, Germany	350	Communications, office equipment, medical imaging
Aachen, Germany	250	Fiber optics, X-ray systems
Paris, France	350	Microprocessors, chip materials, design
Brussels, Belgium	50	Artificial intelligence
Briarcliff Manor, New York	35	Optical systems, television, superconductivity, defense
Sunnyvale, California	150	Integrated circuits

Source: Philips, in *Business Week,* March 21, 1988, p. 156.

Finally, van der Klugt continued the effort to build efficient, specialized, multi-market production facilities by closing 75 of the company's 420 remaining plants worldwide. He also eliminated 38,000 of its 344,000 employees—21,000 through divesting businesses, shaking up the myth of lifetime employment at the company. He anticipated that all these restructurings would lead to a financial recovery by 1990. Unanticipated losses for that year, however—more than 4.5 billion Dutch guilders ($2.5 billion)—provoked a class-action lawsuit by angry American investors, who alleged that positive projections by the company had been misleading. In a surprise move, on May 14, 1990, van der Klugt and half of the management board were replaced.

Timmer Reorganization, 1990

The new president, Jan Timmer, had spent most of his thirty-five-year Philips career turning around unprofitable businesses. With rumors of a takeover or a government bailout swirling, he met with his top 100 managers and distributed a hypothetical—but fact-based—press release announcing that Philips was bankrupt. "So what action can you take this weekend?" he challenged them.

Under "Operation Centurion," headcount was reduced by 68,000, or 22%, over the next 18 months, earning Timmer the nickname "The Butcher of Eindhoven." Because European laws required substantial compensation for layoffs—Eindhoven workers received fifteen months' pay, for example—the first round of 10,000 layoffs alone cost Philips $700 million. To spread the burden around the globe and to speed the process, Timmer asked his PD managers to negotiate cuts with NO managers. According to one report, however, country managers were "digging in their heels to save local jobs." But the cuts came—many from overseas operations. In addition to the job cuts, Timmer vowed to "change the way we work." He established new performance rules and asked hundreds of top managers to sign contracts that committed them to specific financial goals. Those who broke those contracts were replaced—often with outsiders.

To focus resources further, Timmer sold off various businesses, including integrated circuits to Matsushita, minicomputers to Digital, defense electronics to Thomson, and the remaining 53% of appliances to Whirlpool. Yet profitability was still well below the modest 4% on sales he promised. In particular, consumer electronics lagged with slow growth in a price-competitive market. The core problem was identified by a 1994 McKinsey study that estimated that value added per hour in Japanese consumer electronic factories was still 68% above that of European plants. In this environment, most NO managers kept their heads down, using their distance from Eindhoven as their defense against the ongoing rationalization.

After three years of cost-cutting, in early 1994 Timmer finally presented a new growth strategy to the board. His plan was to expand software, services, and multimedia to become 40% of revenues by 2000. He was betting on Philips' legendary innovative capability to restart the growth engines. Earlier, he had recruited Frank Carrubba, Hewlett-Packard's director of research, and encouraged him to focus on developing 15 core technologies. The list, which included interactive compact disc (CD-i), digital compact cassettes (DCC), high-definition television (HDTV), and multimedia software, was soon dubbed "the president's projects." Over the next few years, Philips invested over $2.5 billion in these technologies. But Timmer's earlier divestment of some of the company's truly high-tech businesses and a 37% cut in R&D personnel left it with few who understood the technology of the new priority businesses.

By 1996, it was clear that Philips' analog HDTV technology would not become industry standard, that its DCC gamble had lost out to Sony's Minidisc, and that CD-i was a marketing failure. And while costs in Philips were lower, so too was morale, particularly among middle management. Critics claimed that the company's drive for cost-cutting and standardization had led it to ignore new worldwide market demands for more segmented products and higher consumer service.

Boonstra Reorganization, 1996

When Timmer stepped down in October 1996, the board replaced him with a radical choice for Philips—an outsider whose expertise was in marketing and Asia rather than technology and Europe. Cor Boonstra was a fifty-eight-year-old Dutchman whose years as CEO of Sara Lee, the U.S. consumer products firm, had earned him a reputation as a hard-driving marketing genius. Joining Philips in 1994, he headed the Asia Pacific region and the lighting division before being tapped as CEO.

Unencumbered by tradition, he immediately announced strategic sweeping changes designed to reach his target of increasing return on net assets from 17 to 24% by 1999. "There are no taboos, no sacred cows," he said. "The bleeders must be turned around, sold, or closed." Within three years, he had sold off 40 of Philips' 120 major businesses—including such well known units as Polygram and Grundig. He also initiated a major worldwide restructuring, promising to transform a structure he described as "a plate of spaghetti" into "a neat row of asparagus." He said:

How can we compete with the Koreans? They don't have 350 companies all over the world. Their factory in Ireland covers Europe and their manufacturing facility in Mexico serves North America. We need a more structured and simpler manufacturing and marketing organization to achieve a cost pattern in line with those who do not have our heritage. This is still one of the biggest issues facing Philips.

Within a year, 3,100 jobs were eliminated in North America and 3,000 employees were added in Asia Pacific, emphasizing Boonstra's determination to shift production to low-wage countries and his broader commitment to Asia. And after three years, he had closed 100 of the company's 356 factories worldwide. At the same time, he replaced the company's twenty-one PDs with seven divisions, but shifted day-to-day operating responsibility to 100 business units, each responsible for its profits worldwide. It was a move designed to finally eliminate the old PD/NO matrix. Finally, in a move that shocked most employees, he announced that the 100-year-old Eindhoven headquarters would be relocated to Amsterdam with only 400 of the 3,000 corporate positions remaining.

By early 1998, he was ready to announce his new strategy. Despite early speculation that he might abandon consumer electronics, he proclaimed it as the center of Philips' future. Betting on the "digital revolution," he planned to focus on established technologies such as cellular phones (through a joint venture with Lucent), digital TV, digital videodisc, and web TV. Furthermore, he committed major resources to marketing, including a 40% increase in advertising to raise awareness and image of the Philips brand and de-emphasize most of the 150 other brands it supported worldwide—from Magnavox TVs to Norelco shavers to Marantz stereos.

While not everything succeeded (the Lucent cell phone JV collapsed after nine months, for example), overall performance improved significantly in the late 1990s. By 2000, Boonstra was able to announce that he had achieved his objective of a 24% return on net assets.

Kleisterlee Reorganization, 2001

In May 2001, Boonstra passed the CEO's mantle to Gerard Kleisterlee, a fifty-four-year-old engineer (and career Philips man) whose turnaround of the components business had earned him a board seat only a year earlier. Believing that Philips had finally turned around, the board challenged Kleisterlee to grow sales by 10% annually and earnings 15%, while increasing return on assets to 30%.

Despite its stock trading at a steep discount to its breakup value, Philips governance structure and Dutch legislation made a hostile raid all but impossible. Nonetheless, Kleisterlee described the difference as "a management discount" and vowed to eliminate it. "Our fragmented organization makes us carry costs that are too high," he said. "In some production activities where we cannot add value, we will outsource and let others do it for us."

The first sign of restructuring came within weeks, when mobile phone production was outsourced to CEC of China. Then, in August, Kleisterlee announced an agreement with Japan's Funai Electric to take over production of its VCRs, resulting in the immediate closure of the European production center in Austria and the loss of 1,000 jobs. The CEO acknowledged that he was seeking partners to take over the manufacturing of some of its other mass-produced items such as television sets.

But by 2001, a slowing economy resulted in the company's first quarterly loss since 1996, and by year's end the loss had grown to 2.6 billion euros compared to the previous year's 9.6 billion profit. Many felt that these growing financial pressures—and shareholders' growing impatience—were finally leading Philips to recognize that its best hope of survival was to outsource even more of its basic manufacturing and become a technology developer and global marketer. It believed it was time to recognize that its thirty-year quest to build efficiency into its global operations had failed.

Matsushita: Background

In 1918, Konosuke Matsushita (or "KM," as he was affectionately known), a twenty-three-year-old inspector with the Osaka Electric Light Company, invested ¥100 to start production of double-ended sockets in his modest home. The company grew rapidly, expanding into battery-powered lamps, electric irons, and radios. On May 5, 1932, Matsushita's fourteenth anniversary, KM announced to his 162 employees a 250-year corporate plan broken into 25-year sections, each to be carried out by successive generations. His plan was codified in a company creed and in the "Seven Spirits of Matsushita" (see Exhibit 4), which, along with the company song, continued to be woven into morning assemblies worldwide and provided the basis of the "cultural and spiritual training" all new employees received during their first seven months with the company.

In the postwar boom, Matsushita introduced a flood of new products: TV sets in 1952; transistor radios in 1958; color TVs, dishwashers, and electric ovens in 1960. Capitalizing on its broad line of 5,000 products (Sony produced 80), the company opened 25,000 domestic retail outlets. With more than six times the outlets of rival Sony, the ubiquitous "National Shops" represented 40% of appliance stores in Japan in the late 1960s. These not only provided assured sales volume, but also gave the company direct access to market trends and consumer reaction. When postwar growth slowed, however, Matsushita had to look beyond its expanding product line and excellent distribution system for growth. After trying many tactics to boost sales—even sending assembly line workers out as door-to-door salesmen—the company eventually focused on export markets.

The Organization's Foundation: Divisional Structure

Plagued by ill health, KM wished to delegate more authority than was typical in Japanese companies. In 1933, Matsushita became the first Japanese company to adopt the divisional structure, giving each division clearly defined profit responsibility for its product. In addition to creating a "small business" environment, the product division structure generated internal competition that spurred each business to drive growth by leveraging its technology to develop new products. After the innovating division had earned substantial profits on its new product, however, company policy was to spin it off as a new division to maintain the "hungry spirit."

Under the "one-product-one-division" system, corporate management provided each largely self-sufficient division with initial funds to establish its own development, production, and marketing capabilities. Corporate treasury operated like a commercial bank, reviewing divisions' loan requests, for which it charged slightly higher-than-market interest, and accepting interest-bearing deposits on their excess funds. Divisional profitability was determined after deductions for central services such as corporate R&D and interest on internal borrowings. Each division paid 60% of earnings to headquarters and

Exhibit 4

Matsushita Creed and Philosophy (excerpts)

Creed   Through our industrial activities, we strive to foster progress, to promote the general welfare of society, and to devote ourselves to furthering the development of world culture.

Seven Spirits of Matsushita

Service through Industry

Fairness

Harmony and Cooperation

Struggle for Progress

Courtesy and Humility

Adjustment and Assimilation

Gratitude

KM's Business Philosophy (Selected Quotations)

"The purpose of an enterprise is to contribute to society by supplying goods of high quality at low prices in ample quantity."

"Profit comes in compensation for contribution to society. . . . [It] is a result rather than a goal."

"The responsibility of the manufacturer cannot be relieved until its product is disposed of by the end user."

"Unsuccessful business employs a wrong management. You should not find its causes in bad fortune, unfavorable surroundings or wrong timing."

"Business appetite has no self-restraining mechanism. . . . When you notice you have gone too far, you must have the courage to come back."

Source: "Matsushita Electric Industrial (MEI) in 1987," Harvard Business School Case No. 388-144.

financed all additional working capital and fixed asset requirements from the retained 40%. Transfer prices were based on the market and settled through the treasury on normal commercial terms. KM expected uniform performance across the company's thirty-six divisions, and division managers whose operating profits fell below 4% of sales for two successive years were replaced.

While basic technology was developed in a central research laboratory (CRL), product development and engineering occurred in each of the product divisions. Matsushita intentionally underfunded the CRL, forcing it to compete for additional funding from the divisions. Annually, the CRL publicized its major research projects to the product divisions, which then provided funding in exchange for technology for marketable applications. While it was rarely the innovator, Matsushita was usually very fast to market—earning it the nickname "Manishita," or copycat.

Matsushita: Internationalization

Although the establishment of overseas markets was a major thrust of the second 25 years in the 250-year plan, in an overseas trip in 1951 KM had been unable to find any American company willing to collaborate with Matsushita. The best he could do was a technology exchange and licensing agreement with Philips. Nonetheless, the push to internationalize continued.

Expanding Through Color TV

In the 1950s and 1960s, trade liberalization and lower shipping rates made possible a healthy export business built on black and white TV sets. In 1953, the company opened its first overseas branch office—the Matsushita Electric Corporation of America (MECA). With neither a distribution network nor a strong brand, the company could not access traditional retailers and had to resort to selling its products through mass merchandisers and discounters under their private brands.

During the 1960s, pressure from national governments in developing countries led Matsushita to open plants in several countries in Southeast Asia and Central and South America. As manufacturing costs in Japan rose, Matsushita shifted more basic production to these low-wage countries, but almost all high-value components and subassemblies were still made in its scale-intensive Japanese plants. By the 1970s, an East-West trade war mentality forced the company to establish assembly operations in the Americas and Europe. In 1972, it opened a plant in Canada; in 1974, it bought Motorola's TV business and started manufacturing its Quasar brand in the United States; and in 1976, it built a plant in Cardiff, Wales, to supply the Common Market.

Building Global Leadership Through VCRs

The birth of the videocassette recorder (VCR) propelled Matsushita into first place in the consumer electronics industry during the 1980s. Recognizing the potential mass-market appeal of the VCR—developed by Californian broadcasting company Ampex in 1956—engineers at Matsushita began developing VCR technology. After six years of development work, Matsushita launched its commercial broadcast video recorder in 1964 and introduced a consumer version two years later.

In 1975, Sony introduced the technically superior "Betamax" format, and the next year JVC launched a competing "VHS" format. Under pressure from MITI, the government's industrial planning ministry, Matsushita agreed to give up its own format and adopt the established VHS standard. During Matsushita's twenty years of VCR product development, various members of the VCR research team spent most of their careers working together, moving from central labs to the product division's development labs and eventually to the plant producing VCRs.

The company quickly built production to meet its own needs as well as those of OEM customers like GE, RCA, Philips, and Zenith, who decided to forgo self-manufacture and outsource to the low-cost Japanese. Between 1977 and 1985, capacity increased thirty-three-fold to 6.8 million units. Increased volume enabled Matsushita to slash prices 50% within five years of product launch, while simultaneously improving quality. In parallel, the company aggressively licensed the VHS format to other manufacturers, including Hitachi, Sharp, Mitsubishi, and, eventually, Philips. By the mid-1980s, VCRs accounted for 30% of total sales—over 40% of overseas revenues—and provided 45% of profits.

Changing Systems and Controls

In the mid-1980s, Matsushita's growing number of overseas companies reported to the parent in one of two ways: wholly owned, single-product global plants reported directly to the appropriate product division, while overseas sales and marketing subsidiaries and overseas companies producing a broad product line for local markets reported to Matsushita Electric Trading Company (METC), a separate legal entity. (See Exhibit 5 for METC's organization.)

Throughout the 1970s, the central product divisions maintained strong operating control over their offshore production units. Overseas operations used plant and equipment designed by the parent company, followed manufacturing procedures dictated by the center, and used materials from Matsushita's domestic plants. By the 1980s, growing trends toward local sourcing gradually weakened the divisions' direct control, so instead of controlling inputs they began to monitor measures of output (for example, quality, productivity, inventory levels).

About the same time, product divisions began receiving the globally consolidated return on sales reports that had previously been consolidated in METC statements. By the mid-1980s, as worldwide planning was introduced for the first time, corporate management required all its product divisions to prepare global product strategies.

Headquarters-Subsidiary Relations

Although METC and the product divisions set detailed sales and profits targets for their overseas subsidiaries, local managers were told they had autonomy on how to achieve the targets. "Mike" Matsuoko, president of the company's largest European production subsidiary in Cardiff, Wales, however, emphasized that failure to meet targets forfeited freedom: "Losses show bad health and invite many doctors from Japan, who provide advice and support."

In the mid-1980s, Matsushita had over 700 expatriate Japanese managers and technicians on foreign assignment for four to eight years, but defended that high number by describing their pivotal role. "This vital communication role," said one manager,

Organization of METC, 1985

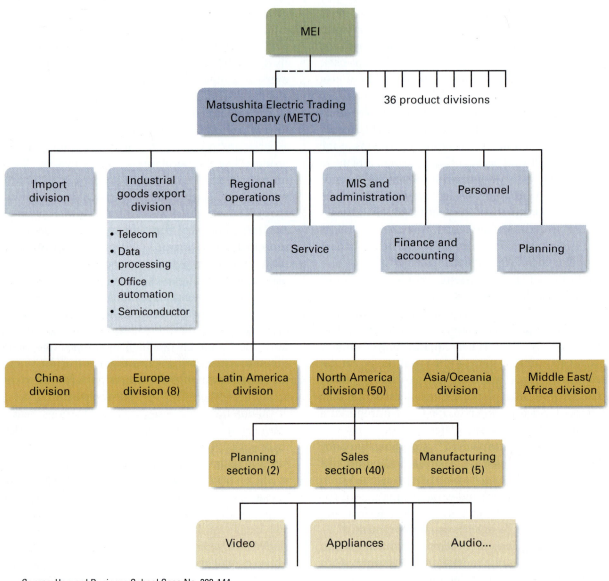

Source: Harvard Business School Case No. 388-144.
Note: ( ) = number of people.

"almost always requires a manager from the parent company. Even if a local manager speaks Japanese, he would not have the long experience that is needed to build relationships and understand our management processes."

Expatriate managers were located throughout foreign subsidiaries, but there were a few positions that were almost always reserved for them. The most visible were subsidiary general managers, whose main role was to translate Matsushita philosophy abroad. Expatriate accounting managers were expected to "mercilessly expose the truth" to corporate headquarters, and Japanese technical managers were sent to transfer product and process technologies and provide headquarters with local market information. These expatriates maintained relationships with senior colleagues in their divisions, who acted as career mentors, evaluated performance (with some input from local managers), and provided expatriates with information about parent company developments.

General managers of foreign subsidiaries visited Osaka headquarters at least two or three times each year—some as often as every month. Corporate managers reciprocated these visits, and on average, major operations hosted at least one headquarters manager each day of the year. Face-to-face meetings were considered vital: "Figures are important," said one manager, "but the meetings are necessary to develop judgment." Daily faxes and nightly phone calls between headquarters and expatriate colleagues were a vital management link.

Yamashita's Operation Localization

Although international sales kept rising, as early as 1982 growing host country pressures caused concern about the company's highly centralized operations. In that year, newly appointed company president Toshihiko Yamashita launched "Operation Localization" to boost offshore production from less than 10% of value-added to 25%, or half of overseas sales, by 1990. To support the target, he set out a program of four localizations—personnel, technology, material, and capital.

Over the next few years, Matsushita increased the number of local nationals in key positions. In the United States, for example, U.S. nationals became the presidents of three of the six local companies, while in Taiwan the majority of production divisions were replaced by Chinese managers. In each case, however, local national managers were still supported by senior Japanese advisors, who maintained a direct link with the parent company. To localize technology and materials, the company developed its national subsidiaries' expertise to source equipment locally, modify designs to meet local requirements, incorporate local components, and adapt corporate processes and technologies to accommodate these changes. And by the mid-1980s, offshore production subsidiaries were free to buy minor parts from local vendors as long as quality could be assured, but still had to buy key components from internal sources.

One of the most successful innovations was to give overseas sales subsidiaries more choice over the products they sold. Each year the company held a two-week internal merchandising show and product planning meeting where product divisions exhibited the new lines. Here, overseas sales subsidiary managers described their local market needs and negotiated for change in features, quantities, and even prices of the products they wanted to buy. Product division managers, however, could overrule the sales subsidiary if they thought introduction of a particular product was of strategic importance.

President Yamashita's hope was that Operation Localization would help Matsushita's overseas companies develop the innovative capability and entrepreneurial initiatives that he had long admired in the national organizations of rival Philips. (Past efforts to develop such capabilities abroad had failed. For example, when Matsushita acquired Motorola's TV business in the United States, the U.S. company's highly innovative technology group atrophied as American engineers resigned in response to what they felt to be excessive control from Japan's highly centralized R&D operations.) Yet despite his four localizations, overseas companies continued to act primarily as the implementation arms of central product divisions. In an unusual act for a Japanese CEO, Yamashita publicly expressed his unhappiness with the lack of initiative at the TV plant in Cardiff. Despite the transfer of substantial resources and the delegation of many responsibilities, he felt that the plant remained too dependent on the center.

Tanii's Integration and Expansion

Yamashita's successor, Akio Tanii, expanded on his predecessor's initiatives. In 1986, feeling that Matsushita's product divisions were not giving sufficient attention to international development—in part because they received only 3% royalties for foreign production against at least 10% return on sales for exports from Japan—he brought all foreign subsidiaries under the control of METC. Tanii then merged METC into the parent company in an effort to fully integrate domestic and overseas operations. Then, to shift operational control nearer to local markets, he relocated major regional headquarters functions from Japan to North America, Europe, and Southeast Asia. Yet still he was frustrated that the overseas subsidiary companies acted as little more than the implementing agents of the Osaka-based product divisions.

Through all these changes, however, Matsushita's worldwide growth continued generating huge reserves. With $17.5 billion in liquid financial assets at the end of 1989, the company was referred to as the "Matsushita Bank," and several top executives began proposing that if they could not develop innovative overseas companies, they should buy them. Flush with cash and international success, in early 1991 the company acquired MCA, the U.S. entertainment giant, for $6.1 billion with the objective of obtaining a media software source for its hardware. Within a year, however, Japan's bubble economy had burst, plunging the economy into recession. Almost overnight, Tanii had to shift the company's focus from expansion to cost containment. Despite his best efforts to cut costs, the problems ran too deep. With 1992 profits less than half their 1991 level, the board took the unusual move of forcing Tanii to resign in February 1993.

Morishita's Challenge and Response

At fifty-six, Yoichi Morishita was the most junior of the company's executive vice presidents when he was tapped as the new president. Under the slogan "simple, small, speedy and strategic," he committed to cutting headquarters staff and decentralizing responsibility. Over the next eighteen months, he moved 6,000 staff to operating jobs. In a major strategic reversal, he also sold 80% of MCA to Seagram, booking a $1.2 billion loss on the transaction.

Yet the company continued to struggle. Japan's domestic market for consumer electronics collapsed—from $42 billion in 1989 to $21 billion in 1999. Excess capacity drove down prices, and profits evaporated. And although offshore markets were growing, the rise of new competition—first from Korea, then China—created a global glut of consumer electronics, and prices collapsed.

With a strong yen making exports from Japan uncompetitive, Matsushita's product divisions rapidly shifted production offshore during the 1990s, mostly to low-cost Asian countries like China and Malaysia. By the end of the decade, its 160 factories outside Japan employed 140,000 people—about the same number of employees as in its 133 plants in Japan. Yet, despite the excess capacity and strong yen, management seemed unwilling to radically restructure its increasingly inefficient portfolio of production facilities or even lay off staff due to strongly held commitments to lifetime employment. Despite Morishita's promises, resistance within the organization prevented his implementation of much of the promised radical change.

In the closing years of the decade, Morishita began emphasizing the need to develop more of its technology and innovation offshore. Concerned that only 250 of the company's 3,000 R&D scientists and engineers were located outside Japan, he began investing in R&D partnerships and technical exchanges, particularly in fast emerging fields. For example, in 1998 he signed a joint R&D agreement with the Chinese Academy of Sciences, China's leading research organization. Later that year, he announced the establishment of the Panasonic Digital Concepts Center in California. Its mission was to act as a venture fund and an incubation center for the new ideas and technologies emerging in Silicon Valley. To some it was an indication that Matsushita had given up trying to generate new technology and business initiatives from its own overseas companies.

Nakamura's Initiatives

In April 2000, Morishita became chairman and Kunio Nakamura replaced him as president. Profitability was at 2.2% of sales, with consumer electronics at only 0.4%, including losses generated by one-time cash cows, the TV and VCR divisions. (Exhibit 6 provides the financial history for Matsushita.) The new CEO vowed to raise this to 5% by 2004. Key to his plan was to move Matsushita beyond its roots as a "super manufacturer of products" and begin "to meet customer needs through systems and services." He planned to flatten the hierarchy and empower employees to respond to customer needs, and as part of the implementation, all key headquarters functions relating to international operations were transferred to overseas regional offices.

But the biggest shock came in November, when Nakamura announced a program of "destruction and creation," in which he disbanded the product division structure that KM had created as Matsushita's basic organizational building block sixty-seven years earlier. Plants, previously controlled by individual product divisions, would now be integrated into multi-product production centers. In Japan alone, 30 of the 133 factories were to be consolidated or closed. And marketing would shift to two corporate marketing entities, one for Panasonic brands (consumer electronics, information and communications products) and one for National branded products (mostly home appliances).

Exhibit 6

Matsushita—Summary Financial Detail, 1970–2000[a]

	2000	1995	1990	1985	1980	1975	1970
In billions of yen and percent:							
Sales	¥7,299	¥6,948	¥6,003	¥5,291	¥2,916	¥1,385	¥932
Income before tax	219	232	572	723	324	83	147
As % of sales	3.0%	3.3%	9.5%	13.7%	11.1%	6.0%	15.8%
Net income	¥100	¥90	¥236	¥216	¥125	¥32	¥70
As % of sales	1.4%	1.3%	3.9%	4.1%	4.3%	2.3%	7.6%
Cash dividends (per share)	¥14.00	¥13.50	¥10.00	¥9.52	¥7.51	¥6.82	¥6.21
Total assets	7,955	8,202	7.851	5,076	2,479	1,274	735
Stockholders' equity	3,684	3,255	3,201	2,084	1,092	573	324
Capital investment	355	316	355	288	NA	NA	NA
Depreciation	343	296	238	227	65	28	23
R&D	526	378	346	248	102	51	NA
Employees (units)	290,448	265,397	198,299	175,828	107,057	82,869	78,924
Overseas employees	143,773	112,314	59,216	38,380	NA	NA	NA
As % of total employees	50%	42%	30%	22%	NA	NA	NA
Exchange rate (fiscal period end; ¥/$)	103	89	159	213	213	303	360
In millions of dollars:							
Sales	$68,862	$78,069	$37,753	$24,890	$13,690	$4,572	$2,588
Operating income before depreciation	4,944	6,250	4,343	3,682	1,606	317	NA
Operating income after depreciation	1,501	2,609	2,847	2,764	1,301	224	NA
Pretax income	2,224	2,678	3,667	3,396	1,520	273	408
Net income	941	1,017	1,482	1,214	584	105	195
Total assets	77,233	92,159	49,379	21,499	11,636	4,206	2,042
Total equity	35,767	36,575	20,131	10,153	5,129	1,890	900

[a]Data prior to 1987 are for the fiscal year ending November 20; data 1988 and after are for the fiscal year ending March 31.

Source: Annual reports; Standard & Poors' *Compustat;* Moody's Industrial and International Manuals.

In February 2001, just three months after raising his earnings estimate for the financial year ending March 2001, Nakamuta was embarrassed to readjust his estimate sharply downward. As Matsushita's first losses in thirty years accelerated, the new CEO announced a round of emergency measures designed to cut costs. When coupled with the earlier structural changes, these were radical moves, but in a company that even in Japan was being talked about as a takeover target, observers wondered if they were sufficient to restore Matsushita's tattered global competitiveness.

Case 8

Mired in Corruption—Kellogg Brown & Root in Nigeria

This case was prepared by Charles W. L. Hill, the University of Washington.

In 1998, the large Texas-based oil and gas service firm Halliburton acquired Dresser Industries. Among other businesses, Dresser owned M. W. Kellogg, one of the world's largest general contractors for construction projects in distant parts of the globe. After the acquisition, Kellogg was combined with an existing Halliburton business and renamed Kellogg Brown & Root, or KBR for short. At the time, it looked like a good deal for Halliburton. Among other things, Kellogg was involved in a four-firm consortium that was building a series of lique-fied natural gas (LNG) plants in Nigeria. By early 2004, the total value of the contracts associated with these plants had exceeded $8 billion.

In early 2005, however, Halliburton put KBR up for sale. The sale was seen as an attempt by Halliburton to distance itself from several scandals that had engulfed KBR. One of these concerned allegations that KBR had systematically overcharged the Pentagon for services it had provided to the U.S. military in Iraq. Another scandal centered on the Nigerian LNG plants and involved KBR employees, several former officials of the Nigerian government, and a mysterious British lawyer named Jeffrey Tesler.

The roots of the Nigerian scandal date back to 1994, when Kellogg and its consortium partners

were trying to win an initial contract from the Nigerian government to build two LNG plants. The contract was valued at around $2 billion. Each of the four firms held a 25% stake in the consortium, and each had veto power over its decisions. Kellogg employees held many of the top positions at the consortium, and two of the other members, Technip of France and JGC of Japan, have claimed that Kellogg managed the consortium (the fourth member, ENI of Italy, has not made any statement regarding management).

The KBR consortium was one of two to submit a bid on the initial contract, and its bid was the lower of the two. By early 1995, the KBR consortium was deep in final negotiations on the contract. It was at this point that Nigeria's oil minister had a falling out with the country's military dictator, General Abacha, and was replaced by Dan Etete. Etete proved to be far less accommodating to the KBR consortium, and suddenly the entire deal looked to be in jeopardy. According to some observers, Etete was a tough customer who immediately began to use his influence over the LNG project for personal gain. Whether this is true or not, what is known is that the KBR consortium quickly entered into a contract with Tesler. The contract, signed by a Kellogg executive, called on Tesler to obtain government permits for the LNG project, maintain good relations with government officials, and provide advice on sales strategy. Tesler's fee for these services was $60 million.

Tesler, it turned out, had long-standing relations with some twenty to thirty senior Nigerian government and military officials. In his capacity as a lawyer, for years Tesler had handled their London affairs, helping them to purchase real estate and set up financial accounts. Kellogg had a relationship with Tesler that dated back to the mid-1980s, when it had employed him to broker the sale of Kellogg's minority interest in a Nigerian fertilizer plant to the Nigerian government.

What happened next is currently the subject of government investigations in France, Nigeria, and the United States. The suspicion is that Tesler promised to funnel big sums to Nigerian government officials if the deal was done. Investigators base these suspicions on a number of factors, including the known corruption of General Abacha's government; the size of the payment to Tesler, which seemed out of all proportion to the services he was contracted to provide; and a series of notes turned up by internal investigators at Halliburton. The handwritten notes, taken by Wojciech Chodan, a Kellogg executive, document a meeting between Chodan and Tesler in which they discussed the possibility of channeling $40 million of Tesler's $60 million payment to General Abacha.

It is not known whether a bribe was actually paid. What is known is that in December 1995, Nigeria awarded the $2 billion contract to the KBR consortium. The LNG plant soon became a success. Nigeria contracted to build a second plant in 1999, two more in 2002, and a sixth in July 2004. KBR rehired Tesler in 1999 and again in 2001 to help secure the new contracts, all of which it won. In total, Tesler was paid some $132.3 million from 1994 through early 2004 by the KBR consortium.

Tesler's involvement in the project might have remained unknown were it not for an unrelated event. Georges Krammer, an employee of the French company Technip, which along with KBR was a member of the consortium, was charged by the French government with embezzlement. When Technip refused to defend Krammer, he turned around and aired what he perceived to be Technip's dirty linen. This included the payments to Tesler to secure the Nigerian LNG contracts.

This turn of events led French and Swiss officials to investigate Tesler's Swiss bank accounts. They discovered that Tesler was "kicking back" some of the funds he received to executives in the consortium and to subcontractors. One of the alleged kickbacks

was a transfer of $5 million from Tesler's account to that of Albert J. "Jack" Stanley, who was head of M. W. Kellogg and then Halliburton's KBR unit. Tesler also transferred some $2.5 million into Swiss bank accounts held under a false name by the Nigerian oil minister, Dan Etete. Other payments include a $1 million transfer into an account controlled by Wojciech Chodan, the former Kellogg executive whose extensive handwritten notes suggest the payment of a bribe to General Abacha, and $5 million to a German subcontractor on the LNG project in exchange for "information and advice."

After this all came out in June 2004, Halliburton promptly fired Jack Stanley and severed its long-standing relationship with Jeffery Tesler, asking its three partners in the Nigerian consortium to do the same. The U.S. Justice Department took things further, establishing a grand jury investigation to determine if Halliburton, through its KBR subsidiary, had been in violation of the Foreign Corrupt Practices Act. In November 2004, the Justice Department widened its investigation to include payments in connection with the Nigerian fertilizer plant that Kellogg had been involved with during the 1980s under the leadership of Jack Stanley. In March 2005, the Justice Department also stated that it was looking at whether Jack Stanley had tried to coordinate bidding with rivals and fix prices on certain foreign construction projects. As of late 2006, the investigation was still ongoing. As for Halliburton's plans to sell KBR, these too had come to naught. In April 2006, Halliburton announced that it would spin off KBR to investors, but a lack of interest in the offering resulted in a delay, and it was not clear when Halliburton would be able to complete the planned transaction.

SOURCES

Gold, R. "Halliburton to Put KBR Unit of Auction Block," *New York Times,* January 31, 2005, p. A2.

Gold, R., and C. Flemming. "Out of Africa: In Halliburton Nigeria Inquiry, a Search for Bribes to a Dictator," *Wall Street Journal,* September 29, 2004, p. A1.

Halliburton 10-K and 10-Q documents for 2005 and 2006, filed with the Securities and Exchange Commission.

Ivanovich, D. "Halliburton: Contracts Investigated," *Houston Chronicle,* March 2, 2005, p. 1.

Sawyer, T. "Citing Violations, Halliburton Cuts Off Former KBR Chairman," *ENR* (June 28, 2004): 16.

Notes

Chapter 1

Text Source Notes

1. There are several different ratios for measuring profitability, such as return on invested capital, return on assets, and return on equity. Although these different measures are highly correlated with each other, finance theorists argue that the return on invested capital is the most accurate measure of profitability. See Tom Copeland, Tim Koller, and Jack Murrin, *Valuation: Measuring and Managing the Value of Companies* (New York: Wiley, 1996).

2. Trying to estimate the relative importance of industry effects and firm strategy on firm profitability has been one of the most important areas of research in the strategy literature during the past decade. See Y. E. Spanos and S. Lioukas, "An Examination of the Causal Logic of Rent Generation," *Strategic Management Journal* 22:10 (October 2001): 907–934; and R. P. Rumelt, "How Much Does Industry Matter?" *Strategic Management Journal* 12 (1991): 167–185. See also A. J. Mauri and M. P. Michaels, "Firm and Industry Effects Within Strategic Management: An Empirical Examination," *Strategic Management Journal* 19 (1998): 211–219.

3. This view is known as "agency theory." See M. C. Jensen and W. H. Meckling, "Theory of the Firm: Managerial Behavior, Agency Costs and Ownership Structure," *Journal of Financial Economics* 3 (1976): 305–360; and E. F. Fama, "Agency Problems and the Theory of the Firm," *Journal of Political Economy* 88 (1980): 375–390.

4. K. R. Andrews, *The Concept of Corporate Strategy* (Homewood, IL: Dow Jones Irwin, 1971); H. I. Ansoff, *Corporate Strategy* (New York: McGraw-Hill, 1965); C. W. Hofer and D. Schendel, *Strategy Formulation: Analytical Concepts* (St. Paul, MN: West, 1978). Also see P. J. Brews and M. R. Hunt, "Learning to Plan and Planning to Learn," *Strategic Management Journal* 20 (1999): 889–913; R. W. Grant, "Planning in a Turbulent Environment," *Strategic Management Journal* 24 (2003): 491–517.

5. http://www.microsoft.com/mscorp/mission/.

6. Andrews, *The Concept of Corporate Strategy;* Ansoff, *Corporate Strategy;* Hofer and Schendel, *Strategy Formulation.*

7. For details, see R. A. Burgelman, "Intraorganizational Ecology of Strategy Making and Organizational Adaptation: Theory and Field Research," *Organization Science* 2 (1991): 239–262; H. Mintzberg, "Patterns in Strategy Formulation," *Management Science* 24 (1978): 934–948; S. L. Hart, "An Integrative Framework for Strategy Making Processes," *Academy of Management Review* 17 (1992): 327–351; G. Hamel, "Strategy as Revolution," *Harvard Business Review* 74 (July–August 1996): 69–83; R. W. Grant, "Planning in a Turbulent Environment," *Strategic Management Journal* 24 (2003): 491–517; and G. Gaveti, D. A. Levinthal, and J. W. Rivkin, "Strategy Making in Novel and Complex Worlds: The Power of Analogy," *Strategic Management Journal* 26 (2005): 691–712.

8. This is the premise of those who advocate that complexity and chaos theory should be applied to strategic management. See S. Brown and K. M. Eisenhardt, "The Art of Continuous Change: Linking Complexity Theory and Time Based Evolu-

tion in Relentlessly Shifting Organizations," *Administrative Science Quarterly* 29 (1997): 1–34; and R. Stacey and D. Parker, *Chaos, Management and Economics* (London: Institute for Economic Affairs, 1994). See also H. Courtney, J. Kirkland, and P. Viguerie, "Strategy Under Uncertainty," *Harvard Business Review* 75 (November–December 1997): 66–79.

9. Hart, "An Integrative Framework"; Hamel, "Strategy as Revolution."

10. See Burgelman, "Intraorganizational Ecology of Strategy Making and Organizational Adaptation"; and Mintzberg, "Patterns in Strategy Formulation."

11. R. A. Burgelman and A. S. Grove, "Strategic Dissonance," *California Management Review* (Winter 1996): 8–28.

12. C. L. Hill and F. T. Rothaermel, "The Performance of Incumbent Firms in the Face of Radical Technological Innovation," *Academy of Management Review* 28 (2003): 257–274.

13. This story was related to the author by George Rathmann, who at one time was head of 3M's research activities.

14. H. Mintzberg and A. McGugh, "Strategy Formulation in an Adhocracy," *Administrative Science Quarterly* 30: 2 (June1985).

15. This viewpoint is strongly emphasized by Burgelman and Grove, "Strategic Dissonance."

16. C. C. Miller and L. B. Cardinal, "Strategic Planning and Firm Performance: A Synthesis of More Than Two Decades of Research," *Academy of Management Journal* 37 (1994): 1649–1665. Also see P. R. Rogers, A. Miller, and W. Q. Judge, "Using Information Processing Theory to Understand Planning/Performance Relationships in the Context of Strategy," *Strategic Management Journal* 20 (1999): 567–577; and P. J. Brews and M. R. Hunt, "Learning to Plan and Planning to Learn," *Strategic Management Journal* 20 (1999): 889–913.

17. H. Courtney, J. Kirkland, and P. Viguerie, "Strategy Under Uncertainty," *Harvard Business Review* 75 (November–December 1997): 66–79.

18. P. J. H. Schoemaker, "Multiple Scenario Development: Its Conceptual and Behavioral Foundation," *Strategic Management Journal* 14 (1993): 193–213.

19. P. Schoemaker, P. J. H. van der Heijden, and A. J. M. Cornelius, "Integrating Scenarios into Strategic Planning at Royal Dutch Shell," *Planning Review* 20:3 (1992): 41–47; I. Wylie, "There Is No Alternative to . . . ," *Fast Company* (July 2002): 106–111.

20. "The Next Big Surprise: Scenario Planning," *Economist* (October 13, 2001): 71.

21. G. Hamel and C. K. Prahalad, *Competing for the Future* (New York: Free Press, 1994).

22. See G. Hamel and C. K. Prahalad, "Strategic Intent," *Harvard Business Review* (May–June 1989): 64.

23. See C. R. Schwenk, "Cognitive Simplification Processes in Strategic Decision Making," *Strategic Management Journal* 5 (1984): 111–128; and K. M. Eisenhardt and M. Zbaracki, "Strategic Decision Making," *Strategic Management Journal* 13 (Special Issue, 1992): 17–37.

24. H. Simon, *Administrative Behavior* (New York: McGraw-Hill, 1957).

25. The original statement of this phenomenon was made by A. Tversky and D. Kahneman, "Judgment Under Uncertainty: Heuristics and Biases," *Science* 185 (1974): 1124–1131. Also see D. Lovallo and D. Kahneman, "Delusions of Success: How Optimism Undermines Executives' Decisions," *Harvard Business Review* 81 (July 2003): 56–67; J. S. Hammond, R. L. Keeny, and H. Raiffa, "The Hidden Traps in Decision Making," *Harvard Business Review* 76 (September–October 1998): 25–34; and N. N. Taleb, *Fooled by Randomness* (New York: Random House, 2005).

26. Schwenk, "Cognitive Simplification Processes."

27. B. M. Staw, "The Escalation of Commitment to a Course of Action," *Academy of Management Review* 6 (1981): 577–587.

28. Taleb, *Fooled by Randomness*.

29. N. J. Hiller and D. C. Hambrick, "Conceptualizing Executive Hubris: The Role of (Hyper) Core Self-Evaluations in Strategic Decision Making," *Strategic Management Journal* 26 (2005): 297–320.

30. R. Roll, "The Hubris Hypotheses of Corporate Takeovers," *Journal of Business* 59 (1986): 197–216.

31. See R. O. Mason, "A Dialectic Approach to Strategic Planning," *Management Science* 13 (1969): 403–414; R. A. Cosier and J. C. Aplin, "A Critical View of Dialectic Inquiry in Strategic Planning," *Strategic Management Journal* 1 (1980): 343–356; and I. I. Mintroff and R. O. Mason, "Structuring III—Structured Policy Issues: Further Explorations in a Methodology for Messy Problems," *Strategic Management Journal* 1 (1980): 331–342.

32. Mason, "A Dialectic Approach."

33. Lovallo and Kahneman, "Delusions of Success."

34. For a summary of research on strategic leadership, see D. C. Hambrick, "Putting Top Managers Back into the Picture," *Strategic Management Journal* 10 (Special Issue, 1989): 5–15. See also D. Goldman, "What Makes a Leader?" *Harvard Business Review* (November–December 1998): 92–105; H. Mintzberg, "Covert Leadership," *Harvard Business Review* (November–December 1998): 140–148; and R. S. Tedlow, "What Titans Can Teach Us," *Harvard Business Review* (December 2001): 70–79.

35. N. M. Tichy and D. O. Ulrich, "The Leadership Challenge: A Call for the Transformational Leader," *Sloan Management Review* (Fall 1984): 59–68; F. Westley and H. Mintzberg, "Visionary Leadership and Strategic Management," *Strategic Management Journal* 10 (Special Issue, 1989): 17–32.

36. E. Wrapp, "Good Managers Don't Make Policy Decisions," *Harvard Business Review* (September–October 1967): 91–99.

37. J. Pfeffer, *Managing with Power* (Boston: Harvard Business School Press, 1992).

38. Goldman, "What Makes a Leader?"

Box Source Notes

a. "How Big Can It Grow?" *Economist* (April 17, 2004): 74–78; "Trial by Checkout," *Economist* (June 26, 2004): 74–76; Wal-Mart 10-K, 2007, www.walmartstores.com; Robert Slater, *The Wal-Mart Triumph* (New York: Portfolio Trade Books, 2004); "The Bulldozer from Bentonville Slows: Wal-Mart," *Economist* (February 17, 2007): 70.

b. Based on interviews conducted by Charles Hill.

c. M. Maynard and N. Bunkley, "A Reversal of Fortune at Chrysler Too," *New York Times,* September 20, 2006, p. C1; Gail Edmondson and K. Kerwin, "Stalled: Is the DaimlerChrysler Deal a Mistake?" *Business Week* (September 29, 2003): 55–56; N. Boudette and S. Power, "Gearing Down: Chrysler Turnaround Falters as Unsold Gas Guzzlers Fill Lots," *Wall Street Journal,* September 20, 2006, p. A1; "Divorced: Chrysler," *Economist* (May 19, 2007): 72; B. Simon, "Chrysler's Shift in Strategy Accelerates," *FT.com,* October 11, 2007, p. 1.

Chapter 2

Text Source Notes

1. E. Freeman, *Strategic Management: A Stakeholder Approach* (Boston: Pitman Press, 1984).

2. C. W. L. Hill and T. M. Jones, "Stakeholder-Agency Theory," *Journal of Management Studies* 29 (1992): 131–154; and J. G. March and H. A. Simon, *Organizations* (New York: Wiley, 1958).

3. Hill and Jones, "Stakeholder-Agency Theory."

4. I. C. Macmillan and P. E. Jones, *Strategy Formulation: Power and Politics* (St. Paul, MN: West, 1986).

5. John P. Kotter and James L. Heskett, *Corporate Culture and Performance* (New York: Free Press, 1992).

6. http://www.kodak.com/US/en/corp/careers/why/valuesmission.html.

7. These three questions were first proposed by P. F. Drucker, *Management—Tasks, Responsibilities, Practices* (New York: Harper & Row, 1974), pp. 74–94.

8. D. F. Abell, *Defining the Business: The Starting Point of Strategic Planning* (Englewood Cliffs, NJ: Prentice-Hall, 1980).

9. P. A. Kidwell and P. E. Ceruzzi, *Landmarks in Digital Computing* (Washington, DC: Smithsonian Institute, 1994).

10. http://www.rsis.com/rsis-corporate/RSIS/About-RSIS/Corporate-Vision-Statement.cfm, accessed October 17, 2007.

11. See G. Hamel and C. K. Prahalad, "Strategic Intent," *Harvard Business Review* (May–June 1989): 64.

12. J. C. Collins and J. I. Porras, "Building Your Company's Vision," *Harvard Business Review* (September–October 1996): 65–77.

13. http://www.nucor.com.

14. M. D. Richards, *Setting Strategic Goals and Objectives* (St. Paul, MN: West, 1986).

15. E. A. Locke, G. P. Latham, and M. Erez, "The Determinants of Goal Commitment," *Academy of Management Review* 13 (1988): 23–39.

16. C. Y. Baldwin, *Fundamental Enterprise Valuation: Return on Invested Capital,* Harvard Business School Note 9-801-125, July 3, 2004; and T. Copeland et al., *Valuation: Measuring and Managing the Value of Companies* (New York: Wiley, 2000).

17. R. E. Hoskisson, M. A. Hitt, and C. W. L. Hill, "Managerial Incentives and Investment in R&D in Large Multiproduct Firms," *Organization Science* 3 (1993): 325–341.

18. R. H. Hayes and W. J. Abernathy, "Managing Our Way to Economic Decline," *Harvard Business Review* (July–August 1980): 67–77.

19. M. C. Jensen and W. H. Meckling, "Theory of the Firm: Managerial Behavior, Agency Costs and Ownership Structure," *Journal of Financial Economics* 3 (1976): 305–360.

20. Jensen and Meckling, "Theory of the Firm"; E. F. Fama, "Agency Problems and the Theory of the Firm," *Journal of Political Economy* 88 (1980): 375–390.

21. Hill and Jones, "Stakeholder-Agency Theory."

22. For example, see R. Marris, *The Economic Theory of Managerial Capitalism* (London: Macmillan, 1964); and J. K. Galbraith, *The New Industrial State* (Boston: Houghton Mifflin, 1970).

23. E. F. Fama, "Agency Problems and the Theory of the Firm."

24. A. Rappaport, "New Thinking on How to Link Executive Pay with Performance," *Harvard Business Review* (March–April 1999): 91–105.

25. R. Kirkland, "The Real CEO Pay Problem," *Fortune* (July 10, 2006): 78–82.

26. D. Henry and D. Stead, "Worker vs CEO: Room to Run," *Business Week* (October 30, 2006): 13.

27. For academic studies that look at the determinants of CEO pay, see M. C. Jensen and K. J. Murphy, "Performance Pay and Top Management Incentives," *Journal of Political Economy* 98 (1990): 225–264; Charles W. L. Hill and Phillip Phan, "CEO Tenure as a Determinant of CEO Pay," *Academy of Management Journal* 34 (1991): 707–717; H. L. Tosi and L. R. Gomez-Mejia, "CEO Compensation Monitoring and Firm Performance," *Academy of Management Journal* 37 (1994): 1002–1016; and Joseph F. Porac, James B. Wade, and Timothy G. Pollock, "Industry Categories and the Politics of the Comparable Firm in CEO Compensation," *Administrative Science Quarterly* 44 (1999): 112–144.

28. Andrew Ward, "Home Depot Investors Stage a Revolt," *Financial Times*, May 26, 2006, p. 20.

29. Kirkland, "The Real CEO Pay Problem."

30. For recent research on this issue, see Peter J. Lane, A. A. Cannella, and M. H. Lubatkin, "Agency Problems as Antecedents to Unrelated Mergers and Diversification: Amihud and Lev Reconsidered," *Strategic Management Journal* 19 (1998): 555–578.

31. E. T. Penrose, *The Theory of the Growth of the Firm* (London: Macmillan, 1958).

32. G. Edmondson and L. Cohn, "How Parmalat Went Sour," *Business Week* (January 12, 2004): 46–50; "Another Enron? Royal Dutch Shell," *Economist* (March 13, 2004): 71.

33. O. E. Williamson, *The Economic Institutions of Capitalism* (New York: Free Press, 1985).

34. Fama, "Agency Problems and the Theory of the Firm."

35. S. Finkelstein and R. D'Aveni, "CEO Duality as a Double Edged Sword," *Academy of Management Journal* 37 (1994): 1079–1108; B. Ram Baliga and R. C. Moyer, "CEO Duality and Firm Performance," *Strategic Management Journal* 17 (1996): 41–53; M. L. Mace, *Directors: Myth and Reality* (Cambridge, MA: Harvard University Press, 1971); S. C. Vance, *Corporate Leadership: Boards of Directors and Strategy* (New York: McGraw-Hill, 1983).

36. W. G. Lewellen, C. Eoderer, and A. Rosenfeld, "Merger Decisions and Executive Stock Ownership in Acquiring Firms," *Journal of Accounting and Economics* 7 (1985): 209–231.

37. C. W. L. Hill and S. A. Snell, "External Control, Corporate Strategy, and Firm Performance," *Strategic Management Journal* 9 (1988): 577–590.

38. The phenomenon of back-dating stock options was uncovered by academic research and then picked up by the SEC. See Erik Lie, "On the Timing of CEO Stock Option Awards," *Management Science* 51 (2005): 802–812.

39. G. Colvin, "A Study in CEO Greed," *Fortune* (June 12, 2006): 53–55.

40. D. Henry and M. Conlin, "Too Much of a Good Incentive?" *Business Week* (March 4, 2002): 38–39.

41. CBS News, "Boycott Nike," *48 Hours*, October 17, 1996; D. Jones, "Critics Tie Sweatshop Sneakers to Air Jordan," *USA Today*, June 6, 1996, p. 1B; S. Greenhouse, "Nike Shoeplant in Vietnam Is Called Unsafe for Workers," *New York Times*, November 8, 1997.

Box Source Notes

a. "Money Well Spent: Corporate Parties," *Economist* (November 1, 2003): 79; "Tyco Pair Sentencing Expected on September 19," *Wall Street Journal*, August 2, 2005, p. 1; "Off to Jail: Corporate Crime in America," *Economist* (June 25, 2005): 81; N. Varchaver, "What's Ed Breen Thinking?" *Fortune* (March 20, 2006): 135–139.

b. S. Holt, "Wal-Mart Workers' Suit Wins Class Action Status," *Seattle Times*, October 9, 2004, pp. E1, E4; C. Daniels, "Women v. Wal-Mart," *Fortune* (July 21, 2003): 79–82; C. R. Gentry, "Off the Clock," *Chain Store Age* (February 2003): 33–36; M. Grimm, "Wal-Mart Uber Alles," *American Demographics* (October 2003): 38–42; "Wal-Mart Takes Steps to Address Diversity Criticism," *Financial Wire* (April 25, 2006): 1; Andy Serwer, "Bruised in Bentonville," *Fortune* (April 18, 2005): 84–88.

c. Andy Kessler, "Sellout.com," *Wall Street Journal*, January 31, 2006, p. A14; D. Henninger, "Wonderland: Google in China," *Wall Street Journal*, March 10, 2006, p. A18; J. Dean, "Limited Search: As Google Pushes into China It Faces Clashes with Censors," *Wall Street Journal*, December 16, 2005, p. A1; "The Party, the People, and the Power of Cybertalk: China and the Internet," *Economist* (April 29, 2006): 28–30.

Chapter 3

Text Source Notes

1. M. E. Porter, *Competitive Strategy* (New York: Free Press, 1980).

2. J. E. Bain, *Barriers to New Competition* (Cambridge, MA: Harvard University Press, 1956). For a review of the modern literature on barriers to entry, see R. J. Gilbert, "Mobility Barriers and the Value of Incumbency," in R. Schmalensee and R. D. Willig, *Handbook of Industrial Organization*, vol. 1 (Amsterdam: North-Holland, 1989). Also see R. P. McAfee, H. M. Mialon, and M. A. Williams, "What Is a Barrier to Entry?" *American Economic Review* 94 (May 2004): 461–468; and A.V. Mainkar, M. Lubatkin, and W. S. Schulze, "Towards a Product Proliferation Theory of Entry Barriers," *Academy of Management Review* 31 (2006): 1062–1082.

3. N. Cetorelli and P. E. Strahan, "Finance as a Barrier to Entry," *Journal of Finance* 61 (2006): 437–456.

4. A detailed discussion of switching costs and lock-in can be found in C. Shapiro and H. R. Varian, *Information Rules: A Strategic Guide to the Network Economy* (Boston: Harvard Business School Press, 1999).

5. Most of this information on barriers to entry can be found in the industrial organization economics literature. See especially the following works: Bain, *Barriers to New Competition;* M. Mann, "Seller Concentration, Barriers to Entry and Rates of Return in 30 Industries," *Review of Economics and Statistics* 48 (1966): 296–307; W. S. Comanor and T. A. Wilson, "Advertising, Market Structure and Performance," *Review of Economics and Statistics* 49 (1967): 423–440; Gilbert, "Mobility Barriers"; and K. Cool, L.-H. Roller, and B. Leleux, "The Relative Impact of Actual and Potential Rivalry on Firm Profitability in the Pharmaceutical Industry," *Strategic Management Journal* 20 (1999): 1–14.

6. D. J. Bryce and J. H. Dyer, "Strategies to Crack Well-Guarded Markets," *Harvard Business Review* 85 (May 2007): 84–95.

7. For a discussion of tacit agreements, see T. C. Schelling, *The Strategy of Conflict* (Cambridge, MA: Harvard University Press, 1960).

8. M. Busse, "Firm Financial Condition and Airline Price Wars," *Rand Journal of Economics* 33 (2002): 298–318.

9. For a review, see F. Karakaya, "Market Exit and Barriers to Exit: Theory and Practice," *Psychology and Marketing* 17 (2000): 651–668. Also see C. Decker and T. Mellewight, "Thirty Years After Michael E. Porter: What Do We Know About Business Exit?" *Academy of Management Review* 21 (2007): 41–60.

10. P. Ghemawat, *Commitment: The Dynamics of Strategy* (Boston: Harvard Business School Press, 1991).

11. The development of strategic group theory has been a strong theme in the strategy literature. Important contributions include the following: R. E. Caves and Michael E. Porter, "From Entry Barriers to Mobility Barriers," *Quarterly Journal of Economics* (May 1977): 241–262; K. R. Harrigan, "An Application of Clustering for Strategic Group Analysis," *Strategic Management Journal* 6 (1985): 55–73; K. J. Hatten and D. E. Schendel, "Heterogeneity Within an Industry: Firm Conduct in the U.S. Brewing Industry, 1952–71," *Journal of Industrial Economics* 26 (1977): 97–113; Michael E. Porter, "The Structure Within Industries and Companies' Performance," *Review of Economics and Statistics* 61 (1979): 214–227. Also see K. Cool and D. Schendel, "Performance Differences Among Strategic Group Members," *Strategic Management Journal* 9 (1988): 207–233; A. Nair and S. Kotha, "Does Group Membership Matter? Evidence from the Japanese Steel Industry," *Strategic Management Journal* (2001): 221–235; G. McNamara, D. L. Deephouse, and R. A. Luce, "Competitive Positioning Within and Across a Strategic Group Structure," *Strategic Management Journal* (2003): 161–180; and J. C. Short, T. B. Palmer, and G. M. Hult, "Firm, Strategic Group, and Industry Influences on Performance," *Strategic Management Journal* 28 (2007): 147–165.

12. For details on the strategic group structure in the pharmaceutical industry, see K. Cool and I. Dierickx, "Rivalry, Strategic Groups, and Firm Profitability," *Strategic Management Journal* 14 (1993): 47–59.

13. Charles W. Hofer argued that life cycle considerations may be the most important contingency when formulating business strategy. See Hofer, "Towards a Contingency Theory of Business Strategy," *Academy of Management Journal* 18 (1975): 784–810. There is empirical evidence to support this view. See C. R. Anderson and C. P. Zeithaml, "Stages of the Product Life Cycle, Business Strategy, and Business Performance," *Academy of Management Journal* 27 (1984): 5–24; and D. C. Hambrick and D. Lei, "Towards an Empirical Prioritization of Contingency Variables for Business Strategy," *Academy of Management Journal* 28 (1985): 763–788. Also see G. Miles, C. C. Snow, and M. P. Sharfman, "Industry Variety and Performance," *Strategic Management Journal* 14 (1993): 163–177; and G. K. Deans, F. Kroeger, and S. Zeisel, "The Consolidation Curve," *Harvard Business Review* (December 2002): 2–3.

14. The characteristics of declining industries have been summarized by K. R. Harrigan, "Strategy Formulation in Declining Industries," *Academy of Management Review* 5 (1980): 599–604. Also see J. Anand and H. Singh, "Asset Redeployment, Acquisitions and Corporate Strategy in Declining Industries," *Strategic Management Journal* 18 (1997): 99–118.

15. See M. Gort and J. Klepper, "Time Paths in the Diffusion of Product Innovations," *Economic Journal* (September 1982): 630–653. Looking at the history of forty-six products, Gort and Klepper found that the length of time before other companies entered the markets created by a few inventive compa-

nies declined from an average of 14.4 years for products introduced before 1930 to 4.9 years for those introduced after 1949.

16. The phrase was originally coined by J. Schumpeter, *Capitalism, Socialism and Democracy* (London: Macmillan, 1950), p. 68.

17. M. E. Porter, "Strategy and the Internet," *Harvard Business Review* (March 2001): 62–79.

18. *The Economist Book of Vital World Statistics* (New York: Random House, 1990).

19. For a detailed discussion of the importance of the structure of law as a factor explaining economic change and growth, see D. C. North, "Institutions," *Institutional Change and Economic Performance* (Cambridge: Cambridge University Press, 1990).

Box Source Notes

a. A. Kaplan, "Cott Corporation," *Beverage World* (June 15, 2004): 32; J. Popp, "2004 Soft Drink Report," *Beverage Industry* (March 2004): 13–18; L. Sparks, "From Coca-Colinization to Copy Catting: The Cott Corporation and Retailers Brand Soft Drinks in the UK and US," *Agribusiness* (March 1997): 153–157; E. Cherney, "After Faltering Sales, Cott Challenges Pepsi, Coca-Cola," *Wall Street Journal*, January 8, 2003, pp. B1, B8; and C. Terhune, "Market Share Drops at Coca-Cola, Pepsi Co," *Wall Street Journal*, March 7, 2005, p. B6.

b. "How Big Can It Grow?—Wal-Mart," *Economist* (April 17, 2004): 74–76; H. Gilman, "The Most Underrated CEO Ever," *Fortune* (April 5, 2004): 242–247; K. Schaffner, "Psst! Want to Sell to Wal-Mart?" *Apparel Industry Magazine* (August 1996): 18–20.

c. "Pharm Exec 50," *Pharmaceutical Executive* (May 2004): 61–68; J. A. DiMasi, R. W. Hansen, and H. G. Grabowski, "The Price of Innovation: New Estimates of Drug Development Costs," *Journal of Health Economics* 22 (March 2003): 151–170; "Where the Money Is: The Drug Industry," *Economist* (April 26, 2003): 64–65; Value Line Investment Survey, various issues; "Heartburn: Pharmaceuticals," *Economist* (August 19, 2006): 57; and P. B. Ginsberg et al., "Tracking Health Care Costs," *Health Affairs* (October 3, 2006), www.healthaffairs.org.

Chapter 4

Text Source Notes

1. The concept of consumer surplus is an important one in economics. For a more detailed exposition, see D. Besanko, D. Dranove, and M. Shanley, *Economics of Strategy* (New York: Wiley, 1996).

2. However, $P = V$ only in the special case where the company has a perfect monopoly and can charge each customer a unique price that reflects the value of the product to that customer (i.e. where perfect price discrimination is possible). More generally, except in the limiting case of perfect price discrimination, even a monopoly will see most consumers capture some of the value of a product in the form of a consumer surplus.

3. This point is central to the work of Michael Porter. See M. E. Porter, *Competitive Advantage* (New York: Free Press, 1985). See also Chapter 4 in P. Ghemawat, *Commitment: The Dynamic of Strategy* (New York: Free Press, 1991).

4. Harbour Consulting, "Productivity Gap Among North American Auto Makers Narrows in Harbour Report 2006," Press Release, July 1, 2006.

5. M. E. Porter, *Competitive Strategy* (New York: Free Press, 1980).

6. This approach goes back to the pioneering work by K. Lancaster, *Consumer Demand, a New Approach* (New York: Columbia University Press, 1971).

7. D. Garvin, "Competing on the Eight Dimensions of Quality," *Harvard Business Review* (November–December 1987): 101–119; P. Kotler, *Marketing Management* (millennium ed.) (Upper Saddle River, NJ: Prentice-Hall, 2000).

8. "Proton Bomb," *Economist* (May 8, 2004): 77.

9. C. K. Prahalad and M. S. Krishnan, "The New Meaning of Quality in the Information Age," *Harvard Business Review* (September-October 1999): 109–118.

10. See D. Garvin, "What Does Product Quality Really Mean?" *Sloan Management Review* 26 (Fall 1984): 25–44; P. B. Crosby, *Quality Is Free* (New York: Mentor, 1980); and A. Gabor, *The Man Who Discovered Quality* (New York: Times Books, 1990).

11. M. Cusumano, *The Japanese Automobile Industry* (Cambridge, MA: Harvard University Press, 1989); S. Spear and H. K. Bowen, "Decoding the DNA of the Toyota Production System," *Harvard Business Review* (September–October 1999): 96–108.

12. W. Chan Kim and R. Mauborgne, "Value Innovation: The Strategic Logic of High Growth," *Harvard Business Review* (January–February 1997): 102–115.

13. G. Stalk and T. M. Hout, *Competing Against Time* (New York: Free Press, 1990).

14. Stalk and Hout, *Competing Against Time*.

15. Porter, *Competitive Advantage*.

16. H. Luft, J. Bunker, and A. Enthoven, "Should Operations Be Regionalized?" *New England Journal of Medicine* 301 (1979): 1364–1369.

17. S. Chambers and R. Johnston, "Experience Curves in Services," *International Journal of Operations and Production Management* 20 (2000): 842–860.

18. See P. Nemetz and L. Fry, "Flexible Manufacturing Organizations: Implications for Strategy Formulation," *Academy of Management Review* 13 (1988): 627–638; N. Greenwood, *Implementing Flexible Manufacturing Systems* (New York: Halstead Press, 1986); and J. P. Womack, D. T. Jones, and D. Roos, *The Machine That Changed the World* (New York: Rawson Associates, 1990); and R. Parthasarthy and S. P. Seith, "The Impact of Flexible Automation on Business Strategy and Organizational Structure," *Academy of Management Review* 17 (1992): 86–111.

19. B. J. Pine, *Mass Customization: The New Frontier in Business Competition* (Boston: Harvard Business School Press, 1993); S. Kotha, "Mass Customization: Implementing the Emerging Paradigm for Competitive Advantage," *Strategic Management Journal* 16 (1995): 21–42; J. H. Gilmore and B. J. Pine II, "The Four Faces of Mass Customization," *Harvard Business Review* (January–February 1997): 91–101.

20. F. F. Reichheld and W. E. Sasser, "Zero Defections: Quality Comes to Service," *Harvard Business Review* (September–October 1990): 105–111.

21. A. Z. Cuneo, "Call Verizon Victorious," *Advertising Age* (March 8, 2004): 3–5.

22. H. F. Busch, "Integrated Materials Management," *International Journal of Physical Distribution and Materials Management* (1990): 28–39.

23. Stalk and Hout, *Competing Against Time*.

24. See Peter Bamberger and Ilan Meshoulam, *Human Resource Strategy: Formulation, Implementation, and Impact* (Thousand Oaks, CA: Sage, 2000); and P. M. Wright and S. Snell, "Towards a Unifying Framework for Exploring Fit and Flexibility in Human Resource Management," *Academy of Management Review* 23 (October 1998): 756–772.

25. J. Hoerr, "The Payoff from Teamwork," *Business Week* (July 10, 1989): 56–62.

26. T. C. Powell and A. Dent-Micallef, "Information Technology as Competitive Advantage: The Role of Human, Business, and Technology Resources," *Strategic Management Journal* 18 (1997): 375–405; B. Gates, *Business @ the Speed of Thought* (New York: Warner Books, 1999).

27. "Cisco@speed," *Economist* (June 26, 1999): 12; S. Tully, "How Cisco Mastered the Net," *Fortune* (August 17, 1997): 207–210; C. Kano, "The Real King of the Internet," *Fortune* (September 7, 1998): 82–93.

28. Gates, *Business @ the Speed of Thought.*

29. See the articles published in the special issue of the *Academy of Management Review on Total Quality Management* 19:3 (1994). The following article provides a good overview of many of the issues involved from an academic perspective: J. W. Dean and D. E. Bowen, "Management Theory and Total Quality," *Academy of Management Review* 19 (1994): 392–418. Also see T. C. Powell, "Total Quality Management as Competitive Advantage," *Strategic Management Journal* 16 (1995): 15–37.

30. A. Ries and J. Trout, *Positioning: The Battle for Your Mind* (New York: Warner Books, 1982).

31. R. G. Cooper, *Product Leadership* (Reading, MA: Perseus Books, 1999).

32. See Cooper, *Product Leadership;* A. L. Page, "PDMA's New Product Development Practices Survey: Performance and Best Practices," PDMA 15th Annual International Conference, Boston, October 16, 1991; and E. Mansfield, "How Economists See R&D," *Harvard Business Review* (November–December 1981): 98–106.

33. S. L. Brown and K. M. Eisenhardt, "Product Development: Past Research, Present Findings, and Future Directions," *Academy of Management Review* 20 (1995): 343–378; M. B. Lieberman and D. B. Montgomery, "First Mover Advantages," *Strategic Management Journal* 9 (Special Issue, Summer 1988): 41–58; D. J. Teece, "Profiting from Technological Innovation: Implications for Integration, Collaboration, Licensing and Public Policy," *Research Policy* 15 (1987): 285–305; G. J. Tellis and P. N. Golder, "First to Market, First to Fail?" *Sloan Management Review* (Winter 1996): 65–75; G. A. Stevens and J. Burley, "Piloting the Rocket of Radical Innovation," *Research Technology Management* 46 (2003): 16–26.

34. Stalk and Hout, *Competing Against Time.*

35. K. B. Clark and S. C. Wheelwright, *Managing New Product and Process Development* (New York: Free Press, 1993); M. A. Schilling and C. W. L. Hill, "Managing the New Product Development Process," *Academy of Management Executive* 12:3 (August 1998): 67–81.

36. O. Port, "Moving Past the Assembly Line," *Business Week* (Special Issue, Reinventing America, 1992): 177–180.

37. K. B. Clark and T. Fujimoto, "The Power of Product Integrity," *Harvard Business Review* (November-December 1990): 107–118; Clark and Wheelwright, *Managing New Product and Process Development;* Brown and Eisenhardt, "Product Development"; Stalk and Hout, *Competing Against Time.*

38. C. Christensen, "Quantum Corporation—Business and Product Teams," Harvard Business School Case 9-692-023.

39. P. Sellers, "Getting Customers to Love You," *Fortune* (March 13, 1989): 38–42.

40. Sellers, "Getting Customers to Love You."

41. The material in this section relies on the resource-based view of the company. For summaries of this perspective, see J. B. Barney, "Company Resources and Sustained Competitive Advantage," *Journal of Management* 17 (1991): 99–120; J. T. Mahoney and J. R. Pandian, "The Resource-Based View Within the Conversation of Strategic Management," *Strategic Management Journal* 13 (1992): 363–380; R. Amit and P. J. H. Schoemaker, "Strategic Assets and Organizational Rent," *Strategic Management Journal* 14 (1993): 33–46; M. A. Peteraf, "The Cornerstones of Competitive Advantage: A Resource-Based View," *Strategic Management Journal* 14 (1993): 179–191; B. Wernerfelt. "A Resource-Based View of the Company," *Strategic Management Journal* 15 (1994): 171–180; and K. M. Eisenhardt and J. A. Martin, "Dynamic Capabilities: What Are They?" *Strategic Management Journal* 21 (2000): 1105–1121.

42. For a discussion of organizational capabilities, see R. R. Nelson and S. Winter, *An Evolutionary Theory of Economic Change* (Cambridge, MA: Belknap Press, 1982).

43. Kim and Mauborgne, "Value Innovation."

44. This is the nature of the competitive process. For more detail, see C. W. L. Hill and D. Deeds, "The Importance of Industry Structure for the Determination of Company Profitability: A Neo-Austrian Perspective," *Journal of Management Studies* 33 (1996): 429–451.

45. As with resources and capabilities, so the concept of barriers to imitation is also grounded in the resource-based view of the company. For details, see R. Reed and R. J. DeFillippi, "Causal Ambiguity, Barriers to Imitation, and Sustainable Competitive Advantage," *Academy of Management Review* 15 (1990): 88–102.

46. E. Mansfield, "How Economists See R&D," *Harvard Business Review* (November–December 1981): 98–106.

47. S. L. Berman, J. Down, and C. W. L. Hill, "Tacit Knowledge as a Source of Competitive Advantage in the National Basketball Association," *Academy of Management Journal* (2002): 13–33.

Box Source Notes

a. G. P. Pisano, R. M. J. Bohmer, and A. C. Edmondson, "Organizational Differences in Rates of Learning: Evidence from the Adoption of Minimally Invasive Cardiac Surgery," *Management Science* 47 (2001): 752–768.

b. Sam Walton, *Made in America* (New York: Doubleday, 1992); S. Maich, "Wal-Mart's Mid-Life Crisis," *Maclean's* (August 23, 2004): 45; "The People Make It All Happen," *Discount Store News* (October 1999): 103–106; www.walmartstores.com.

c. Starbucks 10-K, various years; C. McLean, "Starbucks Set to Invade Coffee-Loving Continent," *Seattle Times,* October 4, 2000, p. E1; J. Ordonez, "Starbucks to Start Major Expansion in Overseas Market," *Wall Street Journal,* October 27, 2000, p. B10; S. Homes and D. Bennett, "Planet Starbucks," *Business Week* (September 9, 2002): 99–110; J. Batsell, "A Bean Counters Dream," *Seattle Times,* March 28, 2004, p. E1; "Boss Talk: It's a Grande Latte World," *Wall Street Journal,* December 15, 2003, p. B1; C. Harris, "Starbucks Beats Estimates, Outlines Expansion Plans," *Seattle Post Intelligencer,* October 5, 2006, p. C1.

Chapter 5

Text Source Notes

1. Derek F. Abell, *Defining the Business: The Starting Point of Strategic Planning* (Englewood Cliffs, NJ: Prentice-Hall, 1980), p. 169.

2. R. Kotler, *Marketing Management,* 5th ed. (Englewood Cliffs, NJ: Prentice-Hall, 1984); M. R. Darby and E. Karni, "Free Competition and the Optimal Amount of Fraud," *Journal of Law and Economics* 16 (1973): 67–86.

3. Abell, *Defining the Business,* p. 8.

4. Michael E. Porter, *Competitive Advantage: Creating and Sustaining Superior Performance* (New York: Free Press, 1985).

5. R. D. Buzzell and F. D. Wiersema, "Successful Share-Building Strategies," *Harvard Business Review* (January–February 1981): 135–144; L. W. Phillips, D. R. Chang, and R. D. Buzzell, "Product Quality, Cost Position, and Business Performance: A Test of Some Key Hypotheses," *Journal of Marketing* 47 (1983): 26–43.

6. Michael E. Porter, *Competitive Strategy: Techniques for Analyzing Industries and Competitors* (New York: Free Press, 1980), p. 45.

7. Abell, *Defining the Business,* p. 15.

8. Although many other authors have discussed cost leadership and differentiation as basic competitive approaches [e.g., F. Scherer, *Industrial Market Structure and Economic Performance,* 2nd ed. (Boston: Houghton Mifflin, 1980)], Porter's model *(Competitive Strategy)* has become the dominant approach. Consequently, this model is the one developed here, and the discussion draws heavily on Porter's definitions. The basic cost-leadership/differentiation dimension has received substantial empirical support [e.g., D. C. Hambrick, "High Profit Strategies in Mature Capital Goods Industries: A Contingency Approach," *Academy of Management Journal* 26 (1983): 687–707].

9. Porter, *Competitive Advantage,* p. 37.

10. Porter, *Competitive Advantage,* pp. 13–14.

11. D. Miller, "Configurations of Strategy and Structure: Towards a Synthesis," *Strategic Management Journal* 7 (1986): 217–231.

12. Porter, *Competitive Advantage,* pp. 44–46.

13. Charles W. Hofer and D. Schendel, *Strategy Formulation: Analytical Concepts* (St. Paul, MN: West, 1978).

14. W. K. Hall, "Survival Strategies in a Hostile Environment," *Harvard Business Review* 58 (1980): 75–85; Hambrick, "High-Profit Strategies," pp. 687–707.

15. Porter, *Competitive Strategy,* p. 46.

16. Peter F. Drucker, *The Practice of Management* (New York: Harper, 1954).

17. Porter, *Competitive Advantage,* pp. 44–46.

18. J. Brander and J. Eaton, "Product Line Rivalry," *American Economic Review* 74 (1985): 323–334.

19. P. Milgrom and J. Roberts, "Predation, Reputation, and Entry Deterrence," *Journal of Economic Theory* 27 (1982): 280–312.

20. Sharon M. Oster, *Modern Competitive Analysis* (New York: Oxford University Press, 1990), pp. 262–264.

21. Donald A. Hay and Derek J. Morris, *Industrial Economics: Theory and Evidence* (New York: Oxford University Press, 1979), pp. 192–193.

22. Porter, *Competitive Strategy,* pp. 76–86.

23. O. Heil and T. S. Robertson, "Towards a Theory of Competitive Market Signaling: A Research Agenda," *Strategic Management Journal* 12 (1991): 403–418.

24. Scherer, I*ndustrial Market Structure and Economic Performance,* Ch. 8.

25. The model differs from Ansoff's model for this reason.

26. H. Igor Ansoff, *Corporate Strategy* (London: Penguin Books, 1984), pp. 97–100.

27. Robert D. Buzzell, Bradley T. Gale, and Ralph G. M. Sultan, "Market Share—A Key to Profitability," *Harvard Business Re-*

view (January–February 1975): 97–103; Robert Jacobson and David A. Aaker, "Is Market Share All That It's Cracked Up to Be?" *Journal of Marketing* 49 (1985): 11–22.

28. Ansoff, *Corporate Strategy,* pp. 98–99.

29. S. L. Brown, and K. M. Eisenhardt, "Product Development: Past Research, Present Findings, and Future Directions," *Academy of Management Review* 20 (1995): 343–378.

30. Jack Willoughby, "The Last Iceman," *Forbes* (July 13, 1987): 183–202.

Box Source Notes

a. www.walmart.com, 2008.

b. P. Haynes, "Western Electric Redux," *Forbes* (January 26, 1998): 46–47.

c. www.nike.com, 2008.

d. "The New Nike," www.yahoo.com, September 12, 2004; www.nike.com, press release, 2004.

e. A. Wong, "Nike: Just Don't Do It," *Newsweek* (November 1, 2004): 84.

f. www.nike.com, 2008.

Chapter 6

Text Source Notes

1. World Trade Organization, *International Trade Trends and Statistics, 2006* (Geneva: WTO, 2007).

2. World Trade Organization, *International Trade Statistics, 2006* (Geneva: WTO, 2006); United Nations, *World Investment Report, 2006.*

3. P. Dicken, *Global Shift* (New York: Guilford Press, 1992).

4. D. Pritchard, "Are Federal Tax Laws and State Subsidies for Boeing 7E7 Selling America Short?" *Aviation Week* (April 12, 2004): 74–75.

5. I. Metthee, "Playing a Large Part," *Seattle Post Intelligence,* April 9, 1994, p. 13.

6. T. Levitt, "The Globalization of Markets," *Harvard Business Review* (May–June 1983): 92–102.

7. M. E. Porter, *The Competitive Advantage of Nations* (New York: Free Press, 1990).

8. D. Barboza, "An Unknown Giant Flexes Its Muscles," *New York Times,* December 4, 2004, pp. B1, B3.

9. See J. Birkinshaw and N. Hood, "Multinational Subsidiary Evolution: Capability and Charter Change in Foreign-Owned Subsidiary Companies," *Academy of Management Review* 23 (October 1998): 773–795; A. K. Gupta and V. J. Govindarajan, "Knowledge Flows Within Multinational Corporations," *Strategic Management Journal* 21 (2000): 473–496; V. J. Govindarajan and A. K. Gupta, *The Quest for Global Dominance* (San Francisco: Jossey Bass, 2001); T. S. Frost, J. M. Birkinshaw, and P. C. Ensign, "Centers of Excellence in Multinational Corporations," *Strategic Management Journal* 23 (2002): 997–1018; and U. Andersson, M. Forsgren, and U. Holm, "The Strategic Impact of External Networks," *Strategic Management Journal* 23 (2002): 979–996.

10. S. Leung, "Armchairs, TVs and Espresso: Is It McDonald's?" *Wall Street Journal,* August 30, 2002, pp. A1, A6.

11. C. K. Prahalad and Yves L. Doz, *The Multinational Mission: Balancing Local Demands and Global Vision* (New York: Free Press, 1987). Also see J. Birkinshaw, A. Morrison, and J. Hulland, "Structural and Competitive Determinants of a Global Integration Strategy," *Strategic Management Journal* 16 (1995): 637–655.

12. J. E. Garten, "Wal-Mart Gives Globalization a Bad Name," *Business Week* (March 8, 2004): 24.

13. Prahalad and Doz, *The Multinational Mission.*

14. C. J. Chipello, "Local Presence Is Key to European Deals," *Wall Street Journal,* June 30, 1998, p. A15.

15. C. Bartlett and S. Ghoshal, *Managing Across Borders: The Transnational Solution* (Boston: Harvard Business School Press, 1989).

16. Bartlett and Ghoshal, *Managing Across Borders.*

17. This section draws on several studies, including C. W. L. Hill, P. Hwang, and W. C. Kim, "An Eclectic Theory of the Choice of International Entry Mode," *Strategic Management Journal* 11 (1990): 117–128; C. W. L. Hill and W. C. Kim, "Searching for a Dynamic Theory of the Multinational Company: A Transaction Cost Model," *Strategic Management Journal* 9 (Special Issue on Strategy Content, 1988): 93–104; E. Anderson and H. Gatignon, "Modes of Foreign Entry: A Transaction Cost Analysis and Propositions," *Journal of International Business Studies* 17 (1986): 1–26; F. R. Root, *Entry Strategies for International Markets* (Lexington, MA: D. C. Heath, 1980); and A. Madhok, "Cost, Value and Foreign Market Entry: The Transaction and the Company," *Strategic Management Journal* 18 (1997): 39–61.

18. F. J. Contractor, "The Role of Licensing in International Strategy," *Columbia Journal of World Business* (Winter 1982): 73–83.

19. Andrew E. Serwer, "McDonald's Conquers the World," *Fortune* (October 17, 1994): 103–116.

20. B. Kogut, "Joint Ventures: Theoretical and Empirical Perspectives," *Strategic Management Journal* 9 (1988): 319–332.

21. D. G. Bradley, "Managing Against Expropriation," *Harvard Business Review* (July–August 1977): 78–90.

22. C. W. L. Hill, "Strategies for Exploiting Technological Innovations," *Organization Science* 3 (1992): 428–441.

Box Source Notes

a. A. Lillo, "Wal-Mart Says Global Going Good," *Home Textiles Today* (September 15, 2003): 12–13; A. de Rocha and L. A. Dib, "The Entry of Wal-Mart into Brazil," *International Journal of Retail and Distribution Management* 30 (2002): 61–73; "Wal-Mart: Mexico's Biggest Retailer," *Chain Store Age* (June 2001): 52–54; M. Flagg, "In Asia, Going to the Grocery Increasingly Means Heading for a European Retail Chain," *Wall Street Journal,* April 24, 2001, p. A21; "A Long Way from Bentonville," *Economist* (September 20, 2006): 38–39; "How Wal-Mart Should Right Itself," *Wall Street Journal,* April 20, 2007, pp. C1, C5; www.walmart.com.

b. J. Neff, "P&G Outpacing Unilever in Five-Year Battle," *Advertising Age* (November 3, 2003): 1–3; G. Strauss, "Firm Restructuring into Truly Global Company," *USA Today,* September 10, 1999, p. B2; Procter & Gamble 10-K Report, 2005; M. Kolbasuk McGee, "P&G Jump-Starts Corporate Change," *Information Week* (November 1, 1999): 30–34.

c. K. Capell, A. Sains, C. Lindblad, and A.T. Palmer, "IKEA," *Business Week* (November 14, 2005): 96–101; K. Capell et al., "What a Sweetheart of a Love Seat," *Business Week* (November 14, 2005): 101; P. M. Miller, "IKEA with Chinese Characteristics," *Chinese Business Review* (July/August 2004): 36–69; C. Daniels, "Create IKEA, Make Billions, Take Bus," *Fortune* (May 3, 2004): 44.

Chapter 7

Text Source Notes

1. T. J. Peters and R. H. Waterman, *In Search of Excellence* (New York: Harper & Row, 1982).

2. W. H. Davidow and M. S. Malone, *The Virtual Corporation* (New York: Harper & Row, 1992).

3. Davidow and Malone, *The Virtual Corporation*.

4. "The Outing of Outsourcing," *Economist* (November 25, 1995): 57–58.

5. Davidow and Malone, *The Virtual Corporation*; H. W. Chesbrough and D. J. Teece, "When Is Virtual Virtuous? Organizing for Innovation," *Harvard Business Review* (January–February 1996): 65–74.

6. This is the essence of Chandler's argument; see Alfred D. Chandler, *Strategy and Structure* (Cambridge, MA: MIT Press, 1962). The same argument is made by Jeffrey Pfeffer and Gerald R. Salancik, *The External Control of Organizations* (New York: Harper & Row, 1978). See also K. R. Harrigan, *Strategic Flexibility* (Lexington, MA: Lexington Books, 1985); K. R. Harrigan, "Vertical Integration and Corporate Strategy," *Academy of Management Journal* 28 (1985): 397–425; and F. M. Scherer, *Industrial Market Structure and Economic Performance* (Chicago: Rand McNally, 1981).

7. This section is based on the transaction cost approach popularized by Oliver E. Williamson, *The Economic Institutions of Capitalism* (New York: Free Press, 1985).

8. Williamson, *The Economic Institutions of Capitalism*. For recent empirical work that uses this framework, see L. Poppo and T. Zenger, "Testing Alternative Theories of the Firm: Transaction Cost, Knowledge Based, and Measurement Explanations for Make or Buy Decisions in Information Services," *Strategic Management Journal* 19 (1998): 853–878.

9. Williamson, *The Economic Institutions of Capitalism*.

10. Joseph White and Neal Templin, "Harsh Regimen: A Swollen GM Finds It Hard to Stick with Its Crash Diet," *Wall Street Journal*, September 9, 1992, p. A1.

11. Harrigan, *Strategic Flexibility*, pp. 67–87.

12. For a detailed theoretical rationale for this argument, see G. R. Jones and C. W. L. Hill, "A Transaction Cost Analysis of Strategy-Structure Choice," *Strategic Management Journal* 9 (1988): 159–172.

13. This resource-based view of diversification can be traced to Edith Penrose's seminal book *The Theory of the Growth of the Firm* (Oxford: Oxford University Press, 1959).

14. See, for example, Jones and Hill, "A Transaction Cost Analysis"; and Oliver E. Williamson, *Markets and Hierarchies* (New York: Free Press), pp. 132–175.

15. D. J. Teece, "Economies of Scope and the Scope of the Enterprise," *Journal of Economic Behavior and Organization* 3 (1980): 223–247. For recent empirical work on this topic, see C. H. St. John and J. S. Harrison, "Manufacturing Based Relatedness, Synergy and Coordination," *Strategic Management Journal* 20 (1999): 129–145.

16. Michael E. Porter, *Competitive Advantage: Creating and Sustaining Superior Performance* (New York: Free Press, 1985), p. 326.

17. For a detailed discussion, see C. W. L. Hill and R. E. Hoskisson, "Strategy and Structure in the Multi-product Firm," *Academy of Management Review* 12 (1987): 331–341.

18. For example, see C. W. L. Hill, "Diversified Growth and Competition," *Applied Economics* 17 (1985): 827–847; R. P. Rumelt, *Strategy, Structure and Economic Performance* (Boston: Harvard Business School Press, 1974); and Jones and Hill, "A Transaction Cost Analysis," pp. 159–172.

19. For a review of the evidence and some contrary empirical evidence, see D. E. Hatfield, J. P. Liebskind, and T. C. Opler, "The Effects of Corporate Restructuring on Aggregate Industry Specialization," *Strategic Management Journal* 17 (1996): 55–72.

20. O. A. Lamont and C. Polk, "The Diversification Discount: Cash Flows versus Returns, *Journal of Finance* 56 (October 2001): 1693–1721. See also R. Raju, H. Servaes, and L. Zingales, "The Cost of Diversity: The Diversification Discount and Inefficient Investment," *Journal of Finance* 55 (February 2000): 35–80.

21. For example, see A. Schleifer and R. W. Vishny, "Takeovers in the 60s and 80s: Evidence and Implications," *Strategic Management Journal* 12 (Special Issue, Winter 1991): 51–60.

Box Source Notes

a. W. E. Coyne, "How 3M Innovated for Long-Term Growth," *Research Technology Management* (March–April 2001): 21–24.

Chapter 8

Text Source Notes

1. R. Beckhard, *Organizational Development* (Reading, MA: Addison-Wesley, 1969); W. L. French and C. H. Bell, Jr., *Organizational Development*, 2nd ed. (Englewood Cliffs, NJ: Prentice-Hall, 1978).

2. Beckhard, *Organizational Development*.

3. M. Hammer and J. Champy, *Reengineering the Corporation* (New York: HarperCollins, 1993).

4. Hammer and Champy, *Reengineering the Corporation*, p. 39.

5. J. F. McDonnell, "Learning to Think in Different Terms: TQM & Restructuring at McDonnell Douglas," *Executive Speeches* (June/July 1994): 25–28.

6. L. C. Coch and R. P. French, Jr., "Overcoming Resistance to Change," *Human Relations* (August 1948): 512–532; P. R. Lawrence, "How to Deal with Resistance to Change," *Harvard Business Review* (January–February 1969): 4–12.

7. P. Kotter and L. A. Schlesinger, "Choosing Strategies for Change," *Harvard Business Review* (March–April 1979): 106–114.

8. G. Hamel and C. K. Prahalad, *Competing for the Future* (Cambridge, MA: Harvard Business School Press, 1994).

9. D. Leonard Barton and G. Pisano, "Monsanto's March into Biotechnology," Harvard Business School Case 690-009, 1990. See Monsanto's homepage (http://www.monsanto.com) for more information about its genetically engineered seed products.

10. See A. Campbell and R. Park, "Stop Kissing Frogs," *Harvard Business Review* (July–August 2004): 27–29; R. A. Burgelman and L. Valikangas, "Managing Internal Corporate Venture Cycles," *MTI Sloan Management Review* 46:4 (Summer 2005): 30–40; G. Dess et al., "Emerging Issues in Corporate Entrepreneurship," *Journal of Management* 29 (2003): 351–378.

11. See R. Biggadike, "The Risky Business of Diversification," *Harvard Business Review* (May–June 1979): 103–111; R. A. Burgelman, "A Process Model of Internal Corporate Venturing in the Diversified Major Firm," *Administrative Science Quarterly* 28 (1983): 223–244; Z. Block and I. C. Macmillan, *Corporate Venturing* (Cambridge, MA: Harvard Business School Press, 1993); Burgelman and Valikangas, "Managing Internal Corporate Venture Cycles."

12. Biggadike, "The Risky Business of Diversification"; Block and Macmillan, *Corporate Venturing.*

13. R. O. Crockett and C. Yang, "Why Motorola Should Hang Up on Iridium," *Business Week* (August 30, 1999): 46; L. Cauley, "Iridium's Downfall: The Marketing Took a Back Seat to the Science, *Wall Street Journal,* August 18, 1999, p. A1; J. N. Seth and R. Sisodia, "Why Cell Phones Succeeded Where Iridium Failed," *Wall Street Journal,* August 23, 1999, p. A14.

14. I. C. Macmillan and R. George, "Corporate Venturing: Challenges for Senior Managers," *Journal of Business Strategy* 5 (1985): 34–43.

15. See R. A. Burgelman, M. M. Maidique, and S. C. Wheelwright, *Strategic Management of Technology and Innovation* (Chicago: Irwin, 1996), pp. 493–507.

16. I . C. MacMillan and R. G. McGrath, "Nine New Roles for Technology Managers," *Research Technology Management* 47 (2004): 16–25.

17. See Block and Macmillan, Corporate Venturing; and Burgelman, Maidique, and Wheelwright, *Strategic Management of Technology and Innovation.*

18. G. Beardsley and E. Mansfield, "A Note on the Accuracy of Industrial Forecasts of the Profitability of New Products and Processes," *Journal of Business* 23 (1978): 127–130.

19. J. Warner, J. Templeman, and R. Horn, "The Case Against Mergers," *Business Week* (October 30, 1995): 122–134.

20. For evidence on acquisitions and performance, see R. E. Caves, "Mergers, Takeovers, and Economic Efficiency," *International Journal of Industrial Organization* 7 (1989): 151–174; M. C. Jensen and R. S. Ruback, "The Market for Corporate Control: The Scientific Evidence," *Journal of Financial Economics* 11 (1983): 5–50; R. Roll, "Empirical Evidence on Takeover Activity and Shareholder Wealth," in *Knights, Raiders and Targets,* ed. J. C. Coffee, L. Lowenstein, and S. Rose (Oxford: Oxford University Press, 1989); A. Schleifer and R. W. Vishny, "Takeovers in the 60s and 80s: Evidence and Implications," *Strategic Management Journal* 12 (Special Issue, Winter 1991): 51–60; and T. H. Brush, "Predicted Changes in Operational Synergy and Post Acquisition Performance of Acquired Businesses," *Strategic Management Journal* 17 (1996): 1–24.

21. D. J. Ravenscraft and F. M. Scherer, *Mergers, Selloffs, and Economic Efficiency* (Washington, DC: Brookings Institution, 1987).

22. S. B. Moeller, F. P. Schlingemann, and R. M. Stulz, "Wealth Destruction on a Massive Scale? A Study of Acquiring Firm Returns in the Recent Merger Wave," *Journal of Finance* 60:2 (2005): 757–783.

23. See J. P. Walsh, "Top Management Turnover Following Mergers and Acquisitions," *Strategic Management Journal* 9 (1988): 173–183.

24. See A. A. Cannella and D. C. Hambrick, "Executive Departure and Acquisition Performance," *Strategic Management Journal* 14 (1993): 137–152.

25. R. Roll, "The Hubris Hypothesis of Corporate Takeovers," *Journal of Business* 59 (1986): 197–216.

26. J. Duffy, "Qwest Moves On After MCI Rejection, *Network World* 22:18 (May 9, 2005): 10–11.

27. P. Haspeslagh and D. Jemison, *Managing Acquisitions* (New York, Free Press, 1991).

28. For views on this issue, see L. L. Fray, D. H. Gaylin, and J. W. Down, "Successful Acquisition Planning," *Journal of Business Strategy* 5 (1984): 46–55; C. W. L. Hill, "Profile of a Conglomerate Takeover: BTR and Thomas Tilling," *Journal of*

General Management 10 (1984): 34–50; D. R. Willensky, "Making It Happen: How to Execute an Acquisition," *Business Horizons* (March–April 1985): 38–45; Haspeslagh and Jemison, *Managing Acquisitions;* and P. L. Anslinger and T. E. Copeland, "Growth Through Acquisition: A Fresh Look," *Harvard Business Review* (January–February 1996): 126–135.

29. See K. Ohmae, "The Global Logic of Strategic Alliances," *Harvard Business Review* (March-April 1989): 143–154; G. Hamel, Y. L. Doz, and C. K. Prahalad, "Collaborate with Your Competitors and Win!" *Harvard Business Review* (January–February 1989): 133–139; W. Burgers, C. W. L. Hill, and W. C. Kim, "Alliances in the Global Auto Industry," *Strategic Management Journal* 14 (1993): 419–432; P. Kale, H. Singh, and H. Perlmutter, "Learning and Protection of Proprietary Assets in Strategic Alliances: Building Relational Capital," *Strategic Management Journal* 21 (2000): 217–237.

30. "Asia Beckons," *Economist* (May 30, 1992): 63–64.

31. C. Souza, "Microsoft Teams with MIPS, Toshiba," *EBN* (February 10, 2003): 4.

32. Kale, Singh, and Perlmutter, "Learning and Protection of Proprietary Assets in Strategic Alliances."

33. R. B. Reich and E. D. Mankin, "Joint Ventures with Japan Give Away Our Future," *Harvard Business Review* (March-April 1986): 78–90.

34. J. Bleeke and D. Ernst, "The Way to Win in Cross-Border Alliances," *Harvard Business Review* (November–December 1991): 127–135.

35. E. Booker and C. Krol, "IBM Finds Strength in Alliances," *B to B* (February 10, 2003): 3, 27.

36. W. Roehl and J. F. Truitt, "Stormy Open Marriages Are Better," *Columbia Journal of World Business* (Summer 1987): 87–95.

37. "Cambridge Antibody Technology: Astra Zeneca to Buy 19.9% Stake," *Wall Street Journal,* November 23, 2004, p. A1.

38. See T. Khanna, R. Gulati, and N. Nohria, "The Dynamics of Learning Alliances: Competition, Cooperation, and Relative Scope," *Strategic Management Journal* 19 (1998): 193–210; and Kale, Singh, and Perlmutter, "Learning and Protection of Proprietary Assets in Strategic Alliances."

39. Kale, Singh, and Perlmutter, "Learning and Protection of Proprietary Assets in Strategic Alliances."

Box Source Notes

a. www.sap.com, 2006.
b. www.oracle.com, 2006.

Chapter 9

Text Source Notes

1. J. R. Galbraith, *Designing Complex Organizations* (Reading, MA: Addison-Wesley, 1973).

2. J. Child, *Organization: A Guide for Managers and Administrators* (New York: Harper & Row, 1977), pp. 50–72.

3. R. H. Miles, *Macro Organizational Behavior* (Santa Monica, CA: Goodyear, 1980), pp. 19–20.

4. Galbraith, *Designing Complex Organizations.*

5. V. A. Graicunas, "Relationships in Organizations," in *Papers on the Science of Administration,* ed. L. Gulick and L. Urwick (New York: Institute of Public Administration, 1937), pp. 181–185; J. C. Worthy, "Organizational Structure and Company Morale," *American Sociological Review* 15 (1950): 169–179.

6. Child, *Organization,* pp. 50–52.

7. G. R. Jones, "Organization-Client Transactions and Organizational Governance Structures," *Academy of Management Journal* 30 (1987): 197–218.

8. H. Mintzberg, *The Structuring of Organizations* (Englewood Cliffs, NJ: Prentice-Hall, 1979), p. 435.

9. B. Woolridge and S. W. Floyd, "The Strategy Process, Middle Management Involvement, and Organizational Performance," *Strategic Management Journal* 9 (1990): 231–241.

10. Child, *Organization,* p. 51.

11. R. Carzo Jr. and J. N. Yanousas, "Effects of Flat and Tall Organization Structure," *Administrative Science Quarterly* 14 (1969): 178–191.

12. A. Gupta and V. Govindardan, "Business Unit Strategy, Managerial Characteristics, and Business Unit Effectiveness at Strategy Implementation," *Academy of Management Journal* 27 (1984): 25–41; R. T. Lenz, "Determinants of Organizational Performance: An Interdisciplinary Review," *Strategic Management Journal* 2 (1981): 131–154.

13. W. H. Wagel, "Keeping the Organization Lean at Federal Express," *Personnel* (March 1984): 4.

14. J. Koter, "For P&G Rivals, the New Game Is to Beat the Leader, Not Copy It," *Wall Street Journal,* May 6, 1985, p. 35.

15. G. R. Jones, "Task Visibility, Free Riding and Shirking: Explaining the Effect of Organization Structure on Employee Behavior," *Academy of Management Review* 4 (1984): 684–695.

16. R. L. Daft, *Organizational Theory and Design,* 3rd ed. (St. Paul, MN: West, 1986), p. 215.

17. J. R. Galbraith and R. K. Kazanjian, *Strategy Implementation: Structure System and Process,* 2nd ed. (St. Paul, MN: West, 1986); Child, Organization; R. Duncan, "What Is the Right Organization Structure?" *Organizational Dynamics* (Winter 1979): 59–80.

18. O. E. Williamson, *Markets and Hierarchies: Analysis and Antitrust Implications* (New York: Free Press, 1975).

19. Alfred D. Chandler, *Strategy and Structure* (Cambridge, MA: MIT Press, 1971); Williamson, *Markets and Hierarchies;* L. Wrigley, "Divisional Autonomy and Diversification," PhD dissertation, Harvard Business School, 1970.

20. R. P. Rumelt, *Strategy, Structure, and Economic Performance* (Boston: Division of Research, Harvard Business School, 1974); B. R. Scott, *Stages of Corporate Development* (Cambridge, MA: Harvard Business School, 1971); Williamson, *Markets and Hierarchies.*

21. The discussion draws on each of the sources cited in endnotes 10–17 and on G. R. Jones and C. W. L. Hill, "Transaction Cost Analysis of Strategy-Structure Choice," *Strategic Management Journal* 9 (1988): 159–172.

22. H. O. Armour and D. J. Teece, "Organizational Structure and Economic Performance: A Test of the Multidivisional Hypothesis," *Bell Journal of Economics* 9 (1978): 106–122.

23. Alfred Sloan, *My Years at General Motors* (New York: Doubleday, 1983), Ch. 3.

24. P. R. Lawrence and J. Lorsch, *Organization and Environment* (Homewood, IL: Irwin, 1967), pp. 50–55.

25. Galbraith, Designing Complex Organizations, Ch. 1; Galbraith and Kazanjian, *Strategy Implementation,* Ch. 7.

26. Henry Mintzberg, *The Nature of Managerial Work* (Englewood Cliffs, NJ: Prentice-Hall, 1973), Ch. 10.

27. Lawrence and Lorsch, *Organization and Environment,* p. 55.

28. R. Simmons, "Strategic Orientation and Top Management Attention to Control Systems," *Strategic Management Journal* 10 (1991): 49–62.

29. W. G. Ouchi, "The Transmission of Control Through Organizational Hierarchy," *Academy of Management Journal* 21 (1978): 173–192; W. H. Newman, *Constructive Control* (Englewood Cliffs, NJ: Prentice-Hall, 1975).

30. Williamson, *Markets and Hierarchies;* W. G. Ouchi, "Markets, Bureaucracies, and Clans," *Administrative Science Quarterly* 25 (1980): 109–141.

31. Mintzberg, The Structuring of Organizations, pp. 5–9.

32. L. Smirich, "Concepts of Culture and Organizational Analysis," *Administrative Science Quarterly* 28 (1983): 339–358.

33. Ouchi, "Markets, Bureaucracies, and Clans," p. 130.

34. G. R. Jones, *Organizational Theory, Design, and Change,* 6th ed. (Upper Saddle River, NJ: Prentice-Hall, 2007).

Box Source Notes

a. "Union Pacific to Reorganize," cnnfn.com, August 20, 1998; Union Pacific, Press Release, www. unionpacific.com, 1998.

b. B. Koenig, "Ford Reorganizes Executives Under New Chief Mulally," www.bloomberg.com, December 14, 2006.

c. www.ford.com, December 14, 2006.

Test Prepper Answers

Chapter 1

1. True	9. a
2. True	10. b
3. False	11. a
4. True	12. c
5. True	13. a
6. False	14. c
7. True	15. b
8. c	

Chapter 2

1. True	9. c
2. False	10. c
3. False	11. b
4. True	12. a
5. True	13. a
6. True	14. a
7. True	15. a
8. a	

Chapter 3

1. True	9. b
2. True	10. a
3. True	11. d
4. True	12. a
5. False	13. c
6. True	14. b
7. False	15. b
8. d	

Chapter 4

1. True	9. b
2. True	10. c
3. False	11. c
4. True	12. b
5. False	13. d
6. True	14. e
7. True	15. c
8. d	

Chapter 5

1. False	9. b
2. False	10. b
3. True	11. b
4. True	12. b
5. True	13. c
6. False	14. b
7. False	15. b
8. a	

Chapter 6

1. True	9. b
2. False	10. e
3. True	11. c
4. True	12. b
5. True	13. b
6. False	14. b
7. True	15. a
8. e	

Chapter 7

1. True	9. d
2. True	10. a
3. True	11. a
4. False	12. a
5. False	13. d
6. True	14. c
7. True	15. a
8. d	

Chapter 8

1. True	9. c
2. False	10. d
3. False	11. c
4. True	12. a
5. True	13. c
6. True	14. a
7. True	15. a
8. c	

Chapter 9

1. True	9. a
2. True	10. a
3. True	11. b
4. False	12. b
5. True	13. b
6. True	14. c
7. True	15. c
8. c	

Index

Absolute cost advantage, 55
Accounting principles, generally agreed-on, 33
ACE system, 185–186
Acquisition, 164
    restructuring strategy and, 176, 180
    strategic change and, 200–204
Acquisition and restructuring strategy, 176, 180
Advanced Micro Devices (AMD), 63–64
Agency problem, 32–36
Agency relationship, 32
Agency theory, 32
Agent, 32–36
Airline industry
    in decline stage, 68
    deregulation of, 72
    price wars in, 68
Alcan, 170–171
Alcoa, 170–171, 220
Allard, Jay, 12
Altria Group, 130. *See also* Philip Morris
Aluminum industry, 170–171
Amazon.com
    case on, C33–C43
    consolidation and, 122
    customization at, 100
AMD, 63–64
Analogy, reasoning by, 18
Analyses. *See* External analysis; Internal
        analysis; SWOT analysis
Andreesen, Mark, 12
Anticompetitive behavior, 41–42
Antitrust law, 40, 167
Apple Computer
    case on, C17–C31
    innovation at, 97
    vertical integration at, 169
Arthur Andersen, 39
Asset, specialized, 171
AstraZeneca, 208
AT&T, 181
Auditors, 38–39
Auto industry
    bargaining power in, 61
    competive advantage in, 79
    local responsiveness and, 145–146, 150
    product proliferation in, 124
Autonomous action, 11

Baby boomers, 71
Backward vertical integration, 169, 172–173
Banana industry, 172–173
Bankruptcy regulations, 59
Bargaining power
    of buyers, 60–61
    horizontal integration and, 166–167
    of Intel, 63–64

of suppliers, 61–63
    of Wal-Mart, 62
Barriers
    to entry, 54–57, 170–171, 200
    to exit, 59–60, 129
    to imitation, 102–103
    to mobility, 65
BEA Systems, 211
Behavior, anticompetitive, 41–42
Behavior control, 238–242
Bell, Alexander Graham, 13
Bias
    cognitive, 17–18
    prior hypothesis, 17
Bidding strategy, 202–203
Blockbuster, case on, C44–C58
Board of directors, 33, 36–37, 47
Boeing
    case on, C1–C15
    ethics at, 43
    globalization of production at, 138
    stock options and, 38
Bombardier, 147
Bonds, junk, 182
Bottom-up change, 193
Bowerman, Bill, 134
Brand loyalty, 55, 116
Breen, Edward, 35
Broad differentiator, 115
Budget, operating, 239
Buffet, Warren, 38
Burgelman, Robert, 11
Business ethics, 40–41
Business-level managers, 6
Business-level strategy, 9–10, 192
    competitive positioning and, 110–111,
        120–132
    distinctive competence and, 111, 115–116,
        117–118
    at Nike, 134–135
    obstacles to change and, 192
    types of, 111–120
    at Wal-Mart, 113
Business practice officer, 46–47
Business process, 189
Business unit, 6
Buyers' bargaining power, 60–61, 62

Cambridge Antibody Technology, 208
Canon, 193, 194
Capabilities, 101–102
Capacity, excess, 59–60, 125
Capital
    relational, 208
    return on invested, 2
    risk, 32

Capital productivity, 81
Carrefour, 141
Caterpillar
    customer responsiveness at, 85, 100
    fit model and, 16
Cellular phone industry, 66
Centralization, 219, 221
CEOs, 4–6
    agency problem and, 32–36
    board of directors and, 37
    characteristics of good, 19–21
Cerberus, 23
Cereal industry, 124
Chaining strategy, 121
Chief executive officers. *See* CEOs
Chrysler
    bargaining power of, 61
    strategy making at, 23–24
Cifra, 140
Cisco Systems
    information systems at, 92
    innovation at, 83
Citicorp, 179
Citigroup, 179
Coca-Cola
    business definition and, 53
    entry barriers and, 56
    imitation at, 103
    product development at, 127–128
Code of ethics, 46
Cognitive bias, 17–18
Commitment
    credible, 207–208
    escalating, 17
Communication problems, 222
Company infrastructure, 86, 93
Compaq, 165, 166
Compensation
    pay-for-performance, 92
    stock-based, 37–38
Competence, distinctive. *See* Distinctive
        competence
Competition, nonprice, 126–127
Competitive advantage, 2. *See also*
        Competitive positioning
    building blocks of, 77–84. *See also*
        Value chain
    business-level strategies and,
        110–111
    distinctive competences and,
        100–103
    functional-level strategies and,
        86–100
    superior performance and, 2–3
    sustained, 2, 78
    of Wal-Mart, 4–5

Competitive positioning. *See also* Business-level strategy
in different industry environments, 120–132
nature of, 110–111
of Nike, 134–135
Competitors. *See also* Five forces model
definition of, 53
potential, 54–57
Concentration on a single industry, 163–168
Conglomerate, 180, 185
Conseco, 202
Consolidated industry, 57, 58
Contract law, 40
Control
illusion of, 18
organizational, 230–242
span of, 217
Convergys, 168
Cooper, Robert, 96
Cooperative outsourcing relationships, 175
Core competence. *See* Distinctive competence
Corporate governance, 26. *See also* Board of directors; CEOs
ethics and, 47
strategy and, 31–39
Corporate-level managers, 4–6, 197–198. *See also* CEOs
Corporate-level strategy, 10, 191–192
Corruption, 44
Cost advantage, absolute, 55
Cost conditions, industry, 59
Cost-leadership strategy, 111–114, 116–118
Cost reductions, pressures for, 144–145, 148, 158
Costco, 4, 5
Costs
fixed, 59, 87, 129
operating, 165, 230
switching, 55–56
Cott Corporation, 56
Coyne, William, 178
Credible commitment, 207–208
Cross-functional product development teams, 98–99
Culture, organizational, 30, 44–46
Currency exchange rates, 70
Customer defection rates, 89
Customer needs, 53, 99–100, 110, 145
Customer-oriented business definition, 28, 29–30, 53
Customer response time, 83–84
Customer responsiveness, 77, 80, 83–84, 85, 99–100
Customization, 88, 100

DaimlerChrysler, 23, 117
David, George, 180, 185, 186
Davidson, Dick, 220
Decentralization, 219–220
Decentralized planning, 15–16
Decision making, strategic, 17–19, 46
Declining industry, 68, 128–132

Defection rates, customer, 89
Delegation, 20
Deliberate strategy, 13–14
Dell Computers, 166, 223, 224
Demand, industry, 58–59
Demographic forces, 71
Devil's advocacy, 18
Dialectic inquiry, 18
Differentiation, 216. *See also* Product differentiation
horizontal, 216, 221–230
integration and, 233–234
vertical, 216–221
Differentiation strategy
cost leadership and, 117–118
explanation of, 114–116
Differentiator, broad, 115
Digital Equipment, 171
Directors, 33, 36–37, 47
Discount, diversification, 181
Disney, Walt, 240
Distinctive competence
business-level strategy and, 111, 115–116, 117–118
competitive advantage and, 100–103
diversification and, 177–178
entry mode and, 156–158
strategic change and, 193–195
at Wal-Mart, 113
Diversification
creating value through, 175–180
as entry mode, 163, 175
internal governance and, 176–177
related vs. unrelated, 180
restructuring and, 181–182
at 3M, 178
Diversification discount, 181
Diversified company, 175
Divestment, 182
Divestment strategy, 129, 131–132
Divisional-level strategy. *See* Business-level strategy
Domino's Pizza, 99
Downsizing, 181–183
DuPont, 233
Dyment, Roy, 99

eBay, 122
Economies, location, 142–143
Economies of scale, 55, 87, 142
Economies of scope, 179–180
EDS, 167
Efficiency, 77, 80–81, 87–94
Electronic Data Systems (EDS), 167
Elevonic 401, 185
Ellison, Larry, 210, 211
Embryonic industry, 66
Emergent strategy, 13–14
Emotional intelligence, 20–21
Empire building, 34
Employee productivity, 81, 90–92

Empowerment, 20
Enron, 35, 36, 39
Entry
barriers to, 54–57, 70–71, 200
modes of, 152–158
Environment
industry, 9
macro-, 9, 69–72
national, 9
Environmental degradation, 44
Escalating commitment, 17
Ethical dilemmas, 40
Ethics, 40
business, 40–47
code of, 46
Ethics officer, 46–47
Excess capacity, 59–60, 125
Exchange rates, currency, 70
Exit barrier, 59–60, 129
Exit strategies, 182–183
Exploitation, opportunistic, 42–43
Exporting, 152–153
Express mail delivery industry
exit barriers in, 60
fixed costs in, 59
External analysis, 7, 8, 9, 52–53
of industry life cycle, 65–69
of industry structure, 53–63
of macroenvironment, 69–72
strategic groups and, 63–65
External stakeholders, 27, 192
Exxon, 33

Federal Trade Commission (FTC), 167
FedEx
excess capacity and, 60
fixed costs of, 59
vertical differentiation and, 218
Fill in the blanks, 194
Financial control, 236–237, 242
Financial statements, 38–39
Fiorina, Carly, 166
Fit model of strategy planning, 16, 17
Five forces model, 53–63, 69, 114
Fixed costs, 59, 87, 129
Flat structure, 217
Flexible manufacturing technology, 88
Focus strategy, 112, 117–119
Ford, 208, 237
48 Hours, 40
Forward vertical integration, 169, 173
Four Seasons hotel chain, 99
Fragmented industry, 57–58, 121–122
Franchising, 122, 154–155
FTC, 167
Fuji, 155
Full integration, 173–174
Functional-level managers, 3, 6–7
Functional-level strategy, 9, 10
competitive advantage and, 86–100
obstacles to change and, 192
Functional structure, 221–223

GAAP, 33
Galvin, Christopher, 197
Gates, Bill, 11, 12, 19, 240
GE. *See* General Electric
General Electric (GE), 19
    decentralization at, 220
    ivory tower approach and, 15
    managers of, 5–7
    strategic alliance and, 207
General managers, 3–4. *See also specific types*
General Motors (GM), 16, 33
    imitation at, 102
    innovation at, 97
    market segmentation and, 110
    multidivisional structure of, 227, 229
    vs. Toyota, 79
    vertical integration at, 173
Generalization, 18
Generally agreed-on accounting principles
    (GAAP), 33
Geographic structure, 225–226
Gillette, 127
Global environment, 70, 138–139
    choosing strategy for, 147–152
    competitive pressures in, 144–147
    entry modes in, 152–158
    increasing profitability through,
        139–143
Global standardization strategy, 10, 148, 151,
    152
GM. *See* General Motors
Goal, 30–31. *See also specific control systems*
Goldman, Daniel, 20, 21
Governance mechanisms, 33, 36–39,
    176–177
Government regulation, 55–57
Green Tree Financial, 202
Grove, Andy, 11, 103
Growth industry, 66–67, 121–122
Growth rate, 34–35

H. J. Heinz, 113
Hallmark Cards, 189
Hamel, Gary, 16, 17, 193–194, 195
Hanson PLC, 203
Harvest strategy, 129, 131, 183
Heavyweight project manager, 98
Hewlett, Bill, 45
Hewlett-Packard
    horizontal integration and, 165, 166
    working conditions at, 45
Hiring, and ethics, 45
Holdup, risk of, 172
Home Depot, 34
Horizontal differentiation, 216, 221–230
Horizontal integration, 164–167
Horizontal merger, 122
HP Way, The, 45
HTML, 12
Hubris hypothesis, 18
Human resources strategy, 86, 90–92
Hypertext markup language (HTML), 12

IBM
    location economies and, 143
    mission of, 29–30
    vertical integration at, 169, 171
IKEA, 160
Illusion of control, 18
Imitation, barriers to, 102–103
Immelt, Jeffrey, 6, 238
Industry, 53
    analyzing structure of, 53–63
    concentration on a single, 163–168
    consolidated, 57, 58
    cost conditions of, 59
    declining, 68, 123–132
    demand in, 58–59
    environment of, 69–72
    fragmented, 57–58, 121–122
    growth, 66–67, 121–122
    life cycle of, 65–69, 123–128
Inflation, price, 70
Information asymmetry, 32–33
Information distortion, 218–219,
    229
Information manipulation, 41
Information systems, 86, 92
Infrastructure, company, 86, 93
Innovation, 77, 80
    increasing, 96–99
    process, 83
    product, 83, 96–97
    at 3M, 100–101
Inputs, 80–81
Inside directors, 36–37
Intangible resources, 101, 103
Integration, 216
    acquisition and, 203–204
    differentiation and, 233–234
    full, 173–174
    horizontal, 164–167
    managers and, 233
    organizational control and, 230–234
    postacquisition, 201
    taper, 173–174
    vertical, 162–163, 168–175
Intel, 11
    bargaining power of, 63–64
    innovation in, 83
Intellectual property law, 40
Intelligence, emotional, 20–21
Intended strategy, 13–14
Intent, strategic, 16–17
Internal analysis, 7, 8, 9
Internal governance, 176–177
Internal new ventures, 195–199
Internal stakeholders, 27, 192
International licensing, 153–154
International strategy, 151, 152
Internet, and fragmented industries,
    122
Internet Explorer, 12, 42
Inventory system, JIT, 90, 95
Iridium project, 197

Ito, Yuzuru, 185
Iverson, Ken, 19
Ivory tower approach, 15–16

Java, 12
JIT inventory system, 90, 95
Joint venture, 155, 204
Joseph Schlitz Brewing Company, 114
Junk bonds, 182
Just-in-time (JIT) inventory system, 90, 95

Kahneman, Daniel, 18, 19
Kamprad, Ingvar, 160
KBR, case on, C100–C101
Kelleher, Herb, 19
Kellogg Brown & Root (KBR), case on,
    C100–C101
Klippan loveseat, 160
Kmart, 64
Knight, Phil, 134
Kodak
    mission of, 28, 29
    vertical integration at, 173
Kozlowski, Dennis, 35
Kroc, Ray, 20

LaSorda, Thomas, 23
Laws, business, 40, 167
Leadership
    price, 126
    strategic, 19–21, 45–46, 99. *See also specific*
        leaders
Leadership strategy, 129, 130
Lean production, 83, 88
Learning effects, 88, 89
Legal/political forces, 71–72
Liaison role, of manager, 231
Licensing, 153–154
Life cycle, industry, 65–69
Liquidation strategy, 183
Loblaws, 56
Local responsiveness, pressures for, 144,
    145–148, 149–150
Localization strategy, 149–150, 151, 152
Location, and organization structure, 223
Location economies, 142–143
Logistics, 86, 90
Long-term contracting, 182
Low cost structure, 80, 82, 94, 96

Macroeconomic forces, 69–70
Macroenvironment, 9, 69–72
Management buyout (MBO), 182
Managers
    business-level, 6
    corporate-level, 4–6, 197–198. *See also*
        CEOs
    functional-level, 3, 6–7
    heavyweight project, 98
    integration and, 233
    liaison role of, 231
    motivation of, 219

Market development, 128
Market niche, 117. *See also* Focus strategy
Market segmentation, 110–111, 112
Marketing, 85, 88–90
Marketing penetration, 127
Marketing strategy, 88
Mass customization, 88
Materials management, 86, 90
Matrix structure, 227–228
Matsushita
    case on, C85–C99
    TQM at, 185
Mature industry, 68, 123–128
Maytag, 224
Mazda, 208
MBO, 182
McDonald's
    franchising and, 154
    global expansion at, 142, 143
    strategic leadership at, 20
    vertical integration at, 173
MCI Communications, 201
McKinnell, Hank, 34
Measurement systems, 223
Mega-opportunities, 195
Mercedes-Benz, 23
Mercer Management Consulting, 200
Merger, 122, 164. *See also specific mergers*
Microsoft, 19
    economies of scale and, 87, 142
    ethics at, 41–42
    flexible strategic planning at, 11, 12
    international strategy and, 151
    mission of, 8
    organizational values at, 240
    permanent teams at, 233
    stock options and, 38
    strategic alliance and, 205
Mintzberg, Henry, 13, 232
Mission, 28–30
Mission statement, 8, 28–31
Mobility barriers, 65
Model T Ford, 87
Monaghan, Tom, 99
Monsanto, 195, 196
Moral courage, 47
Mosaic, 12
Motivation, and organization structure, 219
Motorola, 197, 204–205, 207
MTV, 150
Mulally, Alan, 237
Multidivisional company, 3–4, 226–230
Murdoch, Rupert, 164, 203

Nardelli, Bob, 23, 34
National environment, 9
Naval, 131
Needs, customer, 53, 99–100, 110, 145
Neighborhood Market, 199
Neiman Marcus, 225–226
Netscape Navigator, 12
News Corp, 164, 203

News industry
    acquisition strategy and, 204
    horizontal integration and, 164
    technical change in, 71
Niche strategy, 129, 131
Nike
    business-level strategies at, 134–135
    ethics at, 40
    outsourcing and, 167
Noblesse oblige, 41
Nonprice competition, 126–127
Nordstrom, 79–80
Norms, organizational, 240
Nucor Steel
    distinctive competence of, 101
    human resources at, 90–91
    leadership of, 19
    values of, 30

Odle, Stephanie, 42–43
On-the-job consumption, 33
O'Neill, Paul, 220
Operating budget, 239
Operating costs
    horizontal integration and, 165
    organization structure and, 230
Operating responsibility, 228
Opportunistic exploitation, 42–43
Opportunities, 52, 151, 195. *See also specific opportunities*
Oracle Corporation, 210–211
Organization structure, 215–216
    horizontal differentiation in, 221–230
    operating costs and, 230
    role of, 215–216
    vertical differentiation in, 216–221
Organizational control
    integration and, 230–234
    nature of, 234–242
Organizational culture, 30
    behavior controls and, 240–241
    ethics and, 44–46
    at Wal-Mart, 242
Organizational design, 214. *See also* Organization structure; Organizational control
Organizational norms, 240
Organizational values, 240
Output, 80–81
Output control, 238
Outside directors, 36, 37
Outside view, 18–19
Outsourcing, 167–168, 174–175, 190

Packard, David, 45
Palm, 83
Partner selection, 206
Patents, 103
Pay-for-performance compensation, 92
PeopleSoft, 210
PepsiCo
    entry barriers and, 56
    product development at, 127–128

Permanent teams, 233
Perrier, 85
Personal computer industry
    bargaining power in, 62–63
    horizontal integration in, 166
    price signaling in, 125–126
    value-added chain in, 169–170
Personal ethics, 44, 45
Pfeffer, Jeffery, 20
Pfizer, 34
Pharmaceutical industry
    bargaining power in, 61
    global expansion in, 146–147
    strategic groups in, 63–64, 65
Philip Morris, 71, 130, 177
Philips, case on, C85–C99
Planning
    scenario, 14–15
    strategic, 7–10, 11, 12, 16, 17, 223, 228–230
Polaroid, 101
Political/legal forces, 71–72
Porsche, 118
Porter, Michael E., 53, 80. *See also* Five forces model
Portfolio of core competences, 193–195
Positioning strategy, 97
Postacquisition integration, 201
Prahalad, C. K., 16, 17, 193–194, 195
Premier plus 10, 194
Premium price, 114
Price
    cutting of, 124–125
    inflation of, 70
    reservation, 78
    stock, 236–237
Price leadership, 126
Price signaling, 125–126
Price war, 58, 68
Pricing, transfer, 230
Primary activities, 84–85
Principal, 32–36
Principle of the minimum chain of command, 218
Prior hypothesis bias, 17
Process, business, 189
Process innovation, 83
Procter & Gamble
    economies of scope at, 179
    global expansion at, 140, 141, 142, 149, 151
    market penetration and, 127
    vertical differentiation and, 218
Product
    bundling of, 165
    development of, 127–128. *See also* Innovation; Research and development
    quality of. *See* Quality, product
    structure of, 223–224
    substitute, 63
Product development team, 98–99
Product differentiation, 80, 82, 94, 96, 110, 112, 165
Product innovation, 83, 96–97

Product-oriented business definition, 28–30
Product proliferation, 123–124, 128
Product-team structure, 224–225
Production, in value chain, 85
    efficiency and, 87–88
    globalization of, 138
Productivity
    capital, 81
    employee, 81, 90–92
Profitability, 2, 37
    global expansion and, 139–143
    long-run. *See specific strategies*
    revenue growth rates and, 34–35
    scale of entry and, 196, 197
Promotion, 45

Quality, product, 77, 80, 81–82, 128
    franchising and, 154
    increasing, 94–96
    protecting, 122–123
    vertical integration and, 172
Quality as excellence, 81, 95–96
Quality as reliability, 81, 94–95
Quantum Corporation, 99
Qwest, 201

Raymond, Lee, 33
RCA, 154
Realized strategy, 13–14
Reasoning by analogy, 18
Reengineering, 189–190
Related diversification, 180
Relational capital, 208
Representativeness, 18
Research and development, 84–85, 87, 198–199
    efficiency and, 87
    organization structure and, 230
Reservation price, customer's, 78
Resources
    competition for, 230
    intangible, 101, 103
    tangible, 101–102
Responsibility, strategic, 228
Restructuring, 181–183, 190
Retail industry
    competitive advantage in, 79–80
    strategic groups in, 64
Return on invested capital (ROIC), 2
Return on investment (ROI), 237
Richardson Electronics, 130
Risk capital, 32
Risk of holdup, 172
Rivalry, 57–60, 166
ROI, 237
ROIC, 2
Roll, Richard, 18
Royal Crown Cola, 56, 127
Royal Dutch Shell, 14, 15

Sales, in value chain, 85
Sam's Choice, 56
Sam's Club, 5

SAP, 210, 211
Sarbanes-Oxley Act, 37, 39
Scale, economies of, 55, 87
Scale of entry, 196, 197
Scenario planning, 14–15
Scenarios, "what if," 14–15
Schrempp, Jurgen, 23
Schultz, Howard, 106
Scope, economies of, 179–180
SEC, 33, 38–39
Securities law, 40
Security and Exchange Commission (SEC), 33, 38–39
Segmentation, market, 110–111, 112
Self-dealing, 41
Self-managing team, 92
Shakeout stage, of industry, 67
Siebel Systems, 210
Signaling, price, 125–126
Singapore Airlines, 95
Sinofsky, Steve, 12
Six Sigma methodology, 94–95
SKUs, 62
Sloan, Alfred, 229
Smith Corona, 29
Snecma, 207
Social forces, 71
Soft drink industry
    entry barriers in, 56
    structure of, 53
Southwest Airlines, 19, 90
Span of control, 217
Specialization, 87
Specialized asset, 171
Spinoff, 182
Stakeholders, 26
    rights of, 40–41
    types of, 27–28. *See also specific types*
Standardization, 239
Starbucks, 105–106, 142
Steel industry, 68, 128, 129
Stock keeping units (SKUs), 62
Stock options, 37–38
Stock price, 236–237
Stockholders, 31–32
Strategic alliances, 204–208
Strategic change, 186–193
    through acquisitions, 200–203
    distinctive competences and, 193–195
    through internal new ventures, 195–199
    through strategic alliances, 203–208
Strategic control systems, 234–236
Strategic fit, 16, 17
Strategic groups, 63–65
Strategic intent, 16–17
Strategic leadership, 19–21. *See also specific leaders*
    customer focus and, 99
    ethics and, 45–46
Strategic managers, 3–7. *See also specific types*

Strategic planning, 7–10
    fit model of, 16, 17
    at Microsoft, 11, 12
    organization structure and, 223, 228–230
Strategic responsibility, 228
Strategy, 2. *See also specific strategies*
    corporate governance and, 31–39
    in declining industries, 128–132
    as emergent process, 10–14
    ethics and, 40–47
    process for planning, 7–10
Strategy formulation, 7
Strategy implementation, 7, 10
Structure(s)
    analyzing industry, 53–63. *See also specific types*
    flat, 217
    functional, 221–223
    geographic, 225–226
    low cost, 80, 82, 94, 96
    matrix, 227–228
    multidivisional, 3–4, 226–230
    product, 223–224
    product-team, 224–225
    tall, 217–219
Stuck in the middle, 119
Substandard working conditions, 43–44
Substitute products, 63
Sun Microsystems, 12
Sundown rule, Wal-Mart's, 91
Sundstrand, 186
Suppliers' bargaining power, 61–63
Support activities, 86
Sustained competitive advantage, 2, 78
Swartz, Mark, 35
Switching costs, 55–56
SWOT analysis, 7, 8, 9–10, 191

Takeover constraint, 39
Tall structure, 217–219
Tangible resources, 101–102
Taper integration, 173–174
Target, 4, 5
Target screening, 202
Task force, 232–233
Teams
    permanent, 233
    self-managing, 92
Technological change, 70–71
Telephone industry, 56–57
Texas Instruments, 87
ThinkPad, 143
Threats, 52, 191. *See also specific threats*
3M, 12
    case on, C69–C83
    diversification at, 178
    innovation at, 100–101
Tie-in sales, 42
Tit-for-tat strategy, 125–126
Titanium Metals Corporation, 43

Tobacco industry
  in decline stage, 128
  social forces and, 71
Top-down change, 193
Tort laws, 40
Toshiba, 204–205, 207
Total quality management (TQM), 94,
    189–190
Toyota
  global expansion at, 140, 141, 142
  vs. GM, 79
  lean production system of, 83
  market segmentation and, 110
  quality and, 81–82
  strategic intent at, 16
TQM, 94, 189–190
Transfer pricing, 230
Transnational strategy, 150, 151, 152
Travelers, 179
TRW Systems, 207
Tyco, 35

Unilever
  code of ethics at, 47
  working conditions at, 46
Union Pacific, 220
Unit, business, 6
United States Steel Industry Association, 72
United Technologies Corporation (UTC),
    46–47, 180, 185–186
Universal needs, 145
Unrelated diversification, 180
UPS, 60

U.S. Immigration and Customs Enforcement
    Agency, 43
UTC, 46–47, 180, 185–186

Vacuum tube industry, 129, 130
Value chain, 84–86, 169–170
Value creation, 78–80. *See also specific functions*
  through diversification, 175–176
  through horizontal integration, 164–167
  through vertical integration, 162–163,
    168–175
Values, 30, 240
Verizon, 201
Verizon Wireless
  customer defection rates and, 90
Vertical differentiation, 216–221
Vertical integration, 162–163, 168–175
Virtual corporation, 167
Vision, 30
Volvo, 96

Wal-Mart
  bargaining power of, 62
  competitive advantage of, 4–5
  as cost leader, 113
  distinctive competence at, 113
  efficiency at, 90
  employees of, 91
  entry barriers and, 56
  global expansion at, 140–141, 143, 145
  internal venturing at, 199
  leadership of, 19, 20. *See also* Walton, Sam
  organizational culture of, 242

profitability of, 2
  support activities in, 86
  working conditions at, 42–43
Walton, Sam, 4–5, 19, 20, 42, 62, 91, 113, 242
Welch, Jack, 19, 220
Western Union, 13
"What if" scenarios, 14–15
White space, 194
Whole Foods, case on, C60–C67
Wholly owned subsidiary, 155–156
Wilson, Charles, 33
Windows, 42, 87
Wireless telecommunications industry
  customer defection rates in, 89–90
  infrastructure differences in, 146
Wookey, John, 211
Working conditions
  at Hewlett-Packard, 45
  at Nike, 40, 44
  substandard, 43–44
  at Unilever, 46
  at Wal-Mart, 42–43
World cars, 145–146
Wrapp, Edward, 20

Xbox, 11
Xerox, 16
  international strategy and, 151, 152, 155
  strategic intent and, 16

Yahoo!, 178

Zetsche, Dieter, 23